The Animal Ethics Reader

The Animal Ethics Reader is the first comprehensive, state-of-the-art anthology of readings on this substantial area of study and interest. Covering a subject that regularly captures the headlines, the book is designed to appeal to anyone interested in tracing the history of animal ethics, as well as providing a powerful insight into the debate as it has developed. The recent wealth of material published in this area has not, until now, been collected in one volume.

Readings are arranged thematically, carefully presenting a balanced representation of the subject as it stands. It will be essential reading for students taking a course in the subject as well as being of considerable interest to the general reader. Articles are arranged under the following headings:

Theories of Animal Ethics　　　　**Ethics and Wildlife**
Animal Capacities　　　　　　　　**Zoos, Aquariums, and Animals in**
Primates and Cetaceans　　　　　　　**Entertainment**
Animals for Food　　　　　　　　**Animal Companions**
Animal Experimentation　　　　　**Animal Law/Animal Activism**
Animals and Biotechnology

Readings from leading experts in the field including Mary Midgley, Bernard E. Rollin, and Peter Singer are featured as well as selections from Marc Bekoff, J. Baird Callicott, R. G. Frey, Jane Goodall, Donald R. Griffin, F. Barbara Orlans, and Tom Regan. There is an emphasis on balancing classic and contemporary readings with a view to presenting debates as they stand at this point in time.

Each chapter is introduced by the editors and followed by study questions and an annotated bibliography. The foreword has been written by Bernard E. Rollin.

Susan J. Armstrong is Professor of Philosophy and Women's Studies at Humboldt State University and has published widely on this and affiliated subjects. **Richard G. Botzler** is Professor of Wildlife, also at Humboldt State University, and a leading published expert in the field. Together they have edited *Environmental Ethics* (2003).

The
ANIMAL

ETHICS READER

Edited by

Susan J. Armstrong
and Richard G. Botzler

Routledge
Taylor & Francis Group

LONDON AND NEW YORK

Dedicated to:

my animal friends and to

S. L. Svarvari, D.V.M. and J. R. Hight, D.V.M.,
veterinarians *extraordinaire*

S.J.A.

Dedicated to my children:

Emilisa, Tin, Dorothy, Sarah, and Thomas,
with love and pride

R.G.B.

First published 2003
by Routledge
11 New Fetter Lane, London EC4P 4EE

Simultaneously published in the USA and Canada
by Routledge
29 West 35th Street, New York, NY 10001

Routledge is an imprint of the Taylor & Francis Group

© 2003 Selection and editorial material, Susan J. Armstrong and Richard G. Botzler.
Individual contributions, the authors.

Typeset in Sabon and Univers by Refinecatch Ltd
Printed and bound in Great Britain by
TJ International Ltd, Padstow, Cornwall

British Library Cataloguing in Publication Data
A catalogue record for this book is available from the British Library

Library of Congress Cataloging in Publication Data
The animal ethics reader / [edited by] Susan J. Armstrong and Richard G. Botzler.
 p. cm
Includes bibliographical references and index.
 1. Animal welfare—Moral and ethical aspects. 2. Animal rights. I. Armstrong,
Susan J. (Susan Jean) II. Botzler, Richard George, 1942– . III. Botzler, Richard G.
 HV4708.A548 2003
 179'.3—dc21   2003043202

ISBN 0–415–27588–1 (hbk)
ISBN 0–415–27589–x (pbk)

Contents

IV   Animals for Food

V   Animal Experimentation

IX Animal Companions

X Animal Law/Animal Activism

Foreword

Although I have been writing, lecturing, and otherwise actively working in the field of animal ethics since 1975, and had written in the 1970s that social interest in animal treatment would inevitably increase, I could not have anticipated the degree to which this issue would seize the popular imagination. A few examples can serve to underscore the impact of these concerns.

In the spring of 2002, the German Parliament included the protection of animals in the German Constitution. The amendment affirms that "the state takes responsibility for protecting the natural foundations of life and animals." There is widespread belief among German scientists that this amendment will have major implications for animal research by making invasive research far more difficult. Equally impressive is the fact that most Western countries now have strong laws protecting research animals despite strong and vigorous opposition from the research community. In the United States, for example, in the 1980s, although research animal protection legislation was categorically rejected by those who speak for the research community, as potentially impeding human health, the U.S. public overwhelmingly supported its passage. And, in many countries, legislation requires that research animals suffering intractable pain *must* be immediately euthanized. (In the weaker U.S. law, they *may* be euthanized.)

In short, citizens have felt sufficiently strongly about the moral status of research animals (the overwhelming majority of which are rats and mice) to place significant constraints on medical research despite its patent advantage to humans.

According to both the U.S. National Cattlemen's Beef Association and the National Institutes of Health (the latter being the source of funding for the majority of biomedical research in the United States), both groups not inclined to exaggerate the influence of animal ethics, by the mid-1990s Congress had been consistently receiving more letters, phone calls, faxes, e-mails, and personal contacts on animal-related issues than on any other topic.

Whereas five years ago one would have found no bills pending in the U.S. Congress relating to animal welfare, the last five to six years have witnessed 50–60 such bills annually, with even more proliferating at the state level. The federal bills range from attempts to prevent duplication in animal research, to saving marine mammals from becoming victims of tuna fishermen, to preventing importation of ivory, to curtailing the parrot trade. State laws passed in large numbers have increasingly prevented the use of live or dead pound animals for biomedical research and training and have focused on myriad other areas of animal welfare. Numerous states have abolished the steel-jawed leghold trap. When Colorado's politically appointed Wildlife Commission failed to act on a recommendation from the Division of Wildlife to abolish the spring bear-hunt (because hunters were liable to shoot lactating mothers, leaving their orphaned cubs to die of starvation), the general public ended the hunt through a popular referendum. Seventy percent of Colorado's population voted for that constitutional amendment. In Ontario, the environmental minister stopped a similar hunt by executive fiat in response to social ethical concern. California abolished the hunting of mountain lions, and state fishery management agencies have taken a hard look at catch-and-release programs on humane grounds.

In fact, wildlife managers have worried, in academic journals, about "management by referendum." According to the director of the American Quarter Horse Association, the number of state bills related to horse welfare filled a telephone-book-sized volume in 1998 alone. Public sentiment for equine welfare in California carried a bill through the state legislature making the slaughter of horses or shipping of horses for slaughter a felony in that state. Municipalities have passed ordinances ranging from the abolition of rodeos, circuses, and zoos to the protection of prairie dogs and, in the case of Cambridge, Massachusetts (a biomedical Mecca), the strictest laws in the world regulating research. Some thirty-five states have elevated animal cruelty from a misdemeanor to a felony.

Many animal uses seen as frivolous by the public have been abolished without legislation. Toxicological testing of cosmetics on animals has been truncated; companies such as the Body Shop have been wildly successful internationally by totally disavowing such testing, and free-range egg production is a growth industry across the world. Greyhound racing in the U.S. has declined, in part for animal welfare reasons, with the Indiana veterinary community spearheading the effort to prevent greyhound racing from coming into the state. Zoos that are little more than prisons for animals (the state of the art during my youth) have all but disappeared, and the very existence of zoos is being increasingly challenged, despite the public's unabashed love of seeing animals. And, as George Gaskell and his associates' work has revealed, genetic engineering has been rejected in Europe not, as commonly believed, for reasons of risk but for reasons of ethics; in part for reasons of animal ethics. Similar reasons (i.e., fear of harming cattle) have, in part, driven European rejection of bovine somatotropin (BST). Rodeos such as the Houston Livestock Show have, in essence, banned jerking of calves in roping, despite opposition from the Professional Rodeo Cowboys Association, who themselves never show the actual roping of a calf on national television.

Inevitably, agriculture has felt the force of social concern with animal treatment—indeed, it is arguable that contemporary concern in society with the treatment of farm animals in modern production systems blazed the trail leading to a new ethic for animals. As early as 1965, British society took notice of what the public saw as an alarming tendency to industrialize animal agriculture by chartering the Brambell Commission, a group of scientists under the leadership of Sir Roger Brambell, who affirmed that any agricultural system failing to meet the needs and natures of animals was morally unacceptable. Though the Brambell Commission recommendations enjoyed no regulatory status, they served as a moral lighthouse for European social thought. In 1988, the Swedish Parliament passed, virtually unopposed, what the *New York Times* called a "Bill of Rights" for farm animals, abolishing in Sweden, in a series of timed steps, the confinement systems currently dominating North American agriculture. Much of northern Europe has followed suit, and the European Union is moving in a similar direction. Very recently, activists in the United States have begun to turn their attention to animal agriculture, and it is reasonable to expect U.S. society to eventually demand changes similar to those that have occurred in Europe. Dozens of law schools now teach courses in animal law, and many legal scholars are developing strategies to raise the legal status of animals from property.

Although the Western social ethic has always, from Biblical times onward, contained provisions relating to animals, these have been very minimalistic, basically forbidding overt deliberate, purposeless, sadistic cruelty and egregious neglect. Why have the last three decades witnessed the proliferation of concern about all areas of animal use and treatment and seen a correlative demand for a new ethic that goes well beyond cruelty?

There are, I believe, five reasons for this phenomenon. First, traditional animal use was largely husbandry agriculture, where producers did well if and only if animals did well. Thus producers put animals into optimal conditions for which the animals were biologically suited and supplemented their ability to survive with food during famine, water during drought, protection from predation, etc., so proper animal treatment followed from self-interest! Only the anti-cruelty ethic was needed to supplement self-interest by flagging sadists and psychopaths who hurt animals for no reason. The rise of industrialized agriculture and biomedical research after World War II made traditional moral categories for animals obsolete. For both of these pursuits were not husbandry, both caused animal suffering, yet were not initiated by motives of cruelty. Confinement agriculturalists sought cheap and plentiful food in the face of rising population and shrinking agricultural land; researchers sought knowledge of disease. Yet both led to suffering on a scale far greater than cruelty, necessitating a new ethical vocabulary.

Second, the last fifty years have witnessed a major increase in ethical sensitivity toward disenfranchised humans—black people, third world people, women, the handicapped, children. This sentiment inevitably grew to include animals, with many leaders in the animal movement coming from other social movements.

Third, fewer and fewer people make their living directly from animals, with far less than 2 percent of the public engaged in animal production. Correlatively, the social paradigm for an animal has changed from a cow or horse (i.e., a work or food animal) to a companion animal. Most of the public professes to see their pets as "members of the family".

Fourth, an increasingly urban public has an endless fascination with animals and their behavior and treatment. Thus one finds animal stories occupying the greatest amount of television time during a week. "Animals sell papers," as one reporter said to me.

Finally, extremely bright and articulate people have sensed the need for a new ethic for animals, and attempted to provide one. Though largely philosophers, this group also includes scientists like Marc Bekoff and Jane Goodall. And, in a departure from usual philosophical practice, these philosophers have written books aimed not so much at other philosophers, as at the public. Such thinkers as Peter Singer, Tom Regan, Mary Midgley, David DeGrazia, Andrew Linzey, Steve Sapontzis, and Evelyn Pluhar have written persuasively and intelligently, articulating a new ethic, though with some family disagreements. Singer's *Animal Liberation* has been steadily in print since 1975; my *Animal Rights and Human Morality* since 1981.

This anthology is far and away the best, most comprehensive, and readable introduction to a full range of issues associated with the new thinking and concern about animal treatment. Drawing from the best writing by both philosophers and scientists, Professors Armstrong and Botzler have created a book that provides a firm conceptual basis for anyone interested in issues of animal treatment and animal ethics. Excellent and comprehensive as it is, this book should help create many new college and university courses in animal ethics by providing a wonderful assembly of relevant readings and suggestions for additional readings in an accessible format. In addition, it should be required reading for those people who use animals and wish to understand this powerful new social movement having direct impact on their livelihood. This book is no slapdash assembly of obvious readings hurriedly gathered together to take advantage of an increasing market, but rather a true product of intensive scholarship and reflection. I applaud the editors for undertaking this difficult and much-needed project, and for achieving their goals in such a masterful way.

Bernard E. Rollin, University Distinguished Professor, Professor of Philosophy, Professor of Animal Sciences, Professor of Biomedical Sciences, University Bioethicist.

Colorado State University

Acknowledgments

Snyder, G. "Gatha for all threatened beings," *Left Out in the Rain: New Poems 1947–1985*, North Point Press. Copyright 1986 Gary Snyder. Reprinted with permission of the author.

Part I   Theories of Animal Ethics

1 Regan, T. (1983) *The Case for Animal Rights*, pp. 151–4, 235–9, 242–5, 248, 280, 303–8, 324. Copyright 1983 The Regents of the University of California. Reprinted with the permission of University of California Press.
2 Cohen, C. "Reply to Tom Regan," from *The Animal Rights Debate*, C. Cohen and T. Regan (eds). Copyright 2001 Rowman & Littlefield. Reproduced with permission of Rowman & Littlefield.
3 Cavalieri, P. "For an Expanded Theory of Human Rights," Copyright 2001 Paola Cavalieri. Used by permission of Oxford University Press, Inc.
4 Singer, P. (1993) *Practical Ethics*, 2nd ed., pp. 56–72, 78, 80–1, 119–22. Copyright Cambridge University Press, 1993. Reprinted with the permission of Cambridge University Press.
5 Donovan, J. excerpt from "Animal Rights and Feminist Theory," from *Signs*. Copyright University of Chicago. All rights reserved. Reprinted with permission of the University of Chicago Press.
6 Frey, R.G. excerpt from "Rights, Interests, Desires and Beliefs," from *American Philosophical Quarterly* 16. 3. Copyright 1979 North American Philosophical Publications. Reprinted with permission of University of Illinois Press.
7 DeGrazia, D. "Equal Consideration and Unequal Moral Status," *The Southern Journal of Philosophy* 31. 1. Copyright 1993 Southern Journal of Philosophy. Reprinted with permission of the Southern Journal of Philosophy.

Part II   Animal Capacities: Pain, Emotion, Consciousness

8 Rollin, B. "Scientific Ideology, Anthropomorphism, Anecdote, and Ethics," reprinted from *New Ideas in Psychology* 13: 109–18. Copyright 2000, with permission from Elsevier Science.
9 Smuts, B. "Reflections," in *The Lives of Animals*, J.M. Coetzee (ed.), pp. 108–14. Copyright 1999 Princeton University Press. Reprinted by permission of Princeton University Press.

10 Bermond, B. "The Myth of Animal Suffering," in *Animal Consciousness and Animal Ethics*, Marcel Dol *et al.* (eds), pp. 125–30, 135–6. Copyright 1997 Van Gorcum Publishers.

11 Rollin, B. "Animal Pain: The Ideology Cashed Out," from *The Unheeded Cry*. Copyright 1998 Iowa State University Press. Reprinted by permission of Iowa State University Press.

12 Varner, G. "How Facts Matter," in *Pain Forum* 8 (2): 85–6. Reprinted with permission of W.B. Saunders, an imprint of Elsevier Science (USA).

13 Dawkins, M.S. "Animal Minds and Animal Emotions," in *American Zoologist* 40: 883–8. Used by permission of *American Zoologist*. Copyright 2000.

14 Moss, C. "A Passionate Devotion," in *The Smile of a Dolphin*, M. Bekoff (ed.) Copyright 2000 Discovery Communications, Inc. Reproduced with permission of Marc Bekoff.

15 Panskepp, J. "The Rat Will Play," from *The Smile of a Dolphin*, Marc Bekoff (ed.). Copyright 2003 Marc Bekoff. Reproduced with permission of Marc Bekoff.

16 Lawrence, D.H. "Love Was Once a Little Boy". Copyright 1925 Centaur Press, copyright renewed 1953 by Frieda Lawrence Ravaglia, from *Phoenix II: Uncollected Papers of D.H. Lawrence*, edited by W. Roberts and H.T. Moore. Excerpt pp. 446–7. Used by permission of Viking Penguin, a division of Penguin Putnam Inc. Reprinted by permission of Pollinger, Ltd and the estate of Frieda Lawrence Ravagli.

17 Griffin, D. "In Favor of Animal Consciousness" pp. 11–19 in *Animal Minds: Beyond Cognition to Consciousness*, Chicago: University of Chicago Press. Copyright 1992, 2001 the University of Chicago. Reprinted with permission of the University of Chicago Press.

Part III   Primates and Cetaceans

18 Bekoff, M. "Deep Ethology, Animal Rights, and the Great Ape/Animal Project: Resisting Speciesism and Expanding the Community of Equals," in *Journal of Agricultural and Environmental Ethics* 10: 269–96. Reprinted with kind permission of Kluwer Academic Press.

19 Savage-Rumbaugh, S., Fields, W.M., and Taglialatela, J. "Ape Consciousness – Human Consciousness: A Perspective Informed by Language and Culture," in *American Zoologist* 40: 910–21.

20 Whiten, A. *et al.* "Cultures in Chimpanzees," in *Nature*, 1999 vol. 399: 682–5. Reprinted with permission of Macmillan publishers.

21 Gómez, J.C. excerpt from "Are Apes Persons? The Case for Primate Intersubjectivity," from *Etica and Animali*. Copyright 1998 Juan Carlos Gomez and Paola Cavalieri. Reprinted with permission of Juan Carlos Gomez and Paola Cavalieri.

22 Peavey, F. "The Chimpanzee at Stanford," from *Heart Politics*. Copyright 1986 Fran Peavey. Reprinted with the permission of Fran Peavey.

23 Goodall, J. "Foreword. Problems Faced by Wild and Captive Chimpanzees: Finding Solutions", pp. xiii–xxiv in *Great Apes and Humans: The Ethics of Coexistence*, B.B. Beck, T.S. Stoinksi, M. Hutchins, T.L. Maple, B.G. Norton, A. Rowan, E.F Stevens, and A. Arluke (eds). Reprinted with permission of Smithsonian Institution Press.

24 Rendell, L. and Whitehead, H. "Culture in Whales and Dolphins," in *Behavioral and Brain Sciences* 24: 2, pp. 309–19, 322–4. Reprinted with permission of Cambridge University Press.

25 Herman, L.M. "Exploring the Cognitive World of the Bottlenosed Dolphin," in *The*

Cognitive Animal: Empirical and Theoretical Perspectives on Animal Cognition, M. Bekoff, C. Allen and G.M. Burkhardt (eds). Copyright Massachusetts Institute of Technology. Reprinted with the permission of MIT Press.

26 Midgley, M. "Is a Dolphin a Person?" in *Utopias, Dolphins and Computers*. Copyright Mary Midgley. Reprinted with the permission of Mary Midgley.

Part IV Animals for Food

27 DeGrazia, D. "Meat-Eating," reprinted from DeGrazia, D. *Animal Rights: A Very Short Introduction*. Copyright 2002 David DeGrazia. Reprinted by permission of Oxford University Press.

28 Grandin, T. "Thinking Like Animals" from *Intimate Nature*, L. Hogan, L. Metzger and B. Peterson (eds). Copyright 1998 Temple Grandin. Reprinted with permission of Temple Grandin.

29 Grandin, T. "Progress in Livestock Handling and Slaughter Techniques in the United States, 1970–2000," in *The State of Animals 2001*, Salem, D.J. and Rowan, A.N. (eds), published by Humane Society Press, Washington D.C. Copyright The Humane Society of the United States. Reprinted with permission of the Humane Society of the United States.

30 Animal Agriculture Alliance. "Myths and Facts," copyright 1998 Animal Industry Foundation. Reprinted with the permission of the Animal Agriculture Alliance.

31 Wemelsfelder, F. "Lives of Quiet Desperation," from *The Smile of a Dolphin*, M. Bekoff (ed). Copyright 2000 Discovery Communications, Inc.

32 Stephens, W.O. "Five Arguments for Vegetarianism," from *Philosophy in the Contemporary World* 1,4: 25–39 (excerpted). Used with permission of William O. Stephens.

33 Adams, C.M. "The Rape of Animals, the Butchering of Women" from *Sexual Politics of Meat: A feminist-vegetarian critical theory*." Copyright 1990 Continuum Publishing Company. Reproduced with permission of Continuum Publishing Company.

34 George, K.P. excerpt from "A Feminist Critique of Ethical Vegetarianism," reprinted by permission from *Animal, Vegetable, or Woman? A Feminist Critique of Ethical Vegetarianism* by Kathryn Paxton George, the State University of New York Press copyright 2000, State University of New York. All rights reserved.

35 Solomon, N. "Judaism," in *Attitudes to Nature*, Holm. J, (ed.). London: Pinter, pp. 109–10. Reprinted with permission from Norman Solomon and Jean Holm.

36 Fuchs, Rabbi S. "Enhancing the Divine Image," from *Rabbis and Vegetarianism: An Evolving Tradition*. Copyright 1995 Micah Publications. Reproduced with permission of Micah Publications.

37 Linzey, A. Revised version of "The Bible and Killing for Food," originally published in Dan Cohn-Sherbok (ed.) *Using the Bible Today*, Bellew Publishing, copyright 1991 and 2002 Andrew Linzey. Reprinted with permission of Andrew Linzey.

38 Forward, M. and M. Alam, "Islam," in *Attitudes to Nature*, J. Holm (ed.), reprinted with permission of Martin Forward and Jean Holm.

39 Fox, M.W. "India's Sacred Cow: Her Plight and Future," copyright Michael W. Fox. Reprinted with permission of Michael W. Fox.

Part V Animal Experimentation

40 Regan, T. *The Case for Animal Rights*, pp. 151–4, 235–9, 242–5, 248, 280, 303–8, 324.

Copyright 1983 University of California. Reprinted with permission of University of California Press.

41 DeGrazia, D. "The Ethics of Animal Research: What are the Prospects for Agreement?" from *Cambridge Quarterly of Healthcare Ethics* (1999) 8: 23–34. Copyright 1999 Cambridge University Press. Reprinted with the permission of Cambridge University Press.

42 Brody, B.A. "Defending Animal Research: An International Perspective." Reprinted from Ellen Frankel Paul and Jeffrey Paul (eds), *Why Animal Experimentation Matters: The Use of Animals in Medical Research* (New Brunswick, NJ: Transaction Publishers and the Social Philosophy and Policy Foundation, 2001), pp. 131–47. Reprinted with the permission of Transaction Publishers, the Social Philosophy and Policy Foundation and Baruch A. Brody.

43 Farnsworth, E.J. and Rosovsky, J. "The Ethics of Ecological Field Experimentation," in *Conservation Biology* 7: 463–72. Copyright Society for Conservation Biology. Reprinted with permission of Blackwell Publishing Ltd.

44 Emlen, S.T. "Ethics and Experimentation: Hard Choices for the Field Ornithologist," in *The Auk* 110: 406–9.

45 Orlans, F.B. "Ethical Themes of National Regulations Governing Animal Experiments," pp. 131–47. From *Applied Ethics in Animal Research: Philosophy, Regulation and Laboratory Applications*. Copyright Purdue University Press. Reprinted by permission. Unauthorized duplication not permitted.

46 Balcombe, J. "Summary of Recommendations," pp. 81–3 in *The Use of Animals in Higher Education: Problems, Alternatives and Recommendations* published by the Humane Society Press, Washington, D.C. Copyright 2000 The Humane Society of the United States.

47 Petto, A.J. and K.D. Russell, "Humane Education: The Role of Animal-based Learning." Excerpts from pp. 167–85 in *Attitudes to Animals: Views in Animal Welfare*. Copyright Cambridge University Press. Reprinted with permission of Cambridge University Press.

Part VI Animals and Biotechnology

48 Bruce, D. and A. Bruce "Genetic Engineering and Animal Welfare," from *Engineering Genesis: The Ethics of Genetic Engineering in Non-Human Species*. Copyright 1998 Science, Religion and Technology Project. Reprinted with permission of Kogan Page Publishers.

49 Smith, K. "Animal Genetic Manipulation: A Utilitarian Response," from *Bioethics* 16 (1): 55–71. Published by Blackwell Publishing Ltd. Reprinted with permission of Blackwell Publishing Ltd.

50 Burkhardt, J. "The Inevitability of Animal Biotechnology? Ethics and the Scientific Attitude," from *Animal Biotechnology and Ethics*, A. Holland and A. Johnson (eds). Copyright Kluwer Academic/Plenum Publishers. Reprinted with kind permission from Kluwer.

51 Rollin, B. "On Telos and Genetic Engineering," pp. 156–87 in *Animal Biotechnology and Ethics*, A. Holland and A. Johnson (eds). Copyright Kluwer Academic/Plenum Publishers. Reprinted with kind permission from Kluwer.

52 Bovenkerk, B., Brom, F.W.A. and van den Bergh, B.J. "Brave New Birds: The Use of Integrity in Animal Ethics". *Hastings Center Report* 32(1): 16–22. Copyright Hastings Center. Reprinted with permission of the Hastings Center.

53 Frey, R.G. "Organs for Transplant: Animals, Moral Standing, and One View of the

Ethics of Xenotransplantation," pp. 190–208 in *American Biotechnology and Ethics*, A. Holland and A. Johnson (eds). Copyright Kluwer Academic/Plenum Publishers. Reprinted with kind permission from Kluwer.

54 Francione, G.L. "Xenografts and Animal Rights," in *Transplantation Proceedings* 22(3): 1044–6. Copyright 1990. Reprinted with permission from Elsevier Science.

55 Ryder, O. A. "Cloning Advances and Challenges for Conservation," from *Trends in Biotechnology* vol. 20, pp. 231–3. Copyright 2002, with permission from Elsevier Science.

Part VII   Ethics and Wildlife

56 Callicott, J.B. "The Philosophical Value of Wildlife," in *Valuing Wildlife: Economic and Social Perspective*, D.J. Decker and G.R. Goff (eds), Copyright D.J. Decker. Reprinted with permission of D.J. Decker.

57 Leopold, A. Extract from "A Sand County Almanac: And Sketches Here and There," copyright 1949, 1977 by Oxford University Press, Inc. Used by permission of Oxford University Press, Inc.

58 Kheel, M. "The Killing Game: An Ecofeminist Critique of Hunting," *Journal of the Philosophy of Sport* 23: 30–44. Used by permission of the Human Kinetics Publishers.

59 Gunn, A. "Environmental Ethics and Trophy Hunting," in *Ethics and the Environment* 6: 68–95. Copyright Indiana University Press. Reprinted with permission of Indiana University Press.

60 Varner, G. "Can Animal Rights Activists be Environmentalists?" from *Environmental Philosophy and Environmental Activism*, D.E. Marietta and L. Embree (eds). Copyright Rowman and Littlefield.

61 Albrecht, G. "Thinking Like an Ecosystem: The Ethics of the Relocation, Rehabilitation and Release of Wildlife," from *Animal Issues*. Reprinted with permission of G. Albrecht.

62 Duke, G.E. "Wildlife Rehabilitation: Is it Significant?" in *Proceedings of the National Wildlife Rehabilitation Symposium* 6: 141–4. Reprinted with permission of the National Wildlife Rehabilitators Association, copyright 1987.

63 Hettinger, N. "Exotic Species, Naturalisation, and Biological Nativism," *Environmental Values* 10: 193–224. Copyright The White Horse Press, Cambridge, UK. Reprinted by permission of The White Horse Press.

Part VIII   Zoos, Aquariums, and Animals in Entertainment

64 Eaton, R.L. "Orcas and Dolphins in Captivity," in *The Orca Project – A Meeting of Nations: An Anthology*, copyright 1998 Randall Eaton. Reprinted with permission of Randall Eaton.

65 Regan, T. "Are Zoos Morally Defensible?" pp. 38–51 in *Ethics of the Ark: Zoos, Animal Welfare and Wildlife Conservation*, B.G. Norton, M. Hutchins, E.F. Stevens and T.L. Maple (eds), copyright Smithsonian Institution Press. Used by permission of Smithsonian Institution Press.

66 Hutchins, M. Dresser, B and Wemmer, C. "Ethical Considerations in Zoos and Aquarium Research," in *Ethics of the Ark: Zoos, Animal Welfare and Wildlife Conservation*, B.G. Norton, M. Hutchins, E.F. Stevens and T.L. Maple (eds), copyright Smithsonian Institution Press. Used by permission of Smithsonian Institution Press.

67 Lindburg, D.G. "Zoos and the Rights of Animals," from *Zoo Biology* 1999: 18. Copyright 1999 Lindburg. This material is used by permission of Wiley-Liss, Inc., a subsidiary of John Wiley & Sons, Inc.

68 Wemmer, C. "Opportunities Lost: Zoos and the Marsupial that Tried to be a Wolf", from *Zoo Biology* 2002:21. Copyright 2002 Wemmer. This material is used by permission of Wiley-Liss, Inc., a subsidiary of John Wiley & Sons, Inc.

69 Preece, R. and Chamberlain, L. "Animals in Entertainment: Racing, Riding, and Fighting," from *Animal Welfare and Human Values*, pp. 161–84. Copyright 1993 Wilfrid Laurier University Press. Reprinted with permission of Wilfrid Laurier University Press.

70 Rollin, B.E. "Rodeo and Recollection – Applied Ethics and Western Philosophy," in *Journal of the Philosophy of Sport* 23: 1–9. Used by permission of the Human Kinetics Publishers.

Part IX   Animal Companions

71 Lorenz, K. "Affection's Claim," from *Man Meets Dog* by Konrad Lorenz. Copyright for the English translation: 1999 Deutscher Taschenbuch Verlag, Munchen.

72 Rollin, B. E. and Rollin, M.D.H. "Dogmatisms and Catechisms: Ethics and Companion Animals," in *Anthrozoos*, vol. 14, no. 1, pp. 4–11. Reprinted with permission of the International Society for Anthrozoology (ISAZ).

73 Shepard, P. "The Pet World," in *The Other: How Animals made us Human* copyright 1996 Paul Shepard.

74 Merz, A. "Hand Raising a Rhino in the Wild," from *Intimate Nature* Hogan, L., Metger, D. and Peterson, B. (eds), pp. 291–4. Copyright 1998 Anna Merz. Reprinted with permission from Anna Merz.

75 Mathews, F. "Living with Animals," in *Animal Issues* 1.1: 1–18. Excerpt reprinted with permission of Freya Mathews.

76 Garbarino, J. "Protecting Children and Animals from Abuse: A Trans-Species Concept of Caring," from *Child Abuse, Domestic Violence and Animal Abuse*. Copyright 1999 Purdue University Press. Reprinted by permission.

77 Serpall, J.A, Coppinger, R. and Fine, A.H. "The Welfare of Assistance and Therapy Animals: An Ethical Comment," in *Handbook on Animal-assisted Therapy*. Reprinted with permission.

78 Brown, S.W. and Strong, V. "The Use of Seizure-Alert Dogs" in *Seizure: European Journal of Epilepsy* 10.1: 30–41, Copyright 2001, WB Saunders. Reprinted by permission of the publisher WB Saunders.

Part X   Animal Law/Animal Activisim

79 Wise, S.M. "The Great Shout: Legal Rights for Great Apes," from *Great Apes and Humans: The Ethics of Coexistence*, B.B. Beck, T.S. Stoinksi, M. Hutchins, T.L. Maple, B.G. Norton, A. Rowan, E.F. Stevens, and A. Arluke (eds). Copyright 2001 by Smithsonian Institution Press. Reprinted with permission of Smithsonian Institution Press.

80 Posner, R.A. "Book Review: *Rattling the Cage*: *Toward Legal Rights for Animals* by Steven M. Wise". Reprinted with permission of The Yale Law Journal Company and William S. Hein Company from *The Yale Law Journal*, vol. 110, pages 527–41.

81 Epstein, R.A. "The Dangerous Claims of the Animal Rights Movement," from *The*

Responsive Community, copyright 2000 Richard Epstein. Reprinted with permission of Richard Epstein.

82 Jamison, W.V., Wenk, C. and Parker, J.V. "Every Sparrow that Falls: Understanding Animal Rights Activism as Functional Religion," in *Society and Animals* 8.3. Copyright 2000 Brill Academic Publishers. Reprinted with permission of Brill Academic Publishers.

83 Regan, T. "Understanding Animal Rights Violence," in *Defending Animal Rights* Regan, T. (ed). Used with permission.

84 Dillard, C.L. "Civil Disobedience: A Case Study in Factors of Effectiveness", in *Society and Animals* 10.1, pp. 47–62. Copyright 2002 Brill Academic Publishers. Reprinted with permission of Brill Academic Publishers.

85 DeRose, C. *In Your Face: From Actor to Activist*. Copyright 1997 Los Angeles: Duncan Publishing. Reprinted with permission of Chris DeRose.

86 Singer, P. "Ten Ways to Make a Difference," in *Ethics into Action*, pp. 184–92. Copyright Rowman and Littlefield Publishers, Inc. Reprinted with permission.

Every effort has been made to trace all copyright holders. If any have been inadvertently overlooked, the publishers will be pleased to make the necessary arrangements at the first opportunity.

Gatha[1] for All Threatened Beings

Ah Power that swirls us together
Grant us Bliss
Grant us the great release
And to all Beings
Vanishing, wounded
In trouble on earth,
We pass on this love
May their numbers increase.
                    Gary Snyder

[1] "Gatha" is a Sanskrit word meaning "a small instructive verse"

General Introduction

Animal Ethics: A Sketch of How it Developed and Where it is Now

> ... We have thought too little about the shape and sources of our most basic attitudes.
>
> James Turner *Reckoning with the Beast* (1980: 140)

Historians estimate that the "hunter-gatherer" stage of human societies began around 500,000 years ago and lasted until about 11,000 years ago (Serpell 1999: 40). While there are problems with using living or recent hunter-gatherers as representatives of our pre-agricultural ancestors, a "remarkable degree of consistency" in attitudes and beliefs toward animals exists among present-day hunter-gatherer societies. Animals are perceived as being fully rational, sentient, and intelligent, with bodies animated by non-corporeal spirits or souls (Serpell 1999: 40). Hunted animals must therefore be treated with proper respect and consideration. Serpell (1999: 41) locates the origin of contemporary hunting rules and rituals in these beliefs.

Agriculture and animal husbandry began roughly 11,000 years ago, producing a "dramatic shift in the balance of power between humans and the animals they depended on for food." At first animal guardian spirits were elevated to the status of "zoomorphic gods" (Serpell 1999: 43). For example, the first known written expression of prohibition to cruelty to animals is found in ancient Egypt, and this prohibition seems to be at least partly based on the belief that "all creatures were manifestations of the divine" (LaRue 1991: 3). Some gods assumed animal form. The list of sacred animals included "the vulture, hawks, swallows, turtles, scorpions, serpents" (LaRue 1991: 3). Chapter 125 of the Egyptian *Book of the Dead* prohibited mistreatment of animals (LaRue 1991: 34). While the ancient Egyptians ate animals, humans were expected to treat other creatures with respect and kindness, "for in the afterlife the treatment of animals would be included in actions to be judged" (LaRue 1991: 35). Cattle, particularly bulls, were the pre-eminent models for power and fertility. In Egypt, as well as other ancient civilizations, both dogs and snakes were strongly associated with death and healing. In early Mesopotamia, sheep began to fulfill an important surrogate religious role as substitute cattle (Schwabe 1994: 48–9).

This respectful relationship was not to last. As Serpell (1999: 43) points out, over time the connections between the gods and animals became more and more tenuous. The gods became increasingly associated with the agricultural cycle, and wholesale animal sacrifice was used as a way to please them. Religious belief systems became increasingly hierarchical.

This change was slow and complex, as can be seen in the intermittent history of vegetarianism (Dombrowski 1984: 1–2). Vegetarian communities may have existed as long as 8,000 years ago in the Mesolithic period.[1] Ryder affirms that by the time of the Middle Kingdom in Egypt, vegetarianism was common at least among priests, and neither pork nor beef were widely eaten (Ryder 1998: 6). The Greek poet Hesiod told of a Golden Age in which the first race of human beings were free from all sorrow, toil, grief, and evil. They were fed out of a boundless cornucopia of fruit. This Age of Cronus was followed by other less idyllic ages, but the nostalgia for earlier times remained into the time of the pre-Socratic philosopher Empedocles

(495–435 BCE), who said that to kill an animal for food or sacrifice was "the greatest abomination among men" (Dombrowski 1984: 19–22).

The mathematic genius and mystic Pythagorus most probably lived in the sixth century BCE. He seems to have based his vegetarianism on the religious belief in transmigration of souls between animals and human beings, concerns for health, and ethical concerns. Even in moments of great mathematical achievements, Pythagorus remained true to his vegetarian principles: it is related that he once sacrificed an ox made of dough when he found the square of the hypotenuse of a right triangle equal to the sum of the squares of the other sides (Dombrowski 1984: 38). Pythagorus' ethical concerns were founded on a principle of moderation. He believed that we have no right to cause unnecessary suffering. Animals have the same soul as we do; those who senselessly kill animals are murderers (Dombrowski 1984: 46).

While Socrates (470–399 BCE) was generally indifferent to what he ate (Dombrowski 1984: 55), Plato (428–347 BCE), strongly influenced by Pythagorus, affirmed both that those living in the age of Cronus were vegetarians and that philosophers should be vegetarians (Dombrowski 1984: 58ff). Animals share with humans the part of the soul which is mortal but not intrinsically irrational (*Timaeus* 69c–77c, 90e–92c). Nevertheless Plato does not condemn hunting, butchering, or raising livestock for consumption.

Aristotle (384–322 BCE) not only permitted meat-eating, but seems to have been opposed to vegetarianism (Dombrowski 1984: 65–6). While he affirmed that in each animal "there is something natural and beautiful," (*On the Parts of Animals* Bk. I, ch. 5), Aristotle contended that because animals lacked reason they had no moral status. Augustine and Thomas Aquinas both followed Aristotle in this view, thus greatly influencing the development of the Christian view of animals (Ryder 1998: 8).

Beginning in the first century CE, Stoic philosophers believed that logos (reason) was both divine and a cosmic law, and that everything serves some purpose. Thus animals cannot be members of our moral community because they lack reason; nevertheless, their usefulness to human beings reflects divine intention (Boersema 2001: 202–3). While the Romans Seneca and Ovid advocated vegetarianism, animals simply did not count morally for most Romans (Dombrowski 1984: 85).

Plutarch (45–125 CE) was a Greek priest at Delphi. Dombrowski notes that he may have been the first to advocate vegetarianism on grounds of universal benevolence, rather than on the basis of transmigration of souls (Dombrowski 1984: 86–7). He strove to convince the Stoics that animals are indeed rational, and he was the only early thinker whose beliefs have had a demonstrable influence in later ages (Boersema 2001: 208). Plutarch suggested that sentiency is a matter of degree (Dombrowski 1984: 88). For Plutarch the difference between domesticated and wild (and harmful) animals is morally significant; we may not harm harmless animals. "Plutarch challenged his antagonists to use their teeth to rend a lamb asunder and consume it raw, as true carnivores do" (Boersema 2001: 209). Overall, Plutarch exhibited a love of animals, "but never at the expense of the human race" (Boersema 2001: 210).

The great neo-Platonic philosopher Plotinus (204–270 CE) as well as his distinguished pupil Porphyry (232–c.305 CE) were vegetarians. Plotinus affirmed transmigration of souls and animals' capacity for suffering. But Porphyry went far beyond these affirmations. According to Dombrowski, he deserves recognition for having provided "the most comprehensive and subtly reasoned treatment of vegetarianism by an ancient philosopher" (Dombrowski 1984: 107). He not only offers the best possible reasons for vegetarianism but he collects the best reasons against it (Dombrowski 1984: 109–19). Nevertheless, despite the views of thinkers such as Plutarch and Porphyry, the attitude toward nature and animals in ancient cultures was largely dependent upon whether nature or the animals in question were perceived as helpful or harmful to human beings.

Western European culture has been largely shaped by Christianity, in the broad sense of a tradition which includes the heritage of classical antiquity and the Middle East (Boersema 2001: 231). Thus throughout the medieval period the influences of Greek philosophers, in particular Aristotle, and of the Stoics continued to be felt, in addition to more narrowly conceived Christian themes.[2] The importance of animals was taken for granted, and as a consequence animal symbolism was pervasive. But just as in our own contemporary times, medieval society was deeply ambivalent toward animals: clerical culture attempted to distance the human from the animal as far as possible, whereas lay culture attributed to animals human traits and feelings (Cohen 1994: 68). Animals were kept as pets, considered to possess human virtues, and even tried by the courts and convicted of crimes. Ryder cites the case of a greyhound, unjustly executed after rescuing a child in twelfth century France, which acquired the name Saint Guinefort. Miracles were performed at his tomb until the cult was suppressed by Dominicans. Masses were said for horses, and sick animals were shown the eucharistic bread to cure them (Ryder 1998: 14). Many early Christian saints showed deep concern for animals, for example, in rescuing animals from hunters, talking with animals, sharing their food, and caring for sick or wounded animals. St Benedict (c. 480–547) the founder of the Benedictine order, stated that monks should not eat meat except when sick. (This rule was ignored, however, after the reinterpretation of Christianity by Thomas Aquinas in the thirteenth century.) The Hermit of Eskedale was killed in 1159 after sabotaging a hunt (Ryder 1998: 34–5). St Francis of Assisi (c. 1181–1226) saw all creatures as mirrors of the creator. Legend tells of him prevailing upon a wolf to stop eating townspeople (Ryder 1989: 33).

The sixteenth and seventeenth centuries in Europe were a time of great social change. The confluence of early capitalism, the beginnings of modern science, the dualistic thinking expressed by René Descartes (1596–1650) and others, as well as the emergence of Protestantism, helped ensure that Christians ended any lingering deification of nature. Humans asserted their own importance, throwing off their medieval belief in the unity of creation and seeking to deny their own animal natures by emphasizing the boundaries between man and animals. Renaissance writers insisted on the uniqueness and importance of human beings. Nature, including animals, was no longer an organic whole but dead, soulless matter, indeed a machine, from which the minds and immortal souls of human beings were entirely distinct. All things were created principally for the benefit and pleasure of "man." According to Descartes and many others, human beings were distinguished from animals by the possession of speech, reason, the capacity for moral responsibility, and an immortal soul. Bestiality became a capital offense in 1534, and, except for a brief period, remained so until 1861 (Thomas 1983: 30). Cruel medieval practices such as bearbaiting and persecution of cats continued, to be joined by the dissection of living animals (vivisection) for scientific purposes.

Thomas asserts that "the most powerful argument for the Cartesian position was that it was the best possible rationalization for the way man actually treated animals" (1983: 34). The view that there was a total qualitative difference between humans and animals was "propounded in every pulpit" and underlay everyone's behavior (Thomas 1983: 35–6). Yet there were prominent dissenters throughout these centuries, including the vegetarian Leonardo da Vinci, who purchased birds in the marketplace to free them, the essayist Michel de Montaigne who attacked cruelty in his essays of 1580, and William Shakespeare, who vividly depicted the suffering of animals. Martin Luther and John Calvin expressed concern for God's creatures. Sir Isaac Newton (1642–1727) invented cat flaps, and the great English philosopher John Locke (1632–1704) affirmed that children should be brought up to show kindness to animals. British Chief Justice Sir Matthew Hale wrote in 1661 that "I have ever thought that there was a certain degree of justice due from man to the creatures, as from man to man" (Ryder 1998: 13–14). And in 1683 Thomas Tyron, a Christian theologian, produced what may be the first printed use of the term "rights" in connection with animals (Munro 2000: 9).

Despite these examples of compassion for animals, in the seventeenth century the most common view held by intellectuals was that "beasts" had an inferior kind of reason which included sensibility, imagination, and memory but no power of reflection (Thomas 1983: 32–3). Thus, perhaps not surprisingly, the reform movements of the sixteenth and seventeenth centuries were based on the same ideology of human domination as were the oppressions they sought to reform. Slavery was attacked because people were being treated like animals, but the slavery of animals was taken for granted. The main dispute during this period was thus between those who held that all humanity had dominion over the creatures, and those who believed that this dominion should be confined to a privileged group of humans (Thomas 1983: 48–9).

But at the same time there were social changes which worked against the idea of human dominion. For example, pet keeping had been fashionable among the well-to-do as well as among religious orders in the Middle Ages, but it was in the sixteenth and seventeenth centuries that pets seemed to have established themselves as a normal feature of the middle-class household (Thomas 1983: 110). Pets included monkeys, tortoises, otters, rabbits, and squirrels, as well as hares, mice, hedgehogs, bats, and toads. Cage-birds were also common, including canaries as well as wild birds of every kind. Gradually, the idea that tamed animals were property was developed. Pets were distinguished by being allowed into the house and by going to church with their human companions, by being given individual personal names, and by never being eaten. The spread of pet-keeping created the psychological foundation for the view that some animals were entitled to moral consideration (Thomas 1983: 110–19).

In England, the growth of towns and the emergence of an industrial order in which animals became increasingly marginal to production were significant factors in the development of concern for animals' rights (Thomas 1983: 181). The reformist movements were expressed either by well-to-do townspeople or by educated country clergymen (Thomas 1983: 182). The professional middle classes were unsympathetic to the warlike traditions of the aristocracy, which had valued hunting because it simulated warfare, and cock-fighting and bearbaiting because they represented private combat (Thomas 1983: 181). By the later seventeenth century the human-centered (anthropocentric) tradition itself was being eroded. According to Thomas, this erosion is one of the great revolutions in modern Western thought, a revolution to which many factors contributed (Thomas 1983: 166).

Thomas cites factors such as the growth of natural history, which gradually resulted in classifications of animals according to the animals' structure alone, as well as a delight in the world's diversity at least somewhat independent of human standards. Second, people's actual experience of animals on the farms and in their houses conflicted with the theological orthodoxies of the time. Animals were everywhere and consequently were often thought of as individuals, since herds were small. Shepherds knew the faces of their sheep and some farmers could trace stolen cattle by distinguishing their hoof prints (Thomas 1983: 95). Anthropocentrism was still the prevailing outlook, but by the eighteenth century non-anthropocentric sensibilities became much more widely dispersed and were more explicitly supported by the religious and philosophical teaching of the time (Thomas 1987: 174–5). Cruelty to animals began to be regularly denounced. Ryder speculates that one reason for this moral awakening was the extreme cruelty which had been practiced in England for centuries (Ryder 1998: 16). English reformists targeted bullbaiting and bearbaiting, the treatment of horses, the treatment of cattle being driven to slaughter through the streets of London, and the traditional Shrove Tuesday sport of tying a cockerel to a stake and stoning him to death (Ryder 1998: 16). The campaign against cruelty to animals was enhanced by a new emphasis on sensation and feeling as the true basis of moral status (Thomas 1983: 180), as expounded in the utilitarianism of Jeremy Bentham. Once it had been accepted that animals had feelings and therefore should be treated with kindness, it seemed increasingly repugnant to kill them for meat (Thomas 1983: 288). From about 1790 there developed a highly articulate vegetarian movement (Thomas 1983: 295). An increasing number of people felt uneasy about killing animals for food, and so slaughter-houses were concealed from the public eye (Thomas 1983: 300).

By the later eighteenth century the most common view was that animals could indeed think and reason, though in an inferior way. A number of thinkers affirmed the kinship between man and "beast." Humphry Primatt published his dissertation on *The Duty of Mercy and the Sin of Cruelty to Brute Animals*, which presented almost all the arguments used in later centuries (Munro 2000: 10). There was an increasing tendency to credit animals with reason, intelligence, language and almost every other human quality (Thomas 1983: 129). Perhaps most decisive was the revelation by comparative anatomy of the similarity between the structure of human and animal bodies (Thomas 1983: 129). The growing belief in the social evolution of humankind encouraged the view that humans were only animals who had managed to better themselves (Thomas 1983: 132). A substantial number of biblical commentators took the view that animals would be eventually restored in heaven to the perfection they had enjoyed before the Fall (Thomas 1983: 139). The idea of animal immortality made more headway in England than anywhere else during this period (Thomas 1983: 140–1).

Courts in both Germany and Britain began to punish cruelty to animals on the basis that while animals themselves had no rights, maltreatment of animals violated the direct duty to God (Maehle 1994: 95–8). Eighteenth-century American writers Thomas Paine and Hermann Daggett affirmed the moral status of animals. British politicians introduced a bill to outlaw bullbaiting in 1800, but the bill was defeated. The Lord Chancellor Thomas Erskine, who had once physically attacked a man he found beating a horse, joined with Richard Martin to produce a successful bill in 1822 to make it an offense to wantonly beat, abuse or ill-treat any horse, donkey, sheep, cow or other cattle (unless it was the property of the offender). "Known as Martin's Act, this was the first national law against cruelty to animals enacted by full parliamentary process," according to Richard Ryder, though bullbaiting was not stopped until 1835 (1998: 19).

The organized animal welfare movement emerged at this time. One reason for the timing of this emergence was that after the Reformation in northern Europe "good works became increasingly secularized" (Ryder 1998: 25). Also the new general affluence of the period, teamed with increasing democracy, allowed compassionate people to institutionalize their concerns, whether it be opposed to the slave trade or to ill-treatment of animals. In addition, the Industrial Revolution was reducing the dependence on animals, particularly on horses and dogs (Boersema 2001: 237).

In 1824 a group of Members of Parliament as well as three churchmen met to establish two committees: one to publish literature to influence public opinion and the other to adopt measures for inspecting the treatment of animals. In its first year the Society for the Prevention of Cruelty to Animals (SPCA) brought "150 prosecutions for cruelty and engaged in campaigns against bullbaiting, dogfighting, the abuse of horses and cattle and the cruelties of the main London meat market at Smithfield" (Ryder 1998: 21). The society also condemned painful experiments on animals. Shortly thereafter societies were formed elsewhere in northern Europe. In 1840 Queen Victoria "granted the society the *royal* prefix," so that it became known as the "Royal Society for the Prevention of Cruelty to Animals" (RSPCA). Four of the society's founders were already well-known reformers who opposed slavery; two opposed the death penalty for minor offenses (Ryder 1998: 21–2). Kalechofsky (1992: 64) notes that throughout the nineteenth century there were "porous boundaries between the various reform causes, and those involved in anti-slavery, prison reform, and child abuse reform were often the same people involved in the women's movement, anti-vivisection, slum clearance, and the hygiene or sanitary movement . . . ." This observation works against the thesis argued by Turner (1980: 36–8) and still widely accepted, that concern for animals arose as a displaced compassion for human suffering. Finsen and Finsen name Turner's view the "Displacement Thesis" and propose instead the "Extension Thesis": namely, that those who are concerned about one exploited group will often extend that concern to other groups (1994: 28ff).

The greatest campaign of the Victorian era in Britain was against the use of live animals in experiments. Such campaigns started as an outcry against demonstrations on cats and dogs by a French experimenter, and were augmented by reports of unanesthetized horses being tied down and slowly dissected by students. Protests were made to French authorities. In England the Cruelty to Animals Act was passed in 1876, requiring licenses and certificates from the government. The bill was an inconvenience to researchers, though few prosecutions under the act were successful. After much public agitation, a Royal Commission recommended some improvements to the administration of the Act (Ryder 1998: 26–8).

Women were prominent in this anti-vivisection movement, beginning with Descartes' niece, Catherine, who famously rejected his doctrine of the "animal-machine" (Kalechofsky 1992: 61). To undermine women's effectiveness, nineteenth-century scientists viewed women as infantile, animal-like, and belonging to nature rather than to civilization. In contrast, the scientific "intellectual edifice" was identified as masculine, logical, and rational; anyone who opposed animal research was considered irrational, sentimental, and "womanly." These views were shown to be false by the many knowledgable and intellectually powerful women who combated the scientific cruelty of the time (Kalechofsky 1992: 70).

Finsen and Finsen point to the antivivisection movement as the ancestor of the animal rights movement, because the antivivisection movement, in contrast to the humane movement as represented by the RSPCA, "challenged an entire institution" (1994: 38). However, at the same time, the medical profession was attaining greater political power due to the successes in experimental medicine in the 1890s in connection with medical microbiology. The medical microbiology revolution required numerous forms of animal experimentation (Finsen and Finsen 1994: 39). For these and other reasons, as detailed by Finsen and Finsen, "the antivivisection movement ceased to be a vital and mass movement after the turn of the century," since it based its case not only on the immorality of vivisection but on its scientific worthlessness (1994: 41).

While much of the U.S. concern for animals derives from British precedents, a body of laws protecting animals had in fact been approved by the Massachusetts Bay Colony in 1641. Anticruelty laws were passed early in the nineteenth century in several states, but organizations did not form until the 1866 birth of the American Society for the Prevention of Cruelty to Animals (ASPCA). Its founder, Henry Bergh, "rapidly became notorious for defending abused and overworked carriage horses in the streets of New York City." Bergh achieved many successful prosecutions, including those for cruel treatment of livestock, cock-fighting, and dog-fighting. George Angell founded the Massachusetts SPCA, with an emphasis on humane education. Societies modeled on Bergh's soon cropped up all over the country. Shortly thereafter the American Society for the Prevention of Cruelty to Children was formed. And, as was the case in England, many of the American animal welfare pioneers were active in the antislavery movement.

However, the American antivivisection movement was unsuccessful. It appears that proponents of animal research had learned from the British lesson, and formed an effective lobbying force for vivisection (Finsen and Finsen 1994: 48–9). Some vivisectors portrayed themselves as rational men of science whose work was being retarded by "middle-class, city-based female 'cranks' in humane societies" (Munro 2000: 18). Ryder speculates that the pioneering spirit of America may have welcomed the innovations of science more enthusiastically than did British culture. He notes also that American antivivisectionists lacked the equivalent of royal support (Ryder 1998: 28). During this same period, as Munro explains, the animal protection movement in Australia had begun with the 1873 formation of the Animal Protection Society of New South Wales. Due to circumstances peculiar to Australia, the animal protection movement developed in concert with the environmental movement, the first joint campaign being the elevation of the koala from vermin and commercial fur source to "national pet" (Munro 2000: 14).

Vegetarianism was adopted by some during this period in both Britain and America, the word itself being coined in 1842. By the end of the century vegetarianism was established among a "minority of the middle class," including Percy Shelley, Henry David Thoreau, George Bernard Shaw, Anna Kingsford, Howard Williams, and Henry Salt. Mohandas Gandhi in the twentieth century attributed his commitment to vegetarianism to reading Henry Salt's *Plea for Vegetarianism* (1897) (Finsen and Finsen 1994: 25).

After World War I the animal welfare movement seemed to lose its mass appeal in both the U.S. and Britain. There were undoubtedly several reasons for this decline. It may be that incorporating meat into the diet during periods of disease and war was thought to be important for human health. Ryder comments that wars tend to revive the view that worrying about suffering is cowardly; compassion is dismissed as weakness and effeminacy. In any case, those who called for bans on the exploitation of animals tended to be regarded as cranks or extremists (Ryder 1998: 28–9). Animal welfare organizations in Britain and America declined into charities for lost or abandoned dogs and cats, ignoring the "steady increase in the applied technology of cruelty in the laboratory, meat and wild-killing industries" (Ryder 1998: 29), Henry Salt (1851–1939) in Britain being an exception.[3] Although the National Antivivisection Society was founded in 1929, significant progress in the U.S. did not occur until the 1950s, when the Animal Welfare Institute and the Humane Society of the United States were founded. The Society for Animal Protective Legislation, founded in 1955, achieved the passage of the Humane Slaughter Act and the 1959 Wild Horses Act. During this period the International Society for Animal Rights and the Fund for Animals also came into being. In general, however, the postwar period in both Britain and the United States saw little progress in improving conditions for animals. Finsen and Finsen (1994: 3) assert that one reason for this lack of progress was that the humane movement had "promoted kindness and the elimination of cruelty without challenging the assumption of human superiority or the institutions that reflect that assumption," but they also note that the political climate was very conservative during this period.

Beginning with the 1960s in Britain, the humane concern for animals began to be transformed into the animal rights movement, which insists on justice and fairness in our treatment of animals. Guither (1998: 4–5) argues that the modern animal rights movement is "radically different" from the earlier antivivisection groups and the traditional humane societies. While this may be an overstatement, it is certainly true that many advocates of animal rights affirm the moral status of animals and oppose all ways in which animals are confined and used by human beings (1998: 4–5). One expression of this demand for justice was the formation of the Hunt Saboteurs in 1963. This British group "appears to be the first organization to speak openly and uncompromisingly of members as proponents of rights of animals in the modern sense" (Finsen and Finsen 1994: 55). The group employed confrontational tactics of direct action; it also represented a significant broadening of the animal movement to the working class. In 1964 Ruth Harrison published *Animal Machines,* a book which initiated much of the public concern for the welfare of farm animals. She is believed to have been the first to label confinement livestock and poultry production as "factory farming," calling attention to the fact that animal agriculture had come to be conducted behind closed doors (Ryder 1998: 30). In response to these concerns, the British Parliament set up an official committee of inquiry made up of scientists and concerned citizens, which issued the influential Brambell Report in 1965. The Report recommended certain mandatory standards and called for the government to establish regulations defining animal suffering; it has set the stage for animal welfare reform in the United Kingdom and other northern European countries.

A powerful collection of essays titled *Animals, Men and Morals* was published in 1971 by a group of young philosophers and sociologists at Oxford, employing the new term "species-ism," coined by Richard Ryder. Peter Singer reviewed the book and was invited to expand his review into a book of his own. The resulting work was *Animal Liberation*, published in 1975, known as the first philosophic text to include recipes—vegetarian, of course. The book included clear and powerful argumentation together with well-documented descriptions of the conditions of animals in factory farms and research laboratories. Parliamentarian Douglas Houghton with others led the struggle to "put animals into politics," a campaign which issued in the (British) Animals (Scientific Procedures) Act of 1986 (Ryder 1998: 33).

Overall there was a marked increase in direct action, both legal and illegal, during the 1970s and 1980s. Ronnie Lee launched the Animal Liberation Front (ALF) in England in 1972, leading to raids on animal laboratories, factory farms, and abattoirs all over Europe and North America, and the International Fund for Animal Welfare broadened the move to include wildlife (Ryder 1998: 34). However, the climate of opinion changed in Britain during the years of Margaret Thatcher as Prime Minister, and the animal rights movement began to be looked at as a subversive threat to capitalism (Ryder 1998: 35). Acts of violence by groups such as the ALF led to a backlash within the animal rights movement as well as to long prison terms (Finsen and Finsen 1994: 101–2).

In the 1990s the British-led European movement again became active. Partly due to the effectiveness of the organization Compassion in World Farming, farm animals succeeded laboratory animals as the main focus among European animal welfarists in the 1990s. "Massive protests in British ports in 1994 against the exports of sheep and calves . . . escalated into self-sustaining grassroots local movements that continued for over a year" (Ryder 1998: 35). Prime Minister John Major invited animal welfarists to Downing Street, and the European Union Commission voted to phase out by 2006 the keeping of calves in crates in Europe. By 1995 4.5 percent of the British population was vegetarian (Ryder 1998: 37).

In the United States, Peter Singer and Tom Regan emerged as strong voices for animal liberation and animal rights, respectively, in the 1970s and 1980s. A number of organizations formed, among them People for the Ethical Treatment of Animals (PETA), Trans-Species Unlimited, Farm Animal Reform Movement, Mobilization for Animals, and In Defense of Animals.The principal target of reform in the 1980s in the U.S. was the use of animals in laboratories. Two scandals in 1981 and 1984 helped lead to the upgrading of the oversight of research facilities and some reduction of pain and distress in procedures. Henry Spira led effective protests against the seizure of unwanted dogs from pounds for use in research laboratories.

The U.S. Animal Liberation Front (ALF) is a group of loosely knit cells which has conducted controversial direct-action, using illegal tactics. In the United States the ALF has consistently held to a distinction between property damage and violence toward living beings. However, there have been ALF actions in which the methods used placed people in danger, and researchers who have been targeted claim psychological and professional harm (Finsen and Finsen 1994: 98–106). Finsen and Finsen point out that, whether or not one agrees with the tactics of the ALF, the information brought to light has in fact increased public attention to what happens in some laboratories (1994: 106). Nevertheless, the cost is high, not only in property damage but in deaths among some released animals and, in a few cases, physical injury to humans.

Ryder observes (1998: 41) that disputes between those supporting animal rights versus those supporting animal welfare have sapped some of the movement's energies in the United States. Meanwhile, the factory-farming industry has rapidly expanded in both the United States and the world. Billions of farm animals are raised indoors in "conditions largely unknown to the general public" (Finsen and Finsen 1994: 5). Fortunately, not all of these changes in animal agriculture are negative for animal welfare, though many are (Fraser, *et al.* 2001: 93–4). Overall, the U.S. animal welfare movement is a collection of national and local organizations that often do not work together due to concerns for organizational sovereignty and program purity. Kim Stallwood is developing a new Institute for Animals and Society in order to help the animal welfare movement become more effective.[4]

Contemporary concerns and future directions

Ryder (1998: 42) notes that those concerned with animals have come to see the fates of these animals as increasingly determined by the "moral blindness" found in the policies of many multinational corporations and international structures such as the World Trade Organization (Ryder 1998: 42). But there are other significant factors. One important element is the view of the relationship between the divine and animal realms in the various world religions; new attitudes and scriptural interpretation are emerging. Many now believe that the Abrahamic traditions are properly understood not as being anthropocentric, but as theocentric: God, not man, is at the center as the ultimate source of meaning (Patton 2000: 408). Despite the fact that the Jewish and Christian traditions have affirmed that only human beings are created in God's image, numerous passages from the Hebrew and Islamic scriptures convey God's "fierce and tender devotion" to animals. (Patton 2000: 409–13, 434). In Patton's felicitous phrase, animals display a "joyous devotion to the One who brought them into being" (Patton 2000: 434). Patton recounts the Russian Orthodox Father Thomas Hopko's affirmation of the "rabbithood of God": "there is an aspect of God's Self that at creation expressed itself as a rabbit, and nothing can better reveal that particular aspect of the divine nature than a real, living rabbit" (Patton 2000: 427). Novel reflections such as these may eventually prove to have a powerful effect on the treatment of animals.

In terms of philosophy, David DeGrazia (1999: 125–9) has identified several areas of "unrealized potential" for the future of animal ethics. One such area is found in the work of feminist theorists, who can contribute their powerful moral opposition to oppression as well as their incisive ability to analyze the ideology of speciesism and the various rationalizations for practices which harm animals. DeGrazia also affirms the value of a virtue ethics approach to animal ethics, developed at length so far only by Steve Sapontzis.[5] Virtue ethics emphasizes the importance of character and attitudes: our actions express what kind of people we are. For example, disrespectful treatment of animals may not always involve harm to an animal but rather may express our own insensitivity and coarseness (DeGrazia 1999: 125–9). A recent example can be found by the creation in 2000 of a transgenic rabbit that glows in the dark.[6] The artist, Eduardo Kac, a professor at the School of the Art Institute of Chicago, teamed up with French geneticists to produce the rabbit by injecting rabbit zygotes with a fluorescent protein gene derived from jellyfish. Such use of a living creature as a "new art form" seems to many to be disrespectful and sensationalist.

Finsen and Finsen (1994: 257) comment that the animal rights movement has had some impact to date, in the process "arousing intense opposition from [extremely powerful] industries with vested economic interests in the status quo." They join a number of other writers in identifying the reform/abolition split as the crucial distinction among members of the animal rights movement. This split is often summarized in the question: should we work for larger cages or empty cages? The reformists usually want to work within the system to improve the conditions for animals, whereas the abolitionists work to eliminate all uses of animals that they see as causing pain and suffering (Guither 1998: 10). In the Foreword to this book, Bernard Rollin allies himself with reform, affirming that the animal ethics movement is dynamic, growing, and influential.

The reason for our treatment of animals has never been a mystery. As Ryder comments in his recent book *The Political Animal*, "the simple truth is that we exploit the other animals and cause them suffering because we are more powerful than they are" (1998: 51). The editors hope that this anthology will stimulate reflection on the misuse as well as the appropriate use of human power. Such reflection will both enrich the human relationship with the nonhuman world and contribute to better lives for animals.

Notes

1 Thomas points out that the tradition that humans were originally vegetarian is ancient and worldwide. He states that it "may reflect the actual practice of our remote ancestors, for apes are largely vegetarian" (1983: 288–9).
2 For articles discussing Christian, Jewish, and Islamic interpretations of scripture as it relates to animals, see Part IV of this volume. See also Paul Waudau's discussion of traditional Christian views in *The Specter of Speciesism: Buddhist and Christian Views of Animals* (2002) New York: Oxford University Press.
3 Both Peter Singer and Tom Regan have identified Henry Salt as an important influence on their thought.
4 The Institute for Animals and Society, c/o Animal Rights Network Inc./The Animals' Agenda, 3500 Boston St., Suite 325, Baltimore, Md. 21224. Tel: 410–675–4566. email: office@animalsagenda.org.www.animalsagenda.org. The mission of the Institute is to advance animal advocacy issues in public policy development by conducting scholarly research and analysis, providing education and training, and fostering cooperation with other social justice movements and interests.
5 S.F. Sapontzis (1987) *Morals, Reason and Animals*, Philadelphia: Temple University Press.
6 <http://cseserv.engr.scu.edu/nquinn/ENGR019_299Fall2000/StudentWebSites/Evans/ethic.html #Ethical>

Bibliography

Boersema, J.J. (2001) *The Torah and the Stoics on Humankind and Nature*, Leiden: Brill.
Cohen, E. (1994) "Animals in Medieval Perceptions: The Image of the Ubiquitous Other." In A. Manning and J. Serpell (eds) *Animals and Human Society: changing perspectives,* London and New York: Routledge, pp. 59–80.
DeGrazia, D. (1999) "Animal Ethics Around the Turn of the Twenty-First Century." *Journal of Agricultural and Environmental Ethics* 11.2: 111–29.
Dombrowshi, D.A. (1984) *The Philosophy of Vegetarianism*, Amherst: University of Massachusetts Press.
Finsen, L. and Finsen, S. (1994) *The Animal Rights Movement in America*, New York: Twayne Publishers.
Fraser, D., Mench, J. and Millman, S. (2001) "Farm Animals and Their Welfare." In D. M. Salem and A. N. Rowan (eds) (2001) *The State of the Animals 2001*, Washington, D.C.: Humane Society Press.
Guither, H.D. (1998) *Animal Rights: History and Scope of a Radical Social Movement*, Carbondale: So. Illinois University Press.
Jasper, J.M. and Nelkin, D. (1992) *The Animal Rights Crusade: The Growth of a Moral Protest*, New York: Macmillan.
Kalechofsky, R. (1992) "Dedicated to Descartes' Niece: The Women's Movement in the Nineteenth Century and Anti-Vivisection." *Between the Species* 8.2: 61–71.

Larue, G.A. (1991) "Ancient Ethics." In Singer, P. (ed.) *A Companion to Ethics*, Oxford: Blackwell.

Maehle, A. (1994) "Cruelty and Kindness to the Brute Creation: Stability and Change in the Ethics of the Man–animal Relationship, 1600–1850." In Manning and Serpell, pp. 81–105.

Manning, A. and Serpell, J. (eds) (1994) *Animals and Human Society: changing perspectives*, London and New York: Routledge.

Munro, L. (2000) *Compassionate Beasts: the quest for animal rights*, Westport, Conn.: Praeger.

Patton, K.C. (2000) "He Who Sits in the Heavens Laughs": Recovering Animal Theology in the Abrahamic Traditions." *Harvard Theological Review* 93.4: 401–34.

Ritvo, H. (1994) "Animals in Nineteenth-Century Britain: Complicated Attitudes and Competing Categories." In Manning and Serpell, 106–26.

Rowlands, M. (1998) *Animal Rights: a philosophical defence*, New York: St. Martin's Press.

Ryder, R. (1989) *Animal Revolution: Changing Attitudes toward Speciesism*, Oxford: Basil Blackwell.

—— (1998) *The Political Animal: The Conquest of Speciesism*, Jefferson, N.C.: McFarland.

Schwabe, C.W. (1994) "Animals in the Ancient World." In Manning and Serpell.

Serpell, J.A. (1999) "Working Out the Beast: An Alternative History of Western Humaneness." In F.R. Ascione and P. Arkow (eds) *Child Abuse, Domestic Violence, and Animal Abuse*, West Lafayette, Ind.: Purdue University Press.

Serpell, J.A. and Manning, A. (1994) *Animals and Human Society: Changing perspectives*, pp. 36–58. London and New York: Routledge.

Singer, P. (ed.) (1991) *A Companion to Ethics*, Oxford: Basil Blackwell.

Sorabji, R. (1993) *Animal Minds and Human Morals: The origins of the Western debate*, Ithaca, N.Y.: Cornell University Press.

Thomas, K. (1983) *Man and the Natural World: Changing Attitudes in England 1500–1800*, Magnolia: Peter Smith.

Turner, J. (1980) *Reckoning with the Beast: Animals, Pain, and Humanity in the Victorian Mind,* Baltimore: Johns Hopkins University.

PART I

Theories of Animal Ethics

Introduction

Animal ethics is involved with arguments over several key issues. The most basic issue concerns the basis of the moral value or moral status of animals. Why should animals count morally? This Part includes excerpts from several influential theorists in the field of animal ethics.

Tom Regan's answer as well as that of Paola Cavalieri is based on the concepts of rights, of what a being is entitled to. While there are significant differences between their theories, both thinkers provide a deontological moral theory, derived from that of Immanuel Kant. Carl Cohen rejects Regan's argument. While Cohen does not deny that animals have rudimentary desires and interests, he does deny that having interests is relevant to having moral rights. Animals are "subjects-of-a-life" for Regan, or "intentional beings" for Cavalieri. They have desires, intentions, feelings, and a psychological identity over time—there is "someone home" in an animal. Animals should be included in our moral community as beings with rights.

Peter Singer rests his argument on the moral principle of the equal consideration of interests, the utilitarian principle which affirms that all sentient individuals, individuals who can experience pleasure or pain, must be considered when we are contemplating an action. Singer advocates preference utilitarianism, a form of utilitarianism which takes into account what an individual wishes to do. He does not advocate equal treatment but rather equal consideration of animals' interests. Singer states that we have different obligations toward animals which are rational and self-conscious as contrasted with those which are not.

Josephine Donovan critiques the over-reliance on reason by Regan and Singer, a reliance which dismisses the significance of emotions and sentiment. Donovan affirms the value of cultural feminism as a source of a holistic concept of life, and provides examples of women artists and feminist theorists who point to a more reciprocal relationship with other creatures.

R.G. Frey critiques Regan and Singer from a different perspective. He maintains that animals, because they lack language, do not have interests in the sense of having desires; thus it is not necessary for Frey to address what relationship there might be between interests and rights.

David DeGrazia accepts the relationship between having interests and having moral rights, but he does not believe that the principle of equal consideration of interests is clear and unproblematic. He demonstrates some of the difficulties in comparing the interests of various organisms, and argues that a better approach is to recognize that individuals matter morally to various degrees.

1

Tom Regan

The Case for Animal Rights

This selection is from the influential *The Case for Animal Rights*, published in 1983. Regan explains his concept of "subject-of-a-life" as the basis for inherent value, the distinction between moral agents and moral patients, and two principles to be used in cases of unavoidable conflicts between subjects-of-a-life.

[. . .]

Moral agents and moral patients

A helpful place to begin is to distinguish between moral agents and moral patients [. . .]. Moral agents are individuals who have a variety of sophisticated abilities, including in particular the ability to bring impartial moral principles to bear on the determination of what, all considered, morally ought to be done and, having made this determination, to freely choose or fail to choose to act as morality, as they conceive it, requires. Because moral agents have these abilities, it is fair to hold them morally accountable for what they do, assuming that the circumstances of their acting as they do in a particular case do not dictate otherwise.

[. . .]

In contrast to moral agents, *moral patients* lack the prerequisites that would enable them to control their own behavior in ways that would make them morally accountable for what they do. A moral patient lacks the ability to formulate, let alone bring to bear, moral principles in deliberating about which one among a number of possible acts it would be right or proper to perform. Moral patients, in a word, cannot do what is right, nor can they do what is wrong. Granted, what they do may be detrimental to the welfare of others—they may, for example, bring about acute suffering or even death; and granted, it may be necessary, in any given case, for moral agents to use force or violence to prevent such harm being done, either in self-defense or in defense of others. But even when a moral patient causes significant harm to another, the moral patient has not done what is wrong. Only moral agents can do what is wrong. Human infants, young children, and the mentally deranged or enfeebled of all ages are paradigm cases of human moral patients. More controversial is whether human fetuses and future generations of human beings qualify as moral patients. It is enough for our purposes, however, that some humans are reasonably viewed in this way.

Individuals who are moral patients differ from one another in morally relevant ways. Of particular importance is the distinction between (a) those individuals who are conscious and sentient (i.e., can experience pleasure and pain) but who lack other mental abilities, and (b) those individuals who are conscious, sentient, and possess the other cognitive and volitional abilities discussed in previous chapters (e.g., belief and memory). Some animals, for reasons already advanced, belong in category (b); other animals quite probably belong in category (a).

[. . .]

Our primary interest, in this and in succeeding chapters, concerns the moral status of animals in category (b). When, therefore, the notion of a *moral patient* is appealed to in the discussions that follow, it should be understood as applying to *animals in category (b) and to those other moral patients like these animals in the relevant respects*—that is, those who have desires and beliefs, who perceive, remember, and can act intentionally, who have a sense of the future, including their own future (i.e., are self-aware or self-conscious), who have an emotional life, who have a psychophysical identity over time, who have a kind of autonomy (namely, preference-autonomy), and who have an experiential welfare. Some *human* moral patients satisfy these criteria—for example, young children and those humans who, though they suffer from a variety of mental handicaps and thus fail to qualify as moral agents, possess the abilities just enumerated. Where one draws the line between those humans who have these abilities and those who do not is a difficult question certainly, and it may be that no exact line can be drawn. But how we should approach the question in the case of human beings is the same as how we should approach it in the case of animals. Given any human being, what we shall want to know is whether his/her behavior can be accurately described and parsimoniously explained by making reference to the range of abilities that characterizes animals (desires, beliefs, preferences, etc.). To the extent that the case can be made for describing and explaining the behavior of a human being in these terms, to that extent, assuming that we have further reasons for denying that the human in question has the abilities necessary for moral agency, we have reason to regard that human as a moral patient on all fours, so to speak, with animals. As previously claimed, some human beings *are* moral patients in the relevant sense, and *it is only those individuals who are moral patients in this sense (who have, that is, the abilities previously enumerated), whether these individuals be human or nonhuman, who are being referred to, in this chapter and in the sequel, when reference is made to " 'moral patients.' "*

Moral patients cannot do what is right or wrong, we have said, and in this respect they differ fundamentally from moral agents. But moral patients can be on the receiving end of the right or wrong acts of moral agents, and so in this respect resemble moral agents. A brutal beating administered to a child, for example, is wrong, even if the child herself can do no wrong, just as attending to the basic biological needs of the senile is arguably right, even if a senile person can no longer do what is right. Unlike the case of the relationship that holds between moral agents, then, the relationship that holds between moral agents, on the one hand, and moral patients, on the other, is not reciprocal. Moral patients can do nothing right or wrong that affects or involves moral agents, but moral agents can do what is right or wrong in ways that affect or involve moral patients.

[. . .]

Individuals as equal in value

The interpretation of formal justice favored here, which will be referred to as *equality of individuals*, involves viewing certain individuals as having value in themselves. I shall refer to this kind of value as *inherent value* and begin the discussion of it by first concentrating on the inherent value attributed to moral agents.

The inherent value of individual moral agents is to be understood as being conceptually distinct from the intrinsic value that attaches to the experiences they have (e.g., their pleasures or preference satisfactions), as not being reducible to values of this latter kind, and as being incommensurate with these values. To say that inherent value is not reducible to the intrinsic values of an individual's experiences means that we cannot determine the inherent value of individual moral agents by totaling the intrinsic values of their experiences. Those who have a more pleasant or happier life do not therefore have greater inherent value than those whose lives are less pleasant or happy. Nor do those who have more "cultivated" preferences (say, for arts and letters) therefore have greater inherent value. To say that the inherent value of individual moral agents is incommensurate with the intrinsic value of their (or anyone else's) experiences means that the two kinds of value are not comparable and cannot be exchanged one for the other. Like proverbial apples and oranges, the two kinds of value do not fall within the same scale of comparison. One cannot ask, How much intrinsic value is the inherent value of this individual worth—how much is it equal to? The inherent value of any given moral agent isn't equal to any sum of intrinsic values, neither the intrinsic value of that individual's experiences nor the total of the intrinsic value of the experiences of all other moral agents. To view moral agents as having inherent value is thus to view them as something different from, and something more than, mere receptacles of what has intrinsic value. They have value in their own right, a value that is distinct from, not reducible to, and incommensurate with the values of those experiences which, as receptacles, they have or undergo.

The difference between the utilitarian-receptacle view of value regarding moral agents and the postulate of inherent value might be made clearer by recalling the cup analogy. On the receptacle view of value, it is *what goes into the cup* (the pleasures or preference-satisfactions, for example) that has value; what does not have value is the cup itself (i.e., the individual himself or herself). The postulate of inherent value offers an alternative. The cup (that is, the individual) has value *and* a kind that is not reducible to, and is incommensurate with, what goes into the cup (e.g., pleasure). The cup (the individual) does "contain" (experience) things that are valuable (e.g., pleasures), but the value of the cup (individual) is not the same as any one or any sum of the valuable things the cup contains. *Individual moral agents themselves have a distinctive kind of value*, according to the postulate of inherent value, but not according to the receptacle view to which utilitarians are committed. It's the cup, not just what goes into it, that is valuable.

[...]

All that is required to insure just treatment, on utilitarian grounds, is that the preferences (pleasures, etc.) of all affected by the outcome be considered and that equal preferences (pleasures, etc.) be counted equally. But if moral agents have a value that is *not* reducible to or commensurate with the value of their own or everyone else's valuable experiences, then how moral agents are to be treated, if they are to be treated justly, cannot be determined *merely* by considering the desires, and the like, of all involved, weighting them equitably, and then favoring that option that will bring about the optimal balance of goods over evils for all involved. To suppose otherwise is to assume that questions of just treatment can be answered by ignoring the value of the individual moral agent, which, if moral agents are viewed as equal in inherent value, simply is not true. Moreover, because all moral agents are viewed as equal in inherent value, if any have such value, what applies to how some may be justly treated applies to all, whatever their race, say, or sex. Given the postulate of inherent value, no harm done to *any* moral agent can possibly be justified merely on the grounds of its producing the best consequences for all affected by the outcome. Thus are we able to avoid the counterintuitive implications of act utilitarianism if we deny the receptacle view of moral agents and postulate their equal inherent value.

[. . .]

It might be suggested that *being-alive* is a *sufficient* condition of an individual's having inherent value. This position would avoid the problems indigenous to the view that being-alive is a necessary condition, but it stands in need of quite considerable analysis and argument if it is to win the day. It is not clear why we have, or how we reasonably could be said to have, direct duties to, say, individual blades of grass, potatoes, or cancer cells. Yet all are alive, and so all should be owed direct duties if all have inherent value. Nor is it clear why we have, or how we reasonably could be said to have, direct duties to collections of such individuals—to lawns, potato fields, or cancerous tumors. If, in reply to these difficulties, we are told that we have direct duties only to some, but not to all, living things, and that it is this subclass of living things whose members have inherent value, then not only will we stand in need of a way to distinguish those living things that have this value from those that do not but more importantly for present purposes, the view that being-alive is a sufficient condition of having such value will have to be abandoned. Because of the difficulties endemic both to the view that being-alive is a necessary condition of having inherent value and to the view that this is a sufficient condition, and granting that moral agents and moral patients share the important characteristic of being alive, it is extremely doubtful that the case could be made for viewing this similarity as the relevant similarity they share, by virtue of which all moral agents and patients have equal inherent value.

Inherent value and the subject-of-a-life criterion

An alternative to viewing being-alive as the relevant similarity is what will be termed *the subject-of-a-life criterion*. To be the subject-of-a-life, in the sense in which this expression will be used, involves more than merely being alive and more than merely being conscious. To be the subject-of-a-life is to be an individual whose life is characterized by those features explored in the opening chapters of the present work: that is, individuals are subjects-of-a-life if they have beliefs and desires; perception, memory, and a sense of the future, including their own future; an emotional life together with feelings of pleasure and pain; preference- and welfare-interests; the ability to initiate action in pursuit of their desires and goals; a psychophysical identity over time; and an individual welfare in the sense that their experiental life fares well or ill for them, logically independently of their utility for others and logically independently of their being the object of anyone else's interests. Those who satisfy the subject-of-a-life criterion themselves have a distinctive kind of value—inherent value—and are not to be viewed or treated as mere receptacles.

[. . .]

The subject-of-a-life criterion identifies a similarity that holds between moral agents and patients. Is this similarity a relevant similarity, one that makes viewing them as inherently valuable intelligible and nonarbitrary? The grounds for replying affirmatively are as follows: (1) A relevant similarity among all those who are postulated to have equal inherent value must mark a characteristic shared by all those moral agents and patients who are here viewed as having such value. The subject-of-a-life criterion satisfies this requirement. *All* moral agents and *all* those moral patients with whom we are concerned *are* subjects of a life that is better or worse for them, in the sense explained, logically independently of the utility they have for others and logically independently of their being the object of the interests of others. (2) Since inherent value is conceived to be a categorical value, admitting of no degrees, any supposed relevant similarity must itself be categorical. The subject-of-a-life criterion satisfies this requirement. This criterion does not assert or imply that those who meet it have the status of subject of a life to a greater or lesser degree, depending on the degree to which they have or lack some favored ability or virtue (e.g., the ability for higher mathematics or those virtues associated with artistic excellence). One either *is* a subject of a life, in the sense explained, or one *is not*. All those who are, are so equally. The subject-of-a-life criterion thus demarcates a categorical status shared by all moral agents and those moral patients with whom we are concerned. (3) A relevant similarity between moral agents and patients must go some way toward illuminating why we have direct duties to both and why we have less reason to believe that we have direct duties to individuals who are neither moral agents nor patients, even including those who, like moral agents and those patients we have in mind, are alive. This requirement also is satisfied by the subject-of-a-life criterion. Not all living things are subjects of a life, in the sense explained; thus not all living things are to be viewed as having the same moral status, given this criterion, and the differences concerning our confidence about having direct duties to some (those who are subjects) and our not having direct duties to others (those who are not subjects) can be at least partially illuminated because the former meet, while the latter fail to meet, the subject-of-a-life criterion. For these reasons, the subject-of-a-life criterion can be defended as citing a relevant similarity between moral agents and patients, one that makes the attribution of equal inherent value to them both intelligible and nonarbitrary.

[. . .]

Justice: the principle of respect for individuals

[. . .]

If individuals have equal inherent value, then any principle that declares what treatment is due them as a matter of justice must take their equal value into account. The following principle (*the respect principle*) does this: *We are to treat those individuals who have inherent value in ways that respect their inherent value*. Now, the respect principle sets forth an egalitarian, nonperfectionist interpretation of formal justice. The principle does not apply only to how we are to treat some individuals having inherent value (e.g., those with artistic or intellectual virtues). It enjoins us to treat *all* those individuals having inherent value in ways that respect their value, and thus it requires respectful treatment of all who satisfy the subject-of-a-life criterion. Whether they are moral agents or patients, we must treat them in ways that respect their equal inherent value.

[. . .]

It is not an act of kindness to treat animals respectfully. It is an act of justice. It is not "the sentimental interests" of moral agents that grounds our duties of justice to children, the retarded, the senile, or other moral patients, including animals. It is respect for their inherent value. The myth of the privileged moral status of moral agents has no clothes.

[. . .]

Comparable harm

[. . .]

A distinction [can be] drawn between those harms that are inflictions and those that are deprivations. Harms that are deprivations deny an individual opportunities for doing what will bring satisfaction, when it is in that individual's interest to do this. Harms that are inflictions diminish the quality of an individual's life, not just if or as they deprive that individual of opportunities for satisfaction, though they usually will do this, but because they detract directly from the individual's overall welfare.

[. . .]

[We can now] give content to the notion of comparable harm. Two harms are comparable when they detract equally from an individual's welfare, or from the welfare of two or more individuals. For example, separate episodes of suffering of a certain kind and intensity are comparable harms if they cause an equal diminution in the welfare of the same individual at different times, or in two different individuals at the same or different times. And death is a comparable harm if the loss of opportunities it marks are equal in any two cases.

[. . .]

The miniride principle

By making use of the notion of comparable harm, the rights view can formulate two principles that can be appealed to in order to make decisions in prevention cases. The first principle (*the minimize overriding principle*, or *the miniride principle*) states the following:

> Special considerations aside, when we must choose between overriding the rights of many who are innocent or the rights of few who are innocent, and when each affected individual will be harmed in a prima facie comparable way, then we ought to choose to override the rights of the few in preference to overriding the rights of the many.

This principle is derivable from the respect principle. This latter principle entails that all moral agents and patients are directly owed the prima facie duty not to be harmed and that all those who are owed this duty have an equally valid claim, and thus an equal prima facie moral right, against being harmed. Now, *precisely because* this right is equal, no one individual's right can count for any more than any other's, when the harm that might befall either is prima facie comparable. Thus, A's right cannot count for more than B's, or C's, or D's. However, when we are faced with choosing between options, one of which will harm A, the other of which will harm B, C, and D, and the third of which will harm them all, and when the foreseeable harm involved for each individual is prima facie comparable, then numbers count. *Precisely because* each is to count for one, no one for more than one, we cannot count choosing to override the rights of B, C, and D as neither better nor worse than choosing to override A's right alone. Three are more than one, and when the four individuals have an equal prima facie right not to be harmed, when the harm they face is prima facie comparable, and when there are no special considerations at hand, then showing equal respect for the equal rights of the individuals involved requires that we override the right of A (the few) rather than the rights of the many (B, C, D). To choose to override the rights of the many in this case would be to override an equal right three times (i.e., in the case of three different individuals) when we could choose to override such a right only once, and *that* cannot be consistent with showing equal respect for the equal rights of all the individuals involved.

To favor overriding the rights of the few in no way contravenes the requirement that each is to count for one, no one for more than one; on the contrary, special considerations apart, to choose to override the rights of the many rather than those of the few would be to count A's right for more than one—that is, as being equal to overriding the rights of three relevantly similar individuals. Accordingly, because we must not allow any one individual a greater voice in the determination of what ought to be done than any other relevantly similar individual, what we ought to do in prevention cases of the sort under consideration is choose to override the rights of the fewest innocents rather than override the rights of the many. And since this is precisely what the miniride principle enjoins, that principle is derivable from the respect principle.

[. . .]

The worse-off principle

[. . .]

Recall the earlier prevention case where we are called upon to choose between harming A quite radically (–125), or harming a thousand individuals modestly (–1 each), or doing nothing

[. . .]

The miniride principle, since it applies *only* in prevention cases where harms are prima facie comparable, cannot be relied on in cases, such as this one, where the harm all the innocents face is not prima facie comparable. The rights view thus requires a second principle, distinct from but consistent with the miniride principle, and one that is distinct from and not reducible to the minimize harm principle. The following principle (*the worse-off principle*) meets these requirements.

[. . .]

Special considerations aside, when we must decide to override the rights of the many or the rights of the few who are innocent, and when the harm faced by the few would make them worse-off than any of the many would be if any other option were chosen, then we ought to override the rights of the many.

Unfinished business

Two issues deferred in earlier discussions may now be addressed. The first is the lifeboat case [. . .] There are five survivors: four normal adults and a dog. The boat has room enough only for four. Someone must go or else all will perish. Who should it be? Our initial belief is: the dog. Can the rights view illuminate and justify this prereflective intuition? The preceding discussion of prevention cases shows how it can. All on board have equal inherent value and an equal prima facie right not to be harmed. Now, the harm that death is, is a function of the opportunities for satisfaction it forecloses, and no reasonable person would deny that the death of any of the four humans would be a greater prima facie loss, and thus a greater prima facie harm, than would be true in the case of the dog. Death for the dog, in short, though a harm, is not comparable to the harm that death would be for any of the humans. To throw any one of the humans overboard, to face certain death, would be to make that individual worse-off (i.e., would cause *that* individual a greater harm) than the harm that would be done to the dog if the animal was thrown overboard. Our belief that it is the dog who should be killed is justified by appeal to the worse-off principle.

[. . .]

Thus has the case for animal rights been offered. If it is sound, then, like us, animals have certain basic moral rights, including in particular the fundamental right to be treated with the respect that, as possessors of inherent value, they are due as a matter of strict justice.

[. . .]

2

Carl Cohen

"Reply to Tom Regan"

In the following passage Carl Cohen analyzes Regan's use of "subject-of-a-life" and "inherent value" as the foundation for moral rights for animals. According to Cohen, Regan's fallacious logic can be clearly demonstrated.

Why "subjects-of-a-life"?

Regan's need is to create some *link* between the imputed subjective experience of animals and the alleged rights of those animals. To this end a class of beings is marked off that Regan calls "subjects-of-a-life." These are the beings who are believed to have some subjective awareness of their own lives, and for whom, as a result, it may be said that things "fare well or badly." Of course we may not conclude, from the fact that things fare well or badly for an animal, that it can formulate the proposition expressing this, or can even grasp that notion in some sub-linguistic way. The judgment that "things are faring well *for me* these days" is not likely to be among the repertoire of chicken reflections. But some crude subjective experience there must be, since the chicken is drawn toward the food tray and runs away from the fox. This indicates, says Regan, that the chicken (like every "subject-of-a-life") has *interests*.

The strategy here is to devise some category into which both animal lives and human lives may be assimilated. Within this newfound category, since it is designed to include humans too, some of the lives led (the human ones) are plainly moral. From this he will go on to infer that *all* the lives in that class, lives so categorized by virtue of his definition, are moral. But this maneuver could succeed only if the criteria for admission to the newly invented category were themselves intrinsically moral—which of course they are not.

"Subjects-of-a-life" is a category of beings that Regan defines by his own stipulation; membership in that class requires only the crudest subjective experience. Having devised the category by fastening upon certain kinds of primitive experience that rats and humans do share, he goes on to assume that moral rights, possessed by humans, arise from just those interests. Some human interests (e.g., in food and sex) are no different in essence from those of rats, and since we all agree that humans do have rights, he infers that rats must have them, too.

In the sense that a sentient animal—even an octopus or a trout—seeks to avoid pain, it does indeed have interests; many animals obviously have interests in that sense. Were Regan to leap directly from the possession of interests to the claim that such interests establish moral rights, his argument—like [the] far-fetched claims of Bernard Rollin and Steven Sapontzis would be a transparent failure.[1] To avoid this transparency Regan takes a more convoluted path.

A closer look at inherent value

The rights that are to be established flow, Regan contends, from the "*inherent value*" of rats and chickens, and their inherent value is held to be a consequence of their being "subjects-of-a-life." So he makes the passage from interests to rights *by way of* "subjects-of-a-life" and then "inherent value." Both these concepts, as in his 1983 book, are critical links for him: what has subjective experience must have inherent value, and what has inherent value must have rights.[2] This can explain, he argues, why moral respect is owed to rats and chickens.

Reasoning in this way supposes that the rights of rats and chickens are *derived* from the primitive capacities that give them interests. Like Rollin and Sapontzis, Regan is at bottom convinced that rights are the product of animal interests, that a being has rights because it has interests—and he cannot fathom how we could assert of humans, who surely do have interests, that their rights could flow from anything else.

But the conviction that human rights flow from human interests (a conviction shared expressly or tacitly by virtually all animal rights advocates) is one for which there is simply no foundation. The lives we humans lead are indeed moral lives, pervaded by duties and rights. But this moral character of our lives is not a byproduct of our subjective awareness. Our rights are not ours because we experience our lives as our own. Nonhuman creatures may have subjective interests like ours in survival and reproduction, and they may be supposed to have subjective experience of some sort. But from those interests moral rights cannot be inferred.

The plausibility of Regan's reasoning depends on the inference that animals have "inherent value" and then on what may be inferred from the possession of such value. The failure of the argument is a consequence of the fact that the "inherent value" that he infers from the reality of subjective experience is not the same "inherent value" from which rights are later derived. An academic shell game is afoot, in which readers are the marks. Having given our assent to what is plausible in one sense of the expression "inherent value," we are told that dramatic conclusions follow respecting rights. But these conclusions do *not* follow from the inherent value that we may have assented to in animals, although they may follow from inherent value in a very different sense of that term.

[. . .]

What is true of inherent value in the one sense is not true of inherent value in the other sense, and by slipping from one to the other meaning of the phrase Regan commits an egregious fallacy.

We earlier distinguished:

1   Inherent value in the very widely applicable sense that every unique life, not replaceable by other lives or things, has some worth in itself. In this sense every rat, and every octopus too, has inherent value. This value may be minimal; it certainly has no awesome moral content—but it is fair to say that, being irreplaceable and unique, even primitive living things ought not be destroyed for no reason whatever.

2   Inherent value in the far narrower sense arises from the possession of the capacity to make moral judgments, the value of beings with duties and the consciousness of duties. This is the rich philosophical sense of value made famous by Immanuel Kant and employed by many moral thinkers since; it is the sense of inherent worth flowing from the special *dignity* of those who have a moral will. The value of agents who have a moral will does indeed *inhere* in them and entitles them to be treated as ends,

and never as means only. Beings with value in this sense—human beings, of course—have rights.

Now it is plain that most beings with inherent value in the first sense—live creatures in the wild, for example—although they may merit some protection, do not begin to possess inherent value in the second, moral sense. Trees and rats have value in the common sense, and we may plausibly call that value "inherent"—but that is no ground for ascribing/moral agency to them. The gap in the argument is here exposed: subjective experiences of rats and chickens lead us to conclude that they really do have interests, but subjective experiences cannot serve to justify the claim that they have rights.

[. . .]

Human beings, on the other hand, have inherent value in both senses. We have worth in that second, Kantian sense, to be sure, but value also in the simpler, common sense as well. [. . .] [The] slippage between these two senses of the same phrase [. . .] is obscured by reaching rights from subjectivity *through* the concept "subject-of-a-life." Within that category lie beings with inherent value in both senses (humans), and beings with inherent value in the first sense only (rats). The stage is set for slippage.

We humans are subjects of our own lives, of course, so we have inherent value in that simple first sense; and surely we do have moral rights. Regan then asks: if the rat is the subject of its own life, must it not also have the same "inherent value" that we have? In the first sense of inherent value it does. And if it does have inherent value as we do, does it not also have moral rights as we do? No, not at all! By moving *into* the concept of "inherent value" in the first sense (in which that value is shared), then drawing inferences *from* inherent value in the second sense (in which it is not shared), Regan pulls the rabbit from the hat, miraculously extending the realm of moral rights to include the rats and the chickens.

Underlying his equivocation is the tacit supposition that we humans have rights only as a *consequence* of our being "subject-of-a-life." But this is false, and we have not the slightest reason to think it true. Having assumed it true, Regan and his friends take themselves to have *amalgamated* the world of human moral experience with the world of rodent experience. That cannot be done with words, or with anything else.

The argument step by step

Here follow the steps of Regan's argument, essentially as he sets them forth, with brief comment on each. Close scrutiny will show that his critical steps rely on double meanings, his objectives reached by using whichever sense of the equivocal term is convenient for the purpose at hand.

1   Humans and rats are both "subjects-of-a-life."
    Comment: If all that is being said here is that other animals as well as humans have subjective interests and awareness, this premise is not in dispute. In having subjective interests "non-human animals are like us," Regan says. Yes, in the sense that they also have appetites, feel pain, and so on.
2   Beings that are "subjects-of-a-life" are beings having inherent value.
    Comment: This is the introduction of the central equivocal phrase. Animals with subjective experience do indeed have "inherent value" in the common sense

that all living things, including humans, are unique and irreplaceable. But the vast majority of beings having subjective experiences do *not* have "inherent value" in the Kantian sense that would be needed to ground moral rights.

3   Since rats, like humans, have inherent value because they are "subjects-of-a-life," the inherent value that rats possess is essentially no different from the inherent value that humans possess.

Comment: The distinction between the two very different senses of inherent value being here ignored or obscured, it seems plausible for Regan to assert here what is true (but innocuous) if the words are taken in one way, yet false (and very harmful) if taken in another. In the common sense both rats and humans do have inherent value. But this "inherent value" possessed by them both (sense 1) is profoundly different from the "inherent value" that is bound up with human moral agency (sense 2).

Regan writes, "The relevant similarity shared by humans who have inherent value is that we are subject-of-a-life" (p. 211). No, that similarity is not relevant to moral matters at all. On the contrary, we may say that the relevant *dissimilarity* between humans and rats is that, although both may have value as lives, only humans have inherent value in the sense from which rights may be inferred. Regan conflates the two very different senses of value, referring to both with the same words, and his argument depends upon this conflation.

5   The inherent value that we humans possess is what accounts for our moral rights. (In his words: "All those who possess inherent value possess the equal right to be treated with respect.")

Comment: So long as we understand that it is Kantian inherent value (sense 2) here referred to, the claim that from it great moral consequences flow is not in dispute.

6   Since rats possess inherent value for the same reasons that humans do, rats must have moral rights just as humans do.

Comment: Not at all! Here the switch is cashed out. Rats possess inherent value *in sense 1* for the same reason humans do, because they have subjective interests as humans also have. But from these primitive interests no moral rights can be inferred. Regan writes, "Relevantly similar cases should be judged similarly" (p. 212). But the circumstances of rats and humans are in the most essential matters *not* relevantly similar. Indeed, with regard to moral status they could hardly be more sharply dissimilar. The argument thrives on repeated equivocation.

7   Regan concludes, "It follows that all those human beings and all those animal beings who possess inherent value share the equal right to respectful treatment" (p. 212).

Comment: Not on your life! The inherent value shared is value in the common sense, but what can entail respect for rights is *not* shared by rats. What is true of both rats and humans is the fact that they are living beings, the life of each unique, each having interests of its own. From this, nothing about moral rights may be validly inferred.

Infected throughout by the equivocation between inherent value that "subjects-of-a-life" may possess and the entirely different sense of inherent value that may indeed ground human rights, the argument is worthless. The lives of rats and chickens are indeed like the lives of humans in some primitive ways, but it certainly does not follow from those likenesses that rats and chickens share membership in the community of moral beings. Repeatedly we encounter the same fallacious passage from the premise that animals have interests to the conclusion that animals have rights.

[. . .]

Notes

1   Rollin, B. (1992) *Animal Rights and Human Morality*, Amherst: Prometheus Books. Sapontzis, S.F. (1987) *Morals, Reason and Animals*, Philadelphia: Temple University Press.
2   Regan, T. (1983) *The Case for Animal Rights*, Berkeley: University of California Press.

3

Paola Cavalieri

"For an Expanded Theory of Human Rights"

Paola Cavalieri argues that basic human rights should be expanded to include all "intentional beings": those with goals and desires. Her theory is deontological, disallowing the sacrifice of one for the benefit of others or the use of a hierarchical scale of value. Justice requires that society be reorganized to prohibit all use of animals as mere instruments for human use.

We may briefly summarize the discussion [of human rights] as follows. Human rights tend to cover the domain of morality in the narrow sense and are therefore essentially negative rights, or rights to non-interference. They are, moreover, institutional in character, in the sense that the model of both their implementation and their violation is based on the organization and the action of the state.

Within the moral community, human rights define the sphere of beings endowed with full moral status and, on the basis of their most convincing line of defense, the comparative criterion for access to such sphere is simply the fact of being an agent, that is, the fact of being an intentional being that has goals and wants to achieve them.

Given that the beings that fulfill the requisite of intentionality are characterized by the capacity to enjoy freedom and welfare, as well as life which is a precondition for them, both directly and as prerequisites for action, the specific rights claimed concern freedom, welfare, and life. Such rights are equal for all their holders, because the value of the goods they protect is equal, and, as a consequence of this, the sphere characterized by full moral status is homogenous rather than stratified.

In this light, it is clear that, on the basis of the very doctrine that establishes them, human rights are not human. On the one hand, the more or less avowed acceptance of the idea that species membership is not morally relevant [de facto eliminates] from the best foundation of the theory any structural reference to the possession of a genotype Homo sapiens. And, on the other, the will to secure equal fundamental rights to all human beings, including the non-paradigmatic ones, implies that the characteristics appealed to in order to justify the ascription of such rights can no longer be those (seen as) typically human but should instead lie at a cognitive-emotive level accessible to a large number of non-human animals.

Which, exactly, among nonhuman animals meet the requisites for inclusion in the privileged area of full moral status is a problem that cannot yet be settled in detail. However, among the beings that an expanded theory of human rights should cover there undoubtedly are mammals and birds, and probably vertebrates in general. I do not deem it necessary to restate here the cumulative case for this claim, which is supported by common sense as well.[1]

Since the doctrine is centered on non-interference, it does not involve distributive problems which might imply the necessity of attributing differential value to the beings involved. [Moreover], as the resort to the language of rights makes clear, the perspective within which the theory roots is deontological rather than consequentialist. Given that rights are side constraints on possible forms of utilitarian aggregation, it is evident that any form of maximizing sacrifice is excluded a priori. Since, therefore, nobody can be permissibly sacrificed for the benefit of others, the problem of a possible attribution of differential value does not arise in this respect either. Finally, the fact that the doctrine refers to the institutional level—that it deals, that is, with codified or official violations—implies that the problem of possible inter-individual conflicts is set aside in order to focus only on the relationship between social power and the individuals who make up the collectivity.

[Within such a framework,] it is plausible to claim that the egalitarian thesis proves to be the most intuitive. For none of us holds that slavery could be prohibited in the case of individuals with a high IQ but be permissible in the case of individuals with a lower IQ; or that a massacre of intellectuals is a more serious violation of human rights than a massacre of intellectually disabled children. When it comes to official violations of basic rights, we deem any hierarchical scale morally repugnant.

The fundamental step

In a recent volume, the American legal scholar Gary Francione claimed that the characterization of nonhumans—from now on, I shall use this term to refer only to nonhumans endowed with intentionality—as property is the main obstacle placed in the way of any attempt to extend basic rights beyond the boundaries of the species Homo sapiens.[2] In the light of this, he has argued that the first right to be afforded in such a context is the right not to be treated as mere means to others' ends.

The application of the line of reasoning so far developed to the current situation of our societies leads to a like conclusion. With an important difference, however: that the removal of nonhumans from the category of things or items of property is not seen as the implementation of a particular right but rather as the essential condition for a translation at the social level of the implications of the expanded theory. Within the framework of the feminist debate on equality, it has been emphasized that in case of serious disparity in access to rights, the fundamental step to be made regards what could be defined as juridical equality as a legal principle in itself.[3] If, so far as women are concerned, this takes the form of a law on equality which may play an active role in fostering social transformation, in the case of nonhumans what is in question is instead a legal change aimed at removing in the status of property the basic obstacle to the enjoyment of the denied rights. In this sense, the shift from the condition of objects to that of subjects of legal rights does not appear as a point of arrival but rather as the initial access to the circle of possible beneficiaries of that "egalitarian plateau" from which contemporary political philosophy starts in order to determine any more specific individual right.[4]

In order to better understand this point, consider the current situation. Billions of non-human animals are tortured, confined, and killed for our benefit. In a real sense, the actual parallel for the condition of these beings is slavery, that is, the practice by which human beings are reduced to assets in the strict meaning of that term ("live articles of property" was the telling Aristotelian definition of slaves.)[5] In nineteenth century United States, for example, slaves were institutionally dispossessed of their own goals, and their welfare, their freedom, and their lives were under the control of others. Only with the abolition of slavery through the Thirteenth Amendment to the Constitution was the fundamental inequality precluding access to nearly any other moral and legal protections removed. A reorganization of society along the lines of the expanded theory likewise requires the constitutional abolition of the status of mere assets of nonhuman animals, and the prohibition of all the practices that are today made possible by such status, from raising for food to scientific experimentation to the most varied forms of commercial use and systematic extermination.[6]

These are the conclusions to which we are led by an argument that is neither contingent nor eccentric but is the necessary dialectical derivation of the most universally accepted among contemporary ethical doctrines—human rights theory. In this sense, the normative force of the demands of the expanded theory entails a commitment not only to avoid participating in, but also to oppose, present discrimination.[7] And this because the institutional denial of fundamental rights to beings that are entitled to them does not simply deprive the victims of the objects of their rights, but is a direct attack on those very rights themselves. In other words, such a denial subverts not merely what is right, but the very idea of justice.

Notes

1   For a synthesis of the argument see for example David DeGrazia, *Taking Animals Seriously: Mental Life and Moral Status* (Cambridge: Cambridge University Press, 1996), chap. VI and pp. 166–72.
2   Gary L. Francione, *Animals, Property and the Law* (Philadelphia: Temple University Press, 1995), p. 10.
3   Catharine A. MacKinnon, "Crimes of War, Crimes of Peace," in *On Human Rights*, ed. Stephen Shute and Susan Hurley (New York: Basic Books, 1993), p. 103.
4   The notion of egalitarian plateau is Ronald Dworkin's. For an analysis of its role in the contemporary debate, see Will Kymlicka, *Contemporary Political Philosophy: An Introduction* (Oxford: Clarendon Press, 1990), p. 5.
5   Aristotle, *Politics*, I, 2, 1253 b.
6   Only if, and when, the decisive step of the abolition of any sort of official discrimination has included nonhuman animals among the beneficiaries of the protection the expanded theory affords, will it become possible to deal with the problem of specific transactions between individual right-holders, and with the ways of settling unavoidable conflicts of interests. For though a commitment to the rights envisaged by the expanded theory does not coincide with an interactional commitment, it is not entirely separate from such an idea, because the claim that societies ought to be organized so that the individuals living in them should not endure discriminatory or degrading treatment is naturally connected with a more inclusive concern for the protection of individuals. A seminal attempt at immediately coupling the two commitments can however be found in Paola Cavalieri and Peter Singer, *The Great Ape Project: Equality beyond Humanity*, eds Paola Cavalieri and Peter Singer (New York: St Martin's Press, 1994).
7   For this statement, as well as for the following one, cf. Thomas Pogge, "How Should Human Rights Be Conceived?", *Jahrbuch für Recht und Ethik*, vol. 3 (1995), p. 116 and p. 109. Such analysis seems to disprove the distinction between individual morality and political morality which has been drawn, with variations, by Jean-Yves Goffi in *Le philosophe et ses animaux: du statut éthique de l'animal* (Nîmes: Éditions Jaqueline Chambon, 1994), and by Ursula Wolf in *Das Tier in der Moral* (Frankfurt: Vittorio Klostermann, 1990).

4

Peter Singer

Practical Ethics

Peter Singer states that there is no moral justification for refusing to take animal suffering seriously. He calls for a boycott of the meat industry on the basis of equal consideration of interests. Singer affirms that experiments on animals should only be carried out if experimenters would be willing to also use human beings at an equal or lower level of consciousness. He then responds to common objections to his views. In a concluding section he presents a strong case against the killing of rational and self-conscious animals such as the great apes.

The argument for extending the principle of equality beyond our own species is simple, so simple that it amounts to no more than a clear understanding of the nature of the principle of equal consideration of interests.[1] We have seen that this principle implies that our concern for others ought not to depend on what they are like, or what abilities they possess (although precisely what this concern requires us to do may vary according to the characteristics of those affected by what we do). It is on this basis that we are able to say that the fact that some people are not members of our race does not entitle us to exploit them, and similarly the fact that some people are less intelligent than others does not mean that their interests may be disregarded. But the principle also implies that the fact that beings are not members of our species does not entitle us to exploit them, and similarly the fact that other animals are less intelligent than we are does not mean that their interests may be disregarded.

[. . .] [M]any philosophers have advocated equal consideration of interests, in some form or other, as a basic moral principle. Only a few have recognised that the principle has applications beyond our own species, one of the few being Jeremy Bentham, the founding father of modern utilitarianism. In a forward-looking passage, written at a time when African slaves in the British dominions were still being treated much as we now treat non-human animals, Bentham wrote:

> The day may come when the rest of the animal creation may acquire those rights which never could have been withholden from them but by the hand of tyranny. The French have already discovered that the blackness of the skin is no reason why a human being should be abandoned without redress to the caprice of a tormentor. It may one day come to be recognised that the number of the legs, the villosity of the skin, or the termination of the *os sacrum*, are reasons equally insufficient for abandoning a sensitive being to the same fate. What else is it that should trace the insuperable line? Is it the faculty of reason, or perhaps the faculty of discourse? But a fullgrown horse or dog is beyond comparison a more rational, as well as a more conversable animal, than an infant of a day, or a week, or even a month, old. But

suppose they were otherwise, what would it avail? The question is not, Can they *reason?* nor Can they *talk?* but, *Can they suffer?*[2]

In this passage Bentham points to the capacity for suffering as the vital characteristic that entitles a being to equal consideration. The capacity for suffering – or more strictly, for suffering and/or enjoyment or happiness – is not just another characteristic like the capacity for language, or for higher mathematics. Bentham is not saying that those who try to mark 'the insuperable line' that determines whether the interests of a being should be considered happen to have selected the wrong characteristic. The capacity for suffering and enjoying things is a prerequisite for having interests at all, a condition that must be satisfied before we can speak of interests in any meaningful way. It would be nonsense to say that it was not in the interests of a stone to be kicked along the road by a schoolboy. A stone does not have interests because it cannot suffer. Nothing that we can do to it could possibly make any difference to its welfare. A mouse, on the other hand, does have an interest in not being tormented, because mice will suffer if they are treated in this way.

If a being suffers, there can be no moral justification for refusing to take that suffering into consideration. No matter what the nature of the being, the principle of equality requires that the suffering be counted equally with the like suffering – in so far as rough comparisons can be made – of any other being. If a being is not capable of suffering, or of experiencing enjoyment or happiness, there is nothing to be taken into account. This is why the limit of sentience (using the term as a convenient, if not strictly accurate, shorthand for the capacity to suffer or experience enjoyment or happiness) is the only defensible boundary of concern for the interests of others. To mark this boundary by some characteristic like intelligence or rationality would be to mark it in an arbitrary way. Why not choose some other characteristic, like skin colour?

Racists violate the principle of equality by giving greater weight to the interests of members of their own race when there is a clash between their interests and the interests of those of another race. Racists of European descent typically have not accepted that pain matters as much when it is felt by Africans, for example, as when it is felt by Europeans. Similarly those I would call 'speciesists' give greater weight to the interests of members of their own species when there is a clash between their interests and the interests of those of other species. Human speciesists do not accept that pain is as bad when it is felt by pigs or mice as when it is felt by humans.

That, then, is really the whole of the argument for extending the principle of equality to nonhuman animals; but there may be some doubts about what this equality amounts to in practice. In particular, the last sentence of the previous paragraph may prompt some people to reply: 'Surely pain felt by a mouse just is not as bad as pain felt by a human. Humans have much greater awareness of what is happening to them, and this makes their suffering worse. You can't equate the suffering of, say, a person dying slowly from cancer, and a laboratory mouse undergoing the same fate.'

I fully accept that in the case described the human cancer victim normally suffers more than the nonhuman cancer victim. This is no way undermines the extension of equal consideration of interests to nonhumans. It means, rather, that we must take care when we compare the interests of different species. In some situations a member of one species will suffer more than a member of another species. In this case we should still apply the principle of equal consideration of interests but the result of so doing is, of course, to give priority to relieving the greater suffering. A simpler case may help to make this clear.

If I give a horse a hard slap across its rump with my open hand, the horse may start, but it presumably feels little pain. Its skin is thick enough to protect it against a mere slap. If I slap a baby in the same way, however, the baby will cry and presumably does feel pain, for the baby's skin is more sensitive. So it is worse to slap a baby than a horse, if both slaps are administered with equal force. But there must be some kind of blow – I don't know exactly what it would be, but perhaps a blow with a heavy stick – that would cause the horse as much pain as we cause a baby by a simple slap. That is what I mean by 'the same amount of pain' and if we consider it wrong to inflict that much pain on a baby for no good reason then we must, unless we are speciesists, consider it equally wrong to inflict the same amount of pain on a horse for no good reason.

There are other differences between humans and animals that cause other complications. Normal adult human beings have mental capacities that will, in certain circumstances, lead them to suffer more than animals would in the same circumstances. If, for instance, we decided to perform extremely painful or lethal scientific experiments on normal adult humans, kidnapped at random from public parks for this purpose, adults who entered parks would become fearful that they would be kidnapped. The resultant terror would be a form of suffering additional to the pain of the experiment. The same experiments performed on nonhuman animals would cause less suffering since the animals would not have the anticipatory dread of being kidnapped and experimented upon. This does not mean, of course, that it would be *right* to perform the experiment on animals, but only that there is a reason, and one that is not speciesist, for preferring to use animals rather than normal adult humans, if the experiment is to be done at all. Note, however, that this same argument gives us a reason for preferring to use human infants – orphans perhaps – or severely intellectually disabled humans for experiments, rather than adults, since infants and severely intellectually disabled humans would also have no idea of what was going to happen to them. As far as this argument is concerned, nonhuman animals and infants and severely intellectually disabled humans are in the same category; and if we use this argument to justify experiments on nonhuman animals we have to ask ourselves whether we are also prepared to allow experiments on human infants and severely intellectually disabled adults. If we make a distinction between animals and these humans, how can we do it, other than on the basis of a morally indefensible preference for members of our own species?

There are many areas in which the superior mental powers of normal adult humans make a difference: anticipation, more detailed memory, greater knowledge of what is happening, and so on. These differences explain why a human dying from cancer is likely to suffer more than a mouse. It is the mental anguish that makes the human's position so much harder to bear. Yet these differences do not all point to greater suffering on the part of the normal human being. Sometimes animals may suffer more because of their more limited understanding. If, for instance, we are taking prisoners in wartime we can explain to them that while they must submit to capture, search, and confinement they will not otherwise be harmed and will be set free at the conclusion of hostilities. If we capture wild animals, however, we cannot explain that we are not threatening their lives. A wild animal cannot distinguish an attempt to overpower and confine from an attempt to kill; the one causes as much terror as the other.

It may be objected that comparisons of the sufferings of different species are impossible to make, and that for this reason when the interests of animals and humans clash, the principle of equality gives no guidance. It is true that comparisons of suffering between members of different species cannot be made precisely. Nor, for that matter, can comparisons of suffering between different human beings be made precisely. Precision is not essential. As we shall see shortly, even if we were to prevent the infliction of suffering on animals only when the interests of humans will not be affected to anything like the extent that animals are affected, we would be forced to make radical changes in our treatment of animals that would involve our diet, the farming methods we use, experimental procedures in many fields of science, our approach to wildlife and to hunting, trapping, and the wearing of furs, and areas of entertainment like circuses, rodeos, and zoos. As a result, the total quantity of suffering caused would be greatly reduced; so greatly that it is hard to imagine any other change of moral attitude that would cause so great a reduction in the total sum of suffering in the universe.

So far I have said a lot about the infliction of suffering on animals, but nothing about killing them. This omission has been deliberate. The application of the principle of equality to the infliction of suffering is, in theory at least, fairly straightforward. Pain and suffering are bad and should be prevented or minimised, irrespective of the race, sex, or species of the being that suffers. How bad a pain is depends on how intense it is and how long it lasts, but pains of the same intensity and duration are equally bad, whether felt by humans or animals. When we come to consider the value of life, we cannot say quite so confidently that a life is a life, and equally valuable, whether it is a human life or an animal life. It would not be speciesist to hold that the life of a self-aware being, capable of abstract thought, of planning for the future, of complex acts of communication, and so on, is more valuable than the life of a being without these capacities. (I am not saying whether this view is justifiable or not; only that it cannot simply be rejected as speciesist, because it is not on the basis of species itself that one life is held to be more valuable than another.) The value of life is a notoriously difficult ethical question, and we can only arrive at a reasoned conclusion about the comparative value of human and animal life after we have discussed the value of life in general. This is a topic for a separate chapter. Meanwhile there are important conclusions to be derived from the extension beyond our own species of the principle of equal consideration of interests, irrespective of our conclusions about the value of life.

Speciesism in practice

Animals as food

For most people in modern, urbanised societies, the principal form of contact with non-human animals is at meal times. The use of animals for food is probably the oldest and the most widespread form of animal use. There is also a sense in which it is the most basic form of animal use, the foundation stone on which rests the belief that animals exist for our pleasure and convenience.

If animals count in their own right, our use of animals for food becomes questionable – especially when animal flesh is a luxury rather than a necessity. Eskimos living in an environment where they must kill animals for food or starve might be justified in claiming that their interest in surviving overrides that of the animals they kill. Most of us cannot defend our diet in this way. Citizens of industrialised societies can easily obtain an adequate diet without the use of animal flesh. The overwhelming weight of medical evidence indicates that animal flesh is not necessary for good health or longevity. Nor is animal production in industrialised societies an efficient way of producing food, since most of the animals consumed have been fattened on grains and other foods that we could have eaten directly. When we feed these grains to animals, only about 10 per cent of the nutritional value remains as meat for human consumption. So, with the exception of animals raised entirely on grazing land unsuitable for crops, animals are eaten neither for health, nor to increase our food supply. Their flesh is a luxury, consumed because people like its taste.

In considering the ethics of the use of animal flesh for human food in industrialised societies, we are considering a situation in which a relatively minor human interest must be balanced against the lives and welfare of the animals involved. The principle of equal consideration of interests does not allow major interests to be sacrificed for minor interests.

The case against using animals for food is at its strongest when animals are made to lead miserable lives so that their flesh can be made available to humans at the lowest possible cost. Modern forms of intensive farming apply science and technology to the attitude that animals are objects for us to use. In order to have meat on the table at a price that people can afford, our society tolerates methods of meat production that confine sentient animals in cramped, unsuitable conditions for the entire duration of their lives. Animals are treated like machines that convert fodder into flesh, and any innovation that results in a higher 'conversion ratio' is liable to be adopted. As one authority on the subject has said, 'Cruelty is acknowledged only when profitability ceases.' To avoid speciesism we must stop these practices. Our custom is all the support that factory farmers need. The decision to cease giving them that support may be difficult, but it is less difficult than it would have been for a white Southerner to go against the traditions of his society and free his slaves; if we do not change our dietary habits, how can we censure those slaveholders who would not change their own way of living?

These arguments apply to animals who have been reared in factory farms – which means that we should not eat chicken, pork, or veal, unless we know that the meat we are eating was not produced by factory farm methods. The same is true of beef that has come from cattle kept in crowded feedlots (as most beef does in the United States). Eggs will come from hens kept in small wire cages, too small even to allow them to stretch their wings, unless the eggs are specifically sold as 'free range' (or unless one lives in a relatively enlightened country like Switzerland, which has prohibited the cage system of keeping hens).

These arguments do not take us all the way to a vegetarian diet, since some animals, for instance sheep, and in some countries cattle still graze freely outdoors. This could change. The American pattern of fattening cattle in crowded feedlots is spreading to other countries. Meanwhile, the lives of free-ranging animals are undoubtedly better than those of animals reared in factory farms. It is still doubtful if using them for food is compatible with equal consideration of interests. One problem is, of course, that using them as food involves killing them – but this is an issue to which, as I have said, we shall return when we have discussed the value of life in the next chapter. Apart from taking their lives there are also many other things done to animals in order to bring them cheaply to our dinner table. Castration, the separation of mother and young, the breaking up of herds, branding, transporting, and finally the moments of slaughter – all of these are likely to involve suffering and do not take the animals' interests into account. Perhaps animals could be reared on a small scale without suffering in these ways, but it does not seem economical or practical to do so on the scale required for feeding our large urban populations. In any case, the important question is not whether animal flesh *could* be produced without suffering, but whether the flesh we are considering buying was produced without suffering. Unless we can be confident that it was, the principle of equal consideration of interests implies that it was wrong to sacrifice important interests of the animal in order to satisfy less important interests of our own; consequently we should boycott the end result of this process.

For those of us living in cities where it is difficult to know how the animals we might eat have lived and died, this conclusion brings us close to a vegetarian way of life. I shall consider some objections to it in the final section of this chapter.

Experimenting on animals

Perhaps the area in which speciesism can most clearly be observed is the use of animals in experiments. Here the issue stands out starkly, because experimenters often seek to justify experimenting on animals by claiming that the experiments lead us to discoveries about humans; if this is so, the experimenter must agree that human and nonhuman animals are similar in crucial respects. For instance, if forcing a rat to choose between starving to death and crossing an electrified grid to obtain food tells us anything about the reactions of humans to stress, we must assume that the rat feels stress in this kind of situation.

People sometimes think that all animal experiments serve vital medical purposes, and can be justified on the grounds that they relieve more suffering than they cause. This comfortable belief is mistaken. Drug companies test new shampoos and cosmetics they are intending to market by dripping concentrated solutions of them into the eyes of rabbits, in a test known as the Draize test. (Pressure from the animal liberation movement has led several cosmetic companies to abandon this practice. An alternative test, not using animals, has now been found. Nevertheless, many companies, including some of the largest, still continue to perform the Draize test.) Food additives, including artificial colourings and preservatives, are tested by what is known as the LD50 – a test designed to find the 'lethal dose', or level of consumption that will make 50 per cent of a sample of animals die. In the process nearly all of the animals are made very sick before some finally die and others pull through. These tests are not necessary to prevent human suffering: even if there were no alternative to the use of animals to test the safety of the products, we already have enough shampoos and food colourings. There is no need to develop new ones that might be dangerous.

In many countries, the armed forces perform atrocious experiments on animals that rarely come to light. To give just one example: at the U.S. Armed Forces Radiobiology Institute, in Bethesda, Maryland, rhesus monkeys have been trained to run inside a large wheel. If they slow down too much, the wheel slows down, too, and the monkeys get an electric shock. Once the monkeys are trained to run for long periods, they are given lethal doses of radiation. Then, while sick and vomiting, they are forced to continue to run until they drop. This is supposed to provide information on the capacities of soldiers to continue to fight after a nuclear attack.

Nor can all university experiments be defended on the grounds that they relieve more suffering than they inflict. Three experimenters at Princeton University kept 256 young rats without food or water until they died. They concluded that young rats under conditions of fatal thirst and starvation are much more active than normal adult rats given food and water. In a well-known series of experiments that went on for more than fifteen years, H. F. Harlow of the Primate Research Center, Madison, Wisconsin, reared monkeys under conditions of maternal deprivation and total isolation. He found that in this way he could reduce the monkeys to a state in which, when placed among normal monkeys, they sat huddled in a corner in a condition of persistent depression and fear. Harlow also produced monkey mothers so neurotic that they smashed their infant's face into the floor and rubbed it back and forth. Although Harlow himself is no longer alive, some of his former students at other U.S. universities continue to perform variations on his experiments.

In these cases, and many others like them, the benefits to humans are either nonexistent or uncertain, while the losses to members of other species are certain and real. Hence the experiments indicate a failure to give equal consideration to the interests of all beings, irrespective of species.

In the past, argument about animal experimentation has often missed this point because it has been put in absolutist terms: would the opponent of experimentation be prepared to let thousands die from a terrible disease that could be cured by experimenting on one animal? This is a purely hypothetical question, since experiments do not have such dramatic results, but as long as its hypothetical nature is clear, I think the question should be answered affirmatively – in other words, if one, or even a dozen animals had to suffer experiments in order to save thousands, I would think it right and in accordance with equal consideration of interests that they should do so. This, at any rate, is the answer a utilitarian must give. Those who believe in absolute rights might hold that it is always wrong to sacrifice one being, whether human or animal, for the benefit of another. In that case the experiment should not be carried out, whatever the consequences.

To the hypothetical question about saving thousands of people through a single experiment on an animal, opponents of speciesism can reply with a hypothetical question of their own: would experimenters be prepared to perform their experiments on orphaned humans with severe and irreversible brain damage if that were the only way to save thousands? (I say 'orphaned' in order to avoid the complication of the feelings of the human parents.) If experimenters are not prepared to use orphaned humans with severe and irreversible brain damage, their readiness to use nonhuman animals seems to discriminate on the basis of species alone, since apes, monkeys, dogs, cats, and even mice and rats are more intelligent, more aware of what is happening to them, more sensitive to pain, and so on, than many severely braindamaged humans barely surviving in hospital wards and other institutions. There seems to be no morally relevant characteristic that such humans have that nonhuman animals lack. Experimenters, then, show bias in favour of their own species whenever they carry out experiments on nonhuman animals for purposes that they would not think justified them in using human beings at an equal or lower level of sentience, awareness, sensitivity, and so on. If this bias were eliminated, the number of experiments performed on animals would be greatly reduced.

Other forms of speciesism

I have concentrated on the use of animals as food and in research, since these are examples of large-scale, systematic speciesism. They are not, of course, the only areas in which the principle of equal consideration of interests, extended beyond the human species, has practical implications. There are many other areas that raise similar issues, including the fur trade, hunting in all its different forms, circuses, rodeos, zoos, and the pet business. Since the philosophical questions raised by these issues are not very different from those raised by the use of animals as food and in research, I shall leave it to the reader to apply the appropriate ethical principles to them.

Some objections

I first put forward the views outlined in this chapter in 1973. At that time there was no animal liberation or animal rights movement. Since then a movement has sprung up, and some of the worst abuses of animals, like the Draize and LD50 tests, are now less widespread, even though they have not been eliminated. The fur trade has come under attack, and as a result fur sales have declined dramatically in countries like Britain, the Netherlands, Australia, and the United States. Some countries are also starting to phase out the most confining forms of factory farming. As already mentioned, Switzerland has prohibited the cage system of keeping laying hens. Britain has outlawed the raising of calves in individual stalls, and is phasing out individual stalls for pigs. Sweden, as in other areas of social reform, is in the lead here, too: in 1988 the Swedish Parliament passed a law that will, over a ten-year period, lead to the elimination of all systems of factory farming that confine animals for long periods and prevent them carrying out their natural behaviour.

Despite this increasing acceptance of many aspects of the case for animal liberation, and the slow but tangible progress made on behalf of animals, a variety of objections have emerged, some straightforward and predictable, some more subtle and unexpected. In this final section of the chapter I shall attempt to answer the most important of these objections. I shall begin with the more straightforward ones.

How do we know that animals can feel pain?

We can never directly experience the pain of another being, whether that being is human or not. When I see my daughter fall and scrape her knee, I know that she feels pain because of the way she behaves – she cries, she tells me her knee hurts, she rubs the sore spot, and so on. I know that I myself behave in a somewhat similar – if more inhibited – way when I feel pain, and so I accept that my daughter feels something like what I feel when I scrape my knee.

The basis of my belief that animals can feel pain is similar to the basis of my belief that my daughter can feel pain. Animals in pain behave in much the same way as humans do, and their behaviour is sufficient justification for the belief that they feel pain. It is true that, with the exception of those apes who have been taught to communicate by sign language, they cannot actually say that they are feeling pain – but then when my daughter was very young she could not talk, either. She found other ways to make her inner states apparent, thereby demonstrating that we can be sure that a being is feeling pain even if the being cannot use language.

To back up our inference from animal behaviour, we can point to the fact that the nervous systems of all vertebrates, and especially of birds and mammals, are fundamentally similar. Those parts of the human nervous system that are concerned with feeling pain are relatively old, in evolutionary terms. Unlike the cerebral cortex, which developed fully only after our ancestors diverged from other mammals, the basic nervous system evolved in more distant ancestors common to ourselves and the other 'higher' animals. This anatomical parallel makes it likely that the capacity of animals to feel is similar to our own.

It is significant that none of the grounds we have for believing that animals feel pain hold for plants. We cannot observe behaviour suggesting pain – sensational claims to the contrary have not been substantiated – and plants do not have a centrally organised nervous system like ours.

Animals eat each other, so why shouldn't we eat them?

This might be called the Benjamin Franklin Objection. Franklin recounts in his *Autobiography* that he was for a time a vegetarian but his abstinence from animal flesh came to an end when he was watching some friends prepare to fry a fish they had just caught. When the fish was cut open, it was found to have a smaller fish in its stomach. 'Well', Franklin said to himself, 'if you eat one another, I don't see why we may not eat you' and he proceeded to do so.

Franklin was at least honest. In telling this story, he confesses that he convinced himself of the validity of the objection only after the fish, was already in the frying pan and smelling 'admirably well'; and he remarks that one of the advantages of being a 'reasonable creature' is that one can find a reason for whatever one wants to do. The replies that can be made to this objection are so obvious that Franklin's acceptance of it does testify more to his love of fried fish than to his powers of reason.[3] For a start, most animals who kill for food would not be able to survive if they did not, whereas we have no need to eat animal flesh. Next, it is odd that humans, who normally think of the behaviour of animals as 'beastly' should, when it suits them, use an argument that implies that we ought to look to animals for moral guidance. The most decisive point, however, is that nonhuman animals are not capable of considering the alternatives open to them or of reflecting on the ethics of their diet. Hence it is impossible to hold the animals responsible for what they do, or to judge that because of their killing they 'deserve' to be treated in a similar way. Those who read these lines, on the other hand, must consider the justifiability of their dietary habits. You cannot evade responsibility by imitating beings who are incapable of making this choice.

Sometimes people point to the fact that animals eat each other in order to make a slightly different point. This fact suggests, they think, not that animals deserve to be eaten, but rather that there is a natural law according to which the stronger prey upon the weaker, a kind of Darwinian 'survival of the fittest' in which by eating animals we are merely playing our part.

This interpretation of the objection makes two basic mistakes, one a mistake of fact and the other an error of reasoning. The factual mistake lies in the assumption that our own consumption of animals is part of the natural evolutionary process. This might be true of a few primitive cultures that still hunt for food, but it has nothing to do with the mass production of domestic animals in factory farms.

Suppose that we did hunt for our food, though, and this was part of some natural evolutionary process. There would still be an error of reasoning in the assumption that because this process is natural it is right. It is, no doubt, 'natural' for women to produce an infant every year or two from puberty to menopause, but this does not mean that it is wrong to interfere with this process. We need to know the natural laws that affect us in order to estimate the consequences of what we do; but we do not have to assume that the natural way of doing something is incapable of improvement.

[. . .]

Ethics and reciprocity

[. . .]

[I]f the basis of ethics is that I refrain from doing nasty things to others as long as they don't do nasty things to me, I have no reason against doing nasty things to those who are incapable of appreciating my restraint and controlling their conduct towards me accordingly. Animals, by and large, are in this category. When I am surfing far out from shore and a shark attacks, my concern for animals will not help; I am as likely to be eaten as the next surfer, though he may spend every Sunday afternoon taking potshots at sharks from a boat. Since animals cannot reciprocate, they are, on this view, outside the limits of the ethical contract.

[. . .]

When we turn to the question of justification, we can see that contractual accounts of ethics have many problems. Clearly, such accounts exclude from the ethical sphere a lot more than nonhuman animals. Since severely intellectually disabled humans are equally incapable of reciprocating, they must also be excluded. The same goes for infants and very young children; but the problems of the contractual view are not limited to these special cases. The ultimate reason for entering into the ethical contract is, on this view, self-interest. Unless some additional universal element is brought in, one group of people has no reason to deal ethically with another if it is not in their interest to do so. If we take this seriously we shall have to revise our ethical judgments drastically. For instance, the white slave traders who transported African slaves to America had no self-interested reason for treating Africans any better than they did. The Africans had no way of retaliating. If they had only been contractualists, the slave traders could have rebutted the abolitionists by explaining to them that ethics stops at the boundaries of the community, and since Africans are not part of their community they have no duties to them.

Nor is it only past practices that would be affected by taking the contractual model seriously. Though people often speak of the world today as a single community, there is no doubt that the power of people in, say, Chad, to reciprocate either good or evil that is done to them by, say, citizens of the United States is limited. Hence it does not seem that the contract view provides for any obligations on the part of wealthy nations to poorer nations.

Most striking of all is the impact of the contract model on our attitude to future generations. 'Why should I do anything for posterity? What has posterity ever done for me?' would be the view we ought to take if only those who can reciprocate are within the bounds of ethics. There is no way in which those who will be alive in the year 2100 can do anything to make our lives better or worse. Hence if obligations only exist where there can be reciprocity, we need have no worries about problems like the disposal of nuclear waste. True, some nuclear wastes will still be deadly for a quarter of a million years; but as long as we put it in containers that will keep it away from us for 100 years, we have done all that ethics demands of us.

These examples should suffice to show that, whatever its origin, the ethics we have now does go beyond a tacit understanding between beings capable of reciprocity. The prospect of returning to such a basis will, I trust, not be appealing. Since no account of the origin of morality compels us to base our morality on reciprocity, and since no other arguments in favour of this conclusion have been offered, we should reject this view of ethics.

[. . .]

Conclusions

[T]here is no single answer to the question: 'Is it normally wrong to take the life of an animal?' The term 'animal' – even in the restricted sense of 'non-human animal' – covers too diverse a range of lives for one principle to apply to all of them.

Some non-human animals appear to be rational and self-conscious, conceiving themselves as distinct beings with a past and a future. When this is so, or to the best of our knowledge may be so, the case against killing is strong, as strong as the case against killing permanently intellectually disabled human beings at a similar mental level. (I have in mind here the direct reasons against killing; the effects on relatives of the intellectually disabled human will sometimes – but not always – constitute additional indirect reasons against killing the human.)

In the present state of our knowledge, this strong case against killing can be invoked most categorically against the slaughter of chimpanzees, gorillas, and orangutans. On the basis of what we now know about these near-relatives of ours, we should immediately extend to them the same full protection against being killed that we extend now to all human beings. A case can also be made, though with varying degrees of confidence, on behalf of whales, dolphins, monkeys, dogs, cats, pigs, seals, bears, cattle, sheep, and so on, perhaps even to the point at which it may include all mammals – much depends on how far we are prepared to go in extending the benefit of the doubt, where a doubt exists. Even if we stopped at the species I have named, however – excluding the remainder of the mammals – our discussion has raised a very large question mark over the justifiability of a great deal of killing of animals carried out by humans, even when this killing takes place painlessly and without causing suffering to other members of the animal community. (Most of this killing, of course, does not take place under such ideal conditions.)

When we come to animals who, as far as we can tell, are not rational and self-conscious beings, the case against killing is weaker. When we are not dealing with beings aware of themselves as distinct entities, the wrongness of painless killing derives from the loss of pleasure it involves. Where the life taken would not, on balance, have been pleasant, no direct wrong is done. Even when the animal killed would have lived pleasantly, it is at least arguable that no wrong is done if the animal killed will, as a result of the killing, be replaced by another animal living an equally pleasant life. Taking this view involves holding that a wrong done to an existing being can be made up for by a benefit conferred on an as yet non-existent being. Thus it is possible to regard non-self-conscious animals as interchangeable with each other in a way that self-conscious beings are not. This means that in some circumstances – when animals lead pleasant lives, are killed painlessly, their deaths do not cause suffering to other animals, and the killing of one animal makes possible its replacement by another who would not otherwise have lived – the killing of non-self-conscious animals may not be wrong.

Is it possible, along these lines, to justify raising chickens for their meat, not in factory farm conditions but roaming freely around a farmyard? Let us make the questionable assumption that chickens are not self-conscious. Assume also that the birds can be killed painlessly, and the survivors do not appear to be affected by the death of one of their numbers. Assume, finally, that for economic reasons we could not rear the birds if we did not eat them. Then the replaceability argument appears to justify killing the birds, because depriving them of the pleasures of their existence can be offset against the pleasures of chickens who do not yet exist, and will exist only if existing chickens are killed.

As a piece of critical moral reasoning, this argument may be sound. Even at that level, it is important to realise how limited it is in its application. It cannot justify factory farming, where animals do not have pleasant lives. Nor does it normally justify the killing of wild animals. A duck shot by a hunter (making the shaky assumption that ducks are not self-conscious, and the almost certainly false assumption that the shooter can be relied upon to kill the duck instantly) has probably had a pleasant life, but the shooting of a duck does not lead to its replacement by another. Unless the duck population is at the maximum that can be sustained by the available food supply, the killing of a duck ends a pleasant life without starting another, and is for that reason wrong on straightforward utilitarian grounds. So although there are situations in which it is not wrong to kill animals, these situations are special ones, and do not cover very many of the billions of premature deaths humans inflict, year after year, on animals.

In any case, at the level of practical moral principles, it would be better to reject altogether the killing of animals for food, unless one must do so to survive. Killing animals for food makes us think of them as objects that we can use as we please. Their lives then count for little when weighed against our mere wants. As long as we continue to use animals in this way, to change our attitudes to animals in the way that they should be changed will be an impossible task. How can we encourage people to respect animals, and have equal concern for their interests, if they continue to eat them for their mere enjoyment? To foster the right attitudes of consideration for animals, including non-self-conscious ones, it may be best to make it a simple principle to avoid killing them for food.

[. . .]

Notes

1   My views on animals first appeared in *The New York Review of Books*, 5 April 1973, under the title 'Animal Liberation'. This article was a review of R. and S. Godlovitch and J. Harris (eds), *Animals, Men and Morals* (London, 1972). A more complete statement was published as *Animal Liberation*, 2nd ed. (New York, 1990).
2   Bentham's defence of animals, quoted in the section 'Racism and Speciesism' is from his *Introduction to the Principles of Morals and Legislation*, chap. 18, sec. 1, n.
3   The source for the anecdote about Benjamin Franklin is his *Autobiography* (New York, 1950), p. 41. The same objection has been more seriously considered by John Benson in 'Duty and the Beast', *Philosophy*, vol. 53 (1978): 545–7.

5

Josephine Donovan

"Animal Rights and Feminist Theory"

In this essay Josephine Donovan points to the "hyper-rationality" of thinkers such as Tom Regan and Peter Singer. She notes that this rationalism, paradoxically, has been a major theoretical justification for animal abuse. While not maintaining that women's value systems are inherently superior, she does identify a number of recent feminist theorists who articulate a world view based on reciprocity rather than domination.

Peter Singer prefaces his groundbreaking treatise *Animal Liberation* (1975) with an anecdote about a visit he and his wife made to the home of a woman who claimed to love animals, had heard he was writing a book on the subject, and so invited him to tea. Singer's attitude toward the woman is contemptuous: she had invited a friend who also loved animals and was "keen to meet us. When we arrived our hostess's friend was already there, and . . . certainly was keen to talk about animals. 'I do love animals,' she began . . . and she was off. She paused while refreshments were served, took a ham sandwich, and then asked us what pets we had."[1] Singer's point is not only to condemn the woman's hypocrisy in claiming to love animals while she was eating meat but also to dissociate himself from a sentimentalist approach to animal welfare. Speaking for his wife as well, he explains: "We were not especially 'interested in' animals. Neither of us had ever been inordinately fond of dogs, cats, or horses. . . . We didn't 'love' animals. . . . The portrayal of those who protest against cruelty to animals as sentimental, emotional 'animal lovers' [has meant] excluding the entire issue . . . from serious political and moral discussion." In other words, he fears that to associate the animal rights cause with "womanish" sentiment is to trivialize it.

Singer's concerns about the image and strategies of animal rights activists are shared by another major contemporary theorist of animal rights, Tom Regan. In his preface to *The Case for Animal Rights* (1983) Regan stresses that "since all who work on behalf of the interests of animals are . . . familiar with the tired charge of being 'irrational,' 'sentimental,' 'emotional,' or worse, we can give the lie to these accusations only by making a concerted effort not to indulge our emotions or parade our sentiments. And that requires making a sustained commitment to rational inquiry."[2] In a later article Regan defends himself against charges of being hyperrational by maintaining that "reason—not sentiment, not emotion—reason compels us to recognize the equal inherent value of . . . animals and . . . their equal right to be treated with respect."[3] Regan's and Singer's rejection of emotion and their concern about being branded sentimentalist are not accidental; rather, they expose the inherent

This article is dedicated to my great dog Rooney (1974–87), who died as it was being completed but whose life led me to appreciate the nobility and dignity of animals.

bias in contemporary animal rights theory toward rationalism, which, paradoxically, in the form of Cartesian objectivism, established a major theoretical justification for animal abuse.

Women animal rights theorists seem, indeed, to have developed more of a sense of emotional bonding with animals as the basis for their theory than is evident in the male literature. Mary Midgley, for example, another contemporary animal rights theorist, urges, "What makes our fellow beings entitled to basic consideration is surely not intellectual capacity but emotional fellowship." Animals, she notes, exhibit "social and emotional complexity of the kind which is expressed by the formation of deep, subtle and lasting relationships."[4] Constantia Salamone, a leading feminist animal rights activist, roundly condemns the rationalist, masculinist bias of current animal rights theory.[5] In the nineteenth century, women activists in the antivivisection movement, such as Frances Power Cobbe, viewed as their enemy the "coldly rational materialism" of science, which they saw as threatening "to freeze human emotion and sensibility. . . . Antivivisection . . . shielded the heart, the human spirit, from degradation at the hands of heartless science."[6]

Yet Singer's anecdote points up that one cannot simply turn uncritically to women as a group or to a female value system as a source for a humane relationship ethic with animals. While women have undoubtedly been less guilty of active abuse and destruction of animals than men (Virginia Woolf observes in *Three Guineas:* "The vast majority of birds and beasts have been killed by you; not by us"),[7] they nevertheless have been complicit in that abuse, largely in their use of luxury items that entail animal pain and destruction (such as furs) and in their consumption of meat. Charlotte Perkins Gilman, an animal welfare crusader as well as a feminist, criticized such hypocrisy decades before Singer in her "A Study in Ethics" (1933). Condemning women's habit of wearing "as decoration the carcass of the animal," Gilman remarks the shocking inconsistency that

> civilized Christian women, sensitive to cruelty, fond of pets, should willingly maintain the greatest possible cruelty to millions of harmless little animals. . . . Furs are obtained by trapping. Trapping means every agony known to an animal, imprisonment, starvation, freezing, frantic fear and pain. If one woman hung up or fastened down hundreds of kittens each by one paw in her backyard in winter weather, to struggle and dangle and freeze, to cry in anguish and terror that she might 'trim' something with their collected skins . . . she would be considered a monster."[8]

Recognizing that such problems are involved in women's historical relationship with animals, I believe that cultural feminism, informed by an awareness of animal rights theory, can provide a more viable theoretical basis for an ethic of animal treatment than is currently available.

[. . .]

Cultural feminism has a long history. Even during feminism's "first wave," thinkers otherwise as diverse as Margaret Fuller, Emma Goldman, and Charlotte Perkins Gilman articulated a critique of the atomistic individualism and rationalism of the liberal tradition.[9] They did so by proposing a vision that emphasized collectivity, emotional bonding, and an organic (or holistic) concept of life.

[. . .]

In the second wave of feminist theory there have been a few articles specifically linking feminism with animal rights: in the 1970s Carol Adams's articles on vegetarianism and more recently Constantia Salamone's piece in *Reweaving the Web of Life* (1982).[10] There have been a number of other works that link feminism more generally with ecology, such as those by Susan Griffin, Carolyn Merchant, Rosemary Radford Ruether, Marilyn French, Paula Gunn Allen, Chrystos, and Ynestra King.

From the cultural feminist viewpoint, the domination of nature, rooted in postmedieval, Western, male psychology, is the underlying cause of the mistreatment of animals as well as of the exploitation of women and the environment. In her pathbreaking study, *The Death of Nature: Women, Ecology, and the Scientific Revolution*, Carolyn Merchant recognizes that "we must reexamine the formation of a world view and a science that, by reconceptualizing reality as a machine rather than a living organism, sanctioned the domination of both nature and women."[11]

[. . .]

Recent cultural feminist theorists have identified alternative epistemological and ontological modes that must, I believe, replace the mode of sadomasochistic control/dominance characteristic of patriarchal scientific epistemology. Ruether, for example, urges the development of new ways of relating to nature and to nonhuman life-forms. "The project of human life," she says, "must cease to be seen as one of 'domination of nature.' . . . Rather, we have to find a new language of ecological responsiveness, a reciprocity between consciousness and the world systems in which we live and move and have our being."[12] In *Sexism and God-Talk* (1983), Ruether suggests that human consciousness be seen not as different from other life-forms but as continuous with the "bimorphic" spirit inherent in other living beings.

> Our intelligence is a special, intense form of . . . radial energy, but it is not without continuity with other forms; it is the self-conscious or "thinking dimension" of the radial energy of matter. We must respond to a "thou-ness" in all beings. This is not romanticism or an anthropomorphic animism that sees "dryads in trees," although there is truth in the animist view. . . . We respond not just as "I to it," but as "I to thou," to the spirit, the life energy that lies in every being in its own form of existence. The "brotherhood of man" needs to be widened to embrace not only women but also the whole community of life.[13]

Ruether calls for "a new form of human intelligence," one based on a relational, affective mode popularly called "right-brain thinking," which moves beyond the linear, dichotomized, alienated consciousness characteristic of the "left-brain" mode seen in masculinist scientific epistemology. Linear, rationalist modes are, Ruether enjoins, "ecologically dysfunctional."[14] What is needed is a more "disordered" (my term—if order means hierarchical dominance) relational mode that does not rearrange the context to fit a master paradigm but sees, accepts, and respects the environment.

In *The Sacred Hoop: Recovering the Feminine in American Indian Traditions* (1986), Paula Gunn Allen finds in those traditions attitudes toward nature that are quite different from the alienation and dominance that characterize Western epistemology and theology. God and the spiritual dimension do not transcend life but rather are immanent in all life-forms. All creatures are seen as sacred and entitled to fundamental respect. Allen, herself a Laguna Pueblo-Sioux, recalls that "when I was small, my mother often told me that animals, insects, and plants are to be treated with the kind of respect one customarily accords to high-status adults." Nature, in her culture, is seen "not as blind and mechanical, but as aware and organic." There is "a seamless web" between "human and nonhuman life."[15]

Rather than linear, hierarchical, mechanistic modes, Allen proposes a return to the achronological relational sensibility characteristic of her people. Recognizing that "there is some sort of connection between colonization and chronological time," Allen observes that

"Indian time rests on a perception of individuals as part of an entire gestalt in which fitting-ness is not a matter of how gear teeth mesh with each other but rather how the person meshes with the revolving of the seasons, the land, and the mythic reality that shapes all life into significance. . . . Women's traditional occupations, their arts and crafts, and their literatures and philosophies are more often accretive than linear, more achronological than chrono-logical, and more dependent on harmonious relationships of all elements within a field of perception than Western culture in general. . . . Traditional peoples perceive their world in a unified-field fashion."[16]

In her recent study of contemporary women's art, *Women as Mythmakers* (1984), Estella Lauter has identified the contours of a new myth that involves women and nature. "Many of these artists accept the affinity between woman and nature as a starting point—in fact, creating hybrid images of woman/animal/earth until the old distinctions among the levels in the Great Chain of Being seem unimportant."[17] Recognizing Susan Griffin's *Woman and Nature* (1978) as prototypical, Lauter detects in contemporary women's literature and art "an image of relationships among orders of being that is extremely fluid without being disintegrative."[18]

[. . .]

The women artists and the feminist theorists cited here point to a new mode of relation-ship; unlike the subject-object mode inherent in the scientific epistemology and the rationalist distancing practiced by the male animal rights theorists, it recognizes the varieties and differ-ences among the species but does not quantify or rank them hierarchically in a Great Chain of Being. It respects the aliveness and spirit (the "thou") of other creatures and understands that they and we exist in the same unified field continuum. It appreciates that what we share—life—is more important than our differences. Such a relationship sometimes involves affection, sometimes awe, but always respect.

[. . .]

It is interesting that numerous women scientists and naturalists who have worked with and observed animal life for years—such as Jane Goodall, Dian Fossey, Sally Carrighar, Francine Patterson, Janis Carter—exhibit this ethic implicitly: a caring, respecting attitude toward their "subjects."[19]

[. . .]

It may be objected that this ethic is too vague to be practicable in decisions concerning animals. My purpose here, however, is not to lay out a specific practical ethic but, rather, to indicate ways in which our thinking about animal/human relationships may be reoriented. Some may persist: suppose one had to choose between a gnat and a human being. It is, in fact, precisely this kind of either/or thinking that is rejected in the epistemology identified by cultural feminism. In most cases, either/or dilemmas in real life can be turned into both/ands. In most cases, dead-end situations such as those posed in lifeboat hypotheticals can be prevented. More specifically, however, it is clear that the ethic sketched here would mean feminists must reject carnivorism; the killing of live animals for clothing; hunting; the trap-ping of wildlife for fur (largely for women's luxury consumption); rodeos; circuses; and factory farming; and that they must support the drastic redesigning of zoos (if zoos are to exist at all) to allow animals full exercise space in natural habitats; that they should reject the use of lab animals for testing of beauty and cleaning products (such as the infamous "LD-50" and Draize tests) and military equipment, as well as psychological experimentation such as that carried out in the Harlow primate lab at the University of Wisconsin; that they should support efforts to replace medical experiments by computer models and tissue culture; that they should condemn and work to prevent further destruction of wetlands, forests, and other natural habitats. All of these changes must be part of a feminist reconstruction of the world.

Natural rights and utilitarianism present impressive and useful philosophical arguments for the ethical treatment of animals. Yet, it is also possible—indeed, necessary—to ground that ethic in an emotional and spiritual conversation with nonhuman life-forms. Out of a women's relational culture of caring and attentive love, therefore, emerges the basis for a feminist ethic for the treatment of animals. We should not kill, eat, torture, and exploit animals because they do not want to be so treated, and we know that. If we listen, we can hear them.

Notes

1   Peter Singer, *Animal Liberation* (New York: Avon, 1975), ix–x.
2   Tom Regan, *The Case for Animal Rights* (Berkeley and Los Angeles: University of California Press, 1983), xii.
3   Tom Regan, "The Case for Animal Rights," in *In Defense of Animals*, ed. Peter Singer (New York: Basil Blackwell, 1985), 24.
4   Mary Midgley, "Persons and Non-Persons," in Singer, ed., 60.
5   Constantia Salamone, xeroxed from letter, July 1986.
6   James Turner, *Reckoning with the Beast: Animals, Pain and Humanity in the Victorian Mind* (Baltimore: Johns Hopkins University Press, 1980), 101, 103.
7   Virginia Woolf, *Three Guineas* (1938; reprint, New York: Harcourt Brace, 1963), 6. Woolf's note to this passage indicates she had done some research on the issue.
8   Charlotte Perkins Gilman, "A Study in Ethics" (Schlesinger Library, Radcliffe College, Cambridge, Mass., 1933, typescript). Published by permission of the Schlesinger Library. It must be noted that the women criticized by Singer and Gilman are guilty of sins of omission rather than commission; they are not actively conducting atrocities against animals. Their failure is due to ignorance and habit, traits that are presumably correctable through moral education. In this article I focus mainly on the rationalist ideology of modern science because it is the principal contemporary legitimization of animal sacrifice and because its objectifying epistemology, which turns animals into "its," has become the pervasive popular view of animals, thus legitimizing other forms of animal abuse such as factory farming.
9   For a full discussion, see Donovan, *Feminist Theory: "The Intellectual Traditions of American Feminism"* (New York: Unger, 1985), 31–63.
10 Carol Adams, "The Oedible Complex: Feminism and Vegetarianism," in *The Lesbian Reader*, ed. Gina Covina and Laurel Galana (Oakland, Calif.: Amazon, 1975), 145–52, and "Vegetarianism: The Inedible Complex," *Second Wave* 4, no. 4 (1976): 36–42; Constantia Salamone, "The Prevalence of the Natural Law: Women and Animal Rights," in *Reweaving the Web of Life: Feminism and Nonviolence*, ed. Pam McAllister (Philadelphia: New Society, 1982), 364–75.
11 Carolyn Merchant, *The Death of Nature: Women, Ecology, and the Scientific Revolution* (New York: Harper & Row, 1980).
12 Ruether, *New Woman/New Earth*, 83, New York. Seabury, 1975.
13 Ruether, *Sexism and God-Talk*, (Boston: Beacon, 1983), 87.
14 Ibid., 89–90.
15 Paula Gunn Allen, *The Sacred Hoop: Recovering the Feminine in American Indian Traditions* (Boston: Beacon, 1986), 1, 80, 100; see also 224.
16 Ibid., 154, 243, 244.
17 Estella Lauter, *Women as Mythmakers: Poetry and Visual Art by Twentieth-Century Women* (Bloomington: Indiana University Press, 1984), 18.
18 Lauter, 19.
19 See Jane Goodall, *In the Shadow of Man* (Boston: Houghton Mifflin, 1971). *The Chimpanzees of Gombe: Patterns of Behavior* (Cambridge, Mass.: Harvard University Press, 1986); Dian Fossey, *Gorillas in the Mist* (Boston: Houghton Mifflin, 1983); and Sally Carrighar, *Home to the Wilderness* (Boston: Houghton Mifflin, 1973). See Eugene Linden, *Silent Partners* (New York: Times Books, 1986), on Patterson and Carter. Janis Carter spent eight years trying to reintroduce Lucy, a chimpanzee who had learned sign language, to the wild in West Africa. She tells her moving story in "Survival Training for Chimps," *Smithsonian* 19, no. 5 (June 1988): 36–49.

6

R.G. Frey

"Rights, Interests, Desires and Beliefs"

R.G. Frey argues that the key question is whether animals are the kind of beings who can have rights. He distinguishes two senses of "interest" and maintains that animals have interests only in the sense that things can be good or bad for them, as oil is good or bad for a tractor. Animals do not have desires, because having desires requires the having of beliefs. Beliefs require that the creature be able to distinguish between true and false beliefs, and for this distinction language is required.

[. . .]

[T]he question is not about *which* rights animals may or may not be thought to possess or about *whether* their alleged rights in a particular regard are on a par with the alleged rights of humans in this same regard but rather about the more fundamental issue of whether animals—or, in any event, the "higher" animals—are a kind of being which can be the logical subject of rights. It is this issue, and a particular position with respect to it, that I want critically to address here.

The position I have in mind is the widely influential one which links the possession of rights to the possession of interests. In his *System of Ethics*, Leonard Nelson is among the first, if not the first, to propound the view that all and only beings which have interests can have rights,[1] a view which has attracted an increasingly wide following ever since. [. . .] For Nelson, [. . .] it is because animals have interests that they can be the logical subject of rights, and his claim that animals *do have* interests forms the minor premiss, therefore, in an argument for the moral rights of animals: "All and only beings which (can) have interests (can) have moral rights; Animals as well as humans (can) have interests; Therefore, animals (can) have moral rights."

[. . .]

[I]t is apparent that the minor premiss is indeed the key to the whole matter. For given the truth of the major premiss, given, that is, that the possession of interests *is* a criterion for the possession of rights, it is nevertheless only the truth of the minor premiss that would result in the inclusion of creatures other than human beings within the class of right-holders. This premiss is doubtful, however, and the case against it a powerful one, or so I want to suggest.

[. . .]

To say that "Good health is in John's interests" is not at all the same thing as to say that "John has an interest in good health." The former is intimately bound up with having a good or well-being to which good health is conducive, so that we could just as easily have said "Good health is conducive to John's good or well-being," whereas the latter—"John has an interest in good health"—is intimately bound up with wanting, with John's wanting good health. That these two notions of "interest" are logically distinct is readily apparent: good health may well be in John's interests, in the sense of being conducive to his good or well-being, even if John does not want good health, indeed, even if he wants to continue taking hard drugs, with the result that his health is irreparably damaged; and John may have an interest in taking drugs, in the sense of wanting to take them, even if it is apparent to him that it is not conducive to his good or well-being to continue to do so. In other words, something can be *in* John's interests without John's *having* an interest in it, and John can *have* an interest in something without its being *in* his interests.

If this is right, and there are these two logically distinct senses of "interest," we can go on to ask whether animals can have interests in either of these senses; and if they do, then perhaps the minor premiss of Nelson's argument for the moral rights of animals can be sustained.

Do animals, therefore, have interests in the first sense, in the sense of having a good or well-being which can be harmed or benefited? The answer, I think, is that they certainly do have interests in this sense; after all, it is plainly not good for a dog to be fed certain types of food or to be deprived of a certain amount of exercise. This answer, however, is of little use to the Nelsonian cause; for it yields the counter-intuitive result that manmade/manufactured objects and even things have interests, and, therefore, on the interest thesis, have or at least are candidates for having moral rights. For example, just as it is not good for a dog to be deprived of a certain amount of exercise, so it is not good for prehistoric cave drawings to be exposed to excessive amounts of carbon dioxide or for Rembrandt paintings to be exposed to excessive amounts of sunlight.

[. . .]

Do animals, therefore, have interests in the second sense, in the sense of having wants which can be satisfied or left unsatisfied? In this sense of course, it appears that tractors do not have interests; for though being well-oiled may be conducive to tractors being good of their kind, tractors do not *have an interest* in being well-oiled, since they cannot *want* to be well-oiled, cannot, in fact, have any wants whatever. But farmers can have wants, and they certainly have an interest in their tractors being well-oiled.

What, then, about animals? Can they have wants? By "wants," I understand a term that encompasses both needs and desires, and it is these that I shall consider.

If to ask whether animals can have wants is to ask whether they can have needs, then certainly animals have wants. A dog can need water. But *this* cannot be the sense of "want" on which having interests will depend, since it does not exclude things from the class of want-holders. Just as dogs need water in order to function normally, so tractors need oil in order to function normally.

[. . .]

This, then, leaves desires, and the question of whether animals can have wants as desires. I may as well say at once that I do not think animals can have desires. My reasons for thinking this turn largely upon my doubts that animals can have beliefs, and my doubts in this regard turn partially, though in large part, upon the view that having beliefs is not compatible with the absence of language and linguistic ability. I realize that the claim that animals cannot have desires is a controversial one; but I think the case to be made in support of it, complex though it is, is persuasive.

[. . .]

Suppose I am a collector of rare books and desire to own a Gutenberg Bible: my desire to own this volume is *to be traced* to my belief that I do not now own such a work and that my rare book collection is deficient in this regard. By "to be traced" here, what I mean is this: if someone were to ask *how* my belief that my book collection lacks a Gutenberg Bible is connected with my desire to own such a Bible, what better or more direct reply could be given than that, without this belief, I would not have this desire? For if I believed that my rare book collection *did* contain a Gutenberg Bible and so was complete in this sense, then I would not desire a Gutenberg Bible in order to make up what I now believe to be a notable deficiency in my collection.

[. . .]

The difficulty in the case of animals should be apparent: if someone were to say, e.g., "The cat believes that the door is locked," then that person is holding, as I see it, that the cat holds the declarative sentence "The door is locked" to be true; and I can see no reason whatever for crediting the cat or any other creature which lacks language, including human infants, with entertaining declarative sentences and holding certain declarative sentences to be true.

[. . .]

If what is believed is that a certain declarative sentence is true, then no creature which lacks language can have beliefs; and without beliefs, a creature cannot have desires. And this is the case with animals, or so I suggest; and if I am right, not even in the sense, then, of wants as desires do animals have interests, which, to recall, is the minor premiss in the Nelsonian argument for the moral rights of animals.

But is what is believed that a certain declarative sentence is true? I think there are three arguments of sorts that shore up the claim that this *is* what is believed.

First, I do not see how a creature could have the concept of belief without being able to distinguish between true and false beliefs.

[. . .]

Second, if in order to have the concept of belief a creature must be possessed of the difference between true and false belief, then in order for a creature to be able to distinguish true from false beliefs that creature must—simply must, as I see it—have some awareness of, to put the matter in the most general terms, how language connects with, links up with the world; and I see no reason to credit cats with such an awareness.

[. . .]

Third, I do not see how a creature could have an awareness or grasp of how language connects with, links up with the world, to leave the matter at its most general, unless that creature was itself possessed of language; and cats are not possessed of language.

[. . .]

It may be suggested, of course, that there might possibly be a class of desires—let us call them simple desires—which do not involve the intervention of belief, in order to have them, and which do not require that we credit animals with language. Such simple desires, for example, might be for some object or other, and we as language-users might try to capture these simple desires in the case of a dog by describing its behavior in such terms as "The dog simply desires the bone".

[. . .]

Suppose, then, the dog simply desires the bone: is the dog aware that it has this simple desire or not? If it is alleged to have this desire but to be unaware that it has it, to want but to be unaware that it wants, then a problem arises. In the case of human beings, unconscious desire can be made sense of, but only because we first make sense of conscious desire; but where no desires are conscious ones, where the creature in question is alleged to have only unconscious desires, what cash value can the use of the term "desire" have in such a case?

[. . .]

There is nothing the dog can do which can express the difference between desiring the bone and being aware of desiring the bone. Yet, the dog would have to be capable of expressing this difference in its behavior, if one is going to hold, *on the basis of that behavior*, that the dog is aware that it has a simple desire for the bone, aware that it simply desires the bone.

Even, then, if we concede for the sake of argument that there are simple desires, desires which do not involve the intervention of belief in order to have them, the suggestion that we can credit animals with these desires, without also having to credit them with language, is at best problematic.

[. . .]

I conclude, then, that the Nelsonian position on the moral rights of animals is not a sound one: the truth of the minor premiss in his argument—that animals have interests—is doubtful at best, and animals must have interests if, in accordance with the interest thesis, they are to be a logical subject of such rights. For animals either have interests in a sense which allows objects and things to have interests, and so, on the interest thesis, to have or to be candidates for having moral rights or they do not have interests at all, and so, on the interest thesis, do not have and are not candidates for having moral rights. I have reached this conclusion, moreover, without querying the correctness of the interest thesis itself, without querying, that is, whether the possession of interests *really* is a criterion for the possession of moral rights.

Note

1   Leonard Nelson, *System of Ethics*, tr. by Norbert Guterman (New Haven, 1956), Part I, Section 2, Chapter 7, pp. 136–44.

7

David DeGrazia

"Equal Consideration and Unequal Moral Status"

David DeGrazia argues that it is not enough to articulate the principle of equal consideration of interests, because the interpretation of this principle involves many difficulties. He demonstrates some of the problems with comparing well-being, freedom, and the desire to live between different human and non-human animals. He argues that many thinkers maintain the principle of equal consideration and yet routinely hold that moral status is a matter of degree.

[. . .]

Relevantly similar interests

Introduction

It is one thing to articulate the principle of equal consideration, another to determine what it comes to. To do so is surprisingly difficult. But I do not wish to continue in the tradition of those who defend equal consideration, while ignoring or only casually exploring the complexities of interpreting this principle.[1] If the latter is to have any use, that which is to be given equal consideration must be clarified. What does it mean for interests to be relevantly similar? [. . .] I intend to demonstrate how far we are from having a truly adequate conception of equal consideration, while clarifying what remains to be worked out.

Experiential well-being

First consider experiential well-being, the interest in having a favorable experiential welfare. For simplicity, I consider the more specific interest in avoiding suffering; I think other components of experiential well-being are treatable in similar fashion. It seems reasonable that *A's interest in avoiding suffering of intensity I and duration D is relevantly similar to B's interest in avoiding suffering of I and D, regardless of who A and B are* (so long as both can experience such suffering). The same thing seems to be at stake for A and B.

[. . .]

Now it might be objected that the *kind* of suffering should also be specified, that A's suffering of intensity I, duration D, *and kind K* is identical to B's suffering only if the latter is of I, D, and K. Thus we might distinguish a human's "existential" suffering in the face of death—say, anguish over leaving his children fatherless and never completing his life project—from a cat's suffering, even if both are of I and D. Then we might roughly state our criterion thus: *Experiential well-being interest S is relevantly similar to experiential well-being interest T if and only if the experiences involved are similar (experientially).* Without insisting on this point, I suspect that consideration of K can be dropped if two experiences of suffering are, overall, equally aversive—for aversiveness seems to be precisely what is at stake. And the conjunction of intensity and duration seems to capture the dimensions of aversiveness.[2]

[...]

Freedom (and the possibility of values of special weight)

Let us consider freedom. All purposive agents—beings with certain kinds of beliefs and desires who are capable of acting intentionally—desire to do certain things at certain times. They therefore have an interest (special circumstances aside) in freedom, which is a necessary condition for the satisfaction of action-related interests. Assuming that at least normal mammals are purposive agents, are the freedom of a human and that of a cat relevantly similar interests? Is the same thing at stake?

Let us start with "negative freedom," the absence of external constraints. Purposive agents have an interest in negative freedom (at least) because it is necessary for the satisfaction of other, action-related interests. But the sorts of things for which different beings need negative freedom vary enormously. Confining a mouse in a small cage restricts its movement, thereby thwarting many of its desires. But confining a human to a proportionally sized space, say a room, thwarts, in most cases, nearly every action-related desire she has.

It seems *possible* that many of the kinds of things a human typically desires to do have more value than the kinds of things a mouse desires to do. Perhaps such things as deep personal relationships, living autonomously, real accomplishment, and esthetic enrichment have special weight.[3] R.G. Frey has proposed *richness* as a criterion for determining the value of particular activities and the lives that include them.[4] It is important to see that the comparative claim is about *prudential* value, not moral value. To be sure, Frey and others (cited below) who make this claim might maintain that a normal human life has more value to *others* than a mouse life has (however that is determined). But they all contend that the human loses more, in dying, than does the mouse. If a utilitarian were to compare two actions, A and B, that had identical consequences, except that A caused a human death while B caused a rodent death, she would judge B to have more net value (less disvalue)—on the special weight hypothesis. While Frey's and similar proposals merit further exploration, they take us well beyond the scope of this paper.

However, one very important but commonly missed point about such proposals is worth making. Attributing special weight to certain features of lives in making *cross-individual comparisons, where not all of the individuals' lives have such features,* probably requires the attribution of objective, intrinsic value to them. (As I use these terms, X has objective, as opposed to subjective, value if X's value does not depend on its being valued or desired by any particular individual; X has intrinsic, as opposed to instrumental, value if its value does not depend on the value of anything else.[5]) Consider the major alternatives. *Strength* of desires for such things as real accomplishment would not explain such special weight, because a mouse might have equally strong desires, though for different things. Nor would the *centrality* of an interest in one's own system of interests (i.e., its tendency to support other interests), because some of a mouse's interests must be similarly central. Following Mill one might, in comparing two experiences or activities, "ask those who have experienced both." But the problematic cases involve comparative value judgments applying to individuals at least one of whom has not "experienced both."[6] The "special weight" hypothesis appears to implicate objective, intrinsic value. At least anyone who disagrees had better explain how the claim of special weight can be made intelligible and plausible.

At present it is unclear whether the view that some interests have special (cross-individual) weight can be convincingly defended. But it is at least not obvious that things of the same value are at stake with the negative-freedom interests of mice, or other animals, and humans. More and better work in interspecific value theory is necessary.

What about other aspects of freedom, other components of what is needed to act with some prospect of successful action? Besides negative freedom, some minimal experiential well-being (see above) is necessary, as are some nonexperiential components. Nonexperiential conditions of "positive freedom" presumably include bodily functioning (and, therefore, e.g., food) and mental functioning (and, therefore, e.g., a relatively stable environment). Whether instances of each of these interests are relevantly similar, regardless of who has them, is an extremely complicated question.

[. . .]

If we can determine that things of different value are at stake, though, it would be natural to say that two beings, A and B, may be *harmed* to differing degrees by restrictions of their freedom. Equal consideration, then, would not require giving equal moral weight to A's freedom and B's freedom. Because things of different value would be at stake, A's freedom and B's freedom would count as relevantly different interests.

But perhaps the components of freedom are interests not only for being instrumental for the satisfaction of other interests, but also because they themselves are desired. Can animals desire such things as physical functioning and mental functioning *in themselves*, i.e., apart from the experiences that the presence or absence of such functioning affects? I will remain agnostic on this issue. The clearest way in which the components of freedom constitute interests for animals is in their instrumental role, as just discussed.

Life—and conclusion

Consider finally the interest of life or remaining alive. One position is that A has an interest in life only if A has a desire to continue living, requiring the possession of a conception of oneself enduring over time.[7] In contrast, I hold that (special circumstances aside) all beings with interests have an interest in life, a precondition for the satisfaction of almost every other possible interest.[8] If this is correct and both humans and mice have interests in life, are their interests relevantly similar? Is the same thing at stake for both of them?

For some beings, including normal humans and possibly some animals, life is an interest in part because it is the object of a desire (usually a very strong one). But for all beings with an interest in life, a great part of its raison d'être is its role as a condition for the satisfaction of other interests. This fact renders uncertain the claim that all interests in life are relevantly similar. As with freedom, relevantly different things may be at stake. A mouse's interest in life would seem to be an interest in living a particular sort of life, or a life involving interests P, Q, R . . .; a normal human's interest would be an interest in living a different sort of life, involving different interests. And it seems quite possible that the respective (prudential) values of what is at stake are not equal. Thus some—like Singer, Regan, Frey, and Rachels—will deny that equal consideration of relevantly similar interests requires giving equal moral weight to different sorts of lives. Others have attacked this inegalitarian line.[9] Rather than take up the issue here, I simply conclude that it is unclear that equal consideration entails giving equal moral weight to the lives of all morally considerable beings.

Our investigations into experiential well-being, freedom, and life demonstrate that we cannot simply assume that interests that can be grouped under a single heading, such as "life," are relevantly similar—and, therefore, subject to equal consideration.

[. . .]

Equality of moral status

Having explored the principle of equal consideration in some depth, let us turn to moral status and, then, to equal moral status. Of the two, moral status is easier to clarify, because it is more familiar. A has moral status if and only if A's interests have some moral weight, independently of their effects on other beings who have moral status. Normal adult human beings are the paradigm.

[. . .]

Does the concept of moral status entail that those who have it have it equally? Or does it admit of degrees, so that it is intelligible to say that fetuses have moral status but less than pregnant women, or that dogs have moral status but less than normal humans? I submit that the concept of moral status is not sufficiently sharp and univocal to answer this question definitively. Therefore I will propose a reconstruction of the concept that fairly plausibly organizes our linguistic intuitions in a way that is useful for our moral investigations.

But, first, a motivating thought. Who has moral status? Following an impressive list of theorists,[10] I hold that a being has moral status if and only if that being has interests. [. . .] However it is defended, given this assumption and the fact that some animals have interests, it follows that some animals have moral status.

[. . .]

My own experience suggests that, among ethical theorists and lay-persons alike, many who hold that animals are subject to some fundamental principle of equality (e.g., equal consideration) nevertheless hold that normal humans and animals are different in morally significant ways. It is this vague but powerful intuition that I wish to capture in speaking in terms of unequal moral status. The mere possibility that this intuition is right suggests that we need a concept of moral status that admits of degrees.[11]

Now for the hard part. What would it mean to say A has less moral status than B? Well, consider the sorts of judgments that might motivate such a claim—without contradicting an assumption of equal consideration (since I want to show that this assumption and unequal moral status are compatible).

First, a utilitarian might argue as follows. Equal consideration requires that we regard a certain amount (duration and intensity) of suffering as equally bad, whatever the sufferer's species. Due to the suffering typically caused in animal research, the fact that the hoped-for benefits are in most cases not forthcoming and often marginal when they do come, and other considerations, most animal research is unjustified. However, in the present epidemic we really must test possible cures, even though such testing will cost some subjects their lives. Although there is no reason to discount animal suffering because it is animal, normal human lives and cat lives do seem relevantly different—justifying less of a moral presumption against taking cat lives. [. . .] Thus we will use a small number of cats, and no humans, to test possible cures until we find one.

Second, a tribe of normally vegetarian bushpeople live in a part of South Africa quite remote from any city. The tribe has no commerce with cityfolk at all. One winter the fruits, nuts, and crops the bushpeople gather are so scarce that several children are in danger of starvation. Like the bushpeople of *The Gods Must Be Crazy*, a tribemember strikes an antelope with a spear anointed with a substance that immediately puts the animal to sleep. With apologies to the sleeping animal, several adults kill it for the meat that will allow a few children to survive. (They would never kill a human for such a purpose.) While I will not imagine that these people are familiar with Western moral philosophy, their attitudes seem consistent with a rights theory that grants all sentient animals a right not to be harmed needlessly. If we allow that the lives of humans and animals are relevantly different, to kill an antelope when necessary to prevent the death of a human child could plausibly be considered "needful" harm.

Third, I have a Great Dane and my neighbor has a rowdy eight-year-old girl. The two of them often get into trouble outside. Sometimes the dog knocks over the girl; sometimes the girl pulls the dog's ears or tackles him roughly. Each is sometimes hurt, though neither appears in danger of death or disability. My neighbor's talks with his daughter do not succeed in preventing hurts and minor harms to either of them. We jointly decide that my dog should not be allowed outside in the hours when the girl most likes to play (unless he is on a leash). Though committed to equal consideration, I accept this decision, believing that this restriction of my dog's freedom is less of a loss to him than a similar restriction of the girl's freedom would be to her.

I take it that the ethical judgments in these three examples are fairly plausible.

[. . .]

Thus we come to a reconstruction of the concept of moral status that admits of degrees: *Moral status is the degree (relative to other beings) of moral resistance to having one's interests—especially one's most important interests—thwarted.* More positively, *moral status is the degree of moral protectability a being enjoys (vis-à-vis other beings).* [. . .] [E]qual consideration is consistent with justifying some significant harms in cases like those above. And if any harm is, in fact, justified in such conflict cases, it is not against humans.

Thus while equal consideration, on any plausible interpretation, largely condemns current animal-harming practices, this principle is logically compatible with the recognition of some significant moral differences. These differences may be conveniently expressed in the language of (unequal) moral status.

[. . .]

Notes

1   See, e.g., Singer, *Animal Liberation*, and Rachels, *Created from Animals*. The levity of their exploration of what equal consideration means is perhaps best seen in their casual defense of the claim that equal consideration does not entail that all lives are of equal value (*Animal Liberation*, pp. 19–21; *Created from Animals*, pp. 208–9).
2   A reviewer for *The Southern Journal of Philosophy* questioned whether the aversiveness of suffering is exhausted by intensity and duration, arguing that a strong person might find suffering of I and D less aversive than a weak person would. But remember that one's own emotional reaction to suffering can involve further suffering (in the form of anxiety, fear, depression, or other states). What is likely is that the weak person would suffer more in the end for being less able to bear the initial suffering. Therefore the two individuals would not be experiencing the same intensity and duration of suffering, all told, a conclusion consistent with the strong person's finding her experiences less aversive.
3   James Griffin argues for the special importance of these goods, with the exception of esthetic enrich-

ment, in *Well-Being: Its Meaning, Measurement and Moral Importance* (Oxford: Clarendon Press, 1986).

4   R.G. Frey, "Animal Parts, Human Wholes." R.G. Frey, "Animal Parts, Human Wholes: On the Use of Animals as a Source of Organs for Human Transplants," in James M. Humber and Robert A. Almeder (eds), *Biomedical Ethics Reviews 1987* (Clifton, New Jersey: Humana Press, 1987), pp. 89–107.

5   X with objective value may or may not have inherent value. For X to have inherent value is for X to be valuable even if no one in the universe values or desires X.

6   One might still push the Millian proposal by developing a line of thought of Singer's (*Practical Ethics*, p. 90). Imagine that you could live the life of a normal mouse and have all its experiences, before being transformed into a species-less but rational state in which you could remember both human and mouse experiences. Would you not prefer real accomplishment (or whatever) to anything available in the mouse's life, if you could live a life with any of the experiences available to a human or a mouse? A desire for real accomplishment in this thought-experiment might justify assigning it special value, without speaking of objective, intrinsic value.

While this proposal is more promising than the others I surveyed, it raises formidably difficult issues in the philosophy of mind, and might not even be intelligible. For one thing, to avoid human bias, I must really "get into the mouse's shoes" when imagining the mouse's experiences; it is irrelevant that I would not like to be a *human* chasing bugs, living in cupboards, etc. But in order to be sufficiently neutral, I must, presumably, not bring *anything* peculiar to my mental life into my new evaluations. But then it is not obvious that I can even make evaluations. It is not enough to imagine being a mouse and having mouse experiences (no small epistemological feat). I must compare the mouse's experiences to a human's. Is there enough of a self—indeed, any self—left to make comparisons? On what basis are they to be made, if none of my particular preferences can get them off the ground? While I cannot enter into all of the issues raised by this proposal, I am sceptical about it. (I am even doubtful that Millian preference orderings provide an adequate account of value for humans.)

7   This is implied by the version of preference-utilitarianism that holds that only the objects of actual preferences (desires) are interests.

8   Does life also have objective, intrinsic value—so that it has some positive value even if one does not desire to remain alive and being alive does not have instrumental value (due to, say, an existence full of pain and absent of functioning)? For that matter, does freedom have some positive value even if not desired and lacking in instrumental value (say, because one is so vulnerable that freedom imperils one)? These questions are beyond the scope of this paper and do not affect my tentative conclusions about freedom and life.

9   See, e.g., S.F. Sapontzis, *Morals, Reason and Animals* (Philadelphia: Temple University Press, 1987), pp. 216–22, and Edward Johnson, "Life, Death, and Animals," in Harlan B. Miller and William H. Williams (eds), *Ethics and Animals* (Clifton, New Jersey: Humana Press, 1983), pp. 123–33.

10 See, e.g., Joel Feinberg, "The Rights of Animals and Unborn Generations," in W. T. Blackstone (ed.), *Philosophy and Environmental Crisis* (Athens, Georgia: University of Georgia Press, 1974), pp. 43–60; Peter Singer, *Animal Liberation*; Bernard Rollin, *Animal Rights and Human Morality* (New York: Prometheus Books, 1981); and S. F. Sapontzis, *Morals, Reason and Animals*.

11 In this paper I have, again, assumed the principle of equal consideration. But even an explicit rejection of the idea that animals are to be accorded equal consideration would demonstrate the utility of a concept of moral status that admitted of degrees, assuming animals would still be accorded some moral status. For they would then have less than humans.

Annotated Further Reading

Carruthers, P. (1992) *The Animals Issue*, Cambridge: Cambridge University Press. Carruthers strongly argues that animals' mental states are unconscious and hence that animals have no moral status. However the case is weakened by insufficient consideration of available scientific data.

Cavalieri, P. (2001) *Why Non-human Animals Deserve Human Rights*, New York: Oxford University Press. A powerful argument based on the logic of the universal human rights doctrine.

Col, M., *et al.* (eds) (1997) *Animal Consciousness and Animal Ethics: Perspectives from the Netherlands*, Van Gorcum. Useful and carefully written essays.

DeGrazia, D. (1998) *Taking Animals Seriously: Mental Life and Moral Status*, Cambridge: Cambridge University Press. Excellent, empirically informed account arguing for the principle of equal consideration of all beings which have interests.

—— (1998) "Animal Ethics Around the Turn of the Twenty-First Century." *Journal of Agricultural and*

Environmental Ethics 11:111–29. DeGrazia reviews four recent books, including his own argument for the principle of equal consideration.

Dollins, F.L. (ed.) (1999) *Attitudes to Animals: Views in Animal Welfare*, Cambridge: Cambridge University Press. Excellent anthology with a good mix of American and British authors.

Dombrowski, D. (1998) "Rawls and Animals." *International Journal of Applied Philosophy* 12.1:63–77. Argues that Rawls' work is somewhat ambivalent concerning animals but basically anthropocentric.

Donovan, J. and Adams, C.J. (eds) (1996) *Beyond Animal Rights: A Feminist Caring Ethic for the Treatment of Animals*. New York: Continuum. An excellent collection.

Engelhardt, Jr., Tristram, H. "Animals: their Right to be Used." In E.F. Paul and J. Paul (eds) *Why Animal Experimentation Matters*, New Brunswick: Transaction Publishers.

Franklin, A. (1999) *Animals and Modern Cultures: A Sociology of Human-Animal Relations in Modernity*. London: Sage. Changes in human-animal relations in the context of social and cultural change.

Goldman, M. (2001) "A Transcendental Defense of Speciesism." *The Journal of Value Inquiry* 35: 59–69. Uses the principle that primary moral consideration should be extended to beings with whom we are able to cooperate in social reproductive efforts.

Gruzalski, B. (1996) "Autonomy and the Orthodoxy of Human Superiority," with Response by R.G. Frey, *Between the Species* 12. 1 and 2: 1–18. Clear and important arguments.

Jamieson, D. (ed.) (1999) *Singer and his Critics*. Oxford: Blackwell. A collection of highly useful critical essays with responses by Singer.

Kistler, J.M. (2000) *Animal Rights: A Subject Guide, Bibliography, and Internet Companion*, Westport, Conn.: Greenwood Press. A comprehensive, annotated resource.

Kruse, C.R. (1999) "Gender, Views of Nature, and Support for Animal Rights." *Society and Animals* 7.3: 179–98. A sociological study.

Linzey, A. and Yamamoto, D. (1998) *Animals on the Agenda*. Urbana: University of Illinois. Christian perspectives from a wide range of thinkers.

Machan, T.R. (2002) "Why Human Beings May Use Animals." *The Journal of Value Inquiry* 36: 9–14. Argues that human beings are more valuable than other animals.

Meyer, M. (2001) "The Simple Dignity of Sentient Life: Speciesism and Human Dignity." *Journal of Social Philosophy* 32.2: 115–26. An interesting argument for a hierarchy of dignities.

Midgley, M. (1998) *Animals and Why They Matter*. Athens, Ga.: University of Georgia Press. Clear and convincing analysis.

Miller, M. (1998) "Descartes' Distinction between Animals and Humans: Challenging the Language and Action Tests." *American Catholic Philosophical Quarterly* 73.3: 339–70. Descartes is motivated by his belief in the uniqueness and immateriality of human souls, not by a well-grounded assessment of animal abilities.

Nuyen, A.T. (1998) "Hume on Animals and Morality." *Philosophical Review* 57.2: 93–106. Hume's denial of animal morality is not inconsistent with the rest of his thought.

Pluhar, E. (1995) *Beyond Prejudice: The Moral Significance of Human and Nonhuman Animals*. Durham, N.C.: Duke University Press. Careful argument for a rights view drawing on Alan Gewirth's idea of moral agents. Emphasizes (human) marginal cases.

Rachels, J. (1990) *Created from Animals: The Moral Implications of Darwinism*, Oxford: Oxford University Press. Darwinism provides a new ethic without the idea that human beings are special.

Regan, T. (1995) "Obligations to Animals are Based on Rights." *Journal of Agricultural and Environmental Ethics* 8.2: 171–80. Regan responds to criticisms of rights theory from authors affirming the care ethic.

—— (1994) *Defending Animal Rights*, Urbana and Chicago: University of Illinois Press. Many valuable essays, including responses to feminist criticisms and those of Jamieson, Frey, and Narveson.

Robinson, W.S. (1997) "Some Nonhuman Animals Can Have Pains in a Morally Relevant Sense." *Biology and Philosophy* 12: 51–71. Affirms an intrinsic theory of consciousness and points out inadequacies in Carruther's relational theory.

Rollin, B.E. (1992) *Animal Rights and Human Morality*, Amherst: Prometheus Books. An excellent presentation of the issues, accessible to the general reader.

—— (1999) *An Introduction to Veterinary Medical Ethics: Theory and Cases*. Ames, Iowa: Iowa University Press. Clear exposition of ethical theory teamed with 82 intriguing cases.

Rowlands, M. (1997) "Contractarianism and Animal Rights." *Journal of Applied Philosophy* 14.3: 235–47. Presents an argument for animal rights on contractarian grounds.

Rudd, R. (1990) *Biology, Ethics and Animals*. Oxford: Clarendon. Biologically informed, with valuable proposals for alternatives to harmful use of sentient animals in research.

Sapontzis, S.F. (1987) *Morals, Reason and Animals*, Philadelphia, Pa.: Temple University Press. A precisely crafted argument, addressing Frey in detail.

Skidmore, J. (2001) "Duties to Animals: The Failure of Kant's Moral Theory." *The Journal of Value Inquiry* 35: 541–59. Kant's account of the indirect duties of human beings to animals lacks a plausible explanation.
Steeves H.P. (ed.) (1999) *Animal Others: On Ethics, Ontology and Animal Life*. Albany: SUNY. The first anthology based on continental philosophy. Suitable for advanced students.
Waldau, P. (2002) *The Specter of Speciesism: Buddhist and Christian Views of Animals*. New York: Oxford. The most thorough analysis of speciesism yet published, which concludes that both Buddhism and mainline Christianity have been and are speciesist, but not irretrievably so.
Warren, M.A. (1997) *Moral Status: Obligations to Persons and Other Living Things*, Oxford: Clarendon Press. An account of moral status using multiple criteria.
—— (1992) "The Rights of the Nonhuman World." *The Animal Rights/Environmental Ethics Debate*, Hargrove, E.C. (ed.). Albany: SUNY, pp. 185–98. An argument for combining environmentalist and animal rights perspectives; also argues that animals do not have rights equal to those of human beings.
Wilson, M.D. (1995) "Animal Ideas." Presidential address, *Proceedings and Addresses of the American Philosophical Association* 69.2: 7–25. While Descartes didn't know much about nonhuman animal behavior, at least he offered reasoning in support of his views.
Wilson, S. (2001) "Carruthers and the Argument from Marginal Cases." *Journal of Applied Philosophy* 18.2: 135–47. Argues that both animals and marginal cases have direct moral status.

Study Questions

1   Tom Regan bases his argument on the concept of "subject-of-a-life." Do you agree that this concept identifies the crucial difference between a being with moral status and one without moral status? Explain your reasoning.
2   Test the usefulness of Regan's worse-off and miniride principles by applying them to an emergency situation (of your choice) in which the interests of humans conflict with those of animals.
3   Carl Cohen identifies what he believes to be an equivocation in Regan's use of "inherent value." Do you agree with Cohen's point? Why or why not?
4   What might be some advantages of Cavalieri's emphasis on institutional discrimination as opposed to Regan's individualistic approach?
5   Peter Singer uses the principle of equal consideration of interests to guide our practice concerning animals. Do you find this principle more or less convincing than Tom Regan's use of the equal inherent value of moral agents and moral patients? Explain your choice.
6   Do you agree with Donovan that Regan and Singer place too much emphasis on reason? Justify your view.
7   Frey argues that having desires requires having the capacity for language-based beliefs. Do you agree? Why or why not?
8   DeGrazia illustrates some difficulties in comparing the interests of different organisms. Choose animals of two different species and compare them with regard to how one would evaluate their well-being, need for freedom, and desire to live. Do you agree with him that we can recognize moral differences and still give animals equal consideration?
9   In your view, which of the authors in this Part presents the best approach to the moral status of animals? Are there significant modifications you would make in the view of the author you chose?

PART II

Animal Capacities: Pain, Emotion, Consciousness

Introduction

The capacities of nonhuman animals to experience pain, to have a sense of consciousness embedded with cognitive abilities, and to have emotional lives is a challenging and controversial set of topics. On the one hand, a seemingly boundless set of examples of complex behaviors of these animals that correspond to sophisticated human behaviors are regularly reported by people with interest in and experience with individual animals, including pet owners, zoo personnel, farmers, and ranchers. On the other hand, scientists have often struggled to understand these topics in light of contemporary understandings of neurology, anatomy, biochemistry, physiology, ethology, and behavioral ecology of representatives of these various animal groups. Slowly some coherent pictures are emerging.

The first two authors, Rollin and Smuts, discuss methods of gaining insights on animal capacities. Rollin stresses the importance of the scientific community becoming more accepting of anecdotal data and anthropomorphic interpretations as key elements in understanding and interpreting animal capacities. Smuts found it essential to become immersed in the lives of the baboons she studied over a period of years, coming to know the animals on an individual basis.

Three authors address the notion of pain in animals. Bermond takes the more conservative view that the essential anatomy to fully experience pain is lacking in most animals, with the possible exception of apes and dolphins. In contrast, Rollin addresses what he believes to be the scientific incoherence of denying pain in animals and of denying moral consideration to them. Varner briefly addresses the taxonomic distribution of pain capacity and concludes that all vertebrates, including fish, probably feel pain, whereas most invertebrates probably do not.

Several authors address emotional experiences in animals. Dawkins argues that consciousness and emotional awareness still are elusive ideas, but that if awareness of pleasure and pain reflect consciousness, then emotional awareness may be an evolutionarily old and common quality among animals. Moss, Panskepp, and Lawrence each give individual experiences involving elephants, rats, and a cow, respectively, that reflect some of the richer animal emotional experiences described.

Griffin addresses the complex topics of animal cognition and consciousness. He argues that humans and other animals probably differ both in the content and richness of their conscious experiences. He also recognizes that animal communication is much richer than previously understood.

Methods of Study

8

Bernard E. Rollin

"Scientific Ideology, Anthropomorphism, Anecdote, and Ethics"

Rollin addresses the ability to understand animal mentation through science. He argues that if science denies the ability to access animal mentation through anecdotal data and anthropomorphic locutions, it removes itself from addressing the key ethical questions about animal well-being that have emerged in society. Rollin believes that anthropomorphic locutions based on ordinary empathetic experiences of animals' lives are needed to make meaningful claims about what animals experience.

It is virtually impossible to emerge from a training program in the biological or biomedical sciences without developing a well-honed skepticism about and distaste for anthropomorphic attribution of mental states to animals. Equally suspect is the attempt to evidence such states by appeal to anecdotal information of the sort routinely accepted by ordinary common sense.

The incorporation of this skepticism into nascent scientists is a major part of what I have elsewhere termed the common sense of science (Rollin, 1989), the set of foundational or philosophical assumptions taught as fact along with the empirical material constitutive of the scientific discipline in question. In the case of animal mentation, this philosophical stance may be epitomized as follows: Science can only deal with what can be directly observed or what is subject to experimental verification. It is argued that failure to mark this precept historically led to a science fraught with speculation, metaphysics, and even theology—witness the elan vital of Bergson, the entelechies of Driesch, and various theological teleologies which have perennially attempted to capture biology, from Paley to Creationism, Now it is evident, the argument continues, that thoughts, feelings, concepts, desires, intentions in animals are not the sorts of things which can be either perceived or explored experimentally. Thus such material is not a legitimate object of study. This position, implicit in some versions of positivism, found clear expression in Watson's formulation of behaviorism, and exerted major influence even on thinkers otherwise inimical to behaviorism, such as Lorenz and Tinbergen. (Thus the 1948 volume, *Instinctive Behavior*, which chronicled the first encounter between behaviorists and ethologists, stressed the absolute concord between both groups regarding the methodological need for eschewing talk of animal mentation. The two factions in fact agreed on little else.) (Schiller, 1957).

If mentation talk is thus ruled out by fiat, it is a fortiori the case that such talk cannot rely on anecdotal evidence, which often tends to be anthropomorphic in substance. Indeed, even if we allow for the possibility of scientific talk about mental states in animals, the common sense of science asserts that such anecdotal evidence ought to be suspect on other grounds. Anecdotes depict events which are unique, non-repeatable, described by naive observers, and which are often reported by observers biased in favor of what they report. Furthermore, they tend to employ anthropomorphic categories of description, and such categories may famously (a) be inappropriate to the species in question (as in the lay-person's tendency to attribute larceny to a pack rat) or (b) be so wildly speculative as to be absurd, as when ordinary people are all too wont to say that their dog knows his birthday is coming.

With such a formidable arsenal of arguments arrayed against talking anthropomorphic-ally of mental states in animals and buttressing such claims anecdotally, one can understand scientists' reluctance to countenance such talk, and it is indeed the case that such talk virtu-ally disappeared from scientific literature during most of the twentieth century. Nonetheless, the issue has once again been thrust forward into the scientific arenas.

Why has this occurred? There are in fact a multiplicity of historical vectors which have militated in favor of softening the positivistic/behavioristic skepticism about animal consciousness, which I have detailed elsewhere (Rollin, 1989, chapters 7 and 10). But one in particular is worth recounting here: Ordinary common sense, as distinct from the common sense of science, has of course never cavilled at mentalistic attribution to ani-mals—indeed, as Hume point out, few things are more repugnant to ordinary common sense than skepticism about animals' mind (Hume, 1960). But, until recently, ordinary common sense cared little about the implausibility of scientific common sense; if scientists wanted to believe that animals have no mind—fine; scientists believed many strange things!

A major clash between these two competing common senses has therefore only arisen in the last two decades. For it is only in that period that ordinary common sense has begun to draw any significant *moral* implications from the presence of thought and feeling in animals. Although ordinary common sense certainly never doubted that animals could feel pain, fear, etc., it drew no moral conclusions from this, largely because animal exploitation was invis-ible to daily life in virtue of the nature of animal use. Science, on the other hand, insulated itself from the moral implications of its own activity with animals not only by the denial of animal mentation but by another mainstay of scientific ideology—the claim that science is value-free, and thus can make no moral claims and take no moral positions, since moral judgments, too, are unverifiable.

Of late, however, ordinary common sense has grown increasingly conscious of our moral obligations to animals, and increasingly unwilling to let science go its own way. The reasons for this change in public attention to animal treatment—and to science's agnostic attitude thereto—are largely moral ones, growing out of profound changes in animal use that have arisen in the past 50 years. Prior to World War II, and indeed for virtually all of human history, the overwhelming use of animals in society was agricultural—animals were reared for food, fiber, locomotion, and power. The key to successful animal production was *hus-bandry*, an ancient term derived from the old Norse word "hus/bond"—bonded to the household. Husbandry meant putting one's animals into the optimal environment in which they were biologically suited to thrive by virtue of natural and artificial selection, and further augmenting their natural ability to survive and flourish by provision of protection from predation, medical attention, protection from extremes of climate, provision of food and water during times of famine and drought, etc.

[. . .]

The husbandry imperative was thus an almost perfect amalgam of prudence and ethics. It was self-evident that the wise man took care of his animals—to fail to do so was to harm oneself as well as one's animals. Husbandry was assured by self-interest, and there was thus no need to place heavy ethical emphasis on proper care of animals. The one exception was the ancient prohibition against overt cruelty and outrageous neglect, designed to cover those rare sadists and psychopaths unmoved by self-interest.

Proper treatment of animals, then, for most of human history, was not heavily stressed in social ethics, since it was buttressed by the strongest of motivations—self-interest. Husbandry agriculture—the overwhelming use of animals in society—was about putting square pegs in square holes, round pegs in round holes, and generating as little friction as possible while doing so. Animal agriculture—historically virtually *all* of animal use—was thus a fair contract between humans and animals, with both sides benefitting from the ancient contract represented by domestication.

This ancient and fair compact changed dramatically in the mid-twentieth century with the rise of high-technology agriculture. With the advent of "technological sanders"— antibiotics, vaccines, hormones, etc.,—one was no longer constrained in one's agriculture by the animals' biological natures. One could now force square pegs into round holes, round pegs into square holes, with the attendant animal suffering irrelevant to profit. The connection between animal welfare and animal productivity was severed. Similarly, with the rise of massive amounts of research and toxicity testing on animals beginning at approximately the same time, animal use could benefit us while harming them in unprecedented ways— inflicting disease, wounds, burns, fear, pain, etc., on animals so we could study them, with no compensatory benefits to the animal subjects. For the first time in history, the welfare of animals used by humans became a moral issue. By the late 1970s, European and North American society were demanding that animal use be modified in research and agriculture so that suffering be mitigated and animal well-being be assured.

In this way scientific ideology, agnostic about animal consciousness, clashed with ever-increasing social concern about animal treatment. The new social tendency to concern itself about animal welfare forces upon science what I have called "the reappropriation of ordinary common sense" about animal thought and feeling. Thus, for example, in the face of federal law which mandates control of pain and suffering in laboratory animals, it is obviously inappropriate for scientists to express total skepticism about our ability to know what animals think and feel (Rollin, 1987). Thus scientific ideology is threatened, and must bend to accommodate ordinary common sense. And this is precisely what has occurred. Take, for example, the symposium on animal pain and suffering convened by the American Veterinary Medical Association in 1987, and its attendant Panel Report on Animal Pain (Panel Report, 1987). The Report acknowledges that animals do feel pain, pointing out that pain research which is extrapolated to humans is after all done on animals! (Traditional scientific common sense had explained pain research as research into pain mechanisms and behavior, and ignored any talk of the subjective experiential dimension. See for example, the majority of papers in Kitchell and Erickson, 1983). Indeed, the report continues quite reasonably, all animal research which is used to model human beings is based in a tacit assumption of anthropomorphism; and if one can in principle extrapolate from animals to humans, why not the reverse as well?

But a hard-line proponent of the common sense of science would very likely remain unmoved by our discussion, and might respond as follows: Granted that political pressure forces upon us the need to behave as if animal consciousness is scientifically knowable and affirmable. But, in fact, it is not, for the reasons detailed above.

[. . .]

Science is, of course, our vehicle for knowing about the world. If science denies our ability to access animal mentation through anecdotal data and anthropomorphic locutions, it removes itself from answering or helping to answer the key ethical questions about animal well-being that have emerged in society. To address questions of animal treatment, welfare, acceptable environments, pain and suffering, etc., we must be able to make meaningful claims about what the animals experience and feel. To do this, we must in turn be allowed to use anthropomorphic locutions based in our ordinary empathetic experience of animals' lives. Indeed, the psychologist Hebb showed that when zoo-keepers were not allowed to use anthropomorphic, anecdotally based locutions about their animal charges, they reported themselves unable to do their jobs (Hebb, 1946). My animal agriculture students, when taught animal behavior by a mechanistic who refused to use mentalistic locutions about animals, similarly reported ignoring the professor's teachings when they went home to their ranches. [. . .] Our ability to work with animals, anticipate their behaviors, and meet their needs rests foursquare on such locutions. Scientific common sense's agnosticism about such locutions therefore in essence removes questions of animal welfare from the realm of legitimate empirical investigation. Thus, it becomes necessary to briefly examine the logical tenability of the common sense of science if one wishes to guarantee that the admission of some animal mentation into science represents something more than sullen and minimal acquiescence to the vagaries of public opinion.

[. . .]

Philosophically, as soon as one has given up a hard-line verificationism which only admits direct observables into science, and one has admitted that certain non-verifiable beliefs are admissible on the grounds of plausibility (e.g. of an external world independent of observers and commonly accessible), one has replaced a rigid logical criterion for scientific admissibility with a pragmatic one, in which one needs to *argue for* exclusion of certain notions from science, rather than simply apply a mechanical test. And, of course, this is what has in fact occurred in the history of science—science talked of all sorts of entities and processes which were not directly verifiable or directly tied to experiment, from gravitation to black holes. Indeed, contemporary physics, traditionally cited as the hardest of hard science, has positively proliferated notions which violate the common sense of science (see the papers in Kitchener, 1988). Such theoretical notions are accepted, of course, because they help us understand reality far better than we do without them.

Talk of mind in animals has a similar justification. We have already mentioned Hebb's point that we could not interpret animal behavior in ordinary life without imputing such notions as pain, fear, anger, affection to animals—all of which have a mentalistic component in addition to a behavioral one (Hebb, 1946). For saying that a dog is in pain means only that the dog is exhibiting a certain range of behaviors or responses does not explain its cringing or loss of appetite unless we also assume that it is *feeling* something—hurt—which is functionally equivalent to what we feel when we hurt. This assumption is in fact, as the AVMA Pain Panel said, presuppositional to doing pain research and analgesia screening animals and extrapolating the results to people—what we are interested in is a *feeling* common to both, not merely similarity in plumbing and groaning.

We have thus far attempted to establish that the traditional scientific skepticism about animal mind is wrong-headed. Furthermore, using the example of pain, we have argued that, in at least some cases, scientific attribution of mentation is inevitable and based in anthropomorphism as presuppositional to its intelligibility.

It is now relevant to introduce the notion of anecdote as a source of information about animal mentation, and assess its relevance to science. An excellent place to begin, for it retains the simple case of pain we have been using, is a famous article by Griffiths and Morton, which appeared in the *Veterinary Record* (Morton and Griffiths, 1985). This article was one of the first papers addressing the recognition and alleviation of pain in animals. It is noteworthy that while the authors do provide criteria for assessing pain and its degree in animals, they stress that the best sources of information about animal pain are farmers, ranchers, animal caretakers, trainers—in short, those whose lives are spent in the company of animals and who make their living through animals. Given the plausibility criterion discussed earlier, such a move is patent. Whereas scientists could get on perfectly well in highly artificial laboratory situations professing agnosticism about animal pain and other mentation, those who live with and depend on animals could not. If you fall into the latter class, and do not recognize pain, fear anger, etc., in your animals, you will lose your livelihood, be highly vulnerable to injury, unable to control or train your charges, etc. Thus, given that science specifically disavowed the reality of animal thought, and made no attempt to study it, it is perfectly proper to look to those who have been *compelled* to understand animal thought for millennia. To be sure, such information will be "anecdotal"—i.e., not obtained in laboratory experiments and not analyzed, but that does not mean it is illegitimate.

Thus we have seen that, in the simple case of pain, the common sense of science is wrong, and that one can talk of what animals experience; that one must use a measure of anthropomorphism (even as we use our own individual experiences as a guide to understanding that of other humans); and that one must depend (at least currently) on anecdotal information. (Indeed, an even more striking argument can be made regarding the concept of suffering, which does not even appear in the scientific literature with regard to humans; let alone animals.) One can also buttress these arguments with others. Similar physiological mechanisms for pain in humans and animals, similar behavioral responses, similar neurochemistry, and the plausibility of phylogenetic continuity all militate in favor of attributing felt pain to animals, as does the fact that humans who do not *feel* pain, for congenital or acquired reasons, do not fare well (Rollin, 1989).

One could respond to the argument we have developed thus far in this way: As long as you focus on simple, fundamental, primitive mental experiences like pain, your argument is unexceptionable. But as soon as one leaves sensation and begins to talk of higher mental processes in animals, one cannot accept anecdotal anthropomorphic evidence. Ordinary common sense and its discourse are far too disposed to exaggerate animal intelligence, planning, reasoning, emotional complexity, and to jump to unwarranted conclusions by seeing animals as little humans. Indeed, it was precisely such romantic, unbounded anthropomorphism and exaggerated anecdotes which abounded in the nineteenth century that led in part to the behavioristic/positivistic reaction against animal thought!

How does one reply to such an objection? In the first place one might argue (as did Buytendijk) that the ability to feel (and respond appropriately) to pain bespeaks mental sophistication beyond mere sensation (Buytendijk, 1943). Thus, pain in and of itself would be of little value if it was not coupled with some ability to choose among alternative strategies of response, e.g. fight or flight, hide, evade, etc. Thus the evolutionary utility of pain consists in the ability of the noxious stimulus to evoke not only motivation to alleviate it, but strategies to deal with it as well. It is in fact this insight which led pain physiologist Ralph

Kitchell to conjecture that animals may well suffer pain more profoundly than humans do (Kitchell and Guinan, 1989).

[. . .]

Be that as it may, I should rather respond by affirming that the argument and strategy we have constructed for using anecdotal and anthropomorphic information to identify pain is in principle no different from using the same approach to understand "higher" (or other) mental processes. The relevant distinction is not pain (or sensation) versus thought (or higher mental processes): it is rather good versus bad anthropomorphism, reasonable versus unreasonable anecdote.

Once again, the key notion for our analysis is *plausibility*, the same sort of measure we use when we attribute thoughts, plans, feelings, and motives to other humans, be it in daily life or when serving on a jury. Let us recall that we do not experience other people's mental states and that language can be used to conceal and deceive. How, then, do we judge other humans' mental states? What we do is use a combination of weighing of evidence and what we might call "me-thropomorphisms"—extrapolations from our own mental lives to others.

[. . .]

My claim [. . .] is that anecdote is, in principle, just as plausible a source of knowledge about animal behavior as it is about human behavior, provided it is tested by common sense, background knowledge, and standard canons of evidence.

[. . .]

More difficult cases occur when the anthropomorphic anecdote concerns a species of animal with which we do not enjoy [. . .]familiarity [. . .], though here the problem is in principle no different than when we deal with people who come from cultures significantly different from ours.

[. . .]

Thus it would seem to me that once one has in principle allowed the possibility of anthropomorphic, anecdotal information about animal mentation, one must proceed to distinguish between plausible and implausible anecdotes (the latter of which may nonetheless turn out to be true, though we are right to be skeptical) and likewise between plausible and implausible anthropomorphic attributions. The fact that many people tell outrageous anecdotes, or interpret them in highly fanciful or unlikely ways, and even publish such nonsense, should no more blind us to the plethora of plausible anecdotes and reasonable interpretations thereof forthcoming from people with significant experience of the animals in question, than should the presence of outlandish stories about or outrageous interpretations of human behavior cause us to doubt all accounts of human behavior.

[. . .]

Anecdotes and their interpretation may obviously be judged by many [. . .] principles. [. . .] Does the anecdote cohere with other knowledge we have of animals of that sort? Have similar accounts been given by other disinterested observers at other times and in other places? Does the interpretation of the anecdote rely upon problematic theoretical notions? (Cf. imputing a grasp of "birthday" to the dog.) How well does the data license the interpretation? Does the person relating the anecdote have a vested interest in either the tale or its interpretation? [. . .] What do we know of the teller of the anecdote—Konrad Lorenz or

Baron Münchausen? One can—and we do—set up plausible rules for judging anecdotal data, be it about humans or about animals. The alternative is to create total nihilistic skepticism about the common sense experience that has given us most of our social knowledge of the behavior of people and animals.

One fascinating point which has escaped notice is that anecdotes are logically no worse off than reports of scientific experiments and their interpretation—in some ways the latter may be more suspect. [. . .] In the final analysis, any report of an experiment is by definition an anecdote, not a confirmed hypothesis. The following question should be mulled over by anyone interested in these issues: Is it more unreasonable to trust the account of a disinterested lay observer or a scientist who must get results to survive? Is the multiplicity of theoretical biases which scientists carry in virtue of their training any less or more or equally pernicious to their observational capacity than the theoretical biases built into a non-scientifically trained, but intelligent observer?

For purposes of winding up this discussion, let us conclude with, appropriately enough, an anecdote which is very interesting to lay people and to students of animal behavior. The story was in fact reported, in detail, on Denver television accompanied by videotaped pictures of the events described. In the story, an African elephant at the Denver Zoo had gone down and refused to get up, a condition known to lead to fatality if not corrected. All efforts to get the elephant to stand up—including bringing in a hired crane—had failed. By chance, the Asian elephants were herded past the afflicted elephant. The Asian elephants broke ranks, approached the fallen elephant, and nudged and poked him until he stood up. They then supported him until he stood on his own.

Thus far, we have an anecdotal narrative, with little or no theoretical bias obtruding, and no interpretation offered. As data relevant to the study of elephant behavior, the story is surely relevant. Although the TV station has a vested interest in dramatic stories, it filmed the events and its account was buttressed by other observers.

The common sense interpretation of the data offered by the station, and by the average observer, was that the elephants were altruistically *helping* another elephant, albeit a different species. Such an interpretation is more problematic than the simple reportage of the events, since "help" is ambiguous and speculative. The events are certainly open to other interpretations. When, however, one juxtaposes that story with the many other stories of elephants showing helpful behavior to other elephants, together with the extensive data we have on problem solving ability and the social nature of elephants, the interpretation gains in plausibility.

To preclude data on (and interpretations of) animal behavior a priori simply because the data was not garnered in laboratories (which are in any case highly unnatural conditions for animals) or not observed by "accredited scientists" is against the spirit of what science should be. To be sure, common sense is "theory laden" with often problematic categories and interpretations, but so too is science. It is at least as hard to see how intelligent, educated scientists bought whole-hog into behaviorism for most of this century as it is to see how ordinary people can buy into astrology today.

As Feyerabend suggests, science should be democratic in its admission of data sources, but stricter in the theories or explanations it graduates. Mentalistic attribution to animals provides a very plausible theoretical structure for explaining and predicting animal behavior. Anthropomorphism, if tested against reasonable canons of evidence, is another plausible—and indeed inevitable—theoretical approach to assessing animal behavior. And finally, since there are and always have been far more ordinary people out observing animals than there are scientists engaged in the same activity, it would be a pity to rule out anecdote, critically assessed, as a potentially valuable source of information—and interpretation—of animal behavior. In fact, ever-increasing social-ethical concern about animal treatment essentially requires information about what matters to animals as the raw material for formulating social policy. Since the common sense of science has morally castrated the language it uses to describe animal behavior, eschewing, for example, morally laden descriptions of animals as expressing pain in favor of "neutral" locutions like "vocalizing", the gap must be filled by the language of ordinary common sense, replete as it is with morally relevant locutions about animal experience.

References

Buytendijk, F. J. J. (1943). *Pain: Its modes and functions*. Chicago: University of Chicago Press (repr. 1961).

Hebb, D. O. (1946). Emotion in man and animal. *Psychology Review, 53*, 88–106.

Hume, D. (1960). In L. A. Selby-Bigge. *A treatise of human nature* (p. 272). Oxford: Oxford University Press.

Kitchell, R. L., Erickson, H. H. (eds) (1983). *Animal pain: Perception and alleviation*. Bethesda, MD: American Physiological Society.

Kitchell, R. and Guinan, M. J. (1989). The nature of pain in animals. In Rollin, B. E. and Kesel, M. L. *The experimental animal in biomedical research*, vol. 1 (pp. 185–205), Boca Raton, FL: CRC Press.

Kitchener, R. F. (Ed.) (1988). The world view of contemporary physics. Albany: SUNY Press

Morton, D. B. and Griffiths, P. H. M. (1985). Guidelines on the recognition of pain, distress and discomfort in experimental animals and an hypothesis for assessment. *Veterinary Record, 20*, 431–36.

Panel Report on the Colloquium on Recognition and Alleviation of Pain and Distress. (1987). *Journal of the American Veterinary Medical Association 191*, 1186–92.

Rollin, B. E. (1987). Laws relevant to animal research in the United States. In A. A. Tuffery, *Laboratory animals* (pp. 323–33). London: Wiley.

Rollin, B. E. (1989). The unheeded cry: Animal consciousness, animal pain, and science. Oxford: Oxford University Press (Chapter 1).

Schiller, C. H. (ed.) (1957). Instinctive behavior. New York: International Universities Press.

9

Barbara Smuts

"Reflections"

Smuts reports on her studies with baboons, including the process of exploring the complex topic of human–baboon intersubjectivity. She came to know the 140 baboons in the troop as individuals, with characteristic things to communicate, favorite foods, favorite friends, and unique bad habits. She describes in elegant detail some of the personal relationships she experienced with this troop of baboons.

[. . .]

The heart, [. . .] is "the seat of a faculty, *sympathy*, that allows us to share . . . the being of another." For the heart to truly share another's being, it must be an embodied heart, prepared to encounter directly the embodied heart of another. I have met the "other" in this way, not once or a few times, but over and over during years spent in the company of "persons" like you and me, who happen to be nonhuman.[1]

These nonhuman persons include gorillas at home in the perpetually wet, foggy mountaintops of central Africa, chimpanzees carousing in the hot, rugged hills of Western Tanzania, baboons lazily strolling across the golden grass plains of highland Kenya, and dolphins gliding languorously through the green, clear waters of Shark Bay.[2] In each case, I was lucky to be accepted by the animals as a mildly interesting, harmless companion, permitted to travel amongst them, eligible to be touched by hands and fins, although I refrained, most of the time, from touching in turn.

I mingled with these animals under the guise of scientific research, and, indeed, most of my activities while "in the field" were designed to gain objective, replicable information about the animals' lives. Doing good science, it turned out, consisted mostly of spending every possible moment with the animals, watching them with the utmost concentration, and documenting myriad aspects of their behavior. In this way, I learned much that I could confidently report as scientific findings. [. . .] When I first began working with baboons, my main problem was learning to keep up with them while remaining alert to poisonous snakes, irascible buffalo, aggressive bees, and leg-breaking pig-holes. Fortunately, these challenges eased over time, mainly because I was traveling in the company of expert guides—baboons who could spot a predator a mile away and seemed to possess a sixth sense for the proximity of snakes. Abandoning myself to their far superior knowledge, I moved as a humble disciple, learning from masters about being an African anthropoid.

Thus I became (or, rather, regained my ancestral right to be) an animal, moving instinctively through a world that felt (because it was) like my ancient home. Having begun to master this challenge, I faced another one equally daunting: to comprehend and behave according to a system of baboon etiquette bizarre and subtle enough to stop Emily Post in her tracks. This task was forced on me by the fact that the baboons stubbornly resisted my feeble but sincere attempts to convince them that I was nothing more than a detached observer, a neutral object they could ignore. Right from the start, they knew better, insisting that I was, like them, a social subject vulnerable to the demands and rewards of relationship. Since I was in their world, they determined the rules of the game, and I was thus compelled to explore the unknown terrain of human-baboon intersubjectivity. Through trial and embarrassing error, I gradually mastered at least the rudiments of baboon propriety. I learned much through observation, but the deepest lessons came when I found myself sharing the being of a baboon because other baboons were treating me like one. Thus I learned from personal experience that if I turned my face away but held my ground, a charging male with canines bared in threat would stop short of attack. I became familiar with the invisible line defining the personal space of each troop member, and then I discovered that the space expands and contracts depending on the circumstances. I developed the knack of sweetly but firmly turning my back on the playful advances of juveniles, conveying, as did the older females, that although I found them appealing, I had more important things to do. After many months of immersion in their society I stopped thinking so much about what to do and instead simply surrendered to instinct, not as mindless, reflexive action, but rather as action rooted in an ancient primate legacy of embodied knowledge.

Living in this way with baboons, I discovered what Elizabeth Costello means when she says that to be an animal is to "be full of being," full of "joy." Like the rest of us, baboons get grouchy, go hungry, feel fear and pain and loss. But during my times with them, the default state seemed to be a lighthearted appreciation of being a baboon body in baboon-land. Adolescent females concluded formal, grown-up-style greetings with somber adult males with a somersault flourish. Distinguished old ladies, unable to get a male's attention, stood on their heads and gazed up at the guy upside down. Grizzled males approached balls of wrestling infants and tickled them. Juveniles spent hours perfecting the technique of swinging from a vine to land precisely on the top of mom's head. And the voiceless, breathy chuckles of baboon play echoed through the forest from dawn to dusk.

During the cool, early morning hours, the baboons would work hard to fill their stomachs, but as the temperature rose, they became prone to taking long breaks in especially attractive locales. In a mossy glade or along the white-sanded beach of an inland lake, they would shamelessly indulge a passion for lying around in the shade on their backs with their feet in the air. Every now and then someone would emit a deep sigh of satisfaction. Off and on, they would concur about the agreeableness of the present situation by participating in a chorus of soft grunts that rippled through the troop like a gentle wave. In the early days of my fieldwork when I was still preoccupied with doing things right, I regarded these siestas as valuable opportunities to gather data on who rested near whom. But later, I began to lie around with them. Later still, I would sometimes lie around without them—that is, among them, but while they were still busy eating. Once I fell asleep surrounded by 100 munching baboons only to awaken half an hour later, alone, except for an adolescent male who had chosen to nap by my side (presumably inferring from my deep sleep that I'd found a particularly good resting spot). We blinked at one another in the light of the noonday sun and then casually sauntered several miles back to the rest of the troop, with him leading the way.

There were 140 baboons in the troop, and I came to know every one as a highly distinctive individual. Each one had a particular gait, which allowed me to know who was who, even from great distances when I couldn't see anyone's face. Every baboon had a characteristic voice and unique things to say with it; each had a face like no other, favorite foods, favorite friends, favorite bad habits. Dido, when chased by an unwelcome suitor, would dash behind some cover and then dive into a pig-hole, carefully peeking out every few moments to see if the male had given up the chase. Lysistrata liked to sneak up on an infant riding on its mother's back, knock it off (gently), and then pretend to be deeply preoccupied with eating some grass when mom turned to see the cause of her infant's distress. Apié, the alpha male, would carefully study the local fishermen from a great distance, wait for just the right moment to rush toward them, take a flying leap over their heads to land on the fish-drying rack, grab the largest fish, and disappear into the forest before anyone knew what was happening.

I also learned about baboon individuality directly, since each one approached his or her relationship with me in a slightly different way. Cicero, the outcast juvenile, often followed me and sat quietly a few feet away, seemingly deriving some small comfort from my proximity. Leda, the easygoing female, would walk so close to me I could feel her fur against my bare legs. Dakar, feisty adolescent male, would catch my eye and then march over to me, stand directly in front of me, and grab my kneecap while staring at my face intently (thanks to Dakar, I've become rather good at appearing calm when my heart is pounding). Clearly, the baboons also knew me as an individual. This knowledge was lasting, as I learned when I paid an unexpected visit to one of my study troops seven years after last being with them. They had been unstudied during the previous five years, so the adults had no recent experience with people coming close to them, and the youngsters had no such experience at all. I was traveling with a fellow scientist whom the baboons had never met, and, as we approached on foot from a distance, I anticipated considerable wariness toward both of us. When we got to within about one hundred yards, all of the youngsters fled, but the adults merely glanced at us and continued foraging. I asked my companion to remain where he was, and slowly I moved closer, expecting the remaining baboons to move away at any moment. To my utter amazement, they ignored me, except for an occasional glance, until I found myself walking among them exactly as I had done many years before. To make sure they were comfortable with me, as opposed to white people in general, I asked my friend to come closer. Immediately, the baboons moved away. It was I they recognized, and after a seven-year interval they clearly trusted me as much as they had on the day I left.

Trust, while an important component of friendship, does not, in and of itself, define it. Friendship requires some degree of mutuality, some give-and-take. Because it was important, scientifically, for me to minimize my interactions with the baboons, I had few opportunities to explore the possibilities of such give-and-take with them. But occasional events hinted that such relations might be possible, were I encountering them first and foremost as fellow social beings, rather than as subjects of scientific inquiry. For example, one day, as I rested my hand on a large rock, I suddenly felt the gentlest of touches on my fingertips. Turning around slowly, I came face-to-face with one of my favorite juveniles, a slight fellow named Damien. He looked intently into my eyes, as if to make sure that I was not disturbed by his touch, and then he proceeded to use his index finger to examine, in great detail, each one of my fingernails in turn. This exploration was made especially poignant by the fact that Damien was examining my fingers with one that looked very much the same, except that his was smaller and black. After touching each nail, and without removing his finger, Damien glanced up at me for a few seconds. Each time our gaze met, I wondered if he, like I, was contemplating the implications of the realization that our fingers and fingernails were so alike.

I experienced an even greater sense of intimacy when, in 1978, I had the exceptional privilege of spending a week with Dian Fossey and the mountain gorillas she had been studying for many years. One day, I was out with one of her groups, along with a male colleague unfamiliar to the gorillas and a young male researcher whom they knew well. Digit, one of the young adult males, was strutting about and beating his chest in an early challenge to the leading silverback male. My two male companions were fascinated by this tension, but after a while I had had enough of the macho energy, and I wandered off. About thirty meters away, I came upon a "nursery" group of mothers and infants who had perhaps moved off for the same reasons I had. I sat near them and watched the mothers eating and the babies playing for timeless, peaceful moments. Then my eyes met the warm gaze of an adolescent female, Pandora. I continued to look at her, silently sending friendliness her way. Unexpectedly, she stood and moved closer. Stopping right in front of me, with her face at eye level, she leaned forward and pushed her large, flat, wrinkled nose against mine. I know that she was right up against me, because I distinctly remember how her warm, sweet breath fogged up my glasses, blinding me. I felt no fear and continued to focus on the enormous affection and respect I felt for her. Perhaps she sensed my attitude, because in the next moment I felt her impossibly long ape arms wrap around me, and for precious seconds, she held me in her embrace. Then she released me, gazed once more into my eyes, and returned to munching on leaves.

[. . .]

Notes

1   The term *person* is commonly used in two different ways: first, as a synonym for human, and, second, to refer to a type of interaction or relationship of some degree of intimacy involving actors who are individually known to one another, as in "personal relationship," knowing someone "personally," or engaging with another "person to person." Here I use the word in the second sense, to refer to any animal, human, or nonhuman, who has the capacity to participate in personal relationships, with one another, with humans, or both. I return to the concept of animal "personhood" later in the essay.

2   Shark Bay is off the coast of Western Australia, the site of a research project on wild bottlenose dolphins.

Pain

10

Bob Bermond

"The Myth of Animal Suffering"

Bermond reviews the literature for insights on the ability of nonhuman animals to suffer and experience pain. He concludes that to experience suffering, both a well developed prefrontal cortex and a right neocortical hemisphere are needed. Since the prefrontal cortex is phylogenetically the most recent structure, it is likely that most animals are unable to experience suffering. He concludes that emotional experiences of animals, and therefore suffering, may only be expected in anthropoid apes and possibly dolphins.

Introduction

Over the last few years, there have been increasingly vociferous requests to treat animals humanely. Animal protectionists and animal welfare action groups have claimed that there is scientific proof that animals can experience suffering. With the heightened pressure from these circles, and with the appearance of publications claiming that all vertebrates and even some mollusks are able to experience suffering (Aldridge *et al.*, 1991; Bateson, 1992; Rivas and Rivas, 1993; Van Putten, 1986; Verheijen and Buwalda, 1988), it is high time the scientific value of these claims is investigated.

The question

Suffering is the experience of pain and of negative emotions such as fear, anxiety, sorrow and guilt. The experience of pain is also an emotion (Bard, 1934; Jennet, 1989; Kalat, 1992; Menges, 1992). Therefore, the two-pronged question posed above (suffering and pain) can be reduced to a single question: are animals capable of experiencing negative emotions? In posing this question, we must not forget that pain and suffering are conscious experiences. After all, it would be nonsensical to talk of experiences if those experiences failed to reach the domain of the consciousness. The question regarding suffering in animals, therefore, primarily addresses the issue of whether animals have a consciousness.

Animal suffering, methods and starting principles

In literature, the idea that animals can experience suffering is based on

1   Romanes's analogy postulate (Bateson, 1991; Rivas and Rivas, 1993; Verheijen and Buwalda, 1988) and,

2   five research strategies. I would like to deal with the latter first, before discussing the analogy postulate.

2.1 In the first research strategy, one studies the physiological responses in the animal after the animal has been placed in an 'emotion-inducing' situation; the assumption is made that if 'emotional physiological responses' are shown, the animal will also experience subjective emotional experiences (Verheijen and Buwalda, 1988).

2.2 One studies the behaviour of animals, and if the behaviour recorded by the observer can be described as emotional behaviour, then one assumes that this behaviour is also bound to subjective feelings (Verheijen, 1988, 1992; Verheijen and Buwalda, 1988; Wiepkema and Koolhaas, 1992).

2.3 One conditions animals using either positive or negative reinforcements, and if it proves possible to condition the animal, one assumes that the animal must have experienced the reinforcement as a reward or a punishment, as comforting or discomforting (De Cock Buning, 1992).

2.4 One investigates whether an animal is prepared to overcome a barrier in order to leave a specific situation, or to enable it to reach another environment, and if this proves to be the case, one assumes that the animal has experienced a negative feeling in the initial situation, and experiences the new situation as positive, or less negative (Bateson, 1991; Dawkins, 1990).

2.5 One investigates whether an animal is capable of information processing on a, not further specified, high level, and if this is the case, then one assumes that this higher cognition refers to consciousness (Bateson, 1991; Dawkins, 1993).

The idea behind the last method is that higher cognitive processes require consciousness. It has, however, been demonstrated that complicated human learning processes, such as the acquisition of complex procedural knowledge, the acquisition of knowledge and application of the grammar of one's mother tongue or of an artificial grammar, finding new solutions for a mathematical or specific problem, and the learning processes which control our actions indicate situations can take place entirely unconsciously (Baeyens *et al.*, 1990; Greenwald, 1992; Lewicki, 1985, 1986; Penrose, 1989; Van Heerden, 1982). Nevertheless, it has been demonstrated that consciousness has no direct access to the cognitive processes which determine human behaviour. The results of these cognitive processes may reach consciousness, but this does not invariably happen. Just the conclusions, the results of these cognitive processes, can reach consciousness, but this does not invariably happen. In such cases the unconscious conclusion still regulates our behaviour, while consciousness simply fills the information gap with confabulations (Farthing, 1992; Gazzaniga and LeDoux, 1978; Nisbett and Wilson, 1977; Van Heerden, 1982). The reasoning behind the fourth method is as follows: if, for example, an animal is prepared to walk over a hot plate in order to reach food, the animal must have experienced hunger to such a degree that the animal was prepared to undergo this painful experience. This method can never show that a specific animal is capable of experiencing any emotional feeling, after all, the emotional experience (hunger) is deduced on the basis of the assumption of another emotional experience (pain/discomfort) which automatically leads to an endless circular argument. The third method, that of conditioning, is also invalid. First, the idea that reinforcements induce emotional feelings in human beings is incorrect; the two may be linked, but this need not necessarily be so (Kalat, 1992). Furthermore, it has also been shown (Mayes, 1992) that amnesia patients can be conditioned whilst finally, studies amongst human beings have shown that in order for conditioning to succeed, conscious awareness of neither the conditioning process itself nor of the changes which occur as a result of the conditioning are necessary (Baeyens *et al.*, 1990; Eelen, 1992; Vroon, 1992). These results demonstrate that the possibility of conditioning may never serve as proof for consciousness or emotional experiences.

The common element in the first two methods is the assumption that four elements of the emotional process: appraisal (registration of the emotional stimulus as an emotional stimulus), emotional behaviour, emotional physiological response and emotional experience, necessarily occur together such that the experience of emotion may be assumed to be present if one or more of the other components of the emotional process can be shown to be present. This idea normally derives from the layman's theory of emotional which states that the emotional experience is the first element of the emotional process to appear, and that the emotional behaviour and emotional physiological responses are produced in reaction to the primary experience. These assumptions are in conflict with the general rule of parallel processing by the brain (Dennett, 1991; Neafsey, 1990) and are, as will be shown later, incorrect. Indeed, once the emotional experience is present it is but one of the factors regulating behaviour, although it is not the only factor nor is it the first emotional element to appear. In addition, it would not be true to say that genuine emotional behaviour could not be produced without emotional feelings. Moreover, in those cases in which the emotional feeling remains absent, the emotional behaviour is often disinhibited (Bermond, 1995). Finally, psychology can present examples which indicate the incorrectness of the above assumption. Fits of strong emotional behaviour without any subjective experience have been described by Dana (1921), Lashley (1938), and Ross and Rush (1981); pain behaviour without any sensory experience has been described in spinal cord lesioned patients (Jennett, 1989); and there is also evidence of congenital indifference to pain (Kalat, 1992; Krystal and Raskin, 1970). In addition, simple hypnotic suggestions can suppress pain experience to a fully unconscious level (Trigg, 1970). Psychologists are familiar with the phenomenon of alexithymia. This term describes a disorder whereby otherwise normal people are incapable of experiencing subjective emotional feelings (Fricchione and Howanitz, 1985; Nemiah, 1975; Nemiah and Sifneos, 1970; Sifneos *et al.*, 1977), although they regularly show strong emotional behaviour and physiological responses (Krystal, 1988). Emotional physiological responses without conscious perception of the inducing stimuli are described in prosopagnosia sufferers, people blinded in a portion of the visual field, and also in normal people in reaction to subliminal stimuli presented to the right hemisphere (Cowey and Stroerig, 1992; Làdavas *et al.*, 1993; Tranel and Damasio, 1985). Furthermore, it has been demonstrated that exogenously induced increases of materials which are normally secreted or otherwise produced in response to stress or emotions very rarely cause normal people to experience emotions (Cannon, 1927; Marañon, 1924; Peabody *et al.*, 1921; Pitts and Allen, 1980; Tyrer, 1976, 1985). The opposite scenario, i.e., no or considerably reduced production and/or perception of emotional physiological responses, and non-reduced subjective emotional experiences has been described for spinal cord lesioned patients (Bermond *et al.*, 1987, 1991). There is no reason to assume that peripheral feedback has any effect on the strength of the emotional feeling (Bermond and Frijda, 1987). The fact that the various elements of the emotional process can occur in dissociation demonstrates that all the studies into the emotional behaviour, and/or emotional physical responses in animals, are of no value in connection with the question being discussed here. Therefore none of the research strategies is valid in this context.

Could we have expected any other conclusion? Indeed not, because we have merely repeated a discussion which led, half a century ago, to precisely the same conclusion. Cannon (1927), Papez (1937), Bard (1928, 1934), Lashley (1938) and MacLean (1949) already described that emotional experience and emotional behaviour can be separated from one another and added that emotional experience was of cortical origin, whilst emotional behaviour was of subcortical origin. The leading proponents of neurophysiology at the time therefore suggested that not only the elements of the emotional process could be dissociated from one another, but also that these elements were determined at different periods in evolution. According to this reasoning, the assumption that the possible emotional experience in animals can be derived from the emotional behaviour or emotional physiological responses cannot be correct. After all, given the idea that these matters were determined at different moments in evolution, whereby it is suggested that experience as a (neo)cortical product was the last to be determined, animals must exist or have existed which do show emotional behaviour and physiological responses, but which have no experience of emotion.

The analogy postulate of Romanes

Now that we have shown that the study methods are unsuitable for the question posed, all that remains is the analogy postulate (an unproved statement) of Romanes which states that:

> A greater or lesser degree of similarity in the subjective experience of a certain animal (certain animal species) and of the human being may be assumed, relative to the degree of similarity between the structure of the sensory nervous system of that animal species with the human sensory nervous system, and relative to the degree of similarity between the reaction shown by the animal to a specific stimulus and the human reaction to the same stimulus.
>
> (Verheijen and Buwalda, 1988, p. 2)

This idea does attract us; intuitively most people agree with it. It is, therefore, worth investigating the extent to which the assumptions behind the postulate are correct and which conclusions emanate from this postulate. There are however two problems with the postulate. First, the word 'analogy' is used by Romanes in the sense that, on basis of similarity in some features, similarity in other features may be assumed. This meaning of analogy deviates from its current meaning in biology. Nowadays analogy stands for convergent evolutionary developments: independent developments in different species which have resulted in comparable functions, although these species do not share a common ancestor with that function. This meaning of analogy does not apply to Romanes's postulate since that which has to be proven (similarity in function) then forms part of the assumptions. The power of thinking in analogies stands and falls with the choice of features in which similarities has to be proven. Using present day knowledge, similarity in brain structures has to be defined by homology. Neural structures in different species are called homologues when they are located in more or less the same locality in the brain, have comparable connections with other homologous structures and were developed in a common ancestor. Romanes's postulate has to be used in this way, since otherwise, in the absence of clear criteria as to what 'similarity in the sensory nervous system of human beings and animals' means, the analogy postulate becomes nothing more than a 'magic formula' with which all things weird and wonderful can be claimed.

The second problem is the core assumption of the analogy itself, the idea that on the basis of similarity in some features, similarity in other features may be assumed. In this case, this means that one assumes that the functions of the respective homologous neural structures have not fundamentally altered during evolution. Although comparative neuro-anatomy permits us to see that the evolutionary development of the central nervous system consisted mainly in adding new functional structures to what was already there, it is also clear that the phylogenetic older neural structures have not completely remained unchanged. These structures have, for instance, established links with phylogenetic more recently developed neural structures. It is, furthermore, known that the relative size of subcortical structures can vary from species to species. These two facts suggest that there has been some change in function. The central issue here is, however, whether these changes are of funda-mental importance to the question whether animals have a mental life. This question cannot be answered by neuro-anatomical data. The only way to break this deadlock is to accept for the time being the assumption that the functions of phylogenetic older structures have not changed in a fundamental way as being correct and to check the conclusions which emanate from the analogy postulate with other arguments. The conclusions generated by the analogy postulate thus need to be validated or repudiated using other arguments. Since the analogy postulate assumes that animals have subjective experiences on the basis of 1) comparison of the animal neural system with the human neural system and 2) similarity in behaviour between humans and nonhuman animals, and since subjective experiences can only be studied directly in human beings (they are the only creatures which can be asked whether or not they have feelings), one must first answer the following questions: which elements of the human central nervous system and which human behaviours are prerequisites for the human subjective emotional feelings? Subsequently, one must check whether the neural structures and behaviours in question are also found in animal species.

[. . .]

Conclusions to be drawn from the neuro-anatomical analysis of the analogy postulate

1   Spontaneous emotional behaviour and emotional physiological responses can occur without accompanying emotional feelings. The emotional experience is, therefore, neither a prerequisite for emotional behaviour nor for emotional physiological responses.

2   The right neocortex and the prefrontal neocortex are both prerequisites for emotional experience.

3   The above-mentioned neural structures are not required for the production of emotional behaviour nor for the production of emotional physiological responses.

4   Although a prefrontal cortex can be identified in many mammal species, only higher apes show a well developed frontal lobe (Kolb and Whishaw, 1990; Kupfermann, 1991); in addition, some parts of the prefrontal cortex are specifically human (Luria, 1980). For this reason, and because the prefrontal lobe and the right hemi-sphere fulfill, beside emotional functions, various other functions, the group of higher mammals represents a gray area from a neuro-anatomical point of view with respect to the question of possible emotional experiences.

Discussion

[...]

A critical review of the literature inevitably leads to the conclusion that the claims for suffering in animal species, other than in anthropoid apes and possibly dolphins, are incorrectly substantiated. Such claims are the products of anthropomorphic projections.

References

Aldridge, W.N., Balls, M., Bateson, P., Bisset, G.W., Boyed, K.M., Byrne, P., Cromie, B.W., Dworkin, G., Dunstan, G.R., Ewbank, R., Frey, R.G., Harrison, F.A., Hollands, C., Jonson, E.S., Morton, D.B., Purchase, I.F.H., Smith, J.A., and Tavernor, D. (1991). *Lives in the balance: The ethics of using animals in biomedical research. The report of a working party of the institute of medical ethics.* Oxford: Oxford University Press.

Baeyens, F., Eelen, P., and Van den Berg, O. (1990). 'Contingency awareness in evaluative conditioning a case for unaware affective-evaluative learning'. *Cognition and Emotion*, 4, 3–18.

Bard, P.A. (1928). 'Diencephalic mechanism for the expression of rage with special reference to the sympathetic nervous system.' *American Journal of Physiology*, 84, 490–515

Bard, P. (1934). 'On emotional expression after decortication with some remarks on certain theoretical views.' *The Psychological Review*, 41, 309–29.

Bateson, P. (1991). 'Assessment of pain in animals'. *Animal Behaviour*, 42, 827–39.

—— (1992). 'Do animals feel pain?' *New Scientist*, 25 April, 30–3.

Bermond, B. (1995). Alexithymie, een neuropsychologische benadering. *Nederlands tijdschrift voor psychiatric*, 37, 717–27.

Bermond, B. and Frijda, N.H. (1987). 'The intensity of emotional feelings: Product of peripheral emotional responses or cognitions?' *Communication and Cognition*, 20, 191–206.

Bermond, B., Nieuwenhuijse, B., Fassoti, L., and Schuerman, J. (1991). 'Spinal cord lesions, peripheral feedback, and intensities of emotional feelings.' *Cognition and Emotion*, 5, 201–20.

Bermond, B., Schuerman, J., Nieuwenhuijse, B., Fassoti, L., and Elshout, J. (1987). 'Spinal cord lesions: Coping and mood states'. *Clinical Rehabilitation*, 1, 111–17.

Cannon, W.B. (1927). 'The James-Lange theory of emotions: A critical examination and an alternative theory'. *American Journal of Psychology*, 39, 106–24.

Cowey, A. and Stroeng, P. (1992). 'Reflections on blind sight'. In A.D. Milner, and M.D. Rugg (eds), *The Neuro-psychology of Consciousness* (pp. 11–37). London. San Diego, New York, Boston, Sydney, Tokyo, Toronto: Academic Press.

Dana, C.I. (1921). 'The anatomic seat of emotions: A discussion of the James Lange theory'. *Archives of Neurology and Psychiatry*, 6, 634–9.

Dawkins, M. (1990). 'From an animal's point of view: Motivation, fitness, and animal welfare'. *Behavioural and Brain Sciences*, 13, 1–9.

Dawkins, M.S. (1993). *Through our eyes only?* Oxford, New York, Heidelberg: W.H. Freeman Spectrum.

De Cock Buning, T. (1992). 'Pijn bij dieren.' *NRC. Handelsblad 4 mei.*

Dennett, D.C. (1991). *Consciousness explained.* Boston: Little, Brown and Company.

Denny-Brown, D., Meyer, J.S., and Horenstein, S. (1952). 'The significance of perceptual rivalry resulting from parietal lesion'. *Brain*, 75, 433–71.

Eelen, P. (1992). 'Leerpsychologie en gedragstherapie Overdruk' uit: *Handbook gedragstherapie* (pp. F.3–57 t/m F.3–6–2). Bohm Stafleu Van Loghum.

Farthing, G.W. (1992). *The psychology of consciousness.* Englewood Cliffs, New Jersey: Prentice Hall, Inc.

Fricchione, G., and Howanitz, E. (1985). 'Aprosodia and Alexithymia: A case report'. *Psychotherapy and Psychosomatics*, 43, 156–60.

Gazzaniga, M., and LeDoux, J.E. (1978). *The integrated mind.* New York: Plenum.

Greenwald, A.G. (1992). 'Unconscious cognition reclaimed'. *American Psychologist*, 47, 766–79.

Jennett, S. (1989). *Human physiology.* Edinburgh, London, Melbourne and New York: Churchill Livingstone.

Kalat, J.W. (1992). *Biological Psychology.* Belmont, California: Wadsworth Publishing Company.

Kolb, B. and Whishaw, I.Q. (1990). *Fundamentals of human neuropsychology. Third edition.* New York: W.H. Freeman & Company.

Krystal, H. (1988). *Integration and self-healing. Affect-trauma-alexithymia.* The Analytic Press: distributed by Lawrence Erbaum Associates, Inc. Publishers.

Krystal, H. and Raskin, H.A. (1970). *Drug dependence: aspects of ego functions*. Detroit: Wayne State University Press.

Kupflerman, I. (1991). 'Localization of higher cognitive and affective functions: The association cortices.' In E.R. Kandel, J.H. Schwartz, and T.M. Jessell (eds), *Principles of neural science, third edition* (pp. 823–38). New York, Amsterdam, London, Tokyo: Elsevier.

Làdavas, E., Camatti, D., Del Pesce, M. and Tuozzi, G. (1993). 'Emotional evaluation with and without conscious sumulus identification: Evidence from a split-brain patient.' *Cognition and Emotion, 7*, 95–114.

Lashley, K.S. (1938). 'The thalamus and emotion'. *The Psychological Review, 45*, 21–61.

Lewicki, P. (1985). 'Non conscious biasing effects of single instances on subsequent judgments'. *Journal of Personality and Social Psychology, 48*, 563–74.

Lewicki, P. (1986). 'Information about covariation that cannot be articulated'. *Journal of Experimental Psychology. Learning, Memory, and Cognition, 12*, 135–46.

Luria, A.R. (1980). *Higher cortical functions in man. Second edition, revised and expanded*. New York: Plenum Publishing Corporation.

MacLean, P.D. (1949). 'Psychosomatic disease and the "visceral brain": Recent developments bearing on the Papez theory of emotion'. *Psychosomatic Medicine, 11*, 338–53.

Marañon, G. (1924). 'Contribution a l'étude d'action émotive de l'adrenaline.' *Revue Française de Endocrinologie, 2*, 301–25.

Mayes, A.R. (1992). 'Automatic memory processes in amnesia: How are they mediated?' In A.D. Milner, and M.R. Rugg (eds), *The neuropsychology of consciousness* (pp. 235–61). London, San Diego, New York, Boston, Sydney, Tokyo, Toronto: Academic Press.

Menges, L.J. (1992). *Over pijn gesproken*. Kampen: J.H. Kok.

Neafsey, E.J. (1990). 'Prefrontal cortical control of autonomic nervous system. Anatomical and physiological observations'. *Progress in Brain Research, 85*, 147–56.

Nemiah, J.C. (1975). 'Denial revisited: Reflections on psychosomatic Theory'. *Psychotherapy and Psychosomatics, 2*, 140–47.

Nemiah, J.C., and Sifneos, P.E. (1970). 'Psychosomatic illness: A problem in communication.' *Psychotherapy and Psychosomatics, 18*, 154–60.

Nisbett, R., and Wilson, T. (1977). 'Telling more than we can know: Verbal reports on mental process'. *Psychological Review, 84, 3*, 231–59.

Papez, J.W. (1937). 'A proposed mechanism of emotion.' *Archives of Neurological Psychiatry, 38*, 725–43.

Peabody, F.W., Sturgis, C.C., Tomkins, E.M., and Wearn, J.T. (1921). 'Epinephrine hypertensiveness and its relation to hyperthyroidism'. *American Journal of Medical Science, CLXI*, 508–17.

Penrose, R. (1989). *The emperor's new mind*. Oxford: Oxford University Press.

Pitts, F.N., and Allen, R.E. (1980). 'Beta-adrenal blockade in the treatment of anxiety'. In R.J. Mathew (ed.), *The Biology of Anxiety* (pp. 134–61). New York: Brunner Mazel.

Rivas, E., and Rivas, T. (1993). 'Zijn mensen de enige dieren met bewustzijn'. *Prana, 17*, 83–8.

Ross, E.D., and Rush, A.J. (1981). 'Diagnosis and neuroanatomical correlates of depression in brain-damaged patients: Implications for a neurology of depression'. *Archives of General Psychiatry, 38*, 1344–54.

Sifneos, P.E., Apfel-Savitz, R., and Frankel, F.H. (1977). 'The phenomenon of alexithymia observations in neurotic and psychosomatic patients'. *Psychotherapy and Psychosomatics, 28*, 47–57.

Tranel, D., and Damasio, A.R. (1985). 'Knowledge without awareness: An autonomic index of facial recognition by prosopagnosics'. *Science, 228*, 1453–4.

Trigg, R. (1970). *Pain and emotion*. Oxford: Clarendon Press.

Tyrer, P. (1976). *The role of feelings in anxiety*. Oxford: Oxford University Press.

Tyrer, P. (1983). 'What do betablockers tell us about anxiety?' Lecture at the fourth international conference on biological psychiatry, Philadelphia, USA.

Van Heerden, J. (1982). *De zotgelijke staat van het onvewuste*. Proefschrift Universiteit Amsterdam, Meppel, Boom.

Van Putten, G. (1986). 'Ethologisch enderzock naar pijn en lijden.' *Biotechniek, 25, 4*, 61–3.

Verheijen, F.J. (1988). 'Pijn and angst bij een aan de haak geslagen vis.' *Biovisie, 68*, 166–7.

Verheijen, F.J. (1992). *Levend aas. NRC Handelsblad 26 maart*.

Verheijen, F.J., and Buwalda, R.J.A. (1988). *Doen pijn en angst een gehaakte en gedrilde karper lijden?* Publicatie van de Rijks Universiteit Utrecht.

Vroon, P. (1992). *Wolfshlem: De evolutie van het menselijk gedrag*. Baarn: Ambo.

Wiepkema, P.R. and Koolhaas, J.M. (1992). 'The emotional brain.' *Animal Welfare, 1*, 13–18.

11

Bernard E. Rollin

"Animal Pain"

Rollin summarizes the rationale for asserting the scientific incoherence of denying pain in animals, the observability of mental states in animals, the common sense nature of mentation in animals, and the application of morality to animals in light of these understandings. He then points out how the human benefits derived from animals facilitated the rejection of ascribing moral worth to their treatment.

The scientific incoherence of denying pain in animals

[. . .]

[A]s Darwinians recognized, it is arbitrary and incoherent, given the theories and information current in science, to rule out mentation for animals, particularly such a basic, well-observed mental state as pain.

[. . .]

One can well believe that only by thinking of animal pain in terms of Cartesian, mechanical processes devoid of an experiential, morally relevant dimension could scientists have done the experimental work which has created the sophisticated neurophysiology we have today. But given that science, the neurophysiological analogies that have been discovered between humans and animals, certainly at least the vertebrates, are powerful arguments against the Cartesianism which made it possible. In a dialectical irony which would surely have pleased Hegel, Cartesianism has been its own undoing, by demonstrating more and more identical neurophysiological mechanisms in humans and animals, mechanisms which make it highly implausible that animals are merely machines if we are not.[1]

Pain and pleasure centres, like those found in humans, have been reported in the brains of birds, mammals, and fish; and the neural mechanisms responsible for pain behaviour are remarkably similar in all vertebrates. Anaesthetics and analgesics control what appears to be pain in all vertebrates and some invertebrates; and, perhaps most dramatically, the biological feedback mechanisms for controlling pain seem to be remarkably similar in all vertebrates, involving serotonin, endorphins and enkephalins, and substance P. (Endorphins have been found even in earthworms.) The very existence of endogenous opiates in animals is powerful evidence that they feel pain. Animals would hardly have neurochemicals and pain-inhibiting systems identical to ours and would hardly show the same diminution of pain signs as we do if their experiential pain was not being controlled by these mechanisms in the same way that ours is. In certain shock experiments, large doses of naloxone have been given to traumatized animals, reversing the effect of endogenous opiates, and it has been shown that animals so treated die as a direct result of uncontrolled pain.[2] In 1987, it was shown that bradykinin antagonists control pain in both humans and animals.

Denial of pain consciousness in animals is incompatible not only with neurophysiology, but with what can be extrapolated from evolutionary theory as well. There is reason to believe that evolution preserves and perpetuates successful biological systems. Given that the mechanisms of pain in vertebrates are the same, it strains credibility to suggest that the experience of pain suddenly emerges at the level of humans. Granted, it is growing increasingly popular, following theorists like Gould and Lewontin, to assume the existence of quantum leaps in evolution, rather than assume that all evolution proceeds incrementally by minute changes. But surely such a hypothesis is most applicable where there is evidence of a morphological trait which seems to suddenly appear in the fossil record. With regard to mental traits, this hypothesis might conceivably apply to the appearance of language in humans, if Chomsky and others are correct in their argument that human language differs in kind, as well as degree, from communication systems in other species. But in other areas of mentation – most areas apart from the most sophisticated intellectual abilities – and surely with regard to basic mental survival equipment like that connected with pain, such a hypothesis is both *ad hoc* and implausible. Human pain machinery is virtually the same as that in animals, and we know from experience with humans that the ability to *feel* pain is essential to survival; that people with a congenital or acquired inability to feel pain or with afflictions such as Hansen's disease (leprosy), which affects the ability to feel pain, are unlikely to do well or even survive without extraordinary, heroic attention. The same is true of animals, of course – witness the recent case of Taub's deafferented monkeys (monkeys in which the sensory nerves serving the limbs have been severed) who mutilated themselves horribly in the absence of the ability to feel. *Feeling* pain and the motivational influence of feeling it are essential to the survival of the system, and to suggest that the system is purely mechanical in animals but not in man is therefore highly implausible. If pain had worked well as a purely mechanical system in animals without a subjective dimension, why would it suddenly appear in man *with* such a dimension? (Unless, of course, one invokes some such theological notion as original sin and pain as divine punishment – hardly a legitimate scientific move!) And obviously, similar argument would hold for discomfort associated with hunger, thirst, and other so-called drives, as well as with pleasures such as that of sexual congress.

So not only does much scientific activity presuppose animal pain, as we have seen *vis-à-vis* pain research and psychological research, it fits better with neurophysiology and evolutionary theory to believe that animals have mental experiences than to deny it. Outside positivistic-behaviouristic ideology, there seems little reason to deny pain (or fear, anxiety, boredom – in short, all rudimentary forms of mentation) to animals on either factual or conceptual grounds. (Indeed, research indicates that all vertebrates have receptor sites for benzodiazepine, which, in turn, suggests that the physiological basis of anxiety exists in all vertebrates.)[3] One may cavil at attributing higher forms of reason to animals, as Lloyd Morgan did, but that is ultimately a debatable, and in large part empirically decidable, question.

The alleged unobservability of mental states

The one lingering doubt which positivism leaves us with concerns the ultimate unobservability of mental states in animals. After all, we cannot experience them, even in principle. Perhaps there is something fundamentally wrong with admitting such unobservable entities to scientific discourse, for would we not be opening a Pandora's box containing such undesirable notions as souls, demons, angels, entelechies, life forces, absolute space, and the rest? Would we not be giving up the hard-won ground by which we demarcate science from other forms of knowing, and opening ourselves to a dissolution of the line between science and metaphysics, science and speculation? Surely that consideration must far outweigh any benefit of admitting animal mentation into legitimate scientific discourse.

Since this is the key (official) reason behind the common sense of science's refusal to talk about animal mentation, it is worth examining in some detail. The first assumption behind this view is obviously that science is, or can be, and surely ought to be, totally empirical – in other words, that science ought to make no assumptions, postulate no entities, and countenance no terms which cannot be cashed empirically. This is, indeed, a mainstay of classical, hard-line positivism.

[. . .]

Mental states as a perceptual category

[T]here is no good 'scientific' reason for acquiescing to positivism's demand that only observables be permitted in science; first, because that demand cannot itself be observationally proved, and second, because it would exclude all sorts of basic things like other people and intersubjective physical objects in which science has much stake. Furthermore, it has become increasingly clear since Kant that there is no good reason for believing that facts can be gathered or even observations made independently of a theoretical base. Kant showed that sensory information must be 'boxed' before it becomes an object of experience, that even the notions of 'object' and 'event' are brought to sensation, rather than emerging from it. Indeed, examples demonstrating the role of theory in the broadest sense in perception are endless. To see a fracture or a lesion on a radiograph requires an enormous amount of theoretical equipment and a great deal of training, for which the radiologist is very well paid; though he gets the same sensations on his retina as you or I do, he doesn't see the same thing as we do. This is equally true of the woodland tracker, who spots a trail or some sign of an animal's passage; the artist, who sees dozens of colours in a person's face, whereas most of us see only 'flesh colour'; the horse *aficionado* who sees a thoroughbred, while we see only a horse. And what we see in the standard ambivalent figures like the one which can be seen as a vase or as two faces or the duck-rabbit or the young-old woman depends on what we are thinking about, expecting, hypothesizing, and the like.

Indeed, returning to our main concern, what we perceive or observe in science or consider worthy of calling a fact must be in large measure determined by our metaphysical commitments and their associated values. Aristotle saw the world as an array of facts of function and teleology. Galileo saw a mathematical machine. In so far as common sense has a metaphysics and an epistemology, it surely maintains that we perceive the mental states of others. Contrary to the stories that many philosophers have told in the twentieth century, and which we discussed earlier, I do not believe that common sense uses mental terms like 'happy', 'afraid', 'bored', and so on only to refer to overt behaviour in appropriate contexts. Nor do I believe that common sense simply *infers* mental states by analogy from overt behaviour. I think, rather, that common sense *perceives* mental states in others in exactly the way that it perceives physical states or objects.

[. . .]

On this view, perceiving in terms of mentation is one of the categories by which we commonsensically process reality, and mentation is a fundamental plank upon which our common-sense metaphysics is built. And the reason why this notion is so geographically and historically pervasive is because it works so well. Nothing can disconfirm our attribution of mentation to other humans *in general*, because mentation is a (if not *the*) fundamental cognitive category by which we map other humans.

[. . .]

When we use words attributing passion, rage, sadness, joy, depression, and the like to other people, we surely do not do so in the absence of behaviour relevant to and expressive of these mental states. On the other hand, we are not just talking about the behaviour; we are unavoidably referring to what the behaviour is directly and essentially tied to – namely, a feeling which, while perhaps somewhat unlike mine, serves the same function in the other person's life as the feeling in question does in mine.

[. . .]

Morality and the perception of mental states

There are doubtless a number of major reasons for our ubiquitous presumption of subjective experiences in others. Most obvious is the fact that without this presumption, we could not as readily predict or understand the actions of others. Second, in so far as we are taught moral concern for others, such concern is cogent only on the presumption that others have subjective experiences, that we can more or less know them, that their subjective states matter to them more or less as mine matter to me, and that my actions have major effects on what matters to them and on what they subjectively experience. If we genuinely didn't believe that others felt pain, pleasure, fear, joy, and so on, there would be little point to moral locutions or moral exhortations. Morality presupposes that the objects of our moral concern have feelings. And, what is logically equivalent, if there is no presumption of the possibility of feeling in an entity, there is little reason to speak of it 'in the moral tone of voice'.

Of course, the presumption of feeling is only a necessary condition for moral concern, not a sufficient one. One must also believe that the feelings of others warrant our attention. For most people, the mere realization that others experience negative feelings in the same way that they themselves do is enough to generate a stance of moral concern. . . .

[T]he attribution of mental states, especially those associated with pleasure and pain, joy and misery, is connected irrevocably with the possibility of morality. For this reason, only a science with blinders to the moral universe, and, most especially, only a *psychology* provided with such blinders could ever deny not only the legitimacy of talking about mental states, but their fundamental place in the world, which a genuine psychology must seek to explain.

[. . .]

Application of this theory to animals

But what of animals? Clearly, common sense and ordinary language have traditionally extended the presumption of mentation to animals. (In some cultures, this was explained by viewing animals as reincarnated humans.) Probably the major reason for doing so was that it works. By assuming that animals feel and have other subjective experiences, we can explain and predict their behaviour (and control it as well). Why beat a dog if it doesn't hurt him?

Why does a lion hunt if it isn't hungry? Why does a dog drool and beg for scraps from the table if they don't taste good? Why does a cat in heat rub up against the furniture if it doesn't feel good? Why do animals scratch if they don't itch? Again, common sense continued to think in this way regardless of what scientific ideology dictated, and scientists continued to think in this way in their ordinary moments.

The moral reason for presuming consciousness and mental states in animals does not loom nearly so large. It is an interesting fact that although most cultures in most times and places have attributed mentation to animals, few have clearly set out moral rules for their treatment, and for many, animals do not enter the moral arena. For some philosophers, granting moral status to animals is highly problematic, which is why so many of them have been concerned, like Descartes, to prove that animals are really automata. For others, like Hume, who deem it absurd to deny the full range of mental experience to animals, and who are highly cognizant of the connection between morality and feeling, the question of moral treatment of animals nevertheless does not arise. For ordinary people, though their presumption of mentation in animals is strong, their application of moral notions to animals is minimal or non-existent. Only thus can one explain why for centuries animals were held morally and legally responsible for their actions, subject to trial, punishment, and death, yet at the same time had no legal protection whatever.[4]

Why is this the case? Why has common sense (and until recently the legal system as well) studiously avoided coming to grips with our moral obligations to other creatures?[5] For that matter, why has philosophy, which has notoriously concerned itself with all sorts of questions and which has explored all aspects of ethical theory, been virtually blind to questions concerning animals? (There are, of course, notable exceptions, such as the Pythagoreans; but here we must recall that their concern grew out of the doctrine of transmigration of human souls.) There is no certain answer to this question. Perhaps part of an answer lies in the influence of our theological traditions, most especially the Christian tradition, which has stressed that the proper study of man is man. More plausibly perhaps, a key part of the answer lies in a remark made to me by one of my veterinary students at the end of an ethics course in which I put great stress on moral questions pertaining to animals. 'If I take your teaching seriously', she said,

> no part of my life is untouched, and all parts are severely shaken. For if I ascribe moral status to animals, I must worry about the food I eat, the clothes I wear, the cosmetics I use, the drugs I take, the pets I keep, the horses I ride, the dogs I castrate and euthanize, and the research I do. The price of morality is too high – I'd rather ignore the issue.

Perhaps in a culture which has no choice but to exploit animals in order to survive, one cannot even begin to think about these questions, or even see them as moral choices rather than pragmatic necessities. Or perhaps because the use of animals for our purposes without consideration of their interests is so pervasive and our dependence upon it so great, it becomes invisible to us, in much the same way that exploitation of women and minorities was invisible for too long. Indeed, it is interesting that moral interest in these long-neglected areas arose at virtually the same historical time and place, a point to which we will return.

If I am at all correct, the traditional common-sense view of animals went something like this. On the one hand, common sense took it for granted that animals were conscious and experienced pain, fear, sadness, joy, and a whole range of mental states. Indeed, at times common sense probably gave too much credit to the mental lives of many animals, falling into a mischievous anthropomorphism. Yet in the same breath, common sense consistently ignored the obvious moral problems growing out of attributing thought and feeling to animals, since it had an unavoidable stake in using them in manners which inevitably caused them pain, suffering, and death, and thus, ordinary common sense had its own compartmentalization in this area. Indeed, such animal use was often directed not only at satisfying basic needs such as food and clothing, but more frivolous ones, such as entertainment, as in bear- and bull-baiting, fox-hunting, falconry, bull-fighting, cock-fighting, dog-fighting, gladiatorial contests, and indiscriminate bird shoots. (If the moral issue *was* ever raised, the 'Nature is red in tooth and claw anyway' and 'Animals kill each other' responses quickly dismissed it.)

In this way, though common sense and Darwinism reinforced one another, in general, neither felt the need to draw out the obvious moral implications of its position (allowing, of course, for a few exceptions like M. P. Evans and Henry Salt).[6] And when what we have called the ideology or common sense of science arose, at about the same time that animal experimentation became a crucial part of scientific activity, it had both an ideological and a vested interest in perpetuating blindness to moral issues. Hence, though it violated both common sense and the evolutionary theory which it continued to accept by its denial of animal consciousness, positivistic-behaviouristic ideology, with its denial of the legitimacy of asking moral questions in and about science, buttressed, reinforced, and even to some extent justified and grounded common sense and Darwinism's systematic disregard of moral issues surrounding animal use and exploitation. Though common sense might balk at science's denial of consciousness to animals, it had no problem at all with science's rejection of moral concern for animals, since scientific use of animals was, after all, like agricultural and other uses of animals, one more area of human benefit. Even lurid, periodic newspaper accounts of 'vivisection' aroused in most people not so much moral indignation as aesthetic revulsion – 'I don't want to know about that.' (Most people still react that way to slaughterhouses and packing plants.) Thus, for a long time, there was little social moral opposition to scientific denial or ignoring of animal pain, suffering, and mentation, even as common sense might have objected to the strangeness of quantum theory, but certainly had no moral qualms about it. So for science, convenience and ideology went hand in hand, and both were unchecked by common sense, which mostly didn't care much about what scientists did. Though it thought their activities odd, it certainly didn't worry about them morally, most especially in biomedical areas, which promised – and delivered – many glittering advances of direct benefit to all of us. And, as we have seen, common sense's tolerant attitude towards biomedical research was not limited to animal subjects; it extended for a long time to human subjects as well, especially when the subjects were not 'us', but 'them' – prisoners, indigents, primitives, lunatics, retarded persons, and the like.

Notes

1   Stephen Walker's recent book *Animal Thought* elegantly documents the neurophysiological similarity between humans and animals.
2   M. Fettman *et al.*, 'Naloxone therapy in awake endotoxemic Yucatan minipigs'.
3   J. A. Gray, *The Neuropsychology of Anxiety.*
4   M. P. Evans, *Criminal Prosecution and Capital Punishment of Animals.*
5   See Rollin, *Animal Rights*, pt. 2.
6   M. P. Evans, *Evolutional Ethics and Animal Psychology*; H. S. Salt, *Animals' Rights Considered in Relation to Social Progress.*

12

Gary Varner

"How Facts Matter"

Varner addresses the question of which animals can feel pain. Based on a literature review, he concludes that all vertebrates, including cold-blooded vertebrates such as fish and herpeto-fauna, probably feel pain whereas most invertebrates do not; however, cephalopods such as octopi and squid may be invertebrates that can experience pain.

[. . .]

Reference of the term "animals"

Almost everyone believes that *some* animals are conscious, but even with protozoa removed, the animal kingdom as understood today includes such simple organisms as corals, sponges, and *Trichoplax adhaerens*. The lattermost, although composed of a few thousand cells, has no specialized systems devoted to sensation, digestion, or even reproduction [4], let alone nociceptors or a central nervous system. There are reasons to doubt that even more complex organisms like flatworms, insects, and crustaceans are conscious of pain. Therefore, it cannot be said flatly that it is absurd to deny that "animals" feel pain.

How could we decide, in a principled way, which kinds of animals are and are not capable of feeling pain? This is surely a complex and difficult question, but the most detailed treatments I have seen (Smith and Boyd [6], Rose and Adams [5], DeGrazia and Rowan [2], and Bateson [1]) have all reached the same conclusion: Probably all vertebrates are capable of feeling pain, but probably not invertebrates (with the likely exception of cephalopods). These studies compared normal adult humans to various vertebrate and invertebrate animals on behavioral and neurophysiological criteria, such as whether the animals in question have a highly developed central nervous system, whether nociceptors are known to be present and connected to it, whether endogenous opiates are present, whether their responses to what would be painful stimuli for us are similar to ours, and whether these responses are modified by analgesia. It is not true that vertebrates score positively on each and every one of these comparisons and invertebrates score negatively. For instance, despite a disciplined search for them, nociceptors have not been isolated in fish or herpetofauna, and endogenous opiates have been found in earthworms and insects. As the working party of the British Institute of Medical Ethics put it, "the most obvious divide is between the vertebrates and the invertebrates" [6] because the comparisons are almost all positive on the former side of the line and almost all negative on the latter side. The case for thinking that all vertebrates can feel pain is thus very strong, while the case for thinking that invertebrates can feel pain is extremely weak by comparison (with the possible exception of cephalopods like octopus and squid, which have stunning learning abilities [3,8], but about whom little is known regarding nociception, endogenous opiates, and responses to analgesics). (On the points made in this paragraph, see generally Varner [7], pp. 51–4.)

If we have such relatively weak evidence for saying that most invertebrates can feel pain, then it is not absurd to deny that *those* animals feel pain. By the same token, if we have relatively strong evidence for saying that all vertebrates can feel pain, then exclusion of the cold-blooded vertebrates from protection under an animal welfare act is unjustifiable. If pain is a bad thing for the individual who suffers it, and we are committed as a society to reducing unnecessary pain, then whether an animal is cold-blooded or scaly, rather than furred or feathered, should not matter. A careful examination of *which* animals can feel pain can give us good reason to think that not every species in the animal kingdom should be of concern to the animal welfarist, but it also suggests that the U.S. Animal Welfare Act should be amended to protect cold-blooded vertebrates, including fish and herpetofauna.

References

1. Bateson P.: Assessment of pain in animals. *Animal Behav.* 42:827–39, 1991.
2. DeGrazia D., Rowan A.: Pain, suffering, and anxiety in animals and humans. *Theoretical Med* 12:193–211, 1991.
3. Fiorito G., Scotto P.: Observational learning in *Octopus vulgaris*. *Science* 256:545–7, 1992.
4. Margulis L., Schwartz K.V.: *Five kingdoms: An illustrated guide to the phyla of life on earth*, 3rd ed. W.H. Freeman and Company, New York, 1998.
5. Rose M., Adams D.: Evidence for pain and suffering in other animals. pp. 42–71. In Gill Langley (ed): *Animal experimentation: The consensus changes.* Chapman and Hall, New York, 1989.
6. Smith J.A., Boyd K.M. (eds): *Lives in the balance: The ethics of using animals in biomedical research.* Oxford University Press, Oxford, 1991.
7. Varner G.: *In nature's interests? Interests, animal rights and environmental ethics.* Oxford University Press, Oxford, 1998.
8. Wells M.J.: *Octopus: Physiology and behavior of an advanced invertebrate.* Chapman and Hall, London, 1978.

Animal Emotions

13

Marian Stamp Dawkins

"Animal Minds and Animal Emotions"

Dawkins notes that consciousness is still an elusive concept. She believes that many animals have a conscious awareness of pleasure and pain analogous to that experienced by humans. Alternatively, she acknowledges that consciousness emerges with the ability to form abstract concepts, plan for the future, or use language. She notes that if the first conscious experiences were awareness of pleasure and pain, then it implies that emotional awareness is evolutionarily very old and possibly very common among animals.

SYNOPSIS. The possibility of conscious experiences of emotions in non-human animals has been much less explored than that of conscious experiences associated with carrying out complex cognitive tasks. However, no great cognitive powers are needed to feel hunger or pain and it may be that the capacity to feel emotions is widespread in the animal kingdom. Since plants can show surprisingly sophisticated choice and "decision-making" mechanisms and yet we would not wish to imply that they are conscious, attribution of emotions to animals has to be done with care. Whether or not an animal possesses anticipatory mechanisms associated with positive and negative reinforcement learning may be a guide as to whether it has evolved emotions.

The search for animal consciousness is frequently seen as the search for higher and higher cognitive abilities in animals. Thus most theories of consciousness emphasise intellectual achievement – the ability to form abstract concepts, for example, to understand and to use language or to be able to plan ahead and work out what to do in novel situations. For this reason, the achievements of animals such as Alex the parrot (Pepperberg, 1999) and Kanzi the Bonobo (Savage-Rumbaugh and Lewin, 1994) are immensely significant. But although these achievements are impressive, too much emphasis on the cognitive and intellectual side of consciousness may lead us to overlook other aspects that are equally important. It does not take much intellectual effort to experience pain, fear or hunger. We can be conscious of a headache or afraid of flying without being able to put the experience into words or reason about it. We may in fact tell ourselves that flying is a relatively safe way of travelling – in other words, we try to dispel a basic emotion with cognitive reasoning.

Might it be, then, that our search for animal consciousness could fruitfully be extended to the realm of the emotions and therefore potentially to a much wider range of animals than just the ones that are outstandingly clever? Might it not be that the conscious experience of emotions is far older in evolutionary time than the ability to form concepts and certainly than that to use language? The purpose of this contribution is to see what the study of animal emotions can tell us about consciousness in animals.

My own interest in animal emotions arose from working for many years on animal welfare, where a central issue is whether and under what circumstances animals suffer – that is, experience strong or persistent negative emotions. These are questions of far more than just theoretical importance. If animals do experience fear and pain and if they experience frustration as a result of being unable to perform their natural behaviour patterns, then this has legal and ethical importance and in turn may have major economic consequences.

Indeed, the really important moral issues in animal welfare arise precisely because of the belief held by many people that animals do have conscious emotional experiences. An early advocate of this idea was Jeremy Bentham (1789) who wrote the often-quoted lines: "The question is not, Can they reason? nor, Can they talk? but Can they suffer?" And such views are echoed by more recent philosophers such as Bernard Rollin. It is thus very important that we have some way of studying suffering – the unpleasant emotions of animals.

There are basically two approaches that have been adopted to studying animal emotions – the functional and the mechanistic. The functional approach means examining the *role* of emotions in human behaviour and then asking whether the function is the same in humans and non-humans. In many cases it is possible to apply Darwinian ideas to emotions and ask how emotions (in us and in other species) contribute to an organism's fitness. Fear, for example, is adaptive and functions to increase fitness both through motivating an animal to remove itself from danger and also to avoid similar situations in the future.

A widely used framework for viewing emotions in a functional context is that described by Oatley and Jenkins (1998) who see emotions as having three stages: (i) *appraisal* in which there is a conscious or unconscious evaluation of an event as relevant to a particular goal. An emotion is positive when that goal is advanced and negative when it is impeded (ii) *action readiness* where the emotion gives priority to one or a few kinds of action and may give urgency to one so that it can interrupt or compete with others and (iii) *physiological changes, facial expression and then behavioural action*. The trouble with this formulation is that it is so general and unspecific that it encompasses almost all behaviour in the sense that almost everything that humans or other animals do would have to involve such stages. Building a robot to behave in an autonomous and useful way would almost certainly involve ensuring that it could evaluate its environment as either beneficial or harmful, give priority to one action that would be beneficial and then carry out the action. Worse, it even seems to apply to plants operating without nervous systems and using the simplest of mechanisms. For example, the parasitic plant, Dodder (*Cuscata europaea*) appears to "choose" which host plants to parasitise on the basis of an initial evaluation of a potential host's nutritional status. Kelly (1992) tied pieces of Dodder stem onto Hawthorn bushes which had been either fed extra nutrients or starved of nutrients. The transplanted growing shoots were more likely to coil on ("accept") host plants of high nutritional status and grow away from ("reject") hosts of poor quality and this acceptance or rejection occurred before any food had been taken from the host. It was thus based on an as yet unknown evaluation by the parasite of the host's potential food value and, within three hours, the growing tips could be seen either growing at right angles away from a rejected stem or coiling around one it would eventually feed from. By changing the time scale (hours rather than minutes) and the mechanism (growth rather than behaviour), we have an organism that shows appraisal, action readiness and action – the supposed functions of emotion without needing a nervous system at all. This suggests that merely defining emotions in a rather vague functional way of what they do in us and then asking whether there is evidence of similar functions in non-human animals is not going to be very fruitful. We need to look in more detail at how the functions are carried out.

The second possible approach to the study of animal emotions is therefore to look at the mechanisms underlying emotions and to see whether they are similar in ourselves and other species. Can we look at what changes both physiologically and behaviourally when we feel happy, sad, etc., and see whether similar changes take in place in non-human animals?

In humans, there are three systems underlying emotions (e.g., Oatley and Jenkins, 1998). These are (i) the cognitive/verbal. People can report on what they are feeling and indeed this is one of the main ways we have of knowing what other people are feeling. (ii) autonomic. These include changes in heart rate, temperature and hormone levels when we experience emotions (iii) behaviour/expressive. Different emotions give rise to different behaviour and different facial expressions.

Although of course we cannot use (i) for non-human species since they cannot tell us what they are feeling, it might be possible to use similarities in (ii) and (iii) to tell us what emotions they might be having. Unfortunately, there are problems since the three emotional systems do not necessarily correlate with each other, even in humans. Sometimes, for example, strong subjective emotions occur with no obvious autonomic changes, as when someone experiences a rapid switch from excitement to fear on a roller coaster. This does not mean that the change in emotional experience has no physiological basis. It just means that it is probably due to a subtle change in brain state rather than the obvious autonomic changes that most physiological methods pick up. At other times, the emotion we experience and report corresponds to several different kinds of autonomic change or one kind of autonomic change such as heart rate can be shown to accompany very different emotions (Wagner, 1989; Frijda, 1986; Cacioppo *et al.*, 1993).

This lack of correlation is not in fact, very surprising. Many of the physiological changes that occur in our bodies when we feel different emotions are related to the actions we are likely to take, such as running. As running occurs when we are afraid and are running away or excited and running towards (chasing) something we want, the same physiological preparations are appropriate for both situations and consequently a range of emotions.

Another reason why the different emotional systems may diverge is that we have 'multiple routes to action' in other words, the same actions can be prompted by instructions from different parts of the brain (Rolls, 1999). An obvious example is breathing. Most of the time we are not conscious of taking breath – it is done automatically. But if we are drowning or told to take deep breaths by a doctor, control shifts to a conscious route. The existence of multiple routes to action makes the comparison with other species particularly difficult, since non-humans could show similar behaviour to ourselves but have it controlled by a pathway that, in ourselves, is just one of the possible routes we can use. The fact that we can, when the occasion demands, become conscious of what we are doing does not, therefore, necessarily mean that other species have all the same circuits that we do. We may have evolved an additional conscious verbal route that is lacking in them. Indeed the evolution of the vertebrate brain has often involved overlaying existing pathways with new ones rather than eliminating existing ones (Panksepp, 1998).

But if neither similarities of function nor similarities of mechanisms between humans and non-humans can be reliably used to tell us about emotions in other species, what can we do? What is needed is a combination of functional and mechanistic approaches that is considerably more specific than the very general approaches I have outlined so far. Only by understanding the very specific mechanisms associated with emotions in ourselves can we hope to be able to know what to look for in other species. As we have already seen, by being too general (emotions are associated with appraisal and action readiness), we include plants and organisms and machines that operate on the very simplest of mechanisms. And by expecting emotions to be reflected in obvious autonomic measures (such as hormonal state and heart rate), we are unable to distinguish the subtleties of emotions even in ourselves.

Let us start with a more specific evolutionary argument. Animals are able to respond to challenges to their health and well-being in various ways and the mechanisms they use can be divided into those that repair damage to the organism's fitness when damage has already occurred and those that enable the organism to anticipate probable damage and take avoiding action so that the damage does not occur at all. The ability to fight off infection with the immune system and to heal wounds are examples of repair mechanisms, whereas most behaviour (drinking before dehydration occurs, hiding before a predator appears) falls into the category of anticipation and pre-emptive action. In fact, we can see the evolution of cognitive abilities in animals as the evolution of more and more sophisticated anticipatory mechanisms, reaching further and further back in time away from the danger itself, until in ourselves we may take out a health insurance policy many years before any damage is done.

The important point about these anticipatory mechanisms, however, is that many of them can be highly effective without the organism being in any way conscious. Where an aspect of the environment is highly predictable (such as the sun rising every day), very accurate anticipation can be achieved by endogenous rhythms or by simple kineses and taxes. The ability of Dodder plants to anticipate which hosts are likely to yield the most food before investing in the coiling and growth needed to extract any nutrients is a very good example of a simple anticipatory mechanism and should serve as an object lesson about the dangers of using words like 'choice' or 'appraisal' to imply similarity to the mechanisms we ourselves use. Just to emphasise this point, we should be equally cautious about the conclusions we draw from choice tests in animals, such as those that show that chickens prefer one kind of flooring to another (Hughes and Black, 1973) or will "work" (squeeze through gaps or push heavy weights) to get at something they like. Even plants will push up through concrete to get at light and air so both simple choice tests and those involving physical obstacles to allow animals to get what they 'want' could be nothing more than the operation of animals being evolved by natural selection to respond to certain sorts of stimuli and to keep on responding even when there are obstacles. Despite some of the claims that have been made (e.g., Dawkins, 1990), persistence in the face of physical difficulties does not imply that animals experience the same emotions that we have when we have to work harder to get what we want.

But some animals, including ourselves, have evolved anticipatory mechanisms that are quite different in kind from anything we find in plants, anticipatory mechanisms that cannot be explained by simple tropisms and taxes, anticipatory mechanisms that may necessitate emotions. The key is reinforcement learning or the ability to change behaviour as a result of experience so that behaviour is controlled by completely arbitrary stimuli, quite unlike anything that natural selection could have built into the organism. I am not speaking here of just any change that may occur as a result of experience. The immune system changes as a result of experience with certain pathogens but this can be done through a preprogrammed (if highly sophisticated) response. There is no need to invoke "emotions" in the way our immune systems change as a result of their experiences of different diseases. Similarly, if an organism (plant or animal) habituates or changes its response as a result of repeated experience, there is no reason to suppose that they have emotions because receptors can be linked (hard-wired) to response mechanisms in predictable ways.

But where an animal learns to perform an arbitrary response to approach or avoid a stimulus, natural selection cannot hard-wire connections between receptor and response mechanisms or evolve simple rules for how responses should change as a result of experience (Rolls, 1999). For example, suppose a rat learns that turning in a right-hand circle gives it food and turning in a left-hand circle gives it an electric shock and then, when the experimenter changes the rules of the experiment, learns to go left to get food and right to avoid a shock. Natural selection could not have led to the evolution of rats able to do this by any simple rules. Hard-wiring or innate response biases could not account for the completely arbitrary response (turning or anything else the irritating human chose to devise) nor for the ability of the animal to change and do something different.

The only way the rat could achieve such a feat would be by having a reward-punishment system which allowed it to associate any action [that] happened to make it "feel better" or "feel worse" and either repeat or avoid such actions in future (Rolls, 1999). Specific rules (such as always turn right or always turn towards red stimuli) would be very much less effective than more general rules (repeat what leads to feeling better or pleasure). General emotional states of pleasure and suffering would enable animals to exploit many more behavioural strategies to increase their fitness than specific stimulus-response links. The point is, however, that without emotions to guide it, an animal would have no way of knowing whether a behaviour never performed before by any of its ancestors should be repeated or not. By monitoring the consequences of its behaviour by whether it leads to "pleasure" or "suffering" it can build up a complex string of quite arbitrary responses. It can learn, for example, that pressing a lever leads to the appearance of a striped box which contains food. By finding the striped box "pleasurable" because it is associated with food and learning to press the lever to obtain this pleasure, the rat learns to obtain food through a route that is not open to an animal totally pre-programmed in its responses. Emotions are therefore necessary to reinforcement learning.

We have thus come full circle. If it is only animals that are clever enough to master certain cognitive tasks (those associated with reinforcement learning) that have emotions, then the apparent distinction between cognition and emotions is illusory. Only certain kinds of task require emotions. Others, including those achieved by plants, do not. At least this gives us a way of excluding plants from our discussion of consciousness and gives us a way of discriminating those organisms that are likely to have emotion from those that probably do not. We can at least do experiments to find out whether a given animal (an insect, say) does or does not have the capacity for arbitrary reinforcement learning.

But does this really solve the problem of the connection between emotion and consciousness? Of course it does not and I have to admit that I have so far blurred a distinction that is of great importance. I am guilty of using the word "emotion" in two quite different senses that must now be clearly distinguished (Dawkins, 1998). The first sense in which we might use the word "emotion" is to refer to strictly observable physiological and behavioural changes that occur under particular circumstances such as the appearance of a predator. But we might also use it in a second sense to refer to the subjective conscious experience (fear) that we know we experience under conditions of danger.

The problem with the word "emotion" is that it tempts us to slip from one meaning to the other, often without realising that we have done so. We start out describing what we can observe – the behaviour and physiology of the animals or people. I have indeed given an account of why emotional states may have evolved, with behavioural criteria for deciding whether they might exist in a given species. I carefully put scare quotes around words such as "pleasure" and "suffering" in describing positive and negative emotional states. But the problem is that issue of whether conscious experiences as we know them accompany these states in other species is a totally separate question. Given the ambiguous nature of the word "emotion", it may not be obvious that it is a separate question because it so easy to believe that once we have postulated a scale of positive to negative reinforcers, once, that is, we have a common currency in which different stimuli can be evaluated to how positive or negative they are on this emotional scale, then we have also [linked] into the conscious experience of pain and pleasure that we all know about from our human perspective. But this would be an error. It is quite possible (logically) for animals to have positive or negative emotional states without it *feeling like* anything. Stimuli could be evaluated as negative, in other words, but they wouldn't necessarily hurt.

Strictly speaking, therefore, consciousness still eludes us. It is my personal view that emotional states defined in the way I have described (using reinforcement value) does imply subjective experience – a conscious awareness of pleasure and pain that is not so very different from our own. But that should be taken for what it is: a personal statement of where I happen to stand, not a view that can be grounded in empirical fact. It is just as valid (and just as open to challenge) as the more widely held beliefs that consciousness "kicks in" with the ability to form abstract concepts or plan ahead or use a language (Rosenthal, 1993; Dennett, 1996).

If, however, consciousness is associated with reinforcement learning and the first conscious experiences that occurred on this planet were the basic ones of pain and pleasure, long before any concepts were thought of or any plans laid for the future, then this does have implications for the way we see other species. It implies that emotional awareness is evolutionarily very old and possibly very widespread in the animal kingdom. As Damasio (1999) and Rolls (1999) have, others have recently emphasised, emotion deserves much more attention than it has had so far.

References

Bentham, J. 1789. *Introduction to the principles of morals and legislation.* 1996 imprint. Clarendon Press, Oxford.

Cacioppo, J. T., D. J. Klein, and E. Hatfield, 1993. The psychophysiology of emotion. In G. C. Berntson, *Handbook of emotions* M. Lewis and J. M. Hatfield (eds), pp. 119–42. Guilford, New York.

Damasio, A. 1999. *The feeling of what happens: Body, emotion and the making of consciousness.* William Heinemann, London.

Dawkins, M. S. 1990. From an animal's point of view: Motivation, fitness and animal welfare. *Behavioral and Brain Sciences* 13:1–61.

Dawkins, M. S. 1998. Evolution and animal welfare. *Quart. Revi. Biol.* 73:305–28.

Dennett, D. C. 1996. *Kinds of minds: Towards and understanding of consciousness.* Weidenfeld & Nicolson, London.

Frijda, N. H. 1986. *The emotions.* Cambridge University Press.

Hughes, B. O. and A- J. Black. 1973. The preference of domestic hens for different types of battery cage floor. *British Poultry Science* 14:615–19.

Kelly, C. K. 1992. Resource choice in *Cuscuta europaea. Proc. Natl. Acad. Sci.* U.S.A. 89:12194–7.

Oatley, K. and J. M. Jenkins, 1998. *Understanding emotions.* Blackwell, Oxford.

Panksepp, J. 1998. *Affective neuroscience: The foundations of human and animal emotions.* Oxford University Press, Oxford.

Pepperberg, I. M. 1999. *The Alex studies: Cognitive and communicative abilities of grey parrots.* Harvard University Press, Cambridge, Mass.

Rollin, B. E. 1989. *The unheeded cry: Animal consciousness, animal pain and science.* Oxford University Press, Oxford.

Rolls, E. T. 1999. *The brain and emotion.* Oxford University Press, Oxford.

Rosenthal, D. 1993. Thinking that one thinks. In M. Davies and G. W. Humphreys (eds), *Consciousness*, pp. 197–223, Blackwell, Oxford.

Savage-Rumbaugh, S. and R. Lewin, 1994. *Kanzi: The ape at the brink of the human mind.* Doubleday, London.

Wagner, H. 1989. The peripheral physiology and differentiation of emotions. In H. Wagner and A. Mainstead (eds) *Handbook of social psychophysiology*, pp. 78–98. John Wiley, New York.

14

Cynthia Moss

"A Passionate Devotion"

Moss describes a mother elephant assisting her young calf to overcome a serious congenital problem or injury associated with birth. Several years later when several veterinarians tried to remove an embedded spear from the calf, the mother elephant again courageously attempted to protect and assist her offspring at considerable risk to herself.

With an animal as slow to reproduce as an elephant, it's not surprising that a mother invests a great deal of time and energy in the single calf that she bears once every four to five years. The evidence is there in the twenty-two months of gestation and in the four years or even more of lactation. What's harder to quantify, if not impossible, is the emotional energy a female expends in her relationship with her calf.

I have no doubt that elephant mothers feel very strongly about their young; the intense attachment is evident in their maternal behavior. But what does the female feel when she suckles her calf, or rescues it when it falls in a water hole, or lifts it to its feet when it's weak, or carries it on her trunk and tusks when it's dying? It's easy to say that she simply reacts instinctively to the calf's vocalizations and behavior. True, but what does she feel when she reacts? Elephants eat when they feel hungry, drink when they feel thirsty, run when they feel frightened, scream when they feel pain. Is it such a leap to say that as an elephant gently touches her calf with her trunk, she feels love?

In 1990, I was making a film in Kenya about a single family of elephants, the EBs, led by a beautiful matriarch, Echo. She was due to have a calf in late February. On the morning of February 28, cameraman Martyn Colbeck and I found the EB family shortly after dawn with a brand new calf. It was a male, and it was Echo's. Martyn started filming, but we soon realized that there was something wrong with the calf. He couldn't stand because his front legs were bent and rigid at the carpal joints. Echo kept reaching her trunk around and under the calf, wedging a toe under him, and lifting. He was big and strong; he could get up on his hind legs. But then all he could do was shuffle around on his "knees" until he collapsed again. Over and over she tried to lift him, but he could not walk.

Eventually, most of the fourteen-member family left, but Echo and one of her daughters, nine-year-old Enid, stayed with the calf. Enid also tried to lift him, but Echo gently pushed her away. Once the calf was half standing, Enid came up beside him and started walking away, looking back, apparently trying to make him follow. He couldn't.

By now it was hot, and the three elephants were out in the open with no shade, no food, and no water. Patiently and very slowly they managed to move to a small mud hole where Echo and Enid splashed themselves and the calf. By midafternoon they were doubtless extremely hungry and thirsty, but neither female would leave. The calf was exhausted; when

Echo tried again to get him to his feet, he screamed. Frequently both Echo and Enid made the low, rumbling contact call to the rest of the family, listened for an answer, then answered in turn. Enid moved off, turned back, moved off again, her behavior suggesting intense conflict. At one point she got about thirty meters away, but just then Echo tried to get the calf to his feet again and he bellowed. Enid spun around and rushed back to him.

By the end of the day we had little hope for the calf. He was just able to reach Echo's breast from an awkward position, but he could not sustain it for long. Amazingly, he survived the night, and over the next two days he learned how to shuffle along on his carpal joints with Echo and Enid on either side, moving slowly, stopping often. On the second day there was a tiny bit of movement in his joints. On the third day Martyn filmed him as he stood for the first time. I don't know what Echo was feeling, but Martyn wept—both for Echo, for her commitment and tenderness, and for the calf, for his courage and determination.

Later I named the calf Ely, and as I write this today he is almost ten years old. He's had several mishaps, but the most serious occurred just after he turned seven. I was having a shower one afternoon when Echo and the family arrived at the little swamp behind me. A friend who came over to watch them noticed that there was something sticking out of Ely's back. She got her binoculars, and we saw that it was a spear made of twisted metal. About a foot was imbedded in his back, and three feet were sticking out. He was bleeding.

The next morning I flew to Nairobi and went straight to the Kenya Wildlife Service headquarters. A few days later they were able to send a vet team to Amboseli to try to treat Ely. What struck everyone during the procedure was Echo's behavior. By now she had another calf, a three-year-old, but her bond with Ely was clearly still very strong. The team had a terrible time keeping her from trying to rescue her son.

The whole family had panicked when Ely went down under a tranquilizer. His kin surrounded him and desperately tried to lift him. The vet team tried to chase them off. After a brave showing, several of the elephants ran. Finally, only Echo and two of her daughters, Enid and Eliot, remained. They refused to leave, even in the face of vehicles driving full-speed toward them and gunshots being fired over their heads. Finally, one of my research colleagues managed to keep Echo at bay with a Land Rover, but she stood right next to his vehicle, making a groove in the door with her tusk while the vets worked on Ely—successfully, I'm happy to report.

Iain Douglas-Hamilton, who was in Amboseli making a documentary, told me that for him, Echo's response, her courage and passion, epitomized all that's extraordinary about elephants. While he watched her risk her life for her calf, he, like Martyn seven years before, had tears running down his face.

15

Jaak Panksepp

"The Rat Will Play"

Panksepp provides a thoughtful and entertaining description of play behavior among rats.

All mammals play spontaneously when they're young. They don't need to learn to play, but they'll do it only when they have a secure emotional base. Some people feel that the lowly rat has no playful nature, nor any other redeeming qualities, but they're so wrong. Anyone who's ever had young rats for pets knows that they're delightful and loving creatures. And if they have no other companions, they enjoy playing with humans very much indeed.

As a student I had a pet rat named Tulip. Coming out to greet me whenever I returned home, she was especially eager for a little game wherein I'd toss her gently from one end of a couch to the other. She'd eagerly scurry back for more and more of this fun. I usually tired of it long before she did.

We've now studied rough-and-tumble play in young rats for a few decades, and we remain delighted by their antics and their deep desire for romping. Indeed, rats even chirp with joy when they're playing. When we started to listen carefully to the sounds they made during play—sounds inaudible to us without special equipment—the air was filled with short, high-frequency vocalizations (~fifty-kilohertz chirps). Rats continue to make such sounds during positive social engagements as adults, but at much lower levels. They also chirp a lot when they're anticipating various treats, including drugs that humans commonly abuse. They make no such sounds when negative events occur; rather, they exhibit prolonged twenty-two-kilohertz "complaints."

A few years ago, we started to suspect that chirping in rats was a kind of primitive laughter. When we tickled our rats, especially at the nape of the neck where they typically initiate play with one another, they chirped at remarkably high levels. They thoroughly enjoyed being tickled and became especially fond of hands that tickled them, while showing no special preference for hands that merely petted them. When we tickled them, the rats also tried to reciprocate—to play with us. They gently nipped our fingers, especially if we paused in our play, apparently in an attempt to solicit more. I've been "bitten" thousands of times by young rats, but never seriously. Just like puppies or kittens, they never break the skin in their playful eagerness. It's through tickling and other play that they get friendly with others and thereby learn a great deal about their social world.

As every young child knows, play is the very source of joy, and there should be little doubt that rats feel such positive emotions, as do all mammals. Just as our human choices are dictated usually by what makes us feel good or bad, every indication is that other animals base their choices on the same criteria. They seek out what makes them feel good, and they avoid what makes them feel bad. This may seem to be a simple and self-evident fact, but it's also a profound truth of nature. It's a pity that so many scientists who use animals in their research often refuse to acknowledge such a fundamental truth. Their research would improve enormously, and our understanding of animals would progress more rapidly, if scientists were more willing to consider that evolution built emotions into the nervous system at the very foundation of that mysterious process we call consciousness. This is not to say, of course, that other animals cognitively appreciate and dwell on their own feelings the way humans do. That may require more cortex in higher brain regions than most other animals have.

16

D. H. Lawrence

"Love Was Once a Little Boy"

Lawrence provides an elegant, beautiful description of his relationship with Susan, a favorite cow. We presume that this piece from a book of his prose, *Phoenix II: Uncorrected, Unpublished and other Prose Works by D.H. Lawrence* (1968, Viking Press) is based on some personal experiences.

[. . .]

How can I equilibrate myself with my black cow Susan? I call her daily at six o'clock. And sometimes she comes. But sometimes, again, she doesn't, and I have to hunt her away among the timber. Possibly she is lying peacefully in cowy inertia, like a black Hindu statue, among the oak-scrub. Then she rises with a sighing heave. My calling was a mere nothing against the black stillness of her cowy passivity.

Or possibly she is away down in the bottom corner, lowing *sotto voce* and blindly to some far-off, inaccessible bull. Then when I call at her, and approach, she screws round her tail and flings her sharp, elastic haunch in the air with a kick and a flick, and plunges off like a buck rabbit, or like a black demon among the pine trees, her udder swinging like a chime of bells. Or possibly the coyotes have been howling in the night along the top fence. And then I call in vain. It's a question of saddling a horse and sifting the bottom timber. And there at last the horse suddenly winces, starts: and with a certain pang of fear I too catch sight of something black and motionless and alive, and terribly silent, among the tree-trunks. It is Susan, her ears apart, standing like some spider suspended motionless by a thread, from the web of the eternal silence. The strange faculty she has, cow-given, of becoming a suspended ghost, hidden in the very crevices of the atmosphere! It is something in her *will*. It is her tarnhelm. And then, she doesn't know me. If I am afoot, she knows my voice, but not the advancing me, in a blue shirt and cord trousers. She waits, suspended by the thread, till I come close. Then she reaches forward her nose, to smell. She smells my hand: gives a little snort, exhaling her breath, with a kind of contempt, turns, and ambles up towards the homestead, perfectly assured. If I am on horse-back, although she knows the grey horse perfectly well, at the same time she *doesn't* know what it is. She waits till the wicked Azul, who is a born cow-punching pony, advances mischievously at her. Then round she swings, as if on the blast of some sudden wind, and with her ears back, her head rather down, her black back curved, up she goes, through the timber, with surprising, swimming swiftness. And the Azul, snorting with jolly mischief, dashes after her, and when she is safely in her milking place, still she watches with her great black eyes as I dismount. And she has to smell my hand before the cowy peace of being milked enters her blood. Till then, there is something *roaring* in the chaos of her universe. When her cowy peace comes, then her universe is silent, and like the sea with an even tide, without sail or smoke: nothing.

That is Susan, my black cow.

And how am I going to equilibrate myself with her? Or even, if you prefer the word, to get in harmony with her?

Equilibrium? Harmony? with that black blossom! Try it!

She doesn't even know me. If I put on a pair of white trousers, she wheels away as if the devil was on her back. I have to go behind her, talk to her, stroke her, and let her smell my hand; and smell the white trousers. She doesn't know they are trousers. She doesn't know that I am a gentleman on two feet. Not she. Something mysterious happens in her blood and her being, when she smells me and my nice white trousers.

Yet she knows me, too. She likes to linger, while one talks to her. She knows quite well she makes me mad when she swings her tail in my face. So sometimes she swings it, just on purpose: and looks at me out of the black corner of her great, pure-black eye, when I yell at her. And when I find her, away down the timber, when she is a ghost, and lost to the world, like a spider dangling in the void of chaos, then she is relieved. She comes to, out of a sort of trance, and is relieved, trotting up home with a queer, jerky, cowy gladness. But she is never *really* glad, as the horses are. There is always a certain untouched chaos in her.

Where she is when she's *in* the trance, heaven only knows.

That's Susan! I have a certain relation to her. But that she and I are in equilibrium, or in harmony, I would never guarantee while the world stands. As for her individuality being in balance with mine, one can only feel the great blank of the gulf.

Yet a relationship there is. She knows my touch and she goes very still and peaceful, being milked. I, too, I know her smell and her warmth and her feel. And I share some of her cowy silence, when I milk her. There *is* a sort of relation between us. And this relation is part of the mystery of love: the individuality on each side, mine and Susan's, suspended in the relationship.

[. . .]

Consciousness and Cognition

17

Donald R. Griffin

Animal Minds: Beyond Cognition to Consciousness

Griffin proposes that animals are best viewed as actors who choose what to do rather than as objects totally dependent on outside influences, although their choices may be constrained to narrow limits. He argues that animal communication is much richer than previously believed. He believes that it is most plausible to assume that the difference between humans and other animals is the *content* of conscious experience, with significant differences, both qualitatively and quantitatively.

[. . .]

Probabilities of consciousness

One helpful approach to the very challenging problems of investigating nonhuman consciousness is to think in terms of likelihood or probability. We can define pA as our estimate of the probability of conscious awareness in a given case. This might be the probability that a given animal was aware of a particular object, event, or relationship, for instance, the likelihood that it sees another animal in the underbrush or that it is a predator stalking potential prey. Or we might think in terms of the probability that a given species is capable of experiencing consciously a certain type of thought or feeling. For example, many scientists believe that animals can be aware of the behavior of others but cannot think about their beliefs and intentions.

If we are absolutely certain that a particular animal is consciously aware of something, pA would be 1.0. If we are equally sure it is not, we would find pA to be 0. If we believe that it is absolutely impossible to make any such judgment, which seems to be the position of many behavioral scientists, we should set pA at precisely 0.5. A cognitive ethologist would ideally like to determine whether pA is 0 or 1 in particular cases. An adamant behaviorist would find it is impossible to assign any value other than 0.5. Realistically, however, we can escape from this dilemma by recognizing that although we cannot yet assign any meaningful quantitative values to pA, we can make reasonable inferences about the general range of values that are most likely to be correct. For instance, when the bonobo Kanzi uses his keyboard to answer spoken questions as to where he wishes to go, and then goes there enthusiastically but resists efforts to lead him in another direction, it is reasonable to estimate that pA is close to 1. And in many other cases observational or experimental evidence makes it very likely indeed that pA is 0.

At present we can only make rough estimates of pA for most intermediate cases. The simplest judgment is whether pA is below or above 0.5, and opinions will of course differ, depending on the relative weight we assign to various types of indicative evidence. But thinking in terms of pA and its plausible value can help clarify our analysis of these extremely difficult issues. It may also be helpful to extend this approach by recognizing that our judgments of pA are necessarily subject to much uncertainty, so that any numbers we choose should be taken as approximations, and such numbers might well always be expressed with some indication of this uncertainty. Attempts to assign quantitative values to pA are rather premature at this time, because we have little firm evidence on which to base them. Perhaps the best we can do in most cases is to think in terms of only three ranges of values for pA: below 0.5, about 0.5, and above 0.5.

Evidence suggesting animal consciousness

There are several types of scientific evidence that provide promising insights into what life is like for various animals. One category of evidence is the versatility with which many animals adjust their behavior appropriately when confronted with novel challenges. Animals encounter so many unpredictable challenges under natural conditions that it would be very difficult if not impossible for any combination of genetic instructions and individual experience to specify in advance the entire set of actions that are appropriate. But thinking about alternative actions and selecting one believed to be best is an efficient way to cope with unexpected dangers and opportunities. In theory such versatility might result from nonconscious information processing in the brain. But conscious thinking may well be the most efficient way for a central nervous system to weight different possibilities and evaluate their relative advantages.

A second major category of promising evidence about animal thoughts and feelings is their communicative behavior.

[. . .]

And a third type of evidence is available from neuropsychology. For what little is known about the neural correlates of conscious, as opposed to nonconscious, thinking does not suggest that there is anything uniquely human about the basic neural structures and functions that give rise to human consciousness.

[. . .]

The "hard problem"

The lack of definitive evidence revealing just what neural processes produce consciousness has led Chalmers (1996) to designate the question of how brains produce subjective awareness as the "hard problem." He and others claim that it is such a difficult problem that normal scientific investigation is unable, in principle, to solve it, and that consciousness must be something basically distinct from the rest of the physical universe. But this view, fortunately, has not seriously interfered with a striking renaissance in the scientific investigation of consciousness. In the 1990s numerous neuroscientists, psychologists, philosophers, and others have taken up active investigation and discussion of consciousness. Even distinguished molecular biologists such as Edelman (1989), Edelman and Tononi (2000), and Crick (1994) have joined the quest. One of the most inclusive of several international conferences devoted to consciousness and related subjects led to two massive volumes edited by Hameroff *et al.* (1996, 1998). General reviews of this reawakened concern with consciousness have been published by Crook (1980, 1983, 1987, 1988), Baars (1988, 1997), Chalmers (1996), Flanagan (1992), and Searle (1992, 1998).

Although much of our behavior takes place without any awareness, and this includes most of our physiological functions and the details of such fairly complex actions as coordinated locomotion, the small fraction of which we *are* aware is certainly important. It is a completely reasonable and significant question whether members of other species experience anything, although the content of their conscious experiences is likely to be quite different from ours. Perhaps we can never discover *precisely* what the content of nonhuman experiences are, because scientific understanding is seldom complete and perfect. But it seems probable that we can gradually reduce our current ignorance about this significant aspect of life.

The comparative analysis of consciousness

Despite the renaissance of scientific and philosophical interest in consciousness, one of the most significant and promising approaches to the general question has been largely neglected. This is what biologists call the comparative method: analyzing an important function in a variety of species in which it occurs, sometimes in simpler forms, in which it can be studied more effectively without the many interacting complications that obscure its basic properties in the more complicated animals. Crick and Koch (1998), leaders in the renewal of scientific studies of consciousness, take it for granted that monkeys are conscious. But they prefer to defer investigating nonhuman consciousness because they claim that "when one clearly understands, both in detail and in principle, what consciousness involves in humans, then will be the time to consider the problem of consciousness in much simpler animals" (97).

Restricting scientific investigation to the most complex of all known brains may be unwise, however, for insofar as consciousness can be identified and analyzed in a variety of animals, certain species might turn out to be especially suitable for investigating its basic attributes. Obvious analogies are the use of fruit flies for investigations of genetics, squid giant axons for analyzing the biophysics of nerve conduction, laboratory rats and pigeons for studies of learning, and *Aplesia* for detailed analysis of the cellular and molecular basis of learning. It would have been unwise for the early investigators of genetics or learning to limit their research to primates, and the same may be true for contemporary and future studies of consciousness.

Perceptual and reflective consciousness

The psychologist Natsoulas (1978) emphasized a major distinction that is often overlooked. One widespread and important meaning is what he designates as Consciousness 3, following the *Oxford English Dictionary*: "the state or faculty of being mentally conscious or aware of anything." This Natsoulas calls "our most basic concept of consciousness, for it is implicated in all the other senses. One's being conscious, whatever more it might mean, must include one's being aware of something" (910). Another important meaning is what Natsoulas, again following the *OED*, calls Consciousness 4, which he defines as "the recognition by the thinking subject of his own acts or affections. . . . One exemplifies Consciousness 4 by being aware of, or by being in a position to be aware of, one's own perception, thought, or other occurrent mental episode" (911). The other shades of meaning analyzed by Natsoulas (1983, 1985, 1986, 1988) are less important for our purposes, but these two impinge directly on the issues that will be discussed in this book.

Natsoulas' Consciousness 3 is similar to conscious perception, although its content may entail memories, anticipations, or imagining nonexistent objects or events, as well as thinking about immediate sensory input. An animal may think consciously about something, as opposed to being influenced by it or reacting to it without any conscious awareness of its existence or effects. It is convenient to call this *perceptual consciousness*. Consciousness 4, as defined by Natsoulas, entails a conscious awareness that one is thinking or feeling in a certain way. This is conveniently called *reflective consciousness*, meaning that one is aware of one's own thoughts as well as the objects or activities about which one is thinking. It is a form of introspection, thinking about one's thoughts, but with the addition of being able to think about the thoughts of others. The distinction between perceptual and reflective consciousness is important for the sometimes confused (and almost always confusing) debate among scientists about animal consciousness. Many scientists use the unqualified term *conscious* to mean reflective consciousness and imply that perceptual consciousness is not consciousness at all. On the other hand, the existence and distribution of relatively simple perceptual consciousness is important in its own right, and when we understand it better we will be in a much better position to investigate whether any animals are also capable of reflective consciousness.

Many behavioral scientists such as Shettleworth (1998) and philosophers such as Lloyd (1989, 186) believe that it is likely that animals may sometimes experience perceptual consciousness but that reflective consciousness is a unique human attribute. The latter would be much more difficult to detect in animals, if it does occur. People can tell when they are thinking about their own thoughts, but it has generally seemed impossible for animals to do so, although animal communication may sometimes serve the same basic function. The very difficulty of detecting whether animals experience reflective consciousness should make us cautious about concluding that it is impossible. Most of the suggestive evidence that will be discussed in this book points toward perceptual rather than reflective consciousness. Those swayed by a visceral feeling that some important level of consciousness *must* be restricted to our species may cling to reflective consciousness as a bastion still defended by many against the increasing evidence that other animals share to a limited extent many of our mental abilities.

[. . .]

The relation between these two general categories of consciousness can be illustrated by considering a class of intermediate cases, namely, an animal's awareness of its own body—for example, the appearance of its feet or the feeling of cold as a winter wind ruffles its fur. This tends to become an intermediate category between perceptual and reflective consciousness, for an animal might be consciously aware not only of some part of its body but also of what that structure was doing. It might not only feel its teeth crunching on food but also realize that it tastes good. Or it might not only feel the ground under its feet but also recognize that it is running in order to escape from a threatening predator. Furthermore, an animal capable of perceptual consciousness must often be aware that a particular companion is eating or fleeing. This means that it is consciously aware of both the action and of who is performing it. These would all be special cases of perceptual consciousness.

This leads to inquiring how likely it is that such an animal would be incapable of thinking that it, itself, was eating or fleeing. If we grant an animal perceptual consciousness of its own actions, the prohibition against conscious awareness of who is eating or fleeing becomes a somewhat strained and artificial restriction. Furthermore, a perceptually conscious animal could scarcely be unaware of its own enjoyment of eating or its fear of the predator from which it is trying desperately to escape. One could argue that perceptually conscious animals are aware of their actions but not of the thoughts and feelings that motivate them. But emotional experiences are often so vivid and intense that it seems unlikely that when an animal is conscious of its actions it could somehow be unaware of its emotions. We might well pause at this point and ask ourselves whether it is really plausible to claim that an animal can consciously experience emotional feelings and simple thoughts but never be aware that it, itself, is having these experiences. Animals must often feel afraid, but are they incapable of thinking about their fear? Are they sometimes conscious of their actions but never of the thoughts and feelings that motivate them?

Consider the case of an animal that barely escapes from the attack of a predator. It was surely frightened at the time, and if it later sees the same predator it presumably remembers both the event and how frightening it was. If so, this memory of its experience of fear would be a case of thinking about one of its emotional experiences. If we grant such an animal the ability to experience perceptual consciousness of a remembered event, how reasonable is it to rule out the possibility of simple reflective awareness of its remembered fear? To continue with this example, suppose that in its previous narrow escape this animal succeeded only because at the last moment it remembered that it could squeeze into a particular cavity. In this emergency it had been perceptually conscious that a certain action, squeezing between the roots of a particular tree, would get it into a safe retreat. Suppose on the following day it sees the same predator in the same area. Our animal would probably remember not only its fear but the tactic that had saved its life the day before. This would be recalling not only the emotional state of fear but also the simple thought of how to escape. If we insist that all animals are incapable of even such simple sorts of reflective consciousness, we are in effect postulating that a perceptual "black hole" encompasses their most intimate and pressing experiences.

Summary

It is self evident that we sometimes think about our situation and about the probable results of various actions that we might take; that is, we plan and choose what to do. This sort of conscious subjective mental experience is significant and useful because it often helps us select appropriate behavior; thus mental experiences are "local causes" of behavior, although of course they, in turn, are influenced by prior events.

Animals are best viewed as actors who choose what to do rather than as objects totally dependent on outside influences, although their choices are often constrained within quite narrow limits. Especially when they try to solve newly arisen challenges by adjusting their behavior in versatile ways, their choices are probably guided by simple conscious thoughts, such as fear of dangers, a desire to get something good to eat, or a belief that food can be obtained in a certain place or by a particular activity.

The difficult but important questions about animal mentality can best be approached from the viewpoint of a materialist who assumes that mental experiences result from physiological processes occurring in central nervous systems. These processes, and relationships among them, are neither tangible objects nor immaterial essences. They appear to be roughly analogous in this respect to homeostasis, which is an important physiological process but one that cannot be pinned down to a specific structure. In the scientific investigation of animal minds there is no need to call on immaterial factors, vitalism, or divine intervention. We know that our central nervous systems are capable of producing conscious experience on occasion, and nothing yet learned about neuroscience precludes the possibility that other nervous systems can achieve something of the same general kind. Of course, this does not mean that all consciousness is identical or that the experiences of other species come close to rivaling the versatility, breadth, and complexity of ours. The great reluctance to consider the possibility that a wide range of animals may experience at least simple conscious thoughts stems in part from a general opinion that consciousness is something immaterial. This helps explain why cognition has come to be accepted but consciousness has not.

Communicative behavior of animals can serve the same basic function as human verbal and nonverbal communication by expressing at least some of an animal's private experiences. Therefore cognitive ethologists can gather verifiable, objective data about some of the private experiences of communicating animals by interpreting the messages that they convey to others. It is often claimed that although language allows us to obtain significant (though imperfect and incomplete) evidence about the thoughts of our human companions, animals lack language and therefore this source of information is not available. But animal communication is much richer than we used to believe, and this supposed barrier crumbles once we are prepared to listen.

In view of the likelihood that all or at least a wide range of animals experience some form of subjective conscious awareness, it is both more parsimonious and more plausible to assume that the difference between human and other brains and minds is the *content* of conscious experience. This content of consciousness, what one is aware of, surely differs both qualitatively and quantitatively by astronomical magnitudes. Rather than an absolute all-or-nothing dichotomy between human brains uniquely capable of producing conscious experience, on one hand, and all other brains that can never do so, on the other, this hypothesis is consistent with our general belief in evolutionary continuity.

Out of all these multiple cross-currents of ideas three categories of evidence stand out as the most promising sources of significant, though incomplete, evidence of conscious thinking by nonhuman animals:

1. Versatile adaptation of behavior to novel challenges [. . .]
2. Physiological evidence of brain functions that are correlated with conscious thinking [. . .]
3. Most promising of all is the communicative behavior by which animals sometimes appear to convey to others at least some of their thoughts [. . .]

References

Baars, B. J. 1988. *A cognitive theory of consciousness*. New York: Cambridge University Press.
——. 1997. *In the theatre of consciousness: The workspace of the mind*. New York: Oxford University Press.
Chalmers, D. I. 1996. *The conscious mind: In search of a fundamental theory*. New York: Oxford University Press.
Crick, F. 1994. *The astonishing hypothesis: The scientific search for the soul*. New York: Simon and Schuster.
Crick, F., and C. Koch. 1998. Consciousness and neuroscience. *Cerebral Cortex* 8:97–107.
Crook, J. H., 1980. *The evolution of human consciousness*. Oxford: Oxford University Press.
——. 1983. On attributing consciousness to animals. *Nature* 303:11–14.
——. 1987. The nature of conscious awareness. In *Mindwaves: Thoughts on intelligence, identity, and consciousness*, ed. C. Blakemore and S. Greenfield. Oxford: Basil Blackwell.
——. 1988. The experiental context of intellect. In *Machiavellian intelligence: Social expertise and the*

evolution of intellect in monkeys, apes, and humans, ed. R. W. Byrne and A. Whiten. Oxford: Oxford University Press.

Edelman, G. 1989. *The remembered present: A biological theory of consciousness*. New York: Basic Books.

Edelman, G., and G. Tononi, 2000. *A universe of consciousness: How matter becomes imagination*. New York: Basic Books.

Flanagan, O. 1992. *Consciousness reconsidered*. Cambridge: MIT Press.

Hamcroff, S. R., A. W. Kaszniak, and A. C. Scott, (eds) 1996. *Toward a science of consciousness: The first Tucson discussions and debates*. Cambridge: MIT Press.

——. 1998. *Toward a science of consciousness II: The second Tucson discussions and debates*. Cambridge: MIT Press.

Lloyd, D. 1989. *Simple minds*. Cambridge: MIT Press.

Natsoulas, T. 1978. Consciousness. *Amer. Psychologist* 33:906–14.

——. 1983. Concepts of consciousness. *J. Mind and Behav.* 4:13–59.

——. 1985. An introduction to the perceptual kind of conception of direct (reflective) consciousness. *J. Mind and Behav.* 6:333–56.

——. 1986. On the radical behaviorist conception of consciousness. *J. Mind and Behav.* 8:1–21.

——. 1988. The intentionality of retroawareness. *J. Mind and Behav.* 9:549–74.

Searle, J. R. 1992. *The rediscovery of the mind*. Cambridge: MIT Press.

——. 1998. How to study consciousness scientifically. *Brain Research Rev.* 26:379–87.

Shettleworth, S. J. 1998. *Cognition, evolution, and behavior*. New York: Oxford University Press.

Annotated Further Reading

Akins, K.A. (1996) "A Bat Without Qualities?" Chapter 23, in *Readings in Animal Cognition*, Marc Bekoff and Dale Jamieson (eds). Cambridge, Mass.: Massachusetts Institute of Technology, pp. 345–58.

Baker, S. (2001) *Picturing the Beast: Animals, Identity, and Representation*. Urbana: University of Illinois. How our perception of animals is affected by their images in politics, entertainment and social interactions.

Barresi, J. and Moore, C. (1996) "Intentional Relations and Social Understanding." *Behavioral and Brain Sciences* 19: 107–54. Most animals do not integrate information about their own desires with that about other agents' desires. Only great apes do, and only human beings represent intentional relations with mental objects.

Bateson, P. (1992) "Do Animals Feel Pain?" *New Scientist* (25 April): 30–3. An approach based on observable signs associated with the subjective sense of pain in human beings.

Bekoff, M. (1994) "Cognitive Ethology and the Treatment of Non-human Animals: How Matters of Mind Inform Matters of Welfare." *Animal Welfare* 3: 75–96.

—— (ed.) (2000) *The Smile of a Dolphin: Remarkable Accounts of Animal Emotions*. New York: Discovery Books, Stories by well-known scientists.

—— (2001) "The Evolution of Animal Play, Emotions, and Social Morality: On Science, Theology, Spirituality, Personhood, and Love." *Zygon: Journal of Religion and Science* 36(4): 615–55. Insightful analysis integrating many disciplines.

—— (2002) *Minding Animals: Awareness, Emotions, and Heart*. New York: Oxford University Press. Foreword by Jane Goodall. A tour of the emotional and mental world of animals, where creatures do amazing things. Accessible to the general reader.

——, Allen, C. and Burghard, G. M. (2002) *The Cognitive Animal: Empirical and Theoretical Perspectives in Animal Cognition*. Cambridge, Mass.: The MIT Press. Many fine articles from prominent researchers.

Ben-Ari, E.T. (1999) "A Throbbing in the Air." *Bioscience* 49: 353–8. Elephant communications.

Bradshaw, R.H. (1998) "Consciousness in Non-human Animals: Adopting the Precautionary Principle." *Journal of Consciousness Studies* 5: 108–14.

Cartmill, M. (2000) "Animal Consciousness: Some Philosophical, Methodological, and Evolutionary Problems." *American Zoologist* 40: 835–46.

—— and Lofstrom, I. (2000) "Introduction to the Symposium; Animal Consciousness: Historical, Theoretical, and Empirical Perspectives." *American Zoologist* 40: 833–44.

Dawkins, M.S. (1995) *Unravelling Animal Behaviour* (2nd ed.). Essex, England: Longman Scientific & Technical. An admirably clear account of basic concepts.

Dennett, D.C. (1995) "Do Animals have Beliefs?" Chapter 6, pp. 111–18. In *Comparative Approaches to Cognitive Science*, Herbert L. Roitblat and Jean-Arcady Meyer (eds). Cambridge, Mass.: The MIT Press. Yes animals have beliefs but so do thermostats, according to Dennett's definition.

Dickinson, A. (1991) "Intentionality in Animal Conditioning." Chapter 12, pp. 305–25. In *Thought Without Language*, L. Weiskrantz (ed.). Oxford: Clarendon Press.

Dixon, B. (2001) "Animal Emotions." *Ethics and The Environment* 6(2): 23–30. The concept of animal emotions has been insufficiently analyzed.

Dol, M. *et al.* (eds) (1997) *Animal Consciousness and Animal Ethics: Perspectives from the Netherlands*. Van Gorcum. Several well-written and useful essays.

Evans, C.S. and Marler, P. (1995) "Language and Animal Communication: Parallels and Contrasts." Chapter 15, pp. 341–82. In *Comparative Approaches to Cognitive Science*, Herbert L. Roitblat and Jean-Arcady Meyer (eds). Cambridge, Mass.: The MIT Press. Focuses on natural communicative systems, illustrating parallels between animal communication and language in categorical perception, referential signaling and audience effects. The most dramatic contrast is provided by syntax.

Frijda, N.H. (1995) "Emotions in Robots." Chapter 20, pp. 501–16. In *Comparative Approaches to Cognitive Science*, Herbert L. Roitblat and Jean-Arcady Meyer (eds). Cambridge, Mass.: The MIT Press.

Gould, J.L. and Gould, C.G. (1994) *The Animal Mind*. New York: Scientific American Library. Bees, bowerbirds, beavers, primates. No isolated aspect of human cognitive ability is unique.

Griffin, D.R. (1998) "From Cognition to Consciousness." *Animal Cognition* 1: 3–16.

—— (2000) "Scientific Approaches to Animal Consciousness." *American Zoologist* 40: 889–92.

—— (2001) *Animal Minds: Beyond Cognition to Consciousness*. Chicago: University of Chicago Press. Expanded and revised from the 1992 classic. An excellent, comprehensive review, though Griffin stops short of discussing moral judgments.

Heinrich, B. (1999) *Mind of the Raven: Investigations and Adventures with Wolf-Birds*. New York: HarperCollins. An engaging book by a world authority on ravens.

—— (2002) "Raven consciousness." Chapter 7, pp. 47–52. In *Cognitive Animal*, M. Bekoff, C. Allen, and G.M. Burghardt (eds). Cambridge, Mass.: The MIT Press.

Horn, G. (1991) "What Can the Bird Brain Tell Us about Thought without Language?" In *Thought Without Language*, L. Weiskrantz (ed.). Oxford: Clarendon Press.

Jamieson, D. and Marc Bekoff (eds) (1996) *Readings in Animal Cognition*. Cambridge, Mass.: The MIT Press.

Kimler, W.C. (2000) "Reading Morgan's Canon: Reduction and Unification in the Foraging of a Science of the Mind." *American Zoologist* 40: 853–61.

Kistler, J.M. (2000) *Animal Rights: A Subject Guide, Bibliography, and Internet Companion*. Westport, Conn.: Greenwood Press. A very useful annotated source.

Lenain, T. (1997) *Monkey Painting*. London: Reaktion Books. Ape painting is both inseparably human and simian and so can no longer be regarded as a pathway to the solution of the problem of the origins of art.

Macer, D. (1998) "Animal Consciousness and Ethics in Asia and the Pacific." *Journal of Agricultural and Environmental Ethics* 10: 249–67.

Masson, J.M. and McCarthy, S. (1995) *When Elephants Weep: The Emotional Lives of Animals*, New York: Delacorte Press. Readable account with many studies and anecdotes.

Mather, J.A. (1995) "Cognition in Cephalopods." *Advances in the Study of Behavior* 24: 317–53. Cephalopods may have considerable information-processing capacity and the ability to make decisions based on visual and tactile cues.

McFarland, D. (1995) "Opportunity Versus Goals in Robots, Animals and People." In *Comparative Approaches to Cognitive Science*, Herbert L. Roitblat and Jean-Arcady Meyer (eds). Cambridge, Mass.: The MIT Press.

Macphail, E.M. (1998) *The Evolution of Consciousness*. New York: Oxford University Press.

Milius, S. (2001) "Finches Figure out Solo how to use Tools." *Science News* 160: 295.

—— (2001) "Crows Appear to make Tools Right-handedly." *Science News* 160: 375.

Mitchell, R.W., Thompson, N.S., and Miles, H. Lyn (eds). (1997) *Anthropomorphism, Anecdotes, and Animals*. Albany, NY: State University of New York Press, 518 pp.

Netting, J. (2000) "U.S. Dispute over Definition of Animal Distress." *Nature* 406: 668. (See also www.aphis.usda.gov/ppd)

Panskepp, J. (1998) *Affective Neuroscience: The Foundations of Human and Animal Emotions*. New York: Oxford University Press. A comprehensive treatment that steers a middle course between reductionism and anti-reductionism.

Pearce, J.M. (1991) "Stimulus Generalization and the Acquisition of Categories by Pigeons." Chapter 6, pp. 132–55. In *Thought Without Language*, L. Weiskrantz (ed.). Oxford: Clarendon Press.

Pepperberg, I.M. (2002) "Cognitive and Communicative Abilities of Grey Parrots." Chapter 31, pp. 247–53. In *Cognitive Animal*, M. Bekoff, C. Allen, and G.M. Burghardt (eds). Cambridge, Mass.: The MIT Press.

—— and Lynn, S.K. (2000) "Possible Levels of Animal Consciousness with Reference to Grey Parrots (*Psittacus erithacus*)." *American Zoologist* 40: 893–901.
Premack, D. (1991) "Minds with and without Language." In *Thought Without Language*, L. Wiskrantz (ed.). Oxford: Clarendon Press. The human-ape difference does not depend upon language.
Ritvo, H. (2000) "Animal Consciousness: Some Historical Perspective." *American Zoologist* 40: 847–52.
Rollin, B. E. (1998) *The Unheeded Cry: Animal Consciousness, Animal Pain and Science*. Ames, Iowa: Iowa State University Press. An important account of the morality of animal use in the sciences, with an historical perspective beginning in the nineteenth century.
—— (1999) "Some Conceptual and Ethical Concerns about Current Views of Pain." *Pain Forum* 8(2): 78–83.
Rutherford, K.M.D. (2002) "Assessing Pain in Animals." *Animal Welfare* 11: 31–53. Qualitative observation by an experienced observer may be the only method capable of capturing the complexity of animal pain.
Shusterman, R.J., Kastak, C.R., and Kastak, D. (2002) "The Cognitive Sea Lion: Meaning and Memory in the Laboratory and in Nature." Chapter 28, pp. 217–28. In *The Cognitive Animal: Empirical and Theoretical Perspectives on Animal Cognition*, M. Bekoff, C. Allen, and G.M. Burghardt (eds). Cambridge, Mass.: The MIT Press. Sea lions have complex abilities, including the learning of rules.
Skutch, A.F. (1996) *The Minds of Birds*. College Station, Texas: Texas A & M University Press. A delightful account stressing birds' capacity for enjoyment.
Staddon, J.E.R. (2000) "Consciousness and theoretical behaviorism." *American Zoologist* 40: 874–82.
Thompson, R.K. (1995) "Natural and Relational Concepts in Animals." Pp. 175–224. In *Comparative Approaches to Cognitive Science*, Herbert L. Roitblat and Jean-Arcady Meyer (eds). Cambridge, Mass.: The MIT Press. A good overview of the evidence that animals categorize their world on the basis of perceptual and sometimes abstract, relational similarities.
Wall, P.D. (1992) "Defining Pain in Animals." Chapter 3, pp. 63–79. In *Animal Pain*, Charles E. Short and Alan van Poznak (eds). New York: Churchill Livingstone.
Weiskranz, L. (ed.) (1991) *Thought Without Language*. Oxford: Clarendon Press. A useful group of essays on learning in pigeons, primates, human infants, and adults with aphasia and dyslexia.

Study Questions

1   To what degree do you believe that Rollin's assertion for the need to use anthropomorphic interpretations of animal experiences is compatible or incompatible with traditional scientific methodology to study animals? Give your reasoning.
2   To what degree do you believe that Smuts' objectivity for describing chimpanzee lives might be affected by her interpersonal relations with them? Justify your thinking.
3   To what degree are Bermond's and Rollin's position on animal experience of pain compatible, and incompatible? Clarify your reasons.
4   Based on Varner's position that cephalopods can feel pain, how do you believe that cephalopods should be treated differently from other invertebrates, if at all? Explain your reasoning.
5   Compare the perspectives on the emotional lives of animals described by Dawkins with that of your own. What themes do they share and how do they differ? How would you respond to Dawkins on the points where you seem to differ?
6   To what degree do the anecdotes described by Moss, Panksepp, and Lawrence change your perceptions of animals?
7   Compare the type and level of consciousness ascribed to animals by Dawkins and Griffin. To what degree are they similar, and how do they differ? Which do you find closer to your own perspective? Explain your reasoning.

Part III

Primates and Cetaceans

Introduction

This Part exhibits some of the issues involved with the great apes and cetaceans. One issue is whether study should be laboratory-based or should be observation of great apes and cetaceans in the wild. A second issue is whether our focus should be on species or on individual animals. And a third issue is whether the moral status of an animal should be related to its cognitive abilities.

In his essay Marc Bekoff argues against line-drawing between animal species; we should avoid "primatocentrism" and focus not on animal cognitive abilities but simply on animal pain and suffering. Individuals count, whatever their species.

The great apes exhibit such extraordinary capacities that a number of thinkers, such as Steven Wise (see Part X), have proposed that they be given basic legal rights. The linguistic capacities and self-awareness of great apes is discussed by Sue Savage-Rumbaugh in her essay. Her pioneering work with chimpanzees and bonobos has been conducted in a laboratory setting, allowing for carefully controlled observations. Juan Carlos Gómez addresses the specific question of whether or not apes are persons. He rejects definitions of personhood such as that of Daniel Dennett which require that persons exhibit levels of cognitive complexity which require linguistic communication. Based on his studies of great apes, Gómez emphasizes the importance of the second-person, of mutual relationships in personhood. Accordingly, we as human beings attain our personhood before we know how to speak. Apes are persons also, though not the same as human persons. The brief account by Fran Peavey of a captive female chimpanzee reaching out for support from human females illustrates this ape's capacity for mutuality.

Andrew Whiten and his co-workers discuss their findings from their observations of chimpanzees in the wild. They present their findings of cultural variations between chimpanzee communities—a feature previously taught to be unique to human communities.

Jane Goodall discusses problems faced by chimpanzees both in their natural habitats and in captivity. Her comments are based on over thirty years of observations of wild chimpanzees. She states that it is because of knowing chimpanzees who are "wild and free and in control of their own lives" that she is concerned not only with chimpanzees as a species but also with individual chimpanzees in whatever circumstances they find themselves.

Luke Rendell and Hal Whitehead have studied bottlenosed dolphins and killer whales extensively in the wild, and report evidence of social learning, imitation and teaching. Louis M. Herman has spent over thirty years studying bottlenosed dolphins using a long-term program of intensive, special education. Herman's work demonstrates that dolphins are capable of understanding syntax, in the sense of word order, as well as semantic rules. Dolphins respond to televised images but understand that the television scene is not the real world. They demonstrate self-awareness through being able to repeat their own behavior.

In her essay Mary Midgley responds to a 1977 trial of two people who freed two bottlenosed dolphins. While the judge found it obvious that the word "person" did not include dolphins, Midgley affirms that on the contrary there are well-established precedents for calling non-human beings "persons." In an approach similar to that of Gómez, Midgley affirms that it is emotional fellowship which is most important in deciding whether or not to call a being a person.

18

———•———

Marc Bekoff

"Deep Ethology, Animal Rights, and The Great Ape/Animal Project: Resisting Speciesism and Expanding the Community of Equals"

Bekoff advocates expanding The Great Ape Project to The Great Ape/Animal Project and acknowledging that all individual animals count and should be admitted into a Community of Equals based on ascribing moral status and rights to them. He argues that limiting this moral status to primates is speciesist. He argues that at least some past animal research and other activities violating their rights must not continue, and that the burden to justify animal research lies on those who wish to conduct it.

[. . .]

In 1993, *The Great Ape Project: Equality Beyond Humanity* (Cavalieri and Singer 1993) was published. This important and seminal project has become known widely as the GAP. I was a proud contributor to the GAP (Bekoff 1993), and strongly supported its ambitious and major goal, namely that of admitting Great Apes (including all humans) to the Community of Equals in which the following basic moral principles or rights, enforceable at law, are granted: (i) the right to life, (ii) the protection of individual liberty, and (iii) the prohibition of torture. [. . .] I believe that the time really has come to expand the GAP to The Great Ape/ Animal Project, or the GA/AP, and to expand the Community of Equals. [. . .]

Narrow-minded primatocentrism must be resisted in our studies of animal cognition and animal protection and rights. [. . .] I and others have previously argued that it is *individuals* who are important (see Rachels 1990 for a discussion of species-neutral *moral individualism* and also Bekoff and Gruen 1993 and Frey 1996 for further discussion). Thus, careful attention must be paid to *within* species individual variations in behavior.

We must not think that monkeys are smarter than dogs for each can do things the other cannot. *Smart* and *intelligent* are loaded words and often are misused: dogs do what they need to do to be dogs—they are dog-smart in their own ways—and monkeys do what they need to do to be monkeys—they are monkey-smart in their own ways—*and neither is smarter than one another.*

[. . .]

[W]hen we are unsure about an individual's ability to reason or to think, then we should assume that they can in their own ways—and certainly when we are uncertain about an individual's ability to experience pain and to suffer, then we must assume that they can. *We must err on the side of the animals.*

[. . .]

People often ask whether "lower" nonhuman animals such as fish or dogs perform sophisticated patterns of behavior that are usually associated with "higher" nonhuman primates. [. . .] In my view, these are misguided questions [. . .] because animals have to be able to do what they need to do in order to live in their own worlds. This type of speciesist cognitivism also can be bad news for many animals. If an answer to this question means that there are consequences in terms of the sorts of treatment to which an individual is subjected, then we really have to analyze the question in great detail (for discussion with respect to fish, see Dionys de Leeuw 1996 and Verheijen and Flight 1997). It is important to accept that while there are species differences in behavior, behavioral differences in and of themselves may mean little for arguments about the rights of animals.

I want to reemphasize that the use of the words "higher" and "lower" and activities such as line-drawing to place different groups of animals "above" and "below" others are extremely misleading and fail to take into account the lives and the worlds of the animals themselves. These lives and worlds are becoming increasingly accessible as the field of cognitive ethology matures. Irresponsible use of these words can also be harmful for many animals. It is disappointing that a recent essay on animal use in a widely read magazine, *Scientific American* (Mukerjee 1997, p. 86), perpetuates this myth—this ladder view of evolution—by referring to animals "lower on the phylogenetic tree." (For discussion see Crisp 1990, Bekoff 1992, Sober 1998, and Verheijen and Flight 1997; in the same issue of *Scientific American* we are told that "In my opinion, the arguments for banning experiments on animals—that there are empirically and morally superior alternatives—are unpersuasive" (Rennie, 1997, p. 4).) There are a number of objections to hierarchical ladder views of evolution, two of which are: (i) a single "ladder view" of evolution does not take into account animals with uncommon ancestries (Crisp 1990); (ii) there are serious problems deciding which criteria for moral relevance should be used and how evaluations of these criteria are to be made, even if one was able to argue convincingly for the use of a single scale (Bekoff 1992). To be sure, ladder views are speciesist.

As I noted above, some primatologists write as if only some nonhuman primates along with human primates have theories of mind. To dismiss the possibility that at least some nonprimates are capable of having a theory of mind many more data need to be collected and existing data about intentionality in nonprimates need to be considered. Furthermore, primatocentric claims are based on very few comparative data derived from tests on very small numbers of nonhuman primates who might not be entirely representative of their species. The range of tests that have been used to obtain evidence of intentional attributions is also extremely small, and such tests are often biased towards activities that may favor apes over monkeys or members of other nonprimate species. However, there is evidence that mice can outperform apes on some imitation tasks (Whiten and Ham 1992). These data do not make mice "special," and I am sure few would claim that these data should be used to spare mice and exploit monkeys. Rather, these results show that it is important to investigate the abilities of various organisms with respect to their normal living conditions. Accepting that there are species differences in behavior, and that behavioral differences in and of themselves may mean little to arguments about the rights of animals, is important, for speciesist cognitivism can be bad news for many animals.

[. . .]

It is important to talk to the animals and let them talk to us; these reciprocal conversations should allow us to *see* the animals for whom they are. To this end, [. . .] Gluck (1997), in stressing the importance of considering what we do to animals from the perspective of the animal, emphasizes the need to go beyond science and to see animals as who they are. Our respect for animals must be motivated by who they are and not by who we want them to be in our anthropocentric scheme of things. As Taylor (1986, p. 313) notes, a switch away from anthropocentrism to biocentrism, in which human superiority comes under critical scrutiny, "may require a profound moral reorientation." So be it.

We are still a long way from having an adequate data-base from which stipulative claims about the taxonomic distribution of various cognitive skills or about the having of a theory of mind can be put forth with any degree of certainty. Furthermore, we still have little idea about the phylogenetic distribution of pain and suffering in animals. We can only hope that adequate funding will be available so that these important studies can be pursued rigorously.

With respect to possible links between the study of animal cognition and the protection of innocent nonconsenting animals, I believe that a "deep reflective ethology" is needed to make people more aware of what they do to nonhumans and to make them aware of their moral and ethical obligations to animals. We must enter into intimate and reciprocal relationships with all beings in this more-than-human world (Abram 1996). In many circles it simply is too easy to abuse animals. I use the term "deep reflective ethology" to convey some of the same general ideas that underlie the "deep ecology" movement, in which it is asked that people recognize that they not only are an integral part of nature, but also that they have unique responsibilities to nature. Most people who think deeply about the troubling issues surrounding animal welfare would agree that the use of animals in research, education, for amusement, or for food needs to be severely restricted, and in some cases simply stopped. Those who appeal to the "brutality of nature" to justify some humans' brutal treatment of nonhumans fail to see that animals are not moral agents and cannot be held responsible for their actions as being "right" or "wrong" or "good" or "bad" (Bekoff and Hettinger 1994). If animals were to be viewed as moral agents (rather than as moral patients), there are a number of cognitive abilities that are correlated with the ability to make moral judgments, the possession of which would make animal abuse even more objectionable. It is essential to accept that most individual nonhuman animals experience pain and do suffer, even if it is not the same sort of pain and suffering that is experienced by humans, or even other nonhumans, including members of the same species. Furthermore, when all individuals are admitted to the Community of Equals, their rights must be vigorously protected regardless of their cognitive skills or of their capacities to experience pain and to suffer.

Deepening ethology also means we need to bond with the animals we study and even name them (Davis and Balfour 1992). Many individual animals come to trust us and we should not breach this trust.

[. . .]

Let me emphasize once again that studying nonhuman animals is a privilege that must not be abused. We must take this privilege seriously. Although some believe that naming animals is a bad idea because named animals will be treated differently—usually less objectively—than numbered animals, others believe just the opposite, that naming animals is permissible and even expected when working closely with at least certain species, especially with the same individuals over long periods of time. Manes (1997, p. 155) notes:

If the world of our meaningful relationships is measured by the things we call by name, then our universe of meaning is rapidly shrinking. No culture has dispersed personal names as parsimoniously as ours ... officially limiting personality to humans ... [and] animals have become increasingly nameless. Some*thing* not some*body*.

It is interesting to note that early in her career, the well-known primatologist, Jane Goodall, had trouble convincing reviewers of one of her early papers that naming the chimpanzees she studied should be allowed. Professor Goodall refused to make the changes they suggested, including dropping names and referring to the animals as "it" rather than "he" or "she," or "which" rather than "who," but her paper was published. It seems noteworthy that researchers working with nonhuman primates and some cetaceans usually name the animals they study; we read about Kanzi, Austin, Sherman, Koko, Phoenix, and Akeakamai and often see pictures of them with their proud human companions. We also read about Alex, an African gray parrot who Irene Pepperberg has studied extensively. Yet most people do not seem to find naming these individuals to be objectionable. Is it because the animals who are named have been shown to have highly developed cognitive skills? Not necessarily, for these and other animals are often named *before* they are studied intensively. Or, in the case of most nonhuman primates, is naming permissible because these individuals are more similar to humans than are members of other species? Why is naming a rat or a lizard or a spider more off-putting than naming a primate or a dolphin or a parrot? We need to know more about why this is so.

The context in which animals are used can also inform attitudes that people have even to individuals of the same species. For example, scientists also show different attitudes toward animals of the same species depending on whether they are encountered in the laboratory or at home; many scientists who name and praise the cognitive abilities of the companion animals with whom they share their home are likely to leave this sort of "baggage" at home when they enter their laboratories to do research with members of the same species. Based on a series of interviews with practicing scientists, Phillips (1994, p. 119) reported that many of them construct a "distinct category of animal, the 'laboratory animal,' that contrasts with namable animals (e.g., pets) across every salient dimension ... the cat or dog in the laboratory is perceived by researchers as ontologically different from the pet dog or cat at home."

We must also pay attention to the oftentimes limited use, success, and even knowledge of animal models (see Lafollette and Shanks 1996 and Shapiro 1997 for detailed discussions) and to the many successes of using non-animal alternatives. (It seems a safe bet that most people would not venture to go to work if they had as little chance of reaching their destination as some models have of helping humans along.) And we must not be afraid of what those successes might mean in the future—the reduction and then the abolition of animal use as models based on computer simulations or work on humans emerge superior.

Everyone must be concerned with the treatment of nonhuman animals, not only the rich and those with idle time on their hands. [. . .] We must not only think of the animals when it is convenient for us to do so. Although the issues are at once difficult, frightening, and challenging, this does not mean they are impossible with which to deal. *Certainly we cannot let the animals suffer because of our inability to come to terms with difficult issues.*

We need to teach our children well for they are the custodians of the future. They will live and work in a world in which increasingly science will not be seen as a self-justifying activity, but as another human institution whose claims on the public treasury must be defended. It is more important than ever for students to understand that to question science is not to be anti-science or anti-intellectual, and that to ask how humans should interact with animals is not in itself to demand that humans never use animals. Questioning science will make for better, more responsible science, and questioning the ways in which humans use animals will make for more informed decisions about animal use. By making such decisions in an informed and responsible way, we can help to insure that in the future we will not repeat the mistakes of the past, and that we will move towards a world in which humans and other animals may be able to share peaceably the resources of a finite planet.

We and the animals who we use should be viewed as partners in a joint venture. We must broaden our taxonomic concerns and funding must be made available for those who choose not to work on nonhuman primates. We must not be afraid of what broadening our taxonomic interests may bring concerning animal cognitive abilities and their ability to feel pain and to suffer. As Savage-Rumbaugh (1997, p. 68) stressed: "I believe it is time to change course. It is time to open our eyes, our ears, our minds, our hearts. It is time to *look* with a new and deeper vision, to *listen* with new and more sensitive ears. It is time to *learn* what animals are really saying to us and to each other" (my emphases). These three L's should be used to motivate us to act on behalf of all animals. Humans can no longer be at war with the rest of the world, and no one can be an island in this intimately connected universe. Nobel laureate, Barbara McClintock, claimed that we must have a feeling for the organisms with whom we are privileged to work. Thus, bonding with animals and calling animals by name are right-minded steps. It seems unnatural for humans to continue to resist developing bonds with the animals who they study. By bonding with animals, one should not fear that the animals' points of view will be dismissed. In fact, bonding will result in a deeper examination and understanding of the animals' points of view, and this knowledge will inform further studies on the nature of human-animal interactions.

What I fear the most is that if we stall in our efforts to take animal use and abuse more seriously and fail to adopt extremely restrictive guidelines and laws, even more insurmountable and irreversible damage will result. Our collective regrets about what we failed to do for protecting animals' rights in the past will be moot. One way to begin is to expand the GAP and implement the GA/AP and admit all animals into the Community of Equals. It should be presupposed that at least some animal research and other activities that violate the rights of animals must not continue—the burden is on those who want to engage in these activities even if in the past they were acceptable.

My overall conclusion remains unchanged from that which I wrote a few years ago (Bekoff 1997). Specifically, if we forget that humans and other animals are all part of the same world—the more-than-human world—and if we forget that humans and animals are deeply connected at many levels of interaction, when things go amiss in our interactions with animals, as they surely will, and animals are set apart from and inevitably below humans, I feel certain that we will miss the animals more than the animal survivors will miss us. The interconnectivity and spirit of the world will be lost forever and these losses will make for a severely impoverished universe.

[. . .]

References

Abram, D., *The Spell of the Sensuous: Perception and Language in a More-than-Human World* (New York: Pantheon Books, 1996).

Bekoff, M., "What is a 'Scale of Life?'," *Environmental Values* 1 (1992), 253–6.

Bekoff, M., "Common Sense, Cognitive Ethology and Evolution," in P. Cavaleri and P. Singer (eds), *The Great Ape Project: Equality Beyond Humanity* (London: Fourth Estate, 1993), pp. 102–8.

Bekoff, M., "Tierliebe in der Wissenschaft," in M. Tobias and K. Solisti (eds), *Ich spürte die Seele der Tiere* (Stuttgart: Kosmos, 1997).

Bekoff, M., and L. Gruen, "Animal Welfare and Individual Characteristics: A Conversation Against Speciesism," *Ethics and Behavior* 3 (1993), 163–75.

Bekoff, M., and N. Hettinger, "Animals, Nature, and Ethics," *Journal of Mammalogy* 75 (1994), 219–23.

Cavalieri, P., and Singer, P., *The Great Ape Project: Equality Beyond Humanity* (London: Fourth Estate, 1993).

Crisp, R., "Evolution and Psychological Unity," in M. Bekoff and D. Jamieson (eds), *Interpretation and Explanation in the Study of Animal Behavior, Volume II: Explanation, evolution, and adaptation* (Boulder, Colorado: Westview Press, 1990), pp. 394–413.

Davis, H., and D. Balfour (eds), *The Inevitable Bond: Examining Scientist-Animal Interactions* (New·York: Cambridge University Press, 1992).

Dionys de Leeuw, A., "Contemplating the Interests of Fish," *Environmental Ethics* 18 (1996), 373–90.

Frey, R. G., "Medicine, Animal Experimentation, and the Moral Problem of Unfortunate Humans," in E. F. Paul, F. D. Miller, Jr., and J. Paul (eds), *Scientific Innovation, Philosophy, and Public Policy* (New York: Cambridge University Press, 1996), pp. 181–211.

Gluck, J. P., "Learning to see the animals again," in H. LaFollette (ed.), *Ethics in Practice: An Anthology* (Cambridge, Massachusetts: Blackwell Publishers, 1997), pp. 160–7.

LaFollette, H., and N. Shanks, *Brute Science: Dilemmas of Animal Experimentation* (New York: Routledge, 1996).

Manes, C., *Other Creations: Rediscovering the Spirituality of Animals* (New York: Doubleday, 1997).

Mukerjee, M., "Trends in Animal Research," *Scientific American* 276 (1997), 86–93.

Phillips, M. T., "Proper Names and the Social Construction of Biography: The Negative Case of Laboratory Animals," *Qualitative Sociology* 17 (1994), 119–42.

Rachels, J., *Created from Animals: The Moral Implications of Darwinism* (New York: Oxford University Press, 1990).

Rennie, J., "The Animal Question," *Scientific American* 276 (1997), 4.

Savage-Rumbaugh. E. S., "Why are We Afraid of Apes with Language?," in A. B. Scheibel and J. W. Schopf (eds), *Origin and Evolution of Intelligence* (Sudbury, Massachusetts: Jones and Bartlett, 1997), pp. 43–69.

Shapiro, K. J., *Animal Models of Human Psychology: Critique of Science, Ethics, and Policy* (Kirkland, Washington: Hogrefe and Huber, 1997).

Sober, E. "Morgan's Canon," in D. Cummins and C. Allen (eds), *The Evolution of Mind* (New York: Oxford University Press, 1998).

Taylor, P. W., *Respect for Nature: A Theory of Environmental Ethics* (Princeton, New Jersey: Princeton University Press, 1986).

Verheijen, F. J., and W. F. G. Flight., "Decapitation and Brining: Experimental Tests Show That After These Commercial Methods for Slaughtering Eel, *Anguilla Anguilla* (L.), Death is not Instantaneous," *Aquaculture Research* 28 (1997), 361–6.

Whiten, A., and R. Ham., "On the Nature and Evolution of Imitation in the Animal Kingdom: Reappraisal of a Century of Research," *Advances in the Study of Behavior* 21 (1992), 239–83.

19

Sue Savage-Rumbaugh, William M. Fields, and Jared Taglialatela

"Ape Consciousness–Human Consciousness: A Perspective Informed by Language and Culture"[1]

Savage-Rumbaugh and her co-workers summarize recent findings that provide insights on the occurrence of consciousness in nonhuman animals. They view consciousness as a fundamental property of the universe, much like space, time, mass, etc. In particular they present the evidence for consciousness in bonobos and the findings that they are capable of comprehending human speech and employing a lexical communication system. They find that bonobos have first "person" accounts to offer of their lives. They affirm the significant power of culture on biology and as a force in evolution.

What is consciousness?

[. . .]

According to John Searle,

> consciousness refers to the state of sentience or awareness that typically begins when we wake from a dreamless sleep and then continues through the day until we fall asleep again, die, go into a coma, or otherwise become unconscious. Dreams are also a form of consciousness, though in many respects they are quite unlike normal waking states
>
> (Searle, 1998)

We accept Searle's description of consciousness and agree with the view that subjective experience must be taken seriously as an object of study. Moreover, we would observe that "consciousness cannot be understood unless it is accurately described and that reductive approaches are inherently inappropriate to this descriptive task" (Velmans, 1998). For the time being, we believe that it is useful to assume that "consciousness may be an irreducible fundamental property of the universe in the same category as space and time or mass and electric charge. [. . .] Our position is a simple assumption: consciousness is a property (Searle, 1992) which the brain manipulates in ways we might conceive of as bending, folding, focusing, or magnifying. Such contouring of consciousness is a function of the brain's typology, which we assert has been fashioned by culture. We suggest that reality is a construction of consciousness molded by forces of the brain shaped by culture.

We use the term culture in the anthropological sense, a variation of Leslie White's famous definition of culture. That is, culture is a force that has emerged which allows adaptation by the species to the environment at a rate which biology alone would not allow. We further argue that culture, language, and tools ride upon a common neural substrate. As forces, language and tools are subsets of culture.

We suggest that consciousness is quite general among animal species. The differences in what we as humans might interpret as degrees of consciousness are dependent upon the power (size) of the neural substrate to fold or bend consciousness into the appropriate reality. Thus, culture and consciousness co-construct the driving force in the evolutionary mechanism acting upon the highly plastic matter of biological life. [. . .]

Given this co-interactive framework, it is only reasonable to suspect that the culture in which an ape is reared will significantly affect the form of consciousness it develops, as well as its communicative expression of that consciousness. If reared in a human culture, ape consciousness will be molded according to a form that human beings can recognize more easily as similar to their own and thus understandable by them. Such cross-cultural rearing studies can be understood as experiments in the grafting of cultural consciousness across biological platforms. Moreover, the expectations of the human participants in such studies will, unwittingly, affect the outcome. This is because the extent to which they extend their activities of "humanness" to permit the incorporation of alternative biological platforms into their group cultural consciousness, will affect the capacity of the developing organism. Thus studies of ape competence on "human tasks" can never be pure measures of ape capacity. The expectancies and culture of the measurer will inevitably affect them. Nonetheless, they inform us with regard to ourselves, the role of our expectancies and the plasticity of apes.

Ape language: insights into human bias and cultural expectation

[. . .]

When the "Lana Project" began, the chimpanzee Washoe had learned some signs, and serious questions were beginning to surface regarding the amount of imitation that underlay her actions (Terrace *et al.*, 1979). Moreover, her signs were often inarticulate and difficult to decipher for all but those who lived and interacted with her on a daily basis. [. . .] The lexical keyboard system proposed by Duane Rumbaugh, provided a potential means of propelling apes beyond the limitations posed by these other methodologies. In addition, it offered a more accurate means of data collection as it was linked to a computer, which recorded all utterances of experimenter and ape. [. . .] The first studies left no doubt that Lana could discriminate lexigrams visually, and that she could learn the simple ordering rules sufficiently well to apply them to novel sequences. Lana could also associate different symbols with various real world people, places, and things (Rumbaugh, 1977) and the computer-collected data demonstrated that imitation was not the basis of her performance.

Like many other novel findings in science, the work with Lana raised more questions than it answered. It was not clear that Lana *always* understood what was said to her through lexigrams, particularly if the requests were somewhat unusual. It was also not clear why she sometimes made what seemed to be incomprehensible errors and formed nonsensical strings. [. . .] Lana's errors were more appropriately characterized as "puzzling" and it was often difficult to figure out what Lana was trying to say.

[. . .]

The second generation of language studies with the lexical-keyboard system attempted to compensate for some of the perceived inadequacies in Lana's semantic performance. Her errors had revealed that while she grasped the combinatorial rules of her syntax, she often did not consistently apply semantic content.

[. . .]

Consequently the ensuing effort, with two young male chimpanzees (Sherman and Austin) was directed toward the careful inculcation of single words and a more objective analysis of both semantic and pragmatic word functions as contrasted with lexical "assignment." The "meaning" of words came under intense focus, and *receptive understanding*, along with object labeling became an important component of the linguistic instruction. The social aspect of language and culture was also enriched far beyond what had been the case for Lana. And lastly, in place of working with a single subject, efforts were concentrated upon communications between two co-reared apes, Austin and Sherman (Savage-Rumbaugh, 1986).

This simple change had profound theoretical implications that are still not widely understood. *It meant that, for the first time in the field of animal language, the experimenter was removed as half of every subject-experimenter interaction.* Such a change fundamentally altered the traditional experimental psychological paradigm in which every action of an animal subject is both preceded by a structured event, (usually termed the "stimulus") and followed by a structured event (usually termed the "reinforcer").

Previous animal work with apes, dolphins, and parrots followed the experimental control paradigm. These paradigms are insufficient for either the inculcation or analysis of functional linguistic phenomena. *Linguistic communication necessarily takes place between individuals in a multiplicity of exchanges that cannot be controlled from the outside either by intentionally setting the stage of the preceding stimulus or effecting a particular reinforcing event.* If there can be said to be a "reinforcing event" for the speaker during normal conversation, it can only be that of the comprehension of the listener. If there can be said to be a stimulus event that prompts the verbal selections of the speaker, it can only be the prior utterances of the listener, which are themselves a reflection of the listener's prior comprehension.

In attempting to analyze linguistic exchanges, one inevitably comes to focus upon the exchange of meaning between participants, in a situation where "meaning" is not controlled either at the level of input, output or reward by any experimentally manipulatable variable. Consequently, as one moves from the experimenter–subject paradigm to the study of communications between two or more participants, the boundaries of the traditional approach to the study of animal behavior are pressed beyond normal limits. Finally, once the exchange of meaning is the focus of investigation, it quickly becomes apparent that what we call "meaning" cannot exist outside of a socio-cultural context. What one party's utterances "mean" to another can only be determined within a socio-culture framework that permits utterances to assume certain inter-individual expectancies and obligations. This leap into the social dynamics of language took the work beyond the "can they talk" phase into something far more complex, and began to open up the issue of what talking is all about as well as how it is that social contracts are constructed. It required new skills on the part of Sherman and Austin, skills that had been missing in Lana, and for which little, if any, behavioral evidence existed.

The work with Sherman and Austin revealed that symbolic communication of a high level, with the use of an abstract code and with mutual understanding and cooperation, was possible between non-human creatures [. . .]. It also revealed that the semantic processing of the symbolic components of the communicative system was not just lexically based and dependent upon stimulus-response associative phenomena. It was instead, semantically grounded and functionally abstract. Finally, it illustrated, for the first time in the field of animal language, the critical components of listener comprehension and listener co-operation.

[. . .]

The next phase of work pressed the boundaries of scientific method in a different way. The findings with Sherman and Austin brought forth a sensitivity to the process of comprehension as an invisible phenomenon, in the process of language acquisition. Consequently, when research efforts with Kanzi, a young bonobo, began, the emphasis was not on production but comprehension. There is no way to reward comprehension, because, in its initial stages, there is no overt behavioral indication of what is taking place. This made it essential to move away from any type of training.

[. . .]

The bonobo's capacity to acquire high level linguistic skills in essentially the same manner as a child, albeit more slowly, revealed that the burden of linguistic development was carried by comprehension not production (Savage-Rumbaugh *et al.*, 1986). It is especially important that comprehension emerged in contextually meaningful situations, with many variables, not in repetitive training sessions with only a few variables characteristic.

Language competency appeared in Kanzi through an osmotic process in which caretakers passed on their linguistic culture without awareness or intent. These findings raised, for the first time, the serious possibility that bonobos possessed a sentience similar in kind, if not degree, to our own. It also followed logically that this sentience had gone unrecognized in field studies simply because we could not easily grasp the highly abstract and symbolic nature of their communications in the wild (Savage-Rumbaugh *et al.*, 1996b).

Because Kanzi's mode of acquisition was very different from that of other linguistically tutored animals, his linguistic output was dramatically changed as well. Analysis of his utterance corpus revealed a basic comprehension of syntactical ordering rules as well as a comprehension of grammatical classes (Greenfield and Savage-Rumbaugh 1991). But more than this, his understanding encompassed all manner of novel events and even of metaphor. His understanding of language informed his interpretation of real world events and his broadened capacity to interpret and appropriately classify real world events informed his linguistic comprehension in a boot strapping effect. An example of this was the ease with which Kanzi learned to flake stone tools given a modicum of both visual and verbal instruction. Similar attempts by other apes required long and arduous conditioning and shaping regimens (Toth *et al.*, 1993).

Because Kanzi's achievements went far beyond the accomplishments of Lana, Sherman and Austin, it became essential to determine the degree to which these remarkable capacities were a function of Kanzi's species versus a function of the unique rearing circumstances surrounding his development. Kanzi's rearing had taken place in a free-form captive environment modeled upon the type of existence a young bonobo might experience in the wild. This contrasted with the formal training regimens encountered by Sherman, Austin and Lana. Kanzi's linguistic accomplishments raised two possibilities. The first was that bonobos and human beings somehow shared a peculiar and unique genetic heritage for linguistic competency, and that studies of wild bonobos had simply failed to reveal the true abstract nature of their communication system. The other possibility was that something about the unstructured socio-cultural approach—with its absence of training and its focus upon comprehension—facilitated language in a manner that classical learning approaches did not and could not.

Kanzi's culture was characterized by many objects and by a variety of participants, including human beings who served as caretakers, but also by many others. There were repairmen who cleaned the lab, fixed the cages, and repaired the bridges in the field. [. . .] But Kanzi's world was not solely a human one; it was also "peopled" by Matata who was raised as a wild bonobo in the Congo. Across time, as Matata produced more offspring, Kanzi's world grew to include many nonlinguistically competent siblings who multiplied in number and began to form a bonobo community.

Kanzi thus developed as a being within a *Pan paniscus/Homo sapiens* socio-cultural world. That is, as a bicultural entity who learned multiple of ways of relating to and communicating with others in both his bonobo and human cultures. His linguistic acts were fully, intimately and irrevocably embedded within both these cultures. Moreover, his behavior indicated an awareness that his biological mother could not fully relate to, or trust, many of his human caretakers. The same was true of the majority of his human caretakers; they could not completely understand or adequately relate to the culture and ways of his bonobo mother. Kanzi served, and continues to serve, as something of a liaison between these two cultures in ways that remain to be adequately documented. He will, for example, often employ the keyboard to request food for his mother and siblings who do not know the lexigrams.

Because Kanzi's language development was enmeshed within a culture, his life and communications evidenced a richness and depth that transcended the symbolic communications of Sherman, Austin and Lana. Kanzi became able to "mean" in a variety of ways. He also appeared to understand that symbolic meaning is something that can be constructed between individuals in the act of social engagement. He seemed to recognize as well that the "meanings" constructed through joint action develop a history, expectancies and even a certain necessity of being, once undertaken in a legitimate fashion. But Kanzi's very existence made it necessary to determine the relative effects that biology and environment had played in his development.

Consequently, the ensuing research project sought to separate the species variable from the environmental variable by co-rearing a bonobo (Panbanisha) and a chimpanzee (Panzee) in an environment that was essentially the same as that encountered by Kanzi. However, unlike Kanzi, these two apes were always together and therefore always inevitably exerting some indeterminable degree of influence over the development of the other. By introducing two additional apes to the environment built around Kanzi, the cultural aspects of the work expanded greatly. In addition, Kanzi himself provided a model for the behavioral and linguistic development that was very different from the one that Matata had provided for him. He could use the keyboard—she could not. Thus it was not really possible to precisely replicate Kanzi's experiences with additional apes. What we did do was to attempt to avoid the structured training, the emphasis upon production and the failure to ground the language within a rich socio-cultural environment that had characterized earlier work with Lana, Sherman and Austin. We concentrated upon comprehension in cultural context, we continued to make natural spoken English the main route of linguistic input and we spent as much time as possible in the natural forest setting.

Like Kanzi, Panbanisha and Panzee experienced a social environment within which keyboard usage was a daily affair by human caretakers. Because Kanzi was already lexically competent, the keyboard, which had begun with only 1 lexigram in his case, had grown to a board of 256 symbols. Thus the keyboard could not grow with Panbanisha and Panzee, as it did with Kanzi. If Kanzi was to be a part of their linguistic world, his 256 symbols had to be present as well. Consequently, Panbanisha and Panzee were exposed to 256 lexi-grams utilized in complex communications from the first week of life. Perhaps for this reason, their acquisition of these symbols was much more rapid than Kanzi's. Similarly, their combinations appeared far earlier and Panbanisha composed more complex utter-ances of greater duration than Kanzi, although Panzee did not. [. . .] Nonetheless, in map-ping onto all the major capacities that were observed in Kanzi, but previously absent in Lana, Sherman and Austin, Panzee clearly demonstrated that Kanzi's skill was not limited to bonobos. Instead, it was a function of his early exposure to the bicultural social environ-ment.

The process by which Kanzi, Panbanisha and Panzee acquired their lexicons include components of rapid mapping of sound to referent, similar to those utilized by human children (Lyn and Savage-Rumbaugh, 2000; Lyn *et al.*, 1998). In addition, it has been found that no interaction with the ape itself is required, it is sufficient to speak to other individuals about a novel object in front of the ape. New words are learned and understood even when the apes appear to be disinterested in the conversation (Lyn and Savage-Rumbaugh, in press; Lyn *et al.*, 1998). The cognitive and social processes that were found in Kanzi's proto gram-matical utterances also characterized those of Panbanisha and Panzee, suggesting that there exist, within the genus *Pan*, basic cognitive processes that permit language acquisition in a human culture (Greenfield *et al.*, in press). Work with wild bonobos supports this position through the finding that bonobos employ intentional alteration of vegetation in a symbolic fashion to communicate to other bonobos who are following them (Savage-Rumbaugh *et al.*, 1996a). These findings are the first to indicate learned non-human intra-species symbolic communication across the domain of time.

Like Kanzi, Panbanisha and Panzee also attempted to produce human-like vocal sounds. Panzee gained far more voluntary motor control over the ability to produce low frequency sounds than either Kanzi or Panbanisha, suggesting that something about the vocal tract of *Pan troglodytes* is more amenable to the lower registrar than the bonobo vocal tract. Recent work has shown that Panbanisha has the ability to decode some sounds produced by Kanzi and to translate them to us.

It was not only the linguistic aspects of the *Pan paniscus/Homo sapiens* culture that were passed on to Panbanisha and Panzee. They acquired many tool-use skills as well. For example, Panbanisha acquired the capacity to flake stone by observing Kanzi. But unlike Kanzi she began, with precision, to employ the technique of bimanual percussion. Even though Kanzi had observed his human models demonstrate this technique, and even though he had attempted to emulate the bimanual technique, he did not become proficient in that skill without passing through a number of phases. [. . .] Whereas Kanzi developed this skill over a two-year period, Panbanisha's bimanual technique was oriented toward the edges of the stone almost from the beginning. It may be that observation of a bonobo model provided the needed input to permit Panbanisha to propel rapidly into direct aimed bimanual percussion.

[. . .]

The fact that a competent bonobo model existed for many aspects of Panbanisha's development, coupled with the observation that in nearly every aspect of language and tool use Panbanisha made more rapid progress than Kanzi, may be attributable to the modeling he provided. However, it should be noted, that Panbanisha did not appear to be motivated to watch Kanzi or to attempt to do things she observed him do in any sort of imitative manner. She preferred to spend her time with human female caretakers and with her bonobo mother Matata and seemed more prone to actively observe and emulate their actions. [. . .] All three apes that are linguistically competent (Kanzi, Panbanisha, and Panzee) have also been shown to exhibit complex skills in planning travel routes (Menzel, in preparation).

PET scans done to compare Lana's linguistic capacity with that of Panzee revealed that Panzee's information processing skills were more highly elaborated and much more human-like than those of Lana. These findings regarding cortical function correspond tightly to the rearing and behavioral differences encountered between Lana and Panzee. They also reveal that the question of "do apes have language" is far too simple. Both Lana and Panzee "have" language to a certain degree, but their functional competencies vary greatly, as does the neurological processing of verbal material.

In sum, the work with Panzee and Panbanisha demonstrated that the powerful variable was that of rearing, not species. In an environment that did not require training, Panzee learned language faster than Sherman, Austin or Lana. She also comprehended spoken English while they did not. She produced more novel combinations and far more spontaneous utterances. Unlike them, she learned lexigrams independently of keyboard position.

The issue is no longer one of data, the adequacy of data, of potential cueing or experimenter effects, or of conditioning. In addition the issue is no longer that of "apes" in the general sense, but rather that one that must take into account, in detail, the socio-cultural experience of *each* ape, in determining how its performance on the continuum of linguistic competency is to be evaluated. The paradigms of the past, in which animal cognition is viewed as riding upon a different substrate than human cognition, are breaking down and the research at LRC has been a component of this change (Tomasello and Call, 1997).

[...]

The importance of the research to date is not only that it offers the basic outline of a new paradigm for understanding the mind of the other, but also in addition it provides techniques and data to support the approach.

The long standing philosophical issue of how meaning emerges has been significantly informed by work with apes, in a manner that could never have occurred, if all language studies were limited to *Homo sapiens* (Savage-Rumbaugh, 1990, 1991; Savage-Rumbaugh *et al.*, 1993). This work has clarified the Quinean problem and laid open the road for new insights into that which we give the name of "language." It is beginning to reveal that "meaning" can be packed into any gesture, glance, lexicon, or printed symbol. The packing of "meaning" requires inter-subjectivity—the mutual attribution of intentionality and a joint history, informed by mutually shared affective experiences. These components of communication are not limited to *Homo sapiens*, nor are they a peculiarity of the human capacity for reason.

[...]

Consciousness in other minds

Detecting consciousness: We agree with Searle's principle of connection between consciousness and the intrinsic intentionality that underpins linguistic meaning. The time has come to break away from views which hold that meaning, reference, and intentionality are not measurable phenomena and hence are closed to scientific investigation. Intentionality is systematically observable. While we do not ignore needs, wants, and desires as matters of intentionality, our current research with great apes emphasizes first the

> measurable sequence[s] of complex monitoring responses in which the [person]:
> (a) checks to see that a listener is present before emitting a communicative signal,

(b) engages the attention of the listener before emitting this signal, (c) emits a signal that requires a specific behavioral or verbal response on the part of the listener. [and] (d) monitors the listener's response visually and auditorially . . .

(Savage-Rumbaugh, 1986).

More importantly, we recognize that intentionality has a dynamic quality when intentional processes emerge between speaker and listener. With respect to our research, we do engage dialogs, i.e., intentional processes between listeners and speakers in which both are human and nonhuman primates.

[. . .]

Regarding the concept of "degree of consciousness" as stated, we reject this notion. We believe that the metaphors of bending and folding that we have applied to consciousness are a process that the neural substrate performs in the creation of reality. We reiterate our introductory remark, culture controls the topology of the neural substrate and therefore we believe culture is driving speciation. If we are correct, the brain of a nonhuman primate like Kanzi, reared in a *Pan/Homo* culture, capable of understanding spoken English and uttering lexical English counterparts, should possess a brain which is morphologically different than a brain of a feral bonobo or a bonobo reared without human language, culture and tools.

Our experience with great apes convinces us that they in fact possess consciousness, for they have first "person" accounts to offer of their lives. As a matter critical to the survival of scientific methodology, "We accept the[se] first person accounts and . . . the irreducible nature of experience, while at the same time refusing both a dualistic concession and a pessimistic surrender" to the debate regarding consciousness issues (Varela, 1998) or animal language research. We emphasize the power of cultural forces upon the neural substrate of biology and the significant role of culture as a force in evolution.

[. . .]

Note

1   From the Symposium *Animal Consciousness: Historical, Theoretical, and Empirical Perspectives* presented at the Annual Meeting of the Society for Integrative and Comparative Biology, 6–10 January 1999, at Denver, Colorado.

References

Greenfield, P., H. Lyn, and E. S. Savage-Rumbaugh. (In press). Semiotic Combinations in Pan: A cross-species comparison of communication in a chimpanzee and a bonobo.

Greenfield, P. M., and E. S. Savage-Rumbaugh. 1991. Imitation, grammatical development and the invention of protogrammar by an ape. In N. Krasnegor, D. M. Rumbaugh, M. Studdert-Kennedy, and R. L. Schiefelbusch (eds.), *Biological and behavioral determinants of language development*, pp. 235–58 Lawrence Erlbaum Associates, Inc, Hillsdale, NJ.

Lyn, H. and E. S. Savage-Rumbaugh, 2000. Observational Word Learning by Two Bonobos. *Language and Communication* 20:255–73.

Lyn, H., E. S. Savage-Rumbaugh, and D. Rumbaugh. 1998. Observational word learning in bonobos (*Pan paniscus*). *American Journal of Primatology*, 45:193 (Abstract).

Rumbaugh, D. M. 1977 *Language learning by a chimpanzee: The Lana project*. Academic Press. NY.

Savage-Rumbaugh, E. S. 1986. *Ape language: From conditioned response to symbol*. Columbia University Press, NY.

Savage-Rumbaugh, E. S. 1990. Language acquisition in a nonhuman species: Implications for the innateness debate. Special Issue: The idea of innateness: Effects on language and communication research. *Developmental Psychobiology* 23(7): 599–620.

Savage-Rumbaugh, E. S. 1991. Language learning in the bonobo: How and why they learn. In Norman A. Krasnegor (ed.), *Biological and behavioral determinants of language development*, pp. 209–33: Lawrence Erlbaum Associates, Inc., Hillsdale, NJ.

Savage-Rumbaugh, E. S., K. McDonald, R. A. Sevcik, W. D. Hopkins, and E. Rubert. 1986. Spontaneous symbol acquisition and communicative use by pygmy chimpanzees (*Pan paniscus*). *J Exp Psychol.* (General), 115(3):211–35.

Savage-Rumbaugh, E. S., J. Murphy, R. A. Sevcik, D. M. Rumbaugh, K. E. Brakke, and S. Williams. 1993. Language comprehension in ape and child. Monographs of the Society for Research in Child Development, 58(233):1–242.

Savage-Rumbaugh, E. S., S. L. Williams, T. Furuichi, and T. Kano. 1996a. Language perceived: Paniscus branches out. In B. McGrew, L. Marchant, and T. Nishida (eds.), *Great ape societies*, pp. 173–84. Cambridge University Press, London.

Savage-Rumbaugh, E. S., S. L. Williams, T. Furuichi, and T. Kano. 1996b. Language perceived: Paniscus branches out. In W. C. McGrew, L. F. Marchant, and T. Nishida (eds.), *Great ape societies*, pp. 173–84. Cambridge University Press, NY.

Searle, 1992. *The rediscovery of the mind*. MIT Press, Cambridge, MA.

Searle, J. 1998. How to study consciousness scientifically. In S. R. Hammeroff, A. W. Kaszniak, and A. C. Scott (eds.). *Toward a science of consciousness II: The second Tucson discussions and debates*, pp. 14–29. MIT Press, Cambridge, MA.

Terrace, H. S., L. A. Petitto, R. J. Sanders, and T. G. Bever, 1979. Can an ape create a sentence? *Science*, 206(4421):891–902.

Tomasello, M. and J. Call. 1997. *Primate cognition*. Oxford University Press, NY.

Toth, N., *et al.* 1993. Pan the tool-maker: Investigations into the stone tool-making and tool-using capabilities of a bonobo (*Pan Paniscus*). *Journal of Archeological Science*. 20:81–91.

Velmans, M. 1998. Goodbye to reductionism. In S. R. Hammeroff, A. W. Kaszniak, and A. C. Scott (eds.). *Toward a science of consciousness II: The second Tucson discussions and debates*, pp. 44–52. MIT Press, Cambridge, MA.

20

A. Whiten, J. Goodall, W.C. McGrew, T. Nishida, V. Reynolds, Y. Sugiyama, C.E.G. Tutin, R.W. Wrangham, and C. Boesch

"Cultures in Chimpanzees"

Whiten and co-workers summarize numerous years of research on chimpanzee culture. They found that 39 different behavior patterns, including tool use, grooming and courtship, were customary in some communities but absent in others; ecological explanations could be discounted. They noted that the combined repertoire of these behavior patterns was a highly distinctive feature found in human cultures, but previously not observed in nonhuman species.

As an increasing number of field studies of chimpanzees (*Pan troglodytes*) have achieved long-term status across Africa, differences in the behavioural repertoires described have become apparent that suggest there is significant cultural variation[1-7]. Here we present a systematic synthesis of this information from the seven most long-term studies, which together have accumulated 151 years of chimpanzee observation. This comprehensive analysis reveals patterns of variation that are far more extensive than have previously been documented for any animal species except human.[8-11] We find that 39 different behaviour patterns, including tool usage, grooming and courtship behaviours, are customary or habitual in some communities but are absent in others where ecological explanations have been discounted. Among mammalian and avian species, cultural variation has previously been identified only for single behaviour patterns, such as the local dialects of song-birds.[12,13] The extensive, multiple variations now documented for chimpanzees are thus without parallel. Moreover, the combined repertoire of these behaviour patterns in each chimpanzee community is itself highly distinctive, a phenomenon characteristic of human cultures[14] but previously unrecognized in non-human species.

Culture is defined in very different ways in different academic disciplines.[15] At one extreme, some cultural anthropologists insist on linguistic mediation, so that culture is constrained to be a uniquely human phenomenon.[16] In the biological sciences, a more inclusive definition is accepted, in which the significance of cultural transmission is recognized as one of only two important processes that can generate evolutionary change: inter-generation transmission of behaviour may occur either genetically or through social learning, with processes of variation and selection shaping biological evolution in the first case and cultural evolution in the second. From this perspective, a cultural behaviour is one that is transmitted repeatedly through social or observational learning to become a population-level characteristic.[17] By this definition, cultural differences (often known as 'traditions' in ethology) are well established phenomena in the animal kingdom and are maintained through a variety of social transmission mechanisms.[18] Well documented examples include dialects in song-birds,[12,13] sweet-potato washing by Japanese macaques (*Macaca fuscata*) at Koshima,[19] and stone handling by Japanese macaques at Arashiyama.[20] However, each case refers to variation in only a single behaviour pattern.

Tabulations of population differences amongst chimpanzees have indicated that multiple behavioural variants may exist.[2-7] However, these tabulations have been based on published reports, which, although they record the presence of behaviours, remain problematic in three respects: they are incomplete; they frequently do not clarify the extent to which each behaviour pattern is habitual in the community; and they do not systematically document the absence of behaviour patterns present elsewhere. We therefore adopted a different strategy in our attempt to provide a definitive assessment of what is now known of chimpanzee cultural variation.

Phase 1 of the study established a comprehensive list of candidate cultural variants, which are behaviours suspected by research workers to be specific to particular chimpanzee populations. Beginning with a list drawn from literature review by A.W. and C.B., the research directors of the major chimpanzee field projects . . . added and defined unpublished candidate patterns. The patterns were then split and lumped as appropriate. This complex, collaborative and iterative process produced a listing of candidate cultural variants that were fully and consensually defined. . . . The scope of this list, differentiating 65 categories of behaviour, represents a unique record of the inventiveness of wild chimpanzees.

In phase 2, the research directors assigned to each of these behaviour categories one of the following six codes, as applicable at their site: (1) customary, for which the behaviour occurs in all or most able-bodied members of at least one age-sex class (such as adult males); (2) habitual, for which the behaviour is not customary but has occurred repeatedly in several individuals, consistent with some degree of social transmission; (3) present, for which the behaviour is neither customary nor habitual but is clearly identified; (4) absent, for which the behaviour has not been recorded and no ecological explanation is apparent; (5) ecological explanation, for which absence is explicable because of a local ecological feature; and (6) unknown, for which the behaviour has not been recorded, but this may be due to inadequacy of relevant observational opportunities. These codings were cross-checked and confirmed by senior colleagues at each site. Our results are for the seven chimpanzee groups with the most long-term observation record, so the 'unknown' code was seldom applicable. These studies bring together a total of 151 years of direct observation (range 8–38 years), so our data summarize the enormous increase in our knowledge of chimpanzee behaviour achieved in the latter half of this century.

[. . .]

The profile of codings of particular interest with respect to cultural variation is that in which behaviours are recorded as customary or habitual in some communities, yet absent at others. Three other classes of profile need to be recognized and discriminated from this.

First, seven behaviours proposed as potential cultural variants in phase 1 were shown instead to be either customary or habitual in all communities. Second, 16 patterns failed to achieve habitual status in any community. The third class includes profiles in which all cases of absence are explicable by local conditions; just three cases were identified. Absence of algae-fishing can be explained by the rarity of algae, and any absence of ground night-nesting by high predator risk. Use of an additional stone to balance an anvil (anvil-prop) occurs only at Bossou, but it is not expected elsewhere because stone anvils are either not used or (at Taï) are embedded in the ground.

The remaining behaviours are absent at some sites but are customary or habitual at others. We have found 39 such behavioural variants, significantly more than previously suspected for chimpanzees.[1-6] We know of no comparable variation in other non-human species, although no systematic study of this kind appears to have been attempted.

We arrive at a similar comparative conclusion when we examine the overall profiles of cultural variants in the different communities. Some customary and habitual patterns are unique to certain communities, but others are shared between two or more communities, so the clusters of variants that characterize each community are not mutually exclusive. Nevertheless, the profiles of each community are distinctively different, each with a pattern comprising many behavioural variants. These patterns vary as much between sites associated with the same subspecies [...] as between subspecies themselves. The only major difference between the western and eastern populations is that nut-cracking occurs only in the west, although the fact that this behaviour terminates abruptly at the Sassandra-N'Zo river within the range of the *verus* subspecies shows that it is culturally, rather than genetically, transmitted.[21] The patterns can thus be seen to resemble those in human societies, in which differences between cultures are constituted by a multiplicity of variations in technology and social customs.[14] It remains to be shown whether chimpanzees are unique in this respect, or whether any other animal species, if studied in the same way, would reveal qualitatively similar patterns.

Other comparisons between human and non-human animal cultures have focused on the cognitive processes involved, arguing that if processes of human cultural transmission, such as imitative learning and teaching, are not found in animals, then culture in animals is merely an analogue of that in humans, rather than homologous with it.[22,23] Our data agree with experimental studies that have shown that chimpanzees copy the methods used by others to manipulate and open artificial 'fruits' designed as analogues of wild foods.[24,25] These experimental designs show differential copying of each of two quite different methods used to process the foods. Similarly, some of the differences between communities described here represent not only the contrast between habitual versus absent, but also the contrast between different versions of an otherwise similar pattern. Examples include cases of tool use, such as two different methods of ant-dip; in the first of these, a long wand is held in one hand and a ball of ants is wiped off with the other, whereas in the second method a short stick is held in one hand and used to collect a smaller number of ants, which are transferred directly to the mouth. Other examples occur in social behaviour, such as the variants used to deal with ectoparasites discovered during grooming, with leaf-squash, leaf-inspect and index-hit occurring in different communities. It is difficult to see how such behaviour patterns could be perpetuated by social learning processes simpler than imitation, the most commonly suggested alternative to which is stimulus enhancement, in which the attention of an observer is merely drawn to a relevant item such as a stick.[26] But this does not mean that imitation is the only mechanism at work. Experimental studies on the acquisition of tool-use and food-processing skills by both children and captive chimpanzees indicate that there is a complex mix of imitation, other forms of social learning, and individual learning.[24,25,27-30]

Our results show that chimpanzees, our closest sister-species, have rich behavioural complexity. However, although this study represents the definitive state of knowledge at present, we must expect that more extended study will elaborate on this picture. Every long-term study of wild chimpanzees has identified new behavioural variants.

Notes

1   McGrew, W. C. and Tutin, C. E. G. Evidence for a social custom in wild chimpanzees? *Man* 13, 234–51 (1978).
2   Goodall, J. *The Chimpanzees of Gombe: Patterns of Behavior* (Harvard Univ. Press, Cambridge. Massachusetts, 1986).

3   Nishida, T. *The Chimpanzees of the Mahale Mountains: Sexual and Life History Strategies* (Tokyo Univ. Press, Tokyo, 1990).
4   McGrew, W. C. *Chimpanzee Material Culture Implications for Human Evolution* (Cambridge Univ. Press, Cambridge, 1992).
5   Sugiyama, Y. in *The Use of Tools by Human and Non-human Primates* (eds Berthelet, A. and Chavaillon, J.) 175–87 (Clarendon, Oxford, 1993).
6   Wrangham, R. W., McGrew, W. C., de Waal, E. B. M. and Heiltne, P. G. (eds) *Chimpanzee Cultures* (Harvard Univ. Press, Cambridge, Massachusetts, 1994).
7   Boesch, C. The emergence of cultures among wild chimpanzees. *Proc. Br. Acad.* 88, 251–68 (1996).
8   Bonner, J. T. *The Evolution of Culture in Animals* (Princeton Univ. Press, New Jersey, 1980).
9   Mundinger, P. C. Animal cultures and a general theory of cultural evolution. *Ethol. Sociobiol.* 1, 183–223 (1980).
10 Lefebvre, L. and Palamets, B. in *Social Learning: Psychological and Biological Perspectives* (eds Zentail, T. and Galef, B. G. Jr) 141–64 (Erlbaum, Hillsdale, New Jersey, 1988).
11 McGrew, W. C. Culture in non-human primates? *Annu. Rev. Anthropol.* 27, 301–28 (1998).
12 Marler, P. and Tamura, M. Song 'dialects' in three populations of white-crowned sparrows. *Science* 146, 1483–86 (1964).
13 Catchpole, C. K. and Slater, P. J. B. *Bird Song: Themes and Variations* (Cambridge Univ. Press, Cambridge, 1995).
14 Murdock, G. P. *Ethnographic Atlas* (Univ. Pittsburgh Press, Pittsburgh, 1967).
15 Kroeber, A. L. and Kluckhohn, C. *Culture: A Critical Review of Concepts and Definitions* (Random House, New York, 1963).
16 Bloch, M. Language, anthropology and cognitive science. *Man* 26, 183–98 (1991).
17 Nishida, T. in *Primate Societies* (eds Smuts, B. B., Cheney, D. L., Seyfarth, R. M., Wrangham, R. W. and Struhsaker, T. T.) 462–74 (Univ. Chicago Press, Chicago, 1987).
18 Whiten, A. and Ham, R. On the nature of imitation in the animal kingdom: reappraisal of a century of research. *Adv. Study Behav.* 21, 239–83 (1992).
19 Imanishi, K. Identification: A process of enculturation in the subhuman society of *Macaca fuscata*. *Primates* 1, 1–29 (1957).
20 Huffman, M. in *Social Learning in Animals: The Roots of Culture* (eds Heyes, C. M. and Galef, B. G.) 267–89 (Academic Press, London, 1996).
21 Boesch, C., Marchesi, P., Marchesi, N., Fruth, B. and Joulian, F., Is nut cracking in wild chimpanzees a cultural behaviour? *J. Hum. Evol.* 26, 325–38 (1994).
22 Galef, B. G. Jr. The question of animal culture. *Hum. Nature* 3, 157–78 (1992).
23 Tomasello, M., Kruger, A. C. and Ratner, H. H. Cultural learning. *Behav. Brain Sci.* 16, 495–552 (1993).
24 Whiten, A., Custance, D. M., Gotner, J.-C., Teixidor, F. and Bard, K. A. Imitative learning of artificial fruit-processing in children (*Homo sapiens*) and chimpanzees (*Pan troglodytes*). *J. Comp. Psychol.* 110, 3–14 (1996).
25 Whiten, A. Imitation of the sequential structure of actions by chimpanzees (*Pan troglodytes*). *J. Comp. Psychol.* 112, 270–81 (1998).
26 Spence, K. W. Experimental studies of learning and the mental processes in infra-human primates. *Psychol. Bull.* 34, 306–50 (1957).
27 Sumita, K., Kitahara-Frisch, J. and Norikoshi, K. The acquisition of stone tool use in captive chimpanzees. *Primates* 26, 168–81 (1985).
28 Tomasello, M., Davis, Dasilva, M., Camak, L. and Bard, K. Observational learning of tool-use by young chimpanzees. *Hum. Evol.* 2, 175–83 (1997).
29 Paquett, D. Discovering and learning tool-use for fishing honey by captive chimpanzees. *Hum. Evol.* 7, 17–30 (1992).
30 Nagell, K., Olguin, K. and Tomasello, M. Processes of social learning in the tool use of chimpanzees (*Pan troglodytes*) and children (*Homo sapiens*). *J. Comp. Psychol.* 107, 174–86 (1993).

21

Juan Carlos Gómez

"Are Apes Persons? The Case for Primate Intersubjectivity"

Gomez argues that apes can perceive others as having intentions (third-person modality) and also can perceive themselves in relationships with others involving mutual intentions (second-person modality). Second-person modality is a feature Gomez believes qualifies apes to be characterized as "persons." He does not argue that apes possess a metarepresentational ability to be aware of their own personhood, but rather possess a special kind of mutual-awareness. They are persons who do not describe themselves as persons, but may act and feel as persons and can recognize themselves and others as individual subjects capable of feeling and behaving intersubjectively.

[. . .]

The philosopher Daniel Dennett (1976) suggests a set of criteria to distinguish persons. His "conditions of personhood" can be summarized into two clusters of cognitive features that are characteristic of persons: a first cluster amounts to being an intentional agent, and a second cluster involves the ability to understand that others are intentional agents as well. Persons are, first of all, *intentional agents*, that is to say, creatures whose behavior is governed, not by external stimuli and blindly learned contingencies of reinforcement or punishment, but by internal representations that allow them to follow *goals* with alternative *means* and generate *expectations* about events, and react to these expectations before the actual events have happened. Apes seem to fare reasonably well in relation to these criteria.

But in Dennett's account, persons must also be capable of understanding that other creatures are intentional agents like themselves; that is to say, a person's representations of the external world should include representations of other creatures' representations; or, in other words, a person should understand that the external world is made, among other things, of the *internal worlds* better known as "minds" of other creatures. This ability of representing representations has come to be known as having a *metarepresentational* ability.

Furthermore, and again following Dennett's detailed discussion, persons should also understand that the representations entertained by their fellow creatures may include representations of other creatures' representations, i.e., that others have a metarepresentational ability too.

[. . .]

Intersubjectivity versus "theory of mind"

Dennett's analysis tries to capture an essential feature of persons: their ability to reciprocally recognize each other's intentionality (or, what is the same, each other's mental states). For him, "recognizing" seems to be synonymous with "representing explicitly" each other's mental states. But would it not be possible to engage in this mutual recognition without explicitly representing the intentions of others as internal mental states? Several authors have tried to explore this possibility and have referred to this form of interpersonal mutuality as *intersubjectivity* (Trevarthen, 1979, 1980; Hobson, 1993). The idea is that subjects (intentional agents, in Dennett's terminology) can coordinate their "subjectivities" (i.e., their mental states) with other creatures' subjectivities (i.e., other creatures' mental states) without having recourse to metarepresentations or any other sort of explicit representation of mental states as internal properties of subjects. For example, Trevarthen (1979, 1980) asserts that during their first year of life human infants achieve intersubjectivity with their caregivers through emotional/expressive interactions that do not require any representations of their underlying mental states. Infants *feel* the subjectivity of others in the emotional and expressive behaviors displayed in their face-to-face interactions with adults. Hobson (1990, 1993) developed a similar view to oppose the "distorting cognitivist frame" advanced by the theory-of-mind approach to intersubjectivity and personhood. In his view, human infants "find themselves relating to people in ways that are special to people" long before they are capable of any metarepresentational ability. Indeed, the metarepresentational understanding of others as persons is built upon the solid foundations provided by this more primitive ability to *relate with* others as persons.

In summary, these authors assert that there is an emotional, expressive, pre-reflective intersubjectivity that precedes the "intellectual", metarepresentational intersubjectivity of Dennett and other students of "theory of mind" abilities (see Gómez, 1999, for a more detailed comparison of approaches). The problem for this approach is to offer a more precise characterization of the mechanisms and features of this earlier form of intersubjectivity. Let me offer you my own version of how this can be achieved in relation to the problem of nonhuman primate intersubjectivity.

As I understand it, this expressive intersubjectivity is not based upon a distinction between external behaviors and internal mental states. For example, an expression of fear is not understood by the young infant as being an index of an internal emotion that causes its external manifestation. Similarly, an expression of attention (e.g., gazing to a target) need not be represented as an indication of an internal mental state that causes that gazing behavior. Fear and attention are experienced as properties of behaviors that are inseparable from those behaviors. They are like colors that are not conceived of as internal essences of objects, but just as properties (dynamic properties, in the case of emotional and cognitive expressions) that may appear or not in the other creatures.

An important characteristic of this intersubjectivity is that it typically appears in face to face interactions. The subjectivity of the other is not understood in an abstract, third-person way, but in a concrete, second-person mode. Others are not understood as persons because we infer from their behaviors that they must have intentions and ideas about other people's intentions, but because we are capable of engaging with them in specific patterns of intersubjective interaction that include emotional and expressive behaviors. What matters is that we are capable not only of engaging with them in intersubjective interactions, but also of representing and understanding them as capable of engaging in these interactions. Persons are capable of representing others as "second persons", i.e., as creatures capable of engaging in intersubjective encounters. Let me clarify what I mean with an example involving apes.

Understanding mental states without metarepresentations

In Gómez (1990) I presented a study in which I claimed to provide an analysis of the emergence of "attention understanding" in a hand-reared gorilla who, in her interactions with human people, developed the skill to look at the eyes of the person at crucial moments of the interaction. There I made it clear that the kind of "understanding of attention" I was attributing to the gorilla was a *practical* one, equivalent to what Piaget (1936) termed "sensorimotor intelligence" in his explanation of early object manipulation and tool use in human infants. This practical understanding of attention implied the gorilla's ability to *see* the expressions of attention of others as causal links that connect her behavior with their behavior. I attributed to the gorilla the possession of a "sensorimotor concept of subjects" not only as entities that are capable of acting by themselves (what some authors call "animacy"), but also as creatures whose executive behavior is causally connected with their perceptual states, as expressed, in this case, in their gaze behavior. Specifically, I proposed that, in the same way that apes seem to understand (in a practical or sensorimotor way) that when using a stick to retrieve an object they must establish physical contact between the tool and the object and apply certain forces to them, they also understand (in a similarly practical or sensorimotor way) that to exert an influence upon other organisms by means of gestures, first they must establish "attention contact" with them and then produce gestures and expressions addressed to their attention. There need be no understanding of the attention of the other as an internal mental state, no understanding of the internal cognitive effects provoked by perception, no abstract conception of intentions and internal mental experiences: all they need is a definite differentiation between physical objects and social subjects, that incorporates not only the understanding of them as animate and goal-directed (cf. Tomasello and Call, 1997), but also as *subjective* entities.

[. . .]

For example, attention is a mental state. It has, however, the interesting property of being indissociable from the behavior of looking. It is impossible that I am visually attending to an object if I am not physically looking at it[1] Visual attention is, therefore, a mental state that closely corresponds to external behaviors. In contrast, knowledge and beliefs can never be directly perceived. There is therefore the possibility that an organism without metarepresentational abilities can nonetheless understand and represent attention as an externally expressed subjective state. Such an organism could generate representations of other organisms attending to particular targets, i.e., being in particular *subjective* relations to a target. Apes may see, remember, represent others intending things and attending to things. This would be equivalent to seeing other creatures as intentional agents. This non-metarepresentational way of perceiving and representing others would capture the most basic property of intentionality: being *about* something. Apes would be perceiving others' actions and attentional and expressive displays as being about objects and targets in general. The intentionality is attributed to, seen in, the actions and bodily attitudes of others, not their minds—those mysterious immaterial entities we humans are used to postulate in our dealings with each other.[2]

This view of what it is like to attribute intentionality without metarepresentation could open the doors of personhood *à la* Dennett to apes—and any other animal that demonstrates the ability to perceive others as subjects in the above sense.

However, there is still an obstacle. According to Dennett, what counts for being a person is not only to be able to see others as intentional agents (or subjects, in my own terminology), but also to see others as capable of adopting the intentional stance in mutual relation to oneself. It is the entry into this recursive circle of mutual intentional attributions that singles out real persons from non-persons. Could creatures endowed exclusively with the sort of non-metarepresentational attribution of intentionality that I have suggested cross the doors of mutual recursive intentionality?

Intersubjectivity in the second person

Let's return to the case of visual attention. In other types of attention (e.g., auditory or olfactive), the act of someone attending to something can only be perceived in a modality that is different from the one in which the organism is displaying its attention: for example, I cannot hear you listening to me. However, the act of attending visually is visually perceivable itself. Thus when we attend to the visual attention of someone, this very act reveals *ipso facto* our own attention; or conversely, when someone attends to our visual attention, his/her own visual attention is overtly displayed for the benefit of any beholder . . . including whoever is his/her current target of attention. Indeed when two organisms happen to be attending to each other's direction of attention, a peculiar pattern is generated in which their respective gazes meet; this pattern is known as *eye contact.*

[. . .]

Evolutionarily, many animals seem to have developed a special sensitivity to eye-contact-like patterns. Curiously enough, usually this sensitivity is expressed in the activation of escape and defensive responses, as if the most adaptive way of responding to being the target of attention of another organism is to fly away (Baron-Cohen, 1995). Nonhuman primates clearly show this sensitivity to eye contact: in many species of monkeys, prolonged eye contact is used as an important component of aggressive displays, and may be quite effective as a threat on its own. But something interesting happens in apes in relation to eye contact: instead of reacting to it in a single, predominantly aggressive/defensive way, they seem to make a more generalized use of it as a pivotal component of different kinds of social inter-actions. For example, for chimpanzees eye contact is not only a component of aggressive displays, but also of their very opposite: reconciliation behaviors. Captive apes have been also reported to use eye contact as part of their interactions with humans (to request food, objects, play bouts, etc.; Gómez, 1991, 1996) and to produce gestures among themselves when the recipients are at least bodily oriented to them (Tomasello *et al.*, 1985).

Of course, the crucial point is not whether apes do or do not make use of eye contact, but how they *understand* eye contact. Do they understand the recursive intentionality embodied in this pattern? I suggest that the answer to this question is "Yes" and "No", depending on what kind of understanding we are asking about. If we are asking about a metarepresentational understanding *à la* Dennett, the answer is probably No; not only for the apes, but also probably for adult humans, who do not seem to understand attention contact in metarepresentational terms either (unless they are cognitive scientists engaging in propositional redescriptions with scientific purposes). However, if we are asking about the ability to perceive and represent eye contact as attention contact in a non-metarepresentational way, the answer is most likely Yes: I suggest that the special use of eye contact made by apes reflects an adaptation to the detection and elicitation of "attention contact" (Gómez, 1996). Apes, and perhaps to some degree other primates, may have discovered and exploited the potentialities of mutual visual attention, as expressed in eye contact, for intersubjective interaction.

[. . .]

Second persons: apes and humans

I suggest that we have evidence in apes of a non-metarepresentational system of intersubjectivity built upon distinctive adaptations to the emotional and cognitive expressions of others
when they are experienced in both a third- and a second-person modality. The third-person
modality allows the perception (and representation) of the behavior of others as oriented to
targets in the environment (i.e., as *intentional* in the fundamental sense of this word); the
second-person modality allows the perception (and representation) of others as intersubjective beings (i.e., as *mutually intentional*). It is this second modality of perception and representation that allows apes to engage in the sort of mutually intentional exchanges that
characterize persons.

[. . .]

In this view, apes are intentional agents (subjects) endowed with brain mechanisms specialized in perceiving and treating others as intentional agents (subjects). In a Dennettian mood,
we could still ask: but do they understand all this? Are they aware that they are perceiving
others as persons and that they themselves are persons? If by "understand" we mean: "Are
they capable of elaborating metarepresentations of themselves holding representations of
others as subjects?", then the answer is most likely "No", because to begin with, they
probably never hold metarepresentations. But this objection would be beside the point. Being
aware of being a person is a different phenomenon from being a person. Dennett states that
what is crucial for personhood is to possess a special kind of self-awareness. I would rather
suggest that what is crucial for personhood is to possess a special kind of *mutual-awareness*.
Apes seem indeed to possess such a special kind of mutual-awareness—one that is expressed
in the mutuality of attention-contact situations (cf. Gómez, 1994).

Apes are capable of adopting a second-person attitude that is devoid of all the metarepresentional noise of human first- and third-person attitudes. Certainly, in humans, metarepresentations may add a new resonance to the basic psychological processes that make us
persons, like the masks of the ancient Greek and Roman actors—the *personae*—could add
resonance to their voices. But these additional artefacts cannot create persons on their own.
The keys of human personhood will never be found in our metarepresentational fireworks.
Apes are not "cheap" versions of persons evolutionarily overcome by the high-tech,
metarepresentational minds of humans who are capable of achieving much more sophisticated versions of consciousness and personhood. Our metarepresentional *personae* are
mounted upon the solid intersubjective foundations that evolution planted before the advent
of *Homo sapiens*. Second-person perceptions and representations are essential parts of ourselves, capable of achieving feats that are not within the reach of third-person representations, that would need to engage in hopeless metarepresentational spirals in a vain attempt to
try to imitate what a second-person system achieves in an immediate and direct way (Gómez,
1994, 1996).

In the personhood of apes we may find some of the keys to escape our stubborn persistence in reducing to first- or third-person terms what belongs to the realm of the second-
person. I am not a person in so far that I think I am a person; I am not a person in so far as
another thinks of me as a person. I am a person in so far as I and another perceive and treat
each other as persons.

But we must, on the other hand, avoid the error of "humanizing" the apes. Their
mentality, including their mentalizing abilities, are related, but not identical to ours. They are
persons that do not describe themselves as persons neither perhaps think of themselves as
persons: they, however, may act and feel as persons in the most essential sense of the word,

which I take to be the ability to recognize others and themselves as individual subjects capable of feeling and behaving intersubjectively. We are not persons because we can claim we are so. Before speaking we already are human persons. Apes, without speaking, perhaps without thinking in the same sense as we do, also are ape persons. We are lucky enough to have a different evolutionary version of persons. Perhaps we, human persons, will be wise enough to preserve and respect these other ape persons.

Notes

1   Some degree of dissociation can be, however, achieved within the scene we are looking at: I may be mentally attending to an object that is in my peripheral vision instead of to the object in front of my eyes, but my visual attention is still constrained by the presence of the object in my visual field. It could be argued that visual attention is, in fact, a combination of two different mental activities: seeing (which would be the one subject to the behavioral constraint of looking) and attending (which could be purely mental and dissociable from external manifestations). The sort of attentiveness I am exploring in the text is the one that remains indifferentiated from the behavior of looking.
2   Cf. Hobson 1993 for a similar account of early infant intersubjectivity.

References

Baron-Cohen, S. (1995), *Mindblindness: an Essay on Autism and Theory of Mind*, MIT Press, Cambridge, MA.

Dennett, D.C. (1976), "Conditions of personhood", in A.O. Rorty (ed.), *The Identities of Persons*, University of California Press, Berkeley. [Reprinted in D.C. Dennett (1978), *Brainstorms*, Penguin, London.]

Gomez, J.C. (1990). "The emergence of intentional communication as a problem-solving strategy in the gorilla", in S.T. Parker and K.R. Gibson (eds), *"Language" and Intelligence in Monkeys and Apes: Comparative Developmental Perspectives*, Cambridge University Press, Cambridge, pp. 333–55.

Gómez, J.C. (1991). "Visual behavior as a window for reading the minds of others in primates", in A. Whiten (ed.), *Natural Theories of Mind: Evolution, Development and Simulation of everyday Mindreading*, Blackwell, Oxford, pp. 195–207.

Gómez, J.C. (1994), "Mutual awareness in primate communication: a Gricean approach", in S.T. Parker, M. Boccia, and R. Mitchell (eds), *Self-recognition and Awareness in Apes, Monkeys and Children*, Cambridge University Press, Cambridge, pp. 61–80.

Gómez, J.C. (1996), "Ostensive behavior in the great apes: the role of eye contact", in A. Russon, S.T. Parker, and K. Bard (eds), *Reaching into Thought: the Minds of the Great Apes*, Cambridge University Press, Cambridge, pp. 131–151.

Gómez, J.C. (1999), "Do concepts of intersubjectivity apply to non-human primates?", in S. Braten (ed.), *Intersubjective Communication and Emotion in Ontogeny: a Source Book*, Cambridge University Press, Cambridge.

Hobson, P. (1990), "On acquiring knowledge about people and the capacity to pretend: responses to Leslie (1987)", *Psychological Review* 1, 97, pp. 114–21.

Hobson, P. (1993), *Autism and the Development of Mind*, LEA, Hove.

Praget, J. (1936), *La naissance de l'intelligence chez l'enfant*, Delachaux et Niestlée, Neuchatel.

Tomasello, M. and Call, J. (1997), *Primate Cognition*, Oxford University Press, Oxford.

Tomasello, M., George, B., Kruger, A., Farrar, J. and Evans, E. (1985), 'The development of gestural communication in young chimpanzees", *Journal of Human Evolution* 14, pp. 175–86.

Trevarthen, C. (1979), "Communication and cooperation in early infancy", in M. Bullowa (ed.), *Before Speech: The Beginnings of Human Communication*, Cambridge University Press, Cambridge, pp. 321–47.

Trevarthen, C. (1980). "The foundations of intersubjectivity: development of interpersonal and cooperative understanding in infants", in D.R. Olson (ed.), *The Social Foundations of Language and Thought*, Norton, New York, pp. 316–42.

22

Fran Peavey

"The Chimpanzee at Stanford"

Peavy provides a brief and poignant anecdote about an interspecies relationship she encountered with a captive female chimpanzee.

One day I was walking through the Stanford University campus with a friend when I saw a crowd of people with cameras and video equipment on a little hillside. They were clustered around a pair of chimpanzees—a male running loose and a female on a chain about twenty-five feet long. It turned out the male was from Marine World and the female was being studied for something or other at Stanford. The spectators were scientists and publicity people trying to get them to mate.

The male was eager. He grunted and grabbed the female's chain and tugged. She whimpered and backed away. He pulled again. She pulled back. Watching the chimps' faces, I began to feel sympathy for the female.

Suddenly the female chimp yanked her chain out of the male's grasp. To my amazement, she walked through the crowd, straight over to me, and took my hand. Then she led me across the circle to the only other two women in the crowd, and she joined hands with one of them. The three of us stood together in a circle. I remember the feeling of that rough palm against mine. The little chimp had recognized us and reached out across all the years of evolution to form her own support group.

23

<hr>

Jane Goodall

"Problems Faced by Wild and Captive Chimpanzees: Finding Solutions"

Goodall provides a brief summary of her work and experiences with chimpanzees, and offers her perspectives on problems faced by these primates in their natural habitats, sanctuaries established by the Jane Goodall Institute to allow orphaned chimpanzees to be raised, the role of zoos, chimpanzees as pets, chimpanzees in circuses or used for entertainment, medical research, and bringing just solutions to "surplus" chimpanzees. She ends with a call to work together to give these animals a good chance to survive and have the best possible quality of life.

In 1960 I began a study of the chimpanzees living in the Gombe National Park in Tanzania. Today I am seldom able to visit more than three or four times a year, for two weeks at a time, but the work continues. Data are collected daily by a team of researchers, making the Gombe project the longest unbroken study of any group of wild animals. Information from this research and from other chimpanzee study sites has provided a wealth of data about these apes. Rich data have also accumulated from studies of gorillas and bonobos in Africa and orangutans in Asia. This information, together with behavioral, psychological, and physiological data from a variety of studies of captive great apes around the world, has served to emphasize their close evolutionary relationship to ourselves. How shocking, then, to learn that these amazing beings are vanishing in the wild and being subjected to abuse in many captive situations.

[. . .]

Chimpanzees show intellectual abilities once thought unique to our own species. They have excellent memories, and they can plan for the immediate future. They are capable of cross-modal transfer of information, generalization and abstraction, and simple problem solving. They are aware of themselves as individuals, and they can interpret the moods and identify the wants and needs of others. They have demonstrated a sense of humor. Moreover, although harder to prove, they undoubtedly feel and express emotions similar to those that we label happiness, sadness, rage, irritation, fear, despair, and mental as well as physical suffering. None of this should surprise us in view of the remarkable similarity between the anatomy of the brain and central nervous system of chimpanzee and human. All of this helps to blur the line, once perceived as so sharp, between humans and the rest of the animal kingdom. Once science admits that it is not, after all, only humans who have personalities, are capable of rational thought, and know emotions similar to happiness, sadness, anger, despair, this should lead to a new respect for other animals with whom we share the planet, especially for the great apes, our closest living relatives. In fact that respect is seldom apparent.

[. . .]

Problems faced by chimpanzees in the wild

There are still some chimpanzees living in utterly remote wilderness areas who seldom if ever encounter humans—for example, those in the Ndoke National Park area in the People's Republic of Congo (Brazzaville). There are a number of areas, spread across the range of the chimpanzee, that have been given protected status to preserve wildlife. In some countries (e.g., Tanzania and Uganda) efforts are made by wildlife authorities to patrol such areas. Protection is also afforded by wildlife research teams working within these forests. Too often, though, poachers with guns, snares, or spears have easy access, and there are many illegal logging operations with pit saws and illegal mining.

[. . .]

The most severe threat to the Gombe chimpanzees is human population growth in the areas around the tiny 30-square-mile national park. The 120 or so chimpanzees, in three different communities, are isolated, cut off from other conspecifics by cultivated hillsides on three sides, the lake on the fourth. Even 15 years ago chimpanzee habitats stretched far along the eastern shore of Lake Tanganyika. Today the trees have gone as more and more desperate people, including large numbers of refugees from Burundi and Congo, try to grow food on the very steep slopes. In the rainy season the precious thin layer of topsoil is washed down into the lake. In some places the shoreline looks like rocky desert, and the fish breeding grounds have become silted up.

How can we hope to save the forest jewel that is the Gombe National Park, and its famous chimpanzees, when the local people are facing starvation? There are now more people living there than the land can support, there is almost nowhere for them to move to, and they mostly cannot afford to buy food from other areas. In many places the women have to dig up the roots of previously cut trees to get wood to cook their food.

The Jane Goodall Institute has initiated a project in the Kigoma region to try to address this problem. Tree nurseries have been established in 33 villages around Gombe and along the lakeshore. Fruit trees and fast growing trees for building poles, firewood, and charcoal are nurtured as seedlings, then planted in the villages. George Strunden, project manager, has picked a team of qualified Tanzanians who introduce the program into the villages. He has also trained women who demonstrate appropriate tree growing methods. Farming methods that help control and prevent soil erosion are introduced. And there is a strong conservation education element that includes taking small groups of secondary school students to Gombe. There is a big push to increase the self-esteem of women, teaching them skills that will enable them to earn money for themselves. A number of scholarships are offered annually to enable girls from primary schools to benefit from further education. A small microcredit program has been introduced based on the Grameen Bank system. By working with the local medical authorities, TACARE (Lake Tanganika Catchment Reforestation and Education Project) is able to bring primary health care to the village women, along with family planning and AIDS education. Most recently we have formed a partnership with UNICEF that will enable us to bring hygenic latrines and freshwater wells to 33 villages in the area. It should be stressed that the villagers are consulted about their needs, and only projects that have their absolute support are introduced.

Only if we work with the villagers, helping to improve the standard of living of some of the poorest people in Tanzania, do we have a chance to protect the Gombe chimpanzees. Without the goodwill of the local people, the last forests within the park itself, and the tiny remnant forests outside, would surely disappear. A significant factor in our battle to save the Gombe chimpanzees is our employing field staff from communities around the park since

1988. These men follow the chimpanzees, make detailed reports, use 8-mm video cameras, and are proud of their work. They talk about it to family and friends. They care about the chimpanzees as individuals. I believe this is why, until the recent influx of refugees from eastern Congo (people who traditionally eat the meat of monkeys and apes), we had only one case of poaching at Gombe.

Across Africa the great apes face problems caused by the relentless growth of human populations, habitat destruction, and fragmentation of populations. Peasants clear-cut forests to create fields for crops and grazing. They cut down hundreds of trees for the charcoal industry. The forest soils are fragile and soon become infertile and barren when the tree cover is destroyed. So the desert spreads.

In some parts of Africa apes are hunted for the live animal trade and for food. In addition they may be caught in the snares set by village hunters for antelopes and bush pigs. They can usually break the wire, but the tightened noose causes great pain and typically results in gangrene and the loss of the affected hand or foot and sometimes ends in death. Between 40 and 50 percent of all adult chimpanzees in the study communities at Budongo and in the Tai Forest have lost a hand or foot in this way.

Wildlife is sometimes endangered as a result of the ethnic violence so tragically prevalent in many parts of the chimpanzees' range. These conflicts may displace hundreds of refugees who flee their homes, as in Liberia, the Democratic Republic of Congo, Sierra Leone, and Rwanda. Typically they are starving and forced to hunt wild animals for food. Those chimpanzees remaining in Cabinda are endangered by the land mines that have been placed throughout the forests in northwest Angola.

The great apes are also threatened by the live animal trade, when dealers pay hunters to shoot females simply to steal their infants for export. This trade is by no means as extensive as it was in the days before the Convention on International Trade in Endangered Species of Wild Fauna and Flora (CITES), but there is still brisk business in some parts of the world, such as the United Arab Emirates, various countries in South America, and parts of eastern Europe. For every infant that arrives at its final destination alive, about ten chimpanzees are estimated to have died in Africa: mothers who escaped only to die later of their wounds, along with their infants; infants killed during capture; other individuals who tried to protect the victims; and captured infants who die of wounds, dehydration, malnutrition, or shock and depression.

Chimpanzees and other wildlife in remote unprotected forests are seriously and increasingly threatened by commercial activities, particularly logging. Even companies that practice sustainable logging have a highly adverse effect on much animal life. Roads made for transportation of logs open up the forests for settlements. People then cut down trees to grow crops, for firewood, for building poles. They set snares to catch antelopes and other animals for food. And they carry human diseases into areas where they have never been before, and the great apes are susceptible to almost all of our infectious diseases. Most serious of all, the roads provide easy access to previously inaccessible areas for commercial hunters who ride the logging trucks. The roads and trucks provide, for the first time, the means for meat, dried or even fresh, to be transported from the heart of the forest to towns far away. Subsistence hunting permitted indigenous people to live in harmony with the forests for hundreds of years. It is the new commercial hunting that threatens the animals of many of the remaining forests. This is the infamous bushmeat trade, exposed by Karl Ammann.

Thus it is clear that wild chimpanzees, gorillas, and bonobos are, only too often, persecuted by their closest relatives, the human apes. The chimpanzee population, that must have numbered more than one million at the beginning of the twentieth century, has been reduced to 200,000 at the very most, spread through 21 countries. It is the rate of decrease of all the great apes that is so alarming. If nothing is done to halt the bushmeat trade, it is estimated that almost no great apes will remain in the Congo Basin in 10 to 15 years. Many organizations have joined The Bushmeat Crisis Task Force in the United States and the Ape Alliance in Europe, which are working on developing methods to slow down and ultimately eliminate this trade.

Sanctuaries

There is not much meat on an infant chimpanzee. Orphans, whose mothers have been shot and sold for meat, are sometimes offered for sale in native or tourist markets. In some areas mothers are shot only so that their infants can be stolen for sale. These pathetic orphans are sometimes bought as pets, to attract customers to a hotel or other place of business, or simply because people feel sorry for them. Paying money for any wild animal for sale serves only to perpetuate a cruel trade. Yet it is hard to turn away from a small infant who looks at you with eyes filled with pain and hopelessness. A solution to this moral dilemma is to persuade government officials to confiscate these victims, because in most African countries there is a law prohibiting the hunting and sale of endangered species, such as the great apes, without a license.

After confiscation, the orphan must be cared for. The Jane Goodall Institute has established sanctuaries in a number of locations. The biggest is in Congo (Brazzaville), where Graziella Cotman cares for 80 at the time of writing (October 2000). The Tchimpounga sanctuary, north of Pointe-Noire on the coast, was built by the petroleum company Conoco, in 1991. It was designed for 25 chimpanzees at most. It has become urgent to add additional enclosures, but we have been delayed by civil war.

In this area, as at Gombe, we employ individuals from the surrounding villages to care for the chimpanzees (and other animals) and as support staff. We also buy fruit and vegetables locally, and this boosts the economy. In addition, we use these orphans as the focus of an environmental education program. The local people are amazed and fascinated when they see the chimpanzees close up. We are trying to establish a wildlife reserve to protect the remaining forest—savanna mosaic in the area. Most of the savanna has been destroyed by eucalyptus plantations, a project of Shell Oil working with a Congolese company, but there is a beautiful unspoiled area around our sanctuary. With permission from the central government we are working with local government officials and also employing ecoguards from each of the seven nearby villages. There are more wild chimpanzees in the area than we believed. When the fighting stops it may be possible to attract tourists and thus bring foreign exchange into the country. Although the building and maintenance of chimpanzee sanctuaries is very expensive, we are not only caring for abandoned orphans but raising awareness through conservation education, and trying to protect the wild chimpanzees.

[. . .]

Zoos

There are approximately 250 chimpanzees living in zoos accredited by the American Zoo and Aquarium Association (AZA) and participating in the chimpanzee Species Survival Plan. There are about 1,700 in all zoos worldwide. There is much controversy regarding zoos, with many animal rights activists believing that they should be closed. Of course, chimpanzees belong in the wild, and if they are lucky enough to live in a protected area, or one remote from people, that is the best life. That life cannot be replicated in captive situations. In the forest they have a great deal of freedom of choice. They can choose whether to travel on their own, in a small group, or to join large excitable gatherings. They can usually choose which individuals to associate with. Females can wander off, with their dependent young, and stay feeding peacefully and grooming together for hours, or even days. Close companions meet often, others may avoid each other. They know the excitement of participating in hunts or boundary patrols, and even aggressive, almost war-like encounters with individuals of neighboring social groups. To survive they must spend much time searching for and sometimes preparing their food—they are occupying their brains, using their skills. They are free. Nevertheless, when compared with the life of chimpanzees living in danger zones in Africa, it sometimes seems to me that those in the really good zoos—those in which there are large enclosures, rich social groups, and an enriched environment—may in fact be better off.

On the other hand, there are still many zoos that should be closed—zoos where chimpanzees are forced to live alone or in pairs in tiny cement-floored, iron-barred, old-fashioned cages. There they suffer terribly from boredom. In African zoos, where sometimes even the keepers can only eat one meal a day, if that, conditions are often appalling for all the animals, and there is much suffering. Lack of water is often a major problem, because there may be no running water and water is delivered very sporadically by keepers who are in the business simply for a job.

[. . .]

The medical research lab

Many ex-pet and ex-entertainment chimpanzees end their days in medical research. It is hard for me to visit the laboratories to see chimpanzees, who have committed no crime, locked into 5 ft × 5 ft × 7 ft high prison cages. They are there because their biology and physiology is so like ours that they can be infected with almost all human diseases. Hundreds have been used in hepatitis and AIDS research. Admittedly some laboratories are improving, developing programs to enrich their prisoners' lives, giving them more space. But there are still hundreds in the United States and other parts of the world in such cells.

Surplus chimpanzees

A major problem today is the so-called "surplus" chimpanzee population. [. . .] The following stories of three chimpanzees, two born in the wild and one in captivity, serve to remind us that, when we talk of the "surplus" problem we are actually talking of the fate of individuals, each with his or her own personality, each having been exploited by humans.

Gregoire was born in the wild, in the northern forests of Congo (Brazzaville). When I met him he was alone in a dark cage, one in a row of similarly caged, solitary primates at the Brazzaville Zoo. Gregoire had been given to the zoo when his owners left the country, and he had been there since about 1949, some 40 years. He was almost hairless, and I could see nearly every bone in his body. Most of the animals at that zoo were starving; it was cheaper to replace animals who died of malnutrition than to buy an adequate diet. I knew I had to help Gregoire even though he had, somehow, survived without help for so long. A small group of people got together and agreed to save up food and deliver it to the zoo. The Jane Goodall Institute employed its own keeper to care for Gregoire and the other primates. Gregoire put on weight and his hair began to grow. Then the Brigitte Bardot Foundation gave us a small grant (after she saw a video of Gregoire), and we were able to build a small "patio" for him. By this time Graziella Cotman was living in Brazzaville, and she was able to introduce three small orphans to the old male. One was a 2-year-old female, whom I named Cherie. A wonderful relationship, a bit like a grandfather and granddaughter, developed between this little girl and old Gregoire. Things were going well, until civil war broke out again. The zoo, near the airport, was in the middle of the war zone. Fortunately Gregoire, his young companions, and the two adult chimpanzees could be airlifted to the Tchimpounga Sanctuary (along with a group of young gorillas and bonobos). When Gregoire arrived his back was raw, apparently because he had rushed under his low bed shelf whenever the shelling got too close. But once again this old man adapted, and his hair grew back. Today he is in a group with two adult females and three youngsters.

Sebastian was brought to Kenya (where there are no wild chimpanzees) from West Africa. He ended up in the orphanage run by the Kenya Wildlife Service. There he lived for more than 20 years, becoming the star attraction. When I met him his quarters consisted of a small indoor and private cage that led into a circular mesh enclosure. He lived alone because he had seriously hurt females who had been introduced to him. He was very gentle with humans whom he liked, and loved to manicure my nails with a piece of twig. But when crowds of visitors arrived, especially when these were children who would make faces and tease him, he would display wildly, back and forth in the enclosure, throwing anything he could find. Yet when he was put in a newly built enclosure that prevented the public from approaching closely, he became seriously depressed and refused to eat. Eventually he was returned to his original home where he quickly recovered. Several years later he again became depressed when the orphanage was temporarily closed for reconstruction. Not until it was again opened to the public, and the daily teasing and displaying sessions resumed, did he recover. Clearly, the crowds provided stimulation and entertainment.

Lucy was born in captivity. As a tiny baby she was adopted by Jane and Maurice Temerlins, a psychoanalyst and his zoologist wife. Lucy was brought up like a human child, clothes and all. The original plan was to find out whether a chimpanzee brought up with love and affection would be able to nurture her first baby despite having no experience of other chimpanzees. But as she reached adolescence the Termerlins decided that their lives had been ruled by Lucy for too long. After considering all options, they decided, with the best of intentions, to give her her freedom, to send her to Africa. Although she went with a trusted human, all that she had learned in her "human" days had to be forgotten. She had learned sign language, but her signs were ignored by the only person she knew, the person with whom, until the nightmare began, she had communicated in sign language. Lucy was introduced to two rambunctious young wild-born chimpanzees. She wanted nothing to do with them. She fell into deep depression. Although she eventually began to behave more like a chimpanzee, I personally believe the exercise was very cruel. Lucy died, years after arriving in Africa and ultimately being released on an island. Her body was found on the island with hands and feet removed. The whole exercise can be compared with taking a middle-class American girl of about 14 years old to live with a group of indigenous people in some far off part of the world. She would leave behind all her clothes, all her comforts, and all her culture. And her American companion would pretend not to understand a word she said.

These three chimpanzees had unnatural life styles to which they adapted. Humans created those situations. We have no right to try to effect change from our arrogant human perspective of "we know what is best." Rather we should try to get inside the mind of the individual chimpanzees and move slowly, a step at a time, toward a solution that is *best for them*.

Conclusions

Clearly chimpanzees today face many problems, both in the wild and in captivity. These problems are all different and need their own unique solutions that take into account all the variables; the country, the different people involved, the resources available, especially financial, and the personalities of the chimpanzees themselves. We cannot draw sweeping conclusions about the correct procedure in all zoos, in all sanctuaries, and in all situations.

Those trying to help the great apes have their own perspectives. There are many differences of opinion. But so long as we all have the same goals—the improvement of conditions for the great apes, in the world and in captivity—we should be able to work together.

[. . .]

I have encountered criticism for starting sanctuaries (they have been called a waste of money to help a few individuals when precious funds are needed to save the species), but for me there was no option. I simply could not look into the eyes of a pathetic orphan and leave it to its fate, because, for so many years, I have been able to look into the eyes of chimpanzees who are wild and free and in control of their own lives.

Let us move forward, united toward our goal of conserving the great apes in the wild, striving for the best treatment for all captive apes, and eliminating them from invasive medical research. Whether we care about the apes as species or as individuals, we all want solutions that will give them a chance to survive and to enjoy the best possible quality of life.

Cetaceans

24

Luke Rendell and Hal Whitehead

"Culture in Whales and Dolphins"

Taking an ethnographic approach, Rendell and Whitehead find evidence for transmission of cultural information among several cetacean species. They note experimental evidence of social learning abilities in bottlenosed dolphins and observations of imitation and teaching among killer whales. They note that the distinct vocal and behavioral characteristics of sympatric groups of killer whales are both complex and stable, and the authors believe that these cetacean cultural characteristics represent an independent evolution of cultural faculties in a species other than humans.

Introduction

[. . .]

The presence of cultural processes in nonhuman animals is an area of some controversy (de Waal 1999; Galef 1992). In this target article we attempt to fuel the debate by reviewing the evidence for cultural transmission in whales and dolphins (order *Cetacea*), a group that has so far received almost no attention from students of animal culture. [. . .]

The logistical difficulties of studying wild cetaceans make the study of culture difficult, and often give rise to information that is incomplete and poor in detail. Nonetheless, we feel it is timely to introduce cetaceans into the wider debate surrounding animal culture for a number of reasons. First, there is growing evidence of cultural transmission and cultural evolution in the cetaceans, some of which is strong, some of which is weaker, but which when taken as a whole make a compelling case for the detailed study of cultural phenomena in this group. [. . .] Second, the evidence now available describes some interesting and rare (in some cases unique outside humans) patterns of behavioural variation in the wild, likely maintained by cultural transmission processes. Third, there is growing evidence that in the complexity of their social systems—the only non-human example of second-order alliances (Connor *et al.* 1998)—and their cognition—data suggest that dolphins can use abstract representations of objects, actions and concepts to guide their behaviour (Herman *et al.* 1993; 1994)—some cetaceans match or exceed all other non-human animals. Since complex social systems and advanced cognitive abilities have been suggested as good predictors of animal culture (Roper 1986), it is pertinent to ask whether these factors are reflected in the cultural faculties of cetaceans. Finally, cetaceans provide an interesting contrast to the study of culture in humans and other terrestrial animals, since they inhabit a radically different environment and perhaps represent an independent evolution of social learning and cultural transmission.

[. . .]

The work of Boyd and Richerson (1985; 1996) has been crucially important in giving the study of cultural transmission and cultural evolution a sound theoretical basis (Bettinger 1991, p. 182). Thus the definitions of culture that they found useful are particularly important, and have heavily influenced our decision on which definition to adopt: "Culture is information or behaviour acquired from conspecifics through some form of social learning" (Boyd and Richerson 1996).

[. . .]

We strongly believe that research on cultural processes is best served by an approach that integrates the sometimes opposing process-and product-oriented perspectives, as well as the laboratory and field approaches, taking good data from each. This cannot be achieved unless both perspectives are understood, and so we shall approach cetacean culture from both in turn. Following this, we will bring our own perspective, as field biologists heavily influenced by evolutionary ecology, to an attempted integration.

[. . .]

Culture in cetaceans

From the ethnographic perspective cultural transmission is deduced from spatial, temporal or social patterns of variation in behaviour that are not consistent with genetic or environmental determination or individual learning. [. . .] We will consider three types of pattern:

1   Rapid spread of a novel and complex form of behaviour through a segment of the population, indicating a largely horizontal—within-generation (Cavalli-Sforza and Feldman 1981)—cultural process.
2   Mother-offspring similarity in a complex form of behaviour, indicating vertical— parent-offspring (Cavalli-Sforza and Feldman 1981)—cultural transmission.
3   Differences in complex behaviour between stable groups of animals that are hard to explain by genetic differences, shared environments, or the sizes or demographic structure of the groups.

[. . .]

We will refer to these as *rapid-spread, mother-offspring* and *group-specific* behavioural patterns, respectively.

[. . .]

On their winter breeding grounds, male humpback whales produce songs, structured sequences of vocalizations cycling with a period of about 5–25 min (Payne and McVay 1971). At any time, all males in a breeding population sing nearly the same song, but the song evolves structurally over time, changing noticeably over a breeding season, substantially over periods of several years, but remaining stable over the largely nonsinging summer months (Payne and Payne 1985). Males sing virtually identical songs on breeding grounds thousands of kilometres apart and the songs on these different grounds evolve as one.

[. . .]

Humpback song is homogenous over entire ocean basins compared to the sharp variation over short distances in both bird species, and thousands of individual humpbacks share the same song compared to the colony- or locale-specific birdsongs (Cerchio 1993). [. . .] [T]he differences in scale make humpback songs a so far unique instance among non-humans of a continuously evolving conformist culture in a large and dispersed population.

[. . .]

Cultural innovations can also spread quite rapidly on humpback feeding grounds where they spend the summer months. In the southern Gulf of Maine, a novel complex feeding technique, "lobtail feeding," was first observed in 1981, and by 1989 had been adopted by nearly 50 per cent of the population (Weinrich *et al.* 1992). This feeding method is apparently a modification of "bubble-cloud" feeding, a complex but common form of feeding in humpbacks in which prey schools are enveloped in clouds of bubbles formed by exhaling underwater; . . . the behaviour is modified by slamming the tail-flukes onto the water (termed lob-tailing) prior to diving.

[. . .]

The spread of novel feeding methods through a population has been documented for a number of terrestrial and avian species (Roper 1986). Two of the most famous cases are milk-bottle top opening by birds in Britain (Fisher and Hinde 1949), and washing sweet potatoes by Japanese macaques (*Macaca fuscata*) (Kawai 1965). In both cases, the spread was thought to be due to imitation, but more recent work has cast doubt on this (Sherry and Galef 1984; Whiten 1989). Rates of spread of the innovations were similar to those observed for the lobtail-feeding humpbacks: Milk-bottle opening took 20 years to spread across London and potato washing spread through almost all the band of macaques in nine years.

[. . .]

Genetic and photo-identification studies have shown that young beluga (*Delphinapterus leucas*) and humpback whales follow their mothers on initial migrations between breeding and feeding grounds, and then repeat them faithfully throughout their lives (Katona and Beard 1990: O'Corry-Crowe *et al.* 1997).

[. . .]

Bottlenose dolphins in Shark Bay, Australia, carry sponges on their rostra (Smolker *et al.* 1997). The exact function of "sponging" is not known; it is thought to be a foraging specialisation (Smolker *et al.* 1997).

[. . .]

Several species of cetaceans live in stable social groups (Connor *et al.* 1998); of these the best known is the killer whale, particularly those that live around Vancouver Island. There are at least two different forms of killer whale in this area, which are sympatric but can be distinguished by diet, morphology, behaviour, social structure, and genetics (Baird 2000). Although they are known as *residents* and *transients*, this terminology does not really reflect the habits of the two forms (Baird and Dill 1995). Best known is the fish-feeding, resident, form. Residents live in highly stable matrilineal *pods* averaging 12 animals (Bigg *et al.* 1990); there is no known case of individuals changing pods in over 21 years of study (Baird 2000). [. . .]

The strongest evidence lies in the vocal dialects of resident pods; each pod has a distinctive set of 7–17 *discrete* calls (Ford 1991; Strager 1995). These dialects are maintained despite extensive associations between pods. Some pods share up to 10 calls (Ford 1991), and pods that share calls can be grouped together in acoustic *clans* (Ford 1991), suggesting another level of population structure. Ford (1991) found four distinct clans within two resident communities, and suggested that the observed pattern of call variation is a result of dialects being passed down through vocal learning and being modified over time.

[. . .]

Between-pod variation is also evident in other aspects of killer whale behaviour, particularly foraging. There are strong indications that different sympatric resident pods specialise on different salmon species (*Oncorhynchus* spp.), evidenced by correlations in the abundance of different salmon species and killer whale pods at various locations. It has been suggested that accumulated knowledge of salmon distribution results in the traditional use of specific areas by different pods (Nichol and Shackleton 1996).

Other behavioural patterns vary among higher-level groups of killer whales. Off Vancouver Island, there are community-specific "greeting ceremonies" observed when resident pods of one community meet (Osborne 1986); the two pods line up facing each other and stop in formation for 10–30 seconds before approaching and mingling. Some pods of another community engage in "beach-rubbing," and again there is variability between pods in the preferred locations for rubbing (Hoyt 1990).

[. . .]

Sperm whales make distinctive, stereotyped patterns of 3 to > 12 clicks called *codas*, which are thought to function in communication (Watkins and Schevill 1977). Distinctive coda dialects (consisting of very different proportional use of about 30 different types of coda) are a feature of partially matrilineal, but interacting, groups of about 20 female sperm whales (Weilgart and Whitehead 1997). Given the wide-ranging movements of these animals—on the order of 1,000 km (Dufault and Whitehead 1995)—these dialects are effectively sympatric.

[. . .]

In addition to these group-specific patterns of killer and sperm whales, there are some local behavioural patterns of cetaceans that do not live in such stable groups. Bottlenose dolphins at Laguna off the coast of Brazil have an unusual group-specific feeding technique which seems to date from 1847 and have been transmitted within a matrilineal community since at least three generations of dolphin are involved (Pryor *et al.* 1990). The 25–30 dolphins and local fishers follow a strict protocol—involving no training or commands from the fishermen—that allows the humans and dolphins to coordinate their actions. The dolphins drive fish into the nets of human fishermen, indicating as they do so by performing a distinctive rolling dive when the humans should cast their nets. The humans can also pick up from how much of the body comes out of the water on this roll an idea of how many fish are present—it is entirely unclear whether this cue is given intentionally or not—and then feed off the fish that are stunned or missed by the net (Pryor *et al.* 1990). There are other bottlenose dolphins in the area that do not participate in the cooperative fishing and sometimes try to disrupt it (Pryor *et al.* 1990); hence, again, behavioural variation is sympatric. Only young adults whose mothers took part in the fishing later adopted it themselves, although not all the offspring of fishing mothers did so (Pryor *et al.* 1990).

[. . .]

Group-specific, culturally transmitted behavioural patterns have parallels in other animal taxa, but in some respects these cetacean cultures, in particular those of the killer whale, appear unique outside humans.

[. . .]

[D]ifferent cultural variants of killer and sperm whales, as well as the cooperative fishing traditions of bottlenose dolphins, are sympatric, and animals with different cultures often interact. Thus, members of these species are repeatedly exposed to a wide range of cultural variations but maintain their own group-specific culture. [. . .] [T]he behavioural complexes seen in killer whales appear to encompass both vocal *and* physical behaviours; such complex multicultural societies where culture encompasses both the vocal and motor domains are otherwise known only from humans. However, it should be noted that in no cetacean example is there evidence of such broad suites of cultural behaviours as have been found in chimpanzees, where 39 behaviour patterns have been shown to vary culturally (Whiten *et al.* 1999).

A second remarkable attribute of some of the group-specific cultural traits of cetaceans is in their stability. Killer whale dialects are highly stable, known to persist for at least six generations, and it has been suggested, much longer (Ford 1991).

[. . .]

There is less direct evidence for social learning in the other good example of group-specific cetacean dialects, the sperm whale coda repertoire. However, in the remarkable *echocodas*, two animals precisely interleave their click patterns, giving rise to two overlapping codas, identical in temporal pattern to within a few milliseconds, offset by about 50–100 msec (Weilgart 1990). This duetting suggests that sperm whales may be matching codas in a similar way to bottlenose dolphins matching signature whistles (see Tyack 1986b); such matching would require imitative learning in some form.

[. . .]

Adult killer whales have been observed pushing their young up the beach, then back down the beach, directing them towards prey, helping them out when they become stuck by creating wash, helping them back to deep water after a successful capture (Guinet and Bouvier 1995), and throwing prey at juveniles (Lopez and Lopez 1985)—hence they modify their behaviour in the presence of naïve observers. Adults are more successful at hunting in the absence of juveniles (Hoelzel 1991); at the extreme, they throw away already captured prey (Lopez and Lopez 1985)—hence there is a demonstrable cost. Pushing juveniles onto beaches and pushing them towards prey is clearly encouragement.

[. . .]

The question of cetacean culture

Does the evidence we present here legitimately allow us to attribute culture to cetaceans? We recognise that how one defines culture will inevitably affect how one attributes it, and we also recognise that we have chosen a broad definition of culture. [. . .] [W]e have adopted a definition that has allowed significant progress to be made in developing a theoretical basis for understanding culture and is not tied to any particular species or any particular form of culture. Such a broad definition allows us to concentrate on comparing cultures across species, and relating these comparisons to ecology.

[. . .]

Here is the central problem with an experimental approach to cetacean culture: It can freeze the question by demanding that which will never occur (i.e., experimental studies). In our view, it is not reasonable to postpone discussion on this semipermanent basis, because other rigorous and conceptually sound approaches are available. [. . .]

The field-based approach to culture is exemplified by Boesche *et al.*'s (1994) and Whiten *et al.*'s (1999) work on chimpanzee culture, Grant and Grant's (1996) work on Darwin's finches and Warner's (1988) work on bluehead wrasse. The approach is clear; systematic field observation (and manipulation of natural populations in Warner 1988) enables the elimination of ecological and genetic factors potentially causing behavioural variation; what is left must be cultural. The resulting conclusions are weak in that the transmission process remains unproven but strong in that they are firmly rooted in how the animals actually behave in the wild. Since cultural learning is *social* learning, we can only fully appreciate its complexity and functional usage in animals when it is studied in a naturalistic *social* setting.

The effects of culture: gene-culture coevolution and nonadaptive behaviour

The two features in which killer and probably sperm whale cultures seem to differ from those of virtually all other non-human animals, stability and multiculturalism, are prerequisites for cultural processes to have much effect on genetic evolution. To affect genetic evolution, cultures must usually be stable over many generations (Laland 1992), and if cultural variants rarely interact, they will generally have only local effects (Whitehead 1998). There have been two suggestions that substantial gene-culture coevolution has occurred in whales and dolphins; since both involve historical explanation, neither can be empirically proven. However, this is no different from posited cases of gene-cultures co-evolution in humans (Feldman and Laland 1996). Both Baird (2000) and Boran and Heimlich (1999) propose that culturally transmitted group-specific foraging techniques initiated the divergence of the forms of killer whale, which now show genetic and morphological differences, and may well be in the process of speciation given the apparent reproductive isolation of the two forms (Baird *et al.* 1992). This is a plausible explanation for the ongoing sympatric speciation; however, since the genetic differences between the two forms are now so evident (Hoelzel *et al.* 1998), it cannot be proven that culture was responsible for the divergence.

Conformist traditions can lead to cultural group selection (Boyd and Richerson 1985). Group conformity increases both homogeneity within groups and heterogeneity among groups and thus elevates variation in behavioural phenotype to the group level (Boyd and Richerson 1985; Richerson and Boyd 1998); hence we would expect selection on behavioural phenotype to act at this level. For species that forage cooperatively, particularly within kin-based groups (e.g., killer whales), competition for resources may occur largely between rather than within groups, which would significantly increase the adaptive value of conformist traditions, reinforcing the whole system. Similarly, predator-prey arms races can be a potent driver of both genetic evolution (Dawkins and Krebs 1979) and, as is very apparent in human history, cultural evolution. For most whales and dolphins, the most formidable and important natural predator is another cetacean, the killer whale (Jefferson *et al.* 1991), and the predatory techniques of killer whales appear to be largely determined by cultural processes. Thus, it is possible to envisage cultural arms races between killer whales and their cetacean prey.

Theoretical studies also suggest that during the evolution of group-specific cultures, behaviour that is not adaptive can easily arise (Boyd and Richerson 1985). There is one

behavioural pattern seen in group-living cetaceans that is individually maladaptive but could
have arisen within a system of conformist traditions: mass stranding. Cetaceans of several
species fatally strand en masse. In contrast to individual strandings, most of the animals
involved in these mass strandings appear healthy, but when individually pulled back to sea,
turn around and restrand (Sergeant 1982).

[. . .]

Culture may also have had effects on the evolution of life history. Menopause is known
in killer and short-finned pilot whales (*Globicephala macrorhynchus*), and there are indications of its occurrence in other cetacean species (Marsh and Kasuya 1986; Olesiuk *et al.*
1990). Like humans, and unlike any other mammal, female killer and short-finned pilot
whales may live decades after the birth of their last offspring. Within-group cultural processes may have played a part in this phenomenon, if, for instance, the role of older females in
cultural transmission is very important. Menopause could be highly adaptive if the role of
older females as a source of information significantly increases the fitness of her descendants,
and reproduction towards the end of her life decreases survival (Boran and Heimlich 1999;
see also Norris and Pryor 1991). Guinet and Bouvier (1995) note that the juvenile killer
whales they observed learning the difficult and dangerous technique of self-stranding in
order to catch pinnipeds spent at least six years closely associated with their mothers; one
calf was not observed to capture prey itself until it was six years old and even then required
assistance in handling the prey.

Although it has not been experimentally demonstrated in any case, observations of
cetaceans in the wild strongly suggest that cultural transmission is important in some species. Theoretical work indicating the widespread adaptiveness of culture, coupled with a
dearth of empirical examples suggest there are important obstacles to the evolution of
cultural transmission, obstacles which both humans and some cetaceans appear to have
overcome. What ecological and social factors were common in the histories of both groups
to enable this evolutionary leap? Our review suggests stable matrilineal groups as an
important social factor, and environmental variability and mobility (c.f. Boesch 1996) as
important ecological factors.

References

Baird, R. W. (2000) The killer whale: Foraging specializations and group hunting. In: *Cetacean societies: Field
    studies of dolphins and whales*, eds., J. Mann, R. C. Connor, P. I. Tyack and H. Whitehead. University of
    Chicago Press.
Baird, R. W., Ahrams, P. A. and Dill, L. M. (1992) Possible indirect interactions between transient and
    resident killer whales: Implications for the evolution of foraging specializations in the genus *Orcinus*.
    Oecologia 89:125–32.
Baird, R. W. and Dill, L. M. (1995) Occurrence and behavior of transient killer whales: Seasonal and
    pod-specific variability, foraging behavior and prey handling. *Canadian Journal of Zoology*
    73:1300–11.
Bettinger, R. L. (1991) *Hunter-gatherers: Archaeological and evolutionary theory*. Plenum Press.
Bigg, M. A., Olesiuk, P. F., Ellis, G. M., Ford, J. K. B. and Balcomb, K. C. (1990) Social organization and
    genealogy of resident killer whales (*Orcinus orca*) in the coastal waters of British Columbia and
    Washington State. *Reports of the International Whaling Commission* 12:383–405.
Boesch, C. (1996). The emergence of cultures among wild chimpanzees. *Proceedings of the British Academy*
    88:251–68.
Boesch, C., Marchesi, P., Marchesi, N., Fruth, B. and Joulian, F. (1999) Is nut-cracking in wild chimpanzees a
    cultural behaviour? *Journal of Human Evolution* 26:325–38.
Boran, J. R. and Heimlich, S. L. (1999). Social learning in cetaceans: Hunting, hearing and hierarchies.
    Symposia of the Zoological Society (London) 73:282–307.

Boyd, R. and Richerson, P. J. (1985) *Culture and the evolutionary process*. Chicago University Press.

—— (1996) Why culture is common but cultural evolution is rare. *Proceedings of the British Academy* 88:77–93.

Cavalli-Sforza, L. L. and Feldman, M. W. (1981) *Cultural transmission and evolution: A quantitative approach*. Princeton University Press.

Cerchio, S. (1993). Geographic variation and cultural evolution in songs of humpback whales (*Megaptera novaeangliae*) in the Eastern North Pacific. Master of Science thesis, Moss Landing Marine Laboratories, San Jose State University, California.

Connor, R. C., Mann, J., Tyack, P. L. and Whitehead, H. (1998) Social evolution in tooth whales. *Trends in Ecology and Evolution* 13:228–32.

Dawkins, R. and Krebs, J. R. (1979) Arms races between and within species. *Proceedings of the Royal Society of London B* 205:489–511.

De Waal, F. B. M. (1999) Cultural primatology comes of age. *Nature* 399:635–6.

Dufault, S. and Whitehead, H. (1995) The geographic stock structure of female and immature sperm whales in the South Pacific. *Reports of the International Whaling Commission* 45:401–5.

Feldman, M. W. and Laland, K. N. (1996) Gene-culture coevolutionary theory. *Trends*

Fisher, J. and Hinde, R. A. (1949) The opening of milk bottles by birds. *British Birds* 42:347–57.

Ford, J. K. B. (1991) Vocal traditions among resident killer whales (*Orcinus orca*) in coastal waters of British Columbia. *Canadian Journal of Zoology* 69:1454–83.

Galef, B. (1992) The question of animal culture. *Human Nature* 3:157–78.

Grant, B. H. and Grant P. R. (1996) Cultural inheritance of song and its role in the evolution of Darwin finches. *Evolution* 50:2471–87.

Guinet, C. and Bouvier, J. (1991) Development of intentional stranding hunting techniques in killer whale (*Orcinus orca*) calves at Crozet Archipelago. *Canadian Journal of Zoology* 73:27–33.

Herman, L. M., Pack, A. A. and Morrel-Samuels, P. (1993) Representational and conceptual skills of dolphins. In: *Language and communication: Comparative perspectives*, eds. H. L. Roitblat, L. M. Herman and P. E. Nachtigall. Lawrence Erlbaum.

Herman, L. M., Pack, A. A. and Wood, A. M. (1994) Bottlenosed dolphins can generalize rules and develop abstract concepts. *Marine Mammal Science* 10:70–80.

Hoelzel, A. R. (1991) Killer whale predation on marine mammals at Punta Norte. Argentina; food sharing, provisioning and foraging strategy. *Behavioral Ecology and Sociobiology* 29:197–204.

Hoelzel, A. R., Dahlheim, M. and Stern, S. J. (1998) Low genetic variation among killer whales (*Orcinus orca*) in the eastern North Pacific, and genetic differentiation between foraging specialists. *Journal of Heredity* 89:121–5.

Hoyt, E. (1990) *Orca: The whale called killer*. Hale.

Jefferson, T. A., Staevy, P. J. and Bairel, R. W. (1991) A review of killer whale interactions with other marine mammals. Predation to co-existence, *Mammal Review* 4:151–80.

Katona, S. K. and Beard, J. A. (1990) Population size, migrations and feeding aggregations of the humpback whale (*Megaptera novaeangliae*) in the western North Atlantic Ocean. *Reports of the International Whaling Commission* 12:295–305.

Kawai, M. (1965) Newly acquired pre-cultural behavior of natural troop of Japanese monkeys on Koshima Islet. *Primates* 1:1–30.

Laland, K. N. (1992) A theoretical investigation of the role of social transmission in evolution. *Ethology and Sociobiology* 13:87–113.

Lopez, J. C. and Lopez, D. (1985) Killer whales (*Orcinus orca*) of Patagonia, and their behavior of intentional stranding while hunting nearshore. *Journal of Mammalogy* 66:181–3.

Marsh, H. and Kasuya, T. (1985) Evidence for reproductive senescence in female cetaceans. *Reports of the International Whaling Commission* 8:37–74.

Nichol, J. M. and Shackleton, D. M. (1996) Seasonal movements and foraging behavior of northern resident killer whales (*Orcinus orca*) in relation to the inshore distribution of salmon (*Oncorhynchus* spp.); in British Columbia. *Canadian Journal of Zoology*, 14:983–91.

O'Corry-Crowe, G. M., Suydam, R. S., Russenberg, A., Frost, K. J. and Diann, A. F. (1997) Phylogeography, population structure and dispersal patterns of the beluga whale *Delphinapterus leucas* in the western Nearctic revealed by mitochondrial DNA. *Molecular Ecology* 6:955–70.

Olesiuk, P., Bigg, M. A. and Ellis, G. M. (1990) Life history and population dynamics of resident killer whales (*Orcinus orca*) in the coastal waters of British Columbia and Washington State. *Reports of the International Whaling Commission* 12:209–43.

Osborne, R. W. (1986) A behavioral budget of Puget Sound killer whales. In: *Behavioral biology of killer whales*, eds., B. C. Kirkevold and J. S. Lockard. Alan R. Liss.

Payne, K. and Payne, B. S. (1985) Large-scale changes over 17 years in songs of humpback whales in Bermuda. *Zeitschrift für Tierpsychologie* 68:89–114.

Payne, R. and McNay, S. (1971) Songs of humpback whales. *Science* 173: 587–97.

Pryor, K. W., Lindbergh, J., Lindbergh, S. and Milano, R. (1990) A dolphin-human fishing cooperative in Brazil. *Marine Mammal Science* 6:77–82.

Richerson, P. J. and Boyd, R. (1998) The evolution of human ultrasociality. In: *Indoctrinability, ideology and warfare*. eds. I. Eibl-Eibesfeldt and F. K. Salter. Berghahn Books.

Roper, T. J. (1986) Cultural evolution of feeding behaviour in animals. *Science Progress* 70:571–83.

Sergeant, D. E. (1982) Mass strandings of toothed whales (*Odontoceti*) as a population phenomenon. *Scientific Reports of the Whales Research Institute* 34:1–47.

Sherry, D. F. and Galef, B. G. (1984) Cultural transmission without imitation: Milk bottle opening by birds. *Animal Behaviour* 32:937–8.

Smolker, R. A., Bicharls, A. F., Connor, H. C., Mann, J. and Berggren, F. (1997) Sponge-carrying by Indian Ocean bottlenose dolphins: Possible tool-use by a dolphinid. *Ethology* 103:454–65.

Strager, H. (1995) Pod-specific call repertoires and compound calls of killer whales (*Orcinus orca*, Linnaeus 1758) in the waters off Northern Norway: *Canadian Journal of Zoology*, 73:1037–47.

Tyack, P. (1986) Whistle repertoires of two bottlenosed dolphins, *Turstops truncatus*: Mimicry of signature whistles? *Behavioural Ecology and Sociobiology* 15:251–7.

Warner, R. R. (1988) Traditionality of mating-site preferences in a coral reef fish. *Nature* 335:719–21.

Watkins, W. A. and Schevill, W. E. (1977) Sperm whale codas. *Journal of the Acoustical Society of America* 62:1486–90.

Weilgart, L. S. (1990) Vocalizations of the sperm whale (*Physeter macrocephalus*) off the Galapagos Islands as related to behavioral and circumstantial variables. Doctoral dissertation, Dalhousie University, Halifax, Nova Scotia, Canada.

—— (1997) Group-specific dialects and geographical variation in coda repertoire in South Pacific sperm whales. *Behavioural Ecology and Sociobiology* 40:277–85.

Weinrich, M. T., Schilling, M. R. and Belt, C. R. (1992) Evidence for acquisition of a novel feeding behaviour: Lobtail feeding in humpback whales, *Megaptera novaeangliae*. *Animal Behaviour* 44:1059–72.

Whitehead, H. (1998) Cultural selection and genetic diversity in matrilineal whales. *Science* 282:1709–11.

Whiten, A. (1989) Transmission mechanisms in primate cultural evolution. *Trends in Ecology and Evolution* 4:61–2.

Whiten, A., Goodall, J., McGrew, W. C., Nishida, T., Reynolds, V., Sugyama, Y., Tutin, C. E. G., Wrangham, R. W. and Boesch, C. (1999) Cultures in chimpanzees, *Science* 399:682–5.

25

Louis M. Herman

"Exploring the Cognitive World of the Bottlenosed Dolphin"

Herman and his research team conducted studies on sensory abilities, cross-modal matching, memory, conceptual processes, vocal and motor mimicry, language understanding, self-awareness, and the underlying mental representations. Among their many findings are that dolphins are capable of extensive vocal and behavioral mimicry and understand imitation as a concept, understand grammatical structure of language, and can understand symbolic references to absent objects.

An exceptionally large brain, a high degree of sociability, and easy trainability make the bottlenosed dolphin (*Tursiops truncatus*) an ideal species for studying intellectual processes and potential. Accordingly, our long-term research program into dolphin cognition, now spanning some 30 years, with as many as 22 years of study of individual animals, has been directed toward the description and analysis of these processes and potential. The philosophy guiding this approach is that the intellectual potential of a long-lived, presumptively intelligent species (such as the dolphin) is best revealed through a long-term program of intensive, special education in a culture that values education. Since these conditions surely favor the emergence of the full flower of human intellect, can comparable conditions also reveal the intellectual potential of other targeted species? To this end, we have worked intensively with different individual animals, using a broad-brush, multilevel approach that includes studies of sensory processes, cognitive characteristics, and communication. These different areas of study have increased our understanding of the perceptual, cognitive, and social worlds of the dolphin.

The brain of the adult bottlenosed dolphin is about 25 percent heavier than the average adult human brain (Ridgway 1990). Inasmuch as larger mammals tend to have larger brains, a more meaningful metric is to compare actual brain size with that expected for the species body size (i.e., relative brain size) (Jerison 1973). Measures of relative brain size place the bottlenosed dolphin, and two or three other closely related delphinid species, second only to humans and well above the great apes (Marino 1998; Ridgway and Tarpley 1996). The dolphin cortex has a degree of fissurization and a surface area exceeding that of the human brain, although its depth (thickness) (ca. 1.3–1.8 mm) is shallower than that of the human brain (ca. 3.0 mm) (Ridgway 1990). In addition, the size of the cerebellum relative to the total brain is significantly larger in the dolphin than in the human (Marino *et al.* 2000). Recent work has demonstrated that the cerebellum is involved in cognitive processing in addition to its role in motor control (Leiner *et al.* 1995; Fiez 1996).

Language learning

Semantics and syntax are considered the core attributes of any human natural language (Pavio and Begg 1981). Our studies of language comprehension have revealed capabilities in the dolphin for processing both semantic and syntactic information (Herman *et al.* 1984; Herman 1986: Herman and Uyeyama 1999). The primary syntactic device used in our language studies has been word order. The dolphin is capable of understanding that changes in word order change meaning. It can respond appropriately, for instance, to such semantic contrasts as *surfboard person fetch* (take the person to the surfboard) and *person surfboard fetch* (take the surfboard to the person).

In these language studies, the dolphin demonstrated an implicit representation and understanding of the grammatical structure of the language. For example, the language-trained dolphin Akeakamai was able to spontaneously understand logical extensions of a syntactic rule (Herman *et al.* 1984) and was able to extract a semantically and syntactically correct sequence from a longer anomalous sequence of language gestures given by a human (Herman *et al.* 1993). To perform this extraction, the dolphin in some cases had to conjoin nonadjacent terms in the sequence. For example, the anomalous string glossed as *water speaker Frisbee fetch* violates a syntactic rule in that there is no rule that accommodates three object names in a row. However, embedded in this sequence are two semantically and syntactically correct three-item sequences, *water Frisbee fetch* (bring the Frisbee to the stream of water), and *speaker Frisbee fetch* (bring the Frisbee to the underwater speaker). In sequences of this type, the dolphin almost always extracted one or the other of the correct three-item sequences and operated on that implicit instruction. In theory, in responding to these anomalous sequences, the dolphin utilized its implicitly learned mental representation or schema of the grammar of the language to include not only word-order rules but also the semantic rules determining which items are transportable and which are not (neither the stream of water nor the underwater speaker affixed to the tank wall can be transported). No explicit training was given for these rules.

Representation

One of the issues in animal language studies is whether the symbols used to refer to objects or actions function as representations of those things; this is the problem of linguistic reference. For example, when a tutored ape uses a symbol for candy, does it understand that the symbol refers to or represents candy, or does it merely treat the symbol as a means to obtain candy (by using it on seeing candy present)? Much of the early ape language work failed to show that the symbols used were understood referentially (Savage-Rumbaugh 1986). The clearest indication that the dolphin Akeakamai understood the gestural symbols of her language referentially was her ability to report "yes" or "no" (by pressing one or another of two paddles) in response to gestural questions asking whether specific gesturally named objects were or were not present in her tank world (Herman and Forestell 1985). The ability to understand symbolic references to absent objects is one of the clearest indicants that the symbols represent the referent. In addition, the dolphin understood that if an experimenter pointed to a distal object, it was a reference to that object (Herman *et al.* 1999).

Television scenes are representations of the real world and, as humans, we respond to them as we might to the real world but understand that they are not the real world. A cat might respond to a television image of a moving bird in the same way it would respond in the real world, failing to discriminate between the representation and the real world. In other cases, the cat or other animals might simply ignore the television scene, seemingly failing to recognize that anything meaningful or relevant is occurring. The latter behavior has been reported, for example, for language-trained common chimpanzees, who only learned to respond appropriately to television scenes after long periods of watching their human companions responding (Savage-Rumbaugh 1986).

In contrast, all four of our dolphins, on the very first occasion that they were exposed to television, responded spontaneously and appropriately to televised images of people gesturing to them (Herman *et al.* 1990). They responded in the same way as they did to live people, faithfully carrying out the gestural instructions conveyed by the image. ... The dolphins understood, however, that the television scene was not the real world. For example, if the trainer tossed a ball in the air and then gestured to the dolphin to imitate the action, the dolphin did not attempt to retrieve the ball in the television scene, but used one in its real world.

Self-awareness

Self-awareness is a multidimensioned concept that has usually been studied through the mirror self-recognition mark test (Gallup 1970). We chose to ask a different question about self-awareness: was a dolphin aware of its own recent behaviors (Mercado *et al.* 1998)? We taught the dolphin an abstract gesture, which we called "repeat." If this gesture occurred, it signaled the dolphin to do again what it just did: in essence to imitate its own behavior. A behavior was to be repeated only if that particular gesture was given. As an alternative to the repeat signal, some other gesture might be given that called for a behavior different from the one just executed. The demonstrated ability of the dolphin to reliably repeat or not repeat its previous behavior indicated that it maintained a mental representation of the behavior last performed and updated that as each new behavior was performed.

Conclusions

It seems clear that many of the studies we undertook would not have been possible, and many of the dolphin capabilities described would have gone unrevealed, without the implementation of the initial guiding educational philosophy. Immersion in a long-term program of intensive special education results in the accumulation of knowledge, concepts, rules, strategies, and a general level of intellectual sophistication that allows for the understanding and solution of a broad range of increasingly complex problems or tasks. Many of the later studies we carried out were not anticipated earlier (for example, interpretation of television scenes) because the groundwork was not yet in place, and the next step was not evident. The educational approach we used with the dolphin, a species with a life span stretching into the 40s or 50s, is not possible of course with short-lived species, but is applicable to such interesting species for cognitive investigation as elephants and the great apes. The work we have carried out with dolphins has expanded our understanding of the perceptual and cognitive world of this species, and certainly has demonstrated that the dolphin's reputation for intelligence is well earned.

Intelligence is of course a term with many definitions and interpretations, but I prefer to view it as flexibility of behavior (Herman and Pack 1994). By flexibility I mean the ability to organize and carry out behaviors that are appropriate to new situations, new contexts, or new events, and that are not necessarily genetically determined or part of the species' naturally occurring repertoire of behaviors. Flexibility is demonstrated then by the animal's ability to go beyond the boundaries of its naturally occurring behaviors or the context of its natural world.

Perhaps the most daunting task facing potential investigators of dolphin cognition is to find a place where such studies can take place. Facilities such as our Kewalo Basin Marine Mammal Laboratory in Honolulu are rare, and opportunities for research may be limited mainly to oceanaria or marine parks. At such places, however, the investigator may be constrained by the competing uses of the animals for demonstrations or display. This situation may be improving, though, as the benefits of research, its educational value, and even its display value come to be appreciated by the managers of these oceanaria and parks. Given the availability of facilities, and the access to animals, there is almost an unlimited opportunity for new discoveries about dolphin cognition. Topics such as theory of mind, social awareness, imitation, productive language, interanimal communication, and much more, are relatively unstudied and await only the investigator and the opportunity.

[. . .]

References

Fiez, J. A. (1996). Cerebellar contributions to cognition. *Neuron* 16: 13–15.

Gallup. G. G., Jr. (1970). Chimpanzees: Self-recognition. *Science* 167: 86–7.

Herman, L. M. (1986). Cognition and language competencies of bottlenosed dolphins. In *Dolphin Cognition and Behavior: A Comparative Approach*, R. J. Schusterman, J. Thomas, and F. G. Wood, (eds) pp. 221–51. Hillsdale, N.J.: Lawrence Erlbaum Associates.

Herman, L. M. and Forestell, P. H. (1985). Reporting presence or absence of named objects by a language-trained dolphin. *Neuroscience and Biobehavioral Reviews* 9: 667–91.

Herman, L. M. and Pack, A. A. (1994). Animal intelligence: Historical perspectives and contemporary approaches. In *Encyclopedia of Human Intelligence*, R. Sternberg, ed., pp. 86–96. New York: Macmillan.

Herman, L. M. and Uyeyama, R. K. (1999). The dolphin's grammatical competency: Comments on Kako (1998). *Animal Learning & Behavior* 27: 18–23.

Herman, L. M., Richards, D. G., and Wolz, J. P. (1984). Comprehension of sentences by bottlenosed dolphins. *Cognition* 16: 129–219.

Herman, L. M., Morrel-Samuels, P., and Pack, A. A. (1990). Bottlenosed dolphin and human recognition of veridical and degraded video displays of an artificial gestural language. *Journal of Experimental Psychology: General* 119: 215–30.

Herman, L. M., Kuczaj, S. III, and Holder, M. D. (1993). Responses to anomalous gestural sequences by a language-trained dolphin: Evidence for processing of semantic relations and syntactic information. *Journal of Experimental Psychology: General* 122: 184–94.

Herman, L. M., Abichandani, S. L., Elhajj, A. N., Herman, E. Y. K., Sanchez, J. L., and Pack, A. A. (1999). Dolphins (*Tursiops truncatus*) comprehend the referential character of the human pointing gesture. *Journal of Comparative Psychology* 113: 1–18.

Jerison, H. J. (1973). *Evolution of the Brain and Intelligence*. New York: Academic Press.

Leiner, H. C., Leiner, A. L., and Dow, R. S. (1995). The underestimated cerebellum. *Human Brain Mapping* 2: 244–54.

Marino, L. (1998). A comparison of encephalization levels between odontocete cetaceans and anthropoid primates. *Brain, Behavior and Evolution* 51: 230–38.

Marino, L., Rilling, J. K., Lin, S. K., and Ridgway, S. H. (2000) Relative volume of the cerebellum in dolphins and comparison with anthropoid apes. *Brain, Behavior and Evolution* 56: 204–11.

Mercado, E. III, Murray, S. O., Uyeyama, R. K., Pack, A. A., and Herman, L. M. (1998). Memory for recent actions in the bottlenosed dolphin (*Tursiops truncatus*): Repetition of arbitrary behaviors using an abstract rule. *Animal Learning & Behavior* 26: 210–18.

Pavio, A. and Begg, I. (1981). *Psychology of Language*. Englewood Cliffs, N.J.: Prentice-Hall.

Ridgway, S. H. (1990). The central nervous system of the bottlenose dolphin. In *The Bottlenose Dolphin*, S. Leatherwood and R. R. Reeves (eds), pp. 69–97. New York: Academic Press.

Ridgway, S. H. and Tarpley, R. J. (1996). Brain mass comparisons in Cetacea. In *Proceedings of the International Association of Aquatic Animal Medicine*, Vol. 2, pp. 55–7. Philadelphia: University of Pennsylvania Press.
Savage-Rumbaugh, E. S. (1986). *Ape Language: From Conditioned Response to Symbol*. New York: Columbia University Press.

26

Mary Midgley

"Is a Dolphin a Person?"

Midgley explores the question of personhood and addresses the question of whether dolphins might qualify. Midgley argues that what makes creatures our fellow beings entitled to basic consideration is not intellectual capacity, but emotional fellowship. Further weight is given to those creatures that can form deep, subtle, and lasting relationships. She notes that both apes and dolphins share this kind of social and emotional complexity. Finally, Midgley notes that the characteristics of these animals further supports their moral consideration in that they are highly sensitive social beings.

The undoubting judge

This question came up during the trial of the two people who, in May 1977, set free two bottle-nosed dolphins used for experimental purposes by the University of Hawaii's Institute of Marine Biology. It is an interesting question for a number of reasons, and I want to use most of this discussion in interpreting it, and tracing its connection with several others which may already be of concern to us. I shall not go into details of the actual case, but shall rely on the very clear and thoughtful account which Gavin Daws gives in his paper, ' "Animal Liberation" as Crime'.[1]

Kenneth le Vasseur, the first of the two men to be tried, attempted through his counsel what is called a 'choice of evils' defence. In principle the law allows this in cases where an act, otherwise objectionable, is necessary to avoid a greater evil. For this defence to succeed, the act has to be (as far as the defendant knows) the only way of avoiding an imminent, and more serious, harm or evil to himself or to 'another'.

Le Vasseur, who had been involved in the care of the dolphins, believed that their captivity, with the conditions then prevailing in it, actually endangered their lives. His counsel,

> in his opening statement for the defence, spoke of the exceptional nature of dolphins as animals; bad and rapidly deteriorating physical conditions at the laboratory; a punishing regimen for the dolphins, involving overwork, reductions in their food rations, the total isolation they endured, deprived of the company of other dolphins, even of contact with humans in the tank, deprived of all toys which they had formerly enjoyed playing with – to the point where Puka, having refused to take part consistently in experimental sessions, developed self-destructive behaviours symptomatic of deep disturbance, and

finally became lethargic – 'comatose.' Le Vasseur, seeing this, fearing that death would be the outcome, and knowing that there was no law that he could turn to, believed himself authorized, in the interests of the dolphins' well-being, to release them. The release was not a theft in that le Vasseur did not intend to gain anything for himself. It was intended to highlight conditions in the laboratory.

(Daws: 356–67)

But was a dolphin 'another'? The judge thought not. He said that 'another' would have to be another person, and he defined dolphins as property, not as persons, as a matter of law. A dolphin could not be 'another person' under the penal code. The defence tried and failed to get the judge disqualified for prejudice. It then asked leave to go to Federal Court in order to claim that Thirteenth Amendment rights in respect of involuntary servitude might be extended to dolphins. This plea the judge rejected:

Judge Doi said, 'We get to dolphins, we get to orangutans, chimpanzees, dogs, cats. I don't know at what level you say intelligence is insufficient to have that animal or thing, or whatever you want to call it, a human being under the penal code. I'm saying that they're not under the penal code and that's my answer.'

(Daws: 365)

At this point—which determined the whole outcome of the trial—something seemed perfectly obvious to the judge about the meaning of the words 'other' and 'person'. What was it? And how obvious is it to everybody else? In the answer just given, he raises the possibility that it might be a matter of intelligence, but he rejects it. That consideration, he says, is not needed. The question is quite a simple one; no tests are called for. The word 'person' just means a human being.

What are persons?

I think that this is a very natural view, but not actually a true one, and the complications which we find when we look into the use of this interesting word are instructive. In the first place, there are several well-established and indeed venerable precedents for calling non-human beings 'persons'.

One concerns the persons of the Trinity, and indeed the personhood of God. Another is the case of 'legal persons'—corporate bodies such as cities or colleges, which count as persons for various purposes, such as sueing and being sued. As Blackstone says, these 'corporations or bodies politic . . . are formed and created by human laws for the purposes of society and government'; unlike 'natural persons', who can only be created by God. The law, then, can if it chooses create persons; it is not a mere passive recorder of their presence (as indeed Judge Doi implied in making his ruling a matter of law and not of fact). Thirdly, what may look nearer to the dolphins, the word is used by zoologists to describe the individual members of a compound or colonial organism, such as a jellyfish or coral, each having (as the dictionary reasonably puts it) 'a more or less independent life'.[2]

There is nothing stretched or paradoxical about these uses, for the word does not in origin mean 'human being' or anything like it. It means a mask, and its basic general sense comes from the drama. The 'masks' in a play are the characters who appear in it. Thus, to quote the Oxford Dictionary again, after 'a mask', it means 'a character or personage acted, one who plays or performs any part, a character, relation or capacity in which one acts, a being having legal rights, a juridical person'.

[. . .]

I think it will be helpful here to follow out a little further the accepted lines of usage for the word person. How complete is its link with the human bodily form? What, for instance, about intelligent alien beings? Could we call them persons? If not, then contact with them—which is certainly conceivable—would surely require us to coin a new word to do the quite subtle moral job which is done at present by 'person'. The idea of a person in the almost technical sense required by morality today is the one worked out by Kant.[3] It is the idea of a rational being, capable of choice and therefore endowed with dignity, worthy of respect, having rights; one that must be regarded always as an end in itself, not only as a means to the ends of others.

Because this definition deals solely with rational qualities, it makes no mention of human form or human descent, and the spirit behind it would certainly not license us to exclude intelligent aliens, any more than disembodied spirits. The moral implications of the word 'person' would therefore, on our current Kantian principles, surely still have to attach to whatever word we might coin to include aliens. C.S. Lewis, describing a planet where there are three distinct rational species, has them use the word *hnau* for the condition which they all share, and this term is naturally central to the morality of all of them.[4]

Now if intelligence is really so important to the issue, a certain vertigo descends when we ask 'where do we draw the line?' because intelligence is a matter of degree. Some inhabitants of our own planet, including whales and dolphins, have turned out to be a lot brighter than was once thought. Quite how bright they are is not yet really clear to us. Indeed it may never become so, because of the difference in the kind of brightness appropriate to beings with very different sorts of life. How can we deal with such a situation?

[. . .]

When our civilization formed the views on the species barrier which it still largely holds, all the most highly-developed non-human animals were simply unknown. Legend apart, it was assumed that whales and dolphins were much like fish. The great apes were not even discovered till the eighteenth century and no real knowledge of their way of living was acquired until within the last few decades. About better-known creatures too, there was a very general ignorance and unthinking dismissal of available evidence; their sociality was not noticed or believed in. The central official intellectual tradition of our culture never expected to be forced to subtilize its crude, extreme, unshaded dichotomy between man and beast. In spite of the efforts of many concerned thinkers, from Plutarch to Montaigne and from Blake to John Stuart Mill, it did not develop other categories.

If alien beings landed tomorrow, lawyers, philosophers and social scientists would certainly have to do some very quick thinking. (I don't expect the aliens myself, but they are part of the imaginative furniture of our age, and it is legitimate to use them to rouse us from our dogmatic slumbers.) Science fiction, though sometimes helpful, has far too often side-tracked the problem by making its aliens just scientists with green antennae—beings whose 'intelligence' is of a kind to be instantly accepted at the Massachusetts Institute of Technology, only of course a little greater. Since neither dolphins nor gorillas write doctoral theses, this would still let us out as far as terrestrial non-human creatures were concerned. 'Persons' and their appropriate rights could still go on being defined in terms of this sort of intelligence, and we could quietly continue to poison pigeons in the park any time that we felt like it.

The question is, why should this kind of intelligence be so important, and determine the limits of our moral concern? It is often assumed that we can only owe duties to beings capable of speech. Why this should be thought is not altogether clear. At a simple level, Bentham surely got it right: 'The question is not *can they talk?* Nor *can they reason?* But *can they suffer?*'[5] With chimps, gorillas and dolphins, however, there is now a further problem, because people have been trying, apparently with some degree of success, to teach them certain kinds of language. This project might have taught us a great deal about just what new categories we need in our attempt to classify beings more subtly. But unluckily it has been largely obscured by furious opposition from people who still have just the two categories, and who see the whole proceeding as an illicit attempt to smuggle contraband from one to the other.

This reaction is extremely interesting. What is the threat? Articulate apes and cetaceans are scarcely likely to take over the government. What might happen, however, is that it would become much harder to exclude them from moral consideration. In particular, their use as experimental subjects might begin to look very different. Can the frontier be defended by a resolute and unbreakable refusal to admit that these animals can talk?

The meaning of fellowship

It is understandable that people have thought so, but this surely cannot really be the issue. What makes creatures our fellow-beings, entitled to basic consideration, is not intellectual capacity, but emotional fellowship. And if we ask what powers can give a higher claim, bringing some creatures nearer to the degree of consideration which is due to humans, what is most relevant seems to be sensibility, social and emotional complexity of the kind which is expressed by the forming of deep, subtle and lasting relationships. The gift of imitating certain intellectual skills which are important to humans is no doubt an indicator of this, but it cannot be central. We already know that both apes and dolphins have this kind of social and emotional complexity.

If we ask what elements in 'persons' are central in entitling them to moral consideration, we can, I think, get some light on the point by contrasting the claim of these sensitive social creatures with that of a computer of the present generation, programmed in a manner which entitles it, by current controversial usage, to be called 'intelligent' and certainly able to perform calculations impossible to human beings. That computer does not trouble our sleep with any moral claims, and would not do so however much more 'intelligent' it became, unless it eventually seemed to be conscious, sensitive and endowed with emotions.

If it did seem so, we should have the Frankenstein problem in an acute form. (The extraordinary eagerness with which Frankenstein drove his researches to this disastrous point is something which contemporary monster-makers might like to ponder.) But those who at present emphasize the intelligence of computers do not see any reason to want to call them persons, nor to allow for them as members of the moral community. Speech alone, then, would scarcely do this job for the apes. What is at issue is the already glaring fact, which speech would make it finally impossible to deny, that they mind what happens to them—that they are highly sensitive social beings.

These considerations are not, I think, ones confined to cranks or extremists. They seem fairly widespread today, and probably occur at times to all of us, however uncertain we may be what to do about them. If so, and if the law really allows them no possible weight, then we seem to have reached the situation where the law will have to be changed, because it shocks morality. There is an obvious precedent, to which the dolphin-liberators tried to appeal:

When the dolphins were taken from the tanks, a message was left behind identifying the releasers as the 'Undersea Railroad', a reference to the Underground Railroad, the Abolitionists' slave-freeing network of pre-Civil War days. Along the
Underground Railroad in the 1850s, it sometimes happened that juries refused to
convict people charged with smuggling slaves to freedom. That was the kind of
vindication le Vasseur and Sipman were looking for. . . . They did not consider
themselves to be criminals. In fact they took the view that, if there was a crime, it
was the crime of keeping dolphins—intelligent, highly aware creatures with no
criminal record of their own—in solitary confinement, in small, concrete tanks,
made to do repetitious experiments, for life.

(Daws: 362)

If we go back to the alien beings for a moment and consider whether even the most intelligent
of them would have the right to keep any visiting human beings, however stupid, in these
conditions, even those of us least partial to astronauts may begin to see point which le
Vasseur and Sipman were making. It surely cannot be dismissed merely by entrenching the
law round the definition of the word 'person'. We need new thinking, new concepts and new
words, not (of course) just about animals but about our whole relation to the non-human
world. We are not less capable of providing these than people were in the 1850s, so we
should get on with it.

Notes

1   Gavin Daws, ' "Animal Liberation" as Crime' in Harlan B. Miller and William H. Williams (eds), *Ethics and Animals* (Humana Press, Totowa, NJ, 1983).
2   It is also interesting that 'personal identity' is commonly held to belong to continuity of consciousness rather than of bodily form, in stories where the two diverge. Science fiction strongly supports this view, which was first mooted by John Locke, *Essay concerning Human Understanding*, bk 2, ch. 27, sect. 15.
3   See Immanuel Kant, *Foundations of the Metaphysic of Morals* (tr. Lewis White Beck, Bobbs-Merrill, 1959), sect. 428–32, p. 46. In the UK, a more available translation is that called *The Moral Law* (tr. H.J. Paton, Hutchinson, 1948), pp. 90–2.
4   C.S. Lewis, *Out of the Silent Planet* (London, John Lane, 1938).
5   Jeremy Bentham, *Introduction to the Principles of Morals and Legislation*, ch. 17.

Annotated Further Reading

Beck, B.B., Stoinski, T.S., Hutchins, M., Maple, T.L., Norton, B., Rowan, A., Stevens, E.F., and Arluk, A. (eds)
(2001) *Great Apes and Humans: The Ethics of Coexistence*, Washington, D.C. Smithsonian Institution
Press. Important, well-written articles.
Bickerton, D. (2000) "Resolving Discontinuity: A Minimalist Distinction between Human and Non-human
Minds." *American Zoologist* 40: 862–73.
Blum, D. (1995) *The Monkey Wars*, New York: Oxford University Press. Exploration of the controversial use
of primates in research based on Blum's 1992 Pulitzer Prize winning newspaper articles.
Bofysen, S.T. and Hallberg, K.I. (2000) "Primate Numerical Competence: Contributions Toward Under-
standing Nonhuman Cognition." *Cognitive Science* 24.3: 423–43. An historical overview of primate
numerical studies, illustrating complex cognitive skills including a concept of number.
Cavalieri, P. and Singer, P. (eds) (1994) *The Great Ape Project: Equality Beyond Humanity*. New York: St
Martin's Press. This book launched the Great Ape Project (GAP) as an international movement.
—— (eds) (1996) "The Great Ape Project." *Etica and Animali* 8: 1–178. An issue dedicated to developing the
view that nonhuman great apes should have the same basic rights as human beings.
Chimpanzee cultures website: http://chimp.st-and.ac.uk/cultures/ (accessed 12 October 2002).

Coetzee, J.M. (1999) *The Lives of Animals*, Princeton, N.J.: Princeton University Press. A literary, post-modern approach to the question of animal lives.

De Waal, F. (1995) "Bonobo Sex and Society." *Scientific American* 274: 82–8. Well-written account by a prominent researcher.

—— (1996) *Good Natured*, Cambridge, Mass.: Harvard University Press. The beginnings of morality are found in nonhuman primate societies.

—— (2001) *The Ape and the Sushi Master: Cultural Reflections by a Primatologist*, New York: Basic Books. Enjoyable book for the general reader by a central figure in the study of chimpanzees and bonobos.

Fouts, R. (with Mills, S.T.) (1997) *Next of Kin: What Chimpanzees Have Taught Me About Who We Are*, New York: William Morrow. Fouts taught American Sign Language to Washoe, the first chimpanzee to communicate with humans by this means.

Galdikas, B.M.F. and Shapiro, G.L. (1996) "Orangutan Ethics." *Etica & Animalia* 8: 50–67. Fascinating account of wild orangutans.

Great Ape Project website: http://www.greatapeproject.org (accessed 12 October 2002).

Hauser, M.D., Kralik, J., Botto-Manan, C., Garrett, M., and Oser, J. (1995) "Self-recognition in Primates: Phylogeny and the Salience of Species-typical Features." *Proceedings of the National Academy of Science*, USA 92: 10811–14.

Kalin, N.H. (2002) "The Neurobiology of Fear." *Scientific American Special* 12: 77–81. Researchers are identifying the neurochemical mechanisms that give rise to various fears in monkeys.

Matsuzawa, T. (2002) "Chimpanzee Ai and her son Ayumu: An Episode of Education by Master-apprenticeship." In *The Cognitive Animal: Empirical and Theoretical Perspectives on Animal Cognition*, M. Bekoff, C. Allen, and G.M. Burghardt (eds), Cambridge, Mass.: The MIT Press.

—— (ed.) (2001) *Primate Origins of Human Cognition and Behavior*. Tokyo, Japan: Spring. A Japanese view of primates, primate culture, primate science, and the cognitive capacities of chimpanzees and macaques.

National Research Council. (1997) *Chimpanzees in Research: Strategies for Their Ethical Care, Management, and Use*. Washington, D.C.: National Academy Press. Recommendations include a five-year breeding moratorium, not endorsing euthanasia for population control, and assuring lifetime support for the core population of chimpanzees.

—— (1998) *The Psychological Well-being of Nonhuman Primates*, Washington, D.C.: National Academy of Sciences.

New Zealand Animal Welfare Act. (1999) http://rangi.knowledge-basket.co.nz/gpacts/public/text/1999/an/142.html (accessed 12 October 2002). First act to give specific legal protection for nonhuman great apes.

Povinelli, D.J., Bering J.M., and Giambrone, S. (2000) "Toward a Science of Other Minds: Escaping the Argument by Analogy." *Cognitive Science* 24(3): 509–41. Chimpanzees do not reason about seeing or about other mental states.

Savage-Rumbaugh, S. and Brakke, K.E. (1996) "Animal Language: Methodological and Interpretive Issues." Chapter 18, pp. 269–88. In *Readings in Animal Cognition*, Bekoff, M. and Jamieson, D. (eds), Cambridge, Mass.: The MIT Press. Language in 11 apes of the Language Research Center at George State and Yerkes Primate Research Center of Emory University.

Savage-Rumbaugh, S., Fields, W.M., and Taglialatela, J.P. (2001) "Language, Speech, Tools and Writing." *Journal of Consciousness Studies* 8(5–7): 273–92.

Schueller, G.H. (2000) "Hey! Good looking." *New Scientist* 17, June 30–34. Discussion of mirror studies as evidence of self-awareness.

Shumaker, R.W. and Swartz, K.B. (2002) "When Traditional Methodologies Fail: Cognitive Studies of Great Apes." In *The Cognitive Animal: Empirical and Theoretical Perspectives on Animal Cognition*, M. Bekoff, C. Allen, and G.M. Burghardt (eds), Cambridge, Mass.: The MIT Press.

Seyfarth, R.M. and Cheney, D.L. (2000) "Social Awareness in Monkeys." *American Zoologist* 40: 902–9.

Tomasello, M. (2000) "Primate Cognition: Introduction to the Issue." *Cognitive Science* 24(3): 351–61. Argues that human cognition is unique due to its collective nature.

Tyack, P.L. (2000) "Dolphins Whistle a Signature Tune." *Science* 289: 1310–11.

Whiten, A. (2000) "Primate Culture and Social Learning," *Cognitive Science* 24(3): 455–8. Focus on imitation and emulation.

Whiten, A. and Boesch, C. (2001) "The Cultures of Chimpanzees." *Scientific American* 280.1: 60–7. Useful summary.

Wild Chimpanzee Foundation website: http://www.wildchimps.org (accessed 12 October 2002).

Study Questions

1   In your view, is it more important to study animals at the species level or on an individual basis? Explain the reasons for your answer.

2   Do you agree with Marc Bekoff that we should not base our moral treatment of animals on their cognitive abilities?

3   In your view, are apes or dolphins persons? What definition of "person" are you using? Explain why your definition should be adopted.

4   Is the information concerning culture in chimpanzees and in whales and dolphins important for your view of the moral status of these animals? Explain your answer.

5   Should the information concerning consciousness and self-awareness in bonobos presented by Savage-Rumbaugh and her co-workers be taken into account in our treatment of bonobos? If so, in what ways?

PART IV

Animals for Food

Introduction

The use of animals for food is a highly charged topic for many people. For some the emotional lives of animals are reason enough not to eat them. Researcher Françoise Wemelsfelder provides a poignant description of a young female pig in a small barren pen, whose behavior expressed quiet emptiness and despair.

For those who do eat animals, accurate information on how animals for food are raised and slaughtered is important for an informed moral judgment. David DeGrazia describes the conditions of pigs, chickens, and cattle in modern factory farms, which now supply most of the meat and dairy products in the U.S., Great Britain, and most other industrial countries. He argues that factory farming causes more harm to animals than any other human practice.

Temple Grandin has designed 30 percent of the livestock-handling facilities in the U.S. She affirms that we owe animals a decent life and a painless death. Her essay "Thinking like Animals" explains how her life as a person with autism has enabled her to better understand animal emotions. She has found that cattle are sensitive to the same things that disturb people with autism, and has designed restraint chutes for holding cattle for slaughter with the emotional needs of cattle in mind. In "A Major Change" she describes the improvements made in the handling and stunning of animals between 1997 and 1999, the importance of proper transport of cattle and pigs, and the promotion of better stockmanship.

In "Animal Agriculture: Myths and Facts" the Animal Agricultural Alliance presents the view of food producers. The Alliance points out that a very high percentage of U.S. farms are family-owned and operated. The proper housing of animals protects their health and welfare and is scientifically designed for the specific needs of the animal. The Alliance states that all forms of restraint are designed for the welfare of the animal as well as efficiency of production.

Two of the authors in this Part argue for vegetarianism. William O. Stephens describes five different arguments that, taken as a whole, provide a persuasive case for the view that vegetarianism is a morally good practice. In "The Rape of Animals, the Butchering of Women," Carol J. Adams argues that both women and animals are "absent referents," made absent through language and metaphor, and also, in the case of animals, through death. Patriarchal culture transforms women and animals into commodities to be used and consumed.

Kathryn Paxton George presents a feminist critique of ethical vegetarianism in which she points out that the arguments provided by Regan, Singer, and Adams are discriminatory, applying only to most men and some women age 20–50 in industrialized countries. George advocates "feminist aesthetic semivegetarianism," which permits everyone to eat a certain small amount of meat, dairy products, and other animal products as long as animals are well treated and killed as painlessly as possible.

The final five essays in this Part concern the doctrines of some of the world religions with regard to the slaughter and eating of animals. Norman Solomon explains the Jewish tradition. While the Torah does not require vegetarianism, it does demand that one not practice cruelty to animals. Also, the Torah places restraints on which animals may be eaten and on the method of slaughter. In "Enhancing the Divine Image" Rabbi Fuchs explains how his decision to become a vegetarian was based on his understanding of the early chapters of Genesis. The Rev. Andrew Linzey argues for vegetarianism from a Christian perspective, based on his reading of Genesis as well as other books of the Bible.

Martin Forward and Mohamed Alam explain the Islamic view of animals. Few Muslims are vegetarians, but certain animals are forbidden to Muslims, and all creatures used for food must be killed in a prescribed manner. Michael W. Fox describes the situation in India, which has the largest concentration of livestock in the world, many of whom are malnourished or starving. While both Muslims and Hindus oppose the modernization of slaughtering facilities, Fox argues for modernization on the basis of animal welfare.

Animals for Food

27

David DeGrazia

"Meat-Eating"

David DeGrazia describes the conditions endured by chickens, pigs, and cows during their lives and deaths as part of the factory farming system in the U.S., Great Britain, and most other industrialized countries. American farm animals have virtually no legal protection. DeGrazia argues that consumers are morally obliged to make a reasonable effort to not provide financial support to institutions that cause extensive unnecessary suffering.

Hen X begins life in a crowded incubator. She is taken to a 'battery' cage made entirely of wire—and quite unlike the outdoor conditions that are natural for her—where she will live her life. (Having no commercial value, male chicks are gassed, ground up alive, or suffocated.) Hen X's cage is so crowded that she cannot fully stretch her wings. Although her beak is important for feeding, exploring, and preening, part of it has been cut off, through sensitive tissue, in order to limit the damage caused by pecking cage mates—a behaviour induced by overcrowding. For hours before laying an egg, Hen X paces anxiously among the crowd, instinctively seeking a nest that she will not find. At egg-laying time, she stands on a sloped, uncomfortable wire floor that precludes such instinctual behaviours as pecking for food, dust bathing, and scratching. Lack of exercise, unnatural conditions, and demands for extreme productivity—she will lay 250 eggs this year—cause bone weakness. (Unlike many hens, Hen X is not subjected to forced moulting, in which water is withheld for one to three days and food for up to two weeks in order to extend hens' productive lives.) When considered spent at age two, she is jammed into a crate and transported in a truck—without food, water, or protection from the elements—to a slaughterhouse; rough handling causes several weak bones to break. At her destination, Hen X is shackled upside down on a conveyor belt before an automated knife slices her throat. Because the (US) Humane Slaughter Act does not apply to poultry, she is fully conscious throughout this process. Her body, which was extensively damaged during her lifetime, is suitable only for pot pies, soup, and the like.

After weaning at four weeks of age, Hog Y is taken to a very crowded, stacked nursery cage. Due to poor ventilation, he breathes in powerful fumes from urine and faeces. Upon reaching a weight of 50 pounds, he is taken to a tiny 'finishing' pen. It is slatted and has a concrete floor with no straw bedding or sources of amusement. Despite being a member of a highly intelligent and social species, Hog Y is separated from other hogs by iron bars and has nothing to do except get up, lie down, eat, and sleep. He sometimes amuses himself by biting a tail in the next crate—until all the hogs' tails are 'docked' (cut off). Both this procedure and castration are performed without anaesthesia. When he is deemed ready for slaughter, Hog Y is roughly herded into a truck with thirty other hogs. The two-day journey is not pleasant for Hog Y, who gets in fights with other hogs while receiving no food, water, rest, or protection from the summer heat. At the slaughterhouse, Hog Y smells blood and resists prodding from the human handlers. They respond by kicking him and smashing him repeatedly from behind with an iron pipe until he is on the restraining conveyor belt that carries him to the stunner. Hog Y is fortunate in so far as the electric stunning procedure is successful, killing him before his body is dropped in scalding water and dismembered. (Although the Humane Slaughter Act requires that animals other than poultry be rendered unconscious with a single application of an effective stunning device before being shackled, hoisted upside down, and dismembered, many slaughterhouse employees state that violations occur regularly. Fearing that a higher voltage might cause 'bloodsplash' in some carcasses, many slaughterhouse supervisors apparently encourage use of a voltage that is much too low to ensure unconsciousness. Moreover, in numerous slaughterhouses stunners have to stun an animal every few seconds and face extreme pressure not to stop the line of animals.)

Although it is natural for cows and their calves to bond strongly, Cow (then Calf) Z is taken from her mother shortly after birth to begin life as a dairy cow. She never receives colostrum—her mother's milk—which would help her fight disease. She lives in a very crowded 'drylot', which is devoid of grass, and her tail is docked without anaesthesia. In order to produce twenty times more milk than a calf would need, she receives a diet heavy in grain—not the roughage that cows have evolved to digest easily—causing metabolic disorders and painful lameness. And like many dairy cows, she often has mastitis, a painful udder inflammation, despite receiving antibiotics between lactations. To maintain continuous milk production, Cow Z is induced to bear one calf each year. To stimulate additional growth and productivity, she receives daily injections of bovine growth hormone. Her natural life span is twenty or more years, but at age 4 she can no longer maintain production levels and is deemed 'spent'. During transport and handling, Cow Z is fortunate: although deprived of food, water, and rest for over two days, and frightened when prodded, she is not beaten; at the slaughterhouse her instincts—unlike hogs'—allow her to walk easily in a single-file chute. Unfortunately, the poorly trained stun operator has difficulty with the air-powered knocking gun. Although he stuns Cow Z four times, she stands up and bellows. The line does not stop, however, so she is hoisted up on the overhead rail and transported to the 'sticker', who cuts her throat to bleed her out. She remains conscious as she bleeds and experiences some of the dismemberment and skinning process alive. (The federal inspector cannot see what is happening where he is stationed; besides, he's frenetically checking carcasses that whiz by, for obvious signs of contamination.) Cow Z's body will be used for processed beef or hamburger.

The institution of factory farming

The animals portrayed above offer examples of life in modern factory farms, which now supply most of our meat and dairy products in the USA, Great Britain, and most other industrial countries. Since the Second World War, factory farms—which try to raise as many animals as possible in very limited space in order to maximize profits—have driven three million American family farms out of business; over the same time period, Great Britain and other nations have witnessed similar transformations in their agricultural sectors. Scientific developments that have fuelled the emergence of factory farming include the artificial provision of vitamin D (which otherwise requires sunlight for its synthesis), the success of antibiotics in minimizing the spread of certain diseases, and advanced methods of genetic selection for production traits. Since the driving force behind this institution is economic efficiency, factory farming treats animals simply as means to this end—as mere objects with no independent moral importance, or moral status, whatever.

Considering both numbers of animals involved and the extent to which they are harmed, *factory farming causes more harm to animals than does any other human institution or practice*. In the USA alone, this institution kills over 100 million mammals and five billion birds annually. American farm animals have virtually no legal protections. The most important applicable federal legislation is the Humane Slaughter Act, which does not cover poultry—most of the animals consumed—and has no bearing on living conditions, transport, or handling. Moreover, as Gail Eisnitz and others have extensively documented, the Act is rarely enforced. Apparently, the US Department of Agriculture supports the major goal of agribusiness: absolute maximization of profit without hindrance. This is not surprising when one considers that, since the 1980s, most top officials at USDA either have been agribusiness leaders themselves or have had close political and financial ties to the industry.

By contrast, European nations have curbed some of the excesses typified by American factory farming. For example, Great Britain has banned veal crates and limits to fifteen hours the amount of time animals can go without food and water during transport. The European Community and the Council of Europe have developed requirements for the well-being of farm animals that are translated into law in different member nations. These requirements generally provide animals with more space, greater freedom to engage in species-typical behaviours, and more humane living conditions than those of farm animals in the USA. Despite the more humane conditions that are typical in Europe, however, most European animal husbandry remains sufficiently intensive to merit the term 'factory farming'.

So far this discussion has provided a descriptive sense of factory farms primarily through three cases. Therefore it might be objected that the situations of Hen X, Hog Y, and Cow Z do not represent universal features of factory farming. That is correct. But the experiences of these three animals, the evidence suggests, are not atypical—at least in the USA. Still, while a thorough description of factory farms is impossible here, it may be helpful to add a few general remarks about other types of farm animals. The following generalizations are meant to describe the American situation, although some of them accurately describe the experiences of animals in many other countries as well.

Cattle raised specifically for beef are generally better off than the other animals described here. Many have the opportunity to roam outdoors for about six months. After that, they are transported long distances to feedlots, where they are fed grain rather than grass. Major sources of pain or distress include constant exposure to the elements, branding, dehorning, unanaesthetized castration, the cutting of ears for identification purposes, and a sterile, unchanging environment. We may add, of course, the harms associated with transportation to the slaughterhouse and what takes place therein.

Broiler chickens spend their lives in enclosed sheds that become increasingly crowded as tens of thousands of birds grow at an abnormally fast rate. Besides extreme crowding, major sources of concern include cannibalism, suffocation due to panic-driven piling on top of one another, debeaking, and very unhealthful breathing conditions produced by never-cleaned droppings and poor ventilation. Veal calves' deprivations are similar to many of those that hogs experience. Formula-fed veal calves in particular live in solitary crates too small to permit them to turn around or sleep in a natural position. Denied water and solid food, they drink a liquid milk replacer deficient in iron—making possible the gourmet white flesh and resulting in anaemia. This diet and solitary confinement lead to numerous health problems and neurotic behaviours.

Let us now consider the overall picture: *factory farming routinely causes animals massive harm in the form of suffering, confinement, and death*. Regarding suffering—or experiential harm in general—all evidence suggests that factory farm animals, in the course of their lives, typically experience considerable pain, discomfort, boredom, fear, anxiety, and possibly other unpleasant feelings. Furthermore, factory farms by their very nature *confine* animals in our stipulated sense of the term; that is, they impose external constraints on movement that significantly interfere with living well. (For at least part of their lives, cattle raised specifically for beef are not confined in this sense.) And, of course, factory farming ultimately kills animals raised for meat, adding the harm of death—assuming (. . .) that death harms such beings as cows, pigs, and chickens. Then again, death counts as a harm here only if we consider the sorts of lives these animals *could* have under humane treatment. Given animals' current treatment, death would seem to be a blessing, except possibly in the case of beef cattle. In any event, the general thesis that factory farms cause massive harm to animals is undeniable.

Moral evaluation

If the first crucial insight in a moral evaluation of factory farms is that they cause massive harm to animals, the second crucial insight is this: *consumers do not need the products of factory farms*. We cannot plausibly regard any of the harms caused to these animals as *necessary*. Unusual circumstances aside—say, where one is starving and lacks alternatives— we do not need to eat meat to survive or even to be healthy. The chief benefits of meat-eating to consumers are *pleasure*, since meat tastes especially good to many people, and *convenience*, since switching to and maintaining a vegetarian diet requires some effort. Putting the two key insights together brings us to the conclusion that *factory farms cause massive unnecessary harm*. Since causing massive unnecessary harm is wrong if *anything* is wrong, the judgement that factory farming is an indefensible institution seems inescapable.

Note that this condemnation of factory farming does not depend on the controversial assumption that animals deserve equal consideration. Even if one accepts a sliding-scale model of moral status, which justifies less-than-equal consideration for animals, one cannot plausibly defend the causing of massive unnecessary harm. Thus, it appears that if one takes animals at all seriously—regarding them as beings with at least some moral status—one must find factory farming indefensible.

But what about the consumer? She isn't harming animals; she's just eating the products of factory farming. Well, imagine someone who says, 'I'm not kicking dogs to death. I'm just paying someone else to do it.' We would judge this person to act wrongly for encouraging and commissioning acts of cruelty. Similarly, while meat-eaters may typically feel distant from meat production, and may never even think about what goes on in factory farms and slaughterhouses, the purchase of factory-farmed meat directly encourages and makes possible the associated cruelties—so the consumer is significantly responsible. In general, the following moral rule, although somewhat vague, is defensible: *make every reasonable effort not to provide financial support to institutions that cause extensive unnecessary harm*.

By financially supporting massive unnecessary harm, the purchase of factory-farmed meat violates this principle and is therefore, I argue, morally indefensible. Interestingly, we reached this important conclusion without commitment to any specific ethical theory such as utilitarianism or a strong animal-rights view. In any event, while our case against factory farming and buying its products has so far cited considerations of animal welfare, it is further strengthened by considerations of human welfare. How so?

First, animal products—which are high in fat and protein and contain cholesterol—are associated with higher levels of heart disease, obesity, stroke, osteoporosis, diabetes, and certain cancers. Medical authorities now recommend much less meat and more grains, fruits, and vegetables than Americans, for example, typically consume. Second, American factory farming has driven three million family farms out of business since the Second World War, as huge agribusinesses, enjoying billions of dollars in annual government subsidies, have increasingly dominated; while American consumers frequently hear that factory farming lowers meat prices at the cash register, they are rarely reminded of the hidden cost of tax subsidies. In Britain and many other countries, relatively few large agribusinesses have similarly come to dominate, putting many smaller farms out of business. Third, factory farming is devastating for the environment. It excessively consumes energy, soil, and water while causing erosion of topsoil, destruction of wildlife habitat, deforestation, and water pollution from manure, pesticides, and other chemicals. Fourth, factory farming has a perverse effect on the distribution of food to humans. For example, it takes about 8 pounds of protein in hog feed to generate 1 pound of pork for humans and 21 pounds of protein in calf feed to yield 1 pound of beef. Consequently, most US-produced grain, for example, goes to livestock. Unfortunately, wealthy countries' demand for meat makes plant proteins too costly for the masses in the poorest countries. Poor communities often abandon sustainable farming practices to export cash crops and meat, but profits are short-lived as marginal lands erode, causing poverty and malnutrition. There is, in fact, easily enough grain protein, if used sensibly, to feed every human on Earth. Fifth, perhaps especially in the USA, factory farming is cruel to its employees. It subjects them to extreme work pressures—as seen in a worker who cuts up to ninety chickens per minute, or urinates on the workline for fear of leaving it— and to some of the worst health hazards faced by any American workers (for example, skin diseases, respiratory problems, crippling hand and arm injuries, injury from wild, improperly stunned animals)—all for low pay. Finally, deregulation of the American meat industry since the 1980s, combined with extremely fast production lines, have made it virtually impossible to ensure safe meat. . . .

Thus, receiving further support from considerations of human welfare, the case for boycotting factory farm products is extremely powerful. But let us not ignore the following important objection. One might argue that the continuation of factory farming is economically necessary. Putting this industry out of business—say, through a successful boycott— would obviously be devastating for agribusiness owners, but would also eliminate many jobs and possibly harm local economies. These consequences, the argument continues, are unacceptable. Thus, just as factory farming is necessary, so is the extensive harm it inevitably causes to animals—contrary to my charge of massive *unnecessary* harm.

In reply, we may accept the factual assumption about likely consequences while rejecting the claim that they are unacceptable. First, as Peter Singer notes, the negative costs of ending factory farming would have to be borne only once, whereas perpetuating this institution entails that the costs to animals continue indefinitely. Also, considering how badly factory farm employees are treated, it is hard to believe they would be seriously harmed by having to seek alternative employment, as innumerable 'burnt out' employees do anyway. More generally, the various threats to human well-being posed by factory farming—health risks, environmental destruction, inefficient use and perverse distribution of grain proteins, etc.—could be avoided if this industry is eliminated (assuming it is not simply replaced by less intensive animal husbandry, which would perpetuate some of these problems). Avoiding these risks and harms, not once but indefinitely, would seem to counterbalance any short-term economic harm. Finally, I submit that *there are moral limits to what we may do to others in the pursuit of profit or employment—and causing sentient beings massive harm in pursuing these goals oversteps those bounds.* (Cases in which people are forced into prostitution, pornography, or slavery vividly exemplify the violation of such limits.) If that is correct, then factory farming cannot be considered necessary. In conclusion, I suggest that these rebuttals, taken together, undercut the argument from economic necessity.

Traditional family farming

This chapter has focused on factory farms because most of the animal products we consume come from this source. But people also eat animals from other sources, including traditional family farms.

Because they involve far less intensive rearing conditions, family farms cause much less suffering to animals than factory farms do. Family farms may not even confine animals in our sense of imposing constraints on movement that significantly interfere with living well. But, . . . farm animals cannot fully escape harm because they are ultimately killed, entailing the harm of death.

Causing much less harm to animals, and avoiding at least some threats that factory farming poses to human well-being (for example, water pollution, extremely hazardous working conditions), family farming is much more defensible than its dominant competitor. Still, there is a strong moral case against family farming and the practice of buying its products. For one thing, this institution does impose some significant suffering through certain practices: branding and dehorning cattle; castrating cattle and hogs; separating mothers from offspring, which may well cause distress even to birds; and treating animals roughly in transport, handling, and slaughter. And, again, all the animals die. Since meat-eating is—unusual circumstances aside—unnecessary, these harms are unnecessary. It is difficult to defend the routine imposition of unnecessary harm.

A few possible replies, however, may strengthen the case for some forms of family farming. For example, chickens and turkeys can escape most of the harms just described. If a chicken or turkey is able to live a pleasant life—say, with family intact—and is never abused, the only relevant harm would be death.

[. . .]

Alternatively, if one (unlike the present author) accepts the sliding-scale model of moral status, one would grant unequal moral weight to the interests—including the avoidance of suffering—of different beings depending on their cognitive, emotional, and social complexity. Perhaps proponents of this ethical framework would defend practices of family farming that keep the admittedly unnecessary suffering to a minimum. They might argue that it is not always wrong to cause *minimal* unnecessary harm, even to mammals, especially if there are some significant benefits such as employment for farmers. Then again, one would need to consider negative effects on human welfare, such as extremely inefficient use of grain protein, in assessing the plausibility of this line of argument.

Seafood

Much of the meat we consume comes from the sea. Beginning with fish and cephalopods (octopuses and squid), we concluded [in an earlier chapter] that these creatures are sentient, subject to pain and distress; we left somewhat more open whether they can experience suffering in the specific sense: a highly unpleasant emotional state associated with more-than-minimal pain or distress. Now catching fish and cephalopods requires hooking or netting them and causing them to suffocate. Clearly, they experience unpleasant feelings in the process. While traditional fishing methods do not involve confinement—since the animals are at liberty in their natural environment—death is obviously unavoidable. Death harms such creatures to *some degree* on the opportunities-based account of the harm of death, but not on the desire-based view.

There are several ways in which one might argue that fish and cephalopods are harmed only minimally: by claiming that any suffering is very brief; by denying that they suffer at all; or by arguing that the harm of death in their case is negligible to non-existent. Then one might argue that this minimal harm is adequately counterbalanced by certain benefits to humans: pleasure, convenience, rounding out a healthful diet, and employment for fishers. (One who believes that animals have rights in the strongest, utility-trumping sense would reject such reasoning, however.) Naturally, a proponent of the sliding-scale model of moral status will find the production and consumption of seafood easier to defend, since fish and cephalopods would be relatively low in the moral hierarchy.

One complicating factor in our analysis is that many fish today are raised in fish farms. These are so crowded that they amount to confinement and increase the unpleasantness of the fishes' lives. When fish are raised in this way, the case for boycotting these products is stronger.

What about lobsters, crabs, shrimp, and other invertebrates other than cephalopods? Available evidence leaves open the issue of their possible sentience. If they are not sentient, our actions cannot harm them. People might reasonably disagree about whether, in this state of uncertainty, we should give them the benefit of the doubt and assume they are sentient.

As we think about the issue of eating seafood, we must not ignore any harms caused to creatures other than those consumed. For example, suppose you buy tuna fish from a company whose nets often ensnare and kill dolphins—whose cognitive, emotional, and social complexity rivals that of Great Apes. The harms thereby caused to dolphins might make the purchase of tuna from this company as serious a moral matter as buying meat from factory farms.

28

Temple Grandin

"Thinking like Animals"

Temple Grandin describes the similarities between autistic emotion and animal emotion, and explains how she has designed chute systems for handling cattle in slaughter plants to keep cattle calm. She also discusses how important the attitude of the handler is and the growing role of women in slaughter plants. Grandin affirms that life and death are inseparable, and that it is important to accept our own mortality.

Language-based thought is foreign to me. All my thoughts are full-color motion pictures, running like a videotape in my imagination. It was always obvious to me that cattle and other animals also think in pictures. I have learned that there are some people who mainly think in words and I have observed that these verbal thinkers are more likely to deny animals' thought; they are unable to imagine thought without words. Using my visual thinking skills, it is easy for me to imagine myself in an animal's body and see things from their perspective. It is the ultimate virtual reality system. I can imagine looking through their eyes or walking with four legs.

My life as a person with autism is like being another species: part human and part animal. Autistic emotion may be more like an animal's. Fear is the dominant emotion in both autistic people and animals such as deer, cattle, and horses. My emotions are simple and straightforward like an animal's, my emotions are not deep-seated. They may be intense while I am experiencing them but they will subside like an afternoon thunderstorm.

For the last fifteen years I have designed chute systems for handling cattle in slaughter plants. The conveyorized restraint system I designed is used in slaughtering one third of all the cattle in the United States.

Cattle are not afraid of the same things that people fear. The problem is that many people cannot observe this because they allow their own emotions to get in the way. To design a humane system I had to imagine what it would be like if I were the animal. I had to become that animal and not just be a person in a cow costume.

Cattle and people are upset by different things. People are repulsed by the sight of blood, but blood does not bother cattle. They are wary of the things that spell danger in the wild, such as high-pitched noise, disturbances of the dirt, and sudden jerky movements. A high-pitched noise may be a distress cry, and dirt or grass that is displaced may mean that there has been a struggle to avoid being eaten. Abrupt motion may be associated with a predator leaping onto its prey. These are all danger signals.

Many times I have observed cattle balking and refusing to move through a chute at a slaughter plant. They may balk at a jiggling gate, a shadow, a shiny reflection, or anything that appears to be out of place. A coffee cup dropped on the floor can make the cattle stop and turn back. But cattle will walk quietly into a slaughterhouse if the things they are afraid of are eliminated. Solid sides on chutes prevent them from seeing people up ahead and muffling devices lessen the shrill sounds that alarm them.

Cattle are sensitive to the same things that disturb people with autism. Immature development in the lower brain systems causes some people with autism to have a heightened sense of hearing, and an intense fear is triggered when anything in their environment is out of place. A curled-up rug, or a book that is crooked on the shelf, causes the same fear as being stalked by a predator. The autistic brain is acutely aware of details that most other people ignore. Sudden high-pitched sounds in the middle of the night cause my heart to race as if a lion was going to pounce.

Like a wild animal, I recoil when people touch me. A light touch sets off a flight reaction and my oversensitive nerve endings do not tolerate hugging. I want the soothing feeling of being held, but the sensations can be too overwhelming, so I pull away. My need for touch started my interest in cattle.

Puberty began the onslaught of hormones that sensitized my nervous system and started the constant fear and anxiety. I was desperate for relief. At my aunt's ranch I observed that when cattle were placed in a squeeze chute for their vaccinations, the pressure from the side panels squeezing against their bodies relaxed them. Pressure over wide areas of the body has a calming effect on many animals. Pressure applied to the sides of a piglet will cause it to fall asleep. Firm touch has a calming effect, while a light tickle touch is likely to set off a flight reaction.

Many parents of autistic children have observed that their child will seek pressure by getting under sofa cushions or a mattress. Therapists often use deep pressure to calm autistic children. I decided to try the squeeze chute and discovered that the intense pressure temporarily made my anxiety go away. When I returned home from the ranch I built a squeezing machine. Early versions pressed against my body with hard wood. When I first started using the machine I flinched and pulled away from it like a wild animal. As I adjusted to being held I used less intense pressure and I remodeled the side panels with foam rubber padding to make the machine more comfortable.

As I became able to tolerate being held I became more interested in figuring out how the cattle felt when they were handled and held in squeeze chutes at the feed yards. Many of the animals were scared because people were rough with them. They chased them, yelled at them, and prodded them. I found that I could coax most cattle to walk through a chute to be vaccinated by moving them quietly, at a slow walk. When an animal was calm I could observe the things that would catch his eye, like shadows or people leaning over the top of the chute. The leader would look at the things that concerned him. He would stop and stare at a coffee cup on the floor or move his head back and forth in time with a small chain that was swinging in the chute. Before moving forward he had to carefully scrutinize the things that attracted his attention. If the handlers tried to force him to move before he had determined that the chain was harmless, he and all the other cattle would panic. Cattle moved quietly and quickly through the chutes as soon as the swinging chain was removed.

I found that the animals were less likely to resist being held by the squeeze chute if pressure was applied slowly. An animal would panic if suddenly bumped. I also discovered the concept of optimum pressure. The chute must apply sufficient pressure to provide the feeling of being held but not cause pain. Many people make the mistake of mashing an animal too tight when it struggles. And the chute always needs solid sides, so that the cattle do not see people deep inside their flight zone. The flight zone is the animal's safety zone. They become anxious and want to get away when people get too close.

Years later, when I designed a restraint chute for holding cattle for slaughter, I was amazed that the animals would stand still and seldom resist the chute. I found that I could just ease their head and body into position by adjusting the chute. When I got really skilled at operating the hydraulic controls, the apparatus became an extension of my arms and hands. It was as if I could reach through the machine and hold each animal very gently. It was my job to hold the animal gently while the rabbi performed the final deed.

During the last ten years, more and more women have been hired to handle cattle and operate chutes in both feed yards and slaughter plants. At first the men were skeptical that women could do the work, but today progressive managers have found that women are gentler and work well with the animals. Some feed yards now hire only women to doctor sick cattle and vaccinate the new arrivals. In slaughter plants, two of the best operators of kosher restraining chutes are women. They were attracted to the job because they couldn't stand to see the guys abusing cattle.

When I first started designing equipment I thought that all the problems of the rough treatment of animals in slaughter plants could be solved with engineering. But engineering is only part of the equation. The most important thing is the attitude of management. A strong manager acts as the conscience of the employees in the trenches. To be most effective in maintaining high standards of animal treatment the manager has to be involved enough to care, but not so much that he or she overdoses on the constant death. The managers who are most likely to care and enforce humane handling are most likely to have close associations with animals, or are close to the land.

I am often asked how I can care about animals and be involved in their slaughter. People forget that nature can be harsh. Death at the slaughter plant is quicker and less painful than death in the wild. Lions dining on the guts of a live animal is much worse in my opinion. The animals we raise for food would have never lived at all if we had not raised them. I feel that our relationship with animals must be symbiotic. In nature there are many examples of symbiosis. For example, ants raise aphids and use them as "dairy cows." The ants feed the aphids and in return they provide a sugar substance. It is important that our relationship with farm animals is reciprocal. We owe animals a decent life and a painless death.

I have observed that the people who are completely out of touch with nature are the most afraid of death, and places such as slaughter houses. I was moved by Birute Galdikas's book on her research on orangutans. The people in the Borneo rain forests live as a part of nature and have a totally different view of life and death. To the native people, "death is not separate from life." In the jungle they see death every day. Birute states, "For me, as for most middle-class North Americans death was just a tremor far down, far away at the end of a very long road, not something to be lived with every hour of every single day."

Many people attempt to deny the reality of their own mortality. When I designed my first system I had to look my own mortality straight in the eye. I live each day as if I could die tomorrow. I want to make the most of each day and do things to make the world a better place.

29

Temple Grandin

"A Major Change"

In this article Temple Grandin notes that progress has been made in both handling and stunning from 1997 to 1999, largely through the decision of two fast-food companies to audit U.S. plants to make sure they complied with industry guidelines. Grandin describes the animal welfare problems with transporting sick or weak animals. The increase in the numbers of such animals indicates to Grandin that producers may be pushing animals beyond their biological limits. She stresses the importance of continually monitoring animal welfare, using vocalization as an objective measure.

I have worked as a consultant to the meat industry since the early 1970s. I've been in more than 300 slaughter plants in the United States, Canada, Mexico, Europe, Australia, New Zealand, and South America. During the course of my career. I've seen many changes take place, but I'm going to focus in this paper on my work to improve conditions for the slaughter of cattle and calves and later address transport and other animal-handling issues.

[. . .]

I saw more improvement in both handling and stunning from 1997 to 1999 than I had seen previously in my entire career. Two fast-food companies started auditing U.S. plants during 1999 to make sure they complied with the American Meat Institute Guidelines (Grandin 1997c). Both federally inspected beef and pork plants were scored objectively. Many plants now have better stunner maintenance, and electric prod usage has been greatly reduced. One company audited forty-one beef plants in 1999; I was present at about half of the audits. By the end of 1999, 90 percent of beef plants were stunning 95 percent of the cattle they processed with one shot: 37 percent were stunning 99 percent to 100 percent with one shot (Grandin 2000b). If the first shot missed, the animal was immediately restunned. (This was a big improvement over performance noted in the 1996 USDA survey [Grandin 1997a,b].) Large flags were being used to move pigs, and a piece of plastic on a stick was being used to move cattle. These devices had replaced many electric prods.

In beef production, plants were scored on percentage of cattle stunned with one shot, insensibility on the bleed rail, and vocalization during handling. Vocalization (moos and bellows) is a sensitive indicator of welfare-related problems such as excessive electric prod use, slipping and falling, missed stunner shots, and excessive pressure from a restraint device (Grandin 1998a,b).

Researchers have found that vocalization in both cattle and pigs is correlated with physiological indicators of stress (Dunn 1990; Warriss *et al.* 1994; White *et al.* 1995). Vocalization is also correlated with pain (Watts and Stookey 1998; Weary 1998). Vocalization scoring can pinpoint handling problems. Beef plants with good handling practices will have 3 percent or less of their cattle vocalizing during handling in the stunning chute (Grandin 1998b). (To keep scoring simple, vocalization is scored on a "yes" and "no" basis—a cow either vocalizes or it does not. Vocalization in the yards where cattle are standing undisturbed is not scored.) In 1999 74 percent of forty-two U.S. beef plants had vocalization scores of 3 percent or less for cattle. In 1996 only 43 percent of the plants had a vocalization score of 3 percent or less. Excessive electric prod use, due to cattle balking, had raised vocalization scores to as high as 17 percent at some plants.

Vocalization scoring can be used to chart handling improvement within a plant. It also works well on feedlots and ranches. Vocalization scores will often be higher than 3 percent when animals are ear-tagged on ranches or feedlots. In contrast, it is easy to have a 0 percent vocalization rate for animals moving through the chutes, being restrained in the squeeze chute, and being vaccinated.

The presence of distractions, which makes cattle balk, makes a 3 percent or less vocalization score almost impossible. The movement of a small chain hanging in a chute, for example, will make an approaching animal stop and impede the flow of the other animals. Lighting a dark restrainer entrance will often improve animal movement. (Information on debugging systems and removing distractions can be found in Grandin 1998c, 1996.)

People manage the things that they measure. Bad practices become "normal" if there is no standard to which they can be compared. Vocalization scoring can be used to chart progress as a plant improves its equipment and practices.

[. . .]

Dairy and pig industry problems

The number-one transport problem in the 1970s—and the number-one transport problem today—is loading onto a truck animals who are not fit for transport. The dairy industry has some of the worst such problems. Baby dairy calves, who are too young to walk, are not fit for transport. Emaciated or lame dairy cows are not fit for transport. Downer dairy cows, those who are unable to walk, are more prevalent now than in 1994. Numbers of beef cattle downers have decreased slightly (Smith *et al.* 1994, 1995; Roeber 2001). The 1999 audit by Smith *et al.* indicated that 1.5 percent of all culled dairy cows arrived at a slaughter plant down and unable to walk. In the beef industry, 0.77 percent of the cows were downers.

In the past thirty years, although the handling of beef cattle on ranches and feedlots has improved, welfare problems in the transport of old, culled dairy cows have worsened. Genetics is partly to blame. Selection of individuals for milk production has increased the incidence of lameness. John Webster at Bristol University in the United Kingdom states that the typical cow's foot can no longer support its weight. A dairy veterinarian in Florida told me that the incidence and aspects of lameness in dairy cows are horrendous. Leg conformation is heritable, and good conformation will help prevent lameness (Boettcher *et al.* 1998; Van Dorp *et al.* 1998). Slaughter plant managers and truck drivers have reported that dairies that use bovine somatrophin (BST), bovine growth hormone, in their dairy herds sometimes have more thin, weak cows. Administration of BST reduced body condition score (Jordan *et al.* 1991; and West *et al.* 1990). Unless the cow is fed very well, it may lose body condition. The degree of body condition reduction is related to the dose of BST.

Single-trait selection of pigs for rapid growth and leanness has created pigs who are more fragile and likely to die during transport. I have observed that death losses during transport have tripled in the 1990s compared to the 1980s. Some hybrid pigs are very excitable, which makes handling them more difficult (Grandin 2000a). These pigs act as though they have high sympathetic nervous system arousal. A tap on the rump will make them squeal. Normal pigs are much less likely to startle. Pigs who are selected solely for productivity may have a loss of disease resistance. Genetic factors affect susceptibility to disease.

One of my biggest concerns is the possibility that producers are pushing animals beyond their biological limits. The pig industry, for example, has repeated most of the mistakes that the broiler-chicken industry made. Genetic traits are linked in unexpected ways. Some pigs grow so fast that they have very weak bones. These pigs have large bulging muscles but are so fragile that livestock insurance companies will not sell transport insurance to producers to cover them. Fortunately, some breeders are now selecting far more "moderate" pigs, which will have fewer problems. [. . .]

Conclusions

Promoting better stockmanship is essential to improving animal welfare. Large meat-buying customers such as fast-food restaurants in the United States and supermarket chains in the United Kingdom can motivate great change by insisting that suppliers uphold better animal welfare standards, The greatest advances of the last thirty years have been the result of company audits. To maintain such progress, handling and stunning must be continually audited, measured, and managed. Handlers tend to revert to rough handling unless they are monitored and managed. An objective scoring system provides a standard that can be upheld. An overworked employee cannot do a good job of taking care of animals. Good stockmanship requires adequate staffing levels. More efforts are also needed to address problems of faulty stunning equipment, ever-increasing line speed, and enforcement of the Humane Slaughter Act when violations occur.

Attitudes can be changed, and that change can improve both animal welfare and productivity.

References

Boettcher, P.J., J.C. Dekkers, L.O. Warnick, and S.J. Wells. 1998. Genetic analysis of lameness in cattle. *Journal of Dairy Science* 81: 1148–56.

Dunn. C.S. 1990. Stress reactions of cattle undergoing ritual slaughter using two methods of restraint. *Veterinary Record* 126: 522–5.

Grandin, T. 1996. Factors that impede animal movement at slaughter plants. *Journal of the American Veterinary Medical Association* 209: 757–9.

—— 1997a. Assessment of stress during handling and transport. *Journal of Animal Science* 75: 249–57.

—— 1997b. Survey of handling and stunning in federally inspected beef, pork, veal, and sheep slaughter plants. *ARS Research Project No. 3602–32000–002–08G*. Washington, D.C.: U.S. Department of Agriculture.

—— 1997c. *Good management practices for animal handling and stunning*. Washington, D.C.: American Meat Institute.

—— 1998a. Objective scoring of animal handling and stunning practices in slaughter plants. *Journal of the American Veterinary Medical Association* 212: 36–93.

—— 1998b. The feasibility of using vocalization scoring as an indicator of poor welfare during slaughter. *Applied Animal Behavior* Science 56: 121–8.

—— 1998c. Solving livestock handling problems in slaughter plants. In *Animal welfare and meat science*, ed. N.G. Gregory. Wallingford, U.K.: CAB International.

—— 2000a. *Livestock handling and transport*. Second Edition. Wallingford. U.K.: CAB International.

—— 2000b. 1999 Audits of stunning and handling in federally inspected beef and pork plants. Paper presented. American Meat Institute 2000 Conference on Handling and Stunning, Kansas City, Mo.

Jordan, D.C., A.A. Aquilar, J.D. Olson, C. Bailey, G.F. Hartnell, and K.S. Madsen, 1991. Effects of recombinant methionyl bovine somatrophic (sometribove) in high-producing cow's milk three times a day. *Journal of Dairy Science* 74: 220–6.

Roeber, D.L., P.D. Mies, C.D. Smith, K.E. Belk, T.G. Field, J.D. Tatum, J.A. Scanga, and G.C. Smith. 2001. National market cow and bull beef quality audit: 1999: A survey of producer-related defects in market cows and bulls. *Journal of Animal Science* 79: 658–65.

Smith, G.C., J.B. Morgan, J.D. Tatum, C.C. Kukay, M.T. Smith, T.D. Schnell, and G.G. Hilton. 1994. Improving the consistency and competitiveness of non-fed beef: and improving the salvage value of cull cows and bulls. The final report of the National Cattlemen's Beef Association. Fort Collins: Colorado State University.

Smith, G.C., *et al.* 1995. Improving the quality, consistency, competitiveness, and market share of beef: A blueprint for total quality management in the beef industry. The final report of the National Beef Quality Audit. Fort Collins: Colorado State University.

Warriss, P.D., S.N. Brown, and S.J.M. Adams. 1994. Relationship between subjective and objective assessment of stress at slaughter and meat quality in pigs. *Meat Science* 38: 329–40.

Watts, J.M., and J.M. Stookey. 1998. Effects of restraint and branding on rates and acoustic parameters of vocalization in beef cattle. *Applied Animal Behavior Science* 62: 125–35.

Weary, D.M., L.A. Braithwaite, and D. Fraser. 1998. Vocal response to pain in piglets. *Applied Animal Behavior Science* 56: 161–72.

West, J.W., K. Bondair, and J.C. Johnson. 1990. Effect of bovine somatotropin on milk yield and composition, body weight, and condition score of Holstein and Jersey cows. *Journal of Dairy Science* 73: 1062–8.

White, R.G., J.A. DeShazer, C.J. Tressler, G.M. Borcher, S. Davey, A. Waninge, A.M. Parkhurst, M.J. Milanuk, and E.T. Clems. 1995. Vocalizations and physiological response of pigs during castration with and without anesthetic. *Journal of Animal Science* 73: 381–6.

Van Dorp, T.E., J.C.M. Dekkers, S.W. Martin, and J.P., Noordhuizen, T.M. 1998. Genetic parameters of health disorders and relationships with 305-day milk yield and information traits in registered dairy cows. *Journal of Dairy Science* 81: 2264–70.

30

Animal Agriculture Alliance

"Animal Agriculture: Myths and Facts"

The Animal Agriculture Alliance argues that the general population accepts the human right to use animals. Further, farmers and ranchers constantly attend to their animals' welfare, because healthy animals provide a greater return on their investment. Most of the farms in the U.S. are owned by an individual or a married couple. The Alliance goes on to explain the treatment of pigs, dairy cows, laying hens, and veal calves, addressing questions of animal welfare and the use of antibiotics in food animals.

Myths	Facts
Farm animals deserve the same rights as you or I. All creatures deserve to share the planet equally with man.	To believe that man and all other animals exist with the same rights is anthropomorphism, or the "humanizing" of animals. This is a belief held by some vegetarians and animal rights extremists, and is not accepted by the general population. There are theological, scientific and philosophical arguments for why man cares for animals so they may serve him. Certainly, man has the moral obligation to avoid cruelty in dealing with all animals in all situations.
Farmers care less for their animals than they do for the money animals bring them. Agribusiness corporations mislead farmers into using production systems and drugs that mean profits at the cost of animal welfare.	Farmers and ranchers are neither cruel nor naive. One of the main reasons someone goes into farming or ranching is a desire to work with animals. A farmer would compromise his or her own welfare if animals were mistreated. Agriculture is very competitive in the U.S., a career which pays the farmer a slim profit on the animals he cares for. It is in the farmer's own best interest to see the animals in his charge treated humanely, guaranteeing him a healthy, high quality animal, a greater return on his investment, and a wholesome food product.

No advertising campaign or salesman can convince a farmer to use a system or product that would harm an animal. Farmers are always looking for ways to improve their farms to ensure animal welfare and the economics of production.

We must also understand the difference between what an animal may want and what it needs. It is not generally in the best interest of the animal to be left untended. An animal may eat poisonous plants if in the open, or fall prey to predators. An animal may "want" to do these things, but does it "need" to?

Farming in the U.S. is controlled by large corporations which care about profits and not about animal welfare.

Of the 2.2 million farms in the U.S., 87 percent are owned by an individual or a married couple responsible for operating the farm. If partnerships—typically a parent and one or more children or other close relatives—are added to this total, 97 percent of U.S. farms are family-owned and operated, according to the U.S. Department of Agriculture's "1987 Fact Book of U.S. Agriculture." Even those farms which are legally corporations are generally family controlled, with USDA reporting only 7,000 non-family controlled corporate farms in the U.S.

Farm animals are routinely raised on "factory farms," confined in "crowded, unventilated cages and sheds."

Animals are generally kept in barns and similar housing, with the exception of beef cattle, to protect the health and welfare of the animal. Housing protects animals from predators, disease, and bad weather or extreme climate. Housing also makes breeding and birth less stressful, protects young animals, and makes it easier for farmers to care for both healthy and sick animals.

Modern animal housing is well ventilated, warm, well-lit, clean and scientifically designed for the specific needs of the animal, such as the regular availability of fresh water and a nutritionally balanced feed. For instance, a hog barn wouldn't be used for cows, any more than an adult would sleep in a child's crib. Housing is designed to allow the farmer to provide the best animal care and control costs.

Not only are all animals confined, most are held in crates and cages and not allowed to move at all.

Animal behavior is as varied as human behavior. In some cases, animals are restrained to avoid injuring themselves, other animals or the farmer. All forms of restraint are designed for the welfare of the animal as well as efficiency of production.

Breeding sows are helped during breeding so they are not injured by the larger, heavier boar. When a sow is ready to farrow or give birth, she is placed typically for 3–4 weeks in a stall to make her delivery easier, help with veterinary care if necessary, ensure she does not step on or roll over and crush her litter, while allowing her piglets to be near her. Pigs are naturally aggressive and curious, and what has been described as "manic" or abnormal behavior during this protective restraint is currently under study by swine specialists.

Dairy cows are milked in stalls, usually twice a day. This is so farmers can use modern milking equipment, and to protect the cow and the farmer. Placing the cows in these stalls during milking also facilitates medical treatment of an animal weighing more than 1,200 lbs. At other times, most dairy farmers will turn cows out into pasture or into large pens.

Laying hens are kept in cages to ensure adequate feed and water reaches every bird every day and to facilitate egg collection. It allows the farmer to care for more birds efficiently and produce the millions of eggs consumers value each year. Sorting the birds into small groups helps control naturally aggressive behavior, such as pecking and cannibalism, while allowing the birds to interact with their penmates. It takes greater amounts of land, labor and money to raise laying hens in open flocks because of exposure to bad weather, disease, predators, etc. Today, one egg farm may house 50,000–100,000 hens. If layers were not raised in a controlled environment, feeding, cleaning, preventing disease, treating sick birds, and locating where 50,000 birds laid thousands of eggs each day would greatly increase the cost of eggs, and price a valuable food out of the diet of many consumers.

Veal calves may be raised in stalls, hutches, pens or in small groups. The system used by an individual farmer varies by region and climate, type of calf, farmer preference and size of farm. One system cannot arbitrarily be said to be better than another in all situations. Studies comparing these various housing systems are on-going.

Veal calves are generally kept in individual stalls to provide individual attention, improve general health, separate aggressive young bulls from each other, minimize or eliminate injury to the animals and the farmer, and to aid in feeding efficiency and veterinary care.

In modern stall systems, calves can stand, lie down, see, touch and react to other calves in well-lit, sanitary barns. It is not true that veal calves are kept in "boxes" or perpetual darkness. Veal feed is a liquid milk "replacer" product that is specially formulated for baby calves. It is a fortified formula containing minerals, vitamins, and animal health products, including minimum recommended amounts of iron to ensure calf health. The farmer would be compromising his own economic welfare if calves weren't kept healthy.

Beef cattle in large herds or feedlots are restrained generally when being given veterinary care. In cow/calf operations, housing allows for protection from predators and the elements, disease control and ease of handling.

Farm animals are routinely "mutilated" by beak trimming, tail docking, branding, dehorning, castration, and other practices to make it easier for the farmer.

To the inexperienced viewer, some routine farm animal handling practices necessary to the welfare and health of the animal and the insurance of quality food may appear brutal, just as some life-saving human surgical and medical practices may seem brutal to the casual observer. All of these practices are done in a professional manner to ensure the welfare of the animal.

Egg laying hens may have their beaks trimmed—not removed—to avoid injury to each other as a result of the bird's natural cannibalistic tendencies. Claws may be trimmed to avoid injury during mating.

With hogs, piglets may have their needle teeth trimmed shortly after birth to avoid injury to the nursing sow and to litter mates. Tails may be docked or shortened to end a natural tendency toward tail biting that occurs in some swine herds.

Beef cattle, sheep and some dairy cattle may be dehorned when young to avoid injury to each other and to the rancher; castration, or neutering, may be necessary to help control aggressive behaviors in young animals, and to insure the quality meat consumers demand. In sheep, tails may be docked to improve hygiene and prevent fly and parasite infestation.

Permanently identifying animals by ear-marking, tattooing, branding and other means is necessary to maintain accurate health records to prevent the spread of disease to animals and man. It also helps during marketing.

All of these practices are under regular review and new research is done to ensure their necessity and effectiveness, and to ensure the required results are achieved in the most humane, efficient manner.

A vegetarian diet is healthier than a diet that includes meat, milk and eggs.

Both the federal government and the American Heart Association contend a diet containing meat, milk and eggs is appropriate to both groups' dietary guidelines. The Washington Post, reporting on the First International Congress on Vegetarian Nutrition held in Washington in March, 1987, had this to say: "The Congress didn't uncover any earth-shattering findings or recommend that everyone take up bean sprouts full time," the Post reported. Health benefits can be derived by non-vegetarians who follow a prudent diet that is low in fat, sodium, sugar and alcohol. Just as there are nonvegetarian diets that are unhealthy, so too there are poorly planned vegetarian diets. The approach to healthful eating should be common sense.

Farm animals in "confinement" are prone to disease, forcing farmers to routinely use antibiotics, hormones and drugs to keep

Animal scientists, veterinarians and on-farm experience show animals kept in housing are no more likely to get sick than animals kept them alive. This jeopardizes animal and human health.

Grain fed to livestock and poultry could be used to feed the hungry overseas.

The average U.S. farm animal is fed whatever the farmer happens to have available, without regard to what the animal needs for good health.

in the open. In fact, they're generally healthier because they are protected. However, farm animals do sometimes get sick. To prevent illness and to ensure that an animal remains healthy all of its life, farmers will take preventive measures, including the use of animal health products. These products are generally given to the animal in a scientifically formulated feed best suited to the animal's needs. This is the simplest way to make sure each animal gets the care indicated.

Animal health products include animal drugs and vaccines, in addition to vitamins, minerals and other nutrients the animal needs in a balanced diet. Not all animals are given the same treatment in all situations.

Animal drugs include antibiotics to prevent and treat animal disease, and most are not used in human medicine. There are antibiotics used in humans that are also used in animals. There is now an unresolved scientific debate over these uses. Since there is no conclusive scientific proof that the use of human antibiotics in animals—a practice going back 35 years—is a risk to human health, these products are used to prevent and treat illness in some animals, in addition to aiding growth.

Grain fed to livestock and poultry is generally referred to as "feed grade." It is not usually intended for human consumption and is not generally the same quality and nutrient value as grain used in human food production. Animals, in fact, are the most efficient converters of this lower-quality grain and other grasses and forages into high-quality protein.

The average U.S. farm animal, from the standpoint of nutrition, eats better than the average U.S. citizen. There are more than a thousand professional livestock and poultry nutritionists in the U.S.—many are Ph.Ds—who spend much of their professional time determining the needs of each animal for each phase of the animal's life cycle for about 40 basic nutrients. When nutritional research indicates how much of a given nutrient is needed in a given ration, both the feed manufacturer and the farmer who owns the livestock or poultry, have an economic incentive to provide animals with exactly the indicated amount of necessary nutrients for animal health. The result is a healthier animal. While most people don't know how many calories they consume in a day, feed manufacturers and farmers see that each farm animal receives almost precisely the correct amount of such vital nutrients as minerals, vitamins, amino acids, etc.

Many of the ingredients used in animal rations are agricultural by-products of other industries, such as cotton, rice, flour milling, meat packing and alcohol production. Many of these ingredients—high in animal nutrition value—would have little or no value to man were they not used to feed animals. Some of these products would create significant disposal problems were they not used as animal feed ingredients and had to be dumped.

Medical and social benefits of livestock production

Most of us are not aware that the farmer provides us with more than just a healthy, inexpensive diet. Animals raised for food are also invaluable in human medical treatments and in our everyday lives, by providing us with materials which make our lives easier and safer. Listed below by contributing animal category, are just a few of myriad medical and social benefits provided to us by livestock production:

Cattle:

Medical contributions:

Adrenal glands:

Epinephrine is used to relieve some symptoms of hay fever, asthma and some allergies.

It is also used as a heart stimulant in some crisis situations, and by dentists to prolong the effect of local anesthetics.

Blood:

Thrombin from cattle blood helps blood clotting, and is valuable in treating wounds to inaccessible parts of the body. It is also used in skin grafting.

Liver:

Liver extract is sometimes combined with folic acid and injected to treat various types of anemia.

Pancreas:

Perhaps the best known contribution, insulin derived from cattle pancreas is used to treat diabetes. Glucagon helps counteract insulin-shock.

Medical benefits derived from cattle by-products include rennet, epinephrine, thrombin, insulin, heparin, TSH, ACTH, cholesterol, estrogen, thyroid extract.

Product contributions using cattle by-products:

Tires	*Buttons*
Antifreeze	*China*
Upholstery	*Photographic film*
Leather	*Musical instrument*
Sports equipment	*components such*
Surgical sutures	*as strings*
Soaps	*Brushes*
Cosmetics	*Explosives*

31

Françoise Wemelsfelder

"Lives of Quiet Desperation"

Françoise Wemelsfelder describes her impression of a young female pig that had been housed alone in a barren pen. The alert responsiveness normal to a pig had given way to withdrawal, indicating serious suffering.

Biological science tends to assume that we can't know directly what an animal feels, that emotions are hidden within the animal's brain. But I believe this view unnecessarily creates a split between body and mind, between behavior and emotion. Animals are integrated beings whose behavior has an expressive quality, a body language that speaks to us in a meaningful way. Animals can behave fearfully, confidently, apathetically, excitedly, or calmly. In the way in which an animal acts and moves about, its experience of a situation is present for us to observe and share. It's possible, of course, to make mistakes; to correctly interpret an animal's behavioral expression, we have to be well acquainted with a particular creature and with the species it belongs to. With enough experience, however, we can get it right.

In my work I meet mostly pigs, which are naturally inquisitive and alert animals. If I enter a pen with young pigs, after a moment's hesitation they quickly approach and vigorously sniff and nibble my hand. But they're also quick to withdraw; one unexpected movement from me and they back away. Newborn piglets are in danger of being crushed by the sow, so picking up a young pig or holding it for a moment will cause it to scream at the top of its lungs and to frantically wriggle to get away. Such behavior helps the piglet survive, but it also conveys panic and acute despair. For us, this may seem exaggerated in a situation of mild and harmless restraint. From the pig's point of view, however, the despair is very real. That most pigs calm down as soon as they are freed is no reason for us to suspect that the previous moment of despair wasn't intense.

In the highly restrictive and monotonous agricultural environments in which we keep pigs, their alert responsiveness may disappear and give way to drowsy lethargy. I gained a clear impression of this in a young female pig that had been housed alone for many months in a small barren pen. She was sitting on the floor, her hind legs stretched underneath her, her back hunched, her head and ears drooping, and her tongue occasionally hanging out of her mouth. She had been sitting this way for quite some time, and my entrance into the pen had little effect. When I sat down next to her and carefully touched her, she glanced at me but didn't move. As the moments passed, I was struck by the soft, gentle, helpless quality of her passivity, the total absence of hostility, fear, or any other active response. She was present only vaguely, her apathy such a stark contrast to what pigs normally are like.

What I realized that day is that the expression of suffering, in pigs and perhaps in other animals as well, is not necessarily dramatic or assertive. It can take the form of withdrawal, of absence rather than presence, and it can appear in an expression so subtle that we could easily fail to notice it or, having noticed it, ignore its significance. Yet the soft quality of a pig's helplessness signals a suffering that is serious rather than slight. It speaks of a loss of communication, of a lost ability to cope. I found the quiet emptiness emanating from the pig poignant and very sad.

It seems to me that animal suffering is invisible only when we avert our eyes. With prolonged and careful observation, the nature of that suffering is bound to become clear.

32

William O. Stephens

"Five Arguments for Vegetarianism"

William O. Stephens examines five arguments for vegetarianism: the argument from distributive justice, environmental harm, sexual politics, moral consideration for animals, and the prudential argument from health. Stephens argues that the cumulative case succeeds in establishing that vegetarianism is a morally good choice and that it is meat-eaters who have the burden of proof.

Introduction

In this paper I will examine five different arguments for adopting a vegetarian diet. These "arguments" can be viewed as various persuasive strategies directed towards different audiences. Many readers will be familiar with some of these arguments, but I think it is useful to bring them all together and to see them as presenting a cumulative case for vegetarianism. Taken as a whole they lead one in a certain direction regarding the choice of one's diet. Although these arguments may have different degrees of logical persuasiveness and different rhetorical audiences, it is worthwhile to ask whether virtuous persons find in themselves some moral trait that inclines them to respond sympathetically to each argument, and even more sympathetically to the persuasive case taken as a whole. That is, I want to bring these arguments together in order to challenge an otherwise serious, mature human being who wants to be a morally good person. . . . These restrictions all include abstaining from intensively raised, grain-fed, factory-farmed sentient animals such as cattle, pigs, and poultry, and perhaps also lambs (sheep).[1] Thus the dietary goal towards which the arguments lead is not strict veganism which excludes consumption of all animal products, including dairy food and eggs. Nor do the arguments exclude consumption of those fish, crustaceans, mollusks, and other organisms whose sentience is doubtful and which have not been bred, raised, and slaughtered by intensive, factory-farming methods. Moreover, these arguments do not apply universally to all people in all agricultural circumstances. These arguments do not apply to those few people who, out of genuine necessity, must, in order to survive, hunt and/or trap wild animals in remote areas that are unsuitable for raising crops.

[. . .]

The argument from distributive justice

This first argument was advanced as early as 1971 by Frances Moore Lappé, and has been repeated by such philosophers as Peter Singer, James Rachels, Stephen R. L. Clark, Mary Midgley, and mentioned in passing by still others.[2] The argument can be reconstructed as follows:

1   16 to 21 lbs. of grain and soy are needed to produce 1 lb. of beef.
    6 to 8 lbs. of grain and soy are needed to produce 1 lb. of pork.
    4 lbs. of grain and soy are needed to produce 1 lb. of turkey meat.
    3 lbs. of grain and soy are needed to produce 1 lb. of chicken meat.
2   Therefore, converting grain and soy to meat is a very wasteful means of producing food.
3   Every day millions of human beings in the world suffer and die from lack of sufficient grains and legumes for a minimally decent diet.
4   By choosing to eat meat when sufficient grains and vegetables are available for a healthy diet for oneself, one participates in and perpetuates a very wasteful means of producing food.

[. . .]

Basically, the idea here is that eating meat perpetuates a system which indirectly harms other human beings. Therefore, to choose to be a part of this system indicates a disregard for those people, and this in effect contaminates one's moral character.

The argument from environmental harm

This argument is motivated by the interest many who are sensitive to environmental issues have in "treading lightly on the planet." The sources of my reconstruction of this argument are Jeremy Rifkin,[3] Frances Moore Lappé, and the Worldwatch Institute, but it has been mentioned by many others.[4]

[. . .]

Basically, the argument is that with over a billion cows, bulls, and steers worldwide, the cattle industry is responsible, either directly or indirectly, for considerable ecological devastation.

[. . .]

The feminist argument from sexual politics

This third argument is that there is an intimate connection between vegetarianism and feminism, and between male dominance and meat eating. Carol J. Adams[5] argues that "to talk about eliminating meat is to talk about displacing one aspect of male control and demonstrates the ways in which animals' oppression and women's oppression are linked together."[6] Adams calls this connection "the sexual politics of meat." She claims it is overtly acknowledged when we hear that men, and especially soldiers, athletes, and other "working men," need meat to be strong and virile, or when wives report that they could give up meat, but prepare it for their husbands who insist on it.

[. . .]

The basic gist of Adams' Feminist Argument from Sexual Politics is that since meat is a symbol of patriarchal oppression, domination, and violence perpetrated against both non-human animals and women, vegetarianism represents an explicit rejection of our "Meat is king"[7] patriarchal culture.

The argument from moral consideration for animals

This argument is probably the most familiar one to philosophical audiences and has several different formulations,[8] but since the object of moral concern in each is the sentient animals themselves, whether couched in terms of the value of their lives, their moral rights, or their suffering. I group them all together as arguments appealing to moral consideration for animals.

[. . .]

Regan's argument rests on no utilitarian calculation weighing the interests farm animals have in not suffering against the interests meat eaters have in eating meat.[9] Instead, he argues that animals are experiencing subjects of a life, have inherent value, and thus have a *prima facie* right not to be harmed by being raised and slaughtered when we can become vegetarians without being made worse off by doing so.

Both Regan and Singer appeal to the moral consideration we owe the animals them-selves; Singer enjoins us to reduce their pain and suffering, while Regan enjoins us to respect them as beings with inherent value equal to our own. Both contend that we are wronging these animals whom we breed into existence, make to suffer, and slaughter.

The prudential argument from health

The last argument for vegetarianism is perhaps the least philosophically interesting argument because it turns on a simple appeal to self-interest,[10] but it is probably the argument that has succeeded in persuading most people. In recent years many nutritionists have judged eating meat to be unhealthy. [. . .]

Some evidence also suggests that a strict vegan diet is the healthiest diet of all. Thus prudence would seem to dictate eliminating at least all beef, pork, lamb, and poultry from one's diet, and preferably all fish, seafood, eggs, and dairy products as well. As conservative a group as the American Dietetic Association, having reviewed the current literature on the nutritional status of vegetarians, has concluded that "vegetarian diets are healthful and nutritionally adequate when appropriately planned."[11] Thus, since a balanced, meatless diet is healthier than a diet containing meat, there appear to be strong prudential reasons for becoming a vegetarian.

Critical discussion

A critic could object that if each one of these arguments is flawed by weak reasoning, then all I have presented are five poor arguments for vegetarianism. So let's now look briefly at each argument from the standpoint of its relation to a wider persuasive strategy. That is, consider each argument as a logical or rhetorical moment that attempts to build a stronger and stronger case for the *prima facie* virtue of vegetarianism.

Distributive justice or gustatory guilt?

First let's consider the Argument from Distributive Justice. It is certainly true that if an individual American in Omaha refuses to buy and eat a particular hamburger, the hamburger will not magically transform itself into a bowl of porridge large enough to sustain ten hungry Rwandans. The lines of causation that stretch out between the boycotting of meat by Americans, the market effect this will have on international agribusinesses, rising surpluses of grain worldwide, and political decisions to export such surpluses to famine-plagued areas are without question long, complicated, difficult to establish, and even more difficult to predict. One could argue that such tenuous, convoluted causal lines are too easily severed by unforeseen or uncontrollable circumstances. But even granting this in no way concedes that such causal lines are *unreal*. Such a boycott would not be a mere symbolic gesture.[12] Coupled with political action, it could exert real market pressure to undercut the meat industry.

But even if the effects of one discrete human action are negligible in a utilitarian sense, the ethics of individual boycotting can never be generated merely by appeals to overall consequences. If everyone were to act in a certain manner, good consequences might occur. However, boycotts may fail as collective action dissipates or never gets energized in the first place. Action remains the expression of individual virtue. If some action or practice produces widespread suffering or injustice, a virtuous person will not be insensitive to this. By making the *personal* choice to abstain from meat, a virtuous individual would be actively expressing her compassion for famine victims. She would be making a moral exemplar of herself, whether others rally to follow her example in sufficient number to achieve the hoped for market effects or not. It is a matter of moral integrity, not empirical, utilitarian calculations of probable consequences.

[. . .]

Our view of meat consumption might be transformed if we bear in mind that if Americans were to reduce their meat consumption by only 10 percent for one year, it would free at least 12 million tons of grain for human consumption—or enough to feed 60 million starving people. We can see factory-farmed meat as a luxury indulged in predominately by Americans and Europeans at the expense of the poor of developing nations. As such it is a form of wastefulness and selfishness at odds with distributive justice. Thus it betrays a lack of compassion for those who deserve decent food.

Environmental harm or harmless heifers?

Peter Singer observed some time ago that "there would be environmental benefits from ending factory farming, which is energy intensive and leads to problems in disposing of the huge quantities of animal wastes which it concentrates on one site."[13] Here Singer is only concerned with the environmental harm resulting from factory-farming animals on land which could be put to other agricultural uses for humans. He grants that "If a calf, say, grazes on rough pasture land that grows only grass and could not be planted with corn or any other crop that provides food edible by human beings, the result will be a net gain of protein for human beings, since the grown calf provides us with protein that we cannot—yet—extract economically from grass."[14] This suggests a counterargument to the Argument from Distributive Justice. The defender of meat eating could argue that by limiting consumption to those animals (e.g. goats) that graze on unfarmable "rough pasture land that grows only grass" as Singer describes it (e.g. mountain slopes), meat eaters would *not* be depriving hungry people of any grain protein at all.

The first reply to this argument is that it already concedes that farmable land should not be used to support meat production. But the deeper reply is that this argument too quickly assumes that all land "that grows only grass" can and rightly should be used to produce animal protein for humans. This assumption can be challenged by asserting the ecological value such grassland (say, open prairie) has independent of human agricultural use. Peter S. Wenz[15] has argued that if healthy ecosystems are of value, and the value of an ecosystem is positively related to its degree of health, then people have *prima facie* obligations to avoid harming, to repair damage to, and to improve the health of ecosystems. He reasons that using land to grow large quantities of food impairs the health of the ecosystems involved, so people have a *prima facie* obligation to meet their nutritional needs through minimal use of land. Because vegetarianism enables people to do this, Wenz infers, we have a *prima facie* obligation to be vegetarians.

[. . .]

Patriarchy of pork or feminist fuss?

. . . [W]hen I have discussed arguments for vegetarianism with my undergraduate students, my experience has consistently been that a significantly greater number of young women are receptive to vegetarianism than young men.[16] Admittedly, this is not a scientific survey with a sample guaranteed to be representative.

[. . .]

However, some of Adams' assumptions are suspicious. Take for example her labeling of the ideas that "the end justifies the means," "objectification of other beings is a necessary part of life," and "violence can and should be masked" as "patriarchal attitudes." Gandhi and Martin Luther King were pacifists and were men, but surely that would not make pacifism a "patriarchial attitude." Some of the connections Adams tries to establish between meat-advocating discourse and patriarchal culture seem rather strained and somewhat far-fetched. If the Feminist Argument from Sexual Politics were the only argument for vegetarianism, it might not sway the hardened skeptic who could object that there is no logically necessary connection between meat eating and patriarchy. Yet Adams' argument does, I think, retain an interesting degree of plausibility in its own right, and it adds another rhetorical dimension to the cumulative case for vegetarianism.

Concern for animals or soppy sentimentalism?

A common criticism of the utilitarian argument for vegetarianism is that as long as farm animals experience a greater balance of pleasure over pain while they exist, then breeding them into existence, treating them on balance decently, and then killing and eating them to increase the gustatory utility of meat eaters, yields greater net utility than a vegetarian world devoid of all farm animals.[17] One could object that this argument fails to include the loss of utility that would have accrued from the balance of the farm animals' lives had they not been slaughtered. Yet this objection can be countered by the "replaceability argument" discussed by Singer. If one is sympathetic to Regan's view that animals have *inherent* value, then one can reject the very idea that animal lives are "replaceable" at all. Here I do find Regan's position more appealing than Singer's since it strikes me as wrong to view animals as our resources to create, manipulate, slaughter, consume, and replace in the name of maximizing the utility of the class of sentient beings. Perhaps a better criticism of the replaceability argument is that it fails to factor in the number of wild animals that could come into existence on their own once we stopped breeding so many domesticated farm animals into existence. Given the fact that farm animals today are the product of dozens of years of selective breeding by humans, these animals are sentient artifacts that humans have manu-factured for illegitimate purposes. That is why at this point I would part company with Regan and maintain that battery chickens and grain-fed steers have less inherent value than bald eagles and grizzly bears.[18]

[. . .]

I suggest that compassionate persons who had to breed, raise, and slaughter by their own hands the animals they would eat would be greatly disinclined to do so. The anguished cries, terrified struggles, and spurting blood of the farm animals would no doubt deter many people from cutting off the animals' heads in order to make a meal of them. The gory, visceral experience of slaughtering a breathing, feeling animal may trigger the sensitive per-son's latent compassionate impulse enough to make the prospect of a fleshy meal quite unappetizing. The suggestion here is that if a person would be unwilling to perform the labor necessary for producing an item she wants to have (or consume), then that realization should deter the person from having (or consuming) that item even when it is produced by the labor of another.

Prudential health or dietary delusion?

A criticism that has been leveled at all moral arguments for vegetarianism is that while it may be ethically "pure" or "ideal" to abstain from meat, we can have no general duty to become vegetarians because meat is necessary for a healthful diet. Jack Weir has argued that abstain-ing from meat is at best supererogatory and at worst dangerous to one's health, and Steve Sapontzis has offered a critical response to Weir.[19] A more protracted exchange has ensued between Kathryn Paxton George and Evelyn Pluhar, with Gary E. Varner joining the fray.[20] It seems to me that Sapontzis and Pluhar have had the better of these exchanges. Worries about deficiencies from strict vegan diets have ranged from protein, calcium, and iron to zinc and riboflavin. The majority of nutritionists seem to agree that vegans can amply satisfy their needs for these nutrients by eating a variety of grains, legumes, vegetables, and fruits.

[. . .]

While it is true that the specific dietary needs of individuals vary, and that some people are allergic to some plant foods, no one has yet established that even a strict vegan diet cannot be adapted to fulfill each person's dietary needs. Carol Adams' claim that anthropo-logical evidence suggests that humans have predominantly been vegetarians has been confirmed by other authors:

> Studies of tribal Australian aborigines and the Kung-San of South Africa—groups that live under conditions similar to those of our ancestors—show that only about one fourth of their caloric intake derives from animal products. Nuts, seeds, fruits, and vegetables are the staple foods of these groups. A view of early humans as *gatherers* rather than hunters is a more accurate portrayal.[21]

Conclusion

The choice is not between being a moral saint (cum-health fanatic) and being a heartless egoist. I do not think that people who have deliberately chosen to become vegetarians are moral saints. But I do think that receptiveness to the first four arguments is linked to the character trait of compassion.[22] I suggest that the five different arguments for abstaining from intensively raised, grain-fed birds and mammals constitute reasons for vegetarianism that are at least as strong as the reasons for many daily actions that are routinely accepted by most people. My conclusion is that this cumulative case for vegetarianism succeeds in establishing that vegetarianism is, in at least five different respects, a virtuous dietary commitment. If I am correct, then this shifts the burden of proof to meat eaters who believe their dietary choice is without moral taint.[23]

[. . .]

Notes

1   For a singularly unpersuasive argument that one is morally required both to abstain from the flesh of intensively-raised animals *and to eat* the flesh of certain non-intensively raised animals, see Roger Crisp, "Utilitarianism and Vegetarianism," *International Journal of Applied Philosophy* 4 (Spring 1988): 41–7. Peter Singer pointed out to me that sheep are typically not raised intensively in feedlots, but that since intensively raised egg-laying hens are kept in miserable conditions, their eggs ought to be boycotted.

2   Jack Weir, in "Unnecessary Pain. Nutrition, and Vegetarianism," *Between the Species* 7, no. 1 (Winter 1991): 13–26, mentions that "being a vegetarian is good because it . . . strikes a blow against capitalistic injustices" (25); Hud Hudson, in "Collective Responsibility and Moral Vegetarianism," *Journal of Social Philosophy*, 24 no. 2 (Fall 1993): 89–104, mentions that "the moral variety of vegetarianism can arise from . . . a concern for human welfare" (90).

3   Jeremy Rifkin, *Beyond Beef* (New York: Dutton, 1992), 183–230.

4   Peter Singer, "Utilitarianism and Vegetarianism," *Philosophy & Public Affairs* 9, no. 4 (1980): 334; Weir, 21; Hudson, 90. See f.n. 2.

5   Carol J. Adams. *The Sexual Politics of Meat: A Feminist-Vegetarian Critical Theory* (New York: Continuum, 1990).

6   Ibid., 13.

7   Adams writes: "Meat is king: this noun describing meat is a noun denoting male power. Vegetables, a genetic term meat eaters use for all foods that are not meat, have become as associated with women as meat is with men, recalling on a subconscious level the days of Woman the Gatherer. Since women have been made subsidiary in a male-dominated, meat-eating world, so has our food. The foods associated with second-class citizens are considered to be second-class protein. Just as it is thought a woman cannot make it on her own, so we think that vegetables cannot make a meal on their own, despite the fact that meat is only secondhand vegetables and vegetables provide, on the average, more than twice the vitamins and minerals of meat. Meat is upheld as a powerful, irreplaceable item of food. The message is clear: the vassal vegetable should content itself with its assigned place and not attempt to dethrone king meat. After all, how can one enthrone women's foods when women cannot be kings?" (33–4).

8   Bart Gruzalski, "The Case Against Raising and Killing Animals for Food," *Ethics and Animals*, ed. Harian B. Miller and William H. Williams (Clifton, NJ: Humana Press, 1983); 251–63; S. F. Sapontzis, "Animal Liberation and Vegetarianism," *Journal of Agricultural Ethics* 1, no. 2 (1988): 139–53.

9   Tom Regan, *The Case for Animal Rights* (Berkeley: University of California Press, 1983). As Regan emphasizes: "The totem of utilitarian theory (summing consequences for all those affected by the outcome) is the taboo of the rights view" (337).

10 Peter Singer mentioned "the possible reduction a vegetarian diet would bring in human suffering from heart disease and cancer of the stomach and colon" long ago in "Utilitarianism and Vegetarianism" *Philosophy and Public Affairs* 9, no. 4 (1980): 334.

11 "Position of the American Dietetic Association: Vegetarian Diets," *The Journal of the American Dietetic Association* 3 (1988): 351–5: quoted by Pluhar, 204.

12 Cf. Thomas E. Hill. "Symbolic Protest and Calculated Science," *Philosophy and Public Affairs* 9 (1979): 83–102.

13 Singer, *Philosophy and Public Affairs*, 334.

14   Singer, *Animal Liberation*, rev. ed. (New York: Ballantine Books, 1990), 164.
15   Peter S. Wenz. "An Ecological Argument for Vegetarianism," *Ethics and Animals* 5 (March 1984): 2–9.
16   Peter Singer has also reported to me that the memberships of animal welfare/rights organizations have significantly greater majorities of women than men.
17   Frederick Ferré, in "Moderation, Morals, and Meat," *Inquiry* 29 (1986): 391–406 writes that: ". . . *if* conditions for farm animals are good, so that the net balance of the life experience of the typical animal being raised is positive, then it is morally licit to support such practices, even if they lead to the 'premature' deaths . . . of the animals in question. Having respect for inherent value means, among other things, taking a benevolent attitude toward the bringing into existence of as many bearers of inherent value as is reasonably compatible with their collective well being. If people did not eat meat, many fewer bearers of inherent value would be in the world. Therefore under ideal farming conditions, the eating of meat makes possible a larger net good than its opposite" (399: his emphasis).
        Jack Weir, in "Unnecessary Pain, Nutrition, and Vegetarianism," *Between the Species* 7.1 (1991): 13–26. repeats this idea: "But, if no one ate meat, then billions of animals would not exist and would not experience any pleasure. Most food animals could not survive in the wild, and society surely would not pay for their food and veterinary costs. . . . The animals would not exist and would not enjoy any life if they were not to be eaten" (21).
18   Explanations of the shortcomings of these one-sided utilitarian calculations have been offered by S. F. Sapontzis, "Animal Liberation and Vegetarianism," *Journal of Agricultural Ethics* 1, no. 2 (1988): 139–53.
19   Weir, 13–26: Sapontzis, "Reply to Weir: Unnecessary Fear, Nutrition, and Vegetarianism," *Between the Species* 27–32; Weir, "Response," 33–5.
20   Kathryn Paxton George, "So Animal a Human . . ., or the Moral Relevance of Being an Omnivore," *Journal of Agricultural Ethics* 3, no. 2 (1990): 172–86; Pluhar, "Who Can Be Morally Obligated to Be a Vegetarian," 189–215; George, "The Use and Abuse of Scientific Studies," *JAEE* 5, no. 2 (1992): 217–33; Pluhar, "On Vegetarianism, Morality, and Science: A Counter Reply," *JAEE* 6, no. 2 (1993): 185–213; Varner, "What's Wrong with Animal By-products?" 7–17; George, "Discrimination and Bias in the Vegan Ideal," 19–28; Varner, "In Defence of the Vegan Ideal: Rhetoric and Bias in the Nutrition Literature," 29–40; George, "Use and Abuse Revisited: Response to Pluhar and Varner," 41–76; Pluhar, "Vegetarianism, Morality, and Science Revisited," 77–82; Varner, "Rejoinder to Kathryn Paxton George," 83–6; *JAEE* 7, no. 1 (1994).
     See for example Neal Barnard, M.D., *Food for Life* (New York: Harmony Books, 1993) 155–6.
21   Paul R. Amato and Sonia Patridge, *The New Vegetarians: Promoting Health and Protecting Life* (New York: Plenum Press, 1989), 2; they give as their source Gretel H. Pelto and Pertti J. Pelto, *The Human Adventure* (New York: Macmillan, 1976), 203–4.
22   My appeal to the virtue of compassion is inspired by Richard Taylor, *Good and Evil: A New Direction* (New York: Macmillan, 1970), 205–22.
23   Hudson offers a separate argument from collective responsibility that adopting and acting upon "modified moral conditional vegetarianism" is a candidate for being a necessary, or at least sufficient, means of "removing the moral taint which pollutes one's character by virtue of one's membership in, say, the group of non-vegetarian consumers of factory-farmed products" (101).

33

Carol J. Adams

"The Rape of Animals, the Butchering of Women"

In her powerful essay, Carol J. Adams uses the concept of "absent referent" to describe the erasure of both women and animals used for food. Patriarchal culture strengthens oppression by "always recalling other oppressed groups." She points out how patriarchal culture violently transforms living animals to dead consumable ones both literally and conceptually through words of objectification such as "food-producing unit" to refer to a living animal.

The absent referent

Through butchering, animals become absent referents. Animals in name and body are made absent *as animals* for meat to exist. Animals' lives precede and enable the existence of meat. If animals are alive they cannot be meat. Thus a dead body replaces the live animal. Without animals there would be no meat eating, yet they are absent from the act of eating meat because they have been transformed into food.

Animals are made absent through language that renames dead bodies before consumers participate in eating them. Our culture further mystifies the term "meat" with gastronomic language, so we do not conjure dead, butchered animals, but cuisine. Language thus contributes even further to animals' absences. While the cultural meanings of meat and meat eating shift historically, one essential part of meat's meaning is static: One does not eat meat without the death of an animal. Live animals are thus the absent referents in the concept of meat. The absent referent permits us to forget about the animal as an independent entity; it also enables us to resist efforts to make animals present.

There are actually three ways by which animals become absent referents. One is literally: as I have just argued, through meat eating they are literally absent because they are dead. Another is definitional: when we eat animals we change the way we talk about them, for instance, we no longer talk about baby animals but about veal or meat: the word *meat* has an absent referent, the dead animals. [. . .] The third way is metaphorical. Animals become metaphors for describing people's experiences. In this metaphorical sense, the meaning of the absent referent derives from its application or reference to something else.

As the absent referent becomes metaphor, its meaning is lifted to a "higher" or more imaginative function than its own existence might merit or reveal. An example of this is when rape victims or battered women say, "I felt like a piece of meat." In this example, meat's meaning does not refer to itself but to how a woman victimized by male violence felt. That meat is functioning as an absent referent is evident when we push the meaning of the metaphor: one cannot truly *feel* like a piece of meat. Teresa de Lauretis comments: "No one can really *see* oneself as an inert object or a sightless body,"[1] and no one can really feel like a piece of meat because meat by definition is something violently deprived of all feeling. The use of the phrase "feeling like a piece of meat" occurs within a metaphoric system of language.

The animals have become absent referents, whose fate is transmuted into a metaphor for someone else's existence or fate. Metaphorically, the absent referent can be anything whose original meaning is undercut as it is absorbed into a different hierarchy of meaning; in this case the original meaning of animals' fates is absorbed into a human-centered hierarchy. Specifically in regard to rape victims and battered women, the death experience of animals acts to illustrate the lived experience of women.

The absent referent is both there and not there. It is there through inference, but its meaningfulness reflects only upon what it refers to because the originating, literal experience that contributes the meaning is not there.[2] We fail to accord this absent referent its own existence.

Women and animals: overlapping but absent referents

This chapter posits that a structure of overlapping but absent referents links violence against women and animals. Through the structure of the absent referent, patriarchal values become institutionalized. Just as dead bodies are absent from our language about meat, in descriptions of cultural violence women are also often the absent referent. Rape, in particular, carries such potent imagery that the term is transferred from the literal experience of women and applied metaphorically to other instances of violent devastation, such as the "rape" of the earth in ecological writings of the early 1970s. The experience of women thus becomes a vehicle for describing other oppressions. Women, upon whose bodies actual rape is most often committed, become the absent referent when the language of sexual violence is used metaphorically. These terms recall women's experiences but not women.

When I use the term "the rape of animals," the experience of women becomes a vehicle for explicating another being's oppression. Some terms are so powerfully specific to one group's oppression that their appropriation to others is potentially exploitative: for instance, using the "holocaust" for anything but the extermination of Jewish people, or "slavery" for anything but the forced enslavement of black people. Yet, feminists, among others, appropriate the metaphor of butchering without acknowledging the originating oppression of animals that generates the power of the metaphor. Through the function of the absent referent, Western culture constantly renders the material reality of violence into controlled and controllable metaphors.

Sexual violence and meat eating, which appear to be discrete forms of violence, find a point of intersection in the absent referent. Cultural images of sexual violence, and actual sexual violence, often rely on our knowledge of how animals are butchered and eaten. For example, Kathy Barry tells us of "*maisons d'abattage* (literal translation: houses of slaughter)" where six or seven girls each serve 80 to 120 customers a night.[3] In addition, the bondage equipment of pornography—chains, cattle prods, nooses, dog collars, and ropes—suggests the control of animals. Thus, when women are victims of violence, the treatment of animals is recalled.

Similarly, in images of animal slaughter, erotic overtones suggest that women are the absent referent. If animals are the absent referent in the phrase "the butchering of women," women are the absent referent in the phrase "the rape of animals." The impact of a seductive pig relies on an absent but imaginable, seductive, fleshy woman. Ursula Hamdress is both metaphor and joke; her jarring (or jocular) effect is based on the fact that we are all accustomed to seeing women depicted in such a way. Ursula's image refers to something that is absent: the human female body. The structure of the absent referent in patriarchal culture strengthens individual oppressions by always recalling other oppressed groups.

Because the structure of overlapping absent referents is so deeply rooted in Western culture, it inevitably implicates individuals. Our participation evolves as part of our general socialization to cultural patterns and viewpoints, thus we fail to see anything disturbing in the violence and domination that are an inextricable part of this structure. Consequently, women eat meat, work in slaughterhouses, at times treat other women as "meat," and men at times are victims of sexual violence. Moreover, because women as well as men participate in and benefit from the structure of the absent referent by eating meat, neither achieve the personal distance to perceive their implication in the structure, nor the originating oppression of animals that establishes the potency of the metaphor of butchering.

The interaction between physical oppression and the dependence on metaphors that rely on the absent referent indicates that we distance ourselves from whatever is different by equating it with something we have already objectified. For instance, the demarcation between animals and people was invoked during the early modern period to emphasize social distancing. According to Keith Thomas, infants, youth, the poor, blacks, Irish, insane people, and women were considered beastlike: "Once perceived as beasts, people were liable to be treated accordingly. The ethic of human domination removed animals from the sphere of human concern. But it also legitimized the ill-treatment of those humans who were in a supposedly animal condition."[4]

Racism and the absent referent

Through the structure of the absent referent, a dialectic of absence and presence of oppressed groups occurs. What is absent refers back to one oppressed group while defining another. This has theoretical implications for class and race as well as violence against women and animals. Whereas I want to focus on the overlapping oppressions of women and animals, further exploration of the function of the absent referent is needed, such as found in Marjorie Spiegel's *The Dreaded Comparison: Human and Animal Slavery*. Spiegel discusses the connection between racial oppression and animal oppression and in doing so demonstrates their overlapping relationship.[5]

The structure of the absent referent requires assistants who achieve the elimination of the animal, a form of alienated labor. Living, whole animals are the absent referents not only in meat eating but also in the fur trade. Of interest then is the connection between the oppression of animals through the fur trade and the oppression of blacks as slaves rather than Native Americans. Black historians suggest that one of the reasons black people rather than Native Americans were oppressed through the white Americans' institution of slavery is because of the slaughter of fur-bearing animals. As Vincent Harding describes it in *There Is a River: The Black Struggle for Freedom in America*: "One important early source of income for the Europeans in North America was the fur trade with the Indians, which enslavement of the latter would endanger."[6] While the factors that caused the oppression of Native Americans and blacks is not reducible to this example, we do see in it the undergirding of interactive oppressions by the absent referent. We also see that in analyzing the oppression of human beings, the oppression of animals ought not to be ignored. However, the absent referent, because of its absence, prevents our experiencing connections between oppressed groups.

When one becomes alert to the function of the absent referent and refuses to eat animals, the use of metaphors relying on animals' oppression can simultaneously criticize both that which the metaphor points to and that from which it is derived. For instance, when vegetarian and Civil Rights activist Dick Gregory compares the ghetto to the slaughterhouse he does so condemning both and suggesting the functioning of the absent referent in erasing responsibility for the horrors of each:

> Animals and humans suffer and die alike. If you had to kill your own hog before you ate it, most likely you would not be able to do it. To hear the hog scream, to see the blood spill, to see the baby being taken away from its momma, and to see the look of death in the animal's eye would turn your stomach. So you get the man at the packing house to do the killing for you. In like manner, if the wealthy aristocrats who are perpetrating conditions in the ghetto actually heard the screams of ghetto suffering, or saw the slow death of hungry little kids, or witnessed the strangulation of manhood and dignity, they could not continue the killing. But the wealthy are protected from such horror. . . . If you can justify killing to eat meat, you can justify the conditions of the ghetto. I cannot justify either one.[7]

Sexual violence and meat eating

To rejoin the issue of the intertwined oppressions with which this chapter is primarily concerned, sexual violence and meat eating, and their point of intersection in the absent referent, it is instructive to consider incidents of male violence. Men's descriptions of their own violence suggest the structure of overlapping but absent referents. In defense of the "Bunny Bop"—in which rabbits are killed by clubs, feet, stones and so on—sponsored by a North Carolina American Legion post, one organizer explained, "What would all these rabbit hunters be doing if they weren't letting off all this steam? I'll tell you what they'd be doing. They'd be drinking and carousing and beating their wives."[8]

One common form of domestic violence is the killing of a family's pet. Here the absent referent is clearly in operation: the threatened woman or child is the absent referent in pet murders. Within the symbolic order the fragmented referent no longer recalls itself but something else.[9] Though this pattern of killing pets as a warning to an abused woman or child is derived from recent case studies of domestic violence, the story of a man's killing his wife's pet instead of his wife can be found in an early twentieth-century short story. Susan Glaspell's "A Jury of Her Peers" exposes this function of the absent referent and the fact that a woman's peers, i.e., other women, recognize this function.[10]

Generally, however, the absent referent, because of its absence, prevents our experiencing connections between oppressed groups. Cultural images of butchering and sexual violence are so interpenetrated that animals act as the absent referent in radical feminist discourse. In this sense, radical feminist theory participates in the same set of representational structures it seeks to expose. We uphold the patriarchal structure of absent referents, appropriating the experience of animals to interpret our own violation. For instance, we learn of a woman who went to her doctor after being battered. The doctor told her her leg "was like a raw piece of meat hanging up in a butcher's window."[11] Feminists translate this literal description into a metaphor for women's oppression. Andrea Dworkin states that pornography depicts woman as a "female piece of meat" and Gena Corea observes that "women in brothels can be used like animals in cages."[12] Linda Lovelace claims that when presented to Xaviera Hollander for inspection, "Xaviera looked me over like a butcher inspecting a side of beef."[13] When one film actress committed suicide, another described the dilemma she and other actresses encounter: "They treat us like meat." Of this statement Susan Griffin writes: "She means that men who hire them treat them as less than human, as matter without spirit."[14] In each of these examples, feminists have used violence against animals as metaphor, literalizing *and* feminizing the metaphor. Thus, Mary Daly appropriates the word "butcher" to describe lobotomists, since the majority of lobotomies have been performed on women.[15]

Because of this dependence on the *imagery* of butchering, radical feminist discourse has failed to integrate the *literal* oppression of animals into our analysis of patriarchal culture or to acknowledge the strong historical alliance between feminism and vegetarianism. Whereas women may feel like pieces of meat, and be treated like pieces of meat—emotionally butchered and physically battered—animals actually are made into pieces of meat. In radical feminist theory, the use of these metaphors alternates between a positive figurative activity and a negative activity of occlusion, negation, and omission in which the literal fate of the animal is elided. Could metaphor itself be the undergarment to the garb of oppression?

The cycle of objectification, fragmentation, and consumption

What we require is a theory that traces parallel trajectories: the common oppressions of women and animals, and the problems of metaphor and the absent referent. I propose a cycle of objectification, fragmentation, and consumption, which links butchering and sexual violence in our culture. Objectification permits an oppressor to view another being as an object. The oppressor then violates this being by object-like treatment: e.g., the rape of women that denies women freedom to say no, or the butchering of animals that converts animals from living breathing beings into dead objects. This process allows fragmentation, or brutal dismemberment, and finally consumption. While the occasional man may literally eat women, we all consume visual images of women all the time.[16] Consumption is the fulfillment of oppression, the annihilation of will, of separate identity. So too with language: a subject first is viewed, or objectified, through metaphor. Through fragmentation the object is severed from its ontological meaning. Finally, consumed, it exists only through what it represents. The consumption of the referent reiterates its annihilation as a subject of importance in itself.

Since this chapter addresses how patriarchal culture treats animals as well as women, the image of meat is an appropriate one to illustrate this trajectory of objectification, fragmentation, and consumption. The literal process of violently transforming living animals to dead consumable ones is emblematic of the conceptual process by which the referent point of meat eating is changed. Industrialized meat-eating cultures such as the United States and Great Britain exemplify the process by which live animals are removed from the idea of meat. The physical process of butchering an animal is recapitulated on a verbal level through words of objectification and fragmentation.

Animals are rendered being-less not only by technology, but by innocuous phrases such as "food-producing unit," "protein harvester," "converting machine," "crops," and "biomachines." The meat-producing industry views an animal as consisting of "edible" and "inedible" parts, which must be separated so that the latter do not contaminate the former. An animal proceeds down a "disassembly line," losing body parts at every stop. This fragmentation not only dismembers the animal, it changes the way in which we conceptualize animals. In *The American Heritage Dictionary* the definition of "lamb" is illustrated not by an image of Mary's little one but by an edible body divided into ribs, loin, shank, and leg.[17]

After being butchered, fragmented body parts must be renamed to obscure the fact that these were once animals. After death, cows become roast beef, steak, hamburger; pigs become pork, bacon, sausage. Since objects are possessions they cannot have possessions; thus, we say "leg of lamb" not a "lamb's leg." We opt for less disquieting referent points not only by changing names from animals to meat, but also by cooking, seasoning, and covering the animals with sauces, disguising their original nature.

Only then can consumption occur: actual consumption of the animal, now dead, and metaphorical consumption of the term "meat," so that it refers to food products alone rather than to the dead animal. In patriarchal culture, meat is without its referent point. This is the way we want it, as William Hazlitt honestly admitted in 1826:

> Animals that are made use of as food should either be so small as to be impercept-
> ible, or else we should . . . not leave the form standing to reproach us with our
> gluttony and cruelty. I hate to see a rabbit trussed, or a hare brought to the table in
> the form which it occupied while living."[18]

The dead animal is the point beyond the culturally presumed referent of meat.

Notes

1   Teresa de Lauretis, *Alice Doesn't: Feminism, Semiotics, Cinema* (Bloomington: University of Indiana Press, 1984), p. 141.
2   I am indebted to Margaret Homans' discussion of the absent referent in literature for this expanded explanation of the cultural function of the absent referent. See her *Bearing the Word: Language and Female Experience in Nineteenth-Century Women's Writing* (Chicago: University of Chicago Press, 1986), p. 4.
3   Kathy Barry, *Female Sexual Slavery* (Englewood Cliffs, NJ: Prentice Hall, 1979), p. 3.
4   Keith Thomas, *Man and the Natural World: A History of the Modern Sensibility* (New York: Pantheon, 1983), p. 44.
5   Marjorie Spiegel, *The Dreaded Comparison: Human and Animal Slavery* (Philadelphia, PA: New Society Publishers, 1988).
6   Vincent Harding, *There Is a River: The Black Struggle for Freedom in America* (New York: Harcourt Brace Jovanovich, 1981, New York: Vintage Books, 1983), p. 7. Harding's source is Peter H. Wood's *Black Majority: Negroes in Colonial South Carolina from 1670 through the Stono Rebellion* (New York: Alfred A. Knopf, 1974). Wood discusses the reasons that the Proprietors of the Carolina colony protested the enslavement of Indians. They did so not only because they feared "prompting hostilities with local tribes" but also because "they were anxious to protect their peaceful trade in deerskins, which provided the colony's first source of direct revenue to England. With the opening up of this lucrative Indian trade to more people in the 1690s, the European settlers themselves became increasingly willing to curtail their limited reliance upon native American labor." *Black Majority*, p. 39.
7   Dick Gregory, *The Shadow That Scares Me*, ed. James R. McGraw (Garden City, NY: Doubleday & Co., Inc., 1968), pp. 69–70.
8   Commander Pierce Van Hoy quoted in Cleveland Amory, *Man Kind? Our Incredible War on Wildlife* (New York: Harper & Row, 1974), p. 14.
9   Another example of this can be found in the case of Arthur Gary Bishop, a child molester and murderer of five boys, who relived his first murder by buying and killing as many as twenty puppies.
10 Susan Glaspell, *A Jury of Her Peers* (London: Ernest Benn, Ltd., 1927).
11 R. Emerson Dobash and Russell Dobash, *Violence Against Wives: A Case Against the Patriarchy* (New York: The Free Press, Macmillan, 1979), p. 110.
12 Andrea Dworkin, *Pornography: Men Possessing Women* (New York: Perigee Books, 1981), p. 209; Gena Corea, *The Hidden Malpractice: How American Medicine Mistreats Women* (New York: William Morrow and Co., 1977, New York: Jove-Harcourt Brace Jovanovich Books, 1978), p. 129.
13 Linda Lovelace with Mike McGrady, *Ordeal* (New York: Citadel Press, 1980, Berkley Books, 1981), p. 96. Note that this is one woman looking at another as "meat."
14 Susan Griffin, *Rape: The Power of Consciousness* (San Francisco: Harper & Row, 1979), p. 39.
15 Daly defines "butcher" as "a bloody operator, esp. one who receives professional recognition and prestige for his 'successes.' " (*Websters' First New Intergalactic Wickedary of the English Language*

[Boston: Beacon Press, 1987], p. 188.) Her failure to include animals in this definition is all the more notable because her book discusses hunting and vivisection, argues for our ability to communicate with animals, and is dedicated to the late Andrée Collard who had written on violence against animals. (See Andrée Collard with Joyce Contrucci, *Rape of the Wild: Man's Violence against Animals and the Earth* [London: The Women's Press, 1988].)

16   Annette Kuhn remarks: "Representations are productive: photographs, far from merely reproducing a pre-existing world, constitute a highly coded discourse which, among other things, constructs whatever is in the image as object of consumption—consumption by looking, as well as often quite literally by purchase. It is no coincidence, therefore, that in many highly socially visible (and profitable) forms of photography women dominate the image. Where photography takes women as its subject matter, it also constructs 'woman' as a set of meanings which then enter cultural and economic circulation on their own account." (*The power of the image: Essays on representation and sexuality* [London: Routledge and Kegan Paul, 1985], p. 19.) Also see Kaja Silverman, *The Subject of Semiotics* (New York: Oxford University Press, 1983), especially her chapter on "Suture," pp. 194–236.

17   William Morris, ed., *The American Heritage Dictionary of the English Language* (Boston: American Heritage Publishing Co., Inc., and Houghton Mifflin Co., 1969), p. 734.

18   William Hazlitt, *The Plain Speaker* (EL, n.d.), 173, quoted in Keith Thomas, *Man and the Natural World*, p. 300.

34

Kathryn Paxton George

"A Feminist Critique of Ethical Vegetarianism"

Kathryn Paxton George argues that traditional and feminist arguments for vegetarianism fail due to their ignoring differences between the nutritional needs of different people and cultures as well as the differences stemming from the imbalance of power in society. When these needs are considered in the actual contexts in which we eat, it becomes evident that rules about vegetarianism are aesthetic rather than moral. Eating small amounts of meat is appropriate as long as it does not involve cruelty, violence, or waste.

How traditional moral theory fails

Singer, Regan, and virtually all other philosophers defending the moral status of animals claim that animals are our equals and that we may not kill them for food. According to Peter Singer (1975), we may not use their products unless we could be sure that these products are obtained under painless conditions. Singer's utilitarian position would permit some people to eat animals or their products if they have a strong welfare-interest (say, for reasons of ill health), but these would be exceptional cases, on grounds that are apparently the same as offered by Tom Regan (1983).[1] Regan's rights position allows certain people to consume meat as exceptional cases based on what he dubs the Liberty Principle:

> Provided that all those involved are treated with respect, and assuming that no special considerations obtain, any innocent individual has the right to act to avoid being made worse-off even if doing so harms other innocents.
>
> (1983, 333)

Being made to starve or suffer a significant decline in health and vigor would make us worse off, and Regan accedes that if some humans have a strong welfare-interest in consuming meat or animal products, this would excuse them from a duty to be vegetarians. But Regan clearly thinks most people do not fall into such a category. He briefly discusses protein complementation and then dismisses the argument from nutrition:

> Certain amino acids are essential for our health. Meat isn't. We cannot, therefore, defend meat eating on the grounds that we will ruin our health if we don't eat it or even that we will run a very serious risk of doing so if we abstain.
>
> (1983, 337)

The question is, to whom does that "we" refer? Traditional morality claims to prescribe for everyone—not merely for some; its rules are supposed to be universal. Because its rules are universal and rights-holders are equal, the rules should also be impartial. All mature and rational persons regardless of their age, sex, race, and other irrelevant factors are supposed to be able to follow a universal rule—or at least to be capable of being taught to do so. Traditional moral theories assume the moral equality and the general interchangeability of persons regardless of age, sex, race, and so forth. Ethical vegetarians and ethical vegans suppose that all of us could adopt such diets if we choose.

In making these assumptions, ethical vegetarians posit a moral norm that should be consistent with physiological norms. "Moral norms" are rules and standards meant to guide the conduct of beings who have the capacity for morality. Moral norms and physiological norms should not be confused, even though both imply significant value claims. A "physiological norm," as it is intended here, picks out some fact or material aspect about the world, such as, "it is the norm for males to produce more testosterone than estrogen." We might pick out many more traits that are common for the human species. Abnormal physiology need not and should not be taken to mean moral inferiority or even illness, although it will sometimes impair function. People born with webbed fingers or toes, extra fingers or even no fingers at all are neither morally inferior nor ill, although their physical function differs from that usually seen. Nondiscrimination requires that, insofar as possible, society should eliminate moral, social, or legal constraints that will cause extraordinary persons to suffer an increased burden in their attempts to function in society. We provide ramps for those who use wheelchairs, for instance. Nondiscrimination is the attempt by fair-minded people to affirm the equal worth of each member of the moral community. No single group can simply assume that its own practices are the only right ones, or even the best ones. Nondiscrimination also requires that moral norms distribute burdens and benefits equitably among groups. It is wrong, for example, to set out greater punishments for offenders of one race than for another. If the moral norm or rule prescribing vegetarian or vegan diets is truly nondiscriminatory, it should not require greater or very much greater burdens for some groups because of aspects about themselves that cannot be changed and that are thought to be neutral to the interests served by the rule.[2]

The moral rule requiring vegetarianism is quite otherwise. It does systematically impose greater burdens on some. Although most men age 20–50 in industrialized countries can choose to be vegetarians without significant risk or burdens, the same cannot be said for other people identifiable by characteristics over which they have no choice or control: infants, children, adolescents, gestating and lactating women, and some elderly people. Inextricably bound up with this male physiological norm is a presupposed cultural norm that is biased against many people living in ethnic, cultural, economic, and environmental circumstances unlike those in which a vegan ideal can be successfully realized. That cultural norm also presupposes a society largely structured on wealth generated from unsustainable environmental, agricultural, and industrial practices.

In what follows, I explain why arguments for a stringent ethical vegetarianism must suppose that all or almost all ethical vegans and vegetarians have bodies approximating that of an adult male between the ages of twenty and fifty. This is the "male physiological norm" and it is biased against females, children, and the elderly.

[. . .]

In my view "moral" or "ethical" must be conceptually linked to guidance with respect to our relations with others. Although we guide by example, human beings must also learn by instruction. When we instruct, we make choices and express concerns about behaviors, actions, rules, virtues and ideals.

[. . .]

Below I explicate the answer I have come to accept, what I refer to as a feminist aesthetic semivegetarianism. I explore some of the contexts within which we eat and suggest ways of evaluating these particular contexts.

[. . .]

Eating alone

Considering oneself alone and eating without others present, any adult might choose a diet in industrialized countries from veganism to semivegetarianism. Prudence dictates that individuals consider their personal health when deciding on diet. Reasons to take care of ourselves are not simply egocentric. If we do not do so, then we may become overly dependent on others, either for personal care or through use of the health care system.

[. . .]

Eating with others

What should this individual do if she finds herself among others? It seems most consistent to me that she should practice a semivegetarian diet or at least defer to it. Some people really do not wish to consume meat, but there are various symbolic ways to affirm the efforts of pregnant women and parents to provide adequate nutrition to their children through food rather than supplements, for instance. The strict vegetarian might still cut meat for a child.

The good person should not place herself in a position of assuming that she knows or understands the motives and needs of others. For instance, we often do not know the food allergies of our friends much less of the person sitting next to us in a restaurant.

[. . .]

Eating in families

Women and their families live in various contexts. Many families are amalgams of the young and the old, male and female, two or more cultures, two or more species. Families may have many reasons for serving different kinds of food that involve the nutritional needs of its members, health concerns, cultural traditions, and so on. For this example, let us say that our family consists of an adult, a child, and an elderly person. Eating a small amount of meat and using dairy products is defensible for all. Several reasons support this. The first is health; semivegetarian diets are healthy and involve few, if any, of the risks in vegetarian diets. Second, children tend to imitate their parents. If a mother and grandmother do not eat meat or drink milk, then her daughter may not, even if at the daughter's stage of life she is building bones whereas the mother is not. The grandmother may lose bone from inadequate calcium in her diet and become dependent upon the family for care. If a father is not eating any meat or milk, then his son may not even though he too needs to build bone and maintain iron levels.

[. . .]

Eating and parenting

Providing meals for children presupposes a special responsibility. . . . There is no evidence that semivegetarian diets are risky for infants or children (Havala and Dwyer 1988), and semivegetarian diets are likely to be less dependent on supplementation than vegan diets. The traditionalist ethical vegetarian position requires that parents take these risks for their children and put them on vegan diets.[3] But this is to confuse what it is safe to do with what one is morally required to do. Feminist aesthetic vegetarianism would leave it to individual parents to decide whether it is appropriate to move in the direction of moral vegetarianism for a child.

Summary

Does my view mean that people can go on eating meat without concern? No, it does not. Absolutism functions only as an attempt at domination; that is, accept this rule and you won't be required to think ever again! Many good reasons exist to moderate our eating habits to semivegetarian practice. These reasons should count with all of us, and we must decide for ourselves what sort of balance is possible in our own lives.

All things considered—the needs of women and children, the tendencies of young females towards eating disorders, pressures on women to diet in general, the extra burden that is placed on women in preparing different kinds of food for each family member, the conditions under which animals are raised—families and people in general should be semivegetarians. We should write, teach, and actively work for a reduction in animal cruelty, to improve the conditions under which animals are raised, to encourage gratitude for their association with us, and to recognize their membership in a community with us. We should not eat them wastefully but only in a portion that balances the needs of family members sharing the same meal. Feminists need not necessarily drop their vegan or vegetarian lifestyles if they and their families are doing well and living happily on them. But I do think feminists must stop preaching the vegetarian life as a moral imperative. Vegetarianism is not morally required. It is an aesthetic choice that may be personally satisfying and healthful. To argue otherwise is divisive and self-defeating.

Because needs vary, feminist aesthetic semivegetarianism does not prescribe measured amounts of meat or dairy products. But, people in most industrialized countries should drastically reduce their consumption of meat and dairy products. Three of the best reasons to endorse a drastic reduction, but not elimination, in meat eating and dairy use are (1) preserving personal health, (2) establishing a global sustainable environment that produces a long-term supply of adequate food, and (3) restoring domestic animals to a place of greater respect by giving them housing, care, transport, and slaughter that empowers these domestic species to their natural activities. Their lives and suffering count and should not be wasted. Efforts at producing global health require attention to the particular contexts of climate, culture, soils, species, and their systems. A balancing of various goods and interests will be necessary, and preaching the evils of meat eating is more likely to do harm than good.

Traditionalist arguments for ethical vegetarianism collapse because they violate their own central Principle of Equality. If we believe that sexism is wrong and women and men should be equal, then we must *accept* speciesism—animals cannot be the equals of humans because women, men, children, and others have differing nutritional needs. But if we *reject* speciesism, then we must *accept* sexism and the belief that women cannot be the equal of men because their bodies are weaker, vulnerable, and inferior to that of adult males, who can practice vegetarianism with relatively little risk. In the face of this dilemma, traditional moral arguments for the rights and welfare of animals are inconsistent and fail. So, these traditional moral arguments for ethical vegetarianism cannot be integrated into a feminist ethic.

Moreover, specifically feminist arguments for ethical vegetarianism or the vegan ideal also fail. The historical and claimed theoretical link between vegetarianism and feminism is a chimera. The vegan ideal is not at all a feminist ideal. Even the feminist arguments assume that the human norm is male, and women are expected to accommodate themselves to it. I have argued that feminist ethical frameworks have been committed to two basic beliefs that I call the "minimum conception of a feminist ethics." These two beliefs are: First, no ethics can admit of arbitrariness in its prescriptions and theories. Second, any specifically feminist ethic must affirm the value of the female body. Current feminist arguments for ethical vegetarianism would require women to live as if physiologically identical to men and assign arbitrary moral or physical burdens to women, children, and others based on factors that cannot be changed by human choice. Thus, the minimum conception rules out ethical vegetarianism. Therefore, my arguments show that all formulations of ethical vegetarianism, whether traditionalist or feminist, fail.

The "vegan ideal" is not a *moral* ideal at all. It may be adopted as a personal lifestyle, but it cannot be a moral ideal because it would idealize those of a particular age, sex, class, ethnicity, and culture; that is, adult (age 20–50), middle-class, mostly white males living in high-tech societies—the group with the most power in our world.

Feminists should not moralize about food practice, even though it remains appropriate to condemn cruelty and to encourage moderation and semivegetarianism for that reason. Equality remains a central principle of any feminist ethic. Reinterpreting equality to include differences suggests that we should adopt equality on a range from empowerment to acceptance. We should work to understand domesticated animal behaviors and to empower their natures within the human-animal relationship and simultaneously attempt to understand and contribute to acceptance as equality among humans. Certainly, sustained discussion and debate will be necessary in order to determine ways to make these differences cost less for those who live them. Because even Deane Curtin's feminist contextual moral vegetarianism collapses to values clarification and offers no moral guidance, individuals must not focus on vegetarianism as an avenue to moral virtue. Instead, we must look again at how to make ethics and equality *functional*. An aesthetic semivegetarianism *permits* everyone to eat a certain small amount of meat, dairy products and other animal products as long as animals are well treated and killed as painlessly as possibly. It respects a fuzzy boundary between the aesthetic and the moral in this way. That is, the imperative *against* cruelty and violence *limits* how much one may consume. Yet *that* one consumes the meat and animal products is itself aesthetic because it is *permitted* as a matter of taste, health, and context. Each person must decide the divide between the aesthetic and the moral on the basis of her own conscience, but depending on those with whom one eats setting the line too low (veganism) will often be just as wrongful as setting it too high (excessive meat eating). We must fashion our diets within social settings, realizing that personal and global health are intersubjectively valid aesthetic values. In some cases it may be that a person will choose vegetarianism or veganism because that choice will most beautify her life. In more ordinary cases, though, feminists should choose aesthetic semivegetarianism in recognition of the differences among males and females, young and old, humans and nonhumans, and those in other cultures and classes, in an effort to *live* equality as acceptance, and in affirmation of personal and global health as well as strength of character as guiding values.

Notes

1   Singer (1975) relies on the notion that "a vegetarian can expect to be at least as healthy as one who eats meat" (256). Unlike Regan, he does say that such health rests on the ability of the food industry to include supplements in our food. He also counsels pregnant women and other vulnerable groups to take extra care. But he does not notice the male bias in the vegan ideal (see 274–5).

2   That individuals actually carry different burdens in fulfilling their moral responsibilities is not always objectionable, however. For example, under traditional moral theory, all people are expected to keep their promises as a general rule. Some exceptions apply and rights or utilitarian theory can prescribe justifications for these exceptions, but the mere presence of a greater burden does not automatically grant an individual an exception to a valid moral rule. Many people will sometimes find it a greater burden than other people to keep a promise. Traditional moral theory would deny, however, that a valid moral rule or norm would systematically require self-sacrifices not required of others in circumstances beyond one's own control. So, a poor woman who buys a television set, promises to pay for it over time, and then finds she cannot make the payments does have more difficulty than a wealthy person in keeping her promise. But the rule is still impartial and nondiscriminatory if she chose to make the promise and could have refrained from making it. Even though she belongs to a class that makes it more difficult to keep this particular promise, it does not thereby systematically foreclose her ability to make all promises without difficulty.

3   This example also illustrates something else about the presumed norm in traditionalist ethical vegetarianism (that is, Adams, Donovan, Gaard, Gruen, Regan, Singer, Varner): The ideal person has no one else dependent upon him and for whom he must make decisions and no one else's interests to protect but his own. He is not a parent.

References

Havala, Suzanne, and Johanna T. Dwyer. 1988. Position of the American Dietetic Association: Vegetarian diets—Technical support paper. *Journal of the American Dietetic Association* 88:3 (March): 352–5.
Regan, Tom. 1983. *The Case for Animal Rights*. Berkeley: University of California Press.
Singer, Peter. 1975. *Animal Liberation*. New York: Avon.

Religious Perspectives

35

Norman Solomon

"Judaism"

Norman Solomon points out that while Judaism prohibits cruelty to animals, human life is valued above animal life. Harm to animals must be evaluated in the context of what alternatives exist. The passage contains a brief description of the required method of slaughter.

[. . .]

The Torah does not enjoin vegetarianism, though Adam and Eve were vegetarian [And God said, "Behold, I have given you every plant yielding seed which is upon the face of all the earth, and every tree with seed in its fruit; you shall have them for food"] (Gen. 1:29 RSV). Restrictions on meat eating perhaps indicate that it is a concession to human weakness; among the mediaeval Jewish philosophers of the Iberian peninsula, Joseph Albo (1380–1435) wrote that the first people were forbidden to eat meat because of the cruelty involved in killing animals (*Sefer Ha-Iqqarim* 3: 15). Isaac Abravanel (1437–1508) endorsed this in his commentary on Isaiah, Ch. 11 and also taught in his commentary on Genesis, Ch. 2, that when the Messiah comes we would return to the ideal, vegetarian state. Today the popular trend to vegetarianism has won many Jewish adherents though little official backing from religious leaders.

Although the Torah does not insist on vegetarianism, it places considerable restraints on the eating of meat; only the meat of certain animals may be eaten, certain parts may not be eaten at all, the blood must be drained, and there are regulations as to how the animals should be slaughtered. *Shehitah*, the method of slaughter, is by a single sharp cut across the trachaea and oesophagus; this may be performed only by a qualified religious expert, and nowadays there are special pens and procedures to ensure that the animal suffers the minimum of psychological distress as well as the minimum pain. Since in any case the animal very swiftly loses consciousness, generally before the onset of pain from the sharp cut, this is a relatively humane process.

From time to time voices are heard suggesting that *shehitah* is cruel to animals, but the criticisms often concern inessential aspects of *shehitah*, such as the form of casting-pen used, rather than *shehitah* itself. Nevertheless, there is at least a theoretical problem for Jews of what to do should it be demonstrated that the *shehitah* process is to some extent cruel; there would be a contradiction between two equally clear demands of the Torah, that meat not be eaten unless *shehitah* has been correctly performed, and that one should not practise cruelty to animals. Since the only cruelty which could conceivably be demonstrated would be minor, it is probable that the decision reached would be that *shehitah* be continued, and the procedures improved as far as possible; otherwise, orthodox Jews would be forced to be vegetarians. Judaism does not recognise cruelty to animals as an absolute value. Human life is consistently valued above animal life, so that any prima facie instance of harm to animals must be evaluated as to its seriousness and then balanced against alternatives.

[. . .]

36

Rabbi Stephen Fuchs

"Enhancing the Divine Image"

Rabbi Stephen Fuchs explains his vegetarianism as based on the creation story in Genesis, an "exquisite religious poem." Genesis details God's goal, which is to create a caring, compassionate society. Being vegetarian is a way to take our place as a partner with God.

For the past seven years I have been a vegetarian. I do not eat meat, fish or chicken. I do, however, use eggs and dairy products. The criterion for what I eat is simple. I eat nothing that has to die for me to consume it.

The foundation of the vegetarian life-style I have adopted is not medical. Neither does it come from a distaste for the taste of flesh. I am one who loved a good steak or a good hamburger or a piece of roast beef. The memories of our chicken dinners on Friday night or the duck or goose we consumed on special occasions are precious to me. No, my decision to become a vegetarian is not based on a distaste for meat. Quite the contrary.

My decision to become a vegetarian is based on my understanding of the essential message of the early chapters of Genesis. First and foremost is the story of creation. Much has been written about this story over the years. Most people think of it as either the scientific account of how the world was created or a fairy tale which offers little meaningful guidance to us today. From my perspective, both of these interpretations are wrong. In his book, *In the Beginning*, the late science fiction writer Isaac Asimov fell into the trap of viewing the creation story as an obsolete scientific document when he wrote, "The biblical writers did the best they could with the scientific material available to them. If they had written those earlier chapters of Genesis knowing what we know today, we can be certain they would have written it completely differently."[1] No, Mr. Asimov, we cannot be so certain. The biblical authors were not concerned with making a scientific statement any more than Mozart was concerned with writing "Rock 'N Roll" music. The biblical authors were concerned with making a religious statement, and the statement they made continues to inspire people today.

So, the first component of my decision to become vegetarian deals with an interpretation of the creation story. No, it is not bad science. It is simply not science at all. The creation story is, though, an exquisite religious poem, and it has a powerful message for us. The basis of the story is the notion that the creation of the world was a purposeful act—not an accident. In the assertion that creation was purposeful, the creation account in the Torah stands apart from other religious creation stories which see the world as we know it as an incidental by-product of interactions among gods with human qualities such as fear, jealousy and sexuality. [2]

God's purposefulness and intentionality also separate the Genesis account from scientific theories which assume that the world in which we live began as the result of an accident of nature. The Torah's creation story assumes that behind creation is a Creator who set the process in motion. The orderliness and purposefulness of the creation account are apparent from the economy of language, the repetition of certain key phrases and, most significantly, from the way that each succeeding action of creation bases itself on that which precedes it.

Clearly, it is the intent of the biblical author to proclaim humanity as God's highest creative act. Light, land, vegetation, fish, fowl and beasts of the earth were all, the creation poem asserts, created by *fiat*—by the simple proclamation "And God said, 'Let there be . . .' and it was so."

Only in the case of humanity does God ponder the task of creation. Only humanity is given "dominion over the fish of the sea, the birds of the sky, the cattle, the whole earth and all the creeping things that creep on earth (Genesis 1:26). Only in the case of humanity does God depart from the "Let there be . . . and it was so" formula. We human beings alone, the Bible asserts, were created in God's image. Jewish tradition makes clear that God has no form or shape, so that "created in God's image" cannot mean that we look like God. Rather, the expression means that we alone among the acts of creation share some of God's characteristics. "Created in God's image" means that we, more than any other creatures, are responsible for the quality of life on earth.

It is ours to replenish or ruin, to protect or to pollute. That indeed is the ultimate purpose of the story: to remind us that we are in charge. We should not glory in our power, but realize our responsibilities as stewards of creation. To "have dominion" over the fish of the sea, the birds of the air, and the beasts of the earth, does not mean to exploit them mercilessly. For me it means "to be responsible for," to understand that we are the most powerful creatures on earth, and that we can rule with either kindness or cruelty. Kindness toward living creatures is part of my understanding of the message of the creation story.

Among the many rabbinic comments on the opening chapter of Genesis is the one which notes that the word "creation" (*Bereshit*, the first word of the Bible) begins with the letter *beth* because *beth* is the first letter of the word *bracha*, which means "blessing." Creation begins with *beth* to remind us that each person has the potential by her or his actions to make life a blessing for ourselves, for those around us, for the other creatures God created and for future generations.[3]

Chapters two through eleven in Genesis, the chapters which follow the story of creation, tell, as I interpret them, of three attempts on God's part to create what has been from the beginning God's highest goal: a caring, compassionate society. Each of those societies has groundrules.[4] Essentially, though, the first society in Eden was a place of no birth, no death, no sexuality (in my view) and no need to work hard. It was a place in which human beings were given to eat of vegetation only. The second society is one which I label "Post-Eden/Pre-Flood." That society was a place of birth, death, sexuality and the need to work for a living. It didn't work out any better than the other two. The Torah pictures the Almighty as constantly trying to make adjustments, even compromises, with human nature, so that society might work out better.

After the flood, there are new ground rules. First, God promises never to destroy the world again (Genesis 8:22). Second, people are to be responsible for their actions (Genesis 9:6). Third and most important for our discussion, for the first time, after the flood, humanity received permission to eat meat (Genesis 9:3). All of the foregoing, though, shows us that in the first two attempts God made to set up a workable society, human beings were vegetarian. Perhaps it was as a concession to human nature that we are given permission to eat meat in a third attempt to set up a society that would be workable. As we know, that third society didn't work out either, and God made a fourth attempt to set up a caring, compassionate society through the covenant which the Almighty made with Abraham and Sarah. The permission that we received to eat meat is still in force, of course, and subsequent Jewish tradition has curtailed that privilege by reminding us through elaborate rituals of *kashrut* of the magnitude of what we do each time we kill a living being.

I have not been able, though, to shake the notion that if we really wanted to do God's will, we would abstain from meat altogether. In short, I believe I more fully approach my potential as a creature created in God's image when I abstain from eating food that must die so that I might eat it. Though much has changed in the course of history and much has happened to our people, I still believe our purpose as Jews is to be exponents of God's hope to create the caring, compassionate society for which God has yearned since creation. For me, part of that quest has been to abstain from eating meat, not because I don't like it, not because I am worried by its effect on my health, but because I believe it helps me to achieve the divine potential with which God made me. I cannot claim that my analysis of the sources and the basis for my decision provide incontrovertible evidence that God wants us to be vegetarian. I only know that, for me, I feel better about myself and more wholehearted in my attempt to take my place as a covenantal partner with God in fulfilling the charge first made to Abram, "Be a blessing," the blessing God intended in using the letter *beth* to begin the story of creation.

Notes

1   Isaac Asimov, *In the Beginning* (New York: Crown Publishers, 1981), 3.
2   Edward Lavitt and Robert McDowell, *In the beginning . . . Creation Stories for Young People* (New York: The Third Press, 1973). The book contains 35 examples of creation stories from throughout the world which illustrate this point.
3   *Bereshit Raba* 1:10.
4   For a fuller discussion of these ground rules, see my doctoral thesis, *Standing at Sinai: Looking Backward, Looking Forward* (Nashville, Tennessee: Vanderbilt University, 1992), 28–54.

37

Andrew Linzey

"The Bible and Killing for Food"

Andrew Linzey discusses the contradiction between the divine command of vegetarianism in Genesis 1 and the reversal of this command in Genesis 9. He states that Biblical vegetarians should not claim that it has never been justifiable to kill animals, but rather that it is not now necessary, and that a vegetarian life is closer to the biblical ideal of peace. Similarly, Linzey argues that while Jesus ate fish in the context of first-century Palestine, the question for us is what we eat now.

> And God said, 'Behold, I have given you every plant yielding seed which is upon the face of all the earth, and every tree with seed in its fruit; you shall have them for food. And to every beast of the earth, and to every bird of the air, and to everything that creeps on the earth, everything that has the breath of life, I have given every green plant for food.' (Gen. 1:29–30; RSV).
> And God blessed Noah and his sons, and said to them '. . . Every moving thing that lives shall be food for you; as I gave you the green plants, I give you everything.' (Gen. 9:1–4; RSV).

At first glance, these two passages may be taken as epitomizing the difficulty of appealing to scripture in the contemporary debate about animal rights. The sheer contradictoriness of these statements presses itself upon us. Genesis 1 clearly depicts vegetarianism as divine command. Indeed 'everything' that has the breath of life in it, is given 'green plant for food'. Genesis 9, however, reverses this command quite specifically. '(A)s I gave you the green plants, I give you everything' (9:3). In the light of this, the question might not unreasonably be posed: cannot both vegetarians and carnivores appeal to scripture for justification and both with *equal* support?

Food of paradise

In order to unravel this conundrum we have first of all to appreciate that those who made up the community whose spokesperson wrote Genesis 1 were not themselves vegetarians. Few appreciate that Genesis 1 and 2 are themselves the products of much later reflection by the biblical writers themselves. How is it then that the very people who were not themselves vegetarian imagined a beginning of time when all who lived were vegetarian (herbivore to be precise) by divine command?

To appreciate this perspective we need to recall the major elements of the first creation saga. God creates a world of great diversity and fertility. Every living creature is given life and space (Gen. 1:9–10; 24–5). Earth to live on and blessing to enable life itself (1:22). Living creatures are pronounced good (1:25). Humans are made in God's image (1:27) given dominion (1:26–9), and then prescribed a vegetarian diet (1:29–30). God then pronounces that everything was 'very good' (1:31). Together the whole creation rests on the sabbath with God (2:2–3). When examined in this way, we should see immediately that Genesis 1 describes a state of paradisal existence. There is no hint of violence between or among different species. Dominion, so often interpreted as justifying killing, actually precedes the command to be vegetarian. Herb-eating dominion is hardly a licence for tyranny. The answer seems to be then that even though the early Hebrews were neither pacifists nor vegetarians, they were deeply convinced of the view that violence between humans and animals, and indeed between animal species themselves, was not God's original will for creation.

But if this is true, how are we to reconcile Genesis 1 with Genesis 9, the vision of original peacefulness with the apparent legitimacy of killing for food? The answer seems to be that as the Hebrews began to construct the story of early human beginnings, they were struck by the prevalence and enormity of human wickedness. The stories of Adam and Eve, Cain and Abel, Noah and his descendants are testimonies to the inability of humankind to fulfil the providential purposes of God in creation. The issue is made explicit in the story of Noah:

> Now the earth was corrupt in God's sight, and the earth was filled with violence. And God saw the earth, and behold, it was corrupt; for all flesh had corrupted their way upon the earth. And God said to Noah, 'I have determined to make an end of all flesh; for the earth is filled with violence through them.' (Gen. 6:11–14; RSV).

The radical message of the Noah story (so often overlooked by commentators) is that God would rather not have us be at all if we must be violent. It is violence itself within every part of creation that is the pre-eminent mark of corruption and sinfulness. It is not for nothing that God concludes: 'I am sorry that I have made them' (Gen. 6:7).

Ambiguous permission

It is in *this* context—subsequent to the Fall and the Flood—that we need to understand the permission to kill for food in Genesis 9. It reflects entirely the situation of the biblical writers at the time they were writing. Killing—of both humans as well as animals—was simply inevitable given the world as it is and human nature as it is. Corruption and wickedness had made a mess of God's highest hopes for creation. There just had to be some accommodation to human sinfulness. 'Every moving thing shall be food for you; and as I gave you the green plants, I give you everything' (Gen. 9:3). For many students of the Bible this seems to have settled the matter of whether humans can be justified in killing animals for food. In the end, it has been thought, God allows it. And there can be no doubt that throughout the centuries this view has prevailed. Meat eating has become the norm. Vegetarians, especially Christian vegetarians, have survived from century to century to find themselves a rather beleaguered minority. The majority view can be summed up in this beautifully prosaic line of Calvin:

> For it is an insupportable tyranny, when God, the Creator of all things, has laid open to us the earth and the air, in order that we may thence take food as from his storehouse, for these to be shut up from us by mortal man, who is not able to create even a snail or a fly.[1]

What Calvin appears to overlook, however, as has most of the Christian tradition, is that the permission to kill for food in Genesis 9 is far from unconditional or absolute:

> Only you shall not eat flesh with its life, that is, its blood. For your lifeblood I will surely require a reckoning; of every beast I will require it and of man. . . . (Gen. 9:4–5; RSV).

Understanding these lines is far from straightforward. At first sight these qualificatory lines might be seen as obliterating the permission itself. After all, who can take animal life without the shedding of blood? Who can kill without the taking of blood, that is, the life itself? In asking these questions we move to the heart of the problem. For the early Hebrews life was symbolized by, even constituted by, blood itself. To kill *was* to take blood. And yet it is precisely *this* permission which is denied.

It is not surprising then that commentators have simply passed over these verses, suggesting that some ritual, symbolic significance was here entertained but one which in no way substantially affected the divine allowance to kill. But this, I suggest, is to minimize the significance of these verses. Rereading these verses in the light of their original context should go rather like this: The world in which you live has been corrupted. And yet God has not given up on you. God has signified a new relationship—a covenant with you—despite all your violence and unworthiness. Part of this covenant involves a new regulation concerning diet. What was previously forbidden can now—in the present circumstances—be allowed. You may kill for food. But you may kill only on the understanding that you remember that the life you kill is not your own—it belongs to God. You must not misappropriate what is not your own. As you kill what is not your own—either animal or human life—so you need to remember that for every life you kill you are personally accountable to God.[2]

If this reading is correct, and I believe few scholars would now dissent from this interpretation, it will be seen immediately that Genesis 9 does not grant humankind some absolute right to kill animals for food. Indeed, properly speaking, there is no *right* to kill. God allows it only under the conditions of necessity. A recent statement by the Union of Liberal and Progressive Synagogues expresses it this way: 'Only after the Flood (contends Genesis 9:3) was human consumption of animals permitted and that was later understood as a concession, both to human weakness and to the supposed scarcity of edible vegetation.'[3]

To give a more complete account of biblical themes requires us to move on from Genesis 1 and 2, to Isaiah 11. We need to appreciate that while killing was sometimes thought to be justifiable in the present time, biblical writers were also insistent that there would come another time when such killing was unnecessary. This is the time variously known as the 'future hope of Israel' or the 'Messianic Age'. Isaiah speaks of the one who will establish justice and equity and universal peace. One of the characteristics of this future age is the return to the existence envisaged by Genesis 1 before the Fall and the Flood:

> The wolf shall dwell with the lamb, and the leopard shall lie down with the kid, and the calf and the lion and the fatling together, and a little child shall lead them. The cow and the bear shall feed; their young shall lie down together; and the lion shall eat straw like the ox. The sucking child shall play over the hole of the asp, and the weaned child shall put his hand on the adder's den. They shall not hurt or destroy in all my holy mountain; for the earth shall be full of the knowledge of the Lord as the waters cover the sea. (Isa. 11:6–9; RSV).

It seems therefore that while the early Hebrews were neither vegetarians nor pacifists, the ideal of the peaceable kingdom was never lost sight of. In the end, it was believed, the world would one day be restored according to God's original will for all creation. Note, for example, how the vision of peaceable living also extends to relations between animals themselves. Not only, it seems, are humans to live peaceably with animals, but also formerly aggressive animals are to live peaceably with other animals.

We may sum up the main elements of the biblical approach as follows: killing for food appears essential in the world as we now know it, influenced as it is by corruption and wickedness. But such a state of affairs is not as God originally willed it. Even when we kill under situations of necessity we have to remember that the lives we kill do not belong to us and that we are accountable to God. Moreover, God's ultimate will for creation shall prevail. Whatever the present circumstances, one day all creation, human and animal, shall live in peace.

Living without violence

It should now be seen that far from being confused and contradictory, the biblical perspectives on killing for food have not only internal integrity but also enormous relevance to the contemporary debate about animal rights and vegetarianism. There are three ethical challenges in particular that we should grapple with.

The first thing that should be noted is that the Bible does not minimize the gravity of the act of killing animals. So often in our heavily industrialized societies we think of animals, especially farm animals, as merely food machines or commodities that are to be bought or sold for human consumption. This can never be the biblical view. Genesis 1 specifically speaks of animal life as that which 'has the breath of life' (1:30). This life is a gift from God. It does not belong to human beings. It may be used only with the greatest reserve and in remembrance of the One from whose creative hands it comes. Those who wish to use animals frivolously or with no regard for their God-given worth cannot claim the Bible for their support.

[. . .]

The second challenge is that we have no biblical warrant for claiming killing as God's will. God's will is for peace. We need to remember that even though Genesis 9 gives permission to kill for food it does so only on the basis that we do not misappropriate God-given life. Genesis 9 posits divine reckoning for the life of every beast taken even under this new dispensation (9:5). The question may not unnaturally be asked: how long can this divine permission last?

[. . .]

In this respect it is interesting that one highly regarded Talmudic scholar, Abraham Isaac Kook, maintains that the most spiritually satisfying way of reading the practical biblical injunctions concerning killing is in terms of preparation for a new dawn of justice for animals. 'The free movement of the moral impulse to establish justice for animals generally and the claim for their rights from mankind,' he argues, 'are hidden in a natural psychic sensibility in the deeper layers of the Torah.' Given the corruption of humankind, it was natural and inevitable that moral attention had first to be paid to the regulation of human conduct towards other humans. But in Kook's view the various injunctions concerning the selection and preparation of meat (in, for example, Lev. 17:13; Ezek. 16:63; Lev. 22:28 and Deut. 22:26–7) were commandments 'to regulate the eating of meat, in steps that will take us to the higher purpose'. And what is this higher purpose? None other it seems than universal peace and justice. Kook maintains that just as the embracing of democratic ideals came late within religious thinking 'so will the hidden yearning to act justly towards animals emerge at the proper time'.[4]

The third challenge to be grasped is that those who wish now to adopt a vegetarian or vegan lifestyle have solid biblical support. Biblical vegetarians will not say, 'It has *never been* justifiable to kill animals,' rather they should say, 'It is *not now* necessary to kill for food as it was once thought necessary.' The biblical case for vegetarianism does not rest on the view that killing may never be allowable in the eyes of God, rather on the view that killing is always a grave matter. When we have to kill to live we may do so, but when we do not, we should live otherwise. It is vital to appreciate the force of this argument. In past ages many—including undoubtedly the biblical writers themselves—have thought that killing for food was essential in order to live. We now know that—at least for those now living in the rich West—it is perfectly possible to sustain a healthy diet without any recourse to flesh products. This may not have always been true in the past. Conventional wisdom was always that meat was essential to live and to live well. Only during the past 200 years has vegetarianism become a publicly known and acceptable option.

Those individuals who opt for vegetarianism can do so in the knowledge that they are living closer to the biblical ideal of peaceableness than their carnivorous contemporaries. The point should not be minimized. In many ways it is difficult to know how we can live more peaceably in a world driven by violence and greed and consumerism. Individuals often feel powerless in the face of great social forces beyond even democratic control. To opt for a vegetarian lifestyle is to take one practical step towards living in peace with the rest of creation. It has been estimated that over 500 million animals are slaughtered for food in the UK every year. In the US the numbers are 6–9 billion annually. To become vegetarian is to take a practical step to reduce the rate of institutionalized killing in the world today. One fewer chicken eaten is one fewer chicken killed.

Nevertheless, we do well to appreciate the biblical perspective that we do not live in an ideal world. The truth is that even if we adopt a vegetarian or vegan lifestyle, we are still not free of killing either directly or indirectly. Even if we eat only beans and nuts and lentils, we have to reckon with the fact that competing animals are killed because of the crops we want to eat. Even if we decide not to wear dead animal skins, we have to face the fact that alternative substances have been tested for their toxicity on laboratory animals. Even if we eat only soya beans we do well to remember that these have been force fed to animals in painful experiments. As I have written elsewhere, there is no pure land.[5] If we embark on vegetarianism, as I think we should, we must do so on the understanding that for all its compelling logic, it is only *one* small step towards the vision of a peaceful world.

Prince of peace

Before I conclude, there is one major—and some would say conclusive—objection to my pro-vegetarian thesis that should be considered. It is this: Jesus was no vegan and possibly no vegetarian. There are no recorded examples of Jesus eating meat in the Gospels. The only possible exception is the Passover itself, but it is not clear, to say the least, that Jesus ate the traditional Passover meal. Jesus did, however, eat fish if the Gospel narratives are to be believed. How are we to reconcile this to the established Christian view of Jesus as the Prince of Peace? There are four possible answers to this question.

The first is that the canonical Gospels are mistaken and Jesus was actually a vegetarian.

However implausible this view may appear, among those who are pro-animals there have always been a significant number who have never believed that Jesus ate the flesh of other living creatures.[6] Those who take this view argue that 'fish' in the New Testament did not actually mean fish as we know it today. Moreover it is sometimes argued that Jesus was really a member of the Essene sect who were, it seems, strict vegetarians. Indeed there are various 'Essene gospels' in which Jesus is depicted as a committed vegetarian.[7] On the face of it, it does seem highly unlikely that such a convenient view is true and the Essene gospels strike me as of rather doubtful antiquity. Nevertheless, I would like to keep an open mind. It is just conceivable that some of these gospels do somehow contain genuine historical reminiscences (we know so little about the historical Jesus in any case) but I think it is a rather remote possibility.

The second possible answer is that Jesus was not perfect in every conceivable way. Jews and Muslims would, of course, have no difficulty with this proposition but orthodox Christians would surely find this idea difficult. After all traditional Christian belief has always been that Jesus Christ was truly God and truly man. Most Christians would hold that being sinless was an essential part of being God incarnate. Those who argue that Jesus was not wholly perfect, however, are not, of course, wholly without biblical support. The question of Jesus: 'Why do you call me good?' And his answer: 'No one is good but God alone,' is recorded in all three synoptic Gospels (Luke 18:19; Matthew 19:17; Mark 10:18). Moreover, it is not inconceivable that Jesus could have been *both* God incarnate and less than morally perfect in every way. Some scholars, such as John Robinson, have maintained this.[8] Perhaps it could be argued that while Jesus committed no sin of commission (deliberate wrongdoing), it could be argued that of necessity every human being commits some sin of omission (things left undone). However, such a view certainly falls short of traditional Christian doctrine and biblical texts such as Hebrews 4:15 which argues that Jesus 'was tempted as we are, yet without sin'.

The third answer is that the killing of fish is not a morally significant matter or, at least, not as significant as the killing of mammals. There is something to be said for this view. Even those who argue rigorously for animal rights sometimes do so on the basis that animals as God's creatures are 'subjects of a life'—that is they have sensitivity and consciousness and the ability to suffer—but it is not clear that all fish do actually possess all these characteristics. In many cases we simply do not know. This must mean, I think, that their moral status is somewhat different from those animals where self-consciousness and sentience can reasonably be taken for granted. Nevertheless, do not fish merit some benefit of the doubt? Are they not also fellow creatures with some God-given life and individuality which means that wherever possible their lives should be respected?

The fourth answer is that sometimes it can be justifiable to kill fish for food in situations of necessity. Such a situation, we may assume, was present in first-century Palestine where geographical factors alone seem to have suggested a scarcity of protein. Such a view would on the whole be more consistent with the biblical perspective that we may kill but only in circumstances of real need. Hence we may have to face the possibility that Jesus did indeed participate in the killing of some life forms in order to live. Indeed we may say that part of his being a human being at a particular stage and time in history necessitated that response in order to have lived at all.

Of all the four possible responses, I find this last one the most convincing. As I have indicated before, the biblical view is not that killing can never be justified and ought to be avoided at all costs. There are times, for example, when euthanasia may well be the most compassionate response to an individual undergoing unrelievable suffering. But even if we accept that killing for food may be justified in those situations of real necessity for human survival, such as may be argued in the case of Jesus himself, this in no way exonerates us from the burden of justifying what we now do to animals in circumstances substantially different. This last point is centrally important and must not be obscured. There may have been times in the past, or even now in the present, where we have difficulty imagining a life without killing for food. But *where we do have the moral freedom* to live without killing, without recourse to violence, there is a *prima facie* case that we should do so. To kill without the strict conditions of necessity is to live a life with insufficient generosity.

It would be wrong, however, to give the impression that the life and teaching of Jesus is a disappointment as far as the enlightened treatment of animals is concerned. While it is true that there is a great deal we do not know about Jesus's precise attitudes to animals, there is a powerful strand in his ethical teaching about the primacy of mercy to the weak, the powerless and the oppressed. Without misappropriation, it is legitimate to ask: who is more deserving of this special compassion than the animals commonly exploited in our world today? Moreover, it is often overlooked that in the canonical Gospels Jesus is frequently presented as identifying himself with the world of animals. As I have written elsewhere:

> His birth, if tradition is to be believed, takes place in the home of sheep and oxen. His ministry begins, according to Mark, in the wilderness 'with the wild beasts' (1:13). His triumphal entry into Jerusalem involves riding on a 'humble ass' (see Matthew 21:4–5). According to Jesus it is lawful to 'do good' on the Sabbath, which includes the rescuing of an animal fallen into a pit (see Matthew 12:10–12). Even the sparrows, literally sold for a few pennies in his day, are not 'forgotten before God' (Luke 12:6). God's providence extends to the entire created order, and the glory of Solomon and all his works cannot be compared to that of the lilies of the field (Luke 12:27). God so cares for his creation that even 'foxes have holes, and birds of the air have nests; but the Son of Man has nowhere to lay his head' (Luke 9:58).[9]

The significance of these and other verses may be much more than had previously been thought. One small example must suffice. Mark describes Jesus's ministry as taking place first within the context of wild animals (1:13). Richard Bauckham has recently argued that the context in which this verse should be understood is messianic in orientation. Jesus is shown to be in continuity with the Isaianic tradition in seeing the messianic age as bringing about a reconciliation between nature and humanity.[10] If this is true, it may be that Mark is seeking to demonstrate how the Gospel of Jesus has implications for the whole of the created world, and for harmony within the animal world in particular. Those who follow Jesus might argue that in seeking to realize what can now be realized in our own time and space of the messianic age is to live now in conformity with the Spirit of Jesus itself.

In conclusion, reference has already been made to how vegetarians have formed a rather beleaguered minority in times past. But it is worth recalling that not a few of the great figures in Christendom have adopted a vegetarian diet. Among these should not go unnoticed the countless saints who have expressed a particular regard for animals and opposed their destruction. 'Poor innocent little creatures,' exclaimed St Richard of Chichester when confronted with animals bound for slaughter. 'If you were reasoning beings and could speak you would curse us. For we are the cause of your death, and what have you done to deserve it?'[11] There has always been an ascetical strand within Christianity which has insisted that humans should live gently on the earth and avoid luxury food. The rule of life penned by St Benedict for his religious community, for example, expressly forbade the eating of meat. 'Except the sick who are very weak, let all abstain entirely from the flesh of four-footed animals.[12]

Moreover, it often comes as a surprise for Christians to realize that the modern vegetarian movement was strongly biblical in origin. Inspired by the original command in Genesis 1, an Anglican priest, William Cowherd, founded the Bible Christian Church in 1809 and made vegetarianism compulsory among its members. The founding of this Church in the United Kingdom and its sister Church in the United States by William Metcalfe, effectively heralded the beginning of the modern vegetarian movement.[13]

The subsequent, if rather slow, growth of vegetarianism from 1809 to 1970, and its rapid and astonishing growth from 1970 to the present day is testimony that Cowherd may have been right in his view that mainstream biblical theology had overlooked something of importance in Genesis 1. It may be that when the history of twentieth-century cuisine is finally written, the radical changes in diet which we are currently experiencing will be found to be due more to the rediscovery of two biblical verses (Gen. 1:29–30) than anything else. These two verses, we may recall, came into existence by people imagining possibilities in the light of their belief in God the Creator. By rekindling the same vision in our own time, we may be enabled to realize—at least in part—those possibilities which our forebears could only imagine. Forwards, we may say, not backwards to Genesis.

Notes

1 John Calvin, *Commentaries on the First Book of Moses*, vol. 1, ET by John King (Edinburgh: Calvin Translation Society, 1847), pp. 291 f. Extract in Andrew Linzey and Tom Regan (eds) *Animals and Christianity: A Book of Readings* (London: SPCK and New York: Crossroad, 1989), pp. 199–200.

2 This argument is developed at length in Andrew Linzey, *Christianity and the Rights of Animals* (London: SPCK and New York: Crossroad, 1987), especially pp. 141–9.

3 *Where We Stand on Animal Welfare* (London: Rabbinic Conference of the Union of Liberal and Progressive Synagogues, May 1990), p. 1.

4 Abraham Isaac Kook, *The Lights of Penitence, The Moral Principles, Lights of Holiness, Essays, Letters, and Poems*, ET by B. Z. Bokser, preface by J. Agus and R. Schatz, *The Classics of Western Spirituality* (London: SPCK, 1979), pp. 317–23. I am grateful to Jonathan Sacks for this reference.

5 See inter alia *Christianity and the Rights of Animals, ibid*, p. 148.

6 See, e.g., Geoffrey L. Rudd, *Why Kill for Food?* (Cheshire: The Vegetarian Society, 1970), pp. 78–90, and Steven Rosen, *Food for the Spirit: Vegetarianism and the World Religions* (New York: Bala Books, 1987), pp. 33–9.

7 For example, *The Gospel of the Holy Twelve* and *The Essene Humane Gospel of Jesus*, cited and discussed in Rosen, *ibid*.

8 J. A. T. Robinson, "Need Jesus have been Perfect?" in S. W. Sykes and J. P. Clayton (eds) *Christ, Faith and History*, Cambridge Studies in Christology (Cambridge: CUP, 1972), pp. 39–52.

9 "Introduction" to Andrew Linzey and Tom Regan (eds) *Compassion for Animals: Readings and Prayers* (London: SPCK, 1989), p. xv.

10 I am grateful to Richard Bauckham for his recent lecture at Essex University on this theme and for bringing to my attention the significance of this verse. I understand that his work will shortly be published as *Jesus and the Greening of Christianity*.

11 St Richard of Chichester, cited in Butler's *Lives of the Saints*, also extract in *Compassion for Animals: Readings and Prayers, ibid*, p. 66.

12 *The Rule of St Benedict*, ET by Justin McCann, Spiritual Masters Series (London: Sheed and Ward, 1976) chp. 39, p. 46.

13 See Richard D. Ryder, *Animal Revolution: Changing Attitudes Towards Speciesism* (Oxford: Blackwells, 1989), p. 96. For a history of the Church in America see *The History of the Philadelphia Bible-Christian Church, 1817–1917* (Philadelphia: J. B. Lippincott Company, 1922). I am grateful to Bernard Unti for this last reference.

38

Martin Forward and Mohamed Alam

"Islam"

Martin Forward and Mohamed Alam explain the Muslim view of the animal-human relationship. Animals are not to be treated as valueless by human beings, but by God's permission human beings have power over the animals and are entitled to use animals for human purposes. Forward and Alam explain the restrictions under which animals may be eaten and the required ritual method of slaughter.

[. . .]

According to the Qur'ān, 'there is not an animal on earth, nor a bird that flies on its wings — but they are communities like you . . . and they shall all be gathered to their Lord in the end' (6: 38). This means that they fulfil the plan which God has allotted to them in his purpose. They are not to be treated as valueless by human beings. It has not usually been taken by commentators of the Qur'ān or jurists to mean that animals share in the bliss (or torment) of life after death. Human beings are distinguished from animals by their capacity to make moral judgements. Only they, of all species of life, can choose to obey or disobey God, and so earn paradise or hell.

Islam is not a sentimental religion. By God's permission, human beings have power over the animals, as over all creation, and they can be used for various purposes.

[. . .]

Islam forbids the keeping of some animals for domestic purposes. Most Muslims do not have dogs as pets. [. . .] Muhammad did not like dogs. [. . .] However, he did not mean that dogs could be mistreated. A prostitute who saw a thirsty dog hanging around a well one day, gave it water to drink. For this act of kindness, the Prophet pardoned all her sins.

[. . .]

Other traditions of the Prophet forbid treating animals cruelly. They are not to be caged, or beaten unnecessarily, or branded on the face, or allowed to fight each other for human entertainment. They must not be mutilated while they are alive, which forbids vivisection. Muslims are opposed to battery farming, the slaughter of calves for veal, and all other forms of animal-husbandry which are cruel to creatures or which needlessly kill them. These interdicts arise out of the Islamic emphasis that human beings have a moral obligation towards animals.

[. . .]

A very important function of animals is to provide human beings with food. Few Muslims are vegetarians. But certain animals are forbidden to Muslims, and all creatures used for food need to be killed in a prescribed manner.

Islamic law declares certain things permissible (*ḥalāl*) for human beings, and other things harmful (*ḥarām*). This division covers all aspects of life, including what Muslims can eat. Muslims regard all things as *ḥalāl* unless God has commanded otherwise. There are four forbidden categories of food, which are derived from the Qur'ān (5: 4):

1   meat of dead animals
2   blood
3   pigs' flesh
4   meat over which another name than God's has been invoked.

The meat of dead animals is taken to mean a beast or fowl which dies of natural causes, without being slaughtered or hunted by humans. The qur'ānic verse offers five classifications of dead animals:

1   the strangled
2   those beaten to death
3   those fallen from a height
4   those gored by other animals
5   those partly eaten by wild animals.

Scholars have elaborated a number of reasons for this prohibition. The animal might have died of some disease. Muslims should intend to kill an animal for food, offering it to God, and not thoughtlessly make use of a deceased creature. By this ban, God makes food available to other animals and birds.

Islamic law has exempted fish, whales and other sea-creatures from the category of dead animals. The Qur'ān says: 'The game of the sea is permitted to you and so is its food' (5: 99). Traditions relate that the Prophet allowed dead food that comes from the sea to be eaten. One story tells of a group of Muslims sent by Muhammad to ambush his enemies. They became very hungry, until the sea threw out a huge, dead whale. They ate its meat, rubbed their bodies with its fat, and, when one of its ribs was fixed over the ground, a rider passed beneath it (Bukhari, in Khan 1984, vol. 7: 293 f.). Many jurists have amplified this permission so that all marine creatures, those which live in the sea and cannot survive outside it, are *ḥalāl*. It does not matter whether they are taken from the water dead or living, whole or in bits, whether they are caught by a Muslim or someone else.

The interdict on blood is interpreted to mean flowing blood, which was felt by jurists to be repugnant and injurious to health. The law does not forbid eating blood that remains in the animal after the flow has ceased.

Pork is outlawed on a number of grounds. It is dangerous to eat in hot climates, where it quickly goes off. It is regarded as an unclean animal, eating filth and offal, and so its meat is repugnant to decent people. Some scholars have claimed that it incites those who eat it to shameful and lustful thoughts.

Finally, God's name must be invoked when the animal is slaughtered. The man who slits its throat says: *bi-smillāhi, allāhu akbar*, 'in the name of God, God is most great'. It is not acceptable to invoke the name of an idol, as Arab polytheists at the time of Muhammad did. Nor is it all right to say nothing. Killing an animal for food is a devotional act. God gave humans control over all the earth, subjecting animals to them, and allowing them to take an animal's life for food. Pronouncing God's name while killing the creature is a reminder of God's permission and ultimate control over all things.

Other than these four categories, all food can be eaten and enjoyed (2: 172; 6: 119). Indeed, the emphasis in Islam is upon what can be eaten and enjoyed, rather than on what is forbidden. Only a few things are forbidden. There is no virtue in exceedingly strict food laws.

[. . .]

Nowadays, the ritual killing of animals is condemned by many non-Muslim individuals and groups. The bottom line for Muslims is that it is commanded by God, and this order counts for more than the opinions of others. Muslims are not mawkish about such matters. Islam began on the fringes of the desert, where staying alive was the pre-eminent concern of many people, and meat was regarded by them as a necessity, not a luxury. Most Muslims today live in relatively poor countries, where survival counts for more than middle-class values, which can seem excessively indulgent. Islam gives human beings power over, and responsibility for, animals, which should be treated with kindness and consideration, but which, by God's permission, provide food, clothing and transport.

[. . .]

Bibliography

Khalid, F. with O'Brien, J. (eds) (1992) *Islam and Ecology*, London, Cassell.
Khan, M.M. (ed.) (1984) *Sahah Al-Bukhari*, vols 1–9, Delhi, Kitab Bhavan.
Nasr, S.H. (1976) *Islamic Science: an illustrated study*, London, Thames and Hudson.
Robson, J.R. (1970 edn) *Mishkat al-Masibih*, vols 1–2, Lahore, Muhammad Ashraf.
Siddiqi, A.H. (ed.) (1977) *Sahih Muslim*, vols 1–4, Delhi, Kitab Bhavan.
Yusuf Ali, A. (1975 edn) *The Holy Qu'rān: Text, Translation and Commentary*, Leicester, Islamic Foundation.

39

Michael W. Fox

"India's Sacred Cow: Her Plight and Future"

Michael W. Fox explains the plight of some 120 million cows in India today, who are either starving or chronically malnourished due to scarcity of land. He argues that vegetarianism in India is more a matter of personal purity rather than animal welfare, and argues for improvement in animal slaughter in the name of ahimsa (Gandhi's central moral value) and compassion.

[. . .]

India has the largest concentration of livestock in the world, having one-third of the world's cattle on approximately 3 percent of the world's land area.[1] India is the world's second largest milk producer, with over half its milk coming from buffalo. Seventy-six percent of Indian people are rural, living in some 600,000 villages. The economic and social values of cattle are so great that cattle have long been seen as religious symbols and are regarded as sacred.

[. . .]

Sadly, India's sustainable pastoral communities have become almost a thing of the past. There is not enough land for all to share. The combined effects of population growth, rural poverty, and ecological illiteracy have had devastating environmental and socio-economic consequences. Abandoned cattle wander everywhere searching for food, along with other cattle whose urban families are landless. Many are hit by traffic or develop serious internal injuries from consuming plastic bags, wire, and other trash.

India's cattle are extraordinary. They are beautiful. Some bulls are quite awesome. Many are colonial cross-breeds, half Holstein or Jersey. These are subject to more abuse in many ways than the hard working indigenous breeds that will soon become extinct if India goes the way of Western industrial agriculture and sacrifices its rural people and relatively self-reliant communities on the altar of 'progress'. These European cows suffer more because they are less able to cope with the climate and diseases to which local breeds have acquired much resistance over thousands of years. When European cows' productive lives are over and they are turned out to graze, they may starve to death because having been stall-fed their entire lives, they don't know how to forage for themselves.

[. . .]

India now has so many cattle, according to Professor Ram Kumar of the India Veterinary Council, that there is only sufficient feed for 60 percent of the cattle population. This means that of an estimated 300 million calves, bulls, and bullocks, some 120 million of these animals, especially in arid regions, and elsewhere during the dry season and droughts when fodder is scarce, are either starving or chronically malnourished.

[. . .]

This tragic situation is made worse by the taboo in most states against killing cattle, either for food, for population control, or even for humane reasons. While Moslem, Christian, and other Indians eat meat (buffalo, sheep, and goats, whose slaughter is permitted) the majority of Indians are Hindus, for many of whom the killing of cattle and eating of beef is unthinkable because this species is regarded as the most sacred of all creatures. [. . .] Belief in ahimsa (not harming) and in aghnya (not killing) possibly arose as a reaction against the vedic religion and social order that sanctified animal slaughter, the brahmans being the highest priestly cast that supervised the killing. Between the eighth and sixth centuries BC a new wave of philosophical treatises emerged that included references to ahimsa, and also reincarnation and karma, that were not included in the Vedas. These treatises, along with the emergence of the religious traditions Buddhism and Jainism that espoused ahimsa, were a challenge to orthodox Hinduism. [. . .]

Vegetarianism in India, like ahimsa, has as much, if not more, to do with concerns about reincarnation, one's personal degree of purity, and place in society than with concern for animals. The Hindu and Jain sect taboo against killing animals has more to do with personal purity and caste than with the principles of ahimsa and aghnya. In the currency of spiritual merit and advancement, dissociation from being involved in the slaughter of cattle and other animals for consumption leads to vegetarianism. But it is not total vegetarianism, since dairy products are consumed by most Hindus and Jains. Few are pure vegan (eating no animal products). Some Jains have agreed with me that to be consistent with their religious beliefs and with the ecological and economic dictates of the current situation, veganism is an ethical imperative. Abstaining from all dairy products would be more consistent with the principle of ahimsa that they hold so dear, than 'saving' spent dairy cows, calves and bullocks from slaughter and condemning them to slow death by starvation in gowshalas [cow shelters] or pinjrapoles [animal shelters].

Yet it is in Jainism that the principle of ahimsa was first espoused, most notably by Mahavira (599–527 BC), a contemporary of Buddha, although earlier Jain leaders (tirthankaras) well before the time of Buddha, like Parsvanatha (circa 840 BC) renounced the world and established an ascetic community that practiced ahimsa. Some contemporary Jains get around the problem of ahimsa by becoming land owners and having others do the farming, clearing the land and killing wild creatures, ploughing the land and killing worms, and using all manner of pesticides.

[. . .]

For Mohandas Gandhi, cow protection was an important aspect of Indian independence from British colonial rule, figuring in the return to traditional values. He wrote:

> The central fact of Hinduism is cow protection. Cow protection to me is one of the most wonderful phenomenon [sic] in human evolution. It takes the human being beyond his species. The cow to me means the entire subhuman world. Man through the cow is enjoined to realize his identity with all that lives. . . . Protection of the cow means the protection of the whole dumb creation of God. . . . Cow protection is the gift of Hinduism to the world. And Hinduism will live as long as there are Hindus to protect the cow. Hindus will be judged not by their *tilaks*, not by the correct chanting of *mantras*, not by their pilgrimages, not by their most punctilious observance of caste rules but by their ability to protect the cow.[2]

[. . .]

Lodrick, in reviewing this history of animal care and shelters in India, concludes that,

> Buddhism, although the major vehicle for the spread of the ahimsa concept throughout India and indeed throughout much of Asia, never carried the doctrine to the extremes of Jainism. In Buddhist thinking, ahimsa became a positive adjunct to moral conduct stemming from the cardinal virtue of compassion, rather than the all-encompassing negative principle of non-activity of the Jains.[3]

This inference by Lodrick, an Indian himself, may help explain the lack of compassion I have witnessed in a Jain-operated pinjrapole in the Nilgiris, South India, where cattle and other animals were saved from slaughter but allowed to starve to death or die from injuries and diseases that could have been easily treated.

[. . .]

Humanitarian concerns over animal slaughter and attempts to modernize slaughtering facilities to make them more humane, sanitary, less wasteful and causing less pollution have been opposed by both Moslems and Hindus for religious and political reasons. Moslems see it as threatening their religious freedom (by the adoption of pre-slaughter stunning) and many Hindus see slaughter modernization as a threat to traditional values, totems, taboos, and even national identity and security.

Such opposition is reminiscent of the Hindu cow protection movement that arose in opposition to British rule and the proposed slaughter of cattle as part and parcel of economic development and modernization. Now under the pressures of trade liberalization and an emerging global market economy that is being pushed by the World Trade Organization, efforts to modernize livestock slaughter are being renewed; and opposition intensifies.

But in the name of ahimsa and compassion, animal slaughter in India is in urgent need of improvement. It is indeed tragic that religious and political factors should become obstacles to progress in animal welfare and protection in this modern day, and especially ironic since one would expect religious values and democratic principles to advance rather than obstruct such progress.

[. . .]

Notes

1   D.O. Lodrick, *Sacred Cows, Sacred Places* (University of California Press, Berkeley, California, 1979).
2   M. K. Gandhi, *How to Serve the Cow* (Navajivan Publishing House, Ahmedabad, 1954), pp. 3–4.
3   Lodrick, *Sacred Cows, Sacred Places*.

Annotated Further Reading

Appleby, M.C. and Hughes, B.O. (eds) (1997) *Animal Welfare*, New York: CAB International. A useful collection providing specific measures of assessment of well-being of farm animals in the U.K. Written by experts in various fields.
Curnutt, J. (1997) "A New Argument for Vegetarianism." *Journal of Social Philosophy* 28.3: 153–72. An argument avoiding past stalemates and focusing on harm to animals as a defeat of interests.
De Jonge, F.H. (1997) "Animal Welfare? An Ethological Contribution to the Understanding of Emotions in Pigs." in M. Dol, *et al.* (eds) *Animal Consciousness and Animal Ethics: perspectives from the Nether-*

lands, Assen: Van Gorcum. Ethological research indicates that the quality of rearing conditions in early development piglets is crucial.

Dombrowski, D.A. (1984) *The Philosophy of Vegetarianism*, Amherst: University of Massachusetts Press. Well-written historical account from ancient Greeks to contemporary philosophers.

Fox, M.W. (1997) *Eating with Conscience: The Bioethics of Food*, Troutdale, Oregon: New Sage Press. A book for general readership with practical suggestions for eating and agriculture.

Gentle, M.J. (1992) "Pain in Birds." *Animal Welfare* 1: 235–47. Based on anatomical, physiological and behavioral parameters, there are no major differences between mammals and chickens.

Gregory, N.G. with a chapter by Grandin, T. (1998) *Animal Welfare and Meat Science*, New York: CABI Publishing. A straightforward account, sensitive to welfare issues.

Kalechofsky, R. (ed.) (1992) *Judaism and Animal Rights: Classical and Contemporary Responses*, Marblehead, Mass.: Micah.

Kunkel, H.O. (2000) *Human Issues in Animal Agriculture*, College Station, Texas: Texas A & M University Press. Discusses the "producer's dilemma": the maximization of profit while providing animals an existence "as free of suffering as possible."

Masri, A.B.A. (1989) *Animals in Islam*, Hants, England: The Athene Trust. A wide-ranging, balanced account which affirms the value of vegetarianism.

McDonald, B. (2000) "Once You Know Something, You Can't Not Know It: an Empirical Look at Becoming Vegan." *Society and Animals* 8.1: 1–23. In-depth interviews with twelve long-term vegans.

McLean, J.A. (2002) "Welfare of Male and Female Broiler Chickens." *Animal Welfare*, 11:55–73. An exhaustive study indicating that during weeks five and six densities should be reduced closer to the RSPCA Freedom Food Standards.

Nicol., C.J. (1996) "Farm Animal Cognition." *Animal Science* 62: 375–91. There is no evidence for any generally reduced cognitive capacity in domestic animals.

Rollin, B. (1995) *Farm Animal Welfare: Social Bioethical, and Research Issues* Iowa: Iowa State University Press. An informed attempt to find a middle ground.

—— (2001) "Farm factories: The end of animal husbandry," *Christian Century* 118 (35: 10–26). Industrial animal agriculture is a major departure from traditional agriculture and its core values.

Varner, G.E. "In Defense of the Vegan Ideal: Rhetoric and Bias in the Nutrition Literature." *Journal of Agricultural and Environmental Ethics* (1994) 7.1: 29–40.

Walters, K.S. and Portmess, L. (eds) (1999) *Ethical Vegetarianism: From Pythagorus to Peter Singer*, Albany: SUNY. An excellent collection with an appendix with concise arguments against ethical vegetarianism and a bibliography of antivegetarian sources.

Study Questions

1   Do you agree with Paxton that vegetarianism is an aesthetic choice rather than a moral duty?

2   Which (if any) of the five arguments presented by Stevens do you find to be persuasive? Explain your answer.

3   The passages by Solomon and Forward represent the use of a sacred text as prescribing moral behavior toward animals. The passages by Fuchs and Linzey (and implicitly) by Fox represent a reformist approach toward sacred texts. In your view, what is the proper relationship between a sacred text such as the Bible or the Koran and contemporary moral practice?

4   Do you agree with DeGrazia's evaluation of the harm caused to human beings by factory farming? How might this harm be diminished?

5   Based on DeGrazia's discussion of family farming and your own views, what sort of animal food production (if any) is morally acceptable?

6   Is it morally acceptable to eat fish or other seafood? Why or why not?

7   Evaluate the points made by the Animal Agriculture Alliance. How does this information affect your current view on the morality of meat-eating?

8   Which diet(s) do you believe to be morally acceptable: that of an omnivore, a vegan, or a vegetarian? What special circumstances might affect your answer?

PART V

Animal Experimentation

Introduction

In this Part, we focus on some ethical issues in the context of using nonhuman animals as research subjects in laboratory and fieldwork, and as teaching subjects in educational institutions. Collectively the authors address a wide range of ethical issues on these topics.

In addressing traditional use of animals in laboratory studies, Tom Regan clearly articulates why no animals should be used in harmful experiments. In particular, reducing their value to human utility does not afford them the respect they deserve. David DeGrazia explores areas in which those opposing ("animal advocates") and those favoring ("biomedicine") use of animals in scientific research might find common ground; he also identifies several topics on which agreement appears unlikely. Responding to DeGrazia's description of the biomedicine perspective, Baruch Brody articulates a position supporting animal research based on the special obligations humans have to each other, including members of their families, communities, and species.

Elizabeth Farnsworth and Judy Rosovsky explore some of the reasons for a general lack of discussion in the scientific literature about ethical issues associated with the impact of ecological field studies on the organisms, populations, species, and ecosystems affected, and encourage greater attention to these matters. Stephen Emlen provides a case study of some of the issues involved with field work as he responds to criticisms of an earlier study; in his defense he also raises some broader ethical issues associated with ecological field work.

Barbara Orlans assesses the range of legal protection governing animal-based research and briefly summarizes the international variation in levels of animal protection. She also addresses the role of ethical criteria, including animal-harm scales as a means to assess animal research.

On the issue of using animals for educational purposes, Jonathon Balcombe summarizes twenty-eight recommendations advocated by the Humane Society of the United States to both reduce the numbers of animals used in schools, as well as the suffering experienced by these animals. Andrew Petto and Karla Russell explore an innovative strategy of fully involving students in making ethical decisions about using animals in their classrooms, including what work can be conducted appropriately as well as the sources, care, and disposal of all animals used.

Laboratory Studies

40

⸺◦⸺

Tom Regan

The Case for Animal Rights

In *The Case for Animal Rights*, Regan makes a case for total elimination of harmful use of animals in research. He argues that animals have a value that cannot be reduced to their utility to others and that their use in research fails to treat them with the respect they are due.

[. . .]

Routine use of animals in research assumes that their value is reducible to their possible utility relative to the interests of others. The rights view rejects this view of animals and their value, as it rejects the justice of institutions that treat them as renewable resources. They, like us, have a value of their own, logically independently of their utility for others and of their being the object of anyone else's interests. To treat them in ways that respect their value, therefore, requires that we *not* sanction practices that institutionalize treating them as if their value was reducible to their possible utility relative to our interests. Scientific research, when it involves routinely harming animals in the name of possible "human and humane benefits," violates this requirement of respectful treatment. Animals are not to be treated as mere receptacles or as renewable resources. Thus does the practice of scientific research on animals violate their rights. Thus ought it to cease, according to the rights view. It is not enough first conscientiously to look for nonanimal alternatives and then, having failed to find any, to resort to using animals.[1] Though that approach is laudable as far as it goes, and though taking it would mark significant progress, it does not go far enough. It assumes that it is all right to allow practices that use animals as if their value were reducible to their possible utility relative to the interests of others, provided that we have done our best not to do so. The rights view's position would have us go further in terms of "doing our best." *The best we can do in terms of not using animals is not to use them*. Their inherent value does not disappear just because we have failed to find a way to avoid harming them in pursuit of our chosen goals. Their value is independent of these goals and their possible utility in achieving them.

[. . .]

The rights view does not oppose using what is learned from conscientious efforts to treat a sick animal (or human) to facilitate and improve the treatment tendered other animals (or humans). In *this* respect, the rights view raises no objection to the "many human and humane benefits" that flow from medical science and the research with which it is allied. What the rights view opposes are practices that cause intentional harm to laboratory animals (for example, by means of burns, shock, amputation, poisoning, surgery, starvation, and sensory deprivation) preparatory to "looking for something that just might yield some human or humane benefit." Whatever benefits happen to accrue from such a practice are irrelevant to assessing its tragic injustice. Lab animals are not our tasters; we are not their kings.

The tired charge of being antiscientific is likely to fill the air once more. It is a moral smokescreen. The rights view is not against research on animals, if this research does not harm these animals or put them at risk of harm. It is apt to remark, however, that this objective will not be accomplished merely by ensuring that test animals are anesthetized, or given postoperative drugs to ease their suffering, or kept in clean cages with ample food and water, and so forth. For it is not only the pain and suffering that matters—though they certainly matter—but it is the *harm* done to the animals, including the diminished welfare opportunities they endure as a result of the deprivations caused by the surgery, *and* their untimely death. It is unclear whether a *benign* use of animals in research is possible or, if possible, whether scientists could be persuaded to practice it. That being so, and given the serious risks run by relying on a steady supply of human volunteers, research should take the direction away from the use of any moral agent or patient. If nonanimal alternatives are available, they should be used; if they are not available, they should be sought. That is the moral challenge to research, given the rights view, and it is those scientists who protest that this "can't be done," in advance of the scientific commitment to try—not those who call for the exploration—who exhibit a lack of commitment to, and belief in, the scientific enterprise—who are, that is, antiscientific at the deepest level.

[. . .]

The rights view, then, is far from being antiscientific. On the contrary, as is true in the case of toxicity tests, so also in the case of research: it calls upon scientists *to do science* as they redirect the traditional practice of their several disciplines away from reliance on "animal models" toward the development and use of nonanimal alternatives. All that the rights view prohibits is science that violates individual rights. If that means that there are some things we cannot learn, then so be it. There are also some things we cannot learn by using humans, if we respect their rights. The rights view merely requires moral consistency in this regard.

The rights view's position regarding the use of animals in research cannot be fairly criticized on the grounds that it is antihumanity. The implications of this view in this regard are those that a rational human being should expect, especially when we recall that nature neither respects nor violates our rights. Only moral agents do; indeed, only moral agents *can*. And nature is not a moral agent. We have, then, no basic right against nature not to be harmed by those natural diseases we are heir to. And neither do we have any basic right against humanity in this regard. What we do have, at this point in time at least, is a right to fair treatment on the part of those who have voluntarily decided to offer treatment for these maladies, a right that will not tolerate the preferential treatment of some (e.g., Caucasians) to the detriment of others (e.g., Native Americans). The right to fair treatment of our naturally caused maladies (and the same applies to mental and physical illnesses brought on by human causes e.g. pollutants) is an *acquired right* we have against those moral agents who acquire the duty to offer fair treatment because they voluntarily assume a role within the medical profession. But those in this profession, as well as those who do research in the hope that they might improve health care, are not morally authorized to override the *basic rights* of others in the process—rights others have, that is, independently of their place in any institutional arrangement and independently of any voluntary act on the part of anyone. And yet that is what is annually done to literally millions of animals whose services, so to speak, are enlisted in the name of scientific research, including that research allied with medical science. For this research treats these animals as if their value is reducible to their possible utility relative to the interests of others. Thus does it routinely violate their basic right to respectful treatment. Though those of us who today are to be counted among the beneficiaries of the human benefits obtained from this research in the past might stand to lose some future benefits, at least in the short run, if this research is stopped, the rights view will not be satisfied with anything less than its total abolition. Even granting that we face greater prima facie harm than laboratory animals presently endure if future harmful research on these animals is stopped, and even granting that the number of humans and other animals who stand to benefit from allowing this practice to continue exceeds the number of animals used in it, this practice remains wrong because unjust.

[. . .]

A final objection urges that the rights view cannot have any principled objection to using mammalian animals for scientific purposes generally, or in research in particular, before these animals attain the degree of physical maturity that makes it reasonable to view them as subjects-of-a-life, in the sense that is central to the rights view. For example, use of newly born mammalian animals must stand outside the scope of the proscriptions issued by the rights view.

This objection is half right. *If certain conditions are met*, the rights view could sanction the scientific use of mammalian animals at certain stages of their physical development. As has been remarked on more than one occasion in the preceding, however, where one draws the line, both as regards what species of animals contain members who are subjects-of-a-life and as regards when a given animal acquires the abilities necessary for being such a subject, is controversial. We simply do not know, with anything approaching certainty, exactly where to draw the line in either case. Precisely because we are so palpably ignorant about a matter so fraught with moral significance, we ought to err on the side of caution, not only in the case of humans but also in the case of animals. Though during the earliest stages of development it is most implausible to regard a fetal mammalian animal as conscious, sentient, and so on, it becomes increasingly less implausible as the animal matures physically, acquiring the physical basis that underlies consciousness, perception, sentience, and the like. Although throughout the present work attention has been for the most part confined to normal mammalian animals, aged one or more, it does not follow that animals less than one year of age may be treated in just any way we please. Because we do not know exactly where to draw the line, it is better to give the benefit of the doubt to mammalian animals less than one year of age who have acquired the physical characteristics that underlie one's being a subject-of-a-life. The rights view's position concerning those animals, then, is against their use for scientific purposes.

There are Kantian-like grounds that strengthen the case against using newborn and soon-to-be born mammalian animals in science. To allow the routine use of these animals for scientific purposes would most likely foster the attitude that animals are just "models," just "tools," just "resources." Better to root out at the source, than to allow to take root, attitudes that are inimical to fostering respect for the rights of animals. Just as in the analogous areas of abortion and infanticide in the case of humans, therefore, the rights view favors policies that foster respect for the rights of the individual animal, even if the creation of these attitudes requires that we treat some animals who may not have rights as if they have them.

Finally, even in the case of mammalian animals in the earliest stages of fetal development, the rights view does not issue a blank check for their use in science. For though, on the rights view, we do not owe a duty of justice to these fetuses, we do owe justice to those animals who would be enlisted to produce them in the number researchers are likely to desire. Were mature animals used as "fetal machines" and, as a result, were they housed in circumstances conducive to their reproducing at the desired rate, it is most unlikely that the rights of these mature animals would be respected. For example, it is very unlikely that *these* animals would be provided with a physical environment conducive to the exercise of their preference autonomy, or one that was hospitable to their social needs; and it is equally unlikely that they would avoid having their life brought to an untimely end, well in advance of their having reached a condition where killing them could be defended on grounds of pref-erence-respecting or paternalistic euthanasia. Once they had stopped reproducing, they would likely be killed. To the extent that we have reason to believe that these mature mam-mals would be treated as if they had value only relative to human purposes, to that extent the rights view would oppose the scientific use of fetal mammalian animals, not because these latter have rights that would be violated, but because this would be true in the case of the mature animals used as breeders. Those who would use mammalian animals in the earliest stages of their fetal development, then, may do so, according to the rights view, but only if they ensure *both* that (1) the lab animals used to produce the fetuses are treated with the respect they are due *and* that (2) reliance on mammalian fetuses does not foster beliefs and attitudes that encourage scientists to use mature mammalian animals for scientific purposes, including research. It is unclear that science could institute policies that satisfied the first condition. It is clear that a policy could be introduced that satisfied the second. This would be for science to cease using mammalian animals who are subjects-of-a-life in ways that harm them directly, or that put them at risk of harm, or that foster an environment in which their harm is allowed. That is a policy the rights view could allow,[2] but one science has yet to adopt.

[. . .]

The use of animals in science was the final area for which the major implications of the rights view were set forth. For a variety of reasons, the rights view takes a principled stand against the use of animals in educational contexts, in toxicity testing of new products and drugs, and in research. Dissection of living mammalian animals in high school and university lab sections is to be condemned, all the more so since the relevant knowledge obtained by this practice can be secured without engaging in it. To anesthetize these animals will not avoid the rights view's condemnation, since it is the animals' untimely death, not merely their pain or suffering, that is morally relevant. To the objection that most animals used in high school and university labs are not mammals and so do not fall within the scope of the principles advo-cated by the rights view, it was noted that (1) where we draw the line between those animals that are, and those that are not, subjects-of-a-life is far from certain, so that we ought to err on the side of caution, giving animals the benefit of the doubt in many cases, including the present one, and that (2) routine use of even nonmammalian animals fosters beliefs and attitudes that contribute to acceptance of acts and institutions that fail to show respect for, and thus violate the rights of, mammalian animals. Both reasons provide compelling grounds for discontinuing standard lab sections in high school and university courses in the life sciences.

[. . .]

The same call is made by the rights view when it comes to the use of animals in research. To harm animals on the chance that something beneficial for others might be discovered is to treat these animals as if their value were reducible to their possible utility relative to the interests of others, and to do this, not to a few, but to many millions of animals is to treat the affected animals as if they were a renewable resource—renewable because replaceable without any wrong having been done, and a resource because their value is assumed to be a function of their possible utility relative to the interests of others. *The rights view abhors the harmful use of animals in research and calls for its total elimination.* Because animals have a kind of value that is not the same as, is not reducible to, and is incommensurate with their having utility relative to the interests of others, because they are owed treatment respectful of their value as a matter of strict justice, and because the routine use of laboratory animals in research fails to treat these animals with the respect they are due, their use in research is wrong because unjust. The laudatory achievements of science, including the many genuine benefits obtained for both humans and animals, do not justify the unjust means used to secure them. As in other cases, so in the present one, the rights view does not call for the cessation of scientific research. Such research should go on—but not at the expense of laboratory animals. The overarching challenge of scientific research is the same as the similar challenge for toxicology and all other facets of the scientific enterprise: to do science without violating anyone's rights, be they human or animal.

The rights view does not deny in principle that use of mammalian embryos in science, including research, might be justified. Fetuses in the early stages of their development can be used, according to the rights view, if we have good reason to believe that allowing their use will not foster beliefs and attitudes that sanction treatment violative of the rights of those animals who have rights, in particular the rights of those animals used as breeders. Though it is not clear that this challenge can be met, it is clear that it cannot be met if scientists themselves continue to use *both* mammalian embryos *and* mature animals. An essential part of the evidence necessary to justify use of mammalian embryos, therefore, consists in scientists not using mature mammalian animals (or other mammalian animals who, though less than one year old, ought to be given the benefit of the doubt). As such, the rights view will take seriously a defense of the use of mammalian embryos only when scientists themselves cease using mammals at later stages of their life. But not until then. The onus of proof is where it belongs.[3]

Notes

1   This is the view recommended in Jamieson and Regan, "On the Ethics of the Use of Animals in Science" (see chap. 8, n. 23). In disassociating myself from this earlier view, I speak only for myself. I am in no position to speak for Professor Jamieson.

2   Note that replies analogous to those given in the last three paragraphs could be given in response to the view that it is all right to eat farm animals or to hunt or trap wild animals less than one year old, including those who are newly born and soon-to-be-born. Concerning farm animals first, since (1) we do not know with anything approaching certainty that these young animals are not subjects-of-a-life; since (2) whether they are or not, we want to encourage the development of beliefs and attitudes that lead to the respectful treatment of those animals who are subjects-of-a-life; and (3) since the adult animals who would be used as "fetal machines" in agriculture would in all likelihood not be treated with the respect they are due, the rights view opposes this defense of meat eating. Points (1) and (2) apply to hunting and trapping newly born wild animals and are the principal (but not the only) sorts of reason the rights view gives against the slaughter of newly born seals, for example. The rights view offers reasons of the same kind in support of its condemnation of killing nonmammalian animals (e.g., birds and fish of all kinds) in the name of sport or in pursuit of a profit. Even assuming birds and fish are not subjects-of-a-life, to allow their recreational or economic exploitation is to encourage the formation of habits and practices that lead to the violation of the rights of animals who are subjects-of-a-life.

3   Comments by Henry Shapiro, professor of psychology at Bates College, helped me see the relevance and importance of the idea of risk-taking in assessing the morality of our treatment of animals. Helpful discussions about rights with my colleague Donald Van De Veer inched me forward to a better understanding of what rights are.

41

David DeGrazia

"The Ethics of Animal Research: What are the Prospects for Agreement?"

DeGrazia assesses the perspectives of those favoring, and those opposed to, animal research. He identifies ten principles where he believes these two perspectives can agree, and at least four additional issues he believes will serve as continuing points of difference. He then makes ten suggestions for continuing to build on the various points of agreement.

Few human uses of nonhuman animals (hereafter simply "animals") have incited as much controversy as the use of animals in biomedical research. [. . .] However, a healthy number of individuals within these two communities offer the possibility of a more illuminating discussion of the ethics of animal research.

One such individual is Henry Spira. Spira almost single-handedly convinced Avon, Revlon, and other major cosmetics companies to invest in the search for alternatives to animal testing. Largely due to his tactful but persistent engagement with these companies - and to their willingness to change - many consumers today look for such labels as "not tested on animals" and "cruelty free" on cosmetics they would like to buy.

Inspired by Spira, this paper seeks common ground between the positions of biomedicine and animal advocates. (The term "biomedicine" here refers to everyone who works in medicine or the life sciences, not just those conducting animal research. "Animal advocates" and "animal protection community" refer to those individuals who take a major interest in protecting the interests of animals and who believe that much current usage of animals is morally unjustified. The terms are not restricted to animal activists, because some individuals meet this definition without being politically active in seeking changes.) The paper begins with some background on the political and ethical debate over animal research. It then identifies important points of potential agreement between biomedicine and animal advocates; much of this common ground can be missed due to distraction by the fireworks of the current political exchange. Next, the paper enumerates issues on which continuing disagreement is likely. Finally, it concludes with concrete suggestions for building positively on the common ground.

Background on the debate over animal research

What is the current state of the debate over the ethics of animal research? Let us begin with the viewpoint of biomedicine. It seems fair to say that biomedicine has a "party line" on the ethics of animal research, conformity to which may feel like a political litmus test for full acceptability within the professional community. According to this party line, animal research is clearly justified because it is necessary for medical progress and therefore human health – and those who disagree are irrational, antiscience, misanthropic "extremists" whose views do not deserve serious attention. (Needless to say, despite considerable conformity, not everyone in biomedicine accepts this position.)

In at least some countries, biomedicine's leadership apparently values conformity to this party line more than freedom of thought and expression on the animal research issue. (In this paragraph, I will refer to the American situation to illustrate the point.) Hence the unwillingness of major medical journals, such as *JAMA* and *The New England Journal of Medicine*, to publish articles that are highly critical of animal research. Hence also the extraordinary similarity I have noticed in pro-research lectures by representatives of biomedicine. I used to be puzzled about why these lectures sounded so similar and why, for example, they consistently made some of the same philosophical and conceptual errors (such as dichotomizing animal welfare and animal rights, and taking the latter concept to imply identical rights for humans and animals). But that was before I learned of the "AMA [American Medical Association] Animal Research Action Plan" and the AMA's "White Paper." Promoting an aggressive pro-research campaign, these documents encourage AMA members to say and do certain things for public relations purposes, including the following: "Identify animal rights activists as anti-science and against medical progress"; "Combat emotion with emotion (e.g [sic], 'fuzzy' animals contrasted with 'healing' children)"; and "Position the biomedical community as moderate – centrist – in the controversy, not as a polar opposite."[1]

It is a reasonable conjecture that biomedicine's party line was developed largely in reaction to fear – both of the most intimidating actions of some especially zealous animal advocates, such as telephoned threats and destruction of property, and of growing societal concern about animals. Unfortunately, biomedicine's reaction has created a political culture in which many or most animal researchers and their supporters do not engage in sustained, critical thinking about the moral status of animals and the basic justification (or lack thereof) for animal research. Few seem to recognize that there is significant merit to the opposing position, fewer have had any rigorous training in ethical reasoning, and hardly any have read much of the leading literature on animal ethics. The stultifying effect of this cultural phenomenon hit home with me at a small meeting of representatives of biomedicine, in which I had been invited to explain "the animal rights philosophy" (the invitation itself being exceptional and encouraging). After the talk, in which I presented ideas familiar to all who really know the literature and issues of animal ethics, several attendees pumped my hand and said something to this effect: "This is the first time I have heard such rational and lucid arguments for the other side. I didn't know there were any."

As for the animal protection community, there does not seem to be a shared viewpoint except at a very general level: significant interest in animal welfare and the belief that much current animal usage is unjustified. Beyond that, differences abound. For example, the Humane Society of the United States opposes factory farming but not humane forms of animal husbandry, rejects current levels of animal use in research but not animal research itself, and condemns most zoo exhibits but not those that adequately meet animals' needs and approximate their natural habitats.[2] Meanwhile, the Animal Liberation Front, a clandestine British organization, apparently opposes all animal husbandry, animal research, and the keeping of zoo animals.[3] Although there are extensive differences within the animal protection community, as far as our paper topic goes, it seems fair to say that almost everyone in this group opposes current levels of animal research.

That's brief sketch of the perspectives of biomedicine and animal advocates on the issue of animal research. What about the state of animal ethics itself? The leading book-length works in this field exhibit a near consensus that the status quo of animal usage is ethically indefensible and that at least significant reductions in animal research are justified. Let me elaborate.

Defending strong animal rights positions in different ways, Tom Regan and Evelyn Pluhar advocate abolition of all research that involves harming animals.[4] Ray Frey and Peter Singer, by contrast, hold the use of animals to the very stringent utilitarian standard – accepting only those experiments whose benefits (factoring in the likelihood of achieving them) are expected to outweigh the harms and costs involved – where the interests of animal subjects (e.g., to avoid suffering) are given the same moral weight that we give comparable human interests.[5]

Without commiting either to a strong animal rights view or to utilitarianism, my own view shares with these theories the framework of equal consideration for animals: the principle that we must give equal moral weight to comparable interests, no matter who has those interests.[6] But unlike the aforementioned philosophers, I believe that the arguments for and against equal consideration are nearly equal in strength. I therefore have respect for progressive views that attribute moral standing to animals without giving them fully equal consideration. The unequal consideration view that I find most plausible gives moral weight to animals' comparable interests in accordance with the animals' cognitive, affective, and social complexity – a progressive, "sliding scale" view. Since I acknowledge that I might be mistaken about equal consideration, my approach tracks the practical implications both of equal consideration and of the alternative just described.

Arguing from pluralistic frameworks, which are developed in different ways, Steve Sapontzis, Rosemary Rodd, and Bernard Rollin support relatively little animal research in comparison with current levels.[7] Drawing significantly from feminist insights, Mary Midgley presents a view whose implications seem somewhat more accepting of the status quo of animal research but still fairly progressive.[8] Of the leading contributors to animal ethics, the only one who embraces the status quo of animal research and does not attribute significant moral status to animals is Peter Carruthers.[9] (It is ironic that while biomedicine characterizes those who are critical of animal research as irrational "extremists," nearly all of the most in-depth, scholarly, and respected work in animal ethics supports such a critical standpoint at a general level.)

In discussing the prospects for agreement between biomedicine and animal advocates, I will ignore political posturing and consider only serious ethical reflection. In considering the two sides of this debate, I will assume that the discussants are morally serious, intellectually honest, reflective, and well informed both about the facts of animal research and about the range of arguments that come into play in animal ethics. I will not have in mind, then, the researcher who urges audiences to dismiss "the animal rights view" or the animal activist who tolerates no dissent from an abolitionist position. The two representative interlocutors I will imagine differ on the issue of animal research, but their views result from honest, disciplined, well-informed ethical reflection. Clearly, their voices are worth hearing.

Points on which the biomedical and animal protection communities can agree

The optimistic thesis of this paper is that the biomedical and animal protection communities can agree on a fair number of important points, and that much can be done to build upon this common ground. I will number and highlight (in bold) each potential point of agreement and then justify its inclusion by explaining how both sides can agree to it, without abandoning their basic positions, and why they should.

1. **The use of animals in biomedical research raises ethical issues.** Today very few people would disagree with this modest claim, and any who would are clearly in the wrong.[10] Most animal research involves harming animal subjects, provoking ethical concerns, and the leading goal of animal research, promotion of human health, is itself ethically important; even the expenditure of taxpayers' money on government-funded animal research raises ethical issues about the best use of such money. Although a very modest assertion, this point of agreement is important because it legitimates a process that is sometimes resisted: *discussing the ethics of animal research.*

[. . .]

2. **Sentient animals, a class that probably includes at least the vertebrates, deserve moral protection.** Whether because they have moral status or because needlessly harming them strongly offends many people's sensibilities, sentient animals deserve some measure of moral protection. By way of definition, sentient animals are animals endowed with any sorts of feelings: (conscious) sensations such as pain or emotional states such as fear or suffering. [. . .] Lately, strong support has emerged for the proposition that at least vertebrate animals are very likely sentient.[11] This proposition is implicitly endorsed by major statements of principles regarding the humane use of research animals, which often mention that they apply to vertebrates.[12] (Hereafter, the unqualified term "animals" will refer to sentient animals in particular.)

3. **Many animals (at the very least, mammals) are capable of having a wide variety of aversive mental states, including pain, distress (whose forms include discomfort, boredom, and fear), and suffering.** In biomedical circles, there has been some resistance to attributing suffering to animals, so government documents concerned with humane use of animals have often mentioned only pain, distress, and discomfort.[13] Because "suffering" refers to a *highly* unpleasant mental state (whereas pain, distress, and discomfort can be mild and transient), the attribution of suffering to animals is morally significant.

[. . .]

4. **Animals experiential well-being (quality of life) deserves protection.** If the use of animals raises ethical issues, meaning that their interests matter morally, we confront the question of what interests animals have.

[. . .]

Another difficult issue is whether animal well-being can be understood *entirely* in terms of experiential well-being – quality of life in the familiar sense in which (other things equal) pleasure is better than pain, enjoyment better than suffering, satisfaction better than frustration. Or does the exercise of an animal's natural capacities count positively toward well-being, even if quality of life is not enhanced?

[. . .]

Whatever the answers to these and other issues connected with animal well-being, what is not controversial is that animals have an interest in experiential well-being, a good quality of life. That is why animal researchers are normally expected to use anesthesia or analgesia where these agents can reduce or eliminate animal subjects' pain, distress, or suffering.

5. **Humane care of highly social animals requires extensive access to conspecifics.** It is increasingly appreciated that animals have different needs based on what sorts of creatures they are. Highly social animals, such as apes, monkeys, and wolves, need social interactions with conspecifics (members of their own species). Under normal circumstances, they will

develop social structures, such as hierarchies and alliances, and maintain long-term relationships with conspecifics. Because they have a strong instinct to seek such interactions and
relationships, depriving them of the opportunity to gratify this instinct harms these animals.

[. . .]

**6. Some animals deserve very strong protections (as, for example, chimpanzees deserve
not to be killed for the purpose of population control).** Biomedicine and animal advocates
are likely to disagree on many details of ethically justified uses of animals in research, as we
will see in the next section. Still, discussants can agree that there is an obligation to protect
not just the experiential well-being, but also the lives, of at least some animals. This claim
might be supported by the (controversial) thesis that such animals have life interests. On the
other hand, it might be supported by the goal of species preservation (in the case of an
endangered species), or by the recognition that routine killing of such animals when they are
no longer useful for research would seriously disturb many people.[14]

[. . .]

**7. Alternatives should now be used whenever possible and research on alternatives
should expand.** Those who are most strongly opposed to animal research hold that alternatives such as mathematical models, computer simulations, and in vitro biological systems
should replace nearly all use of animals in research. (I say "nearly all" because, as discussed
below, few would condemn animal research that does not harm its subjects.) Even for those
who see the animal research enterprise more favorably, there are good reasons to take an
active interest in alternatives. Sometimes an alternative method is the most valid way to
approach a particular scientific question; often alternatives are cheaper.[15] Their potential for
reducing animal pain, distress, and suffering is, of course, another good reason. Finally,
biomedicine may enjoy stronger public support if it responds to growing social concern
about animal welfare with a very serious investment in nonanimal methods. This means not
just using alternatives wherever they are currently feasible, but also aggressively researching
the possibilities for expanding the use of such methods.

8. Promoting human health is an extremely important biomedical goal. No morally
serious person would deny the great importance of human health, so its status as a worthy
goal seems beyond question. What is sometimes forgotten, however, is that a worthy goal
does not automatically justify all the means thereto. Surely it would be unethical to force
large numbers of humans to serve as subjects in highly painful, eventually lethal research,
even if its goal were to promote human health. The controversy over animal research focuses
not on the worthiness of its principal goal – promoting human health – but rather on the
means, involving animal subjects, taken in pursuit of that goal.

9. There are some morally significant differences between humans and other animals.
[. . .] First, the principle of respect for autonomy applies to competent adult human beings,
but to very few if any animals. This principle respects the self-regarding decisions of individuals who are capable of autonomous decisionmaking and action. Conversely, it opposes
paternalism toward such individuals, who have the capacity to decide for themselves what is
in their interests. Now, many sentient beings, including human children and at least most
nonhuman animals, are not autonomous in the relevant sense and so are not covered by this
principle.[16] Thus it is often appropriate to limit their liberty in ways that promote their best
interests, say, preventing the human child from drinking alcohol, or forcing a pet dog to
undergo a vaccination. We might say that where there is no autonomy to respect, the principles of beneficence (promoting best interests) and respect for autonomy cannot conflict;
where there is autonomy to respect, paternalism becomes morally problematic.

Second, even if sentient animals have an interest, other things [being] equal, in staying alive (as I believe), the moral presumption against taking human life is stronger than the presumption against killing at least some animals. [. . .] Leaders in animal ethics consistently support – though in interestingly different ways – the idea that, ordinarily, killing humans is worse than killing at least some animals who have moral status.

[. . .]

10. Some animal research is justified. [. . .] Let me explain by responding to the three likeliest reasons some animal advocates might take exception to the claim.

First, one might oppose all uses of animals that involve *harming them for the benefit of others* (even other animals) – as a matter of absolute principle – and overlook the fact that some animal research does not harm animal subjects at all. Although such nonharmful research represents a tiny sliver of the animal research enterprise, it exists. Examples are certain observational studies of animals in their natural habitats, some ape language studies, and possibly certain behavioral studies of other species that take place in laboratories but do not cause pain, distress, or suffering to the subjects. And if nonsentient animals cannot be harmed (in any morally relevant sense), as I would argue, then any research involving such animals falls under the penumbra of nonharming research.

Moreover, there is arguably no good reason to oppose research that imposes only *minimal* risk or harm on its animal subjects. After all, minimal risk research on certain human subjects who, like animals, cannot consent (namely, children) is permitted in many countries; in my view, this policy is justified. Such research might involve a minuscule likelihood of significant harm or the certainty of a slight, transient harm, such as the discomfort of having a blood sample taken.

Second, one might oppose all animal research because one believes that none of it actually benefits human beings. Due to physical differences between species, the argument goes, what happens to animal subjects when they undergo some biomedical intervention does not justify inferences about what will happen to humans who undergo that intervention. Furthermore, new drugs, therapies, and techniques must always be tried on human subjects before they can be accepted for clinical practice. Rather than tormenting animals in research, the argument continues, we should drop the useless animal models and proceed straight to human trials (with appropriate protections for human subjects, including requirements for informed or proxy consent).

Although I believe a considerable amount of current animal research has almost no chance of benefitting humans, I find it very hard to believe that no animal research does.[17] While it is true that human subjects must eventually be experimented on, evidence suggests that animal models sometimes furnish data relevant to human health.[18] If so, then the use of animal subjects can often decrease the risk to human subjects who are eventually involved in experiments that advance biomedicine, by helping to weed out harmful interventions. This by itself does not justify animal research, only the claim that it sometimes benefits humans (at the very least human subjects themselves and arguably the beneficiaries of biomedical advances as well).

Note that even if animal research never benefited humans, it would presumably sometimes benefit conspecifics of the animals tested, in sound veterinary research.[19] It can't be seriously argued that animal models provide no useful information about animals! Moreover, in successful *therapeutic* research (which aims to benefit the subjects themselves), certain animals benefit directly from research and are not simply used to benefit other animals. For that reason, blanket opposition to animal research, including the most promising therapeutic research in veterinary medicine, strikes me as almost unintelligible.

Almost unintelligible, but not quite, bringing us to the third possible reason for opposing all animal research. It might be argued that, whether or not it harms its subjects, all animal research involves *using animals (without their consent) for others' benefit*, since – qua research – it seeks *generalizable knowledge*. But to use animals in this way reduces them to *tools* (objects to be used), thereby *disrespecting* the animals.

Now the idea that we may never use nonconsenting individuals, even in benign ways, solely for the benefit of others strikes me as an implausibly strict ethical principle. But never mind. The fact that some veterinary research is intended to benefit the subjects themselves (as well as other animals or humans down the road) where no other way to help them is known shows that such research, on any reasonable view, is *not* disrespectful toward its subjects. Indeed, in such cases, the animals *would* consent to taking part, if they could, because taking part is in their interests. I fully grant that therapeutic veterinary research represents a minuscule portion of the animal research conducted today. But my arguments are put forward in the service of a goal that I think I have now achieved: demonstrating, beyond a shadow of a doubt, that some animal research is justified.

[. . .]

Points on which agreement between the two sides is unlikely

Even if biomedicine and the animal protection community approach the animal research issue in good faith, become properly informed about animal ethics and the facts of research, and so forth, they are still likely to disagree on certain important issues. After all, their basic views differ. It may be worthwhile to enumerate several likely points of difference.

First, disagreement is likely on the issue of *the moral status of animals in comparison with humans*. While representatives of biomedicine may attribute moral status to animals, they hold that animals may justifiably be used in many experiments (most of which are nontherapeutic and harm the subjects) whose primary goal is to promote human health. But for animal advocates, it is not at all obvious that much animal research is justified. This suggests that animal advocates ascribe higher moral status to animals than biomedicine does.[20]

Second, disagreement is likely to continue on the issue of *the specific circumstances in which the worthy goal of promoting human health justifies harming animals*. Biomedicine generally tries to protect the status quo of animal research. Animal advocates generally treat not using animals in research as a presumption, any departures from which would require careful justification. Clearly, animal advocates will have many disagreements with biomedicine over when it is appropriate to conduct animal research.

Third, in a similar vein, continuing disagreement is likely on the issue of *whether current protections for research animals are more or less adequate*. Biomedicine would probably answer affirmatively, with relatively minor internal disagreements over specific issues (e.g., whether apes should ever be exposed to diseases in order to test vaccines). Animal advocates will tend to be much more critical of current protections for research animals. They will argue, for example, that animals are far too often made to suffer in pursuit of less than compelling objectives, such as learning about behavioral responses to stress or trauma.

In the United States, critics will argue that the basic principles that are supposed to guide the care and use of animals in federally funded research ultimately provide very weak protection for research animals. That is because the tenth and final principle begins with implicit permission to make exceptions to the previous nine: "Where exceptions are required in relation to the provisions of these Principles, . . ."[21] Since no limits are placed on permissible exceptions, this final principle precludes any absolute restraints on the harm that may be inflicted on research animals – an indefensible lack of safeguards from the perspective of animal advocates. (Although similar in several ways to these American principles, including some ways animal advocates would criticize, the *International Guiding Principles for Biomedical Research Involving Animals* avoids this pitfall of a global loophole. One of its relatively strong protections is Principle V: "Investigators and other personnel should never fail to treat animals as sentient, and should regard their proper care and use and the avoidance or minimization of discomfort, distress, or pain as ethical imperatives."[22])

Although protections of research animals are commonly thought of in terms of preventing unnecessary pain, distress, and suffering, they may also be thought of in terms of protecting animal life. A fourth likely area of disagreement concerns *whether animal life is morally protectable*. Return to a question raised earlier: whether a contented animal in good health is harmed by being painlessly killed in her sleep. Since government documents for the care and use of research animals generally require justification for causing pain or distress to animal subjects, but no justification for painless killing, it seems fair to infer that biomedicine generally does not attribute life interests to animals. Although I lack concrete evidence, I would guess that most animal advocates would see the matter quite differently, and would regard the killing of animals as a serious moral matter even if it is justified in some circumstances.

The four issues identified here as probable continuing points of difference are not intended to comprise an exhaustive list. But they show that despite the fact that the biomedical and animal protection communities can agree on an impressive range of major points, given their basic orientations they cannot be expected to agree on every fundamental question. Few will find this assertion surprising. But I also suggest, less obviously, that even if both sides cannot be entirely right in their positions, differences that remain after positions are refined through honest, open-minded, fully educated inquiry can be reasonable differences.

What can be done now to build upon the points of agreement

Let me close with a series of suggestions offered in the constructive yet critical-minded spirit of Henry Spira's work for how to build on the points of agreement identified above. For reasons of space, these suggestions will be stated somewhat tersely and without elaboration.

First, biomedical organizations and leaders in the profession can do the following: openly acknowledge that ethical issues involving animals are complex and important; educate themselves or acquire education about the ethical issues; tolerate views departing from the current party line; open up journals to more than one basic viewpoint; and stop disseminating one-sided propoganda.

Second, the more "militant" animal advocates can acknowledge that there can be reasonable disagreement on some of the relevant issues and stop intimidating people with whom they disagree.

Third, biomedicine can openly acknowledge, as NASA recently did in its principles, that animals can suffer and invite more serious consideration of animal suffering.

Fourth, the animal protection community can give credit to biomedicine where credit is due – for example, for efforts to minimize pain and distress, to improve housing conditions, and to refrain from killing old chimpanzees who are no longer useful for research but are expensive to maintain.

Fifth, animal researchers and members of animal protection organizations can be required by their organizations to take courses in ethical theory or animal ethics to promote knowledgeable, skilled, broad-minded discussion and reflection.

Sixth, the animal protection community can openly acknowledge that some animal research is justified (perhaps giving examples to reduce the potential for misunderstanding).

Seventh, more animal research ethics committees can bring aboard at least one dedicated animal advocate who (unlike mainstream American veterinarians) seriously questions the value of most animal research.

Eighth, conditions of housing for research animals can be improved – for example, with greater enrichment and, for social animals, more access to conspecifics.

Ninth, all parties can endorse and support the goal of finding ways to *eliminate* animal subjects' pain, distress, and suffering.[23]

Tenth, and finally, governments can invest much more than they have to date in the development and use of alternatives to animal research, and all parties can give strong public support to the pursuit of alternatives.

Notes

1   American Medical Association. Animal Research Action Plan. (June 1989), p. 6. See also American Medical Association. White Paper (1988).
2   See the Humane Society of the United States (HSUS). *Farm Animals and Intensive Confinement*. Washington, D.C.: HSUS, 1994; *Animals in Biomedical Research*. Washington, D.C.: HSUS, revised 1989; and *Zoos: Information Packet*. Washington, D.C.: HSUS, 1995.
3   Animal Liberation Front. Animal Liberation Frontline Information Service: the A.L.F. Primer. (website)
4   Regan T. *The Case for Animal Rights*. Berkeley: University of California Press, 1983; Pluhar E. *Beyond Prejudice*. Durham, North Carolina: Duke University Press, 1995.
5   Frey R. G. *Interests and Rights*. Oxford: Clarendon, 1980; Singer P. *Animal Liberation*, 2nd ed. New York: New York Review of Books, 1990.
6   DeGrazia D. *Taking Animals Seriously*. Cambridge: Cambridge University Press, 1996.
7   Sapontzis S. F. *Morals, Reason, and Animals*. Philadelphia: Temple University Press, 1987; Rodd R. *Biology, Ethics, and Animals*. Oxford: Clarendon, 1990; and Rollin B. E. *Animal Rights and Human Morality*, 2nd ed. Buffalo, New York: Prometheus, 1992.
8   Midgley M. *Animals and Why They Matter*. Athens, Georgia: University of Georgia Press, 1983.
9   Carruthers P. *The Animals Issue*. Cambridge: Cambridge University Press, 1992.
10 In a letter to the editor, Robert White, a neurosurgeon well known for transplanting monkeys' heads, asserted that "[a]nimal usage is not a moral or ethical issue . . ." (White R. Animal ethics? [letter]. *Hastings Center Report* 1990;20(6):43). For a rebuttal to White, see my letter, *Hastings Center Report* 1991;21(5):45.
11 See Rose M., Adams D. Evidence for pain and suffering in other animals. In: Langley G., ed. *Animal Experimentation*. New York: Chapman and Hall, 1989; 42–71; Smith J. A., Boyd K. M. *Lives in the Balance*. Oxford: Oxford University Press, 1991: ch. 4. See also note 7 Rodd 1990: ch. 3; and DeGrazia D., Rowan A. Pain, suffering, and anxiety in animals and humans. *Theoretical Medicine* 1991;12:193–211.
12 See, e.g., U.S. Government Principles for the Utilization and Care of Vertebrate Animals Used in Testing, Research, and Training. In: National Research Council. *Guide for the Care and Use of Laboratory Animals*. Washington, D.C.: National Academy Press, 1996: 117–8; National Aeronautics and Space Administration. *Principles for the Ethical Care and Use of Animals*. NASA Policy Directive 8910.1, effective 23 March 1998; and Council for International Organizations of Medical Sciences. *International Guiding Principles for Biomedical Research Involving Animals*. Geneva: CIOMS, 1985:18.
13 See note 12, National Research Council 1996; CIOMS 1985.
14 Note that the term "euthanasia," which means a death that is good for the one who dies, is inappropriate when animals are killed because they are costly to maintain or for similarly human-regarding reasons.
15 See note 11, Smith, Boyd 1991: 334.
16 See note 6, DeGrazia 1996: 204–10.

17 That is, except those humans who benefit directly from the conduct of research, such as researchers and people who sell animals and laboratory equipment.
18 See, e.g., note 11, Smith, Boyd 1991: ch. 3.
19 Peter Singer reminded me of this important point.
20 The idea of differences of moral status can be left intuitive here. Any effort to make it more precise will invite controversy. (See note 6, DeGrazia 1996: 256–7.)
21 See note 12, National Research Council 1996: 118.
22 See note 12, CIOMS 1985: 18.
23 This is the stated goal of a new initiative of the Humane Society of the United States, which expects the initiative to expand to Humane Society International.

42

Baruch A. Brody

"Defending Animal Research: An International Perspective"

Brody compares and contrasts legal and attitudinal differences towards the use of experimental animals between the U.S. and Europe. He believes that as humans we have special obligations to ourselves, our family members, our friends, and our fellow citizens, that go beyond our obligations to members of other species. Those special obligations lend support to human use of animals in research.

Introduction

In a recent article, "The Ethics of Animal Research," philosopher David DeGrazia asks the very important question of whether or not there is room for at least some agreement between "biomedicine" and "animal advocates" on the issue of animal research.[1] This is an important question, but one on which we are unlikely to make any progress until the contents of both positions are clearly understood. This essay is devoted to better articulating the position which supports animal research, the position that DeGrazia labels the "biomedicine" position; I leave the analysis of the animal-advocacy position for other occasions.

My reason for adopting this strategy is as follows: There has been in recent years an extensive philosophical discussion of various versions of the animal-advocacy position, and the variations on this position have been analyzed by several authors.[2] Much less attention has been paid to development of the pro-research position. DeGrazia himself describes the articulation of that position in negative terms:

> It seems fair to say that biomedicine has a "party line" on the ethics of animal research, conformity to which may feel like a political litmus test for full acceptability within the professional community. According to this party line, animal research is clearly justified because it is necessary for medical progress and therefore human health. . . . [M]any or most animal researchers and their supporters do not engage in sustained, critical thinking about the moral status of animals and the basic justification (or lack thereof) for animal research.[3]

Whether or not this is fully accurate, this perception of the status of the pro-research position seems to be widespread. It therefore seems important to attempt a better articulation and defense of a reasonable version of that position.

What do I mean by a reasonable pro-research position on animal research, the type of position that I wish to defend? I understand such a position to be committed to at least the following propositions:

1 Animals have interests (at least the interest in not suffering, and perhaps others as well), which may be adversely affected either by research performed on them or by the conditions under which they live before, during, and after the research.

2 The adverse effect on animals' interests is morally relevant, and must be taken into account when deciding whether or not a particular program of animal research is justified or must be modified or abandoned.

3 The justification for conducting a research program on animals that would adversely affect them is the benefits that human beings would receive from the research in question.

4 In deciding whether or not the research in question is justified, human interests should be given greater significance than animal interests.

Some preliminary observations about these propositions are in order. Propositions (1) and (2) commit the reasonable pro-research position to a belief that animal interests are morally relevant, and that the adverse impact of animal research on these interests should not be disregarded. This distinguishes the position I am trying to articulate from positions (such as the classical Cartesian position) that maintain that animals have no interests or that those interests do not count morally.[4] In light of their ability to experience pleasures and pains, it is implausible to deny animals interests or to give those interests no moral significance at all. Propositions (3) and (4) distinguish the pro-research position from the animal-advocacy position by insisting that it is permissible for animals to be adversely affected by legitimate research—they do not have a trumping right not to be used adversely for human benefit.[5] Toward this end, proposition (4) asserts that human benefits have greater significance than harms to animals in determining the legitimacy of the research, as animals have less moral significance than humans.[6]

What is the nature of humans' greater significance? [. . .] The reasonable pro-research position is actually a family of positions that differ both theoretically (on their conceptions of the nature of the priority of human interests) and practically (on the resulting types of justified research). What is needed first is a full examination of this family of positions, an examination that explores the plausibility of different views on the priority of human interests. Once we can identify the more plausible of these views, we can begin the attempt to justify one of them.

[. . .]

The U.S. and European positions

The best statement of the U.S. policy on animal research is found in a 1986 document from the Public Health Service entitled "U.S. Government Principles for the Utilization and Care of Vertebrate Animals Used in Testing, Research, and Training."[7] [. . .] I want to highlight what is and is not present in the U.S. principles; they call upon researchers to:

- use the "minimum number [of animals] required to obtain valid results"
- consider alternatives such as "mathematical models, computer simulation, and in vitro biological systems"
- practice the "avoidance or minimization of discomfort, distress, or pain when consistent with sound scientific practices"
- use "appropriate sedation, analgesia, or anesthesia"

- kill animals painlessly after experiments when the animals "would otherwise suffer severe or chronic pain or distress that cannot be relieved"
- provide living conditions that are "appropriate for their species and contribute to their health and comfort."[8]

All of these principles are compatible with the familiar program, developed by W. M. S. Russell and R. L. Burch in 1959, which has come to be called the 3R program.[9] This program calls for the *replacement* of animal experimentation with other research methods where possible; this is why the U.S. principles request the consideration of alternative research techniques. The program also calls for the *reduction* of the number of animals used; hence, the U.S. principles state a commitment to minimizing the number of animals used as much as is consistent with obtaining scientifically valid results. Finally, the 3R program calls for *refining* both the conduct of the research and the environment in which the research animals live; the aim is to minimize the animals' pain and suffering. This is why the U.S. principles talk about pain relief, euthanasia when necessary, and species-appropriate living conditions.

[. . .]

All of this is very much in the spirit of propositions (1) and (2) of my account of the responsible pro-research position on animal research. It is because animals have interests that may be adversely affected by the research—interests that count morally—that we are called upon to replace, reduce, and refine the use of animals in research. Proposition (3) is also explicitly part of the U.S. principles, which assert that "procedures involving animals should be designed and performed with due consideration of their relevance to human or animal health, the advancement of knowledge, or the good of society."[10] But what about proposition (4)? What sort of greater significance are human interests given over animal interests in the U.S. regulations?

In fact, that question is never directly addressed. This stands in sharp contrast to the U.S. regulations on human subjects in research. These regulations require the minimization of risks, but they also require that the minimized risks be "reasonable in relation to anticipated benefits, if any, to subjects, and the importance of the knowledge that may reasonably be expected to result."[11] Nothing like these strictures occurs in the U.S. principles and regulations governing animal research.

Something else can be inferred from the wording of the U.S. principles on animal research. Discomfort, distress, or pain of the animals should be minimized "when consistent with sound scientific practices." The number of animals used should be minimized to "the number required to obtain valid results." Unrelieved pain necessary to conduct the research is acceptable so long as the animal is euthanized after or during the procedure.[12] What this amounts to in the end is that whatever is required for the research is morally acceptable; the 3R principles are to be applied only as long as they are compatible with maintaining scientifically valid research. There is never the suggestion that the suffering of the animal might be so great—even when it is minimized as much as possible while still maintaining scientific validity—that its suffering might outweigh the benefits from the research. Even when these benefits are modest, the U.S. principles never morally require the abandonment of a research project.

This is a position that gives very strong priority to human interests over animal interests, especially to the human interests that are promoted by scientific research using animals as subjects. Given the wide variety of such animal research projects, which range from developing and testing new life-saving surgical techniques to developing and testing new cosmetics, the human interests that are given this strong priority over animal interests are very diverse.

[. . .]

The European approach to these issues is quite different. [. . .] [T]he Europeans find these principles incomplete and augment them with additional principles that give greater significance to animal interests by disallowing some research because the costs to the animal subjects are too great.

The 1986 Directive from the Council of the European Communities (now called the European Community) [. . .] stipulates that the relevant authority "shall take appropriate judicial or administrative action if it is not satisfied that the experiment is of sufficient importance for meeting the essential needs of man or animal."[13] This is a limited provision, as it involves animal interests outweighing human interests only in the case of severe and prolonged pain. The provision does not clearly specify what the "appropriate" actions in such cases are, and it implies that even severe and prolonged pain is acceptable if the research is of "sufficient importance." Nevertheless, it goes beyond anything in the U.S. principles and regulations by giving somewhat greater significance to animal interests.

This approach is developed in national legislation in several European countries. [. . .] While these national provisions are both broader in application and more explicit in their implications than is the E.C. directive, they still leave a crucial question unanswered.

Consider a whole continuum of positions, ranging from the claim that animal interests and human interests count equally (the *equal-significance position*) to the claim that even though one may attend to animal interests, human interests always take precedence (the *human-priority position*). In moving from the first position to the second, the significance of animal interests in comparison to human interests is gradually discounted. The intermediate positions move from those that discount animal interests modestly (and are therefore increasingly close to the equal-significance position) to those that discount them significantly (and are therefore increasingly close to the human-priority position). The U.S. position is the human-priority end of this continuum, and the animal rights movement's rejection of proposition (4) of the pro-research position puts that movement at the other end. The European positions are somewhere in-between, but there is no way to tell from their regulations where they are on the continuum.

[. . .]

[P]roposition (4) of the pro-research position, the principle of giving greater significance to human interests than to animal interests, is understood very differently in the United States and in Europe. For the United States, the proposition means that human interests in conducting research always take lexical priority over animal interests. This lexical priority is not characteristic of the European positions, which allow for some balancing of interests. But there is no evidence that the Europeans have rejected proposition (4) and adopted the equal-significance position that is characteristic of the animal-advocacy position. They seem, instead, to have adopted some discounting of animal interests in comparison to human interests, with the crucial discount rate being undetermined.

Are there any reasons for supposing that a lexical-priority approach is a more plausible articulation of proposition (4) than is a discounting approach (or vice versa)? This is the question I will examine in the next section of this essay.

Lexical priority versus discounting

There are two arguments I will consider in this section. The first argument, in favor of a lexical-priority approach to proposition (4), argues that the cross-species comparison of interests that is presupposed by the discounting approach is meaningless, and that the discounting approach must, therefore, be rejected in favor of a lexical-priority approach. The second argument, in favor of the discounting approach, asserts that lexical priority is incompatible with significant components of the 3R program, and that pro-research adherents of that program must, therefore, adopt the discounting approach.

[. . .]

   The challenge of the first argument . . . has two components. The first component is the claim that there is no basis for placing animal pain and pleasure (if one defines 'interests' hedonistically) or the satisfaction of animal preferences (if one defines 'interests' in terms of preference-satisfaction) on a common metric with human pain and pleasure or human preference-satisfaction. I will refer to this first component of the challenge as the *incommensurability claim*. The second component is the claim that even if there were such a basis, we do not know enough about the sensations or preferences of animals to make such comparisons; I will call this component the *cross-species ignorance claim*.

[. . .]

   [E]ven if one accepts this two-pronged challenge, it does not necessarily follow from this that we should adopt the lexical-priority approach to proposition (4). Those who oppose the lexical-priority approach on the intuitive grounds that it does not give sufficient significance to animal interests can simply conclude that some other approach, one which captures those intuitions, must be developed. All that does follow from the first argument's two-pronged challenge is that the lexical-priority approach to proposition (4) is more plausible than is the discounting approach (which, if the incommensurability claim is correct, has no plausibility at all).

   But should we grant the challenge's components? I see no reason to accept the incommensurability claim. Human pain and pleasure is quantified on the basis of dimensions such as duration and intensity; animal pain and pleasure can also be quantified on those dimensions. Duration is certainly not conceptually different for different species, and no reason has been offered for why we should treat intensity as differing conceptually for different species. Thus, there is a basis for a common metric for hedonistic comparisons of the impact of research on human and animal interests. I think that the same is true for preference-satisfaction comparisons of the impact of research on human and animal interests, but it is hard to say that with the same degree of confidence, since we still have little understanding of the dimensions on which we quantify preference-satisfaction.

[. . .]

   The cross-species ignorance claim is more serious. [. . .] This issue has been faced most directly by a working party of the British Institute of Medical Ethics (an unofficial but respected interdisciplinary group of scholars) in a report published in 1991.[14] The working party's members took note of the fact that the quantification of interests on a common metric seems to be required by the British Animals Act, and that there are doubts as to whether this can be done. In response to these concerns, they make two observations, which seem to me to be the beginning of a good answer to these concerns. First, they note that not every reliable judgment must be based upon a mathematically quantifiable balancing of values: it is often sufficient to have confidence in "the procedures which have been used to arrive at that judgment, ... upon whether [researchers] have taken into account all the known morally relevant factors, and whether they have shown themselves responsive to all the relevant moral interests."[15] Second, the working party claims that it is possible to identify the moral factors relevant to the assessment of animal research and the degree to which they are present in a given case; this knowledge would allow for reliable judgments about the moral acceptability of proposed protocols for animal research. In fact, the working party goes on to create such a scheme and to show by examples how it might work in a reliable fashion.[16]

[...]

This brings me to the second argument of this section. There are, this second argument suggests, reasons for doubting that the lexical-priority approach is compatible with even the 3R approach to the reasonable pro-research position. Satisfying the 3R principles, even if done in a way that allows the proposed research to proceed, involves considerable costs. These costs mean that other human interests, in research or otherwise, will not be satisfied. If human interests truly take precedence over animal interests, this seems inappropriate. A lexical-priority approach, then, cannot support even the now widely accepted 3R approach to protecting animal interests; this, it seems to me, makes the lexical-priority interpretation of proposition (4) an implausible version of the pro-research position.

Consider, for example, that aspect of the 3R program's refinement plank that calls for modifications in the environment in which research animals live in order to make those environments species-appropriate and not a source of distress or discomfort. Those modifications, now widely required throughout the world, are often quite costly, and these costs are passed on to the researchers as a cost of doing research. Some poorly funded research never takes place because these extra costs cannot be absorbed. Other, better funded, research projects go on, but require extra funding. This extra funding may mean that other research projects are not funded, or that the funded research will not be as complete as originally envisioned. To avoid these outcomes, extra funding would have to be provided to research efforts in general, but this would compromise funding for other human interests. In these ways and others, the adoption of this aspect of the 3R program is not compatible with maintaining the full research effort and/or with meeting other human interests. Hence, human interests are not being given full priority, contrary to the basic premise of the lexical-priority position.

None of this, of course, is a problem for the discounting approach unless the discounting of animal interests is so significant that it approaches the lexical-priority position. If the discounting is not this extensive—if animal interests count a lot, even if not as much as the interests of humans—then it seems reasonable to suppose that the interests of the animals in living in a species-appropriate environment are sufficiently great to justify imposing these burdens on the research effort.

In short, then, those who want a reasonable pro-research position to incorporate the widely adopted 3R program should find the discounting approach more plausible than the lexical-priority approach. But what could possibly justify such a discounting of animal interests? We turn to that question in the next section.

The rationale for discounting

Before attempting to develop an approach to justifying discounting, it is important to be clear as to exactly what is claimed by discounting. [...] Discounting [...] is the claim that the same unit of pain counts less, morally, if it is experienced by an animal than it would if it is experienced by a human being, not because of the human's associated experiences but simply because of the species of the experiencer. Discounting directly denies the equal consideration of interests across species.

I am emphasizing this point to make it clear that *discounting* of animal interests is radically different than the *preference* for human interests that even animal advocates such as Peter Singer accept.

[. . .]

But for Singer and other supporters of the equal-significance position, all that follows from this is that humans may suffer more and that this quantitative difference in the amount of suffering is morally relevant. What discounting affirms, and what they deny, is that even when there is no quantitative difference in the amount of suffering, the human suffering counts more morally.

With this understanding of the claim of discounting, we can easily understand why many would find its claims ethically unacceptable. Why should the moral significance of the same amount of suffering differ according to the species of the sufferer if there are no associated additional differences?

[. . .]

I see no reasonable alternative for the adherent of the discounting position except to challenge the whole idea that we are, in general, morally committed to an equal consideration of interests. This is a plausible move, since equal consideration of interests has come under much challenge in contemporary moral philosophy, totally independently of the debate over the moral significance of the interests of animals. I would trace the beginning of the idea that we should not accept equal consideration of interests to W. D. Ross's contention, as early as 1930, that we have special obligations to ourselves, our family members, our friends, our fellow citizens, etc.[17] Recognizing these special obligations means, of course, giving higher priority to the interests of some (those to whom we have special obligations) than to the interests of others (those to whom we do not). Equally important is the emphasis in the 1980s on the idea that we have a morally permissible prerogative to pay special attention to our own interests in the fulfillment of some of our central projects.[18] Recognizing this prerogative means giving a higher priority to at least some of our interests over the interests of others. Each of these ideas, in separate ways, presupposes a denial of equal consideration of interests, and both are best understood as forms of the discounting of certain interests.

How should we understand the special obligations that we have? One good way of understanding them is that we have special obligations to some people to give a higher priority to their interests than we do to those of others. This may call upon us to promote their interests even at the cost of not promoting the greater interests of strangers. Note, by the way, that it is implausible to see this as a form of lexical priority favoring the interests of those people to whom we have special obligations. When their interests at stake are modest, and when the conflicting interests of strangers are great, we are not obliged to put the interests of those to whom we are specially obligated first; we may not even be permitted to do so. It would appear, then, that special obligations might well be understood as involving a requirement that we discount the interests of strangers when they compete with the interests of those to whom we have special obligations.

The same approach sheds much light upon our prerogative to pursue personal goals even at the cost of not aiding others (or even hindering them) in the pursuit of their interests.

This is, once again, hardly a lexical priority. No matter how important a goal may be to me, I may be morally required to put it aside if the competing interests of others are especially great. Our prerogative may best be understood as involving only a permission to discount the interests of strangers when they compete with our interests in attaining our goals.

Note, by the way, that this means that we really have a whole family of theories about special obligations and about personal prerogatives. Different theories will differ on the acceptable discount rate.

Looked at from this perspective, the discounting approach to the animal research position no longer seems anomalous. Rather than involving a peculiar discounting of the interests of animals, in violation of the fundamental moral requirement of the equal consideration of interests, the approach represents one more example of the discounting of the interests of strangers, a feature that is pervasive in morality.

We can see another way of developing this point if we consider the difference between the following two questions:

1A   Why should the interests of my children count more than do those of others?
1B   Why should the interests of my children count more for me than do those of others?

The former question, asked from an impersonal perspective, is unanswerable. The latter question, which is asked from the personal perspective, is answerable. The same needs to be said about the following pair of questions:

2A   Why should the interests of humans count more than do those of animals?
2B   Why should the interests of humans count more for human beings than do those of animals?

As with the previous pair of questions, what is unanswerable from one perspective may be very answerable from the other perspective.

There is, of course, an important difference between special obligations, even to oneself, and personal prerogatives. The former *require* you to give certain interests priority, while the latter just *permit* you to do so. This difference is helpful in explaining a certain ambiguity in the reasonable pro-research position. While its adherents often seem to be attempting to justify only the permissibility of animal research, they sometimes talk as though they are arguing that such research is required. Consider, for example, the standard Food and Drug Administration requirement that new drugs be tested on animals before they are tested on humans. I would suggest the following: when adherents justify the permissibility of animal research, they are invoking the analogy to prerogatives, but when they want to require this research, they are invoking the analogy to special obligations. On the latter view, we have an obligation to human beings, as part of our special obligations to members of our species, to discount animal interests in comparison to human interests by testing new drugs on animals first.

This defense of animal research on the ground of species solidarity has been developed elsewhere by the British philosopher Mary Midgley, although her emphasis seems to me to be more on psychological bonds and less on the logical structure of the consideration of interests in moral thought.[19]

[. . .]

Further issues

[. . .]

There remain, of course, several aspects of the discounting approach that require fuller development. An appropriate discount rate is yet to be determined; the process of cross-species comparisons of gains and losses in interests must be refined; and the conditions under which discounting is merely permissible as opposed to when it is mandatory need to be defined.

In addition to these necessary developments, there is a fundamental challenge that still needs to be confronted. It is a variation on the issue of equal consideration of interests, and it requires much further theoretical reflection. [. . .] Discounting the interests of members of other races or of the other gender seems to be part of the wrong of racism and sexism. Might one not argue that discounting the interests of the members of other species is equally wrong? That is the wrong of "speciesism."

This point can also be put as follows: The charge of speciesism might just be the charge that discounting animal interests is wrong because it violates the principle of equal consideration of interests. This charge is severely weakened by the challenge to the legitimacy of the equal-consideration principle. But the charge might be the very different claim that discounting animal interests is wrong because it is a *discriminatory* version of discounting; this charge is not challenged by the general challenge to the principle of the equal consideration of interests. This version of the charge is articulated by DeGrazia in a critique of Midgley:

> Can appeals to social bondedness in justifying partiality towards humans be convincingly likened to family-based preferences but contrasted with bigotry? Why are racism and sexism unjustified, if species-based partiality is justified?[20]

It is of interest and importance to note that the examples DeGrazia invokes are of partiality toward family members, on the one hand, and toward members of our race or gender, on the other hand. Left out are partiality toward fellow citizens, fellow believers, and fellow members of an ethnic group. All of these seem, *as long as they are not excessive*, to be within the bounds of acceptable partiality toward our fellows and of acceptable discounting of the interests of others. This is why it is appropriate that so much charitable giving is organized by religions and national groups. This is, also, why it is appropriate that nearly all redistribution is done at the individual-country level rather than at the international level. These examples are important in reminding us that the rejection of the equal consideration of interests principle in common morality is very broad, and covers large-scale groups that are more analogous to species than to family members. Of course, this by itself is not a refutation of the discrimination charge leveled against the pro-research position. It does, however, place the position in the company of partialities and discountings that are widely accepted in moral theory and in public policy.

What my arguments foreshadow is the need for further ethical reflection on these controversial issues. We have seen that morality can legitimately involve the discounting of even other people's interests when one acts from a prerogative or a special obligation. A question that requires much more exploration is what differentiates legitimate discounting from discrimination? Only an answer to this question can fully justify the discounting-based, reasonable pro-research position that I have articulated in this essay.

Notes

1   David DeGrazia, "The Ethics of Animal Research," *Cambridge Quarterly of Healthcare Ethics* 8, no. 1 (Winter 1999): 23–34.
2   For summaries of the extensive literature, see, for example, Tom Beauchamp, "The Moral Standing of Animals in Medical Research," *Law, Medicine, and Health Care* 20, nos. 1–2 (Spring/Summer 1992): 7–16; and David DeGrazia, "The Moral Status of Animals and Their Use in Research: A Philosophical Review," *Kennedy Institute of Ethics Journal* 1, no. 1 (March 1991): 48–70.
3   DeGrazia, "The Ethics of Animal Research," 23–4.
4   For a discussion of Descartes's position on these issues, see F. Barbara Orlans, *In the Name of Science: Issues in Responsible Animal Experimentation* (New York: Oxford University Press, 1993), 3–4.
5   This is in opposition to the position articulated in Tom Regan, *The Case for Animal Rights* (Berkeley: University of California Press, 1983).
6   This is in opposition to the position articulated in Peter Singer, *Practical Ethics*, 2nd ed. (New York: Cambridge University Press, 1993).
7   National Institutes of Health—Office for Protection from Research Risks (NIH-OPRR), *Public Health Service Policy on Humane Care and Use of Laboratory Animals* (Bethesda, MD: NIH-OPRR, 1986).
8   NIH-OPRR, *Policy on Humane Care and Use of Laboratory Animals*, i.
9   W. M. S. Russell and R. L. Burch, *The Principles of Humane Experimental Technique* (London: Methuen, 1959).
10 NIH-OPRR, *Policy on Humane Care and Use of Laboratory Animals*, principle 2, p. i.
11 45 C.F.R. sec. 46.111 (1999).
12 NIH-OPRR, *Policy on Humane Care and Use of Laboratory Animals*, principles 3, 4, and 6, p. i.
13 Council Directive of November 24, 1986, art. 12, sec. 2, reprinted in Baruch Brody, *The Ethics of Biomedical Research: An International Perspective* (New York: Oxford University Press, 1998), 237–40.
14 Jane A. Smith and Kenneth M. Boyd (eds), *Lives in the Balance: The Ethics of Using Animals in Biomedical Research—The Report of a Working Party of the Institute of Medical Ethics* (Oxford: Oxford University Press, 1991).
15 Ibid., 141.
16 Ibid., 141–6.
17 W. D. Ross, *The Right and the Good* (Oxford: Oxford University Press, 1930), chap. 2.
18 Samuel Scheffler, *The Rejection of Consequentialism* (Oxford: Oxford University Press, 1982), chap. 3.
19 Mary Midgley, *Animals and Why They Matter* (Harmondsworth, Middlesex: Penguin Books, 1983).
20 David DeGrazia, *Taking Animals Seriously: Mental Life and Moral Status* (New York: Cambridge University Press, 1996), 64.

Field Studies

43

—⁂—

Elizabeth J. Farnsworth and Judy Rosovsky

"The Ethics of Ecological Field Experimentation"

Farnsworth and Rosovsky note that scientists often avoid ethical discussions about ecological field research and propose that this omission among researchers is due to a) concern about initiating controversies that may endanger opportunities for future research, b) assumptions that resulting increased knowledge from a study will offset short-term harms, c) difficulties in perceiving potential negative impacts of their studies, and, d) tacit assumptions about certain experiments believed to be wrong. The authors encourage further discussion between scientists and moral philosophers on ethical issues.

[. . .]

Introduction

Ecology, like most sciences, entails experimental manipulation of organisms or their physical environment, active observation, and deliberate or inadvertent disturbance of organisms in nature. Destructive sampling, labeling of microsites, removal or transplantation of vegetation, and the collection and sacrifice of specimens are common methods in field research. Occasionally these manipulations involve whole ecosystems, perturb fragile communities, or involve rare or endangered species. Herein lies an ethical dilemma: the same work that would both derive from and support an ethic of conservation also may cause damage to the very biotic systems it seeks to understand. It is time to recognize and question the assumptions that we make in choosing our field sites, study organisms, and experimental designs. In this paper, we ask the following questions:

- Do we as researchers consciously invoke a coherent system of ethics in designing our ecological experiments in the field?
- Are these ethical decisions or constructs anywhere explicitly stated? If not, why not?
- Does the community of field researchers need to discuss and develop a body of experimental ethics, especially before others question or regulate our research activity? What existing sources may we draw from in developing an ethical foundation for our work?

Our inquiry will inevitably generate more questions than it can hope to answer. We raise this issue in the hope that it will stimulate discussion among philosophers and field biologists alike.

[. . .]

Environmental ethics

The past four decades have witnessed the emergence of a variously articulated environmental ethic that espouses a general respect for the earth and urges the wise use of its natural resources (see Leopold 1949; Commoner 1974; Ehrlich and Ehrlich 1981). This major social and political movement has alerted the scientific community to the fact that the objects of our research are a limited and shrinking resource, and that care must be taken in the handling of that resource, be it an organism or an ecosystem. Many environmentalists have found that defending groups of organisms, or the physical habitat they require, entails petitioning sets of values based on enlightened self-interest (utilitarianism) or empathy. Appeals by conservation organizations frequently draw on public concern for charismatic megafauna, from elephants and pandas (Sunquist 1992) to spotted owls. They solicit compassion for organisms (often neotenic mammalian species) with whom humans may identify or find uses. It is intuitively easier to focus ethical concern on the plight of a single, demonstrably sentient organism than it is to engender a sense of moral responsibility for a whole ecosystem (Rolston 1981; Kellert 1986). Respect for "the land" is more difficult to invoke, although numerous writers since Thoreau have evoked a land ethic by conveying a strong sense of place in their writings. It is arguable whether a unit so nebulous as an ecosystem deserves moral consideration at all, because ecosystems show neither overt suffering nor a semblance of interests or free will (Cahen 1988).

Environmental philosophers have attempted to discern what value systems inform humans' feelings toward nature – that is, nonhuman animals, communities, and ecosystems (sometimes spuriously) distinguished from human-based systems.

[. . .]

For our purposes, four encompassing attitudes toward nature (summarized by Kellert 1991) may be most relevant. *Scientistic* value systems view nature as a focus of intellectual curiosity, as potential sources of answers to theoretical or practical problems. These values likely spur much current ecological research. Scientistic postures are commonly seen as value-free, arising from the "objective" pursuit of the scientific method. Anthropomorphic compassion for a study organism may be seen as interfering with the objectivity for which scientific studies strive.

Ecologistic value systems are oriented toward the appreciation and protection of whole ecological systems, informed by a knowledge of how physical and biotic components of ecosystems work together. Field biologists have accrued much information about ecosystem functioning, data that have shaped environmental policy, conservation efforts, and restoration strategies (Jordan *et al.* 1990).

Moralistic attitudes assume that absolute good and wrong govern the treatment of animals and natural systems, and that humans have definite duties to minimize harm. The language of contemporary American conservationists is also commonly couched in terms of the perceived rights of species, and many conservationists have argued that humans have no right per se to cause the extinction of other species (see Muir 1901; Leopold 1949; Ehrlich and Ehrlich 1981; Callicott 1986). Moralistic philosophies are opposed to exploitation or harm, especially when it can be shown to cause pain. Here, the opinions of animal rights moralists and environmental ethicists may coincide, though their directives may diverge.

Utilitarian modes of reasoning arise from the premise that nature provides material benefits that increase the common good of humans, and that it is possible through some common currency to weigh human welfare justly against ecological welfare. Economists are now developing means by which to assign tangible monetary value to ecological systems (see Daly and Cobb 1989). Nature is perceived as valuable if it fulfills a pragmatic human need. Utilitarianism has provided the foundation for cost-benefit and environmental impact analyses used to project the long-term effects of projects with detrimental ramifications for the environment (Rolston 1981, 1985). Utilitarian approaches might also justify short-term harm to a certain community if a greater ecological good (measurable in economic terms) were expected of the action. Thus we gamble with encroachment on an endangered species or territory in hopes that our expanded comprehension of the system will ultimately facilitate its survival, and possibly our own.

The ethics of ecological studies on animals

Concern for the welfare of animals used in research has developed with the growth of modern laboratory science. In recent years the emphasis has shifted from animal welfare to animal rights (a moralistic stance), concerned with the intrinsic right of an animal to be free from pain and constraint (Regan 1983). This viewpoint is often in direct conflict with the perceived rights of biologists, or the rights of human beneficiaries of medical cures or other products of animal experimentation (Dodds and Orlans 1982; Rollin 1985). Abundant cogent discussions of both sides of this volatile issue are available (see Fox and Mickley 1987; Vaughan 1988). Rejoinders from the scientific community vary from justifications of animal use (Miller 1985) to the development of explicitly stated alternatives (Huntingford 1984; Gallup and Suarez 1985) and institutionally imposed guidelines (Association for the Study of Animal Behavior 1981, Moss 1992).

[. . .]

The tacit assumption of a hierarchy of value in organisms is solidly incorporated into our culture. Our very existence as a species has entailed the destruction of habitat and other organisms. Our ethical assumptions regarding the environment and our moral duties to organisms reflect this value hierarchy and dictate both economic agendas and research activity. In field-based research, as with environmental ethics, questions of our responsibilities to our objects of study become more diffuse as we try to address higher levels of biological organization such as the population, community, or ecosystem. [. . .] Field biologists do not currently possess adequate mechanisms to evaluate how often extinction or environmental damage may result from our actions. It is generally left to the judgement of the individual biologist to decide when disturbance due to field practices is justifiable. The paucity of discussion of these issues in the literature makes it difficult to assess how individual scientists make these decisions, or how the sum of these decisions affects the organisms that we study and the science that we do.

Case studies from the ecological literature

It is generally accepted that in situ experiments are necessary to gain ecologically realistic information on the system or organism of study. The scale of experimental treatments can in part determine the long-term effects of the research methods on study organisms and their environment. Examples of traditional field techniques with long-term ramifications include the introduction of non-native predators or other invasive species to islands, the introduction of foreign material to lakes and streams, and the establishment of plots in areas where vegetation recovery time is slow. Collections of sufficient numbers of specimens to make reliable taxonomic distinctions, to satisfy statistical sampling needs, to enable gut content analysis, or to estimate population sizes also may deplete the study population locally. Intensive observations of a population; the use of blinds, radio telemetry, and assorted marking techniques; or manipulations such as introductions, exclosures, selective culling, and ecotoxicity studies can induce changes in animal behavior, survivorship, and community structure. We now examine ethical issues associated with some of these methods.

[. . .]

Observations of animals in the field

Ecologists have long recognized that the simple act of observation may affect the behavior of study organisms. [. . .] Ornithologists have acknowledged that, among birds, human intrusion can influence social interactions, the reproductive performance of adults, and the survivorship of chicks (Ellison and Cleary 1978; Gottfried and Thompson 1978; Nisbet 1978; Duffy 1979; Anderson and Keith 1980; Cooke 1980; Fetterolf 1983; Westmoreland and Best 1985; Belanger and Bedard 1989). [. . .] Methods of marking individuals with colored bird bands, radio collars, subcutaneous implants, paints, or dyes may inflict pain, increase the risk of predation, or affect mate choice and reproductive success. While these methods offer effective means for field identification of animals, they may exert an influence on the organisms' behavior that must be accounted for in research results and in our interpretations of "normal" baseline behavior.

It is possible that any organism that exhibits a negative response to human intrusion will suffer reduced fitness from repeated visits by scientists. Researchers undoubtedly take precautions to prevent or lessen detrimental effects on organisms, but at best such measures are only vaguely implied in the published experimental design. It would be interesting to know how many experiments have been constrained or modified out of concern for the organism itself.

Collection of organisms in the field

Other ethical issues arise when we propose to collect study organisms. The question of when collection is warranted is contentious, especially in shrinking tropical habitats; controversy exists over collection of rare specimens for captive propagation or for taxonomic identification and vouchering. [. . .] Sometimes we may learn of a particular species only when it appears in our mist nets, pitfall traps, or fishing seines. There is an urgent need for data on global species diversity: species counts and the presence of rare species often inform conservation policies (Erwin 1983a; Greene 1988; Gaston 1991). Yet where a species is locally rare or confined only to a tiny habitat such as a single tree, is it tenable to risk reducing the population through collecting (Larochelle and Bousquet 1978; Erwin 1983b)?

[. . .]

Ecosystem-level studies

Finally, ecologists frequently initiate large-scale experiments designed to determine the effects of factors such as toxins, new species, and local extinctions on an existing ecosystem (see Likens 1985 for a review). Such manipulations have greatly increased our knowledge of ecosystem structure and function and provide strong evidence (see Platt 1964) to support or refute ecological theories. The establishment of long-term ecological research sites by the U.S. National Science Foundation and other comprehensive field projects elsewhere have enabled ecologists to institute multi-year experiments encompassing whole watersheds (Likens 1985) to study such phenomena as deforestation, global climate change, and atmospheric pollutant deposition (see Herrick 1988).

Such experiments contain their own limitations, principally "because of the difficulty of replication and the great temporal variability of ecosystems" (Carpenter 1989). [. . .] Yet for all the considerable technical accomplishments of ecosystem-level studies, discourse in the scientific literature of the ethics of altering whole ecosystems such as lakes, streams, and forests appears to be limited to the release of genetically-engineered organisms (Tiedje *et al.* 1989).

[. . .]

Assumptions and the lack of public discourse

Returning to our original three questions, we ask, do we and should we consciously invoke a coherent system of ethics in designing our field experiments? We have seen that elements of both environmental ethics and animal-centered ethics are germane to ecological research, but these considerations alone may not be adequate to encompass non-animals, whole populations, communities, or ecosystems. We may need to devise new ethical systems based on scientific, naturalistic, or utilitarian grounds in order to address these areas of scientific endeavor. We asked whether these ethical decisions or constructs are anywhere explicitly stated. A review of the literature reveals that if field biologists are taking ethical issues into account, they are rarely saying so. Why, in a time when science comes under public fire from activists and government alike, is there little more than cursory mention of ecological ethics? We contend that four considerations have discouraged public discussion of this issue.

First, the community of ecologists may be understandably gun-shy, having witnessed the sometimes violent attacks upon their colleagues by "animal liberationists." Contentious and emotional debate, the prospect of litigation, and the possibility of regulation or sabotage may stifle open discussion among ecologists themselves. Likewise, ecologists conducting research on sensitive species or sites may run the risk of being denied access by wary land owners and managers.

Second, many ecologists may be motivated by the tacit utilitarian assumption that the potential benefits of knowledge acquired will far outweigh the short-term costs of research. This argument is frequently used to defend the use of animals in medical research. It can also be applied to ecology, especially where research may ultimately lead to the conservation or protection of the entire species or the habitat in question. We cannot conserve until we comprehend; thus we identify the expanded knowledge of our system as a good (Short 1986).

Third, it may be more difficult in a field situation to perceive – much less quantify – the negative effects of research activity. We may not directly detect the hardship that our treatments levy upon organisms or sites, and we may be hard-pressed to interpret increased mortality as a direct outcome of our actions, especially because harm was an unintended effect.

[...]

Fourth, we may avoid devising some research protocols on the assumption that "certain experiments are simply wrong to do," but we rarely state why explicitly. [...] Huntingford (1984) represents an exception in the literature. She both states the dilemmas inherent in a particular form of behavioral experimentation and attempts to deal with them in designing a humane protocol. She reduces the potential suffering of her study organisms by (1) ensuring that "trivial" experiments are avoided, (2) encouraging collaborative research to streamline efforts, (3) collecting data on both natural and controlled encounters, (4) substituting models for live animals whenever possible, (5) minimizing sample sizes, and (6) keeping encounters/ runs as brief as possible. Some of her solutions may be applicable only to the science of behavioral ecology, while others may be more broadly implemented. Regardless of the efficacy of her solutions, her approach represents one of the few efforts (outside of ornithology; see Still 1982) to identify, address, and resolve ethical issues a priori, and it has been adopted by others (see Hourigan 1986; Magurran and Girling 1986; Timberlake and Melcer 1988; Perrigo *et al.* 1989).

Questions of regulation and cooperation

Does an ethic apply to ecological research, one that might inform scientific research policy, and is it necessary or possible for the community of field researchers to devise general ethical guidelines for scientific activity? The same lessons that gave rise to an environmental ethic inform us that "nature" – the study organism, the pristine field site – is a limited and shrinking resource. [...] Many ecologists are aware of the duties we assume when we undertake a study in nature, and have a vested interest in controlling the amount of irreversible change inflicted upon our study sites. Data are simpler to interpret if treatments are fastidiously applied and maintained, and it is more feasible to return to sites that have been only minimally damaged or fully restored.

As ecologists ourselves, we begin from the clear premise that ecological research is both needed and valuable, and that some manipulation and observation is required in order to answer questions in a scientifically meaningful way. We believe that it is healthy for a discipline to reflect upon its own assumptions and to acknowledge relevant ethical problems where they arise. Such inquiry is especially critical today, when scientists are increasingly called upon both to justify their research economically and ethically and to advise policy makers on environmental issues.

External regulations

Some guidelines governing field experiments exist (Association for the Study of Animal Behavior 1981; Phillips and Szecher 1989; Moss 1992) or are being developed (Linnartz *et al.* 1990), but no comprehensive standard exists for protecting the integrity of natural systems under the scrutiny of research. [. . .] In the end, the emphasis of these review policies is on potential harm to the study organisms; the majority of field studies are not evaluated with regard to the integrated natural systems in which they occur.

Increased legislation or institutional regulation may not be the most appropriate response, in any case. If the need arises, establishing standards for self-governance under the aegis of the scientific community is a viable possibility. [. . .]

Regulations may involve ranking certain ecosystems on the basis of their rarity, size, diversity, pristineness, resident species, aesthetic and educational values, in addition to their importance to science (see Federal Register 1980; Spicer 1987; Jenkins 1988). Consistent environmental ranking schemes have been notoriously hard to develop for the purposes of protection, and devising new means of identifying appropriate research sites could be problematic.

[. . .]

[N]umerous questions remain for discussion. Is it necessary to regulate ecological research to ensure the proper treatment of ecological systems, or would regulation stifle creativity? Even in the absence of formal regulation, is it advisable for ecologists to develop and articulate their own ethical standards? Should nature, as a limited resource, be rationed for research that is deemed critical? Does peer review adequately address these concerns?

Conclusions: regulating ourselves

Ecological science is poised on the horns of a dilemma created by the unique demands that society places upon it. Sagoff (1985) describes the responsibilities that society attributes to ecology as follows: "Ecologists may apply their science either to manage ecosystems to increase the long-run benefits nature offers man or to protect ecosystems from anthropogenic insults and injuries." These two goals may come into conflict, and the practice of field research may occasionally violate both of the objectives, at least in the short term. While individual ecologists may object to society's sometimes burdensome, stereotypic, and simplistic delineation of our roles, we are nonetheless answerable to an ethic generated by that society. And we are a "discipline with a time limit" (Diamond and May 1985). Programs such as the Sustainable Biosphere Initiative being developed by the Ecological Society of America (Lubchenco *et al.* 1991) illustrate that ecologists are beginning to recognize responsibilities to pursue integrated, basic, and applied research protocols that will ultimately promote the conservation of our study sites and species. Given the urgent and unprecedented threats facing the biosphere, it is timely – even imperative – to develop a consistent ethical foundation on which to base our research.

It is clear that the ecological community is aware of many of the ethical issues that arise in our work. Most discussions of these issues take place as informal conversations among colleagues, and rarely in more public fora. We are advocating more open venues for biologists to air their ethical views and the incorporation of more explicit discussion of "ethical methods" (whatever these may be) into research publications. Can field biologists employ the language of philosophers to clarify our choices of research protocols? There are consequences for biological research. A diversity of opinion among field scientists and philosophers may narrow interdisciplinary rifts and help us begin to resolve some of these issues; such discussion can only serve to educate us all.

[...]

Literature cited

Anderson, D. W., and J. O. Keith. 1980. The human influence on seabird nesting success: Conservation implications. *Biological Conservation* **18**:65–80.

Association for the Study of Animal Behavior. 1981. Guidelines for the use of animals in research. *Animal Behavior* **29**:1–2.

Belanger, L., and J. Bedard. 1989. Responses of staging greater snow geese to human disturbance. *Journal of Wildlife Management* **53**(3):713–19.

Cahen, H. 1988. Against the moral considerability of ecosystems. *Environmental Ethics* **10**:195–216.

Callicott, J. B. 1986. On the intrinsic value of nonhuman species. Pages 138–71 in B. G. Norton, editor. *The preservation of species*. Princeton University Press, Princeton, New Jersey.

Carpenter, S. R. 1989. Replication and treatment strength in whole-lake experiments. *Ecology* **70**:453–63.

Commoner, B. 1974. *The closing circle: Nature, man and technology*. Bantam Books, New York.

Cooke, A. S. 1980. Observations on how close certain passerine species will tolerate an approaching human in rural and suburban areas. *Biological Conservation* **18**:85–8.

Daly, H. E., and J. B. Cobb, Jr. 1989. *For the common good*. Beacon Press, Boston, Massachusetts.

Diamond, J. M., and R. M. May. 1985. A discipline with a time limit. *Nature* **317**:111–12.

Dodds, W. J., and F. B. Orlans, editors. 1982. *Scientific perspectives on animal welfare*. Academic Press, New York.

Duffy, D. C. 1979. Human disturbance and breeding birds. *Auk* **96**:815–16.

Ehrlich, P. R., and A. Ehrlich. 1981. *The causes and consequences of the disappearance of species*. Random House, New York.

Ellison, L. N., and L. Cleary. 1978. Effects of human disturbance on breeding of double-crested cormorants. *Auk* **95**:510–17.

Erwin, T. L. 1983a. Tropical forest canopies: The last biotic frontier. *Bulletin of the Entomological Society of America* **29**:14–19.

—— 1983b. Beetles and other insects of tropical forest canopies at Manaus, Brazil, sampled by insecticidal fogging. Pages 59–75 in S. L. Sutton, T. C. Whitmore, and A. C. Chadwick, editors. *Tropical rain forest: Ecology and management*. Blackwell Scientific Publications, Oxford.

Federal Register. 1980. S1212.5: *Natural landmark criteria. Rules and regulations*, vol. **45**(238):81192. U.S. Government Printing Office, Washington, D.C.

Fetterolf, P. M. 1983 Effects of investigator activity on ring-billed gull behavior and reproductive performance. *Wilson Bulletin* **95**(1):23–41.

Fox, M. W., and L. D. Mickley. 1987. *Advances in animal welfare science* 1986/87. Martinus Nijhoff Publications, Boston.

Gallup, G. G., and S. D. Suarez. 1985. Alternatives to the use of animals in psychological research. *American Psychologist* **40**(10):1104–11.

Gaston, K. J. 1991. The magnitude of global insect species richness. *Conservation Biology* **5**(3):283–96.

Gottfried, B. M., and C. F. Thompson. 1978. Experimental analysis of nest predation in an old-field habitat. *Auk* **95**(2):304–12.

Greene, H. W. 1988. Species richness in tropical predators. Pages 259–80 in F. Almeda and C. M. Pringle, editors. *Tropical rainforests: Diversity and conservation*. California Academy of Sciences, San Francisco, California.

Herrick, C. N. 1988. *Interim assessment: The causes and effects of acidic deposition*. U.S. Government Report. National Acid Precipitation Assessment Program, U.S. Government Printing Office, Washington, D.C.

Hourigan, T. F. 1986. An experimental removal of a territorial Pomacentrid: Effects on the occurrence and behavior of competitors. *Environmental Biology of Fishes* **15**(3):161–9.

Huntingford, F. A. 1984. Some ethical issues raised by studies of predation and aggression. *Animal Behavior* **32**:210–15.

Jenkins, J. 1988. *A guide for evaluating the outstanding rivers and streams of Vermont*. Agency of Natural Resources. Waterbury, Vermont.

Jordan, W. R., M. E. Gilpin, and J. D. Aber. 1990. *Restoration ecology: A synthetic approach to ecological research*. Cambridge University Press, Cambridge, England.

Kellert, S. R. 1986. Social and perceptual factors in the preservation of animal species. Pages 50–73 in B. G. Norton, editor. *The preservation of species*. Princeton University Press, Princeton, New Jersey.

—— 1991. Japanese perceptions of wildlife. Conservation Biology 5(3):297–308.

Larochelle, A., and Y. Bousquet. 1978. Reduction of carabid beetle population through intensive collecting. *Cordulia* 3(3):105–6.

Leopold, A. 1949. *A sand county almanac*. Oxford University Press, New York.

Likens, G. E. 1985. An experimental approach for the study of ecosystems. *Journal of Ecology* 73:381–96.

Linnartz, N. E., R. S. Craig, and M. B. Dickerman. 1990. Land ethic canon. Page 24 in Society of American Foresters Committee on Ethics. *Journal of Forestry*, New York.

Lubchenco, J., A. M. Olson, L. B. Brubaker, S. R. Carpenter, M. M. Holland, S. P. Hubbell, S. A. Levin, J. A. MacMahon, P. A. Matson, J. M. Mellilo, H. A. Mooney, C. H. Peterson, H. R. Pulliam, L. A. Real, P. J. Regal, and P. G. Risser. 1991. The sustainable biosphere initiative: An ecological research agenda. *Ecology* 72:371–412.

Magurran, A. E., and S. L. Girling. 1986. Predator and model recognition and response habituation in shoaling minnows. *Animal Behavior* 34:510–18.

Miller, N. E. 1985. The value of behavioral research on animals. *American Psychologist* 40(4):423–40.

Moss, I. S. 1992. Foresters' ethics. *The Forestry Chronicle* 68:339–41.

Muir, J. 1901. *Our national parks*. Houghton-Mifflin, Boston, Massachusetts.

Nisbet, I. C. T. 1978. Direct human influences: Hunting and the use of birds by man's waste deposits. *Ibis* 120:134.

Perrigo, G., W. C. Bryant, L. Belvin, and F. S. vom Saal. 1989. The use of live pups in a humane, injury-free test for infanticidal behavior in male mice. *Animal Behavior* 38:897–904.

Phillips, M. T., and J. A. Szecher. 1989. *Animal research and ethical conflict*. Springer-Verlag, New York.

Platt, J. R. 1964. Strong inference. *Science* 146:347–53.

Regan, T. 1983. *The case for animal rights*. University of California Press, Berkeley, California.

Rollin, B. E. 1985. The moral status of research animals in psychology. *American Psychologist* 40(8):920–6.

Rolston III, H. 1981. Values in nature. *Environmental Ethics* 3:113–28.

—— 1985. Duties to endangered species. *BioScience* 35:718–26.

Sagoff, M. 1985. Fact and value in ecological science. *Environmental Ethics* 7:99–116.

Short, R. V. 1986. Primate ethics. Pages 34–45 in K. Benirschke, editor. *Primates: The road to self-sustaining populations*. Springer-Verlag, New York.

Spicer, R. C. 1987. Selecting geological sites for National Natural Landmark designation. *Natural Areas Journal* 7(4):157–78.

Sunquist, F. 1992. Who's cute, cuddly and charismatic? *International Wildlife* 22:4–13.

Tiedje, J. M., R. K. Colwell, Y. L. Grossman, R. E. Hodson, R. E. Lenski, R. N. Mack, and P. J. Regal. 1989. The planned introduction of genetically engineered organisms: Ecological considerations and recommendations. *Ecology* 70:298–315.

Timberlake, W., and T. Melcer. 1988. Effects of poisoning on predatory and ingestive behavior toward artificial prey in rats (*Rattus norvegicus*). *Journal of Comparative Psychology* 102(2):182–7.

Vaughan, C. 1988. Animal research: Ten years under siege. *Bioscience* 38(1):10–13.

Westmoreland, D., and L. B. Best. 1985. The effect of disturbance on mourning dove nesting success. *Auk* 102(4):774–80.

44

Stephen T. Emlen

"Ethics and Experimentation: Hard Choices for the Field Ornithologist"

In responding to a critique of an earlier study, Emlen defends his earlier work and also addresses the broader issue of ethical trade-offs in experimental science. He agrees that animal pain and suffering should be minimized in animal research whenever possible and that scientists have a responsibility to carefully compare the value of their research against the harm their work causes. He further argues that some animal experimentation is needed—not just for human interests, but as a benefit to the natural world, and ultimately to minimize pain and suffering among nonhuman species.

Every scientist must make difficult ethical decisions when designing experiments, whether such experiments are conducted in the laboratory or in the field. Typically, these decisions require weighing the likely scientific gain (in terms of new information to be learned) against the animal cost (in terms of suffering of the individuals involved). The question of when the pursuit of knowledge justifies the imposition of suffering on animal subjects is one that should be honestly confronted and constantly reassessed. Most scientific societies have published guidelines to help individual scientists formulate their answers (e.g. Oring *et al.* 1988, Dawkins and Gosling 1992. Anonymous 1987, 1992). However, even with such guidelines, there is no magic "threshold" of agreement. Rather, there is a broad gray area within which different opinions are vehemently expressed. Peer feedback is useful in defining these gray areas and in stimulating discussion about them. It is in this light that I welcome the opportunity to reply to the commentary of Bekoff (1993).

Bekoff (1993) criticized our study (Emlen *et al.* 1989) of experimentally induced infanticide in jacanas on ethical grounds and chastised the American Ornithologists' Union for publishing our article in the *Auk*. As the senior author of the challenged paper, I wish to justify our specific experiments, as well as address the broader issue of ethical trade-offs in experimental science.

If asked, everyone would agree that unnecessary and unnatural pain and suffering in animals should be minimized wherever possible, but there exists a spectrum of opinions on when and whether intervention and experimentation are appropriate. At one end, few would disagree that many birds are kept in captivity under sufficiently inhumane conditions that no degree of scientific justification can excuse their poor care. At the other, field ornithologists routinely witness nestlings suffering from predation and starvation, yet few would advocate intervention to eliminate predators or to provide supplemental food to undernourished chicks. In between these extremes the answers are less clear-cut.

How then should scientists balance the trade-off of knowledge gained versus suffering caused (or permitted, by nonintervention)? Bateson (1986) and Driscoll and Bateson (1988) offered a useful "model" in the form of a decision cube with three dimensions: the certainty of benefit (knowledge gained), the quality of the research, and the amount of animal suffering. In relative terms, animal suffering is justified only when the research is of high quality and has a high certainty of benefit.

But what qualifies as "benefit"? Bateson (1986) and Driscoll and Bateson (1988) couched benefit largely in terms of knowledge that has obvious potential benefit to humans. In his original paper, Bateson used "certainty of *medical* benefit" as his first dimension (emphasis mine). I strongly disagree. In this era of diminishing biodiversity it is imperative that we increase our knowledge of organisms that can serve as general models for larger categories of species. Whether we wish it or not, we are becoming stewards for increasing numbers of threatened species on this planet. To be effective stewards, we must have better knowledge of a wide array of species representing different phylogenetic, ecological, physiological, and behavioral types. Gaining such knowledge frequently requires experimental testing of specific hypotheses.

I suggest that "scientific value" replace Bateson's "certainty of medical benefit" as a critical criterion in the decision of when, and whether, animal suffering can be justified. I further suggest two specific criteria as useful guidelines for assessing the scientific value of any study: (1) the conceptual importance of the question being asked; and (2) the degree to which the results will be generalizable to other species (so that, ultimately, fewer experiments will need to be conducted on other species). These considerations were critical factors in our decision to conduct an experimental test of infanticide in jacanas.

The question of the possible adaptive significance of the infanticidal killing of conspecific young is, in my view, one of considerable conceptual importance. Such behavior occurs commonly in a wide variety of species, including our own (Hrdy 1979, Hausfater and Hrdy 1984). When infanticide was found to be widespread among primates, it aroused considerable scientific interest among both evolutionary biologists and anthropologists. Hrdy (1974, 1977) offered a comprehensive adaptive hypothesis for one form of infanticide, that which occurs when a new male in a harem polygynous primate species displaces a male breeder and "takes-over" the breeder's assemblage of females. Such incoming males frequently kill young that are still dependent upon the female(s). Hrdy (1974, 1977) speculated that such behavior was adaptive to the infanticidal male because the removal of dependent young caused females to come into estrous and to reproduce with the new male much more rapidly than would otherwise be the case. This sexually selected infanticide hypothesis proposed specific benefits (enhanced reproductive success) for the perpetrator and predicted the conditions (following takeovers by new mates) under which it was expected to occur.

Alternative hypotheses were rapidly advanced, including several that considered infanticidal killing to be a nonadaptive behavior, aberrantly expressed under conditions of artificially high population density or excessive human disturbance (Curtin and Dolhinow 1978, 1979, Boggess 1979, Sommer 1987). One of the difficulties in differentiating among these hypotheses has been the scarcity of direct observations of the behavior. Infanticide is usually inferred. And even when infanticide is observed, we are left with descriptive and correlational data only; cause and effect can only be tested experimentally. Although a growing body of data are consistent with Hrdy's predictions (e.g. Hausfater and Hrdy 1984, Sommer 1987), we have only weak inference tests of the hypothesis.

Because of their behavioral role-reversal, jacanas offered a unique opportunity to examine the hypothesis of sexually selected infanticide. Jacanas provide a mirror image of the polygynous mating systems in which infanticide has been reported in mammals. In jacanas it is females that hold "harems" of males and that compete intensively for mates. Jenni and

Collier (1972) reported that males frequently change "ownership" during their lifetime. Stephens (1982, 1984) concurred and speculated that infanticide might occur.

By inducing infanticide experimentally, we were able to confirm the specific predictions of the Hrdy hypothesis with a rigor not possible from descriptive observations alone. Further, by our choice of jacanas as the model species, we were able to extend the applicability of the hypothesis (1) across taxa (to birds as well as mammals) and (2) across sexes (since females, as predicted by theory, are the infanticidal sex under conditions of role reversal). Our results thus provided an unusually robust test of the hypothesis. An adaptive explanation for infanticide was strongly supported, and the generality of the Hrdy hypothesis was greatly extended.

What of Bekoff's specific criticisms? In the experiment, we removed two polyandrously breeding female jacanas and then observed the behavior of the incoming females that competed to take-over the residents' territories and the males that occupied them. Bekoff (1993) questioned: (1) the methods used to remove the two breeding females; and (2) the allowing of the "maiming and killing of seven of their chicks." He also challenged (3) the review process that allowed publication of a paper that he believes violated AOU guidelines. Below I address each of these criticisms.

(1) The females were collected by shooting. According to the AOU guidelines, shooting is the most humane method of collection because individuals are killed outright. Our observations were part of a pilot study to determine the feasibility of a more intensive project on the social behavior and breeding biology of this species. The collected individuals served an additional purpose. Blood and tissue samples from these specimens confirmed the suitability of the molecular method of DNA fingerprinting (Jeffries *et al.* 1985, Westneat 1990) for assignment of paternity in jacanas. We determined that blood samples would be sufficient for later studies of promiscuity and paternity, eliminating any need for collection of additional individuals for tissue samples.

(2) Following the removal of each resident female, neighboring females rapidly expended their territories to encompass the vacated areas (and the resident males they contained). These replacement females actively sought out and attacked the chicks of the former female. The males attempted to defend their young, but were unsuccessful. The behavior was dramatic; it provided clear answers to Hrdy's predictions. It also caused the death of five chicks.

After removal of the second female, I called off further experiments. Our sample sizes were extremely small (three of three incoming females infanticidal; four of four broods attacked; five of nine chicks killed and two evicted); however, the results were sufficiently clear that I did not wish to induce further suffering. By terminating the experiment at two female removals, we were unable statistically to confirm that incoming females are infanticidal (a sample of three females or four broods is too small to achieve significance with a Fisher exact test). Ironically, this trade-off "cost" us the opportunity of publishing the results in an interdisciplinary journal of wider circulation because one reviewer felt that the sample sizes were insufficient.

(3) Did this research violate AOU guidelines? The guidelines state that researchers must "avoid or minimize distress and pain to the animals, consistent with sound research design." The design of this experiment, however, was to test whether infanticidal behavior would be induced under specific conditions. One cannot easily control behavior in field situations. Bekoff questioned why we did not intervene to recapture the injured chicks, nursing them back to health or, if fatally injured, killing them humanely. This was not logistically possible. The remaining way of minimizing suffering is to limit the number of individuals attacked. We did this by terminating the experiment after only two removals.

I have no disagreement with Bekoff that animal pain and suffering are sometimes caused by scientific research, that such pain and suffering should be minimized whenever possible, and that scientists have a moral and ethical obligation to weigh carefully the scientific value of their research against the magnitude of suffering that it might cause. However, he and I differ on how such trade-offs should be decided, and on where the line of justification lies. Medical researchers argue that animal experimentation is required if we are to combat human diseases and avoid pain and suffering in our own species. I would expand their argument to encompass the need for selective animal experimentation to enhance our general knowledge of the behavior and ecology of representative species, knowledge that is required if we are to protect and conserve the diversity of life and, ultimately, to minimize pain and suffering in nonhuman species.

I thank Natalie J. Demong and Douglas J. Emlen for their comments.

Literature cited

Anonymous. 1987. Acceptable field methods in mammalogy: Preliminary guidelines approved by the American Society of Mammalogists. *J. Mammal.* 68(4, suppl):1–18.

Anonymous. 1992. Sigma Xi statement on the use of animals in research. *Am. Sci.* 80:73–6.

Bateson, P. 1986. When to experiment on animals. *New Scientist* 109(1496):30–2.

Bekoff, M. 1993. Experimentally induced infanticide: The removal of birds and its ramifications. *Auk* 110:404–6.

Boggess, J. 1979. Infant killing and male reproductive strategies in langurs (*Presbytis entellus*). Pages 283–310 in *Infanticide: Comparative and evolutionary perspectives* (G. Hausfater and S. Hrdy, eds). Aldine, New York.

Curtin, R. A., and P. Dolhinow. 1978. Primate social behavior in a changing world. *Am. Sci.* 66:468–75.

—— 1979. Infanticide among langurs—A solution to overcrowding? *Science Today* 13:35–41.

Dawkins, M. S., and M. Gosling. 1992. *Ethics in research on animal behavior: Readings from Animal Behavior*. Academic Press, London. Pages 1–64.

Driscoll, J. W., and P. Bateson. 1988. Animals in behavioural research. *Anim. Behav.* 36:1569–1574.

Emlen, S. T., N. J. Demong, and D. J. Emlen. 1989. Experimental induction of infanticide in female Wattled Jacanas. *Auk* 106:1–7.

Hausfater, G., and S. B. Hrdy. 1984. *Infanticide: Comparative and evolutionary perspectives*. Aldine, New York.

Hrdy, S. B. 1974. Male-male competition and infanticide among the langurs (*Presbytis entellus*) of Abu, Rajasthan. *Folia Primatol.* 22:19–58.

—— 1977. Infanticide as a primate reproductive strategy. *Am. Sci.* 65:40–9.

—— 1979. Infanticide among animals: A review, classification, and examination of the implications for the reproductive strategies of females. *Ethol. and Sociobiol.* 1:13–40.

Jeffries, A. J., V. Wilson, and S. L. Thein. 1985. Hypervariable 'minisatellite' regions in human DNA. *Nature* 314:411–20.

Jenni, D. A., and G. Collier. 1972. Polyandry in the American Jacana (*Jacana spinosa*). *Auk* 89:743–65.

Oring, L. W., K. P. Able, D. W. Anderson, L. F. Baptista, J. C. Barlow, A. S. Gaunt, F. B. Gill, and J. C. Wingfield. 1988. Guidelines for the use of wild birds in ornithological research. *Auk* 105(suppl):1a–41a.

Sommer, V. 1987. Infanticide among free-ranging langurs (*Presbytis entellus*) at Jodhpur (Rajasthan/India): Recent observations and a reconsideration of hypotheses. *Primates* 28:163–97.

Stephens, M. L. 1982. Mate takeover and possible infanticide by a female Northern Jacana, *Jacana spinosa*. *Anim. Behav.* 30:1253–4.

—— 1984. Maternal care and polyandry in the Northern Jacana, *Jacana spinosa*. Ph.D. thesis, Univ. Chicago, Chicago.

Westnext, D. F. 1990. Genetic parentage in the Indigo Bunting: A study using DNA fingerprinting. *Behav. Ecol. Sociobiol.* 27:67–76.

Regulating Animal Experimentation

45

F. Barbara Orlans

"Ethical Themes of National Regulations Governing Animal Experiments: An International Perspective"

Among laws governing use of experimental animals, Orlans identifies eight regulatory dimensions ranging from minimal to extensive protections to laboratory animals; she also reviews and compares the international distribution of animal research laws. Orlans argues that public concerns have led to more stringent protections in recent years. She also believes that this increased regulation has stemmed both from animal rights activities and scientific insights on the intellectual and emotional capabilities of animals.

This essay reports on worldwide progress in the enactment of national laws governing the humane use of laboratory animals in biomedical research, testing, and education. During the last one hundred years, national laws to improve the welfare of laboratory animals have become enacted in at least twenty-three countries. I identify here eight ethical themes for discussion: (1) simple provision of basic husbandry requirements and inspection of facilities; (2) control of animal pain and suffering; (3) critical review of proposed experimental protocols; (4) specification of investigator competency; (5) bans on certain invasive procedures, sources of animals, or use of certain species; (6) application of the Three R alternatives—to refine procedures, reduce animal use, or replace animal procedures with nonanimal use where possible; (7) use of ethical criteria for decision making; and (8) mandatory use of animal-harm scales that rank degrees of increasing ethical cost to the animal. Countries in which all eight themes are addressed have the highest standards of animal care and use.

[. . .]

Countries with and without animal protection laws

By 2000 at least twenty-three countries worldwide had enacted laws requiring certain humane standards for experimenting on animals. [. . .] In 1985 the World Health

Organization promulgated *Guiding Principles for Biomedical Research involving Animals*, guidelines designed to provide a framework within which specific legislative or regulatory systems could be built in any country, including less-developed countries. Voluntary acceptance of these modest standards is better than having no provisions at all.

Ethical issues in current laws

The eight issues I have previously listed can be used for comparison among the nations. Within the sequence of this listing is a loose, overall historical pattern. The first enactment of laws in any country typically deals only with the first two topics, basic husbandry requirements and inspection of facilities and control of animal pain and suffering. Only later (in amendments to the law) are refinements addressed that illustrate the next four topics—critical review of protocols, specification of investigator competency, bans on certain activities, and the use of the Three R alternatives. The last two topics, which address the complicated issue of how to justify each specific protocol, represent the cutting edge of new legislation. As yet, they are only found in laws of the most progressive countries concerned with animal welfare.

Husbandry standards, inspections, and record keeping

Husbandry and inspections

A basic ethical concern requires that captive animals be housed and cared for humanely. Official government inspection of research facilities maintains standards of sanitation, provision of food and water, space allocation by species' needs, daily care, and other basic requirements. Usually only minimum husbandry standards are mandated, and the tendency has been for animal facilities to conform to the lowest acceptable standards rather than providing optimal housing.

Inspections by government officials are needed to establish compliance. The frequency and adequacy of inspections vary from country to country, as do the standards required. In the United States, inspections are carried out once per year at each of the approximately 1,500 facilities registered with the controlling governing agency. In some countries, inspections are so infrequent and inadequate that the law exists on paper alone.

Historically, standards for housing space have been inadequate. [. . .] However, housing standards for captive animals have been gradually improving in some countries. Reform has been sparked not only by more sympathetic public attitudes to animals but by research demonstrating that poor housing conditions cause stress to the animal, which can confound the experimental results obtained. Also, research has demonstrated that abnormal, stereotypic behaviors (such as pacing, cage biting, etc.) of laboratory, zoo, and farm animals do not occur if the animals are housed in enriched environments—ones as close as possible to those conditions experienced by free-living animals.

In the United States, Congress enacted an amendment to the Animal Welfare Act in 1985 that requires promotion of the "psychological well-being" of primates. This legal provision sparked new funding for environmental enrichment studies and has been profoundly effective in improving the housing conditions of primates. There is a trend toward increased space allocation, group-housing animals of similar species, and the addition of branches, toys, and exercise apparatus to the cages where appropriate. European countries and Australia have been in the forefront of enriching the housing of many common laboratory species, not only primates but also dogs, cats, rabbits, guinea pigs, and rats.

Record keeping

Public reporting of the numbers and species of animals used is a basic requirement of effective oversight and accountability of animal experiments. The rationale is that the public has a right to know what is happening in this socially controversial area of harming animals for human good. [. . .] Worldwide, estimates of the total number of animals used range as high as fifty to a hundred million annually, since many animals are uncounted.

It is unclear whether the total number of animals used worldwide is declining, as animal advocates hope, or increasing. A few countries, including the Netherlands, have reported a decline. In the United States, very probably the largest user of animals worldwide, inadequate data make trends impossible to assess.

[. . .]

Controls on animal pain and suffering

National laws also require that every effort be made to reduce or eliminate pain and suffering that result from an experimental procedure. Anesthetics, analgesics, and postoperative care should be used wherever needed, and animals in extreme pain should be put to death. It is generally considered a matter of plain humanity that the degree of animal pain and suffering be minimized. Indeed, it is a moral imperative.

But such provisions have not necessarily come with the first enactment of a national law. For instance, in the United States, animal pain was not addressed in 1966 when the law was first passed. Indeed, at that time, whether animals actually perceived pain was widely doubted. Not until 1976 was the Animal Welfare Act, the federal law governing laboratory animals, amended to require for the first time the use of anesthetics and analgesics. As a result, research on animal pain and its alleviation accelerated. Textbooks devoted to the physiology and relief of animal pain were published, new anesthetics and analgesics were developed, and postsurgical care became an important topic. Great progress has been made, and by now it is well recognized in national policies throughout the world that vertebrate animals do indeed feel pain.

Methods of killing of animals represent another aspect of control of pain. In the 1980s, the American Veterinary Medical Association established standards for recommended euthanasia practices to ensure that methods used are as rapid and painless as possible. These standards, which are now law in the United States, have been repeatedly updated, and other countries have adopted similar standards.

Critical review of protocols

Not all countries include legal provisions for review of investigators' proposed protocols. Sometimes investigators are subjected to either no formal procedure for protocol review or review only by their peers within their own discipline (for instance, in departmental review at a university or pharmaceutical company).

Nonetheless, there has been considerable growth in the establishment of oversight review committees that function as gatekeepers for approval of proposed experiments. These committees are variously called Animal Care and Use Committees (ACUCs) or Ethical Committees.

[. . .]

The ethical rationale behind such review is that investigators should be accountable in what they do, not only to their peers but also to the public. These committees may be institutional or regional. They typically operate with considerable autonomy, being only loosely regulated by national bodies. The resulting framework is often characterized as "enforced self-regulation."

The composition of these committees varies among countries, but most include representation of several viewpoints. Committee membership typically includes animal researchers, veterinarians, and lay (nonscientist) members of the public. Representatives from the animal-protection movement should be included because this is the constituency most concerned about humane standards. Experience has shown that to avoid rubber stamping, committee membership should not be dominated by animal researchers, and the chair should be an independent person and not an animal researcher.

The value of public representation on these committees is well established, and most committees would benefit with increased public representation.

[. . .]

The purpose of oversight committee review is to ensure compliance with established standards of care and use by modifying (to improve the animal's welfare) or disapproving proposed projects. This does not necessarily mean that ethical debate that questions the fundamental justification of a project occurs. Indeed, most commonly there is an assumption of fundamental justification of a project. Thus there is room for considerable improvement in the level of debate within most of these oversight committees. I discuss this further in the section "Ethical Criteria for Decision Making."

Specification of investigator competency

The question concerning investigator competency is "What training is required before a person is allowed to conduct *any* animal experiment?" Untrained persons are likely to inflict greater harm on an animal than trained persons attempting the same procedure and furthermore are unlikely to produce experimental results that are of scientific value. So the benefits are less and the harms greater. Establishment of competency standards is important, yet only a few countries have adequately addressed these issues.

[. . .]

In addition to controls over qualifications for persons working in animal-research facilities, several countries place controls over what is permitted by beginning biology students in early stages of their education. [. . .] Historically, a real problem existed in U.S. junior and senior high schools in the 1960s to early 1980s. Youths from age eleven to seventeen sought to impress judges of science-fair competitions by attempting highly invasive experiments on live animals. Often the students conducted these experiments in their homes, and supervision was absent or cursory. Extreme animal suffering occurred. Typical were high school student projects of attempted mammalian surgery, blinding, injection of lethal substances, and starving animals to death. Because the public protested strongly about these abuses, improvements have been made. But still today there is inadequate control over the use of animals in junior and senior high school education in the United States, as well as insufficient encouragement to use nonharmful alternatives. Federal laws do not exist. Unsatisfactory 1995 guidelines (which are voluntary and unenforceable) of the National Association of Biology Teachers include no provisions to ban the infliction of animal pain or suffering on sentient creatures and encourage dissection. Further reforms are still urgently needed.

As for the use of animals in U.S. colleges, there has been limited progress. The 1985 amendment to the Animal Welfare Act required for the first time that oversight committees review the use of animals in undergraduate college courses at some (but by no means all) tertiary educational institutions. [. . .] Rats, mice, and birds, the species most used in college classes, are not covered under the Animal Welfare Act. Thus, a number of colleges fall outside the law, so that much of the use of animals in U.S. biology classes is unregulated.

There are a number of ethical rationales for prohibiting students from harming or killing animals: (1) nonpainful, nonharmful animal projects, nonharmful human studies, and other projects that carry no ethical burden are readily available that are equally or more instructive; (2) because projects at this educational level are primarily demonstrations of known facts, they lack the major ethical justification for harming animals that is based on the reasonable likelihood of obtaining significant, original knowledge; (3) unskilled students are likely to inflict greater harm than trained researchers; and (4) allowing emotionally immature youth to harm animals under the guise of education desensitizes students' feeling of empathy with animals. It can be argued that these points apply not only to primary and secondary school students but also to undergraduate college-level students. It is usually not until graduate school that a student makes a serious career commitment, and even then, not all careers in the biological sciences require expertise in animal experimentation techniques.

Bans on certain activities

Experimental procedures that cause intense and prolonged animal suffering have been the focus of the greatest public protest and demands for prohibition. Even if useful scientific results might be obtained, the lack of justification holds.

Some success in banning such activities has been achieved. A 1986 amendment to a German law, the Animal Protection Act, forbids experimentation on animals for development and testing of weapons, as well as the testing of tobacco products, washing powders, and cosmetics. The Netherlands and the United Kingdom also ban the use of animals for cosmetic testing. Recently, the British government announced its commitment to stop licensing any further testing of tobacco or alcohol products on animals. Indeed, in the whole field of animal testing, with the bans on the notorious LD50 test (the lethal dose that painfully kills 50 percent of the animals) and the Draize eye irritancy test (which can cause blindness in rabbits), considerable progress has been made.

Recently, three European countries (the Netherlands, Switzerland, and the United Kingdom) have banned the use of the ascites method of monoclonal antibody production. This procedure, used on mice, causes considerable suffering, including respiratory distress, circulatory shock, difficulty walking, anorexia, and other disabilities. It is estimated that in the United States up to one million animals a year are killed using this experimental method, but efforts to ban it in the United States have failed.

[. . .]

Another issue, apart from the experimental procedure, is the source of the subject animal. There are three potential sources: former animal pets, either stolen for research or abandoned by their owners; free-living wild animals; or purpose-bred animals (those specifically raised by commercial breeders for research). All sources have come under criticism (antivivisectionists object to every source), but most criticism has focused on the use of one-time companion animals and on the capture of wild animals, especially nonhuman primates.

Of the three possible sources, the use of purpose-bred animals is preferred. The ethical reasoning is that purpose-bred animals are likely to suffer less; they do not have to make a stressful transition from a free life to a life in captivity. Purpose-bred animals know no other life than living in confined quarters; they have been singly caged all their lives with little or no opportunity to make decisions for themselves over what exercise they take, what they eat, whom they spend time with, and so on. But former pets and free-living wild animals are different; they have usually lived rich social lives where they were accustomed to expressing their own free will. To lose this freedom can be traumatic. The period of transition can cause considerable suffering, including the stresses that come with transportation (sometimes for thousands of miles, as with some nonhuman primates, and which can result in death), close confinement, and social and other forms of deprivation.

In addition, the experimental results from purpose-bred animals are more reliable because, unlike former pets and wild animals, their genetic and health backgrounds are known. This reduces the number of variables that can confound experimental results.

[. . .]

Three R alternatives

The Three R principles (refine, reduce, replace), first enunciated by Russell and Burch in 1959, state that experimental procedures should be refined to lessen the degree of pain or distress, that the numbers of animals used should be reduced consistent with sound methodological design, and where possible, that nonanimal methods should be used in preference to those that do use animals. Legal mandates requiring the Three Rs facilitate the acceptance of these concepts by investigators and oversight reviewers. The countries that specifically address all Three Rs in their legislation include the United States, the Netherlands, Sweden, Switzerland, and New Zealand.

The Three R principles are increasingly becoming accepted worldwide by both the humane and scientific communities. Although antivivisectionists focus on replacement alternatives exclusively, others believe that incremental improvements in laboratory animal welfare are best achieved at this time by pursuing all Three Rs.

Promising advancements can be made in refining experimental methods by improving anesthetic and other pain-relieving regimens, using humane experimental end points, and employing only rapid and painless methods of euthanasia. To a lesser extent, reductions in numbers are feasible through the better use of statistics in methodological design. Replacement alternatives may not be applicable, but increasingly, nonanimal alternatives are being developed, especially in animal testing and in teaching biology to students.

[. . .]

Although the concept of the Three Rs is now fairly well accepted on a universal basis as an ideal, it has proved very difficult to persuade regulatory bodies to stop requiring safety tests that involve use of whole animals before a new product can be approved. Although validated nonanimal tests are available in many cases, the regulatory bodies continue to mandate whole-animal testing. The nonanimal tests are thereby unreasonably being held to a much higher standard of validation than animal tests.

The evaluation of progress in implementing the Three Rs is a new topic and is in its infancy; most countries do not have adequate data for analysis. However, the Netherlands provides a unique model. Analysis of official data shows a significant decline in the percentage of total experiments that involve severe animal pain, from 29.3 percent in 1984 to 18.8 percent in 1997 (Orlans 2000). In addition, over the same period, the number of animals used has dropped by about half: in 1984 the total was 1,242,285 and in 1997 it was 618,432 (Orlans 2000).

[. . .]

Ethical criteria for decision making

In general, existing laws do not address the fundamental ethical question, "Should this particular animal experiment be done at all?" The usual presumption of the law is that animal experimentation is justified and that proposed projects should be approved so long as the individual investigator believes that useful scientific knowledge might be gained. Indeed, oversight committees tend to approve almost everything that investigators propose, even highly invasive procedures on primates. Although some projects are modified (typically by application of a refinement), rarely is any proposal totally disapproved. It is thus a step forward when national policies specifically acknowledge that ethical decisions are involved in assessing the justification of an animal experiment, giving credence to the possibility that a proposed work is not justified.

Several countries have taken the lead in requiring a cost-benefit analysis that links animal pain (and other harms) to the scientific worthiness and social significance of the experiment's purpose. [. . .] The concept of making a cost-benefit analysis sounds reasonable but is difficult to apply because the costs and benefits are incommensurable. Almost all the harms fall on the animals and all the benefits on humans. Nevertheless, the cost-benefit view has gained considerable acceptance as a tool for clarifying ethical choices.

[. . .]

Use of animal-harm scales

An important issue on the cutting edge of new reforms in national laws is the requirement to assess and rank the sum total of animal harms for any particular procedure. The ranking systems are variously called severity banding, invasiveness, or more colloquially and inaccurately, pain scales. First mandated in the Netherlands in 1979, such systems are now found in other countries (in chronological order, the United Kingdom, Finland, Canada, Switzerland, and New Zealand). This spread attests to the usefulness of these schemes. Pressure exists in the United States and other countries to adopt similar systems.

According to these systems, the degree of pain or distress is ranked according to a severity banding of either minor, moderate, or severe. For example, in the minor category are such procedures as biopsies or cannulating blood vessels; in the moderate category are major surgical procedures under general anesthesia and application of noxious stimuli from which the animal cannot escape; in the severe category are trauma infliction on conscious animals and cancer experiments with death as an end point. At some point (according to one's point of view), procedures become unethical because of the severity of animal pain.

Mandatory use of these ranking systems forces laboratory personnel to think carefully about the condition of the animal and its state of well-being or adversity throughout the experiment. It also encourages laboratory personnel to learn how to identify clinical signs of well-being and adversity.

In recent years, adoption of harm scales by various countries has acted as a significant stimulus to clinical investigations of animals in assessing signs of well-being and adverse states. A notable contribution that has attracted worldwide attention is that of Mellor and Reid (1994). Their categorization system, which represents a major step forward in assessing the condition of animals, has been adopted with minor modification as national policy in New Zealand and is the gold standard by which other harm rankings should be measured.

Summary

Laboratory animals are much benefited by enforcement of legally established standards for humane care and use. Nonetheless, an absence of laws in many countries where animal experimentation takes place needs to be corrected. New provisions along the lines of the topics discussed here are also needed, as is enforcement of many existing laws. It takes a great deal of effort to enact legal protections for animals, but the value of such laws has been indisputably established, as evidenced by the vast improvements that have come about in the standards of animal care and use found in today's laboratories compared with those of previous years. I also believe that improved conditions that serve to support the welfare of animals serve also to improve immeasurably the quality of the resulting science.

References

Australian Government Publishing Service. 1990. *Australian code of practice for the care and use of animals for scientific purposes*. Canberra: Australian Government Publishing Service.

Mellor, D.J., and C.S.W. Reid, 1994. Concepts of animal well-being and predicting the impact of procedures on experimental animals. In *Improving the well-being of animals in the research environment*, 3–18. Glen Osmond, South Australia: Australian and New Zealand Council for the Care of Animals in Research and Teaching.

National Animal Ethics Advisory Committee. 1988. *Guidelines for institutional animal ethics committees*. September 16–17. Wellington, New Zealand: National Animal Ethics Advisory Committee.

Orlans, F.B. 2000. Public policies on assessing and reporting degrees of animal harm: International perspectives. In *Progress in the reduction, refinement, and replacement of animal experimentation*, edited by M. Balls, A.-M. van Zeller, and M.F. Halder, 1075–82. Amsterdam: Elsevier Science.

Russell, W.M.S., and R.L. Burch. 1959. *The principles of humane experimental technique*. London: Methuen. Reprinted 1992 by Universities Federation for Animal Welfare, 8 Hamilton Close, South Mimms, Potters Bar, Herts, UK ENG 3QD.

World Health Organization, 1985. *Guiding principles for biomedical research involving animals*. Geneva: Council for International Organizations of Medical Sciences.

Animals in Education

46

Jonathan Balcombe

"Summary of Recommendations"

Balcombe provides twenty-eight recommendations on the use of animals for classroom educational purposes. The recommendations are designed to facilitate use of fewer animals in the classroom, reduction in the range of activities for which animals are used, and reduction of suffering among individual animals.

1   Biology teachers should emphasize active, inquiry-based learning and engage their students in the doing of science.
2   Hands-on exercises should be pursued, but not at the expense of animal lives; countless ways exist for achieving exciting, engaging, hands-on exercises for students (e.g., having students study themselves, and outdoor studies of animals and plants).
3   The time required to perform good-quality dissections should be used instead to make room for more pressing life science topics such as cell biology, molecular genetics, evolution, biochemistry, environmental science, and animal behavior.
4   Teacher training should be reformed so that exposure to alternatives is included and dissection of animals is not a training prerequisite for obtaining a science teaching license.
5   Students should be fully involved in ethical decision making in the classroom.
6   Conscientious objection should not be seen as rebelliousness aimed at disrupting a teacher's efforts to teach, but rather, respected as evidence of concern and reflection.
7   Concern for animals should not be labeled as "squeamishness" but should be acknowledged as a legitimate manifestation of empathy for others. "Squeamish" students ought not be pressured or humiliated into participation in exercises they find distasteful.
8   Teachers and students should be made more aware of the connexion between cruelty to animals and interpersonal violence; though mutilation of dissected specimens may only reflect a temporary desensitization, it should not be ignored as a possible sign that a student is prone to antisocial behavior.
9   Ethics should be part of the education of all children, and dissections should not be

conducted in the absence of ethical discussion about the origins of the animals and the moral implications of using them.

10 Animal dissection should be eliminated from the precollege curriculum.

11 All procurement of animals for dissection should be from ethical sources, such as animal shelters, veterinary clinics, and wildlife rehabilitation facilities. Guardian-consent programs should be established so that cats (and other companion animals) who have died or been euthanized for medical or humane reasons can be donated from shelters or veterinary clinics to schools for educational use. These cadavers should replace the supply of cats from random sources, fetal pigs from slaughterhouses, frogs from wetlands, etc.

12 The United States Department of Agriculture (USDA), which is responsible for inspecting biological supply companies (classified by the USDA as "Class B Dealers"), should begin requiring biological supply companies to provide annual reports. These reports should include the numbers and species of animals killed and sold to schools for educational use, and the methods of capturing, transporting, handling, and killing the animals.

13 Biological supply companies should be required to conduct environmental impact assessments prior to collecting from wild animal populations.

14 Students should be informed of the specifics regarding the sources of animals used in the classroom, including methods used for capturing, transporting, handling, and killing the animals.

15 Dissection of species whose populations are known to be overexploited and/or in decline (e.g., leopard frogs, bullfrogs, spiny dogfish sharks) should be discontinued.

16 Students involved in dissections should be provided with gloves, masks, and safety instruction to minimize the hazards of exposure to formaldehyde.

17 Science teacher training should, without exception, include training in the use of computer simulations and other alternatives resources, including alternative databases and loan programs.

18 School exercises that involve killing, undernourishing, or otherwise harming live animals should be replaced with humane alternatives, such as computer simulations, observational and behavioral field study, and benign investigations of the students themselves.

19 The traditional frog- and turtle-pithing exercises should be terminated and replaced with computer packages, which have been shown to save time and money without compromising educational value. Studies that involve the students as investigators and subjects should be more widely adopted.

20 Medical schools still using live terminal dog labs should follow the lead of other schools that have replaced these procedures with humane alternatives.

21 Veterinary schools should accelerate the current trend towards replacement of purpose-bred and/or healthy animals with clinical cases for surgical training, including spay/neuter of shelter animals.

22 Recognizing that perioperative experience, including handling live tissue, is a critical part of a veterinary education, student participation in actual clinical cases coupled with primary surgical experience performing procedures of benefit to the animal (e.g., spay/neuter of shelter animals) should wholly replace traditional "survival" surgeries.

23 For common surgeries that are not medically required by an individual animal, only two options should exist: (1) terminal surgery on anesthetized terminally ill

animals with guardian consent, or (2) cadaver surgery where cadavers are ethically obtained.

24 All science fairs should abide by a policy against inflicting deliberate harm on sentient animals.

25 Laws should be implemented that require a certain level of competency before a person is allowed to conduct animal experiments.

26 All students should have a legally mandated right to use humane alternatives to dissection and other classroom exercises harmful to animals. Currently, fewer than one in five American states have statewide laws or policies mandating student choice in dissection. The result is that some students are granted rights denied to others. States still lacking such laws should make their enactment a high priority.

27 Dissection choice laws should apply to students at all levels of education; currently, such laws apply only to precollege students and exclude post-secondary students even though the validity of conscientious objection is independent of learning level.

28 IACUCs should apply more stringent restrictions on proposals for animal use in instruction and should always look for ways to piggyback teaching exercises that involve animals into ongoing research at the institution.

47

Andrew J. Petto and Karla D. Russell

"Humane Education: The Role of Animal-based Learning"

Petto and Russell address the complex issue of incorporating animal use in education, and outline a process for involving students as well as teachers in making humane decisions about animal studies in the curriculum. Issues addressed by students would include decisions on whether and how animals ought to be introduced into the curriculum, as well as various practical issues such as acquisition, classroom care and use, and disposition of animals at completion of the studies. While oriented toward secondary and early levels of education, many of their suggestions are also applicable to university levels.

[. . .]

Concept of the 'humane'

'Humane' is a cognitive concept for humans and subject to the same constraints as other cognitive concepts held by humans (Atran, 1990). It is universal in the sense that all cultures seem to have a concept that some actions and attitudes toward animals (and toward other humans) are desirable and others are unacceptable. However, often the set of acceptable and proscribed actions towards non-human animals differs greatly from one culture to another, and, even within a culture, attitudes toward treatment of animals can vary by class or socio-economic status (Driscoll, 1992; Löfgren, 1985).

[. . .]

The challenge for anyone trying to describe a process through which one learns about animals and with animals as 'humane education', then, is to focus not only on the final rules for behaviours toward animals, but also to examine the pathways to those rules. There are two main goals of this examination. The first is to find opportunities in the learning process to understand better both the 'natural' and the 'cultural' animal (sensu Lévi-Strauss, 1965) and to discover what we can learn from all the different ways in which our culture and others know these animals. The second is to reline the pedagogical process so that we develop in our students a humane attitude that includes appreciation of the animal's natural life, role in the environment, and the costs (to animals and humans) of its capture and study.

The process of considering these issues for animals in education has three stages. The first stage focuses on pedagogical issues and is generally the domain of the teacher. The main issues in this stage relate to the objectives of the lesson, integration of the animal-based activities with other aspects of the curriculum, the design and presentation of the materials, actions and reactions of the learners, and an evaluation of the learning by each individual as well as of the lesson or activity as a whole. The second stage focuses on the impact on the animals themselves. The main issues in this stage relate to the acquisition, care and use, and disposition of the animals being used for education. Finally, the third stage focuses on the wider social impact. The main issues in this stage relate to the outcome(s) of the process on the educational climate in the schools, the community, and in society in general.

We do not believe that this approach will or must lead to an abolition of animals in the classroom nor that it should do so. Rather, we hold that humane education is embodied in the process of considering a variety of issues including the nature of the lesson to be taught, the opportunities for multiple approaches to that knowledge, the active consideration of the life (sensu Regan, 1993) of the animal subject as an important issue, the conservation of resources, and the outcome of the exercise for the teacher, the student, and the animal.

Our use of the term 'active consideration' throughout this chapter is meant to convey a sense that each choice to use animals in education is explored and investigated by the teachers and students as appropriate to the students' experience and abilities; that this exploration is not merely a perfunctory checklist of health, safety, and physical comfort issues, but an integral part of the educational experience; that the conclusions and choices to be made are not a foregone conclusion before the process begins; and that executing this exploration requires a set of learning activities that may take the student beyond the immediate lesson and classroom environment to do background research, to check sources of information, to document past educational uses and their outcomes, etc. If successful, the members of the learning community – teachers and students – have turned the hit-or-miss experiences of the classroom 'pet' into an integrated, multi-disciplinary exploration of the biology, psychology, economics, and anthropology of educational use of non-human animals.

The experience of this process is the essence of humane education. The absence of real experience with non-human animals in the context of a humane educational setting eliminates an important opportunity to develop the concept of 'humane' in our students. Unless all members of the learning community are actively engaged in learning how information about animals is obtained and used in the classroom, we cannot fully demonstrate to the community in practice how to foster an environment of respect for those animals. We illustrate the values of humane education by accepting the responsibility to think clearly and responsibly about the role(s) that animals may play in our planned educational activities and the impact of those activities on the lives of animals.

Issues in teaching and learning

There are many ways in which animals may appear in an educational setting, but we will be concerned with just two subject areas – biological and behavioural sciences. [. . .] [M]ost of the examples that we will use and most of the discussion will centre on secondary and introductory level university students. We believe that the approach and concepts apply through a lifelong education, but our examples drawn from our own teaching and learning experiences draw us to this more restricted phase in our student's formal education.

The first step in a humane approach to animals in education is for the teacher to identify the best pathway to meet the lesson's objectives. The teacher must take into account the learners' stage of cognitive development, prior or collateral knowledge that the learners bring to the lesson, resources available to plan and execute the lesson, plans for evaluating the success of the lesson and the learners, the internal environment of the classroom, and the

Table 1. Issues in teaching and learning with animals

Learning styles (intelligence)

    Does the proposed activity allow or encourage acquisition and construction of know-ledge by learners in a variety of ways?

    Does this proposed activity engage the learner actively in the process of discovery, learning, evaluation, and assimilation of knowledge?

(Cognitive) developmental stage/age/level

    Is the proposed activity appropriate to the abilities of the learners to understand and assimilate the main points of the lesson?

    Is the proposed activity better performed at an earlier or later developmental stage?

    Has the prior preparation for the proposed activity been adequate and appropriate to both the developmental stage of the learners and to the expected learning outcomes or culminations?

Lesson objectives

    When the lesson objectives and goals are clearly formulated, how does the proposed activity support their attainment? What skills or knowledge are being developed, and how and when are they necessary for future learning?

    What other pathways to the objective might be used and how would they affect the educational outcome of the activities?

    Will the proposed activity be a superficial, one-time event or will it reflect and support the main theme throughout a curriculum unit or longer-term educational effort?

Career stage

    How does the development of specific skills and knowledge translate into a potential for future study or career choices for learners?

    Conversely, how would lack of specific skills inhibit the student's future plans and expectations?

    What are the best ways to learn these skills and to what depth at this stage in the learner's academic career?

---

external environment imposed by systemic or other standard for mastery of life sciences content and concepts at this and subsequent stages of education (see Table 1).

[. . .]

If the lesson or any learning activity will include the use of live animals or animal products, the teacher first should be able to provide a compelling and significant pedagogical justification for such use. That means that the use of animals in the classroom provides an added component to the learning that is non-trivial and unique or unattainable in other ways and that there is substantive evidence to support this assertion.

[. . .]

Most educational uses of live animals or animal tissues are based on the demonstrated value of a practical or 'hands-on' component to the lesson. The power of adding visual and 'bodily-kinaesthetic' components to what Gardner (1993:8) called the 'linguistic' and 'logical-mathematical' biases of nineteenth and twentieth-century education is illustrated in many disciplines. This approach has been most appreciated, perhaps not surprisingly, in arts education (e.g. Petto, 1994; Lowenfeld and Brittain, 1970; Arnheim, 1969). In these disciplines, both learning and its evaluation take into account a rich array of interactions among the teacher, the learner, and the subject matter, including sensory, emotional, spatial, interpersonal, and kinaesthetic.

There is no question that what educators call active learning throughout multiple modalities makes learning better in at least two ways. First, students learn more when they confront learning problems that engage them in inquiry, problem posing, problem solving, and defence of their ideas before their classmates (Peterson and Jungck, 1988; Jungck, 1985). In most cases, teachers are referring to their personal experiences as well as a reflection on their intuitive (emotional or interpersonal, sensu Gardner, 1993, 9) sense that hands-on laboratory activities with animals add significantly to learning biology (e.g. Offner, 1993; Keiser and Hamm, 1991; Mayer and Hinton, 1990). This is not merely a matter of developing manual dexterity or hand–eye co-ordination or facility and self-confidence with some laboratory technique, as some have described it (e.g. Kinzie et al., 1993; Quentin-Baxter and Dewhurst, 1992). Rather, these practical or hands-on lessons provide non-linguistic ways of learning, and for some students the movement, proprioception, and emotional reaction to the learning and to other learners cannot be replaced by linguistic, visual, or symbolic (i.e. logical-mathematical) representations of the problem.

Secondly, this approach to learning engages more students in the process (e.g. Petto, 1994; Gardner, 1993; Markova and Powell, 1992). Such a wider engagement allows more students to participate in, and contribute to, the learning experience and may give them more of a sense of control or self-direction in constructing their own learning. In addition, Petto (1994) reports that the personalization of the learning activity through the incorporation of the emotional response to the activity, materials, and even the other learners is a key factor in both the retention of learned material and the ability of students to relate that material or lesson to other knowledge or life experience. Furthermore, the perspectives of those students whose learning is not primarily linguistic or logical-mathematical contribute insights into the learning that may be overlooked by fellow learners, including the teacher. Even the learners who prefer expository teaching and declarative evaluation of their learning, learn more and better when using multiple modalities, as illustrated in a recent study on reinforcing the lessons learned through dissection by using prior preparation with an interactive video demonstration (Kinzie et al., 1993).

[. . .]

Finally, the main issue in humane education with animals is that biology is the study of the living (Lock, 1994; Orlans, 1991). In teaching and learning about living animals, one might consider, for example, their way of life, social and environmental needs (in nature and in captivity), feeding strategies and nutritional needs, and their role in the ecosystem. [. . .] This approach raises a paradox for the learning community, since almost any proposed educational use of animals will disrupt the animals' lives to varying extents.

One solution to this apparent paradox was proposed by Donnelley and colleagues (1990) under the term 'moral ecology'. Considering the moral ecology of the proposed use of an animal in education (or research) includes asking about the life that the animals (would) lead outside the educational context and how any proposed use would contribute to the educational objectives of the lesson. This is where the educational use of animals becomes humane. First, the teachers and students examine what needs to be learned and how an animal might contribute to that learning. Next, they review the needs of the animals and the impact on that animal of the proposed learning activity, considering, perhaps, alternatives that include using the animals in a different way, using different animals, or using non-animal resources. Then they should discuss the source of the animals, their acquisition, and their disposition after the educational activity.

[. . .]

Such a process places a heavy responsibility, however, on science teachers who may not have had any formal training in bioethics, particularly in exploring complex ethical issues with children (Downie, 1993; Downie and Alexander, 1989). Lock (1993, 114), in particular, points out the responsibility of the teacher to demonstrate 'a caring and humane approach in all their work with living things'. The responsibility for the teacher, then, is to be sure that the students have accurate, up-to-date information from a variety of sources about the animals they propose to study, including information relevant to the moral ecology of the use of particular animals in specific learning activities and projects.

In summary, the justification of any educational use of animals must have a strong pedagogical basis. This justification must include consideration of the choice of species, the type of learning activity, the developmental readiness and scholastic abilities of the students, the necessity for adequate foundations for future study, and advanced preparation and study by the students and teachers. A part of this justification is to balance the needs of, and outcomes for, the learners against the impact of the proposed educational usages on the animals.

Effects on animals

After careful consideration of the pedagogical issues, if the teacher concludes that there is an appropriate educational role for animals in the lesson, then s/he must determine whether there are any animals suitable for the lesson and the classroom environment. The main issues pertain to the acquisition, care and use, and disposition of the animals used in the lesson.

[. . .]

Moral ecology may be viewed as an attempt at operationalization of the 'subject-of-a-life' criterion proposed by Regan (1993). It presents a set of principles against which we might explore by what criteria we may judge the subjective lives of animals and the impact on their 'individual experiential welfare' (Regan, 1993, 203) of various uses of these animals by humans. Moral ecologists recognize that the life's experience and the expectations for future life differ greatly among individuals of the same species (e.g. Sapontzis, 1987; Rodd, 1990). Therefore, the impact upon their individual experiential welfare of their interactions with humans in an educational setting may also be different.

[. . .]

[A] humane approach requires that everyone involved in the educational use of animals explores explicitly the effects of the proposed use on the animal subjects. Indeed, such background research before any classroom activity is a hallmark of the proposed standards for life sciences education from the US National Research Council (NRC, 1994).

[. . .]

The issues in Table 2 expand the sphere of inquiry of the effects of educational use on the animals beyond whether the subject animals will live or die. This process includes learning about their lives before the animals come to the classroom (in nature or in any other environment), how the animals will be cared for and by whom, how the proposed use will

Table 2 Inventory of issues for use of animals in education

Acquisition

    How are the acquisition and use of the animals to be introduced to the students?

    How and from where will the animals be acquired?

    Can they be studied in their natural habitats, or must they be introduced to the classroom?

    Can they be acquired and placed in an appropriate classroom habitat without harm to the animals?

    Does the acquisition pose any harm to the students?

Care and use

    Habitat

    Is the classroom habitat safe for the animal? Are temperature, humidity, appropriate?

    Is proposed classroom activity appropriate to activity cycle?

    Are materials appropriate for digging, nesting, foraging, tunnelling, etc.?

    Does the habitat provide appropriate options for movement, rest?

    Social life

    Is habitat appropriate to the type, frequency, intensity of social contact typical of this species?

    If there is more than one individual in an enclosure, how should they be matched or mixed by age, sex, size, or other important variables?

    Is there adequate opportunity for access to food, water, hiding places for all individuals in a social group?

    Life cycle needs

    Is there adequate opportunity for physical growth and development or social maturation?

    Can normal life cycle functions such as reproduction and birth/hatching be carried out?

    If reproduction is successful, can the offspring survive and thrive in the classroom habitat?

    How and up to what point will this population growth be sustained?

Disposition

    What will happen to the animals after the completion of the lesson(s)?

    Can they return to their natural habitat?

    Is any sort of preparation, training, or rehabilitation required before the animal can return to nature or its previous way of life? Is so, how will this be carried out and by whom?

    How will the disposition of the animal(s) be introduced to and discussed with the students?

affect the animals and the learners, and what the effects of this activity might be on the animal's future life once the project is over. It also requires us to identify and evaluate the sources of this information and to determine what message each of these is bringing to the lesson at hand.

Although no such list can ever include all the issues that could be raised, we believe that the process of considering explicitly the impact of educational usage on the animals themselves is vital to the development of a humane ethic in education. The desire to add other items to the list is a healthy expression of a learning community that takes seriously the need for such a development. Perhaps most importantly, this list is applicable to all animals and to any proposed use in education from behavioural observations of free-ranging animals in the schoolyard to dissection of mammalian species.

(Human) social issues

An important question in the use of animals in education that is often overlooked is the effect on human society and on the learners that experience it. Both the lore of scientific training and the criticisms from the animal rights literature point out the distancing, the deadening of emotion, the objectification of the animals, and the desensitization to suffering and death that educational uses of animals can have on the people who use them (e.g. Davis and Balfour, 1992; Shapiro, 1990, 1991). These emotional 'adaptations' are expected for all uses of animals, but are particularly pronounced when the animal use results in death or dismemberment or involves suffering. These studies argue that being forced to partake in these activities may require a psychological adjustment by the learners that degrades or devalues animal life. Similar reactions to the plight of human subjects in scientific research has been well documented for decades (e.g. Milgram, 1974). Under social pressure from peers and authority figures. experimental assistants new to the project were rather easily convinced to administer what they believed were painful procedures to unseen subjects for the sake of the experimental protocol.

However, the contributors to the volume by Davis and Balfour (1992) demonstrate that this outcome is not unavoidable. Furthermore, researchers and research technicians are frequent contributors to the journal *Humane Innovations and Alternatives* (Petto *et al.*, 1992; Cohen and Block, 1991; O'Neill, 1987). In recent years some winners of the journal's annual recognition award have also been on the research staff in biomedical research facilities (Anon., 1992, 1993).

Furthermore, one may argue that confronting the animal subject of our learning 'face-to-face' can be the basis of a sensitizing process in which the students learn about the real needs of non-human animals and the animals' observable reactions to handling, care, and educational activities of various sorts. The presence of living animals in the classroom can be a valuable way to increase the appreciation of learners for the real animal and its experience of life.

[. . .]

Rather than desensitizing the students to the animals that will enrich their education, this process requires the students to confront the real needs that living animals have in their environments. Direct, personal interactions with living animals provide the best opportunity for the bonding and empathetic responding between student and non-human animal that is universally acknowledged from Davis and Balfour (1992) to Shapiro (1990, 1991) to Weatherill (1993) and Ascione (1992). Because there are real and observable consequences in such a situation for making poorly informed choices about learning activities, habitat construction, or even choice of appropriate animal subject, students and teachers must confront and accept the consequences of their actions through interactions with living animals. Davis and Balfour (1992) argue that these interactions also bring benefits to human scientific and educational activities.

Another consequence of educational animals use is the development of an industry that serves the needs of thousands of schools that will use animals in some way. This is an important issue in Hepner's (1994) examination of the role of animals in education. The sheer volume of animals that must be killed, skeletonized, and/or preserved in some form every year in North America alone would probably surprise most educators. It is not only a matter of volume, but a matter of the effect on our expectations of the educational experience with animals.

[. . .]

If the process to acquire each of the animals supplied from these sources took an approach similar to the one we propose here, then the existence of large, centralized supply houses that kill and preserve millions of animals annually might be somewhat less worrisome. However, the sheer volume of this industry's output should be enough to make us reconsider how our choices to use animals in education relates to this phenomenon. The realities of the animal supply business must be a part of the process of choosing to use animals in education.

If there is a determined need for animals or animal tissues in the classroom, the humane educational process is enhanced by the explicit discussion by teachers and learners of the questions of source and supply. Is it better to use purpose-bred animals, or specimens from slaughter-houses, or body parts from hunters or taxidermists? And, what social, economic, and moral implications does each of these choices have? How should, or could, we decide among them and on what basis?

The process of recognizing the social implications of animal use beyond the classroom adds another important dimension to humane education. The whole learning community makes an informed and conscious choice for specific learning activities in which at least one component is animal based. It is vitally important that the learning community take this discussion beyond the blanket prescription or proscription of animal use.

Conclusions

What we have proposed here is an outline for making the choice to include animals in the curriculum a humane learning activity. All members of the learning community should be actively engaged in the process of constructing the humane ethic that will govern the choice to use animals in the classroom and the decisions on how they will be used. It must be clear from the start that there is a choice to be made. We wish to avoid the phenomenon described by McGinnis (1992) of beginning with the conclusion that animal use in education is automatically either 'noa' or 'taboo' – prescribed or forbidden. When the outcome of this consideration is not a foregone conclusion, the process of making these choices adds a valuable dimension to the educational process for all members of the learning community.

For the whole learning community, this process of considering the various practical issues of acquisition, classroom care and use, and disposition of animals used in educational activities is the essence of humane education, because it requires the students to confront these issues explicitly. In so doing, it shows that the teacher and the school value the animals as entities in themselves worthy of such consideration and not only as a means to an end.

In the end, taking this process seriously may mean, perhaps, that some activities using animals in the classroom will not be done at particular times and places – even when they clearly have pedagogical value. It may mean that there will be several learning activities and that not all students will participate in each of them. It may mean that the curricular activities involving animals will be developed around different choices. However, none of what we have described as the process of humane education means that these learning activities will never be done. In the end 'humane' education is a process that increases, not decreases sensitivity of all the members of the learning community to the impact of their learning. This, we believe, can be accomplished through a process of active consideration of these impacts in the various dimensions that are affected by these choices.

References

Anon. (1992). PSYeta's *Human Innovations and Alternatives* Annual Award, 1992. Viktor Reinhardt. *Humane Innovations and Alternatives*, 6, 317.

Anon. (1993). PSYeta's *Human Innovations and Alternatives* Annual Award, 1993. Peggy O'Neill Wagner. *Humane Innovations and Alternatives*, 7, 423.

Arnheim, V. (1969). *Visual Thinking*. Berkeley: University of California Press.

Ascione, F. R. (1992). Enhancing children's attitudes about the humane treatment of animals: generalization to human-directed empathy. *Anthrozoös*, 5, 176–91.

Atran, S. (1990). *Cognitive Foundations of Natural History: Towards an Anthropology of Science*. New York: Cambridge University Press.

Cohen, P. S. and Block, M. (1991). Replacement of laboratory animals in an introductory-level psychology laboratory. *Humane Innovations and Alternatives*, 5, 221–5.

Davis, H. and Balfour, D. (1992). *The Inevitable Bond: Examining Scientist-Animal Interactions*. New York: Cambridge University Press.

Donnelley, S. (with Dresser, R., Kleinig, J. and Singleton, R.). (1990). Animals in science: the justification issue. In *Animals, Science, and Ethics*, ed. S. Donnelley and K. Nolan, Hastings Center Report, Suppl. 20(3), 8–13.

Downie, R. (1993). The teaching of bioethics in the higher education of biologists. *Journal of Biological Education*, 27(1), 34–8.

Downie, R. and Alexander, L. (1989). The use of animals in biology teaching in higher education. *Journal of Biological Education*, 23(2), 103–11.

Driscoll, J. W. (1992). Attitudes toward animal use. *Anthrozoös*, 5(1), 32–9.

Gardner, H. (1993). *Multiple Intelligences: The Theory in Practice*. New York: Basic Books.

Hepner, L. A. (1994). *Animals in Education: The Facts, Issues, and Implications*. Alberquerque, NM: Richmond Publishers.

Keiser, T. D. and Hamm, R. W. (1991). Forum: dissection: the case for. *The Science Teacher*, 58(1), 13, 15.

Kinzie, M. B., Strauss, R. and Foss, J. (1993). The effects of interactive dissection simulation on the performance of high school biology students. *Journal of Research in Science Teaching*, 30(8), 989–1000.

Jungck, J. R. (1985). A problem-posing approach to biology education. *The American Biology Teacher*, 47(5), 264–6.

Lévi-Strauss, C. (1965). *Le Totémisme Aujourd'hui*. Paris: Presses Universitaires de France.

Lock, R. (1993). Animals and the teaching of biology/science in secondary schools. *Journal of Biological Education*, 27(2), 112–14.

Lock, R. (1994). Biology – the study of living things? *Journal of Biological Education*, 28(2), 79–80.

Löfgren, O. (1985). Our friends in nature: class and animal symbolism. *Ethnos*, 50(3–4), 184–213.

Lowenfeld, V. and Brittain, W. L. (1970). *Creative and Mental Growth*, 5th edn. New York: Macmillan.

Markova, D. and Powell, A. R. (1992). *How Your Child is Smart: A Life-changing Approach to Learning*. Berkeley, CA: Conari Press.

Mayer, V. I. and Hinton, N. K. (1990). Animals in the classroom: considering the options. *The Science Teacher*, 57(3), 27–30.

McGinnis, J. R. (1992). The taboo and the 'noa' of teaching science-technology-society (STS): a constructivist approach to understanding the rules of conduct teachers live by. Paper presented at the annual meeting of the Southeastern Association for the Education of Teachers of Science, Wakulla Springs FL. Feb 14–15.

Milgram, S. (1974). *Obedience to Authority*. NY: Harper and Row.

National Research Council, National Committee on Science Education Standards and Assessment. (1994). *National Science Education Standards*. Washington, DC: National Academy Press.

Offner, S. (1993). The importance of dissection in biology teaching. *The American Biology Teacher*, 55(3), 147–9.

O Neill, P. L. (1987). Enriching the lives of primates in captivity. *Humane Innovations and Alternatives*, **1**, 1–5.

Orlans, F. B. (1991). Forum: dissection: the case against. *The Science Teacher*, 58(1), 12, 14.

Peterson, N. S. and Jungck, J. R. (1988). Problem posing, problem solving, and persuasion in biology education. *Academic Computing*, 2(6), 14–17, 48–50.

Petto, A. J., Russell, K. D., Watson, L. M. and LaReau-Alves, M. L. (1992). Sheep in wolves' clothing: Promoting psychological well-being in a biomedical research facility. *Humane Innovations and Alternatives*, **6**, 366–70.

Petto, S. G. (1994). Time and time again: holistic learning through a multimodal approach to art history. MFA Thesis. Boston University.

Quentin-Baxter, M. and Dewhurst, D. (1992). An interactive computer-based alternative to performing rat dissection in the classroom. *Journal of Biological Education*, **26**(1), 27–33.

Regan, T. (1993). Ill-gotten gains. In *The Great Ape Project: Equality beyond Humanity*. ed. P. Cavalieri and P. Singer. New York: St Martin's Press.

Rodd, R. M. (1990). *Biology, Ethics, and Animals*. Oxford: Oxford University Press.

Sapontzis, S. F. (1987). *Morals, Reason, and Animals*. Philadelphia: Temple University Press.

Shapiro, K. (1990). The pedagogy of learning and unlearning empathy. *Phenomenology and Pedagogy*, **8**, 43–8.

Shapiro, K. (1991). The psychology of dissection. *The Animals' Agenda*, pp. 20–1.

Weatherill, A. (1993). Pets at school: Child animal bond sparks learning and caring. *Inter Actions*, **11**(1), 7–9.

Annotated Further Reading

American Association for Laboratory Animal Science (AALAS). Institutional Animal Care and Use Committees: A comprehensive online resource at: http://www.iacuc.org

American Psychological Association. Committee on Animal Research and Ethics. (1993) *Guidelines for Ethical Conduct in the Care and Use of Animals*. The Association, Washington, D.C. http://www.apa.org/science/anguide.html

Anderson, W.P. and Perry, M.A. (1999) "Australian Animal Ethics Committees: We Have Come a Long Way." *Cambridge Quarterly of Healthcare Ethics* 8: 80–6.

Arluke, A. (1996) "The Well-being of Animal Researchers." In *The Human/Research Animal Relationship*, L. Krulisch, S. Mayer, and R. Simmonds (eds) Greenbelt, MD.: Scientists Center for Animal Welfare.

Bagla, P. (2001) "Animal Care: Report Castigates Indian Lab Practices." *Science* 293: 2186–7.

Barnard, N.D. and Kaufmann, S.R. (1997) "Animal Research is Wasteful and Misleading." *Scientific American* 276: 80–3. Strong focus on biological reasoning and argumentation.

Beauchamp, T.L. (1997) "Opposing Views on Animal Experimentation: Do Animals Have Rights?" *Ethics and Behavior* 7: 113–21.

Bekoff, M. (1993) "Experimentally Induced Infanticide: the Removal of Birds and its Ramifications," *The Auk* 110: 404–6.

Bekoff, M. and Jamieson, D. (1996) "Ethics and the Study of Carnivores: Doing Science While Respecting Animals." Chapter 1, in *Carnivore Behavior, Ecology, and Evolution*, John L. Gittleman (ed.). Comstock Publishing Associates, Ithaca, New York, pp. 15–45.

Bekoff, M., Gruen, L., Townsend, S.E., and Rollin, B.E. (1992) "Animals in Science: Some Areas Revisited." *Animal Behavior* 44: 473–84.

Bishop, L.J. and Nolen, A.L. (2001) "Animals in Research and Education: Ethical Issues." Scope Note 40. *Kennedy Institute of Ethics Journal* 11: 91–112.

Botting, J.H. and Morrison, A.R. (1997) "Animal Research is Vital to Medicine." *Scientific American* 276: 83–5. Strong focus on biological reasoning and argumentation.

Botzler, R.G. and Armstrong-Buck, S.B. (1985) "Ethical Considerations in Research on Wildlife Diseases." *Journal of Wildlife Diseases* 21(3): 341–5.

Canadian Council on Animal Care. (1984) *Guide to the Care and Use of Experimental Animals*. The Council, Ottawa, Ontario, Canada. Online at: http://www.ccac.ca

306 ANDREW J. PETTO AND KARLA D. RUSSELL

Cohen, C. and Regan, T. (2001) *The Animal Rights Debate*. Lanham, MD: Rowan & Littlefield Publishers, Inc.

Drone, J. (1999) "PCRM Steps up Campaign to End Live Animal Laboratories in Medical Education." *Good Medicine* 8(1). Online at http://www.pcrm.org/magazine/GM99Winter/GM99Winter5.html. PCRM: Physicians Committee for Responsible Medicine.

Ebrahim, A.F.M. and Vawda, A.I. (1992) *Islamic Guidelines on Animal Experimentation*. Qualbert, South Africa: Islamic Medical Association of South Africa. Scientists must not subject animals to unnecessary or painful experimentation.

Frey, R.G. (2002) "Ethics, Animals and Scientific Inquiry." In *Applied Ethics in Animal Research: Philosophy, Regulation, and Laboratory Applications*, J.P. Gluck, T. DiPasquale, and F.B. Orlans (eds), pp. 13–24. West Lafayette, Ind.: Purdue University Press. Looks for absolute differences between humans and nonhumans.

Gluck, J.P. and Orlans, F.B. (1997) "Institutional animal care and use committees: A flawed paradigm or work in progress?" *Ethics and Behavior* 7: 329–36.

Gluck, J.P., DiPasquale, T., and Orlans, F.B. (eds) (2002) *Applied Ethics in Animal Research: Philosophy, Regulation, and Laboratory Applications*. West Lafayette, Ind.: Purdue University Press. An excellent collection representing those in the middle ground concerning animal experimentation.

Hardy, D.T. (1990) *America's New Extremists: What You Need to Know About the Animal Rights Movement*. Washington, D.C.: Washington Legal Foundation.

Hart, L.A. (1996) "The Human/Animal Relationship in the Research Setting." in *The Human/research Animal Relationship*, L. Krulisch, S. Mayer, and R.C. Simmonds, (eds), Greenbelt, MD.: Scientists Center for Animal Welfare.

Hefner, H.E. (1999) "The Symbiotic Nature of Animal Research." *Perspectives in Biology and Medicine* 43:128.

Home Office, United Kingdom. (1986) *Draft Guidance on the Operation of the Animals (Scientific Procedure) Act 1986: Consultation*. Online at: http://www.homeoffice.gov.uk/ccpd/cons.htm

Humane Society of the United States. (n.d.) *Animals and Society: A List of Courses (Animal Ethics, Animal Rights, Animal Welfare)*. Online at http://www.hsus.org/programs/research/animals_education.html. Provides summaries and contact information about college (and a few vet school) courses addressing animal ethics, animal rights, and/or animal welfare.

Kassi, N. (1994) "Science, Ethics, and Wildlife Management." Pp. 212–16 in *Northern Protected Areas and Wilderness*, Juri Peepre and Bob Jickling (eds). Proceedings of a Forum on Northern Protected Areas and Wilderness, Whitehorse, Yukon.

LaFollette, H. and Shanks, N. (1996) *Brute Science: Dilemmas of Animal Experimentation*, London: Routledge. Carefully argued, sophisticated, scientifically informed case against the current practices of animal experimentation.

Langley, G.R. (1991) "Animals in Science Education – Ethics and Alternatives." *Journal of Biological Education* 24(4): 274.

Mangan, K.S. (2000) "Can Vet Schools Teach without Killing Animals?" *The Chronicle of Higher Education* 46 (issue of February 4, 2000): 2 pp.

——(2002) "Horse Sense or Nonsense?" *The Chronicle of Higher Education* 48 (issue of July 5, 2000): 3 pp.

Morrison, A.R. (2001) "A Scientist's Perspective on the Ethics of Using Animals in Behavioral Research." In *Animal Research and Human Health*, M. Carroll and J.B. Overmier (eds), Washington, D.C.: American Psychological Association. A strongly pro-experimentation view.

Mukerjee, M. (1997) "Trends in Animal Research." *Scientific American* 276: 86–93.

National Research Council. Institute for Laboratory Animal Resources (1989) "Principles and guidelines for the use of animals in precollege education." Pp. 125–6, in *Fulfilling the Promise: Biology Education in the Nation's Schools*. Washington, D.C.: National Academy Press. Online at http://www4.nas.edu/cls/ilarhome.nsf/web/Principles/

National Research Council. Commission on Life Sciences. Institute for Animal Laboratory Resources. (1996) *Guide for the Care and Use of Laboratory Animals*. Washington, D.C.: National Academy Press, 125 pp.

New England Anti-Vivisection Society Ethical Science and Education Coalition. (n.d.) Online at http://www.neavs.org/esec.html and http://www.neavs.org. Advocates of dissection choice legislation, offers a guide on how to pass a student choice dissection policy in your school district, and prepares a catalogue of dissection alternatives. Protects and advocates for animals used in education through education, legislation, litigation, and direct action campaigns.

Orlans, F.B. (1997) "Ethical Decision Making about Animal Experiments." *Ethics and Behavior* 7: 163–71.

Orlans, F.B., Beauchamp, T.L., Dresser, R., Morton, D.B., and Gluck, J.P. (1998) *The Human Use of Animals: Case Studies in Ethical Choice*. Oxford: Oxford University Press.

Phillips, D.F. (1996) "Conference Explores Ethics of Animal Research with Critical Thinking and Balanced Argument." *Journal of the American Medical Association* 276: 87.

Putnam, R.J. (1996) "Ethical Considerations and Animal Welfare in Ecological Field Studies." Chapter 11, in *Ecologists and Ethical Judgments*, N.S. Cooper and R.C.J. Carling (eds). London: Chapman & Hall, pp. 123–35.

Rowan, A.N. (1997) "The Benefits and Ethics of Animal Research." *Scientific American* 276: 81.

Ryder, R. (1983) *Victims of Science: The Use of Animals in Research.* London: National Anti-Vivisection Society. A powerful argument against animal use.

Serpell, J.A. (1999) "Sheep in wolves' clothing? Attitudes to animals among farmers and scientists." Chapter 3, pp. 26–33, in *Attitudes to Animals: Views in Animal Welfare*, F.L. Dolins (ed.). Cambridge: Cambridge University Press.

Shapiro, K.J. (1998) *Animal Models of Human Psychology*, Seattle, WA: Hogrefe and Huber. Well-informed argument against animal models.

Shapiro, K. and Church, J.H. (2000) "It's Academic: the Growing Field of Animal Studies." In *The Animals' Agenda*. Online at http://www.animalsagenda.org/articledetail._asp?menu=News&N32wID=316

Silverman, J. (1999) "The Use of Animals in Biomedical Research and Teaching: Searching for a Common Goal." *Cambridge Quarterly of Healthcare Ethics* 8:64–72. Advocates full acceptance of sentience of nonhuman animals and ending use of nonhuman animals in biomedical research. Emphasis on mammals.

Smith, A. (1998) *The Regulation of Animal Experimentation in Norway: An Introduction.* Laboratory Animal Unit, Norwegian School of Veterinary Science. 22 pp. http://oslovet.veths.no/booklet/Booklet.pdf

Spinelli, J.S. (1996) "Human/research Animal Relationships: Research Staff Perspective." In L. Krulisch, S. Mayer, and R.E. Simmonds (eds) *The Human/Research Animal Relationship*. Greenbelt, MD.: Scientists Center for Animal Welfare. Takes a sociological, compassionate look at attitudes of researchers and animal workers.

Wuensch, K.L. and Poteat, G.M. (1998) "Evaluating the Morality of Animal Research: Effects of Ethical Ideology, Gender, and Purpose." *Journal of Social Behavior and Personality* 13:139. Ethics position questionnaire. Vote of the majority of respondents to stop the research.

Study Questions

1 Select one of the four issues DeGrazia believes will continue to serve as a point of difference between proponents and opponents of animal use, and explain how you might move the two sides closer together on that issue.

2 How might Brody respond to Regan's claim that animals have a value that cannot be reduced to human utility?

3 Based on Farnsworth and Rosovsky's recommendations that scientists and philosophers have further discussions, give three questions you would pose to initiate fruitful discussions.

4 Emlen asserts that animal experimentation is needed to benefit the natural world, including minimizing suffering in nonhuman animals. To what extent do you agree or disagree with his assertion? Justify your position.

5 In light of Orlan's discussion, what additional laws regulating animal use, if any, do you believe should be adopted by the United States?

6 What constraints do you believe are appropriate for the use of live animals in elementary school education? Clarify your reasoning.

Part VI

Animals and Biotechnology

Introduction

Authors of this Part grapple with some of the very difficult issues associated with biotechnology. Some of the moral issues associated with genetic engineering are addressed in the first four papers. Donald and Ann Bruce are concerned about the impacts of genetic engineering on the welfare of animals and raise a number of concerns about providing adequate safeguards for animals on whom this work is conducted. They also believe that ethical issues should be addressed by monitoring committees and that the public needs to be knowledgeable and accountable for the work that is done. Arguing from a utilitarian perspective, Kevin Smith believes that there is no clear moral mandate against genetic sequence alteration; likewise he argues that within the concept of "replaceability," killing of transgenic animals is acceptable for animals not identified with "personhood." Smith does advocate a general prohibition on studies that entail significant suffering for animals. Using the Maxim to Respect *Telos*, Bernard Rollin argues that there is no clear justification to preclude genetic engineering of animals; he notes that genetic modifications should be assessed in relation to the Principle of Conservation of Welfare. Bernice Bovenkerk, Frans Brom, and Babs van den Bergh respond to Rollin's perspective by introducing the notion of integrity as a set of characteristics of an animal humans believe important to preserve; they call for moral discussion to identify these features and note that, even if there is no full agreement on what constitutes integrity for an animal, the discussions can provide a basis for evaluating existing practices.

Two authors address some of the specific moral issues associated with xenotransplantation: the transfer of tissues or organs grown in one species to a different species. Both authors have reservations on the moral justifications for such procedures. R. G. Frey argues that a moral argument for the use of animals for xenotransplantation for humans could lead to moral consequences entailing the possible use of humans, and that such a step would not be morally acceptable. Gary Francione argues that in an animal rights perspective where it is recognized that animals have a right to exist that is not contingent merely on their instrumental value to humans, the use of animals as a source of xenografts would clearly violate those rights.

Oliver Ryder addresses some of the issues associated with the cloning of animals. He notes that these techniques might be particularly valuable in work with endangered species, and others have raised the possibility of resurrecting extinct animals. He calls for increased research, careful targeting of the technology, and an increase in banking cells for possible future application.

Finally, Jeffrey Burkhardt argues that most of the arguments raised in opposition to biotechnology lack ethical force because most scientists and science policy makers lack the moral education necessary to fully understand the significance of the arguments made. Burkhardt calls for ethical training to become an established part of the training and thinking of scientists and science policy makers.

Ethics of Genetic Engineering

48

Donald Bruce and Ann Bruce

"Genetic Engineering and Animal Welfare"

Donald and Ann Bruce consider the welfare impact of genetic engineering on animals. They note that the main applications are related to biomedical goals rather than enhanced animal production, as originally expected. The authors raise concerns for safeguards needed to protect animals from the rapid and repeated changes brought about by genetic engineering, including controls on the use of recombinant hormones, vaccines, and viruses in animals. They also call for increased public involvement and accountability, as well as advisory monitoring committees to consider ethical questions on animal use.

Introduction

[. . .]

The present paper will consider in detail the implications of genetic engineering for animal welfare. Most ethical evaluations in this area have considered the broader field of biotechnology rather than just genetic engineering. [. . .] There are two points to make about the drawing of boundaries. First, although we are concerned here with the impact of the relatively new technique of genetic engineering we should not assume that the status quo is an ethically acceptable or neutral ground. Indeed, there is no status quo. Selective breeding continues with most of the animals with which we are concerned, and welfare problems have resulted and continue to result from the increasingly sophisticated methods used.

[. . .]

Second, however, concern over new breeding technologies is primarily caused by the fact that effects on welfare may be more rapid and intense than hitherto. In particular, genetic modification has vastly more potential than other techniques for producing sudden change in characteristics relevant to welfare. It is more akin to mutation than to recombination of genes already present. For this reason, this chapter will concentrate on genetic modification of animals and only consider other techniques where necessary. Where relevant it will also mention modification of hormones and vaccines which are then used on animals. Further references may be found in the reviews cited, including that by Appleby.[1]

Effects of techniques used in achieving genetic modification

The techniques used in genetic engineering often cause welfare problems irrespective of the nature of the modification achieved. Some of these problems are associated with husbandry and are similar to those of any other manipulative experimental work. They can be divided into three categories which act separately and in combination. First, human contact may be frightening, for example during handling or due to changes in the predictability of husbandry routines. Second, social conditions are often stressful: isolation is common. Lastly, physical conditions are usually suboptimal, with barren surroundings and diets which can be consumed rapidly. In some countries such problems are being considered more than hitherto under the general licensing procedures for experimental work, but there remains considerable room for improvement. One promising finding, with potential to reduce the ill-effects of forcible restraint in many species, is that pigs and sheep can be trained to enter a restraining device for procedures including blood withdrawal (and hence potentially also for injection of anaesthetic) voluntarily and repeatedly.

Other techniques include cloning to create and copy genetically modified organisms (GMOs) and producing embryos by transferring the nucleus of one cell into another without a nucleus. Embryos resulting from this nuclear transfer have a high rate of mortality and at least some have been unusually large, so that there may be welfare problems for both the offspring and the mother around the time of birth.

The actual techniques of genetic engineering may involve a number of procedures on a number of animals. For example, the following welfare issues are associated with pronuclear injection in mice: hormone injection (to stimulate superovulation), mating (while still only three to four weeks old) and euthanasia (to obtain the fertilised eggs, into which DNA is then injected) of mothers, sterilisation of males (which mate with foster mothers to produce pseudopregnancy), insertion of embryos into foster mothers (done under anaesthetic), mortality of offspring and ear punching or tail tip removal of offspring (to distinguish transgenics).

With some applications, techniques are used only a limited number of times, because once genetically modified lines are established they breed true. This is so, for example, with farm animals used for biomedical products. With other applications, for example research into embryonic development using transgenic mutants, techniques are used repeatedly. With such routine techniques it is important that the precise methods and their implications for welfare should not be taken for granted. It should also be remembered for all applications that there will be welfare problems for animals kept in reserve but not used and those on which the techniques are unsuccessful, as well as for any transgenics produced.

[. . .]

Effects of genetic modification

If genetic modification is successful it will result in changes to the physiology and perhaps the physical structure of the animal concerned. Many of these will have direct implications for welfare, intended or unintended. Modification is also likely to have indirect effects, with the animal being treated in ways which are different to normal husbandry. This section will consider the types of effects which are possible and the following section will discuss the extent to which they actually occur.

Direct effects

No effects

Some modifications appear so far to have no direct implications for welfare. An example is transgenic sheep such as Tracy which have the gene for human alpha-1-antitrypsin (AAT) and produce this protein in the milk.

[. . .]

Planned effects

Some changes may be described as specifically intended to affect welfare, either in a positive or negative way. One positive effect which has been attempted in a number of studies is increased disease resistance in farm animals.

[. . .]

Intentional negative effects on welfare exist where transgenics are used to study disease. This is most often justified by their use as models for similar conditions in humans, and the appropriateness of the model is a major issue here. The approach could perhaps also be used to develop treatments for animals, but this does not appear to have been done to any extent. Animal suffering is an integral aspect of this work, as will be discussed below.

[. . .]

Side effects

These have probably received more attention than any others. [. . .] Sheep with additional growth hormone genes never attained puberty and died before they were one year old. Robinson and McEvoy state that 'In many instances, the site and time of expression of the transferred genes still lack the degree of specificity required and lead to deleterious side effects'.[2]

[. . .]

Some effects arise as side effects but then become subjects for study, as with the Legless mouse, considered in the following category.

Integral effects of other changes

Some modifications have effects on welfare which are not themselves the reason for making the modification but are integral to it and so cannot be considered side effects. The distinction is ethically relevant because if such effects are inherently unavoidable they must be accepted and justified as an inevitable consequence of the modification. Transgenics in which normal immunology or development is disrupted, studied for the insight they provide into normal processes, come into this category. Thus the Legless mouse has major limb and craniofacial abnormalities and dies within 24 hours of birth, and is used in embryological and genetic research.[3] This category would also apply if production of pharmaceuticals in the milk of farm animals had deleterious effects on those animals or if genetic engineering increased [. . .] effects [. . .] such as rapid growth and double muscling.

Indirect effects

Husbandry and related effects

As an indirect result of genetic engineering, many animals are kept or treated in ways which have other advantages or disadvantages for welfare. Transgenics are valuable and their health tends to be looked after particularly well. However, as with other experimental animals, they are often kept in isolation rather than in more natural social groups and the importance of hygiene usually means that they are kept in barren conditions. Indeed, for some purposes they are delivered by caesarean section and kept in sterile or near sterile conditions to keep disease risk to a minimum. By contrast, one concern about the work on disease resistance is that if it is achieved it may make it possible to stock animals at higher densities; this possibility also applies to animals treated with vaccines improved by genetic engineering. Isolation, barren conditions and high stocking density all cause problems for welfare.

[. . .]

Another indirect effect, resulting from the genetically engineered improvement of growth hormones, is increased frequency of injections. [. . .] In addition to restraint of the animals and the pain of the injections themselves, there are also problems with injection site abscesses. Some implants are used, for example lasting two weeks, but these have to be injected with a thick needle which is probably more painful. Work on longer lasting implants continues.

Numbers of animals kept for different uses will change as a consequence of genetic engineering. Some uses may be more efficient and need fewer animals: this is one of the aims of work on growth rate in farm animals. Other uses increase numbers; thus the number of animals used in transgenic research is currently increasing rapidly. There is no simple correlation between the numbers of animals involved and the importance of their welfare, but there is probably a consensus that some association does exist. The overall effect of genetic engineering on welfare will therefore depend on the balance between problems and benefits for the animals' welfare (including problems and benefits which are independent of the genetic modification) and the increase or decrease in their numbers. The three Rs of reduction, refinement and replacement should again be borne in mind here.

Effects on attitudes

Modification of animals is likely to affect attitudes to them and hence other aspects of their treatment; it may also alter attitudes to and treatment of other groups of animals. This applies both to people who have direct influence over animals (such as breeders and producers) and to the public, whose influence is nebulous and rarely focused. Attitudes may be affected by new uses of animals (for example as models for human disease or as suppliers of organs for xenotransplantation) and by changes in their legal status (such as whether particular types of animal can be patented). Implications for welfare are difficult to predict: the effects of attitudes to animals are complex.

Categories of animals

Farm animals used for agricultural products

The main attempts to date to change production characteristics of farm animals by genetic engineering have been insertion of genes for growth hormone into pigs and sheep. There is also similar work on fish. It has been suggested that one possible benefit of biotechnology would be more efficient production leading to the use of fewer animals. In fact there seems to have been little consideration of whether such animals growing faster or further would actually be more efficient economically, in terms of food conversion. In addition, transgenes would need to improve economic performance by 5 to 10 per cent to be useful, because they would take several generations to introduce and meanwhile the performance of other stock could be improved by normal breeding methods. However, use of fewer animals for the same meat production would seem to be an advantage. So far, though, most of these attempts have had gross side effects as described above and it is clear that such modifications will not be used commercially unless these can be avoided.

[. . .]

Cloning by nuclear transfer may be used to increase the specificity and range of genetic modification in breeding stock. It may also be used to copy particularly productive animals. This might seem to give a relative advantage for welfare, because although cloning is associated with welfare problems these are probably less than those of other currently available procedures such as manipulation of growth hormone. However, this does not mean that it is necessarily justifiable. Furthermore, improvements in other lines will continue, so that such clones are unlikely to be the most productive animals for very long.

A cause for concern is the possibility that future work will produce changes with commercial advantage and with side effects which are less obviously unacceptable – similar to those which have been produced by selective breeding – because there will be commercial pressure for such deleterious side effects to be tolerated. This is the situation with the use of BST to enhance milk production of dairy cows, which is practised in the US but currently banned in the EU. This has limited effects on welfare if management is good, but negative effects if management is poor. In some respects it is therefore not a special case, but comparable to other management techniques (such as housing design and feeding regimes) intended to increase the profitability of production. However, it could nevertheless be seen as unwarranted in its application of technology.

Some changes in production characteristics being investigated or sought are likely to be neutral or positive for welfare. Work in the Netherlands has produced Herman the transgenic bull, whose female progeny are intended to produce milk containing the human protein lactoferrin. This would make it more digestible for babies and patients on antibiotics. It is believed that this change will also reduce the risk of mastitis in the cows. Another area of interest is the possibility of producing hens and cows which only have female offspring – for egg production and milk production respectively – avoiding the necessity to kill male chicks or rear unwanted male calves. The unnatural character of such developments concerns some people, but they may nevertheless reduce the incidence of welfare problems.

Optimism about the prospects of increasing disease resistance in farm animals appears to have abated recently. Some of the approaches being investigated were unsuccessful or restricted to very specific experimental circumstances. In addition the technology mostly concerns single genes, whereas the disease organisms concerned are complex, and it is increasingly recognised that any increase in resistance might only be temporary. In many cases a slight change in the organisms (for example, by mutation) would be sufficient to make them infective again. It is true that there are examples of long term resistance of certain species to certain diseases, for example native African cattle to trypanosomiasis (sleeping sickness). This suggests that if it becomes possible in future to change multiple genes rather than just single genes some permanent change in disease resistance might be achieved. However, there are again other ethical issues here.

First, in relation specifically to trypanosomiasis, it has been suggested that the only reason there are still large areas of Africa relatively well populated with wildlife is the incomplete resistance of cattle to this disease. If resistance is increased or a vaccine is developed this will greatly increase the pressure on such areas and make conservation of wild animals much more difficult. Second, some of the diseases prevalent in current production systems have been exacerbated by intensive selection for production and by the techniques used in those systems, for example mastitis in dairy cows. Unless genetic modification of dairy cows for resistance to mastitis reduced incidence of the disease to what it was before the increased production, it could be argued that it would be more appropriate to reverse the changes which have caused the problem. This is particularly true if there are other ill effects of increased production on welfare which these techniques help to perpetuate. Similarly, modifying the animals to prevent disease may increase the tendency to keep animals in poor conditions (such as high stocking density, as mentioned above) which have other disadvantages for welfare.

Farm animals used for biomedical products

Of all applications of genetic engineering, this one currently has most commercial potential. As with animal production, the welfare issues are not wholly new: some farm animals are already used for biomedical products with welfare problems resulting. For example in North America many thousands of mares are kept in stalls too small for them to turn round for the production of oestrogen from their urine. Transgenic animals do at least tend to be kept in conditions which ensure their health, although with other limitations.

[. . .]

The area of work which has received most attention is modification of sheep or goats to produce pharmaceuticals in their milk for human medical use which will be cheaper and safer than those from alternative sources (such as human blood). The changes being made – or, at least, those being publicised – appear to be neutral for welfare. As Loew asks, 'What possible harm to man or beast can arise from a minor change in the composition of goat's milk such that it becomes a cost-effective source of a valuable pharmaceutical?'[4] Yet vigilance is necessary, because certain genes might not be expressed solely in the mammary gland, and because the milk–blood barrier is not complete, so some compounds will be expected to affect the lactating female.

[. . .]

One other area which is receiving increasing publicity is the modification of pigs to allow their organs – heart, kidney or pancreas – to be transplanted into humans. One approach being tried is insertion of a gene for human complement regulators into the pig genome, which will label the surface of pig cells so that hyperacute rejection does not occur when they are transplanted. There is no reason to believe that the welfare of a pig with such a gene will be compromised during its life, but it may be necessary to keep the animals in barren environments.

[. . .]

As with farm animals used for agricultural products, cloning may be used to copy animals which are particularly appropriate for pharmaceutical production or xenotransplantation. Again, this is likely to involve welfare problems, but these may be less than those caused by repetition of the procedures which are otherwise necessary to produce such animals.

Laboratory animals

Most lines of research are still at the exploratory stage, so in that sense all animals involved are laboratory animals, but the term is used here to mean animals – primarily mice – on which work is being done without immediate application in that species.

Many procedures carried out on laboratory animals are disturbing. As indicated above, some involve intentional production of major welfare problems, as in the oncomouse, and others require tolerance of such problems, as with the Legless mouse. However, the issues are clearly complex: one point that was made in the public discussion of the oncomouse (in relation to whether or not it could be patented) was that in a particular study use of such a strain would make it possible to use fewer experimental animals. On the other hand the increasing availability of transgenics is increasing the number of experiments being carried out and the number of experimental animals which are suffering.

[. . .]

The intention behind production of such animals is largely philanthropic – prevention or cure of human diseases – although there is necessarily variation in the applicability of such work. Thus Cameron et al. list the following areas of investigation: gene regulation and development, host-pathogen interactions, immunology research and oncology research.[5] Of these, the first is probably further from application than the others, yet mice studied for this reason probably suffer just as much. This becomes relevant when regulatory bodies decide whether particular research proposals are to be allowed. Laws in the UK, for example, require consideration of both the likely effects on the animals involved and the likely benefits. However, assessment of the balance between these is clearly difficult. Poole has pointed out that animal models of human diseases are sometimes inappropriate: even if the symptoms are similar they may have very different causes and development, and may also exist in combination with other pathologies which do not occur in humans.[6]

The issue of patenting has mostly been concerned with this group of animals. Patenting of a whole animal (such as the oncomouse) is permitted in the US but is still being debated in Europe, while patenting of DNA sequences is permitted in both areas. The issue is important here because patenting may affect welfare. Its effects are likely to be complex, but one confusion should be avoided: patenting does not in itself confer any right to use animals or to condone suffering (these are regulated in the normal way). One point which has been made, though, is that experiments on animals which are restricted by patenting are likely to be done in reputable laboratories, while those on animals which are not so restricted may be carried out in conditions which are less than ideal.

It is likely that more transgenic animals are being produced and are suffering than are needed even for the experiments being carried out, because laboratory animal breeders often keep animals in stock to anticipate demand. It is clear that animals should be bred only for firm orders rather than always being available. Genetic modification of mice to make them prone to disease causes suffering, often severe.

Other animals

[. . .] Genetic engineering is being applied to vaccines and viruses to be used in wild animals which are seen as dangerous or inconvenient to humans. Recombinant vaccines against rabies are being used in foxes, racoons and skunks and are beneficial to those species insofar as they reduce other control measures directed against them. On the other hand genetic engineering is being used to introduce an immunocontraceptive effect to viruses which will then induce sterility in pests such as foxes and rabbits. It is intended to use the myxoma virus for rabbits, which will limit the disease caused to the rabbits because many are now immune to myxomatosis and will simply become sterile. The question of pest control is, of course, a complex one: many issues such as conservation are involved as well as human inconvenience, but it is still appropriate to point out that lack of concern over the welfare of pests is inconsistent with strong concern for the welfare of other animals. In this case there will also be other issues such as the risk of these viruses affecting animals other than the intended ones.

Evaluation

One of the issues arising from the discussion so far is the question of why the work is being done at all. For many applications it is clear that a major driving force behind genetic engineering is commercial exploitation of technology. This is important here because of the complex interaction of economics and welfare, which makes it unlikely that any applications will be unequivocally beneficial to both animals and humans.

If there is to be proper evaluation of the justification for genetic engineering, what will be the contributions of the general public? One contribution, which affects the commercial underpinning of the work, is the willingness of individual people to use the products of the processes we are discussing. People's willingness to buy food from genetically modified animals will be affected by various factors including the group of animals concerned: for example, genetically modified fish may be more acceptable than mammals or birds. Perception of the animals' welfare will also be important and will be affected by the information available. For example, with limited information people may have deep but rather formless concerns about the potential effects of genetic engineering on animal welfare, whereas with full consideration it is at least possible that those concerns will be fewer. There may be an initial impression of dozens of grossly suffering animals like the Beltsville pig going into commercial production which is not borne out by the facts. Nevertheless, it seems reasonable that increased safeguards are necessary.

The other way in which members of the public continue to have an important influence is in relation to such safeguards, because safeguards are put in place by legislators and legislators are influenced by public opinion. In North America and in many countries of Europe, members of the public who are concerned about animal welfare are more vocal than those who are not – joining humane societies, writing letters to the newspapers and expressing strong views in opinion polls. This climate of opinion increases the pressure for ethical evaluation and for the control and legislation of genetic engineering.

Many discussions and conferences on genetic engineering include consideration of ethics, particularly about implications for animal welfare, but such articles often make no practical recommendations. One article which does do so is that by Mepham, on the basis of potential advantages and disadvantages to humans and animals. He provides a framework for cost-benefit analysis of the effects on the animals and on the different groups of people affected by the technology (farmers, consumers, people in less developed countries and so on).[7] As with all cost-benefit analysis, this does not provide quantitative answers but does clarify the relevant questions. In particular, the question recurs of how to assess effects on animals. Perhaps the most practical recommendations in this respect are those by Broom.[8]

[. . .]

Legislation and control

It might be argued that few of the welfare implications discussed above are different in kind from those of other procedures such as selective breeding and hence that additional legislation is not needed. However, against this it must be pointed out that current legislation and welfare codes are not tackling existing problems successfully. [. . .] The inadequacy of current legislation is also likely to be worse with the potentially more rapid or unforeseen effects of other breeding technologies.

For adequate control of such technologies, legislation is necessary which specifies what is permitted rather than what is not. This is particularly necessary for procedures involving genetic modification. To obtain such permission, the proponents of a procedure should have to demonstrate one of two cases. First, the procedure may have no deleterious effects on animal welfare. Alternatively, benefits to humans may outweigh deleterious effects to animals.[9] Arguments for the latter case must be assessed by a properly constituted process such as that used by the UK Home Office under the Animals (Scientific Procedures) Act 1986 for licensing animal operations. Without such rigorous control, it seems likely that genetic engineering will cause more disadvantages than advantages for animal welfare.

The argument in the previous paragraph is currently tautologous in the UK, because all genetic engineering must be done under the Act mentioned. The UK also has regulations on potential release of GMOs, monitored by the Health and Safety Executive. However, not all countries have similar legislation. It is also unclear in the UK whether some procedures will in due course come to be regarded as routine rather than experimental and thus be excluded from the requirements of the Act. Another limitation of this legislation is its low profile. There is little public accountability, and yet it is essential for public confidence in the safeguarding of animal welfare that the procedures of committees concerned with these issues should be well publicised.

[. . .]

Notes

1 Appleby, M. C. (1998) 'Genetic Engineering, Welfare and Accountability', *Journal of Applied Animal Welfare Science*, vol. 1, pp. 255–73.
2 Robinson, J. J. and McEvoy, T. G. (1993) 'Biotechnology: The Possibilities' *Animal Production*, vol. 57, pp. 335–52. Quotation from p. 348.
3 McNeish, J. D., Scott W. J. and Potter, S. S. (jnr) (1988) 'Legless, a Novel Mutation found in PHT1–1 Transgenic Mice', *Science*, vol. 241, pp. 837–9.

4   Loew, F. M. (1994) 'Beyond Transgenics: Ethics and Values', *British Veterinary Journal*, vol. 150, pp. 3–5.
5   Cameron, E. R., Harvey, M. J. A. and Onions, E. E. (1994) 'Transgenic Science', *British Veterinary Journal*, vol. 150, pp. 9–24.
6   Poole, T. B. (1995) 'Welfare Considerations with Regard to Transgenic Animals', *Animal Welfare*, vol. 4, pp. 81–5.
7   Mepham, T. B. (1993) 'Approaches to the Ethical Evaluation of Animal Biotechnologies', *Animal Production*, vol. 57, pp. 353–9.
8   Broom, D. B. (1993) 'Assessing the Welfare of Modified or Treated Animals', *Livestock Production Science*, vol. 36, pp. 39–54.
9   Mepham (1993) op. cit., note 82.

49

Kevin R. Smith

"Animal Genetic Manipulation: A Utilitarian Response"

Smith considers several objections to genetically manipulating animals. He rejects the belief that deliberate genetic sequence change is intrinsically wrong, and the belief that such knowledge will inevitably lead to human genetic manipulation. Smith proposes that the concept of replaceability can justify the killing of transgenic animals, but supports a general prohibition on transgenic studies that entail significant suffering of animals.

Is it morally acceptable to genetically manipulate animals? I shall address this question by outlining the process and outcomes of animal genetic manipulation with reference to its morally salient features, followed by a discussion of various objections to the genetic manipulation of animals.

Background to animal genetic manipulation

[. . .]

Biologists view transgenic animals as essential research tools. This is particularly so for research into complex systems, involving interactions between different cells or organs. Transgenic animals are especially valued for their medical use as models of human disease. Such animal models are valued as means for the exploration of abnormal functioning and as testbeds for new therapies.

The agricultural biotechnology industry uses transgenic research in pursuit of quantitative and qualitative changes in animal products. Potential quantitative changes include more milk, more meat and more wool, while potential qualitative changes include altered milk composition (for example, to make cow's milk more suitable for human babies), leaner meat and pest-resistant wool.

Truly novel uses of transgenic animals are also under development. For example, transgenic animals as 'bioreactors' are able to produce human proteins. Such proteins, produced in the milk, have potential medical uses. Another example is research aimed at producing transgenic animals with human-compatible organs for human transplantation ('xenotransplantation').

A final point concerns the types of animals used for transgenesis. Although transgenesis has been successfully carried out on a very wide range of animals, ranging from insects to primates, more than 99 per cent of transgenic animals currently produced are laboratory mice.

The process of transgenesis

Consideration of the morality of animal genetic manipulation requires an understanding of the actual steps involved in transgenesis. This section aims to furnish such an understanding. Aspects that have moral salience are emphasised, and technical (scientific) language is minimised as far as possible.

General features of transgenesis

Foreign DNA molecules (termed 'transgenes') are introduced to a host embryo such that the resident genetic sequence (the 'genome') of the embryo – and hence that of the resulting animal – is altered by the incoming transgene genetic sequences. In most forms of transgenesis (see below), host embryos must be removed from the reproductive tracts of 'donor' females. Donor females are prepared for embryo collection by a course of hormone injections. Embryos may be collected from large agricultural animals by the relatively non-invasive procedure of 'flushing' the upper portions of the reproductive tract via the vagina. For smaller animals, surgery is used or, as is the case with mice, donor females are killed to allow efficient embryo collection. Genetically manipulated embryos are transferred to the reproductive tract of a 'recipient' female. Recipients must be in a 'pseudopregnant' state; this is induced by hormone injections and/or by mating the recipients with vasecto-mised males. In most animal types, including mice, embryo transfer requires surgery under general anaesthesia. When the potentially transgenic offspring are born, tissue samples (typically blood or skin) must be taken to enable laboratory determination of transgeneity. Most methods of transgenesis are less than 100 per cent efficient: the majority of potentially transgenic offspring test negative for transgene genetic sequences. Such animals are routinely killed. Finally, depending on the degree of precision of genetic manipulation associated with each method of transgenesis, further killing occurs when transgenic animals do not satisfy desired criteria.

Specific methods of transgenesis

There are several available methods for the genetic manipulation of animals. [. . .] See below for a tabulation of transgenic methods and their associated *prima facie* morally salient features (Table 1).

Outcomes of transgenesis

The outcomes of genetic manipulation, comparing transgenic animals with their non-manipulated counterparts fall into three main categories: 1. No physiological changes expected; 2. Physiological changes that do not cause suffering; 3. Physiological changes that are likely to cause suffering.

Some transgenic experiments do not aim to alter physiology. An example would be attempts to direct a transgene to a particular non-essential part of the genome, as part of fundamental studies of gene targeting.

[. . .]

Table 1 Transgenic Methods and Associated *Prima Facie* Morally Salient Features

Method of Transgenesis	Donor Females as Egg/embryo Source?	Physical Manipulation of Host Embryos?	Pseudo-pregnant Females as Recipients?	Killing of Non-Transgenic Offspring?	Wastage through lack of in vitro selection?
Retroviral Transfer	Yes, 8-cell embryos	Not usually required	Yes	Yes, only ca. 30% transgenic	Yes
Pronuclear Microinjection	Yes. one-cell embryos	Yes, by injection into one-cell embryos	Yes	Yes, only ca. 25% transgenic	Yes
ESCs* Transgenesis	Yes, early embryos (and as original source of ESCs)	Yes, by addition of ESCs to embryos	Yes	Yes, only ca. 40% germline transgenic	No
Nuclear Transfer Transgenesis	Yes, unfertilised eggs	Yes, transfer of cell nuclei into enucleated eggs	Yes	No, all selected embryos transgenic	No
Sperm-Mediated Transgenesis	Only for non-AI* methods	Only for ICSI* methods	Only for non-AI methods	Yes, not all animals expected to be transgenic	Yes

* ESCs = Embryonic stem cells; AI = Artificial insemination; ICSI = intra cytoplasmic sperm injection

Transgene-induced physiological changes need not necessarily cause suffering to the host animals. For example, human proteins produced in the milk of transgenic ewes have no detrimental effects on the lactating animals. [. . .] There are many more examples of such transgene-induced physiological changes, in which suffering is not entailed. Utilitarians have no clear grounds for objecting to such outcomes of transgenesis.

[. . .]

Certain transgene-induced physiological changes may cause animal suffering as an inci-dental effect of the purpose of the experimentation. [. . .] Suffering is more certain in animals manipulated to develop a specific disease that, in humans, has pain as a central feature. Many such transgenic disease 'models' have been created. For example, transgenic mice have been produced which reliably develop certain cancers. The induction of pain, such as that result-ing from invasive tumours, is only justifiable to utilitarians if outweighed by the avoidance of a greater amount of suffering elsewhere. Of course, a central defence of transgenic disease models is that 'the end justifies the means', in that animal suffering is claimed to be out-weighed by alleviation of suffering from cancer arising from experiments on transgenic models. I shall take up this issue later.

[. . .]

Moral objections to transgenesis

I am not persuaded by arguments from pro-animal absolutism, and this discussion of objections to transgenesis will start from the assumption, shared by most forms of utilitarianism, that *some* research with animals is morally permissible.

I will consider the following claims:

1   Transgenesis is objectionable because it is intrinsically wrong to deliberately alter genetic sequences;
2   Transgenesis is objectionable because it may lead to the genetic manipulation of humans;
3   Transgenesis is objectionable because it necessitates the killing of animals;
4   Transgenesis is objectionable because it involves the infliction of suffering on animals.

Intrinsic wrongness of deliberate sequence alteration

Genetic manipulation entails the deliberate alteration of genetic sequences within the genome. The same fundamental process of sequence alteration occurs as a result of genetic selection, both natural (as with evolution) and artificial (as with selective breeding of domesticated plants and animals). In terms of sequence alteration, the only significant difference between genetic manipulation and genetic selection is that the former process is very much faster than the latter. Thus, an assault on the ethics of transgenesis based on a notion of the intrinsic wrongness of sequence manipulation would be sustainable only as a subset of a much broader assault on all forms of *deliberate sequence alteration* (DSA). A coherent anti-DSA argument would entail the approval or acceptance of sequence alterations occurring naturally (from evolution) and the rejection of deliberate forms of alteration (breeding and genetic manipulation). Thus, to assume an ethical stance against DSA would be to subscribe to an unsubtle 'naturalistic fallacy'. Further, it is difficult to see how any form of utilitarian argument could be made against DSA in respect of its actual historical consequences, considering the vast expansion of thriving humanity that would not have been possible without centuries of selective breeding of domesticated plants and animals.

[. . .]

Thus, I hold that genetic sequence alteration *per se* is ethically neutral. [. . .] Assuming genetic sequence alteration *per se* to be ethically acceptable, it follows that the genetic sequence alteration inherent in animal transgenesis must also be considered ethically acceptable.

Risks of genetic manipulation being applied to humans

Some people object to transgenic research because they take the view that such work represents the 'thin end of a wedge' towards human genetic manipulation. Without doubt, the spectre of human genetic manipulation raises a plethora of moral questions. However, the fact is that most current transgenic techniques could (in principle) be readily applied to humans. Therefore, if the 'wedge' argument represents a valid objection to transgenesis, time has rendered such an objection passé.

However, the following variant of the 'wedge' objection avoids the charge of out-modedness: If transgenesis is allowed to proceed, it will increasingly be applied to 'higher' animals including primates, until the 'highest' primates—humans—become the next easy step. [. . .] The first premise for this objection is difficult to contest: higher animals *will* undoubtedly be used with increasing frequency, assuming continued progress in transgenic science. In addition, there may well be moral grounds for objecting to (at least some aspects of) transgenesis when particular non-human animals are concerned, where such animals have attributes of 'persons'.

However, the preceding 'wedge' argument depends crucially upon a claimed 'easy step' from non-human to human transgenesis. Is this notion of an 'easy step' valid? It is difficult to make a coherent case in its favour. Peoples of all cultures appear well able to discern a firm human/non-human line in terms of what is deemed permissible within each category.

I conclude that, if transgenesis really is the 'thin end of a wedge' on the way to human genetic manipulation, the onus must rest with the proponents of such a position to come forward with persuasive arguments.

Wrongness from killing

The production of transgenics undoubtedly necessitates the *killing* of many animals (such as animals that either fail to become transgenic or fail to express the transgene appropriately). The argument may be advanced that, since it is wrong *prima facie* to kill, it is wrong to produce transgenics. However, this position is opposed by the 'replaceability argument', which holds that it is not wrong to kill if a death is 'balanced' by the bringing into existence of another (equally happy) life. This situation is generally the case with transgenic science, where animals killed are replaced by breeding.

Assuming that significant suffering is not inflicted from an instance of killing (whether directly to the individual being killed or to others as a 'side-effect'[1]), it is difficult for utilitarians to argue against the replaceability argument. One objection to replaceability runs as follows: replaceability does not apply to humans, therefore to invoke the replaceability argument in the case of non-human animals is speciesist. A more sophisticated variant of this objection is the appeal to 'personhood', which starts by dividing sentient life into 'self-conscious' *vs.* 'non-self-conscious' beings.[2] The designation 'self-consciousness' denotes entities that are aware of themselves as distinct entities with a past and a future—entities that we may readily describe as 'persons'. Human beings (except for those with severe neurological deficits) are undoubtedly self-conscious, while very simple life forms (e.g. insects, assuming these to be sentient) are probably non-self-conscious. Proponents of this approach hold that replaceability may be applied to non-self-conscious entities but not to self-conscious entities—those with personhood. This personhood approach is plausible, but it contains at least two major weaknesses. Firstly, it is difficult to give strong reasons for viewing self-conscious entities as non-replaceable. Possibly the least flawed reason is the 'life as a journey' metaphor, where a self-conscious life is held to be inherently non-replaceable, because to end such a life would be to interrupt a coherent life narrative (complete with plans and hopes for the futures) prior to its completion. However, it is not clear why one such 'journey' may not be potentially replaceable by another, equally enjoyable 'journey', or why one large 'journey' may not be replaced by several smaller 'journeys'.

A second weakness of the personhood approach is the very real problem of attributing personhood. [. . .] [A]t the present time, it is impossible to say with confidence which, if any, of the animals commonly used for transgenesis (i.e. mice, sheep, pigs) merit the designation 'persons'.

Thus, the debate on killing and replaceability has not been resolved. [. . .] [A]n 'intermediate position' is highly desirable, in which a *provisional* line is drawn between animals deemed 'persons' and others not so designated, pending ongoing research into personhood. This provisional division would need to be based on (a) the (few) specific research findings presently available, and (b) on general observations of animal behaviour. On this approach, my own tentative preference would be to attribute personhood to (for example) pigs, rats and all higher primates, and withhold it from (for example) mice, sheep and chickens. However, such preferences are inevitably highly subjective. There is no perfect way to avoid such subjectivity, but a 'jury' approach, in which a group of 'disinterested' people is asked to provisionally attribute/withhold personhood, may be the best way forward.

I conclude that, categorisation difficulties notwithstanding, if the moral validity of personhood is accepted, transgenesis (in so far as killing is concerned) ought to be restricted to non-self-conscious animals.

Wrongness from suffering

I suggest that animal suffering gives the strongest grounds for objection to transgenesis. Specifically, I propose that *prohibition* should be considered in cases where either of the following negative consequences are entailed:

A   Significant suffering arising in any animals used in the process of transgenesis.
B   Significant suffering arising in transgenics from the development of a pathological condition engineered into the animals' genetic makeup.

I use the term '*significant suffering*' to exclude suffering likely to occur to an animal in a non-experimental situation. [. . .] If the extent of suffering unavoidably entailed by a particular transgenic approach is clearly less than that likely to occur inevitably in the life of the animal, utilitarians have no clear grounds for objection.

Other occurrences of suffering may be associated with transgenesis, such as suffering arising from failures in basic welfare provision (unsuitable animal accommodation, lack of veterinary care, etc.), and suffering arising from subsequent experimentation on transgenics (invasive surgery, stressful procedures, etc.). These occurrences of suffering have clear moral content. Moreover, the stringency of steps necessary to genuinely ensure adequate welfare may be formidable. For example, the happiness of some higher primates depends *inter alia* on the existence of environmental features such as extensive climbing opportunities, and on the freedom to engage in social groupings, all of which ought (morally) to be provided for such animals, as a prerequisite for any experimentation. Even laboratory mice require extensive welfare provision, such as adequately large cages with features to allow exploration. However, because such welfare issues are not the special reserve of *transgenic* animal science, I will not consider them in this discussion.

Although I propose that prohibition should be considered for negative consequences A and B (above), this should not be taken to mean transgenic cases entailing A or B ought automatically to be prevented. Rather, it is necessary, at least in principle, to weigh costs (significant suffering) against potential benefits (for example, a contribution to the development of a new anticancer drug).

Conclusion

Although conceptually simple, the calculus described above is notoriously difficult to conduct in practice. In the following sections, I shall consider the methods and outcomes of transgenesis from the perspective of significant suffering. I shall argue that there ought to be a strong presumption in favour of prohibition, in transgenic cases involving significant suffering where the extent, value or likelihood of realisation of a potential benefit is uncertain.

Methods of transgenesis

From the perspective of suffering, there are two key morally salient features of genetic manipulation that can lead to negative mental states, such as pain and fear. These features are (i) invasive procedures to recover and transfer embryos, and (ii) killing of animals involved in or arising from transgenesis.[3]

The first question should be: Can the degree of suffering arising from (i) and (ii) be *reduced*, without jeopardising the scientific purposes of transgenic experiments? An affirmative answer is possible for cases in which one method of transgenesis could be substituted for another. The various methods of transgenesis are not all equal in respect of features (i) and (ii). From Table 1 (above), it is apparent that both the 'traditional' methods of transgenesis (pronuclear microinjection and ESCs) entail features (i) and (ii). This is in contrast with the more 'novel' methods (nuclear transfer and sperm-mediated transgenesis). Given that nuclear transfer transgenesis allows the pre-selection of transgene-positive embryos, this method should largely avoid the need to kill non-transgenic offspring. However, invasive procedures (for the recovery and transfer of embryos) are still necessitated by nuclear transfer transgenesis. Conversely, sperm-mediated transgenesis, coupled with artificial insemination, retains the need for killing while avoiding the need for invasive procedures. Thus, substitution of a 'novel' method of transgenesis for one of the 'traditional' methods may permit a reduction in suffering. If such a substitution can be made without undermining experimental objectives, then it follows that such substitutions ought to be made wherever possible. However, it is important to emphasise that, as discussed previously, nuclear transfer transgenesis is in its infancy and sperm-mediated transgenesis is very far from being established as a viable method. Therefore, reducing suffering by choice of transgenesis method should be seen as a future possibility rather than as a practical proposition at present.

Thus, it seems undeniable that the process of transgenesis inevitably entails *some* (significant) suffering. The question now becomes: is this suffering outweighed by good consequences? I suggest that—assuming impeccable welfare provisions—an affirmative answer should be given. The 'good consequences' arising from transgenesis may be summarised under the heading of 'scientific progress'. As discussed previously, the scientific value of transgenesis can be in no doubt. Most forms of utilitarianism view scientific progress (in terms of an increased understanding of nature, and of the possible beneficial uses from such understanding) as morally desirable. Thus, prevention of transgenic research *per se* would only be justifiable on the grounds of major negative consequences. I contend that the inevitable significant suffering entailed by transgenesis is insufficiently large to outweigh the benefits to society arising from the contribution of transgenesis to scientific progress. The amount of significant suffering implicit in transgenesis cannot be quantified. However, the suffering actually entailed by the invasive procedures and killing used in transgenesis ought to be relatively minimal. Typically, donor and recipient animals are used only once in their life-times: this is in marked contrast to the many protracted experiments that 'ordinary' labora-tory animals endure. Moreover, the procedures themselves are not of a severe nature: at worst (but under proper welfare conditions), embryo collection or transfer is akin to the sterilisation operations commonly used with household pet animals. Similarly, euthanasia is the most frequent fate of pet animals.

In summary: although all possible steps ought to be taken to reduce the amount of suffering entailed in the process of transgenesis, it would be wrong to prohibit animal genetic manipulation *per se*.

Outcomes of transgenesis

As discussed previously, the outcomes of transgenesis that have relevance here are those that are likely to cause suffering. Taking this category of transgenic outcomes in general, the consequences are of the same type as those for transgenesis *per se*, scientific progress is the benefit; and suffering is the cost. However, the degree of suffering implicit in this category of outcomes is greater than is the case for the process of transgenesis. On *prima facie* grounds, I contend that transgenic outcomes that cause significant suffering are contenders for prohib-ition. I suggest that utilitarians take a 'default' position in which experimentation entailing such negative transgenic outcomes is deemed unacceptable, unless (on a case-by-case basis) a watertight argument has been made to the effect that suffering is clearly outweighed by good consequences. For example, the generation of transgenics that develop an analogue of a painful human cancer ought to be permissible only if the experimenters could clearly demon-strate a major, tangible, high probability payoff in terms of a specific advance in cancer treatment. The difficulties in practice of convincingly demonstrating such benefits should not be underestimated: the majority of research using transgenic disease models is *not* expected to yield discernible immediate medical benefits. Moreover, there are many forms of trans-genic experimentation for which a cost-benefit justification is *impossible*: for example, pain research may well fall into this category.

What I am suggesting is that, in the case of protracted or acute significant suffering arising in transgenic animals, the general 'scientific progress' benefit (although undeniable) is simply too nebulous to justify such experimentation. By contrast, there are circumstances in which one might envisage very direct benefits to humans that are both highly probable and highly proximate. In such exceptional cases, where it can be firmly demonstrated that the significant suffering of transgenic animals would be outweighed by the prevention of such suffering in humans (or by the saving of many human lives that would otherwise be lost), the prohibition ought to be lifted.

This 'default prohibition' position has radical implications because its application would entail the proscription of many transgenic experiments. However, unless the mis-conceived equation of utilitarianism with the notion 'the end always justifies the means' is accepted, or speciesism is resorted to, default prohibition appears to be the only coherent position compatible with utilitarianism. The alternative is that we would have to accept the doctrine of 'anything goes' in the name of scientific progress: I assume it axiomatic that no utilitarian would accept such a doctrine.

Notes

1   For example, other animals might become terrified as a consequence of their awareness of a nearby killing.
2   See P. Singer. 1993. *Practical Ethics*, 2nd ed. Cambridge, Cambridge University Press: 110–31.
3   Although killing may in principle be free of suffering, I suggest that this is so difficult to achieve in practice that the safest option is to assume *some* suffering, even under the most humane conditions.

50

Jeffrey Burkhardt

"The Inevitability of Animal Biotechnology? Ethics and the Scientific Attitude"

Burkhardt believes that a moral or ethical re-education of scientists and science policy makers is essential if ethical thinking is to enter the scientific establishment. He further believes that fundamental changes in the scientific attitude would be necessary for any ethical arguments to have force and that there probably will be considerable resistance to inclusion of ethical matters in scientific training. He argues that only when ethics becomes an established part of scientific thinking can the issues of the morality of using animals or the propriety of biotechnology be understood by scientists.

Introduction

Most observers of biotechnology are aware that the main standard critiques of animal bio-technology are based on either animal rights/welfare arguments, ecological-oriented arguments, or socioeconomic consequences arguments. In this chapter, I want to suggest that despite the logic or seeming appropriateness of many of these critiques, they lack *ethical force*. By this I mean that the arguments (and the arguers) are unlikely to actually change the minds of those engaged in biotechnology practices and policy-making (Stevenson, 1944; Olshevsky, 1983). This is because of the orientation or attitude of those entrusted with doing and overseeing biotechnological work with non-human animal species. I will argue that this orientation must change before ethical arguments concerning animal biotechnology, indeed ethics generally (in the philosophical sense as opposed to legalistic or professional courtesy senses), mean anything to the scientific community. [. . .]

There are philosophical reasons, but more important, practical reasons for the proposal in this chapter. Philosophically, while some of the ethical objections to animal biotechnology or to particular biotechnology practices may be justifiable, behind many of them is a mis-placed Platonic assumption that the problem with those engaged in animal biotechnology is that they do not know 'the good'. That is, if the scientists or policy makers knew or under-stood the philosophical objections, then they would stop doing what they are doing. The problem with this assumption is that scientists would have to accept the fundamental criteria for justifiability or reasonableness upon which philosophical argument rests before they would even fathom these criticisms as reasonable ones. This relates to my practical concern.

Practically, the rights/welfare, environment/ecology, and socioeconomic approaches are usually bound to fall on deaf ears. Arguments concerning 'ethics and animal biotechnology' are generally irrelevant, at best, to the actual members of the bioscience community or 'Science Establishment'. Scientists and policy makers may fathom some ethical concerns when their scientific or policy-making 'hats' are off. But to scientists and science-oriented policy makers *qua* scientists and science-oriented policy makers, proponents of animal rights/welfare arguments, environmental/ecological ethics arguments, or social justice arguments, can easily be relegated to the role of 'philosophers crying in the wind' (or howling at the moon). Ethical arguments which do not first assume the *a priori* legitimacy of whatever the scientific enterprise has decided to pursue are bound to be 'external' and 'externalized'. [. . .] My belief is that we should accept the inevitability of continued animal biotechnology research and development, and hope that the legalistic-type controls now in place in many nations continue to work or work even better. In the meantime, we should also 'sympathetically' impress on scientists the value of ethical reflection on their work.

Why the standard ethical critiques fail

Animal welfare, rights, and natural kinds arguments

Animal rights or animal welfare arguments regarding animal biotechnology arise because in all of these biotechnology activities, non-human animals are *involved*. The strongest argument objects to the use of animals *per se*. The rights argument, articulated so forcefully initially by Regan (1985), maintains that individuality and 'subject-of-a-life'-hood of non-human animals (in particular larger mammals) ethically demands their being treated in a quasi-Kantian manner: as ends in themselves, with appropriate stakes in life, liberty and self-actualization. Genetically altering an individual non-human animal, either before or after conception, *ipso facto* intrudes upon the autonomy of the being.

[. . .]

The philosophical underpinnings to the rights objection to animal biotechnology are easily countered by the scientific community. Most direct genetic engineering of animals (i.e. altering an animal's genetic structure) is performed either so early in the fetal developmental process that a distinct individual animal (in terms of moral autonomy) is indiscernible, or, more often, occurs even before conception takes place. Under any or all of Regan's criterion of the animal's having some rudimentary consciousness, or Singer's criterion of sentience, or Fox's criterion of 'telos-possession' (Fox, 1990), there is no 'subject of a life' (Rachels, 1990) whose inherent value or rights or unique purpose are disrespected through the engineering process.

[. . .]

Rights or welfare arguments may be appropriate to an appraisal of some biotechnology techniques, nonetheless. In particular, the use of biotechnologically produced hormones, pharmaceuticals and other agents may be seen as in some way disrespecting animals' rights or may cause a decrease in welfare. Using a chemical which artificially increases milk production in dairy cows, but which also increases incidences of disease (mastitis) and shortens an individual cow's productive life (and by implication, its life), may be bad for the cow in both rights and welfare terms. The issue here is, however, less an animal biotechnology matter than a simple matter of people using cows in dairy production systems.

[. . .]

One final point on the rights/welfare approaches: if any ethical concession is to be made to the fact that animals are used by humans, then some animal biotechnology may in fact be more ethical than some other research and production practices currently employed. If, as various humane societies have argued, better treatment of non-human animals ought to be our goal, biotechnology might be precisely the means to achieve that goal. This would, of course, depend on exactly what is being done with or to the animals, individually or by species (see, for example, NABC, 1992).

The natural kinds argument is the other main kind of animal-based objection to genetic engineering. Rifkin (1983) argued that the very ideology of genetic engineering—'algeny'—challenged the naturalness of those species which were either created by God or evolved through natural selection. Independent of the potentially disastrous ecological consequences of tampering with these longstanding kinds, there is a fundamentally immoral audacity in those people who would 'play God' and change the natural order for whatever purposes they intended.

[. . .]

Again, there are science-based replies to natural kinds arguments. Simply stated, humans have used animals for millennia, and in many respects, the very animal species which they used now exist only because of their use.

[. . .]

In terms of ethical force, the appropriate ethical critiques of animal biotechnology are not, at least as animal biotechnology is currently practised, either the animal rights/welfare sorts of argument, or the natural kinds approach advanced by Rifkin. These kinds of criticisms, which I refer to as 'intrinsic' critiques, can generally be met with reasonable points about either the nature of the practices performed on animals, or the extent to which they produce suffering, or the extent to which they are no different in principle from any other animal-using scientific practice. I suggest that other, 'extrinsic' or consequentialist critiques may be more appropriate and forceful challenges to biotechnology, to the extent that there is science-based (and hence, 'reasonable') evidence to support their claims. I will argue, nevertheless, that these criticisms can also fail because they miss major points about what biotechnology, and animal biotechnology in particular, can potentially do.

Consequentialist critiques and irreversibility arguments

Consequentialist-type arguments regarding animal biotechnology usually focus on ecological or socioeconomic cultural ills associated with biotechnology in general, and animal biotechnology in particular. One common theme among these arguments, and, perhaps, underlying fear among their proponents, is that these consequences are or may tend to be irreversible: that is, once the technology or its products have been developed, adopted, or widely used or released into the world, severe negative effects will obtain which will be difficult or impossible to stop or reverse (Comstock, 1990).

The ecological arguments are most straightforward, though most originally were advanced with respect to microorganisms and plant species with little thought given to (larger) animal implications. According to this line of argument, a genetically altered individual or species of organism is necessarily different from its natural or wild counterpart. In fact, the reason behind genetic engineering is to design plants, animals or organisms with traits which would allow the organism to cope with the environment in ways different from the non-engineered kin, for instance withstand different and hostile climatic conditions, resist pests, better absorb nutrients from the environment. [. . .] These creatures of bio-engineering were intended to perform in their environments in ways to be preferred to those of their natural relatives.

The prime concern of the ecological-ethical critique is that bioengineered organisms, once outside controlled laboratory conditions, might behave in ecologically inappropriate ways. For instance, the engineered species might out-compete its natural relatives to the point of the extinction of the latter; or new predator species might evolve in response to the changes in the original species; or the new species just might grow out of control; or the new species might simply upset the 'biotic community' (Holland, 1990). [. . .] Note that it is again not bioengineering *per se* that is at issue. Rather, it is the *results* of bioengineering.

[. . .]

There may be sound moral premises behind this critique, such as, 'We morally should not risk ecosystemic disruption because of risks to present or future people or to the ecosystem itself'. Once we have allowed these organisms into the environment, we cannot get them back. Even so, there is again a reasonable reply in this case. We risk ecosystemic disruption all the time, and in fact *cause* ecosystemic disruption through many things much more dangerous than genetically engineered animals or animal products. So, unless the point is that we should leave the ecosystem alone, a practical impossibility, these potential ecosystemic disruptions are not necessarily immoral. [. . .] Because we know the genetic makeup of the engineered species even better than that of the non-engineered ones, we are in fact in a better position to control the new species or even eradicate those individuals who begin to get out of control.

[. . .]

Risk and irreversibility are also behind the economic and social consequentialist arguments vis-à-vis biotechnology. The argument here is that, unlike ecosystemic behaviour, we have clear precedents with respect to how new technologies affect social or economic behaviour, relationships, or structures (Burkhardt, 1988). On this basis, it is argued that animal biotechnology is potentially socially disastrous, and hence likely to be immoral in that regard.

[. . .]

Despite the force of ethical precedents, the reply to socioeconomic criticisms is straightforward. [. . .] The objection to biotechnology's socioeconomic consequences is really an objection to technology in general, or perhaps to capitalist socioeconomic arrangements. [. . .] [A]ny [. . .] particular product or process might change socioeconomic relations, but that is not the fault of the technology, only the system into which it is introduced (Burkhardt, 1991).

[. . .]

There is one further consequentialist argument to attend to here. This might be called the 'cultural consequence' argument. [. . .] [W]idespread diffusion of biotechnological products (from altered animals and plants to bioengineered chemicals and food products) might open the door for general public acceptance of the ethical appropriateness of engineering *people*. [. . .] As more biotechnology becomes the norm, a whole culture might come to accept whatever is bioengineered as even morally preferable to the non-engineered. Given *real* slippery slopes in attitudes, and *real* risks to longstanding human values such as freedom of choice and perhaps diversity among people, biotechnology accordingly is a cultural threat.

Like the potential ecological consequences critique, this last concern plays up the element of uncertainty. Unlike the environmental/ecological position, however, it is less a matter of how bioengineered organisms or ecosystems will behave or be affected than a matter of how people will act and react toward biotechnology. The question is whether there are any reasons for the public or policy makers to be concerned about the standard science-based reply to this position, namely, it will not happen. I will argue in the next section that the answer is predicated on whether there is indeed any reason for us to be concerned that biotechnology will continue to be employed without prior or at least concomitant ethical reflection. There may be little reason to fear biotechnology progressing, but only if biotechnology is either regulated and monitored, or ethics becomes an intrinsic part of the scientific attitude—the fundamental ideological/epistemological basis for science.

The biotechnology culture and the scientific attitude

[. . .]

A realistic appraisal of biotechnology, in general, has to begin with this fact: something in the biotechnology area has occurred, and likely will continue to occur. Philosophers and social analysts have long pointed to the power that science has in modern society. This notion was given contemporary expression and force by Rosenberg (1976) in his notion of 'Scientism'—the ideology of science solving all human problems. Scientism, it is argued, has become another dominant '-ism' of our day.

[. . .]

The extent to which Scientism undergirds both the biotechnology enterprise as practised as well as public policy regarding biotechnology is astounding. It is this fact which lends credibility to the cultural critique described above.

[. . .]

In the public policy arena, moreover, we have witnessed a gradual but steady strengthening of the power of biotechnology or bioscience in general (Busch et al., 1991). Even as funding for some specific kinds of basic research (e.g. AIDS) has been questioned by members of the United States' Congress, the general level of support for biotechnology has grown. In addition, much of the regulatory oversight which grew up in the early years of biotechnology—the late 1970s and early 1980s—has gradually devolved (NABC, 1994). Public policy priorities have shifted from concerns about the potential negative effects of biotechnological research to concerns that the advances in bioscience and especially bioengineered products are not coming fast enough. [. . .] [T]here is little reason to believe that anything short of an environmental catastrophe caused by a bioengineered product or experiment gone awry could actually cause a reduction in the enthusiasm with which biotechnology has been embraced at nearly all levels of research management, oversight or policy making.

[. . .]

There are a number of reasons or causes to which the biotechnology craze might be attributed. One might simply be the excitement or enchantment that members of the scientific establishment experience when, as I mentioned above, what was conceivable becomes possible, or what was possible becomes actual.

[. . .]

There are other, perhaps less noble, reasons for the degree of excitement and commitment to biotechnology in general and agricultural (plant and animal) biotechnology in particular. [. . .] The motivation also appears to have been the time element involved: whereas a new plant variety or pharmaceutical product might take several years or even decades to develop under older research methods, the new biotechnologies offered hope for quicker new products and processes. Again, in an increasingly competitive environment, the quicker the better.

Whatever the reason for the interest in and excitement about biotechnology, there is one additional glaring fact about the scientific attitude concerning biotechnology: ethical considerations such as those discussed above matter little, if at all. This orientation has permeated the science establishment. This lack of concern for deeper ethical matters, as opposed to legalities or professional courtesies, may permeate all society as well (save theologians and philosophers trying to conserve older ways of thinking about what is or is not moral). So long as science continues to deliver or at least forecast new promises—for corporations, for policy makers, and ultimately for the general public—ethics is irrelevant.

The scientific attitude

Biologist Frederick Grinnell, in *The Scientific Attitude* (1987), described what I take to be the underlying reason why 'ethics and science' or 'ethics and biotechnology' have been seen as beyond the pale in terms of attitudes and practices of members of the scientific community. [. . . Grinnell] hits on the idea that science must become, for scientists, a 'way of seeing' and a 'way of being'.

By 'way of seeing', Grinnell means that the material with which much physical and biological science operates (though perhaps true of social sciences such as economics as well) is only visible once one has come to appreciate and accept the appropriate theoretical or ideological foundation.

[. . .]

The 'way of being' of the scientist is of more direct and critical concern. For, as Grinnell suggests, this means adopting 'the scientific attitude', which in essence is to come to believe in Scientism: Rosenberg's (1976) book was aptly titled *No Other Gods*. And believing in Scientism means always being willing to act on making what is conceivable possible, and what is possible actual. In other words, to *be* a scientist (in this ideal typology), one must accept the *doctrine* that science defines what is real. Those who do not accept either that reality or its technological ramifications (the tools employed or the products created) are wrong at best, *irrational* at worst. This becomes the crux of the matter.

That this sort of attitude might engender a degree of arrogance or self-righteousness is clear (Feyerabend, 1978). However, not all individual scientists, or even most, need to or do display those personality traits. It is enough that the science establishment—research administrators, policy setters, leading scientific spokespersons—has the power to define what is or is not real, reasonable or rational. This is power in sociologist Stephen Lukes' (1986) sense of a 'third dimension' of power (the first two being physical force and persuasive ability)—the ability to define the terms in which rational discourse takes place. The work, perceptions, and professional communications of members of the scientific community all take as a given the reality and importance of scientific rationality, and whatever emanates from rational scientific work.

Scientists, including biotechnologists, may in fact be quite humble in the face of new problems, new theories, new frontiers. Nevertheless, there is a sort of moral imperative in the widely shared attitude that 'the work (of science) *must go on*' (J. Burkhardt, L. Busch and W. Lacy, personal interview, 1988). Moreover, significantly, whatever appears to impede or constrain the work of science must be based on some irrational or non-scientific force. As such, lack of funding (to the extent that some of this work lacks funding) is unreasonable. Even more unreasonable, and immoral by this doctrine, are rules, regulations, oversight committees, and reporting requirements. [. . .] In a word, constraints are unreasonable.

This characterization of the scientific attitude and Scientism undoubtedly overstates the case, and may even be questioned for grossly caricaturing science and the scientist. However, the ease with which the science establishment, and many individual scientists, can dismiss criticism or the kinds of objections to biotechnology discussed above is telling. There is not only nothing wrong with biotechnology (that is not wrong with any part of science), but to suggest otherwise is to either fail to understand science or simply be irrational. This refers back to my earlier point: any criticism or ethical concern which does not *a priori* assume the legitimacy of the scientific enterprise and the necessity of using science (including bio-technology) to solve problems must be ignored or, better, rendered impotent. One way to emasculate those criticisms is to fall back on the power that the science establishment has long had in Western society: change the terms of the discourse.

The culture of biotechnology

The case of bovine somatotrophin, one of the first commercial animal-affecting products to emerge from the biotechnology enterprise, is a telling example of the power of the bioscience community to actually change the terms of discourse—to the advantage of the biotechnology enterprise, of course. Bovine somatotrophin is a naturally occurring compound, produced in the pituitary glands of cows, which regulates growth and indirectly affects milk production. [. . .] Scientists at a number of United States universities, under grants or contracts with Dow Chemical and Monsanto corporations, became able in the early 1980s to produce the compound using recombinant DNA methods. The product could now be produced in greater quantities, and much more cheaply and efficiently.

Bovine somatotrophin was originally named 'bovine growth hormone' (BGH) when scientists and company representatives began touting the chemical for its potential use in animal agriculture. Quite soon afterwards, however, representatives of the bioscience establishment began to be met with resistance from consumer advocacy groups, and eventually lawsuits were even filed to prevent the US Food and Drug Administration from permitting the use of BGH in agriculture. Emphasis was placed on the nature of this compound as a *hormone*, despite scientists' and the industry's assurances that it was a non-steroidal-type hormone, and would not in any adverse way affect consumers of milk from BGH-treated cows. About the same time, however, the term 'BGH' disappeared from scientific publications and company promotions. Bovine somatotrophin became known by its real abbreviation, 'BST'. The resistance and criticisms of the substance did not disappear overnight, but the bioscience establishment managed to diffuse a significant amount of consumer activists' policy-affecting power by simply redirecting the concern away from a 'hormone' to just another productivity-increasing 'treatment' (Browne, 1987).

The whole BGH/BST story is much more complicated and drawn out (Burkhardt, 1992), but just this name change element in the story is sufficient to suggest my point. With nothing more than a semantic sleight of hand, the bioscience establishment was able to effectively control the public forum as well as public policy agenda. There are undoubtedly many, and more glaring cases of science winning a public relations battle or war. The only times the science establishment does not win hands down, it seems, is when it faces an equally formidable foe, for example the tobacco industry in the US, or organized religion, especially the Roman Catholic Church.

[. . .]

Critics of the agricultural research establishment have for a number of years pointed to a 'circle the wagons' mentality among people in the science establishment (Busch and Lacy, 1983). Always mindful of potential criticisms—from environmentalists, animal-rightists and animal welfarists, and small-farm and labour activists—the establishment (it was claimed) sought to dismiss or ignore the reasonableness of criticisms. In the case of the new generation of the bioscience/biotechnology community, the strategy seems more intended to pre-empt or co-opt criticisms than to ignore or dismiss them. The result is, nevertheless, that critics become marginalized, unless, again, there is significant political or social power behind them. Given the inherent (and self-defined) 'reasonableness' of the views, activities, and arguments of the scientific community, even formidable social challenges are likely to fail.

These points may suggest nothing more than that the bioscience community, including practitioners of animal biotechnology, probably have little or no reason to fear that their activities will be fundamentally challenged in the actual public arena. Moreover, to the extent that the scientific establishment is becoming more sophisticated about 'science education', the likelihood of even a powerful challenge diminishes greatly. Science writers, science popularizers, and spokespersons for universities and corporations are out in force, promoting the legitimacy and safety of biotechnology. Surveys suggest that as the public becomes more 'informed' and 'educated' about science, concern diminishes significantly. Further, as policy makers become more informed and educated as to the relative benefits and risks of biotechnology (as defined by scientists themselves), strong legislative action is unlikely. Indeed, as mentioned above, the result of all this information and education may well be simply greater levels of funding for the biotechnology enterprise. The only conclusion to be reached is that 'the beast will go on'. The spectre of a broader, social 'culture of biotechnology', with attendant human genetic engineering, is real.

Conclusion: ethics by regulation, committee, or (re-)education

In the early 1970s, a gathering of concerned scientists was held in Asilomar, California, to discuss the risks and benefits of genetic engineering. What emerged from those meetings was a set of biosafety guidelines concerning biotechnology. Many of those guidelines made their way into federal regulations and general governmental oversight. Though fairly stringent at the time, the guidelines and subsequent rules have been gradually weakened. Scientists argue that, as their knowledge about bioengineering has grown, what were reasonable concerns are now known to be unfounded fears. Recall that the USDA abolished its biotechnology oversight committee. Apparently it was thought to be an unnecessary public expenditure. Most universities have in-house biosafety committees, and corporations, it has been argued, exercise extreme caution because of the risk of lawsuits or prosecution under environmental or human safety regulations.

[. . .]

The scientific establishment continues to engage in genetic engineering practices involving animals. And, technologies will continue to have impacts, some of them negative, on particular socioeconomic groups in society. Barring some sort of major catastrophe, or major gestalt shift, animal biotechnology, biotechnology in general, and even more generally, technological research and development will undoubtedly continue. If ethical considerations are to fit anywhere in this scientific enterprise, it would seem that it would have to be through the current system of oversight and control, or through the force of higher levels of government action. Given the power of science and Scientism, the latter is unlikely, though not impossible.

One conclusion that can be reached is this: if ethics in a substantive sense is to make its way into the scientific establishment, and the bioscience community in particular, it will have to be at least in part if not exclusively through the moral or ethical re-education of scientists and science policy makers. And the moral or ethical education of young scientists and students would also be a key. Indeed, the ethical force of particular kinds of arguments pertaining to animal biotechnology is dependent on *any* ethical argument having force. And for any ethical argument to have force, fundamental changes in the scientific attitude would be necessary. As Grinnell noted, the way of seeing and way of being of science are *learned* orientations. *Seeing* ethical considerations as inherently part of the scientific enterprise, as well as *being* an ethically aware scientist or policy maker, must also be learned.

Just as there is considerable resistance on the part of the science establishment to external control—to the point of pre-empting *rational* discussion of criticisms—there may also be considerable resistance to the inclusion of ethics as part of the indoctrination into the scientific attitude. Nevertheless, there are enough scientists who do engage in ethical reflection when their scientific 'hats are off' that there is at least some promise for ethics to be a part of the scientific mind-set. Already, there are college and university courses, colloquia, and informal discussion among members of the bioscience community about 'science ethics'. With considerable effort on the part of theologians, philosophers, and social scientists—duly respectful of the ability of science to define the terms of rational discussion—more such inclusion of ethics might continue.

Only when ethics becomes a legitimate—and rational—part of the scientific attitude will concerns about particular aspects of animal biotechnology be taken seriously, or taken at all. Only when ethics is a routine concern among scientists will considerations of whether we should be using animals, or engaging in biotechnology, even be fathomed. I do not believe that we will stop using animals in research (or for food purposes) in the near future. Nor do I believe that the scientific establishment will stop engaging in biotechnology any time soon, if at all. I do believe, however, that any critique which does not first address the need for including discussion of ethics in the very process of 'doing science' is doomed to failure. It does little practical or political good to challenge science from the outside. Rather, rational, informed, science-based discussion of ethical considerations has to be the key to whether continued biotechnological research and development, whether in the animal, plant, or human domains, will simply be inevitable.

Note

A considerable amount of the 'evidence' for the theses in this chapter is based on 'research' performed by the author, a professional philosopher, but whose appointment is in the agricultural science college at a major state university in the US. Although the author wishes to indict no particular scientists or administrators for espousing 'the scientific attitude', or especially indict them for 'ethical insensitivity', both orientations have been found to be extant (though the former far more prevalent) among the physical and biological scientists with whom the author interacts on a daily basis.

References

Browne, W. (1987) Bovine Growth Hormone and the Politics of Uncertainty: Fear and Loathing in a Transitional Agriculture. *Agriculture and Human Values*, 4 (1).

Burkhardt, J. (1988) Biotechnology, Ethics, and the Structure of Agriculture. *Agriculture and Human Values*, 4 (2).

Burkhardt, J. (1991) The Value Measure in Public Agricultural Research, in *Beyond the Large Farm* (eds P. Thompson and W. Stout), Westview Press, Boulder, CO.

—— (1992) On the Ethics of Technical Change: The Case of bST. *Technology and Society*, 14.

Busch, L. and Lacy, W. (1983) *Science, Agriculture, and the Politics of Research*, Westview Press, Boulder, CO.

Busch, L., Lacy, W., Burkhardt, J and Lacy, L. (1991) *Plants, Power and Profit*. Blackwell, Oxford.

Comstock, G. (1990) The Case against bGH, in *Agricultural Bioethics* (eds S. Gendel, A. Kline, D. Warren and F. Yates), Iowa State University Press, Ames.

Feyerabend, P. (1978) *Science in a Free Society*, NLB, London.

Fox, M. (1990) Transgenic Animals: Ethical and Animal Welfare Concerns, in *The Bio-Revolution*, (eds P. Wheale and R. McNally), Pluto Press, London.

Grinnell, F. (1987) *The Scientific Attitude*. Westview Press, Boulder, CO.

Holland, A. (1990) The Biotic Community: A Philosophical Critique of Genetic Engineering, in *The Bio-Revolution* (eds P. Wheale and R. McNally), Pluto Press, London.

Lukes, S. (1986) *Power*, New York University Press, New York.

NABC (National Agricultural Biotechnology Council, USA) (1992) *Animal Biotechnology: Opportunities and Challenges*, NABC Report 4, Ithaca, NY.

—— (1994) *Agricultural Biotechnology and the Public Good*, NABC Report 6, Ithaca, NY.

Olshevsky, T. (1983) *Good Reasons and Persuasive Force*, University Presses of America, New York.

Rachels, J. (1990) *Created from Animals*, Oxford University Press, Oxford.

Regan, T. (1985) *The Case for Animal Rights*, University of California Press, Berkeley, CA.

Rifkin, J. (1983) *Algeny*, Viking Press, New York.

Rosenberg, C.E. (1976) *No Other Gods*, Johns Hopkins University Press, Baltimore, MD.

Stevenson, C. (1944) *Ethics and Language*, Yale University Press, New Haven, CT.

TELOS

51

Bernard E. Rollin

"On *Telos* and Genetic Engineering"

Rollin addresses the notion of *telos*, the essence and purpose of a creature, and proposes that there is no direct reasoning to argue that the notion of *telos* in animals and the Maxim to Respect *Telos* should preclude genetic engineering of animals. He notes that for domestic animals, each proposed modification should be assessed in relation to the Principle of Conservation of Welfare. For non-domestic animals, he believes that such modifications also may be valuable. He exercises proceeding cautiously so as to avoid possible ecological impacts or affecting other animals adversely.

Telos

Aristotle's concept of *telos* lies at the heart of what is very likely the greatest conceptual synthesis ever accomplished, unifying common sense, science, and philosophy. By using this notion as the basis for his analysis of the nature of things, Aristotle was able to reconcile the patent fact of a changing world with the possibility of its systematic knowability. [. . .] Though individual robins come and go, 'robin-ness' endures, making possible the knowledge that humans, in virtue of their own *telos* as knowers, abstract from their encounters with the world. Common sense tells us that only individual existent things are real; reflective deliberation, on the other hand, tells us that only what is repeatable and universal in these things is knowable.

[. . .]

For Aristotle, as for common sense, the fact that animals had *tele* was self-evident—the task of the knower was to systematically characterize each relevant *telos*. [. . .] [T]he notion of *telos* has in fact been refined and deepened by the advent of molecular genetics, as a tool for understanding the genetic basis of animals' physical traits and behavioural possibilities. At the same time, the classical notion of *telos* is seen as threatened by genetic engineering, the operational offspring of molecular genetics. For we may now see *telos* neither as eternally fixed, as did Aristotle, nor as a stop action snapshot of a permanently dynamic process, as did Darwin, but rather as something infinitely malleable by human hands.

Contemporary agriculture

Despite the fact that the concept of *telos* has lost its scientific centrality, there are two major and conceptually connected vectors currently thrusting the notion of *telos* into renewed philosophical prominence, both of which are moral in nature. These vectors are social concern about the treatment of animals, and the advent of practicable biotechnology. The former concern reflects our recently acquired ability to use animals without respecting the full range of their *telos*; the latter concern reflects our in-principle ability to drastically modify animal *telos* in unprecedented ways. There obtain significant conceptual connections between the two concerns, but before these are dealt with one must understand the social conditions militating in favour of a revival of the concept of *telos*.

[. . .]

The overwhelmingly preponderant use of animals in society since the dawn of civilization has unquestionably been agricultural—animals were kept for food, fibre, locomotion and power. Presupposed by such use was the concept of husbandry; placing the animals in environments congenial to their *telos*—the Biblical image of the shepherd leading his animals to green pastures is a paradigm case—and augmenting their natural abilities by provision of protection from predators, food and water in times of famine and drought, medical and nursing attention, etc. In this ancient contract, humans fared well if and only if their animals fared well, and thus proper treatment of animals was guaranteed by the strongest possible motive—the producer's self-interest. Any attempt to act against the animals' interests as determined by their natures resulted in damage to the producers' interests as well. In this contract, both sides benefited—the animals' ability to live a good life was augmented by human help; humans benefited by 'harvesting' the animals' products, power or lives. One could not selectively accommodate some of the animals' interests to the exclusion of others, but was obliged to respect the *telos* as a whole.

[. . .]

All of this changed drastically in the mid-twentieth century with the advent of high-technology agriculture, significantly portended as university departments of animal husbandry underwent a change in nomenclature to departments of 'animal science'. In this new approach to animal agriculture, one no longer needed to accommodate the animal's entire *telos* to be successful. [. . .] Technology has allowed animal producers to divorce productivity from total or near-total satisfaction of *telos*.

High-technology agriculture was not the only mid-twentieth century force significantly deforming the ancient contract with animals. Large-scale animal use in biomedical research and toxicology is, like intensive agriculture, a creature of the mid-twentieth century. Like confinement agriculture, too, successful use of animals in biomedicine does not necessitate accommodating the animals' *tele*.

[. . .]

Thus, both the advent of industrialized agriculture and large-scale animal use in science created an unprecedented situation in the mid-twentieth century by inflicting significant suffering on animals which was nonetheless not a matter of sadism or cruelty. Agriculturalists were trying to produce cheap and plentiful food in a society where only a tiny fraction of the population was engaged in agricultural production; scientists were attempting to cure disease, advance knowledge and protect society from toxic substances. As society became aware of these new animal uses neither bound by the ancient contract nor conceptually captured by the anti-cruelty ethic, and concerned about the suffering they engendered, it necessarily required an augmentation in its moral vocabulary for dealing with animal treatment.

[. . .]

It is th[e] notion of rights, based on plausible reading of the human *telos*, which has figured prominently in mid-century concerns about women, minorities, the handicapped and others who were hitherto excluded from full moral concern. It is therefore inevitable that this notion would be exported, *mutatis mutandis*, to the new uses of animals. In essence, society is demanding that if animals are used for human benefits, there must be constraints on that use, equivalent to the natural constraints inherent in husbandry agriculture. These constraints are based in giving moral inviolability to those animal interests which are constitutive of the animals' *telos*. If we are to use animals for food, they should live reasonably happy lives, i.e. lives where they are allowed to fulfil the interests dictated by their *telos*. [. . .] For the baboon used in biomedicine, this means creating a housing system which, in the words of US law, enhances the animals' 'psychological well-being', i.e. social non-austere containment for these animals that accommodates 'species-specific behaviour' (Rollin, 1989, pp. 177–81). For the zoo animals, it means creating living conditions which allow the animals to express the powers and meet the interests constitutive of its *telos* (Markowitz and Line, 1989).

Thus, *telos* has emerged as a moral norm to guide animal use in the face of technological changes which allow for animal use that does not automatically meet the animals' requirements flowing from their natures. In this way, one can see that the social context for the re-emergence of the notion of *telos* is a pre-eminently moral one: *telos* provides the conceptual underpinnings for articulating social moral concern about new forms of animal suffering. From this moral source emerge epistemological consequences which somewhat work against and mitigate the reductionistic tendencies in science alluded to earlier. For example, it is moral concern for *telos* which is sparking a return of science to studying animal consciousness, animal pain and animal behaviour, areas which had been reduced out of existence by the mechanistic tendencies of the twentieth-century science that affords pride of place to physicochemistry (Rollin, 1989). In an interesting dialectical shift, moral concern for animals helps revive the notion of *telos* as a fundamental scientific concept, in something of a neo-Aristotelian turn.

Genetic engineering

If our analysis of the moral concerns leading to the resurrection of the notion of *telos* is correct, we can proceed to rationally reconstruct the concept and then assess its relevance to the genetic engineering of animals. By rationally reconstruct, I mean first of all provide an articulated account of *telos* which fills the moral role society expects of it. Second, I mean to protect it from fallacious accretions which logically do not fit that role but which have attached, or are likely to attach to it for purely emotional, aesthetic or other morally irrelevant reasons. A simple example of such a conceptual barnacle might be those who would restore the notion of 'Divine purpose' to the concept of *telos*, and then argue that any genetic engineering is wrong simply because it violates that Divine purpose.

What sense can we make out of the notion of *telos* we have offered? In that sense, the *telos* of an animal means 'the set of needs and interests which are genetically based, and environmentally expressed, and which collectively constitute or define the "form of life" or way of living exhibited by that animal, and whose fulfilment or thwarting matter to the animal'. The fulfilment of *telos* matters in a positive way, and leads to well-being or happiness; the thwarting matters in a negative way and leads to suffering (see Rollin, 1992, Part I). Both happiness and suffering in this sense are more adequate notions than merely pleasure and pain, as they implicitly acknowledge qualitative differences among both positive and negative experiences. The negative experience associated with isolating a social animal is quite different from the experience associated with being frightened or physically hurt or deprived of water. Since, as many (but not all) biologists have argued, we tend to see animals in terms of categories roughly equivalent to species, the *telos* of an animal will tend to be a characterization of the basic nature of a species. On the other hand, increased attention to refining the needs and interests of animals may cause us to further refine the notion of *telos* so that it takes cognisance of differences in the needs and interests of animals at the level of subspecies or races, or breeds, as well as of unique variations found in individual animals, though, strictly speaking, as Aristotle points out, individuals do not have natures, even as proper names do not have meaning.

Thus, we may attempt to characterize the general *telos* of the dog as a pack animal requiring social contact, a carnivore requiring a certain sort of diet, etc. At this level we should also characterize gender- and age-specific needs, such as nest-building for sows, or extensive play for puppies and piglets.

[. . .]

This is perfectly analogous to moral notions we use vis-à-vis humans. Our *ur*-concern is that basic human interests as determined by human nature are globally protected—hence the emphasis on general human rights. We may also concern ourselves with refinement of those interests regarding subgroups of humans, although these subgroups are as much cultural as genetic.

[. . .]

Thus, *telos* is a metaphysical (or categorial) concept, serving a moral and thus value-laden function, and is fleshed out in different contexts by both our degree of empirical knowledge of a particular kind of animal and by our specificity and degree of moral concern about the animals in question. For example, the earliest stages of moral concern about the *telos* of laboratory animals focused only on very basic needs: food, ambient temperature, water, etc. As our moral concern grew, it focused on the less obvious aspects of the animals' natures, such as social needs, exercise, etc. As it grew still more, it focused on even less evident aspects.

[. . .]

Thus, the notion of *telos* as it is currently operative is going to be a dynamic and dialectical one, not in the Darwinian sense that animal natures evolve but, more interestingly, in the following sense: as moral concern for animals (and for more kinds of animals) increases in society, this will drive the quest for greater knowledge of the animals' natures and interests, which knowledge can in turn drive greater moral concern for and attention to these animals.

It is not difficult to find this notion of *telos* operative internationally in current society. Increasing numbers of people are seeking enriched environments for laboratory animals, and this is even discussed regularly in trade journals for the research community. Indeed, one top official in the US research community has suggested that animals in research probably suffer more from the way we keep them (i.e. not accommodating their natures) than from the invasive research manipulations we perform. The major thrust of international concern about farm animals devolves around the failure of the environments they are raised in to meet their needs and natures, physical and psychological.

[. . .]

Respect for *telos* and the conservation of well-being

This, then, is a sketch of the concept of *telos* that has re-emerged in society today. Though it is partially metaphysical (in defining a way of looking at the world), and partially empirical (in that it can and will be deepened and refined by increasing empirical knowledge), it is at root a moral notion, both because it is morally motivated and because it contains the notion of what about an animal we *ought* at least to try to respect and accommodate.

What, then, is the relationship between *telos* and genetic engineering? One widespread suggestion that has surfaced is quite seductive (Fox, 1986). The argument proceeds as follows. Given that the social ethic is asserting that our use of animals should respect and not violate the animals' *telos*, it follows that we should not alter the animals' *telos*. Since genetic engineering is precisely the deliberate changing of animal *telos*, it is *ipso facto* morally wrong.

[. . .]

Seductive though this move may be, I do not believe it will stand up to rational scrutiny, for I believe it rests upon a logical error. What the moral imperative about *telos* says is this:

Maxim to Respect *Telos*:
If an animal has a set of needs and interests which are constitutive of its nature, then, in our dealings with that animal, we are obliged to not violate and to attempt to accommodate those interests, for violation of and failure to accommodate those interests matters to the animal.

However, it does not follow from that statement that we cannot change the *telos*. The reason we respect *telos*, as we saw, is that the interests comprising the *telos* are plausibly what matters most to the animals. If we alter the *telos* in such a way that different things matter to the animal, or in a way that is irrelevant to the animal, we have not violated the above maxim. In essence, the maxim says that, given a *telos*, we should respect the interests which flow from it. This principle does not logically entail that we cannot modify the *telos* and thereby generate different or alternative interests.

The only way one could deduce an injunction that it is wrong to change *telos* from the Maxim to Respect *Telos* is to make the ancillary Panglossian assumption that an animal's *telos* is the best it can possibly be vis-à-vis the animal's well-being, and that any modification of *telos* will inevitably result in even greater violation of the animal's nature and consequently lead to greater suffering. This ancillary assumption is neither *a priori* true nor empirically true, and can indeed readily be seen to be false.

Consider domestic animals. One can argue that humans have, through artificial selection, changed (or genetically engineered) the *telos* of at least some such animals from their parent stock so that they are more congenial to our husbandry than are the parent stock. I doubt that anyone would argue that, given our decision to have domestic animals, it is better to have left the *telos* alone, and to have created animals for whom domestication involves a state of constant violation of their *telos*.

By the same token, consider the current situation of farm animals mentioned earlier, wherein we keep animals under conditions which patently violate their *telos*, so that they suffer in a variety of modalities yet are kept alive and productive by technological fixes. As a specific example, consider the chickens kept in battery cages for efficient, high-yield, egg production. It is now recognized that such a production system frustrates numerous significant aspects of chicken behaviour under natural conditions, including nesting behaviour (i.e. violates the *telos*), and that frustration of this basic need or drive results in a mode of suffering for the animals (Mench, 1992). Let us suppose that we have identified the gene or genes that code for the drive to nest. In addition, suppose we can ablate that gene or substitute a gene (probably *per impossibile*) that creates a new kind of chicken, one that achieves satisfaction by laying an egg in a cage. Would that be wrong in terms of the ethic I have described?

If we identify an animal's *telos* as being genetically based and environmentally expressed, we have now changed the chicken's *telos* so that the animal that is forced by us to live in a battery cage is satisfying more of its nature than is the animal that still has the gene coding for nesting. Have we done something morally wrong?

I would argue that we have not. Recall that a key feature, perhaps *the* key feature, of the new ethic for animals I have described is concern for preventing animal suffering and augmenting animal happiness, which I have argued involves satisfaction of *telos*. I have also implicitly argued that the primary, pressing concern is the former, the mitigating of suffering at human hands, given the proliferation of suffering that has occurred in the twentieth century. I have also argued that suffering can be occasioned in many ways, from infliction of physical pain to prevention of satisfying basic drives. So, when we engineer the new kind of chicken that prefers laying in a cage and we eliminate the nesting urge, we have removed a source of suffering. Given the animal's changed *telos*, the new chicken is now suffering less than its predecessor and is thus closer to being happy, that is, satisfying the dictates of its nature.

This account may appear to be open to a possible objection that is well known in human ethics. As John Stuart Mill queried in his *Utilitarianism*, is it better to be a satisfied pig or a dissatisfied Socrates? His response, famously inconsistent with his emphasis on pleasure and pain as the only morally relevant dimensions of human life, is that it is better to be a dissatisfied Socrates. In other words, we intuitively consider the solution to human suffering offered, for example, in *Brave New World*, where people do not suffer under bad conditions, in part because they are high on drugs, to be morally reprehensible, even though people feel happy and do not experience suffering. Why then, would we consider genetic manipulation of animals to eliminate the need that is being violated by the conditions under which we keep them to be morally acceptable?

[. . .]

In the case of animals, [. . .] there are no *ur*-values like freedom and reason lurking in the background. We furthermore have a historical tradition as old as domestication for changing (primarily agricultural) animal *telos* (through artificial selection) to fit animals into human society to serve human needs. We selected for non-aggressive animals, animals that depend on us not only on themselves, animals disinclined or unable to leave our protection, and so on. Our operative concern has always been to fit animals to us with as little friction as possible—as discussed, this assured both success for farmers and good lives for the animals.

If we now consider it essential to raise animals under conditions like battery cages, it is not morally jarring to consider changing their *telos* to fit those conditions in the same way that it jars us to consider changing humans.

Why then does it appear to some people to be *prima facie* somewhat morally problematic to suggest tampering with the animal's *telos* to remove suffering? In large part, I believe, because people are not convinced that we cannot change the conditions rather than the animal.

[. . .]

On the other hand, suppose the industry manages to convince the public that we cannot possibly change the conditions under which the animals are raised or that such changes would be outrageously costly to the consumer. And let us further suppose, as is very likely, that people still want animal products, rather than choosing a vegetarian lifestyle. There is no reason to believe that people will ignore the suffering of the animals. If changing the animals by genetic engineering is the only way to assure that they do not suffer (the chief concern of the new ethic), people will surely accept that strategy, though doubtless with some reluctance.

From whence would stem such reluctance, and would it be a morally justified reluctance? Some of the reluctance would probably stem from slippery slope concerns—what next? Is the world changing too quickly, slipping out of our grasp? This is a normal human reflexive response to change—people reacted that way to the automobile. The relevant moral dimension is consequentialist; might not such change have results that will cause problems later? Might this not signal other major changes we are not expecting?

Closely related to that is a queasiness that is, at root, aesthetic. The chicken sitting in a nest is a powerful aesthetic image, analogous to cows grazing in green fields. A chicken without that urge jars us. But when people realize that the choice is between a new variety of chicken, one *without* the urge to nest and denied the opportunity to build a nest by how it is raised, and a traditional chicken *with* the urge to nest that is denied the opportunity to build a nest, and the latter is suffering while the former is not, they will accept the removal of the urge, though they are likelier to be reinforced in their demand for changing the system of rearing and, perhaps, in their willingness to pay for reform of battery cages. This leads directly to my final point.

The most significant justified moral reluctance would probably come from a virtue ethic component of morality. Genetically engineering chickens to no longer want to nest could well evoke the following sort of musings: 'Is this the sort of solution we are nurturing in society in our emphasis on economic growth, productivity and efficiency? Are we so unwilling to pay more for things that we do not hesitate to change animals that we have successfully been in a contractual relationship with since the dawn of civilization? Do we really want to encourage a mind-set willing to change venerable and tested aspects of nature at the drop of a hat for the sake of a few pennies? Is tradition of no value?' In the face of this sort of component to moral thought, I suspect that society might well resist the changing of *telos*. But at the same time, people will be forced to take welfare concerns more seriously and to decide whether they are willing to pay for tradition and amelioration of animal suffering, or whether they will accept the 'quick fix' of *telos* alteration. Again, I suspect that such musings will lead to changes in husbandry, rather than changes in chickens.

We have thus argued that it does not follow from the Maxim to Respect *Telos* that we cannot change *telos* (at least in domestic animals) to make for happier animals, though such a prospect is undoubtedly jarring. A similar point can be made in principle about non-domestic animals as well. Insofar as we encroach upon and transgress against the environments of all animals by depositing toxins, limiting forage, etc. and do so too quickly for them to adjust by natural selection, it would surely be better to modify the animals to cope with this new situation so they can be happy and thrive rather than allow them to sicken, suffer, starve and die, though surely, for reasons of uncertainty on how effective we can be alone as well as aesthetic reasons, it is far better to preserve and purify their environment.

In sum, the Maxim to Respect *Telos* does not entail that we cannot change *telos*. What it does entail is that, if we do change *telos* by genetic engineering, we must be clear that the animals will be no worse off than they would have been without the change, and ideally will be better off. Such an unequivocally positive *telos* change from the perspective of the animal can occur when, for example, we eliminate genetic disease or susceptibility to other diseases by genetic engineering, since disease entails suffering. The foregoing maxim which does follow from the Maxim to Respect *Telos*, we may call the Principle of Conservation of Well-being. This principle does of course exclude much of the genetic engineering currently in progress, where the *telos* is changed to benefit humans (e.g. by creating larger meat animals) without regard to its effect on the animal. A major concern in this area which I have discussed elsewhere is the creation of genetically engineered animals to 'model' human genetic disease (Rollin, 1995b, Chapter 3).

There is one final caveat about genetic engineering of animals which is indirectly related to the Maxim to Respect *Telos*, and which has been discussed, albeit in a different context, by biologists. Let us recall that a *telos* is not only genetically based, but is environmentally expressed. Thus, we can modify an animal's *telos* in such a way as to improve the animal's *telos* and quality of life, but at the expense of other animals enmeshed in the ecological/environmental web with the animal in question. For example, suppose we could genetically engineer the members of a prey species to be impervious to predators. While their *telos* would certainly be improved, other animals would very likely be harmed. While these animals would thrive, those who predate them could starve, and other animals who compete with the modified species could be choked out. Thus, we would, in essence, be robbing Peter to pay Paul. Furthermore, while the animals in question would surely be better off in the short run, their descendants may well not be—they might, for example, exceed the available food supply and may also starve, something which would not have occurred but for the putatively beneficial change in the *telos* we undertook. Thus, the price of improving one *telos* of animals in nature may well be to degrade the efficacy of others. In this consequential and environmental sense, we would be wise to be extremely circumspect and conservative in our genetic engineering of non-domestic animals, as the environmental consequences of such modifications are too complex to be even roughly predictable (Rollin, 1995a, Chapter 2).

Conclusion

In conclusion, there is no direct reason to argue that the emerging ethical/metaphysical notion of *telos* and the Maxim to Respect *Telos* logically forbid genetic engineering of animals. In the case of domestic animals solidly under our control, one must look at each proposed genetic modification in terms of the Principle of Conservation of Welfare. In the case of non-domestic animals, there is again no logical corollary of the maxim of respect for *telos* which forestalls genetically modifying their *telos*, and, on occasion, such modification could be salubrious. Given our ignorance, however, of the systemic effects of such modifications, it would be prudent to proceed carefully, as we could initiate ecological catastrophe and indirectly affect the functionality of many other animals' *tele*.

References

Fox, M.W. (1986) On the genetic engineering of animals: a response to Evelyn Pluhar. *Between the Species*, **2** (1), 51–2.

Markowitz, H. and Line, S. (1989) The need for responsive environments, in *The Experimental Animal in Biomedical Research*, vol. I (eds B.E. Rollin and M.L. Kesel), CRC Press, Boca Raton, Florida, pp. 153–73.

Mench, J.A. (1992) The welfare of poultry in modern production systems. *Critical Reviews in Poultry Biology*, 4, 107–28.

Rollin, B.E. (1989) *The Unheeded Cry: Animal Consciousness, Animal Pain and Science*, Oxford University Press, Oxford.

Rollin, B.E. (1992) *Animal Rights and Human Morality*, Prometheus Books, Buffalo, NY.

Rollin, B.E. (1995a) *Farm Animal Welfare: Ethical, Social, and Research Issues*, Iowa State University Press, Ames, Iowa.

Rollin, B.E. (1995b) *The Frankenstein Syndrome: Ethical and Social Issues in the Genetic Engineering of Animals*, Cambridge University Press, New York.

52

Bernice Bovenkerk, Frans W.A. Brom, and
Babs J. van den Bergh

"Brave New Birds: The Use of 'Animal Integrity' in Animal Ethics"

Bovenkirk, Brom, and van den Bergh use the terms "integrity" and "naturalness" to address the notions of bioengineering and *telos* raised by Rollin. They note that the concept of integrity refers to a set of characteristics of a species humans define and believe is important to preserve, and that the identity of such characteristics can be elucidated by moral discussion. Even in the absence of full agreement, such discussions can help clarify the issues and evaluate existing practices.

Besides providing us with new biological knowledge and opening up some intriguing possibilities in medicine and agriculture, genetic engineering provides philosophers with some interesting thought experiments. Inspired by Bernard Rollin's remark in *The Frankenstein Syndrome*[1] about the creation of wingless, legless, and featherless chickens, Gary Comstock urges us to imagine just that: the transition of chickens into living egg machines.[2]

[. . .]

What if we could make these animals adjust better to their environment and genetically engineer them into senseless humps of flesh, solely directed at transforming grain and water into eggs. [. . .] Intuitively, treating an animal in this way—or rather creating an animal for these purposes—is morally problematic. This intuition is also prompted by uses of biotechnology that are already feasible and indeed are already in use, but the "brave new birds" provide a paradigmatic case.

In public debate in The Netherlands, these sorts of cases evoke appeals to such notions as integrity and naturalness.[3] In the case of the egg machines, for example, we might say that the chickens' integrity has been violated because we have interfered with their physical makeup, not for their own good, but for ours. We have tampered with the characteristics that make a chicken a chicken.

Why animal integrity?

This intuition that changing chickens into senseless, living egg machines is problematic and cannot be elaborated solely with the help of traditional moral concepts such as animal interests or animal rights.

"Welfarists," like Rollin, take animals to have interests because, and only insofar as, they are sentient. In other words, Rollin holds that animals have interests by virtue of their sentience, and therefore that only welfare matters from a moral point of view.

[. . .]

Since the chickens are senseless, Rollin cannot raise any objection to the use of genetic engineering to turn these animals into machines. But even though Rollin asserts that he "sees no moral problem if animals could be made happier by changing their natures," elsewhere he seems to acknowledge that creating living egg machines is not a desirable course of action. Rather, it is the lesser of two evils "while it is certainly a poor alternative to alter animals to fit questionable environments, rather than alter the environments to suit the animals, few would deny that an animal that does mesh with a poor environment is better off than one that does not." This assertion seems to acknowledge the moral intuition that changing an animal's nature is objectionable, while holding that the circumstances may make it neces-sary. Clearly, however, suffering is not the main issue here. In other words, Rollin's concept of interest is too narrow to analyze our moral intuition.[4]

Animal rights proponents, such as Tom Regan, argue that raising animals for food is wrong not primarily because it causes animal suffering, but because it is wrong in principle. This is because animals, like humans, are valuable in themselves and not only by virtue of their value to others. In other words, they possess inherent value and therefore have moral standing.[5] According to Regan, the basis for this inherent value is that animals are "subjects-of-a-life."[6] Regan regards mammals that possess a certain amount of awareness as para-digmatic subjects-of-a-life. If so, the senseless egg machines in our example are probably not subjects-of-a-life, and it is probably not wrong in principle to change chickens into them.

[. . .]

Animal ethicists in The Netherlands have proposed the notion of animal integrity pre-cisely because of the inability of interests and rights to accommodate the moral intuition that we should adjust the farm environment to the animal and not vice versa. Integrity has been described by Bart Rutgers as the "wholeness and intactness of the animal and its species-specific balance, as well as the capacity to sustain itself in an environment suitable to the species."[7]

Some objections

'Integrity' seems to be helpful because it has an objective, biological aspect. It implies that the animal is intact or whole, which is an attribute of the animal itself, not just some value we have placed on it. Integrity therefore could play an important role in elaborating moral concerns not only about genetic engineering but also about other interventions in animal life, like cross-breeding or intensive animal husbandry.

It is important to note that we would not speak of the violation of integrity in all cases in which an animal's intactness is violated. Rutgers holds that docking a dog's tail for aesthetic reasons constitutes a violation of the dog's integrity, but when the dog's tail must be docked for medical reasons, he claims that its integrity has not been violated. In effect, docking a dog's tail for these two reasons could be regarded as two different actions, depending on the intention with which the action is carried out.

But this raises a problem. If the physiological result of the two different kinds of docking is the same, then it seems that integrity is not a biological aspect of the animal itself after all. The concept then loses its objective, biological character and becomes a moral rather than an empirical notion. It does not refer to a notion of factual intactness or wholeness so much as to a *perceived* intactness. It refers to how we feel an animal *should* be.[8] That leaves us wondering how objective the notion of integrity really is.

A second difficulty with the notion of integrity is the problem of "gradation." If we are to judge the acceptability of, say, a certain scientific experiment on animal subjects, then we need to be able to weigh the moral good against the moral wrong.[9] Only when we can deem one type of experiment more acceptable than another will 'integrity' have meaning in the context of ethical deliberation. If gradation were impossible, then every intervention constituting a violation of integrity would have to be dealt with similarly: either they would all have to be condemned, no matter how trivial the purpose, or none of them could be condemned, no matter how severe the consequences.

Gradation could be achieved in three different ways. First, violations of integrity could be graded based on the good that the violation aims at. The problem with this first position is that all the work has to be done by weighing goals and not by grading the moral wrongs. Integrity itself is not graded at all.

Second, one could consider respect for integrity as a prima facie duty that must be weighed against other prima facie duties. The problem with this strategy is that we must know more about integrity to do the weighing, which leads us back to the question about integrity's content.

The third way would be to describe different kinds of violations of integrity, some more severe than others. The problem with the third way is that, unlike the notions of well-being and health, integrity—conceived of as intactness or wholeness—seems to be an absolute notion.[10] A body is either intact or not, and so either has integrity or not. It's like being pregnant: a woman is either pregnant or she is not; she cannot be more or less pregnant. The *violation* of integrity is not necessarily this absolute. Docking a dog's tail, for instance, does not seem to be as harsh a violation of its integrity as, say, the removal of one of its legs. The question is what basis we have for judging the weight of a violation of integrity. What criteria can we use to establish which of two violations is worse? And what criteria can be used to argue that the violation is bad enough to reject the possible good it constitutes (as in the case of scientific experiments)? We need grounds to make this kind of gradation possible. In other words: how can we measure integrity?

Human integrity

Thus the notion of integrity is problematic. It carries a false pretense of objectivity, of being "empirically determinable," and it is not clear how it can be of practical use, as this would entail criteria to measure it. Do these problems render the concept of animal integrity useless? To answer this question, it is helpful to look at two parallel discussions in which integrity plays a role: human integrity and ecosystem integrity.

A widely shared moral intuition exists that no matter what the benefits, every human being has the right not to be physically violated without his or her consent. The concept of human integrity is often employed to give voice to this intuition.

Physical and mental integrity concerns the inviolability or intactness of a person's body and mind. Historically, the concept originates in the debate about the relationship between the state and its citizens. The most important human right is the right not to be imprisoned arbitrarily or to have the integrity of one's person or body violated in any other way. This right has now been extended to the medical sphere, where it plays a central role in defining the relationship between physicians and their patients, obliging doctors to request the patient's informed consent before carrying out an invasive action.[11] More precisely, informed consent is based on two complexly interrelated pillars—autonomy over and integrity of one's mind and body. Sometimes, but not always, they support each other. Protection from invasive action cannot be lifted without the permission of the patient. However, permission is not always a sufficient condition for integrity not to be violated. The concept of integrity provides some restraint on self-determination: some violations might be objectionable even if the person wants them.

If a patient is not able to give permission for whatever reason, others have to see to the protection of her body from invasive action. This is where integrity becomes most important; it establishes the inviolability of the bodies of people who cannot dispose of their bodies themselves, including children, prisoners, and those who are mentally handicapped or comatose. The same intuition plays a role in decisions about people who out of sheer poverty feel forced to "donate" their organs. Socioeconomic circumstances prevent these people from exercising their autonomy. When we want to argue against allowing them to sell their organs, we could appeal to their physical integrity.

[. . .]

It is important to note that the law not only concerns violations of the body resulting in suffering or in adverse health conditions, but that it also deals with infringements on the body without such detrimental effects. In fact, as with animals, it is this dimension of inviolability that is best expressed by the notion of integrity. Even though the person with Down syndrome who receives a contraceptive injection can hardly be said to suffer a great deal of pain or illness as a result of the injection, the notion of integrity allows one to argue that she has been violated and that the administration of contraceptive injection is—at the very least—morally problematic and in need of justification.

Plainly the concept of integrity is well established in the field of medical ethics as a way of structuring discussions. Yet here, too, it is not free of problems. The problems can be illustrated by considering the implications of Article 11 of the Dutch Constitution, which states that every person has the right, apart from limitations imposed by law, to the inviolability of her body. The clause is part of the right to protection of personal privacy and contains two elements: (1) the right to be protected from harm of and infringement upon the body by a third party, and (2) the right to self-determination of the body. Thus in its explanation of what 'integrity' involves, the law makes a distinction between a person and her body and allows a person to dispose of her body freely.

This distinction is controversial in philosophy, but it is undeniably useful for understanding and regulating the doctor-patient relationship. If the distinction is admitted, however, then protecting the integrity of a *person* can lead to a violation of the integrity of the person's *body*. The right to physical integrity contends that every person has the right to remain free from infringements upon the body by others, but it also states that every person has a right to determine the disposition of one's body.

If the body has integrity of its own that could be violated, then a trans-sexual who undergoes a sex-change may very well be violating her own physical integrity. If we do not want to draw this conclusion, then we must hold that an intervention into the body is not a violation when it is approved of by the person. We could say that as the operation seems to bring the person more in harmony with her body, in the overall picture the person's integrity has not been violated.[12] Integrity as a moral notion can therefore be diametrically opposed to integrity as an empirical notion. Here, as with animal integrity, we see that an intervention constitutes a violation of integrity only if it is *perceived* as such. Clearly the problem of objectivity is present in the domain of human integrity as well as in that of animal integrity.

Ecosystem integrity

The notion of integrity has also been applied within the science of ecology in order to help protect environmental resources. Aldo Leopold employed the concept in relation to eco- systems. In what must be the most quoted passage in ecological ethics, he asserted that "A thing is right when it tends to preserve the integrity, stability, and beauty of the biotic community. It is wrong when it tends to do otherwise."[13]

Ecological integrity refers to the wholeness, unity, or completeness of an ecosystem. Immediately, of course, the question arises what we are to make of the stability and whole- ness of an ecosystem when it is a central feature of ecosystems that they change continuously. Parts of an ecosystem can be destroyed while the ecosystem as a whole seems to flourish. There is an uninterrupted movement through life cycles; some individuals die and others are born, but the ecosystem as a whole remains. How can we determine whether or not the integrity of an evolving ecosystem has been violated?

James Kay's definition of ecosystem integrity takes this dynamic character into account and calls attention to certain processes found within ecosystems. According to Kay, constitu- tive elements of ecosystem integrity are the ability of ecosystems to maintain optimum oper- ations, to cope with environmental stress, and to self-organize.[14] Laura Westra adds a human element to this definition; she asserts that an ecosystem must be able to maintain its "condi- tions as free as possible from human intervention" and to withstand anthropocentric stresses upon the environment.[15] Westra also distinguishes ecosystem integrity from ecosystem health. An ecosystem can be healthy even when it is intensively managed by people, but it possesses integrity only "when it is wild, that is, free as much as possible today from human intervention, when it is an "unmanaged" ecosystem, although not a necessarily pristine one."[16]

When the first European settlers came to Australia in 1788, they encountered a more or less harmonious ecosystem, characterized by native flora and fauna that were well adapted to their environment. Delicate relations between the land and its vegetation and between differ- ent kinds of plants and animals kept all in balance. Understandably, however, the settlers felt homesick in this alien land. Also, it did not at first sight seem to offer very many food crops. Thus the settlers thought it would be a good idea to bring some of their own native plants and animals to Australia, in order both to sustain themselves and to remind them of their homeland. Little did they know what havoc they were to cause by this introduction of exotic species.

[. . .]

Biodiversity was lost, and the ecosystem can no longer be said to be free and unmanaged in Westra's sense. The native vegetation has been overgrown, and animals that fed on the native plants have lost a food source. In effect, an altogether new ecosystem has evolved. The initial ecosystem could not respond well.

Several attempts have been made to put the concept of ecological integrity to practical use. This has proven to be difficult, but it is also very important, as it could help guide policy. For instance, managers of different national parks adhere to different approaches about whether or not to prevent naturally occurring fires. Westra's account of ecosystem integrity gives us some criteria to employ in thinking about this problem. Her account suggests that while the health of a forest might be damaged by naturally occurring fires, its integrity cannot be said to be violated because the effects are not the result of human action.

The problems that beset the concept of ecosystem integrity include those of both objectivity and gradation. There is no easy way of establishing objectively whether or not a violation of an ecosystem has occurred. All that seems clear is that ecosystems' integrity is violated when we destroy the whole world, for then it is quite clear that the ecosystem has not been able to cope with anthropocentric stress. As John Lemons notes, "it could be said that any ecosystem that can maintain itself without collapsing has integrity. . . . There is no scientific reason why a changed ecosystem necessarily has less ability to maintain optimum operations under normal environmental conditions, cope with changes in environmental conditions less effectively, or be limited in its ability to continue the process of self-organisation on an ongoing basis."[17] Thus ecological integrity does not allow us to demarcate precisely which intervention does and which does not violate the integrity of an ecosystem.

Moreover, as with animal integrity, it is difficult to find criteria to determine how severely the ecosystem's integrity has been violated. How, for example, can we determine the severity of the damage caused by blackberries in Australia? A new balance was found between different plants and animals within the ecosystem, and in a sense, optimum operations were restored. It is because we find the change undesirable that we say the ecosystem's integrity has been violated. In short, whether or not an ecosystem's integrity has been violated "must be based on human judgement regarding the acceptability of a particular change."[18]

As we saw before in the case of animal integrity, whether or not such a change is rendered acceptable largely depends on the purpose for which the intervention is carried out. The example of the forest destroyed by naturally occurring fire makes clear that integrity is primarily a moral term, referring to human action. Only when the fire has been lit by humans do we speak of a violation of the forest's integrity. Moreover, setting the forest on fire could actually benefit it,[19] and in that case, even a human-induced fire would probably not be counted as a violation of integrity. It is the ends an act serves that makes us judge it favorably or not.

Flawed but workable

As we have seen, arguments about "integrity" are problematic not only in the animal domain but in parallel discussions as well. The concept refers not to a state of affairs that can be assessed empirically, but rather to our own ideals for a human, an animal, or an ecosystem. Violations of integrity cannot be objectively proven, nor can their severity be established.

Yet despite these problems, "integrity" is used in the ecological and human domains to structure discussions and to reach agreements. In these domains, it serves a useful critical function. It has proven especially valuable in the field of medicine, and at least in continental Europe seems to be widely accepted, alongside the concepts of autonomy and dignity.[20] These other concepts are also rather obscure, but nevertheless they have been translated into principles whose usefulness is widely accepted, despite disputes about their exact meaning.

In the field of environmental policy, too, "integrity" seems to be a sound notion. Appeals to integrity frequently pop up in the management of national parks. Even though it is sometimes hard to establish whether or not a policy will amount to a violation of an ecosystem's integrity, the concept hands policymakers and park managers a tool to structure and clarify their discussion. Here, as in the case of medical interventions, an appeal to integrity gives us the opportunity to criticize certain proposed actions that have repercussions for an ecosystem's functioning. Again, the concept of integrity generates no knock-down arguments, but it nonetheless appears to be quite workable in a practical context. It gives us a way to communicate moral reservations we might have about environmental policies.

When we envision a future in which we buy eggs from a warehouse housing hundreds of rows of flesh-colored humps created from what we once knew as chickens, a feeling of discomfort comes over us. We—or many of us, anyway—have a moral intuition that changing chickens into living egg machines is wrong. The moral notion that gives voice to this intuition is "integrity." Integrity goes beyond considerations of an animal's health and welfare, and it applies not only to present but also to future animals. An animal's integrity is violated when through human intervention it is no longer whole or intact, if its species-specific balance is changed, or if it no longer has the capacity to sustain itself in an environment suitable to its species. However, when the intervention is directed toward the animal's own good, we do not speak of a violation of its integrity.

One of the main appeals of the use of integrity seems to be its objective, biological aspect. As we have shown, however, integrity is not as objective a notion as it appears at first sight. Should we therefore do away with the concept of animal integrity? Not necessarily, or rather, necessarily not. The concept has been introduced to fill a gap between moral theory and moral experience. It is important to do justice to this moral experience, and not to reject the concept too swiftly because of difficulties in setting out precisely what it involves. In the light of ongoing technological developments we are confronted ever more frequently with moral dilemmas that traditional moral concepts cannot deal with, and we have a responsibility to try to refine our moral thinking and to develop criteria that help us act in a morally justifiable way.

So let's take a closer look at the problems with the concept of integrity. We argued that the purpose of potential violation of integrity is crucial for judging whether or not the action actually constitutes a violation of integrity. When we dock a dog's tail, for example, our reason for docking it is decisive in deciding whether the dog's integrity has been violated. The concept of integrity thus does not refer to an objective state of affairs, but to one that *we* feel is important to preserve.

Yet we need not regard the concept as completely subjective, either. While it does not refer to empirically ascertainable biological facts, we can still establish intersubjective criteria for its application. Through moral discussion, we can reach agreement about which sorts of actions do and do not lead to violations of integrity. And even if we could not reach this agreement, the notion of integrity still has an important function, namely to clarify the moral debate and criticize existing practices. Integrity can give opponents of Rollin's thought experiment a way to voice their criticism of the creation of living egg machines without having to appeal to traditional moral concepts like welfare, interests, or rights, none of which seem to capture what is important in Rollin's scenario. "Integrity" should therefore remain a part of our moral discussion. Its content can be continually refined through an ongoing learning process.

References

1   B.E. Rollin, *The Frankenstein Syndrome: Ethical and Social Issues in the Genetic Engineering of Animals* (New York: Cambridge University Press, 1995).
2   G. Comstock, *What Obligations Have Scientists to Transgenic Animals?*, discussion paper by the Center for Biotechnology, Policy and Ethics, 8, College Station, Tex.: Texas A&M University, 1992.
3   In this article we will limit ourselves to a discussion of the former. F.W.A. Brom, J.M.G. Vorstenbosch, and E. Schroten, "Public Policy and Transgenic Animals: Case-by-Case Assessment as a Moral Learning Process," in *The Social Management of Genetic Engineering*, ed. P. Wheale, R. von Schomberg, and P. Glasner (Aldershot: Asgate, 1998), 249–64.
4   Other welfarists, such as Nils Holtug, object to changing animals into senseless machines by arguing that attention to welfare should not be limited to the prevention of suffering, but should also be directed

to the promotion of positive experiences. By making animals senseless we would deny animals the possibility to enjoy positive experiences. See N. Holtug, "Is Welfare All that Matters in our Moral Obligations to Animals?" *Acta Agriculturae Scandinavica* Sect. A, Animal Science Supplement 27 (1996): 16–21. However, welfarists need to invoke an extra premise, not reducible to mere sentience, to explain why positive experiences matter to the animal. See F.W.A. Brom, "Animal Welfare, Public Policy and Ethics," in *Animal Consciousness and Animal Ethics: Perspectives from the Netherlands*, ed. M. Dol *et al.* (Assen: Van Gorcum, 1997), 208–22.

5   T. Regan, *The Case for Animal Rights* (London: Routledge and Kegan Paul, 1983).

6   To be a "subject-of-a-life" is to "have beliefs and desires; perception, memory, and a sense of the future, including their own future; an emotional life together with feelings of pleasure and pain; preference and welfare-interests; the ability to initiate action in pursuit of their desires and goals; a psychophysical identity over time; and an individual welfare in the sense that their experiential life fares well or ill for them, independently of their utility to others." See Regan, *The Case for Animal Rights*, 243.

7   L.J.E. Rutgers, F.J. Grommers, and J.M. Wijsmuller, "Welzijn-Intrinsieke waarde-Integriteit," *in Tijdschrift voor Diergeneeskunde* (1995): 490–4; and L.J.E. Rutgers and F.R. Heeger "Inherent Worth and Respect for Animal Integrity," in *Recognizing the Intrinsic Value of Animals: Beyond Animal Welfare*, ed. M. Dol *et al.* (Assen: Van Gorcum, 1999).

8   F.W.A. Brom, "Animal Welfare," and F.W.A. Brom, "The Good Life of Creatures with Dignity," *Journal for Agricultural and Environmental Ethics* 13, nos. 1–2 (2000): 53–63.

9   We intentionally do not use the terms "benefits" and "advantages" because they imply a utilitarian framework, whereas our discussion depends on a deontological one.

10 J.M.G. Vorstenbosch, "The Concept of Integrity: Its Significance for the Ethical Discussion on Biotechnology and Animals," *Livestock Production Science* 36 (1993): 109–12.

11 T.L. Beauchamp and J.F. Childress, *Principles of Biomedical Ethics*, 4th ed. (New York: Oxford University Press, 1994), 128.

12 On the other hand, as integrity is not an absolute notion, it might well be that it is a violation that is justified, because the appeal to integrity is in this case overruled by an appeal to autonomy. However, we doubt that transsexuals even experience their bodies' integrity as being violated by the sex change.

13 A. Leopold, *A Sand County Almanac* (Oxford: Oxford University Press, 1949), 224–5.

14 J. Kay (1992), quoted in J. Lemons, "Ecological Integrity and National Parks," in *Perspectives on Ecological Integrity*, ed. L. Westra and J. Lemons (Dordrecht: Kluwer Academic Publishers, 1995).

15 Lemons, "Ecological Integrity," 180.

16 L. Westra, "Ecosystem Integrity and Sustainability: The Foundational Value of the Wild," in *Perspectives on Ecological Integrity*, ed. L. Westra and J. Lemons (Dotdrecht: Kluwer Academic Publishers, 1995), 12.

17 Lemons, "Ecological Integrity."

18 Lemons, "Ecological Integrity."

19 This is the case with fire-prone and fire-resistant trees, such as gum trees in Australia, that need fire in order to regenerate. Moreover, if regular burning is not conducted in some Australian forests, a fuel buildup on the forest floor will lead to unintended raging bush fires. See on this subject A.M. Gill, R.H. Groves, and I.R. Noble, eds.; *Fire and the Australian Biota* (Canberra: Australian Academy of Science, 1981).

20 Beauchamp and Childress, *Principles of Biomedical Ethics*.

53

R.G. Frey

"Organs for Transplant: Animals, Moral Standing, and One View of the Ethics of Xenotransplantation"

Frey believes that on issues of pain and suffering, moral standing is a category of being rather than a continuous measure. In contrast, on issues of killing, moral standing is a matter of degree rather than a category of being. When one focuses on issues of killing, xenotransplantation can be justified only by making a case that any and all humans have inherent worth that is greater than the inherent value of any animals on which xenotransplantation might be conducted. Frey believes it would be very difficult to build a persuasive case on this.

Introduction

We commonly use animals as means to certain of our ends. We eat them, use them as experimental subjects, treat them as objects to be observed in zoos, keep them to while away the hours or to forestall loneliness, and so on. It should come as no surprise, therefore, that a case is increasingly being made in the medical research community and among the educated lay public for regarding animals as repositories of organs for transplant into humans. Indeed, this use of animals as spare parts for our bodily renewal will doubtless seem to many a perfectly justified use of them, since the prolongation of human life and the enhancement of its quality will strike many as straightforwardly worthy ends.

[. . .]

Moral concerns

[. . .] I think the fundamental question that serious people want to ask morally about xenotransplantation is whether this use of animals in order to save and/or enhance humans' lives is justified, *whatever the species* of animal used and *however close* in many respects that species may be to our own. That is, I take the fundamental question to be one that does not turn upon species at all but rather upon what we think justifies us in using animals to save or enhance human lives in the first place. To be sure, there may be further moral worries if primates are used for spare parts, but the central moral worry is surely about what justifies us in harvesting the organs of any animal to save or enhance a human life.

Put this way, the central moral worry about xenograft encompasses the lowly mouse, though at the moment more in the experimental and genetic engineering phases of 'designing' animals than in the harvesting phase. For those who frown upon xenograft, it is important that the mouse be covered; for rodents are main experimental and engineered animals, and without the work done in them it is easily imaginable that the stage of actually designing animals to be spare parts will be impeded to some degree or other. Such experimentation can certainly appear necessary for us to reach the stage where we can breed animals 'designed' to have body parts that can be used by the human body, quite apart from any importance that we might attach to testing immunosuppressant drugs in such animals.

All justifications of xenograft that I am familiar with appeal to the enormous benefits for human health that harvesting animal organs can potentially confer. Let us accept that there are these enormous potential benefits so far as the saving and enhancing of human lives is concerned: if xenograft fails with respect to a wide array of organs for practical or empirical reasons, such benefits will not come to pass, and we need not resort to any ethical reasons for urging the discontinuance of the practice. The central moral issue then becomes whether, in order to obtain these significant benefits for human beings, we may breed, 'design', and use animals as spare parts.

This central moral issue is quickly joined. For it is obvious that we could produce the very same benefits that are supposed to justify xenograft through harvesting human organs, and the success rate we have in transplanting organs from human to human can make this seem a path more certain of success than xenograft. Morality is thought, however, to get in the way. While it would be agreed on all sides that to breed and 'design' human beings to make good the shortfall in organs for transplant is morally impermissible, presumably, if saving and/or enhancing human life is to justify xenograft, then to breed and 'design' animals for this purpose is not morally impermissible. What, then, is the moral difference between the two cases?

[. . .]

I am aware that all kinds of differences can be appealed to, in order to try to forge a moral difference between the human and animal cases, and I have in a number of places discussed many of these (Frey, 1980, 1983, 1987a,b, 1988, 1989). Here, I want to consider again what I take to be the most radical difference one can cite in this regard, namely, the claim that humans but not animals are morally considerable, that humans but not animals possess moral standing or membership in the moral community. Put succinctly, it is morally permissible to do to animals what it is morally impermissible to do to humans because animals do not count morally. They lack moral standing or moral status. (I use these notions interchangeably hereafter.)

[. . .]

What might be called the usual or standard way of treating moral status has been to link it to the possession of a characteristic that one takes to be a moral-bearing characteristic. If something possesses this characteristic, then it has moral status.

[. . .]

Bentham's famous link of the capacity to suffer to moral status is of this sort: it is a sufficient condition for the possession of moral standing. It does not follow that beings or things which lack this capacity lack moral status, since they may possess it in virtue of some other characteristic that is regarded as a moral-bearing one; it follows only that having the capacity suffices to confer moral standing on a being or thing. Because so much of the discussion of animal issues following Bentham has made use of his focus on pain and suffering, his view of the moral status of animals has come to be very influential in recent 'animal rights' debates. So far as it goes, I think it correct. But it is by no means the end of the matter. Nor, in other contexts, does it block our using animals to certain of our ends. Just which contexts these are figure below.

What is it about animals that does not count morally? The two obvious candidates that might fill this role are their pains and sufferings and their lives. As for the former, I think something along the Benthamite line is correct. Pain is pain, an evil for any being that can experience it, and certainly the 'higher' animals can experience it. (I am not concerned here with those who deny that the 'higher' animals can feel pain, very much now a minority view, or with those who claim that animals can experience pain but not in a morally significant sense, an even more uncommonly held view. Different arguments address these positions.) Once this is conceded, as I think it must be, the development of the Benthamite line follows a predictable course.

[. . .]

With pain and suffering, this conclusion seems to me to be the truth of the matter. Feel pain, and one has moral standing; feel pain, and one has full-fledged moral standing, as much as any other being that feels pain. There is no matter of degree here: if pain is an evil, and if it is an evil irrespective of who feels it, then the pains of dogs and men are on a par. Thus, in contexts in which pain and suffering are very much to the fore, I see no difference between the moral standing of animals and humans. The pains of both count and count equally. They count because pain is a moral-bearing characteristic for us; they count equally because who feels the pain is irrelevant. Thus, there is nothing speciesist about the position, nothing that inherently discriminates in favour of humans. Of course, strength and intensity of pain enter the picture, but these do not differentiate between dogs and humans.

The value of life

When we turn to the value of lives, however, matters do not appear in a similar light. Here, the vast majority of us think that human life is more valuable than animal life, and I have tried in a number of other places to show why we are right to think this (1993, 1995). One implication of my way of showing this is that, in contexts in which the value of lives is to the fore, and this includes all contexts of killing, moral status is a matter of degree.

[. . .]

I see no reason to give an account of the value of animal life any different from that which I take to govern the value of human life, namely, that the value of a life is bound up with its quality.

[. . .]

I accept that animals—certainly, the 'higher' animals—have subjective experiences, that those experiences determine their quality of life, and that the quality of their lives determines the value of those lives. This is exactly what I accept in the human case. With animals, we use behaviour and behavioural studies to give us access to their inner lives, and what is rough and ready in all this we can come to use with more confidence as empirical studies of animals yield more information about them. Perhaps I can never know exactly what it is like to be a baboon, but I can come to know more and more in this regard, as we learn more about them and their responses to their environment.

Now most of us do not think that animal life is as valuable as human life, and it is plain that a quality of life view of the value of a life can explain why. The richness of normal adult human life vastly exceeds that of animals: our capacities for enrichment, in all their variety, extent, and depth vastly exceed anything that we associate with dogs or even chimps. That dogs have a more acute sense of hearing than we do does not make up for this difference in the variety, extent, and depth of capacities; for that to happen we should have to think that the dog's more acute hearing confers on its life a quality that approximates the quality that all of our capacities for enrichment, along multi-dimensions that appear unavailable to the dog, confer on our lives.

The theses of life

Now I do not need to go further here into a discussion of richness of content to make the point that, quite apart from the question of whether pain and suffering are moral-bearing characteristics for us, animals are members of the moral community because they are experiential creatures with a welfare or well-being that can be affected by what we do to them. But they do not have the same moral standing as normal adult humans, since the value of these human lives far exceeds anything that we associate with the lives of animals. The truth is that not all creatures who have moral standing have the same moral standing. Alas, however, this truth applies to the differences between human lives as well as to the differences between normal adult human life and animal life.

Two theses I draw out of this discussion of how lives have value flow readily out of quality of life views of the value of a life. [. . .] These two theses I call the *greater value thesis* and the *equal value thesis*.

According to the greater value thesis, normal adult human life is more valuable than animal life and for non-speciesist reasons. I have argued for the non-speciesist view that, since value is a function of richness and richness of the capacity or scope for enrichment, then normal adult human life is more valuable than animal life because of the extent, variety, and depth of our capacities for enrichment. [. . .] It will be obvious, however, that this outcome accounts for the greater value of normal adult human life over animal life but not in any way that represents a barrier to the lives of some animals having greater value than the lives of some humans. We are all familiar with tragic human lives, lives whose quality has fallen to such an extent that even those living those lives no longer wish to do so; hence, the increasing attraction of physician-assisted suicide. This leads to the equal value thesis.

According to the equal value thesis, all human lives have the same value. I think that this thesis is plainly false and that the truth of the greater value thesis shows why. There are some human lives of such an appalling quality that no one would wish to live them, and where, in the past, religion maintained that all human lives were equal in value in the eyes of God, such a line rings very much more hollow today, as those who live such lives seek release from them. It seems bizarre in the extreme to insist that, though all of us know there are human lives that no one would pick to live, those lives are as valuable as normal adult human life.

[. . .]

In my view, then, the greater value thesis is true, and for non-speciesist reasons, but the equal value thesis is false. The conjunction of the two leads straightforwardly to the possibility of using humans as we use animals. If we need to perform experiments on retinas in order to enhance human health, and if we still must use living models in order to do so, then we morally must use beings of a lower quality of life to beings of a higher quality of life. Normal adult humans will have a higher quality of life than rabbits, but anencephalic infants, the brain dead, or those in a permanently vegetative state, etc., will not. If a living model has to be used, what then is the case for still using the rabbit? So far as I can see, what we need is something that always ensures, in each and every case without exception, that a human life of any quality whatever, however low, is more valuable than an animal life of any quality whatever, however high. I have dealt in several places with attempts to provide humans with this magical ingredient, from appeals to religion and culture to outright appeals to partiality and affinity; all I have found argumentatively unconvincing (Frey, 1980, 1983, 1987a,b, 1988, 1989, 1996).

[. . .]

The point I want to stress is that, in contexts in which the value of a life is to the fore, moral status is a matter of degree. Some lives have more moral status than others. Normal adult human life, with a very high quality, has moral status in the highest degree. As human lives begin to fall in quality, however, their value and moral status begin to fall; when these lives fall to a disastrously low quality as, for example, in the case of the brain dead or anencephalic infants, their moral status has reached a very low ebb indeed. In fact, on a quality of life view of the value of a life, some lives can fall to a quality so low as to bring into question their continued value at all.

[. . .]

By emphasizing pain and suffering and conferring moral standing through these, utilitarians invite opponents by way of response to focus upon, say, some treatment of animals that does not involve the infliction of pain and suffering or upon a magical ingredient that could dispel any pain or suffering that animals might feel. If the objection to what is being done is the pain and suffering inflicted, what is being done will no longer be objectionable on that score. Then, if what is done is to be objected to, some other ground must be found for the objection. *This* kind of focus, however, does not really get at what seems a deeper problem here. For what one *wants* to make the object of moral concern here is not so much whether what one is doing to animals involves the infliction of pain and suffering, however powerful the case may be for the view that these are moral-bearing characteristics for us, but rather how what we are doing to animals involves using up valuable lives. Even if their lives are not of equal value to normal adult human life, their lives have some value; using up their lives involves the destruction of these things of value, and this remains true even if we had the power completely to eliminate any infliction of pain or suffering. Put differently, using up valuable lives requires justification, and justification is not provided merely through observing that what we did to the animals in question did not involve pain and suffering.

Suppose, then, the argument from benefit now reasserts itself: what justifies using up animal lives in the course of what we do to them, including using them as spare parts, is human benefit. The argument from benefit, however, does not tell us which lives to use up; it needs to be supplemented. The point of my earlier discussion of the greater value and equal value theses should now be apparent: using a quality of life account of the value of life, whereby we find the former thesis to be true but the latter one to be false, it turns out that lives of higher quality have greater value than lives of lower quality and that taking a life of higher quality in preference to a life of lower quality is worse. *This* line of argument thus tells us *which* lives to use up, assuming we have to use up some lives in the first place, in order to realize the human benefits in question. We should use lives of lower rather than higher quality. Typically, lives of lower quality will be animal lives, but we simply cannot guarantee that we shall find this always to be true; in some cases, it seems quite clear that healthy animals will have a higher quality of life than some unfortunate humans. Then, the argument demands that these human lives be used up to produce the benefits in question, if, that is, any lives have to be used up at all, in order to produce the benefits.

Xenotransplantation

Xenotransplantation would appear to fit this argument line exactly. That is, the argument will certainly justify, *if* we employ the argument from benefit, using some animals as spare parts; but it will also justify using some humans, e.g. anencephalic infants, as spare parts. There is nothing strange or peculiar in it so justifying this. For if we can save a life, we save the life of greater value to the life of lesser value; thus, it would be very odd indeed to save a person who was going to die anyway *in preference* to a person who was not going so to die or to save the life of a person in the final agonizing moments of senile dementia *in preference* to the life of a healthy person. The taking of life is simply the reverse of this: we take the life of lesser value in preference to the life of greater value. Most of the time, this will involve us in taking animal lives over human lives; but there will be times when this is not the case, times when there are humans whose lives fall below the quality of lives of the animals involved. Thus, xenotransplantation, to be justified at all, must involve us in using lives of lower rather than higher quality, and I know of nothing whatever that ensures always, in each and every case, that animal lives turn out to be of lower quality than human lives.

While nothing demands that one rely upon the argument from benefit in order to justify xenotransplantation, I have never found any attempt to justify it that did not. Thus, if one appeals to this argument in order to justify xenotransplantation, and if one uses quality of life views of the value of a life, views which are very widespread today, then there are going to be cases in which using certain humans in preference to animals will be indicated. Almost certainly, we will not use these humans. Thus, it will be interesting in the extreme to examine what is cited in order to ensure that all human beings, including those in permanently vegetative states, have a higher quality of life than any animal. Without this, the argument from benefit will only justify xenotransplantation if one is prepared to use humans of a very low quality of life in preference to animals of a higher quality of life; since it is most unlikely that we would ever agree to use these humans, I conclude that the case for anti-vivisectionism is far stronger than is usually believed by those who, like myself, favour continued use of, say, non-primates in medical research. Where killing is concerned, then, the case for using animals to save or enhance human lives is, I believe, harder to make out than is usually thought, by those who appeal to human benefit, who rely upon quality of life views of the value of a life, and who seek to deny animals moral status.

If I am right so far, then I think we can now see the step that defenders of xenotransplantation who rely upon the argument from benefit are going to have to take, a step, it is clear, that places them at odds with what both they and others may well want to maintain in other important cases in medical ethics. For it seems almost required, in order to block the case for using certain humans, that defenders of xenograft give up quality of life views of the value of a life. If the value of human life can be traced to some other source, then perhaps one can argue that a human life, no matter what its condition, no matter how poor its quality, no matter how strongly the human living that life desires to be relieved of it, is always more valuable than an animal life.

[. . .]

What the defender of xenotransplantation requires, then, is an equivalent of what used to be established by appeal to religion behind the Judaic–Christian ethic. As I indicated earlier, one might try in this regard to distinguish the value of a human life from, say, its inherent worth. It might be maintained that, while human lives of different quality may have different value, absolutely all human lives, whatever their quality and so their value, have the same inherent worth. Notice that even if we were to accept some such distinction, it would not, in and of itself, give the defender of xenotransplantation what is desired. For if the lives of animals had inherent worth, then we might be forced to choose between the levels of inherent worth of human and animal lives, in order to decide which creatures' organs to use in a particular case.

So, if defenders of xenotransplantation are going to use talk of the inherent worth of human lives to block arguments that might expose some unfortunate humans to being used in medicine in the way we use animals, then they seem likely to have to maintain either that animal lives have no inherent worth or that the inherent worth of human lives is always greater than the inherent worth of animal lives (irrespective of quality in both cases). But why should we think either of these things? Why should we think that some living things have inherent worth and other living things do not? Indeed, why should we think that *only* living things have inherent worth? Why could not a volcano have such worth? And the claim that human lives have more inherent worth than animal lives seems self-serving, in order both to answer the problem of using humans instead of animals in certain cases of transplant and to make sure that our lives are, as it were, always and inevitably beyond compare with the animal case. These assumptions look too convenient for the human case, even if we were to concede, what seems to me to be highly problematic, that we actually knew what inherent worth was and could state the criteria in terms of which we identified its presence. All criteria I have come across in this regard, such as our exhibiting wonder and awe, fail miserably to suit; for these are things many of us exhibit not only in the case of volcanoes and other parts of nature but also in the case of cars, computers and other human artefacts.

There is, moreover, a further problem with using some distinction between the value and inherent worth of a life, in order to block the kind of argument I have been concerned with above. Suppose for the sake of argument that: (i) we allow that we can make sense of what is meant by the inherent worth of a life; (ii) we know what the criteria are by which to recognize the inherent worth of lives; and (iii) we do not contest the claim that human lives of absolutely abysmal quality are of equal inherent worth with the lives of normal adult humans: nothing whatever about the distinction shows that moral status is to be allied with the inherent worth as opposed to the value of a human life. This, I think, is a crucial point; for if the defender of xenotransplantation hopes to use animals but not humans as sources of organs in part through arguing that all animals lack but all humans have moral status, then it is by no means clear that this is shown by arguing that all humans have inherent moral worth. Nothing as yet ties moral status to inherent worth as opposed to value of the life lived. And it is far from clear that anything *will* tie moral status to inherent worth, since, if the lives of animals have inherent worth (even if less inherent worth than the lives of humans) but the defender of xenotransplantation argues that they lack moral status, then clearly moral status is not turning upon the possession of inherent worth.

With this the case, however, the defender of xenotransplantation seems required to argue that the lives of animals lack inherent worth. But now the criteria for identifying the presence of inherent worth in a being or thing become crucial: what are the criteria for having inherent worth, such that the brain dead, those in a permanently vegetative state, anencephalic infants, those in the very final stages of senile dementia, etc. have it but that all healthy animals with a high quality of life lack it? What could confer inherent worth on an anencephalic infant but not a healthy dog? The mere human appearance? The mere bodily shell? Very far down *this* road, I suspect, and we shall encounter something like earlier religious stories that invest the human body with special religious significance.

Finally, on quality of life views of the value of a life, the content of a life determines the value of it, and most people today concede not only that the content of human lives can vary but also that it can vary massively in a negative and tragic direction. Such lives turn out to be less valuable than normal adult human life, and lives of less value have, in the way indicated, less moral standing. To be sure, one can move to block this kind of account by insisting, through, say, some distinction between the value and inherent worth of a life, that the moral standing a creature has is tied to that creature's inherent worth, not the value of its life. But now another puzzle arises: the value of a life is determined by its content, by the experiences the life contains; unless inherent worth is to reduce to the same thing, it must be determined by something other than the content of the life and be such that a human life, even if devoid of content altogether (or all but the barest content), nevertheless has such worth. What could this worth consist in? In the absence of some story of a religious kind, what could make it the case that a human life of disastrously low quality, a quality so low that we would not wish that life on anyone and would move heaven and earth to avoid such a life for ourselves and our loved ones, had equal inherent worth with the lives of normal adult humans? If we concede that the value of the lives are different, but hold that the inherent worth of them is the same, what could this inherent worth consist in? In the earlier stories, these different lives were equal in that they were equal in the eyes of God; in what way are they equal apart from this sense? The puzzle is this: if moral standing turns upon the value of a being's life, and the value of that life turns upon its quality, and if its quality turns upon the richness of content of the life, then moral standing is going to turn out to be a matter of degree. What degree will be determined by the content of the life actually being lived, and this content will reflect the differences in capacities and scope for enrichment present in different lives in question. This view makes the moral standing and value of a life turn upon the actual content of the life as lived, not upon some metaphysical abstraction that is devoid of any connection with the content of the life lived. It seems odd in the extreme to proffer an account of the value of a life that has nothing to do with the actualities of that life as lived, and that is exactly what some claim of inherent worth would appear to do.

Conclusion

In sum, in contexts in which pain and suffering are to the fore, moral standing is a matter of kind and not of degree; in contexts in which killing is to the fore, moral standing is a matter of degree and not of kind. By focusing upon pain and suffering exclusively, as so many contemporary discussions of animal issues do, including those by utilitarians, we can over-look claims about the value of the lives that the practice of xenotransplantation uses up. Once we focus upon this question of the value of the lives involved, however, we see that xenotransplantation can be justified but only at a human cost, a cost that most people will be unprepared to pay, and to proceed further without moral justification is unthinkable for morally serious people.

References

Frey, R. (1980) *Interests and Rights: The Case Against Animals*, Clarendon Press, Oxford.
—— (1983) *Rights, Killing, and Suffering*, Blackwell, Oxford.
—— (1987a) Autonomy and the Value of Animal Life. *The Monist*, 70, 50–66.
—— (1987b) The Significance of Agency and Marginal Cases. *Philosophica*, 39, 39–46.
—— (1988) Moral Standing, the Value of Lives, and Speciesism, in *Between the Species*, 4, pp. 191–201.
—— (1989) Vivisection, Morals and Medicine, in *Animal Rights and Human Obligations* (eds T. Regan and P. Singer), Prentice-Hall, Englewood Cliffs, NJ, pp. 223–36.
—— (1993) The Ethics of the Search for Benefits: Animal Experimentation in Medicine, in *Principles of Health Care Ethics* (ed. R. Gillon), John Wiley, New York.
—— (1995) The Ethics of Using Animals for Human Benefit, in *Issues in Agricultural Bioethics* (eds T.B. Mepham, G.A. Tucker and J. Wiseman), University of Nottingham Press, Nottingham, pp. 335–44.
—— (1996) Medicine, Animal Experimentation, and The Moral Problem of Unfortunate Humans, *Social Philosophy and Policy*, 13, 181–210.

54

Gary L. Francione

"Xenografts and Animal Rights"

Francione recognizes that under a utilitarian approach, the benefits gained from some xenografts might justify their use. However, he argues that when it is recognized that animals have
rights to exist not contingent on their providing benefit to humans, it becomes evident
that xenografts are morally unjustifiable. Consequences are irrelevant where fundamental
rights are involved.

Introduction

There are many ethical issues raised by xenografts (cross-species transplantations). In this
article I will briefly discuss just one of these ethical issues: the moral status of the use of
nonhuman animals involved in xenografts. In at least one sense, the fact that the animal use
occurs in the context of a xenograft is irrelevant. That is, if one accepts that human animals
may always (or almost always) use nonhumans to serve human purposes, then it should
make no significant difference whether the use is for the purpose of a xenograft, or some
other purpose, such as drug testing or food consumption. Conversely, if one rejects any (or
almost any) exploitation of nonhuman animals, then the purpose of the exploitation will
probably not matter.

In another sense, however, xenografts crystallize the basic moral issue in a rather
dramatic way. To the extent that a xenograft is successful, or will be successful in at least
some cases, one can arguably trace a direct benefit that results from the exploitation of
the nonhuman animal. This ostensibly tangible benefit distinguishes the xenograft from at
least some other instances of vivisection where any benefit is likely to be far more attenu-
ated. Whenever there is an arguably "direct" benefit from vivisection, the character of the
debate seems to change, and some people who would normally oppose animal
exploitation will "balance" in favor of what is perceived to be the human interest. It
would seem, then, that there would be strong moral arguments in favor of at least some
xenografts if the ostensible benefit to humans is weighed only against the harm to
animals.

It is clear that the efforts to perfect xenografts will intensify. But it is also clear that these
efforts will meet with more resistance from what is referred to loosely as the "animal rights"
community. There are at least three reasons why this resistance will intensify. First, more and
more people are rejecting the "balancing" approach as an appropriate way to resolve moral
issues. Second, the concept of animal *rights* is becoming increasingly accepted as the morally
appropriate alternative to the balancing approach. Third, as a general matter, various

groups, including but not limited to the animal rights movement, have begun to question the "objectivity" of science, and see science as a political activity. The remainder of this article will present a (brief) exploration of these three factors.

Balancing interests

Although some early thinkers did ascribe rights to nonhumans, the animal "rights" movement was, until recently, really an animal "welfare" movement. That is, most people, including those very actively involved in trying to ameliorate conditions for animals, accepted that animals could be exploited by humans in various ways, but that humans had an obligation to ensure that animals were not used in trivial ways and that they were treated as well as possible given the particular type of use involved. It was our responsibility to balance human interests and animal interests.

This welfare approach is reflected in virtually all current and proposed legislation concerning animals. For example, consider the changes to the Canadian Criminal Code recently proposed by the Law Reform Commission of Canada. The proposed law criminalizes any *unnecessary* injury or pain inflicted on an animal, and, in the case of research, defines "unnecessary" pain or injury as that "disproportionate to the benefit expected from such research." Whether experimentation meets the proportionality test will, for all purposes, be determined by the research community which, in all but the most extreme cases, will defer to the individual vivisector. In essence, the proportionality test merely restates, and does not explain, the necessity requirement. Far from representing a progressive approach, the proposed law merely codifies a standard that most people—even those who use animals in experiments—would accept as tautologically true—that animals ought not be subjected to unnecessary pain or injury. The proposed law strikes the balance dramatically in favor of human interests and accepts that animals may be used in experiments, as long as there is some benefit expected from the use.

The problem with this type of approach is apparent: As long as those who do the balancing regard virtually any "benefit" to justify animal use, there will be no effective regulation of animal research. Although every person would agree that animals ought not to be used for "trivial" purposes, there are myriad instances of animal use that must be regarded as morally unjustifiable whatever understanding of "trivial" is employed. Nevertheless, the experimenters who performed those experiments would hardly characterize their work as "trivial" and, in most cases, neither did the people who performed the peer review for those experiments.

People do the balancing and until recently, most people have accepted that *species* is a morally relevant criterion to determine membership in the moral community. That is, animal interests have been underestimated systematically in this balancing process because of species discrimination, which is no different from discrimination based on race or sex. This species discrimination, or speciesism, as it is commonly referred to, has resulted in the justification of barbaric cruelty to animals.

But even if we were to be more conscientious about our balancing approach, this method of approaching moral issues would still be inadequate. The reason for this inadequacy is that balancing alone virtually never provides a satisfactory answer. For example, assume that virtually all xenografts would point to the ostensible consequences of improved human health to justify the practice. Those who disfavor xenografts would point to the negative consequences to the nonhuman animals. Although both sides accepted a balancing framework, there would be no agreement on the ultimate issue because an appeal to consequences can never work unless there is some sort of agreement on the valuation of those consequences.

Rights

Despite our resort to the balancing approach to resolve issues about the exploitation of animals, many of us do not use this same approach to resolve other moral issues. For example, very few people are willing to balance interests where the issue is using unwilling humans as donors of organs or as experimental subjects.

This reluctance has to do with the fact that we are unwilling to balance where fundamental rights are involved. That is, most of us believe that human beings possess certain rights. Sometimes the character or extent of these rights will be determined by a balancing process. For example, I may live in a society that grants me a right to medical care, but the scope of that right may be determined by balancing my right against other uses of resources. But there are some rights where such a balancing would not be permitted. For example, I suspect that few would accept as morally justifiable the enslavement of other human beings even if it could be demonstrated that marvelous consequences would ensue for all free people. A right acts as a sort of barrier between the rightholder and everyone else. If I have a right to be free, then, as a general matter, the fact that it will benefit you if I am enslaved is irrelevant.

Until recently, the dispute between those who use animals and those opposed to such use has centered on different concepts of "necessity"—one group would balance in a manner different from another group but both would balance and accept the legitimacy of a balancing approach. Indeed, even the position articulated by Peter Singer must be characterized as a balancing approach. Singer argued that species is not a morally relevant criterion for determining membership in the moral community and that equivalent human and animal interest ought to be accorded the same weight in the balancing process. Although Singer's approach would rule out a great deal of animal exploitation, it does not represent a rights approach (for people or animals).

The theoretical playing field changed dramatically in 1983 with the publication of Tom Regan's theory of animal rights. Regan argued persuasively that some animals have at least some of the same rights that humans have, and Regan explicitly rejects all forms of balancing. Although Regan's arguments are complex, and deserve to be read in their entirety, the thrust of his approach may be characterized as a recognition that animals have some of the same characteristics that lead us to grant rights to humans. In failing to extend the relevant rights to nonhumans, Regan argues, we are merely engaging in species discrimination. Regan's work is now beginning to have a dramatic impact on popular thought, and the concept of animal rights—as opposed to animal welfare—is beginning to take hold.

It is clear that once we accept the concept of animal rights, it no longer is open to us to ask whether the "sacrifice" of a baboon to help Baby Fae is morally justifiable. The baboon is not something that exists for the benefit of Baby Fae any more than Baby Fae exists for the benefit of the baboon. The balancing question becomes irrelevant.

The "objectivity" of science

The third reason for the increased opposition to xenografts (and other forms of vivisection) is that science no longer enjoys a position as epistemologically superior to other forms of knowledge. Despite the seductive simplicity of the traditional empiricist point of view—that science represents "objective" truth, the assumptions supporting this traditional view have been challenged effectively in recent years. Philosophers and sociologists of science have argued persuasively that factual assertions are completely contingent on theoretical assumptions, and that observation itself is subject to interpretation. In addition, the problems that scientists choose to solve are often dictated by political concerns.

This recognition is slowly eroding the pedestal upon which science has presided for many years. More and more people in the animal rights movement, the environmental movement, and the alternative health care movement recognize that science is as value-based as any other activity. Indeed, there is increasing criticism of the fundamental premises of Western medicine.

It is clear that the exploitation of animals in science, whether for xenografts or other purposes, raises ethical issues in addition to any technical issues. Scientists are no better able to cope with the vital ethical issues than are the rest of us.

Conclusion

Once we accept that animals have rights, the framework of our discussion of the morality of xenografts must change. That is not to say that a balancing approach would sanction xenografts. On the contrary, the current level of medical technology and resource allocation is such that a very good argument could be made that at least some xenografts are morally unjustifiable for many reasons. But what if we could be substantially certain that a particular xenograft will work? We would then be faced with a much more difficult decision under a balancing approach. Indeed, under such a set of circumstances, the benefits to be gained would be unlike the supposed benefits that occur in the context of basic research. That is, the prospect of a successful xenograft raises very difficult questions for the consequential moral theorist who balances interests.

But if instead we accept a rights approach (i.e., that a baboon is an individual with a right to exist not contingent on his/her providing a benefit to humans) then it is far less difficult to see why the xenograft is morally unjustifiable. Consequences are irrelevant where fundamental rights are involved.

Cloning of Endangered Species

55

Oliver A. Ryder

"Cloning Advances and Challenges for Conservation"

Ryder points out that recent successes in cloning animals raise the possibility that cloning technology can assist with the management of endangered species. He acknowledges that the reduced fitness of some cloned animals is still problematic, but believes this technique can contribute to conservation efforts. He calls for increased research, targeted application of the technology, and an expanded effort to bank cells to allow for the future success of cloning technology.

> Although controversy surrounds cloning efforts, the cloning of animals to assist efforts to preserve genetic variation in support of endangered species conservation efforts has attracted serious interest. A recent report by Loi *et al.* describing the cloning of a mouflon (a species of wild sheep) in a domestic sheep surrogate points to potential conservation opportunities and additional challenges in the evaluation of appropriate technologies for present and future efforts to conserve gene pools of endangered species.
>
> Published online: 10 April 2002

Each major report about cloning involving somatic nuclei brings new insights and new debates. As the controversy around human cloning expands [1,2] there is a diversity of opinion regarding the potential of cloning for the conservation of endangered species [3–5]. It is important to evaluate separately the issues surrounding human cloning and those of animal cloning.

With respect to predictions for loss of species, technologies for assisted reproduction, such as artificial insemination, embryo transfer and cloning from somatic cells, have been advocated as technologies that could contribute to conservation of biological diversity [6].

Successful cloning of an endangered sheep

Discussion of the application of cloning technology to conservation efforts for endangered species [3] was an immediate result from Ian Wilmut's 1997 report of the cloning of Dolly [7]. Although reports of embryo development [8,9] and newborn animals have appeared as a result of cloning technology, the recent report of surprising success in cloning mouflon (a species of wild sheep) [10] is notable for several reasons. The success rate was much greater than when the domestic sheep, Dolly, was cloned. A higher proportion of embryos (constructed by nuclear transfer to enucleated domestic sheep ova) developed *in vitro* to blastocysts and, subsequently, to pregnancies and live birth in surrogate dams than previously reported [7,11]. It is also noteworthy that the donor nuclei were obtained from dead donor mouflon. These rather unexpected findings might serve as the basis for additional studies to help identify factors contributing to the rate of success. Studies of telomere length were not reported and future work in this area will be of interest.

From a theoretical perspective, there is reason to believe that cloning can assist in the preservation of genetic diversity in precariously small populations. The cloned animals, as individuals, might serve as conduits for the retention of genetic variation otherwise lost. There are many vulnerable and endangered forms of sheep (including forms of argali, urial, desert bighorn and Marco Polo and snow sheep) for which this technology could be considered in defined programs of gene pool preservation.

Objections to the use of cloning technology for conservation focus on inefficiencies of the current process, impracticalities involved in applying these techniques to non-domestic ova donors and surrogate dams, and the lack of fitness for survival of cloned animals in the natural environment. Fitness concerns are heightened owing to the use of domestic surrogates that fail to impart appropriate behavioral attributes for cloned offspring that will interact with others of their species raised by conspecific mothers (i.e. mothers of the same species).

Defects in cloned animals

Abnormal morphology and lack of developmental success in cloned mice is associated with abnormal regulation of imprinted genes [12]. Thus, imprinted genes in successfully (and unsuccessfully) cloned animals have been investigated in detail [13]. As the specific loci subject to imprinting have been modified in the course of mammalian evolution [14,15], further studies of the evolution of imprinting and imprinted genes in mammals might also provide useful insights. Active management of deprogramming differentiated nuclei and epigenetic effects is an area of active investigation that might eventually increase the fitness of cloned animals.

As discussions of the fitness of clones continue, the question is not so much whether Dolly has arthritis as whether her descendants have a reduction in their fitness associated with the deprogramming of her genome that facilitated her development from the nucleus of a differentiated cell. Also, apparently normal cattle have resulted from cloning [16]. The over-arching concern for the genetic continuity of a species rather than for the fitness of a single individual is a crucial difference between application of cloning technologies to endangered animals in comparison to humans.

Cloning as a tool for assisting in conservation of gene pools

When considering the potential role of cloning to help the conservation of endangered species, a crucial point is whether cloning represents a functional technology suitable to the management of gene pools. The changes in gene pools of vulnerable populations becoming endangered will limit viability of some populations with grave prospects for recovery. The potential to modulate loss of genetic variation in small populations undergoing sexual reproduction by incorporating genetic variation from unrelated individuals or individuals of known genotype or phenotype from preserved cell nuclei offers a form of intervention previously unimaginable in the animal breeding or conservation breeding context. Although we would prefer to envision that, if intervention is required, some limited form of management will be sufficient to ensure the viability of populations in protected areas and, indeed, all suitable habitats, we can by no means say that this is assured.

Allelic diversity is lost owing to drift and, in small populations, the persistence of rare alleles becomes vulnerable to chance events. Practical intervention will probably consist of managing retention of genetic variation, including heritable attributes that are most likely yet to be identified. Deleterious loci might need to be detected and their frequencies managed in the population. Haplotype diversity might also be desirable to manage, and evidence for selection for some haplotypes might become apparent as a result of population studies.

Alteration in allele frequencies that could accumulate over generations as a result of differential selection and drift in a captive environment might be mitigated if founder and early generation individuals could be used for breeding to provide individuals for reintroduction and augmentation programs.

Cell banking and research should top the current agenda

We are probably not at the stage where cloning technology is ready to be applied to maintain population viability or conserve species for which the technology is available and, in any case, cloning is no panacea. However, in the struggle to maintain self-sustaining populations cloning might have a future role more significant than present technology suggests. Looking to the future, there will probably be instances in which cloning technology can make a crucial difference for some species. Although it might be decades from now that answers become clear, it is apparent that access to declining levels of genetic diversity is more readily available now than in the future. Additional research should be welcomed and evaluated in the context of conservation.

Anticipation of potential benefits to be derived from the strategic use of cloning technology will require a broad understanding of its limitations in the context of specific conservation goals. For which species might cloning technology be considered? Where might the most significant benefit be derived from initial efforts? Surely, cells that might be later used for a variety of purposes, including cloning, should be collected as opportunity allows—for many species in peril this needs to be done sooner rather than later. We will not be able to explore the potential of cloning without additional studies, which could be focused on development of a strategic tool for conservation management of small populations. Such studies will require access to cells that have been previously banked from species for which loss of genetic variation is considered to be detrimental to the maintenance of a self-sustaining population. There are few sources of such cells because, with a few exceptions, banking cells from small populations of endangered animals has not been undertaken. These exceptional collections offer much in the way of resources that might be used in evaluating the circumstances in which cloning technology might offer practical conservation benefits. Delaying such experimentation will forestall the collection of information crucial to the evaluation of cloning technology for targeted management of small populations for conservation.

Planning for the future

Certainly, a concerted effort involving collaborations of field biologists familiar with the status of threatened and endangered species with reproductive scientists, geneticists and others with expertise and resource banking should be undertaken to match conservation and technological opportunities. Identification of the taxa at risk and the systematic collection of samples as opportunities arise, consistent with the conservation management of threatened and endangered species, offer increased opportunities for preventing extinction and for the preservation of gene pools.

In the future, even if efforts to establish banks of cells from endangered species are viewed as a needlessly pessimistic strategy, these cell banks will be of great use for a variety of biological studies that will increase the understanding of the natural world and its evolution. It has been suggested that an abrogating effect of the effort to bank cells is the establishment of unrealistic and unattainable programs for effective conservation and insufficient diligence to ensure preservation of sufficient natural habitat for conservation of biodiversity. However, an effort in genetic resource banking for endangered species serves the interests of future generations irrespective of the application of cloning technology. Furthermore, cell-banking efforts are not envisaged as efforts *in lieu* of *in situ* conservation but as supporting efficiencies and informed decision making capabilities that assist *in situ* conservation efforts.

Summary

The successful cloning of a mouflon from cells of an animal found dead in the field again raises the possibility that cloning technology can assist with the management of endangered species. Although the fitness of cloned animals remains a subject of controversy, the potential of cloned individuals to contribute to the retention of genetic variation in small populations provides an opportunity for this technology to contribute to conservation efforts. Increased research, targeted application of the technology and an expanded effort to bank cells are indispensable before this technology will make a significant impact on small population management for conservation.

References

1   Jaenisch, R. and Wilmut, I. (2001) Developmental biology – Don't clone humans. *Science* 291, 2552
2   Solter, D. (2000) Mammalian cloning: Advances and limitations. *Nat. Rev. Genet.* 1, 199–207
3   Ryder, O.A. and Benirschke, K. (1997) The potential use of 'Cloning' in the conservation effort. *Zoo Biology* 16, 295–300
4   Loskutoff, N.M. Role of embryo technologies in genetic management and conservation of wildlife. *Symposium on Reproduction and Integrated Conservation Science*. Zoological Society of London. (In press)
5   Critser, J.K. *et al.* Application of nuclear transfer technology to wildlife species. *Symposium on Reproduction and Integrated Conservation Science*. Zoological Society of London. (In press)
6   Lanza, R.P. *et al.* (2000) Cloning Noah's ark. *Sci. Am.* 283, 84–9
7   Wilmut, I. *et al.* (1997) Viable offspring derived from fetal and adult mammalian cells. *Nature* 385, 810–13
8   White, K.L. *et al.* (1999) Establishment of pregnancy after the transfer of nuclear transfer embryos produced from the fusion of argali (*Ovis ammon*) nuclei into domestic sheep (*Ovis aries*) enucleated oocytes. *Cloning* 1, 47–54
9   Chen, D.Y. *et al.* (1999) The giant panda (*Ailuropoda melanoleuca*) somatic nucleus can dedifferentiate

in rabbit ooplasm and support early development of the reconstructed egg. *Science in China Series C-Life Sciences* 42, 346–53

10   Loi, P. *et al.* (2001) Genetic rescue of an endangered mammal by cross-species nuclear transfer using post-mortem somatic cells. *Nat. Biotechnol.* 19, 962–4

11   Galli, C. *et al.* (1999). Mammalian leukocytes contain all the genetic information necessary for the development of a new individual. *Cloning* 1, 161–70

12   Rideout, W.M. *et al.* (2001) Nuclear cloning and epigenetic reprogramming of the genome. *Science* 293, 1093–8

13   Humpherys, D. *et al.* (2001) Epigenetic instability in ES cells and cloned mice. *Science* 293, 95–7

14   Killiam, J.K. (2001a) Monotresse IGF2 expression and ancestral origin of genomic imprinting. *J. Exp. Zool.* 291, 205–12

15   Killam, J.K. (2001b) Divergent evolution in M6P/IGFZR imprinting from the Jurassic to the Quaternary. *Hom. Mol. Genet.* 10, 1721–8

16   Lanza, R.P. *et al.* (2001) Cloned cattle can be healthy and normal. *Science* 294, 1893–4

Annotated Further Reading

Anonymous (1997) "Ethical Aspects of Cloning Techniques." (No. 9) (28 May 1997) http://europa.eu.int/comm/secretariat_general/sgc/ethics/oldversion/en/biotec12.htm

—— (2002) "Xenotransplantation: Promising Advances Cause Excitement, Uneasiness." *American Journal of Veterinary Research* 63(5): 630.

Balls, M. (2001) "Animal Procedures Remain Vital to Biomedical Research: It ain't Necessarily so . . . (Editorial)." *Alternatives to Laboratory Animals* 29: 385–8.

Canadian Council on Animal Care (CCAC) (1997) "CCAC Guidelines: on Transgenic Animals." Online at http://www.ccac.ca/english/gdlines/transgen/transgel.htm

Donnelley, S., McCarthy, C.R., and Singleton, R. (eds). (1994) "The Brave New World of Animal Biotechnology." *Hastings Center Report* 24(1) (Special Supplement) 31 pp.

European Commission Group of Advisers on the Ethical Implications of Biotechnology (1996) "Opinion of the Group of Advisers on the Ethical Implications of Biotechnology to the European Commission." *Ethical Aspects of Genetic Modification of Animals* (No. 7) (21 May 1996) 5 pp. Online at http://europa.eu.int/comm/secretariat-general/sgc/ethics/oldversion/en/biotec10.htm

Fox, M.W. (1999) *Beyond Evolution: the Genetically Altered Future of Plants, Animals, the Earth . . . and Humans.* New York: Lyons Press, 256 pp. Fox urges an approach that treats animal, plant, and human life with more compassion.

Holland, A. and Johnson, A. (eds) (1998) *Animal Biotechnology and Ethics.* London: Chapman and Hall. Excellent anthology covering scientific procedures, social context, ethical, and conceptual issues as well as policy and regulation.

Kaiser, J. (2002) "Cloned Pigs May Help Overcome Rejection." *Science* 295: 25–7.

Kochelkoren, P. and Linskens, M. (1997) "Intrinsic Value of Plants and Animals: from Philosophy to Implementation." In: *The Future of DNA*, Dordrecht: Kluwer Academic Publishers. Discusses the 1997 Dutch legislation on biotechnology on animals.

Loi, P., Barboni, B., and Ptak, G. (2002) "Cloning Advances and Challenges for Conservation." *Trends in Biotechnology* 20(6): 233.

Maclean, N. (ed.) (1994) *Animals with Novel Genes.* Cambridge: Cambridge University Press. Examines actual and potential contributions and ethical concerns related to transgenic animals.

Munro, L. (2001) "Future animals: Environmental and Animal Welfare Perspectives on the Genetic Engineering of Animals." *Cambridge Quarterly of Healthcare Ethics* 10: 314–24.

Rogers, C.P. (2001) "Solution or Stumbling Block: Biological Engineering and the Modern Extinction Crisis." *Georgia Journal of International and Comparative Law* 30(1): 141–63. Scientists could establish a genetic library of endangered species that could later be cloned.

Rollin, B.E. (1995) *The Frankenstein Syndrome: Ethical and Social Issues in the Genetic Engineering of Enimals.* Cambridge, U.K.: Cambridge University Press.

Sagoff, M. (2001) "Genetic Engineering and the Concept of the Natural." *Philosophy and Public Policy Quarterly* 21(2/3): 2–10. Emphasis on plants. The food industry in its advertising conspicuously appeals to the image of nature and insists that all its products are natural. This has made it difficult for the industry to embrace, as it wishes, the efficiencies of genetic engineering.

Senior, K. (2001) "What Next after the First Transgenic Monkey?" *Lancet* 357: 450.

Thompson, P.B. (1997) "Ethics and Genetic Engineering of Food Animals." *Journal of Agricultural and Environmental Ethics* 10: 1–23. Addresses Rollin, Regan, Verhoog, and others, with attention to *telos*.

Thompson, P.B. (1998) "Biotechnology Policy: Four Ethical Problems and Three Political Solutions." In: *Animal Biotechnology and Ethics*, A. Holland and A. Johnson (eds), London: Chapman and Hall.

Tsien, J.Z. (2000) "Building a Brainier Mouse." *Scientific American* 279(4): 62–8. A study working with a particular molecule involved in memory formation.

U.S. Food and Drug Administration. Center for Biologics Evaluation and Research. (1995) Online at http://www.fda.gov/cber/ptc/ptc-tga.txt. Points to consider the manufacture and testing of therapeutic products for human use derived from transgenic animals.

Verhoog, H. (1996) "Genetic Modification of Animals: Should Science and Ethics be Integrated?" *The Monist* 79: 247–63.

Verhoog, H. (1998) "Morality and the 'Naturalness' of Transgenic Animals." *Animal Issues* 2(2): 1–16. We must not lose the qualitative aspects of nature.

Ward, K. (1995) "Transgenic Farm Animals and Enhanced Productivity." Chapter 3, pp. 39–48. In: *Animal Genetic Engineering: of Pigs, Oncomice and Men*, P. Wheale and R. McNally (eds). London: Pluto Press.

Wheale, P., and McNally, Ruth (eds). (1995) *Animal Genetic Engineering: of Pigs, Oncomice and Men*. London: Pluto Press. 293 pp. Conference papers by scientists, civil servants, biotech entrepreneurs, animal welfare advocates, and science philosophers address numerous issues.

Weidensaul, S. (2002) "Raising the Dead." *Audubon* 94: 58–66. Summarizes attempt to recreate a live Tasmanian wolf by cloning.

Study Questions

1   Do you agree with Bruce and Bruce's call for more public involvement in oversight of genetic engineering? If so, how might greater involvement be achieved?

2   Do you believe that increased knowledge of genetic engineering will inevitably lead to increased human genetic manipulation? Justify your response.

3   What is your view on developing genetically engineered animal strains with a *telos* that would make them well adapted to the conditions associated with intensive farming and production?

4   What is your response to Frey's assertion that moral standing is a category of being rather than a continuous measure? Justify your position.

5   Explain why you agree or disagree with Francione's assertion that xenografts are never justifiable.

6   What role do you believe is appropriate for cloning technology in the management of endangered species?

7   In light of Burkhardt's discussion, do you agree that ethical preparation is lacking in scientific education? If so, what approach do you propose for best incorporating ethical training into science education? If not, give your reasons.

Part VII

Ethics and Wildlife

Introduction

In this Part, the authors focus on issues affecting the human relationship to wildlife. J. Baird Callicott first assesses the variety of fashions in which humans value wildlife. He compares instrumental values, in which wildlife is used to fulfill human wants and needs, such as subsistence and economic values, with inherent values, in which wildlife is valued for their own sake. Callicott further assesses the effectiveness of ascribing inherent value through utilitarian (animal liberation) philosophy, theocentric arguments, and ecocentric (biophilia) rationale. He advocates the ecocentric perspective.

Three authors assess moral issues related to the hunting of wild animals. Aldo Leopold provides a very brief summary of some of the intense experiences associated with hunting as well some of the ethical dilemmas he encountered as a young hunter. Marti Kheel challenges the morality of sport hunting and offers a number of thoughtful responses to the justifications given for hunting, including psychological, ecological, and spiritual benefits. Using feminist psychoanalytic theory, she offers a more deep-seated basis for the propensity of men to seek to kill animals as part of the hunting ritual. Alastair Gunn addresses the morality of hunting generally, and then delves more deeply into the issue of trophy hunting and its role in the economy and culture of poorer countries. Despite reservations that he and many feel about trophy hunting, he proposes that it ultimately may be an important strategy to protect the interests of both wildlife and people.

Many of the arguments addressed to these wildlife issues are themes traditionally associated with anthropocentric, individualistic (animal rights, animal liberation), or ecocentric thinking. Gary Varner challenges the notion that these perspectives always need to be incompatible by arguing that they can find common ground in an example such as the "therapeutic hunting" of species whose populations have exceeded the capacity of the land to support them. He addresses other areas in which common concerns might lead to establishing common ground among these philosophies.

Two authors address moral issues surrounding wildlife rehabilitation efforts. Gary Duke assesses wildlife rehabilitation and proposes at least four justifications for their continued efforts: humane treatment of animals, gaining experience applicable to less common and endangered species, allowing permanently injured wildlife to be used in place of healthy wildlife in zoos and education programs, and gaining better insights on the common biomedical problems encountered by wildlife under natural conditions. In contrast, Glenn Albrecht is more reserved about the general value of rehabilitation programs, and cautions that such programs are not successful without a careful evaluation of the availability and health of the habitats for release of these animals.

Ned Hettinger addresses the arguments surrounding introduction of exotic species to new habitats. He addresses different types and degrees of exotic species, discusses the notion of when a species is considered to be naturalized, and clarifies the arguments both of those offering a sympathetic view of exotic species and of those opposed. He also counters the argument that opposition to exotic species may be comparable to a xenophobic response to various cultural and ethnic groups among humans. Hettinger concludes by arguing that the loss of biological purity and the greater homogenization of the earth's biodiversity are compelling reasons to oppose introduction of exotic species.

General Theories

56

J. Baird Callicott

"The Philosophical Value of Wildlife"

Callicott distinguishes the notions of instrumental and inherent value as applied to wildlife and then explores the various philosophical foundations for ascribing inherent value to wildlife. He recognizes the contributions of utilitarian philosophy and theocentric sources of inherent value, but also finds these foundations outmoded and lacking in persuasiveness. Callicott goes on to affirm that Aldo Leopold's ecocentric perspectives best articulate ecologically informed understandings about wildlife, subordinating individual animals to the values of populations, species, and communities.

In "The Land Ethic" of *A Sand County Almanac*, Aldo Leopold wrote: "It is inconceivable to me that an ethical relation to land can exist without love, respect, and admiration for land, and a high regard for its value. By value, I of course mean something far broader than mere economic value; I mean value in the philosophical sense" (1966: 261).

[. . .]

Instrumental and intrinsic value

Philosophers like myself are not accustomed to dealing with value questions in these terms— economic versus philosophical value; rather, philosophers more often oppose instrumental and intrinsic value (Callicott 1986a). The instrumental value of something is its utility as a means to some end. The intrinsic value of something is its inherent worth as an end in itself.

Though nothing is universally accepted in philosophy, in the prevailing traditions of Western moral thought human beings or their states of consciousness (like pleasure or happiness or more recently "preference satisfaction") are generally agreed to be the intrinsically valuable things and everything else to be the instrumentally valuable things (Callicott 1984). [. . .] [W]e human beings have spiritual as well as material needs. And wildlife and nature generally have served as spiritual as well as material resources. Indeed, one major historical conflict in U.S. resource management may be understood as a conflict between the spiritual and material utility of natural resources (Nash 1973). Wild things may be fed, eaten, worn, made into implements, built with, and so on, and/or they may be listened to, watched, studied, worshipped, enjoyed, and so on. [. . .] But my point is that from the prevailing perspective of modern Western philosophy, wildlife and other natural resources remain only instrumentally valuable—whether as a means to satisfy the widest possible range of human spiritual needs or the most narrow range of human material needs.

Economic valuation, ideally conceived, is one clear way—though perhaps not the only or even the best way—to compare and adjudicate conflicts between the different utilities that wildlife and other natural resources represent (Daly 1980). [. . .] However, since real-world economics rarely takes into account the dollar value of the nonconsumptive/nonmaterial utilities of trees on the stump, birds on the wing, ungulates on the hoof, soil in conservancy (to say nothing of pollinators, decomposers, nitrogen fixers, and other members of nature's service industry), the nonmaterial utilities of wildlife and other natural resources are usually excluded by the term *economic value*.

[. . .]

In general, Leopold recommended a wholly unprecedented ethical relationship between people and land—a relationship between ends and ends, not ends and means. And more particularly, he mentioned in the same breath with philosophical value, love, respect, admiration, and high regard—attitudes we reserve for intrinsically valuable beings, not for instrumentally valuable things however noble and ethereal their uses. From the higher utilitarian point of view, we may be delighted by the song of a mockingbird, awed by the size and age of a redwood, arrested by the stoop of a Peregrine falcon, overcome by the sight of a grizzly bear, but we can only love and respect a being whose worth transcends the positive experiences it affords us and other human beings.

So by the philosophical value of wildlife, if we may take Aldo Leopold as our guide and inspiration, we should understand what philosophers themselves would more technically call *intrinsic* or *inherent value*. The burden of this chapter may thus be transposed into the following question: How may we ground or justify Leopold's ethical proposition that in addition to the full spectrum of instrumental values, spiritual as well as material, wildlife possesses intrinsic value?

The conceptual foundations of intrinsic value

Animal liberation

The most visible and vocal contemporary defense of the intrinsic value of wildlife has ironically evolved out of classic utilitarianism (Callicott 1980). According to Jeremy Bentham (1823), founding father of utilitarianism, pleasure is good and pain is evil; and an ethical person should attempt, in choosing courses of action, to maximize the one and minimize the other, no matter whose pain or pleasure may be involved.

[. . .]

This grounding of the intrinsic value of some nonhuman animals—sentient animals—is popularly known as animal liberation and has been recently and most notably espoused by Peter Singer (1975). I have been a resolute philosophical opponent of animal liberation as a serviceable environmental ethic because it provides for no discrimination between wild and domestic animals, or between overabundant and rare animals, or between native and exotic animals (Callicott 1980).

[. . .]

On a deeper level, animal liberation is concerned exclusively with the welfare of individual animals, so much so that should the welfare of individuals conflict with that of a population of them—as is often the case with cervids—animal liberation unhesitatingly gives uncompromising priority to the welfare of individuals, more holistic considerations be damned (Singer 1979).

Most disturbingly, a ruthlessly consistent deduction of the consequences of animal liberation would be a universal predator eradication program as a policy of wildlife management (Callicott 1986b)! Why? Because predators obviously inflict pain and death on their prey. If we should stop humans from hunting, as animal liberationists advocate, then by parity of reasoning, we should also stop other animals from hunting.

[. . .]

Death and often pain are at the heart of nature's economy. To the extent that animal liberation morally condemns pain and death, it is irreconcilably at odds with the ecological facts of wild life. Thus we shall have to look elsewhere for a theory of the intrinsic value of wildlife consistent with the ecological facts of wild life.

Theocentrism

One of wildlife's greatest champions, John Muir, stressed the spiritual utility of wild nature. [. . .] [His] argument for the intrinsic value of wildlife was primarily theological. According to the Bible, God created other forms of life as well as human life, and He declared them all to be "good" (May and Metzger 1966:2). More technically expressed, God created all life forms and either at that time or by a subsequent fiat conferred intrinsic value upon them. [. . .] In Muir's view this Biblical truth—if it is a truth—constitutes the grounds for "the rights of all the rest of the creation" (1916:98).

Muir's theological theory of the intrinsic value of wildlife provides a conceptual context more congenial to an ecologically informed program of wildlife conservation than does Singer's theory. Its intractably individualistic value orientation is the main problem with the animal liberation ethic, from the viewpoint of wildlife conservation (Callicott 1980). On the other hand, Genesis clearly implies that in His acts of creation God established and conferred value upon species primarily, whereas individual specimens are understood to come and go. Nor is there any overriding obligation placed upon us in Genesis or elsewhere in the Bible to try to prevent animals from experiencing pain (though gratuitous cruelty is proscribed). Hence, Muir's theory of the intrinsic value of wildlife is not in direct conflict (as Singer's is) with the more holistic value orientation of wildlife ecology and management.

The main problem with Muir's theocentric axiology is not that its practical implications are inconsistent with an ecologically informed program of wildlife conservation but that its theoretical premises are inconsistent with the scientific foundations of wildlife ecology and conservation. According to science, wildlife species were not created as we find them today; they evolved into their present form. Nature is regarded as autochthonous and autonomous. To the extent that we believe that science gives us a true understanding of nature, a theocentric grounding of the intrinsic value of wildlife simply rests upon false beliefs about the natural world. This deep theoretical inconsistency is rendered more acute and vitiating when we reflect that our appreciation and respect for wildlife are deepened the more science discloses about the origins and interactions of wild things.

[. . .]

Biophilia

Leopold accordingly grounds the intrinsic value of wild things in evolutionary and ecological biology. A theory of the intrinsic value of wildlife grounded exclusively in a scientific world view seems immediately implausible, however. According to the metaphysical foundations of modern science, the natural world, from atoms to galaxies—including the middle-sized organic world—is value free, value neutral. Values, from a general scientific point of view, are subjective: they originate in consciousness and are projected onto objects. If all consciousness were eradicated, there would be no value anywhere in nature; there would remain only brute facts (Callicott 1985).

Leopold appears to respect this objective-fact/subjective-value dichotomy of modern science (Callicott 1984, 1986). Values remain subjective, consciousness dependent in his land ethic. But [. . .] although the value of objective things depends upon some conscious subject valuing them, a conscious subject, at least a human conscious subject, can value them for themselves as well as for what they may do for him or her. Most people, for example, value their children and other loved ones in this way.

For human beings and other social animals, this other-oriented valuational capacity is a product of natural selection. In his second great work Darwin (1871) argued that what he called the "moral sentiments," following David Hume and Adam Smith, were naturally selected as a means to social integration and evolution. In short, social membership increases the inclusive fitness of the individuals of some species. But social membership is impossible without "limitations on freedom of action [in regard to proximate individuals of the same species] in the struggle for existence" (Leopold 1966:238). Among social mammals these requisite limitations have taken the form of other-oriented sentiments—love, respect, admiration, fellow-feeling, sympathy, and high regard. In the final analysis, intrinsic value—the value of something as an end in itself—is a philosophical abstraction from these primitive moral sentiments (Callicott 1985).

Since the moral sentiments and the philosophical value that is ultimately erected upon them originally evolved in conjunction with the evolution of mammalian societies, there is a close correlation among community, perceived social membership, and intrinsic value. In the past only our own clan or tribe and our fellow tribespeople were regarded as ends in themselves, and all other human beings and human groups were treated as mere means (Nash 1977). More recently, for many a sense of community has come to embrace all humankind (Nash 1977). Accordingly, modern humanism affirms the intrinsic value of all human beings regardless of race, creed, or national origin and of all humankind. Aldo Leopold observed that today ecology represents both human beings and wild things as members of [. . .] the biotic community (Leopold 1966:193). Because we now perceive wild creatures as belonging to this expanded ecological society, we are naturally impelled to extend to the biotic community itself and to wild things as members in good standing the same value—philosophical or intrinsic value—once more restrictively reserved for more narrowly defined classes.

In my opinion, therefore, Aldo Leopold's account of the philosophical value of wildlife is the most persuasive of the three alternatives reviewed here. It best articulates our ecologically informed intuitions about the transutilitarian value of wildlife. It subordinates the value of specimens to populations, species, and biocenoses. And it is based neither on an outmoded moral philosophy (utilitarianism) or on an outmoded theology (Judeo-Christian theism), but squarely on modern science.

References

Bentham, J. 1823. *An introduction to the principles of morals and legislation.* Vol. 1. W. Pickering, London. 381pp.

Callicott, J. B. 1980. Animal liberation: a triangular affair. *Environ. Ethics* 2(4):311–38.

—— 1984. Non-anthropocentric value theory and environmental ethics. *Am. Philos. Q.* 21(4):299–309.

—— 1985. Intrinsic value, quantum theory, and environmental ethics. *Environ. Ethics* 7(2):257–75.

—— 1986a. On the intrinsic value of non-human species. Pages 138–72 in B. Norton, ed. *The preservation of species.* Princeton Univ. Press, Princeton, N.J.

—— 1986b. The search for an environmental ethic. Pages 381–424 in T. Regan, ed. *Matters of life and death.* 2nd ed. Random House, New York.

Daly, H. 1980. *Economics, ecology, ethics.* W. H. Freeman and Co., San Francisco. 372pp.

Darwin, C. 1871. *The descent of man and selection in relation to sex*: 2nd ed. J. A. Hill and Co., New York. 314pp.

Leopold, A. 1966. *A sand county almanac.* Ballatine Books, New York. 226pp.

May, H. G., and G. M. Metzger, eds. 1966. Genesis. Pages 1–66 in *The holy bible: revised standard version containing the old and new testaments.* Oxford Univ. Press, New York.

Muir, J. 1916. *A thousand mile walk to the gulf.* Houghton-Mifflin and Co., New York, 220pp.

Nash, R. 1973. *Wilderness and the American mind.* Yale Univ. Press, New Haven, Conn. 300pp.

—— 1977. Do rocks have rights? *Cent. Mag.* 10(6):2–12.

Singer, P. 1975. *Animal liberation: a new ethics for our treatment of animals.* New York Rev., New York, 297pp.

—— 1979. Not for humans only. Pages 191–206 in K. E. Goodpaster and K. M. Sayer, eds. *Ethics and problems of the 21st century.* Univ. Notre Dame Press, Notre Dame, Indiana.

Hunting

57

Aldo Leopold

"Red Legs Kicking"

Leopold recounts one of his earliest experiences as a hunter, eloquently capturing the sense of wonder, delight, and ethical perspective in just a few short paragraphs.

When I call to mind my earliest impressions, I wonder whether the process ordinarily referred to as growing up is not actually a process of growing down; whether experience, so much touted among adults as the thing children lack, is not actually a progressive dilution of the essentials by the trivialities of living. This much at least is sure: my earliest impressions of wildlife and its pursuit retain a vivid sharpness of form, color, and atmosphere that half a century of professional wildlife experience has failed to obliterate or to improve upon.

Like most aspiring hunters, I was given, at an early age, a single-barreled shotgun and permission to hunt rabbits. One winter Saturday, *en route* to my favorite rabbit patch, I noticed that the lake, then covered with ice and snow, had developed a small 'airhole' at a point where a windmill discharged warm water from the shore. All ducks had long since departed southward, but I then and there formulated my first ornithological hypothesis: if there were a duck left in the region, he (or she) would inevitably, sooner or later, drop in at this airhole. I suppressed my appetite for rabbits (then no mean feat), sat down in the cold smartweeds on the frozen mud, and waited.

I waited all afternoon, growing colder with each passing crow, and with each rheumatic groan of the laboring windmill. Finally, at sunset, a lone black duck came out of the west, and without even a preliminary circling of the airhole, set his wings and pitched downward.

I cannot remember the shot; I remember only my unspeakable delight when my first duck hit the snowy ice with a thud and lay there, belly up, red legs kicking.

When my father gave me the shotgun, he said I might hunt partridges with it, but that I might not shoot them from trees. I was old enough, he said, to learn wing-shooting.

My dog was good at treeing partridge, and to forego a sure shot in the tree in favor of a hopeless one at the fleeing bird was my first exercise in ethical codes. Compared with a treed partridge, the devil and his seven kingdoms was a mild temptation.

At the end of my second season of featherless partridge-hunting I was walking, one day, through an aspen thicket when a big partridge rose with a roar at my left, and, towering over the aspens, crossed behind me, hell-bent for the nearest cedar swamp. It was a swinging shot of the sort the partridge-hunter dreams about, and the bird tumbled dead in a shower of feathers and golden leaves.

I could draw a map today of each clump of red bunchberry and each blue aster that adorned the mossy spot where he lay, my first partridge on the wing. I suspect my present affection for bunchberries and asters dates from that moment.

58

⸺ ❖ ⸺

Marti Kheel

"The Killing Game: An Ecofeminist Critique of Hunting"

Kheel addresses the morality of sport hunting and concludes that it lacks justification as a moral activity. She goes on to address the flaws she finds in the various justifications of hunting often cited, including the psychological, moral, and social benefits; ecological benefits; and spiritual benefits. Using feminist psychoanalytic theory, Kheel then proposes that the killing of animals allows the hunter to ritually enact the death of his longing for a return to a primordial female/animal world through death of the animal.

Hunting is an act of violence. And for some, it is a sport. Increasingly, these two facts present hunters with a major public relations problem. While at the turn of the century hunting was considered a praiseworthy activity, today 63 percent of the American public disapproves of hunting for recreation or sport (9).

[. . .]

Hunters have responded to the new public climate by taking refuge in a discourse designed to present what they do as morally laudable. Using a confused amalgam of arguments, they have represented hunting simultaneously as a cultural and spiritual asset, a biological drive, a management tool, and a return to the natural world.

[. . .]

A note about terminology is in order. A growing number of hunters eschew the word "sport hunting," claiming that they hunt for "ecological" or "spiritual" reasons, not merely for "sport." Although I make distinctions among types of hunters based on their self-professed motives for hunting, I hope to demonstrate that these differences are not as pronounced as many hunters would have us believe. Because, in addition, I challenge the validity of the very notion of hunting as a "sport," generally I use the term *hunting* without the qualifying word *sport*. My use of the word *hunter*, however, does not encompass subsistence hunters. Although I do not rule out the possibility that subsistence hunters share some of the characteristics of the hunters in this study, the more complicated nature of their motives places subsistence hunters beyond the scope of this article. This study examines those who hunt out of desire.

Is hunting a sport?

[. . .]

The distinction between sport and play is generally thought to reside in the greater complexity of sport. According to Thomas, "Sport has elements of play but goes beyond the characteristics of play in its rule structure, organization, and criteria for the evaluation of success" (29: p. 18). In addition, although sport is thought to have its basis in play, according to Thomas it has a second distinguishing feature, that is, its agonistic quality. Play, by contrast, is viewed as an inherently "co-operative interaction that has no explicit goal, no end point, and no winners" (11: p. 481).

Caillois (3: pp. 3–10) developed a framework listing six features common to play: (a) Its outcome is uncertain; (b) it is an activity that is freely engaged in; (c) it is unproductive; (d) it is regulated; (e) it takes place in a separate area; and (f) it is make-believe. Although these features are not universally agreed upon, they provide a helpful starting point for evaluating whether hunting conforms to common conceptions of play and sport.

The first of Caillois's features, the notion that play must not have a predetermined outcome, is inherent in the very nature of hunting as an activity. According to Cartmill, hunting is, by definition, "the deliberate, violent killing of unrestrained, wild animals" (4: p. 30).

[. . .]

The notion of competing with an animal, however, raises a moral problem. Because the animal has not consented to the competition, the game lacks symmetry of structure. [. . .] As Schmitz points out, hunting is more like a contest in which there is only one contestant (i.e., the hunter) (25: p. 30). The morality of a sport in which there is only one participant, however, is highly problematic. The animal's experience is obliterated, subsumed under the rules of a game that require the animal's death.

This relates to the second feature of play (i.e., that it is freely engaged in). Sport hunting is, by definition, an activity that is freely engaged in by hunters. The sport hunter typically is contrasted with the subsistence hunter, who hunts out of need, not out of "desire." [. . .] Yet, there is a major logical flaw in the notion of sport hunting as a voluntary activity, in that only one of the "participants" has chosen to compete.

[. . .]

The notion of hunting as a voluntary activity is also closely allied with the third of Caillois's features, that is, the notion of play as unproductive. Sport hunting, like play or sport in general, is an activity that is thought to be its own reward. Unlike work, it is not undertaken for any external reason.

[. . .]

Although this notion may accurately portray the attitude of many hunters (i.e., they may hunt more for the experience of pursuing the animal than for the moment of the kill), there is a moral problem entailed in the idea of pursuing the death of another living being for the opportunity it affords one to engage in an enjoyable experience.

Hunters frequently invoke the fourth of Caillois's features of play (i.e., that hunting has rules, to defend their "sport" from the charge of cruelty). Hunters, it is said, do not hunt indiscriminately: they conform to rules of good conduct (i.e., limitations on the number of animals killed, the season, and the weapons used). Such rules are said to give the animal a "fair chance." [. . .] [A]ccording to Leopold, the ethical value of hunting resides in the fact that hunters are bound not only to the laws about hunting but to their conscience as well (10: p. 212).

The fifth feature of play, that it takes place in a separate area, clearly applies to sport hunting. [. . .] [H]unting must occur outside and, traditionally, in an area that is considered "wild."

The last feature of Caillois's framework, the make-believe aspect of play, interestingly applies to hunting. For many hunters, sport hunting imaginatively recaptures a time when it is believed that men had to hunt for reasons of survival. In their attempt to lure their prey, hunters often describe an imaginary experience in which they feel as though they have become the animal they intend to kill.

[. . .]

The moral problem with the make-believe aspect of hunting is glaring, for the goal of the hunter's "game" is deadly serious. While hunters may play a "game" in which they imaginatively seek to understand another animal, this game has irrevocable consequences that extend beyond the world of make believe. The hunter does not pretend to kill the animal; the death of the animal is quite real.

Whereas the competitive, goal-oriented nature of hunting fits the notion of a sport, the nonvoluntary conscription of the animal into this "game" casts doubt on the validity of this idea. Both the willingness to "play" and the amusement derived from the activity are one sided. Although hunters may *experience* the activity of hunting as a sport, the skewed symmetry of the "game" renders this notion unintelligible. Hunters thus face a conceptual problem. On the one hand, hunting can exist as a sport only by conferring subjective identity on the animal. On the other hand, hunters can only pursue the death of an animal as playful activity by denying the animal's subjective experience and focusing exclusively on their own experience.

Most hunters ignore the question of the animal's subjective experience, defending their actions by reference to the purity of their own motives and desires, and, in particular, by presenting their *desire* to hunt as a *need*. Hunters have used several strategies to justify hunting, which I have categorized by means of a tripartite typology that distinguishes hunters according to the particular need they argue hunting fulfills: the "happy hunter" hunts for the purpose of enjoyment and pleasure, as well as character development (psychological need); the "holist hunter" hunts for the purpose of maintaining the balance of nature (ecological need); and the "holy hunter" hunts in order to attain a spiritual state (religious need). Whereas the happy hunter once gained status by calling hunting a sport, today's holist and holy hunters seek to distance themselves from the notion of sport. What unites the three types of hunters is their claim that hunting provides some redeeming social, moral, or personal value that is not just desirable but necessary.

The happy hunter: psychological need

The happy hunter is an unabashed sport hunter who freely admits to the pleasure that he derives from this "sport." Significantly, the animal is literally called "game." As one hunter proclaimed, "I hunt because it is something I like to do" (cited in 17: p. 20). Or, as another states, "The adrenalin flows. It's a good feeling" (cited in 17: p. 34). And, in Ernest Hemingway's inimitable words, "I think they (birds) were made to be shot and some of us were made to shoot them and if that is not so well, never say we did not tell you that we like it" (8: p. 152). In the United States, the conception of hunting as a pleasurable, recreational activity emerged in the middle of the nineteenth century in response to increased urbanization and leisure time. Like other forms of recreation, sport hunting was also thought to confer particular moral and social benefits. This notion of hunting as a beneficial activity stood in stark contrast to the ideas of the colonial period in New England, where hunting was considered a frivolous pastime of irresponsible young men, permissible only insofar as it was necessary for livelihood.

[. . .]

In the late 1800s, happy hunters helped to institutionalize "rules of fair play" in the form of laws designed to stop the decimation of wildlife by commercial and sport hunters. These laws, which included limitations on time, place, and type of weaponry, were seen as necessary not to preserve the animals in and of themselves, but rather to preserve their "sport."

The early conservationist hunters saw hunting as useful in building character, that is, male character. They argued that hunting was a necessary corrective for men who had become overly feminized by the encroaches of civilization. Theodore Roosevelt represents this view (22: p. 1236). [. . .] Messner explains this turn to competitive sports: "With no frontier to conquer, with physical strength becoming less relevant in work, and with urban boys being raised and taught by women, it was feared that males were becoming 'soft,' that society itself was becoming 'feminized' " (15: p. 14). Thus, sport hunting came to be seen as a necessary release for "man's" instinctual and aggressive drives. The point, however, was not for men to be reduced to the level of the animal world. By complying with the rules of "fair play," sport hunters felt they were able to express their "animal instincts," while also demonstrating their superiority to the animal world.

The notion that hunting is a psychologically beneficial release for man's aggression has persisted into this century. Aldo Leopold claimed that hunting is an instinctual urge, in contrast to golf (10: p. 227). [. . .] The value of hunting, for Leopold, resides in the exercise of this aggressive impulse as well as in its control. Leopold's concern is not the preservation of individual animals, but, rather, the "inalienable right" to hunt and kill them (p. 227). Leopold derives this right from a "fact" of nature, which modern hunting is intended to preserve, namely, the Darwinian notion of conflict or survival of the fittest. As Leopold states, "Physical combat between men and beasts was [once] an economic fact, now preserved as hunting and fishing for sport" (10: p. 269). According to Leopold, "An individual's instincts prompt him to compete for his place in the community, but his ethics prompt him also to cooperate (*perhaps in order that there may be a place to compete for*)" [emphasis added] (10: p. 239).

[. . .]

Happy hunters claim hunting provides a variety of additional psychological benefits. According to Leopold, it stimulates an awareness of history. That is, the hunter is "reenacting the romance of the fur trade." And it promotes a sense of "our dependency on the soil-plant-animal-man food chain, and of the fundamental organization of the biota" (10: p. 212). Another sportsman claims that hunting "renews the traditional kinship between men, wild things, and the land" (13: p. 71). All of these purported benefits have in common the claim that sport hunting helps men to become morally mature.

The holist hunter: ecological need

Whereas the happy hunter is unabashedly anthropocentric, extolling hunting for its psychological benefits for human beings (and in particular for men), the holist hunter claims more altruistic motives. Although hunting journals still openly extol the pleasures of the hunt, increasing numbers of hunters feel compelled to cite less self-serving reasons for hunting. Holist hunters claim that without their services, the animals they kill would die from starvation. Hence, they are performing a laudable ecological role.

Relinquishing the realm of recreation and pleasure, holist hunters have entered the world of business management and science. Using terms such as "population density," "sustainable yield," and the necessity of "culling" or "harvesting" the "excess" animals that would otherwise starve, holist hunters claim the title of "managers" for the biotic community. Their management partners in this undertaking are the federal and state fish and wildlife agencies, which manage both the animals and the hunters themselves. While hunters claim to be responding to nature's unfortunate excesses, the game management journals reveal another story. For example, according to an article in the *Journal of Wildlife Management*. "The primary management plan has been the one directed at increasing the productivity of the whitetail deer through habitat manipulation and harvest regulation . . . to produce optimum sustained deer yields . . . and hunter satisfaction" (16: p. 92). In short, holist hunters are intent on "managing" animals so that sufficient numbers will remain for them to kill.

For holist hunters, it is not the hunter who is the agent of death, but rather nature or ecology. The hunter is merely carrying out nature's inexorable directives, a participant in a "drama" not of his own making. The violence that hunting inflicts merely expresses the reality of violence in the natural world and thus is beyond ethical reproach. The holist hunter believes that not only should hunting not be shunned, but that it should be embraced.

Holist hunters, however, overlook the vast differences between human predation and natural predation. Whereas natural predators prey on the old, the weak, and the sick, human hunters typically select the biggest and healthiest animals to kill. As a consequence, hunters promote what Teale has called a kind of "evolution in reverse" (28: p. 161). Moreover, sport hunters overlook the extent to which their own actions have produced the problems that they claim to resolve. Sport hunters have pursued a deliberate policy of eliminating natural predators in numerous areas throughout the country, precisely so that they can claim the status of predators for themselves.

The alliance between hunting and the science of ecology has been a fortuitous partnership for modern hunters. Responding to a modern public that rejects the conjunction of pleasure and violence, happy hunters have found in the world of science and business a convenient refuge from attack. Armed with the claim that their mental state has been purified of the taint of pleasure, holist hunters contend that their motives are beyond rebuke. Although their official trade journals continue to enumerate the multiple pleasures to be found in the hunt, increasing numbers of happy hunters assume the camouflage of the holist hunt.

The holy hunter: spiritual need

For the holy hunter, hunting is not a means of recreation, nor is it a form of work. For the holy hunter, hunting is a religious or spiritual experience. As James Swan has stated, for many it is their religion (27: p. 35). Holy hunters contrast their spiritual attitude of reverence and respect with the crass and superficial mentality of the typical sportsman or happy hunter.

Although they too emphasize the notion of emotional self-restraint, they see it as a by-product of a transformed world view. Hunting is akin to a religious rite. In the words of Holmes Rolston, "Hunting is not *sport*: it is a *sacrament* of the fundamental, mandatory seeking and taking possession of value that characterizes an ecosystem and from which no culture ever escapes" (21: p. 91).

The spiritual nature of the hunt is thought to derive from a particular type of awareness, often described as a meditative state. As Richard Nelson states, "Hunting for me can be almost hypnotic. It's like a walking meditation" (18: p. 89). And for Ortega y Gassett, "The hunter is the alert man" who achieves a "universal attention, which does not inscribe itself on any point and tries to be on all points" (19: p. 91). [. . .] And according to Ortega y Gassett, hunting entails a "mystical union with the animal" (19: p. 124).

[. . .]

Like the holist hunters, holy hunters draw on the science of ecology not for a management policy, but for the spiritual lessons that it is thought to inspire. As Young explains, "What is religious about hunting is that it leads us to remember and accept the violent nature of our condition, that every animal that eats will in turn one day be eaten" (32: p. 139). Holy hunters claim a humble and submissive attitude, seeking not to conquer nature, but rather to "submit to ecology" (21: p. 92). Once again, desire and necessity are elided. Hunting is seen not as manifestly the desire to kill, but rather as an ecological necessity.

Holy hunters frequently draw on the spiritual traditions of native cultures to bolster the notion of the holy hunt. James Swan cites the "wisdom of native peoples" that claims that "under the right conditions, the success of the hunter is not just a reflection of skill but the choice of the animal" (27: p. 21). [. . .] The association of hunting with spirituality does, in fact, have a long history among subsistence hunters in native cultures. Some, but by no means all, of these cultures promoted the notion of saying a prayer before killing an animal, as well as the idea that the animal "gives" her or his life as a gift to the hunter. However, there are a number of ethical problems with invoking the traditions of native cultures.

First, the spiritual teachings of diverse native cultures cannot accurately be treated as a monolithic model from which to draw on for our own interactions with animals. Second, it is ethically questionable to extirpate a narrative from one cultural context and to graft it onto another. To the extent that native cultures hunted for subsistence reasons, their experience cannot be applied to a culture where this is no longer the case.

[. . .]

In place of the notion of an inherently aggressive drive that must be contained through adherence to a code of conduct, the holy hunter claims to restrain his aggression to the point of nonexistence at least within the holy hunter's mind. Holy hunters do not "kill" animals according to this world view: rather, animals "give" their lives. Nor do holy hunters perpetrate violence; instead they are passive participants in nature's cycles.

The hunt for psychosexual identity

It is time to ask if there are common underlying themes in all three categories of hunters. The association between hunting and masculine self-identity has been a recurring theme throughout history. Many cultures require a young boy to hunt and kill an animal as a symbolic rite of passage into manhood. Significantly, the young boy is frequently sequestered from the world of women as well. Although hunting is not an exclusively male activity, the vast majority of hunting has been performed by men.

[. . .]

The connection between hunting and masculinity is also commonly expressed in the notion that hunting provides an outlet for men's sexual energy. Thus, according to the holy hunter proponent Dudley Young, there is "an almost erotic connection between hunter and hunted," with the emotion-filled kill being analagous to "sexual ecstasy" (32: pp. 138, 134). And, for the holist environmental writer Holmes Rolston, hunting is viewed as a safety valve for sexual energy. In his words, "the sport hunt sublimates the drive for conquest, a drive without which humans could not have survived, without which we cannot be civilized." He concludes that "perhaps the hunting drive, like the sexual urge, is dangerous to suppress and must be reckoned with" (21: p. 91). For these writers, hunting is not simply a desire, but a biological need.

Hunting is also frequently conceptualized as having a narrative structure that resembles a sexual encounter. There is the initial build up of tension in the course of the chase, leading ultimately to the climax of the kill. Hunters can no more eliminate the kill from the narrative structure of the hunt than it would seem that many men can eliminate orgasm as the goal of sex.

[. . .]

Hunters, however, do not typically depict their sport as the crass expression of a sexual drive. More frequently, hunting is portrayed as an urge to achieve intimacy with nature and as the quintessential act of connection. The priest Theodore Vitali argues that "hunting is a direct participation in nature and has the potential of deepening the spiritual and moral bonds between human and subhuman communities" (30: p. 210). Vitali contrasts hunting with activities such as nature photography and hiking, which he considers "virtually voyeuristic" in that they "lack the intimacy with nature that hunting achieves" (p. 211).

[. . .]

The ingestion of the flesh of the conquered animal is also described by a number of writers as an erotic act. According to Shepard, whereas the "ecstatic consummation of love is killing," the "formal consummation is eating" (26: p. 173). Similarly. Nelson states that "I get a great deal of pleasure from knowing that my body is made in no small measure from deer. I am passionately in love with deer but I also kill them. I appreciate the fact that I am made out of the animal I love" (18: p. 92).

[. . .]

The analogy with sex is instructive, however. Sex is both a biological urge and a socially constructed activity. A man who rapes a woman cannot credibly defend his actions by saying he was simply following his "animal instincts." Nor can he claim that the rape provided a much needed outlet for his sexual energy, nor that it builds (male) character, nor that the rape was performed according to rules of good conduct. Rape is wrong because it is a violation of another living being. Significantly, the literature on rape argues that rapists are not motivated by the urge to fulfill a sexual drive, nor are they out of control. On the contrary, rape is designed to establish men's dominance and control (1). Similarly, hunting may be seen as a symbolie attempt to assert mastery and control over the natural world.

[. . .]

Feminist psychoanalytic theory has sought to explain men's greater propensity for violence. According to object relations theorists, the development of identity in boy children is established through a process of negative identification. Unlike girls, who are able to continue the initial, primary identification with the mother figure, boys must not only disidentify with the mother figure, but they must deny all that is female within themselves, as well as their involvement with the female world (5: p. 167). As a consequence, according to Chodorow, "girls emerge from this period with a basis for 'empathy' built into their primary definition of self in a way that boys do not" (p. 167).

Dorothy Dinnerstein extends this analysis to all of nature. As she argues, boys not only establish their identity in opposition to women, but to all of the natural world (6). Having established a second and alienated nature, it appears that men then face a lifelong urge to return to the original state of oneness that they left behind. The return to an original undifferentiated state, however, is precisely what must be avoided because such a return would constitute an annihilation of the masculine self.

The conflict between these two drives may shed light on the hunter's urge to achieve intimacy in death. The pursuit of the animal expresses the hunter's yearning to repossess his lost female and animal nature. The death of the animal ensures that this oneness with nature is not genuinely attained. Violence becomes the only way in which the hunter can experience this sense of oneness while asserting his masculine self-identity as an autonomous human being. By killing the animal, the hunter ritually enacts the death of his longing for a return to a primordial female/animal world.

Beyond the killing game: toward a life-giving play/sport

Psychologists and philosophers note that one of the functions of play is to facilitate the maturation process and the development of self-identity. Significantly, hunters claim this is characteristic of hunting. They argue that hunting helps humans (mostly men) to attain full status as human beings. Like play in general, hunting is thought to be particularly useful for young (male) children, aiding them to attain skills that will help them as adults. According to Shepard, the "play" activity of hunting prepares the young boy for future religious experience (26: p. 200).

Another function of children's games often discussed in the literature is their role in developing feelings of empathy for others. According to George Herbert Mead (14) and Jean Piaget (20), games provide children with a means by which to learn to take the role of the other and to come to see themselves through another's eyes.

Interesting differences appear at a young age between the play of boys and girls, which may shed light on men's propensity to hunt. Building on Piaget's studies on rules of the game. Lever found that boys tended to play far more competitively than girls and were more likely to play at structured games, which accorded importance to being proclaimed the winner (11: p. 479). By contrast, girls tended to "keep their play loosely structured [and played] until they [were] bored" (p. 479). Lever's study also found that girls' games were "mostly spontaneous, imaginative, and free of structure or rules. Turn-taking activities like jump rope may be played without setting explicit goals" (p. 481). In addition, "disputes are not likely to occur" and when they do, the game tends to be stopped (p. 479). Playing in smaller, more intimate groups, Lever found that girls' play tended to foster the development of empathy and sensitivity necessary for taking the role of "the particular other," and pointed toward knowing the other as different from the self.

Hunters claim that in the course of stalking their prey, they imaginatively enter into the life of the animal. But whereas hunters claim that this exercise in imagination helps them develop feelings of empathy for the animal, it is their inability to understand the experience of nonhuman animals that is a prerequisite of their hunt. As we have seen, hunters also emphasize the keen sense of alertness and attention that characterizes their state of mind. It is apparent, however, that if hunters were truly attending to nature, instead of to their own amorphous feelings of "love" and "connection," they would feel the terror and fright of the animal they seek to kill.

[. . .]

Ecofeminist philosophy recognizes a crucial distinction that hunters overlook: it is one thing to accept the reality and necessity of death, and quite another to deliberately kill a living being.

The notion of "attentive love," first used by Simone Weil (31), has been employed by a number of feminist philosophers as a central idea in the development of caring interactions toward others. For Weil, attentive love was a certain form of pure, receptive perceiving, as contrasted to egoistic perception, whereby one asks of the other, "What are you going through?" As Ruddick develops this idea, even the notion of empathy is not devoid of egoistic perception. As she explains, "The idea of empathy, as it is popularly understood, underestimates the importance of knowing another *without* finding yourself in her" (23: p. 121). By contrast, "attention lets difference emerge without searching for comforting commonalities, dwells upon the *other* and lets otherness be (23: p. 122).

The ability to achieve this form of attention entails a kind of playful leap of imagination into another's world. Maria Lugones develops this idea in her notion of an imaginative, playful world traveling, in which we can learn to "travel" into different worlds and realities, identifying with others so that "we can understand what it is to be them and what it is to be ourselves in their eyes" (12: p. 17). Sara Ebenreck has suggested that "awareness of imaginative activity may be especially important for environmental ethics, in which the guidelines for action have to do with response to others who are not human, for whom respectful attention may require of us the probing work of imaginative perception" (7: p. 5).

According to Burke, play is "an activity which is free, complete in itself, and artificial or unrealistic" (2: p. 38). As he elaborates, play's "true significance" lies in the fact that it develops our "creative, imaginative ability," enabling us to "live not only in the 'real' world but also in countless symbolic worlds of [our] own making" (2: p. 42). A problem arises, however, when living beings are forcibly conscripted into an artificial world to play the role of symbols themselves. All too often, women and animals have been relegated to the status of symbols, objects, or props for the construction of masculine self-identity. It is one thing to transcend the reality of the mundane world, and quite another to transcend the experience of other living beings.

Modern Western culture has achieved an unprecedented alienation from nature. For many, the urge to reconnect with nature is, in fact, experienced as a deep spiritual or psychological need. Killing is not the best way, however, to fulfill this need, and certainly not the most compassionate. The cooperative play of young girls would appear to provide a more mature and compassionate model for attaining intimacy with nature than hunting. The Council of All Beings workshops developed by John Seed and Joanna Macy (24) provide an example of a playful and imaginative connection with animals that conforms to the cooperative nature of girls' play. In these councils, participants are asked to imaginatively enter into the world of another species and to then bring their experience back to the group. People express profound feelings of empathy, grief, and rage when they realize the impact of deforestation, factory farming, and hunting on nonhuman animals. Through the expression and sharing of such feelings, people become motivated for a larger context of action.

The root of the word *sport* is "to leap joyously." Perhaps, through playful leaps of imagination such as these, we can learn to engage in a play/sport that affirms with love and compassion a genuine connection to all of life.

Bibliography

1   Brownmiller, Susan. *Against Our Will: Men, Women and Rape*. New York: Simon and Schuster, 1975.
2   Burke, Richard. "Work and Play." *Ethics*, 88 (1971), 33–47.
3   Caillois, Roger. *Man, Play, and Games*. Translated by Meyer Barash. New York: The Free Press of Glencoe, 1961.
4   Cartmill, Matt. *A View to a Death in the Morning: Hunting and Nature Through History*. Cambridge and London: Harvard University Press, 1993.
5   Chodorow, Nancy. *The Reproduction of Mothering*. Berkeley: University of California Press, 1978.
6   Dinnerstein, Dorothy. *The Mermaid and the Minotaur: Sexual Arrangements and Human Malaise*. New York: Harper, 1967.
7   Ebenreck, Sara. "Opening Pandora's Box: The Role of Imagination in Environmental Ethics." *Environmental Ethics*, 18:1 (1996), 3–18.
8   Hemingway, Ernest. "Remembering Shooting-Flying." *Esquire* (February 1935).
9   Kellert, Stephen. *The Value of Life: Biological Diversity and Human Society*. Washington, DC: Island Press, 1996.
10 Leopold, Aldo. *A Sand County Almanac: With Essays on Conservation from Round River*. Oxford: Oxford University Press, 1966.
11 Lever, Janet. "Sex Differences in the Complexity of Children's Play and Games." *American Sociological Review*, 43 (1978), 471–83.
12 Lugones, Maria. "Playfulness, 'World-Traveling' and Loving Perception." *Hypatia* 2 (1987), 3–19.
13 Madson, Chris. "State Wildlife Agencies and the Future of Hunting." *Second Annual Governor's Symposium*. Pierre, SD. August 24–6, (1993), pp. 64–71.
14 Mead, George Herbert. *Mind, Self, and Society*. Chicago: University of Chicago Press, 1934.
15 Messner, Michael A. *Power at Play: Sports and the Problem of Masculinity*. Boston: Beacon, 1992.
16 Mirarchi, Ralfe, Scanloni, Patrick, and Kirkpatrick, Roy L. "Annual Changes in Spermatozoan Production and Associated Organs of White-Tailed Deer." *Journal of Wild-life Management*, 41:1 (1977), 92–9.
17 Mitchell, John G. *The Hunt*. Harmondsworth, England: Penguin, 1981.
18 Nelson, Richard. "Life Ways of the Hunter." In *Talking on the Water: Conversations about Nature and Creativity*. Edited by Jonathan White. San Francisco: Sierra Club Books, 1994, pp. 79–97.
19 Ortega y Gasset, José. *Meditations on Hunting*. Translated by Howard B. Wescott, with a forward by Paul Shepard. New York: Scribner's, 1985.
20 Piaget, Jean. *The Moral Judgement of the Child*. New York: The Free Press, 1968.
21 Rolston, Holmes, III. *Environmental Ethics: Duties to and Values in the Natural World*. Philadelphia: Temple University Press, 1988.
22 Roosevelt, Theodore. "The Value of an Athletic Training." *Harper's Weekly* 37 (23 December, 1893), p. 1236.
23 Ruddick, Sara. *Maternal Thinking: Toward a Politics of Peace*. New York: Ballantine, 1989.
24 Seed, John, Macy, Joanna, Flemming, Pat, and Naess, Arne. *Thinking Like a Mountain: Toward a Council of All Beings*. Philadelphia: New Society Publishers, 1988.
25 Schmitz, Kenneth L. "Sport and Play: Suspension of the Ordinary." In *Sport and the Body: A Philosophical Symposium*. Edited by Ellen W. Gerber. Philadelphia: Lea & Febiger, 1972, pp. 25–32.
26 Shepard, Paul. *The Tender Carnivore and the Sacred Game*. New York: Scribner's, 1973.
27 Swan, James A. *In Defense of Hunting*. San Francisco: HarperCollins, 1995.
28 Teale, Edwin Way. *Wandering Through Winter*. New York: Dodd, Mead and Company, 1966.
29 Thomas, Carolyn E. *Sport in a Philosophic Context*. Philadelphia: Lea & Febiger, 1983.
30 Vitali, Theodore R. "The Dialectical Foundation of the Land Ethic." *Proceedings, Governor's Symposium on North America's Hunting Heritage*, Montana State University. Bozeman, July 16–18, (1992), pp. 203–14.
31 Weil, Simone. "Reflections on the Right Use of School Studies with a View to the Love of God." *Waiting for God*. Translated by E. Craufurd. New York: Harper, 1951.
32 Young, Dudley. *Origins of the Sacred: The Ecstasies of Love and War*. New York: St. Martin's Press, 1991.

59

Alastair S. Gunn

"Environmental Ethics and Trophy Hunting"

Gunn addresses the morality of hunting, including trophy hunting, in relation to animal death, animal suffering, hunting ethics, biodiversity and ecosystems, and human needs. Despite sharing with many sport hunters a distaste for trophy hunting, he argues that from broad-based economic and human survival values, trophy hunting is justified. Using Zimbabwe as a case study, he argues that trophy hunting successfully integrates both conservation and development and may be the only feasible strategy to protect the interests of both wildlife and people.

Introduction

The publication in 1980 of J. Baird Callicott's "Animal Liberation: A Triangular Affair" introduced the conflict for environmental management and policy between animal liberation and environmental ethics. Hunting provides a prime example of this still unresolved controversy.

I have found no published source that condemns hunting per se. There is a spectrum in the environmental literature. At one end is the view that hunting is justified only for self protection and for food, where no other reasonable alternative is available. Most writers also agree that hunting is sometimes justified in order to protect endangered species and threatened ecosystems where destructive species have been introduced or natural predators have been exterminated. Others accept hunting as part of cultural tradition or for the psychological well being of the hunter, sometimes extended to include recreational hunting when practiced according to "sporting" rules. Nowhere in the literature, so far as I am aware, is hunting for fun, for the enjoyment of killing, or for the acquisition of trophies defended. However, as I argue towards the end of this paper, trophy hunting is essential in parts of Africa for the survival of both people and wildlife.

Throughout this paper, I assume that animals have interests, and that we have an obligation to take some account of those interests: roughly, that we are entitled to kill animals only in order to promote or protect some nontrivial human interest and where no reasonable alternative strategy is available. This position is roughly that presented by Donald VanDeVeer (1979). Versions of it are widely defended in the literature, though there are different views about *which* human interests are sufficiently significant to justify killing. I restrict my discussion to cases where the interest in question cannot reasonably be achieved without killing animals.

[. . .]

Wildlife management: the conventional Western view

[. . .]

Anti-hunting organizations present a number of arguments against both hunting in general and specifically the hunting of marine mammals, elephants, large carnivores, great apes, rhinos, and other large ungulates. In this paper, I concentrate particularly on elephants.

Some common arguments against hunting include the following, each of which is discussed in more detail later.

- Hunting wrongfully deprives animals of something that is valuable to them—their lives (Regan 1983, Taylor 1996). Killing, and not merely successful stalking, is recognized by both supporters and opponents as a central feature of hunting. As Roger King (1991) notes, for proponents of hunting such as José Ortega y Gasset (1972) and Paul Shepherd (1973), the central meaning of hunting is killing, and killing is essential to "Participation in the life cycle of nature" (King 1991, 80). Ann Causey says, "The one element that stands out as truly essential to the authentic hunting experience is the kill" (Causey 1989, 332). Some ecofeminists believe that hunting is a prime example of patriarchal oppression of nature: in Mary Daly's terms, of a "necrophiliac" culture (Daly 1978).
- Hunting causes suffering. [. . .] A high proportion of land mammals and ducks are injured rather than being killed instantly; these "cripples" may suffer for days before either recovering or dying.
- Great apes, elephants, whales, and dolphins are special animals. They are highly intelligent; many species have developed elaborate social systems; they exhibit altruistic behavior toward each other and apparently suffer grief at the death of group members; members of some species including the great apes, orca, and some dolphins are sociable towards humans and are even recorded as having saved human lives; some (humpbacked whales) compose and perform music.
- Hunting is unworthy of civilized beings: "The hunter . . . as a "redneck," bloodthirsty villain storming the woods each fall with a massive arsenal . . . hunting [as] a disgusting sport that recalls and rehearses the worst in human behavior" (Vitali 1990, 69).
- Hunting is a threat to biodiversity. It threatens the existence of target species, many of which are already rare, threatened, or endangered. Sport hunting also degrades the gene pool of ungulate species because the most valued targets, dominant males, are the individuals "most fit to pass on the best genes" (Loftin 1984, 69).
- Hunting is not necessary for the fulfillment of important human interests; these interests can be satisfied by other means that do not require killing. Hunting is not economically necessary nor even particularly useful. There are substitutes for all marine and most land mammal products and because whaling, in particular, is probably not a sustainable industry, it cannot make a long-term contribution to the economy (Clark 1973).

Animal deaths

[. . .] The question for sport hunting advocates to address, if it is admitted that the life of an animal is valuable to it and that animals have an interest in continued life, is whether this interest may justly be overridden. The most obviously persuasive argument is that sustainable hunting kills only animals that would die anyway—or more precisely, since we don't know which animals will die from "natural causes," a proportion of the population will die each year, usually much more slowly and painfully through predation. starvation, or disease.

[. . .]

Animal suffering

It is inevitable that some animals that are hunted will suffer. [. . .] Where the target is animals whose numbers are widely agreed to be in need of control, supporters of hunting claim that it causes less suffering than alternative methods. Causey believes that "The genuine sport hunter, due to his earnest regard for his prey, is usually highly sensitive to the animal's pain and suffering, and makes every effort to minimize both. Proper weaponry and hunter training can minimize both" (Causey 1989, 335).

[. . .]

Special status of major target species

The mammals which Western environmentalists especially wish to protect from hunting, and trophy hunters especially wish to bag, are often referred to as "charismatic megafauna." Large land and marine mammals certainly have an appeal to many people, because of their sheer size and presence and in some cases because of special qualities they are said to have.

[. . .]

Claims of intelligence, social structure, altruism, and artistic ability that are comparable to humans, must however be met with some skepticism. Decades of research on humans have failed to obtain widespread agreement on the nature of human intelligence or even on whether there is such a thing as "general intelligence," let alone on how to test it.

[. . .]

Perhaps a case could be made (though not consistently with animal liberation) for giving special protection to species that are particularly intelligent or social or altruistic or which meet a particular standard of aesthetics, but it would need to be a consistent one. Since many species of "lower" mammals, birds, reptiles, fish, and invertebrates meet one or more of these criteria, it follows that we should oppose killing them too.

Hunting as uncivilized

[. . .] "Shooters" who kill for an extrinsic goal are not necessarily blameworthy. They may, for instance, kill pests or overabundant animals in order to protect ecosystems or endangered species, or to feed their families, and this may be morally justifiable or even a duty. From the idealized hunting perspective shooters do not exhibit the virtues promoted by Ortega y Gasset (1972), Shepherd (1973), and Vitali (1990), but this does not make them vicious. Trophy hunters, however, who kill purely for the sake of acquiring prestigious evidence that they have killed an animal, surely act immorally, because they achieve a trivial benefit for themselves at the expense of the life of an animal. Unlike professional cullers, they may also be considered to exhibit serious character defects. They want to control, to have power, to reduce animals to easy targets, to kill, and to brag about it.

[. . .]

Biodiversity and ecosystems

It is certainly true that many hunters seek to kill trophy animals which are precisely the animals that the species can least afford to lose: the "genetically prime animals," as Vitali (1990) puts it. However, he believes that most hunters are "opportunistic . . . They take what they can get, and oftentimes this amounts to the young, the weak, and the disabled," as do stalking animal predators. He also points out that opportunistic predators such as lions kill a large number of prime animals "precisely because of the opportunities the animals themselves provide"—for instance, prime male wildebeest are usually alone and, "during the rut . . . tend to be incautious and thus vulnerable to attack" (Vitali 1990, 70). In any case, controlled trophy hunting that is part of an ecologically sound wildlife management program will not unduly affect the gene pool. This is in contrast to the uncontrolled hunting of the past, which in the case of elephants has led to an alarming increase in tusklessness in many parts of Africa.

[. . .]

Hunting in general is not a major threat to biodiversity. In the past, a number of species have become extinct due to hunting pressure—palaeolithic hunters contributed to the extermination of many species of megafauna (Uetz and Johnson 1974; Martin and Klein 1984), while in recent centuries species such as the great auk appear to have died out entirely due to hunting (Halliday 1980). But the millions of species around the world that are currently at risk are threatened not by hunting but by habitat destruction and pollution, loss of food sources, and human disturbance. Opposition to hunting, on its own, will do little to protect biodiversity. The comparatively few species that are commercially hunted—mostly large mammals—can be sustainably managed. Nor is hunting necessarily a threat to ecosystems. In most of Europe and the United States, for instance, humans have exterminated large predators, but are able to control the populations of ungulates by culling and sustainable hunting. We should not allow opposition to hunting to deflect us from the much greater threat to biodiversity posed by habitat loss and degradation.

[. . .]

Protecting existing wilderness may not require any killing, but the restoration of degraded environments is very different. Conservation agencies in New Zealand have killed literally millions of introduced pests, including rodents, goats, deer, possums, and predators in order to restore damaged environments on both the mainland and off-shore islands.

[. . .]

Gary Varner (1994) has argued that what he calls therapeutic hunting ("hunting motivated by and designed to secure the aggregate welfare of the target species and/or the integrity of its ecosystem") is justified in the case of an obligatory management species ("one that has a fairly regular tendency to overshoot the carrying capacity of its range, to the detriment of future generations of it and other species"). Therapeutic hunting is not merely consistent with animal liberation: it is morally required under certain circumstances, where fewer animals would die "than if natural attrition is allowed to take place" (Varner 1994, 257–8). Animal liberationists, obviously, prefer non-lethal methods of control, but "Wildlife requires management, and hunting is at this time the most efficient means to do it" (Vitali 1990, 70).

Opponents of hunting (and trapping) as methods of pest control often advocate contraception. However, at the time of writing, no such methods exist except for a few species on a small scale. Even if effective methods did exist, the costs would be phenomenal and for years to come the contracepted animals would continue to destroy vegetation and to compete with and prey on other animals.

[. . .]

In many areas that were colonized by Europeans, native animals have suffered from predation, competition, and habitat destruction by feral introduced animals. [. . .] *In these and many other cases the conflict between animal liberation and environmental protection is quite inescapable*: Foxes and lyrebirds, feral dogs and kiwis, mallards and their close relatives absolutely cannot coexist, so whatever we do, we will be responsible for some animals living and others dying. The "do-nothing" option is effectively a choice to allow the introduced animals to kill, directly or indirectly, the native animals, as well as upsetting ecological equilibrium.

[. . .]

I conclude that it is legitimate to kill introduced animals that threaten the livelihood of native species, and that sport hunting, where it is an effective means of control (at no cost to society) is legitimate. More controversially, perhaps. I also believe that trophy hunting is also legitimate in these circumstances, even though I also share sports hunters' low opinion of trophy hunting.

Hunting and human needs

Writers who identify or sympathize with animal liberation (Varner 1994 and 1998 is an exception) usually accept killing only in situations where human survival is at stake. In this view, hunting is regrettable because it causes major harm to animals, or violates their rights, or fails to respect them for their intrinsic or inherent value or intrinsic worth, or deprives them of something (life) that is valuable to them (e.g., Regan 1983; Singer 1975; Taylor 1986). But, as Paul Taylor notes, to insist that even subsistence hunting is wrong is to expect people to sacrifice "their lives for the sake of animals, and no requirement to do that is imposed by respect for nature" (Taylor 1986, 294).

Self-defense is established as a full justification for killing a human attacker, typically by appeal to rights. [. . .] Wild elephants killed 358 people in Kenya between 1990 and 1995 and 53 people in one area of Sri Lanka in 1995; the killing of 43 elephants by the local people in the same year is regrettable, and regretted by the villagers themselves, but hardly blameworthy (Sugg 1996). I take it that this case is uncontroversial.

The self-defense justification is very narrowly conceived where the attacker is human. In contrast, almost everyone would accept the killing of a less direct threat from an animal such as a plague-infected rat or a swarm of locusts, but not an equally infectious human plague sufferer or a crop devastating polluter, which suggests that we don't consider animals' interests to be equal to the like interests of humans. Following Donald VanDeVeer (1979), we might accept that hunting animals (but not humans) to protect one's livelihood is also justified. Laura Westra (1989), who advocates an ethic of respect for animals, accepts that we may kill animals if it is necessary for our survival—it is by restricting our utilization to the meeting of needs that we show respect for both animals and ecosystems. Traditional subsistence hunters are commonly said to show respect for their prey, for instance by refraining from killing totem animals even when food is scarce, explaining to animals why the hunter needs to kill them, asking for their forgiveness, and even mourning their deaths, and are praised for their complete usage of every part of the animal (e.g., Mails 1972).

[. . .]

Conservation: rich and poor nations

The remainder of this paper is concerned with broadly economic issues: I argue that economic considerations (at the extreme, the survival of thousands of people) justify commercial trophy hunting.

First, however, I wish to draw attention to the global economic context in which wildlife management must be discussed. Calls from the North to preserve rainforests, set up national parks, and save endangered species might be more effective if local communities within nations of the South were agreed to have property rights over their fauna and flora (Gunn 1994). Typically, however, genetic resources are appropriated by multinational companies and countries that can afford to research their potential to develop food and industrial and pharmaceutical products. Thus there is little incentive for poor countries to forego the advantages of immediate exploitation (Tietenberg 1990).

[. . .]

Conventional preservation measures will not help poor countries to deal with pressing problems such as malnutrition, poverty, disease, and overcrowding. Indeed, protecting large areas from human encroachment often exacerbates social and economic problems. Nowhere is this more evident than in Africa.

[. . .]

The social and economic costs of preservation are often allocated quite unfairly. For instance, India's "Project Tiger" has possibly—just possibly—saved the species, but according to one report (Chippindale 1984), on average about one person per week is killed by tigers in India. The Amboseli National Park, in Southern Kenya, illustrates the injustice (and also the ineffectiveness) of viewing national parks as "biological islands" which must be preserved from all human use except scientific study and limited tourism. The nomadic Maasai who had traditionally used this region were excluded from it for the benefit of others.

[. . .]

Over the next few decades, wildlife numbers in the "protected" park actually declined, mainly due to illegal hunting. However, a change in land use philosophy in Amboseli NP in the mid 1970s improved both the numbers of wildlife and the economic position of the Maasai. Revenue sharing was introduced, the central government absorbed developmental and recurrent costs of the park, local Maasai were granted title to land outside the Park, to be owned cooperatively as group ranches, and cash compensation was paid for loss of grazing, to cover livestock losses from wildlife migrating outside the Park borders. The Maasai became less dependent on cattle because of these measures and, more importantly, because of the revenue they received from tourist campsites and employment in the Park, with which they were able to build community facilities. Reduction in livestock numbers meant less competition with wildlife, and because the Maasai were now part of the enterprise, illegal hunting greatly declined. As a result, within ten years wildlife numbers had greatly increased (Western 1984).

The economics of hunting

Commercial and sport hunting are economically significant activities in many developed countries. For instance, according to the BFSS (n.d.) 33,000 jobs in the United Kingdom depend on hunting. [. . .] However, the economies of rich countries do not depend significantly on hunting and if it was banned, recreational hunters would simply switch their discretionary spending, thus creating jobs in other sectors of the economy.

The situation is quite different in poorer countries, where wildlife has always been used as a resource and "Use or non-use is not the issue; sustainable use is" (Makombe 1993, 17). The colonial powers, after reducing many species to rarity or extinction, generally adopted policies of strict preservation of wildlife. This was done without regard to the needs of local people who were regarded as poachers even when they engaged in traditional subsistence hunting (Makombe 1993, 18).

Poor countries gain considerable revenue from trophy hunting. The impoverished Mongolian government charges $10,000 for a permit to shoot a snow leopard and a 16-day hunt with one snow leopard costs $25,000 per person; any wolves shot along the way are thrown in for $600. Bulgarian dealers sell falcons in the West for $10,000. Orangutan were sold in Taiwan in the 1980s at $30,000 each, though the local traders in Indonesia received less than $200 each for them—still a very considerable sum by local standards (information from Ghazi 1994, Anon. 1993 and 1994). None of these cases is part of a sustainable management program, but other countries which manage their wildlife effectively have achieved substantial revenues from trophy hunting while maintaining or increasing their wildlife populations.

Zimbabwe: a case study

Wild resources are vital to the survival of millions of Africans. One study estimated that wild resources contributed over $120 million to the Tanzanian economy in 1988 (Kiss 1990); hunting licenses alone yielded $4.5 million in 1990. [. . .] Before Kenya imposed a ban on hunting, the total revenue from sport hunting contributed about 6.5 percent to the total foreign exchange from tourism (Makombe 1993, 28). [. . .] In some countries, a large proportion of household income is derived from wildlife based enterprises—in Malawi, for instance, rural communities derive 2.5 times more cash from wildlife than the market value of their subsistence agricultural products (Makombe 1993, 22). In Zimbabwe, local people are allowed to hunt sustainably both for their own families and to take to market, and a limited number of trophy hunting permits are sold. Zimbabwe—12.7 percent of whose area is devoted to national parks and reserves—also has some of the toughest anti-poaching (in the sense of illegal hunting) units in Africa and spends 0.60 percent of its budget on wildlife (whereas the United States spends only 0.15 percent). This is a substantial commitment in a country which cannot afford to provide adequate health care and education for much of its population and in which 50 percent of the population is unemployed.

[. . .]

Rich countries such as the United States, Australia, and New Zealand which oppose hunting of large animals including whales, and especially trophy hunting, have a very bad reputation in Zimbabwean conservation circles such as Africa Resources Trust (ART) and Zimbabwe Trust (ZIMTRUST). These private organizations strongly support the government CAMPFIRE Association (an acronym for Communal Areas. Management Programme for Indigenous Resources) which was set up by the Zimbabwean Department of National Parks and Wildlife Management in 1986, with the support of the Worldwide Fund for Nature, the Office of USAID, Harare, and the Centre for Applied Social Sciences (CASS) at the University of Zimbabwe. The objectives of CAMPFIRE, "based on the rationale that communities will invest in environmental conservation if they can use their resources on a sustainable basis," are:

- to initiate a programme for the long-term development, management and sustainable utilisation of the natural resources in the communal areas;
- to achieve management of resources by placing their custody and responsibility with the resident communities;
- to allow communities to benefit directly from the exploitation of natural resources within the communal areas; and
- to establish the administrative and institutional structures necessary to make the programme work. (ZIMTRUST 1993)

The communal areas are the marginal and submarginal lands which were created early in the twentieth century when the British colonists "took over the most fertile lands and forced much of the indigenous population into arid and semi-arid areas" which are unsuitable for agriculture because they have insufficient or unreliable rainfall. However, they make excellent wildlife habitat" (Anon 1996). The 1975 Parks and Wildlife Act gave ownership of wildlife (including hunting rights) to all property owners, and in 1982 this was extended to the communal areas through their Rural District Councils (Murphree 1991, 8). Over five million people—almost half the population—live in communal areas, which make up 42 percent of the country. Communities may decide to participate in CAMPFIRE, which around half had done in August 1996.

In 1995, CAMPFIRE generated $2.5 million, a substantial sum given that game wardens are paid as little as $80 per month (CAMPFIRE News 1996). This revenue is gained from hunting safaris, tourism such as photographic safaris, sales of products such as animal products and crocodile eggs (for sale to crocodile farmers), and rafting licenses (ZIMTrust 1993; CAMPFIRE News 1996). Around 90 percent of the revenue is generated from the sale of big game hunting licenses, and 64 percent of this is derived from elephant trophy hunting licenses which in March 1996 cost $9,000 (CAMPFIRE News 1996). Over the period 1989–93, 22 percent of revenue was reinvested in wildlife management and 54 percent devolved to the participating communities on the communal lands. Communities spent their shares on infrastructure development such as water supply, clinic and school development, farm fencing (to keep out crop-destroying elephants, hippos, buffalo, and kudu) and roading, income generating projects, and cash distributions to families for their own use. In some areas, this income amounts to 50 percent of a household's annual income and enables families to pay for items such as school fees (CAMPFIRE News 1996). Masoka Ward, a formerly impoverished area, earned $100,000 in 1994 from a safari hunting concession organized through CAMPFIRE. The ward used the money to build a health clinic, pay game guards, and fund a football team, and each of the 140 households also received more than four times their annual income for drought relief, either in cash or maize (CAMPFIRE News 1996). This revenue, of course, would not be available without the sale of hunting licences. It would be even greater were it not for the ban on international trade in elephant products under the Convention on International Trade in Endangered Species and Their Products (CITES) since 1990.

Zimbabwe's policies are a conservation success. Whereas the total population of African elephants fell by half between 1975 and 1990 (from 160,000 to 16,000 in Kenya), Zimbabwe's elephants have increased steadily—32,000 in 1960, 52,000 in 1989, and over 70,000 in 1993 (Ricciutti 1993). The national trophy off-take is restricted to no more than 0.7 percent per year, which is clearly sustainable. For instance, the elephant population density of the Omay Communal Land, a CAMPFIRE participant, is the same as that in the adjacent Matusadona NP, where hunting is strictly prohibited, and the Omay population grew at 3–4 percent per year from 1982 to 1992, even though, counting "problem" elephants shot by villagers, the average annual off-take was 1.03 percent (Taylor n.d.).

Because they have a stake in sustaining populations of economically valuable game animals, Zimbabweans have a commitment to conservation. As a result, species such as elephants which are rare or extinct in many other countries are thriving in Zimbabwe, along with populations of other animals which benefit from protection of big game habitat. It is sadly ironic that governments of the same European nations that reduced Zimbabwe's elephants to around 4,000 in 1900 (Thomas n.d.) are now highly critical of Zimbabwe's effective and socially equitable sustainable management policies.

It may be claimed that economic benefits could be obtained without the deaths of big game animals, by encouraging wilderness tourism and big game viewing. Norman Myers, who has played an important role in protecting East African wildlife, has argued that animals such as lions are actually much more valuable, economically, than dead ones. He notes (Myers 1981) that a trophy hunter will pay $8,500 to shoot a lion in Kenya, whereas the same animal will generate $7 3/4 million over its lifetime from people such as myself who wish to view and photograph wildlife, not to kill it. But this is unsound economics, for several reasons. First, each lion is substitutable by another lion. Wildlife tourists want to see lions, not any particular lion. So long as there is a reasonably good chance of seeing lions, people will continue to visit parks. Second, the viability of lions as a species, or of a given population, is not threatened by the carefully controlled issue of permits to trophy hunters. Lions reproduce rapidly and the revenue that would have been generated by Myers's hypothetical lion over its lifetime will continue to be generated by other lions. Third, and most importantly, the number of lions—which the tourists want to view and the trophy hunters want to kill—is limited by the carrying capacity of the environment. The available environment is restricted to National Parks and other protected wildlife areas, such as private game lands. When the human population of Africa (and other areas where lions used to live) was small, lions and humans coexisted, if not necessarily happily on the part of either. With rising human populations, and different expectations, it is utterly impossible that lions will ever again exist in any numbers outside protected areas. Therefore, lion numbers will have to be regulated, and if this can be done for the economic benefit of impoverished local people by the issuing of game licenses, why not?

Conclusion

As Africa's population continues to grow, and habitat shrinks, pressure on wildlife will increase. Africans, like Western environmentalists, are entitled to a materially adequate standard of life. They cannot and should not be expected to protect wildlife if it is against their interests to do so. The only feasible strategy to protect the interests of both wildlife and people is one that integrates conservation and development, as in Zimbabwe. Whatever we may think of trophy hunting—and I share the distaste of serious sports hunters for it—at present it is a necessary part of wildlife conservation in Southern Africa.

References

Africa Resources Trust website, www.art.org.uk.
Anon. 1996. *Zimbabwe's CAMPFIRE: Empowering Rural Communities for Conservation and Development*. Harare: Africa Resources Trust and CAMPFIRE Association.
——. 1994. "Cash Quest Could Mean End of Snow Leopard." *New Zealand Herald*, October 10.
——. 1993. "Back to Nature's Bosom." *New Zealand Herald*. September 22.

British Field Sports Society. n.d. "Hunting: The Facts." Website www.countryside-alliance/org/country/foxhunting.html.

Callicott, J. Baird. 1980. "Animal Liberation: A Triangular Affair." *Environmental Ethics* 2: 311–38.

CAMPFIRE News. 1996. Issue 12. Harare: CAMPFIRE Association.

Care for the Wild website: www.cftw@fastnet.co.uk

Causey, Anne S. 1989. "On the Morality of Hunting." *Environmental Ethics* 11: 327–43.

Chippindale, Peter. 1984. "Tigers Too Safe Now." *New Zealand Herald*, March 24.

Clark, Collin W. 1973. "Profit Maximization and the Extinction of Animal Species." *Journal of Political Economy* 81: 950–61.

Daly, Mary. 1978. *Gyn/Ecology: The MetaEthics of Radical Feminism*. Boston: Beacon Press.

Ghazi, Polly. 1994. "Illegal Help at Circuses." *New Zealand Herald*, December 28.

Gunn. Alastair S. 1994. "Environmental Ethics and Tropical Rainforests: Should Greens Have Standing?" *Environmental Ethics* 16: 21–40.

Halliday, Tim. 1980. *Vanishing Birds*. Harmondsworth: Penguin Books.

King, Roger J.H. 1991. "Environmental Ethics and the Case for Hunting." *Environmental Ethics* 13: 59–85.

Kiss, A., 1990. "Living with Wildlife: Wildlife Resource Management with Local Participation in Africa." Washington, DC: World Bank Technical Paper No. 130, Africa Technical Department Series.

Loftin, Robert F. 1984. "The Morality of Hunting." *Environmental Ethics* 6: 241–50.

Mails, T. E. 1972. *The Mystical Warriors of the Plains*. Garden City, NY: Doubleday.

Makombe, Kudzai (ed.) 1993. "Sharing the Land: Wildlife, People and Development in Africa," IUCN/ROSA Environmental Series No. 1. Harare, IUCN/ROSA, and Washington DC, IUCN/SUWP.

Martin, Paul and R.G. Klein (eds) 1984. *Quaternary Extinctions: A Prehistoric Revolution*. Tucson: University of Arizona Press.

Murphree, M.W. 1991. "Communities as Institutions for Resource Management." *Harare: Occasional Paper Series*, Centre for Applied Social Studies, University of Zimbabwe, 1991.

Myers, Norman. 1981. "The Exhausted Earth." *Foreign Policy* 42: 141–55.

Ortega y Gasset, José. 1972. *Meditations on Hunting*. New York: Charles Scribner's Sons.

Regan, Tom. 1983. *The Case for Animal Rights*. Berkeley: University of California Press.

Ricciuti, Edward. 1993. "The Elephant Wars." *Wildlife Conservation* March/April.

Shepherd, Paul. 1973. *The Tender Carnivore and the Sacred Game*. New York: Charles Scribner's Sons.

Singer, Peter. 1975. *Animal Liberation*. New York: New York Review.

Sugg, Ike G. 1996. "Selling Hunting Rights Saves Animals." *Wall Street Journal*, July 24.

Taylor, Paul. 1986. *Respect for Nature*. Princeton: Princeton University Books.

Taylor, Russell. n.d. "From Liability to Asset: Wildlife in the Omay Communal Land of Zimbabwe." Wildlife and Development Series booklet No. 8, published by the International Institute for Environment and Development and CAMPFIRE Collaborative Group for Africa Resources Trust and available on the ART website.

Thomas, Stephen, n.d. "The Legacy of Dualism in Decision-making Within." CAMPFIRE. *Wildlife and Development Series booklet No. 4*, published by the International Institute for Environment and Development and CAMPFIRE Collaborative Group for Africa Resources Trust and available on the ART website.

Tietenberg, T.N. 1990. "The Poverty Connection to Environmental Policy." *Challenge*, Sept/Oct: 26–32.

Uetz, G. and D.L. Johnson. 1974. "Breaking the Web." *Environment* 16: 31–9.

VanDeVeer, Donald. 1979. "Interspecific Justice." *Inquiry* 22: 55–70.

Varner, Gary E. 1998. *In Nature's Interests? Interests, Animal Rights, and Environmental Ethics*. New York: Oxford University Press.

——. 1994. "Can Animal Rights Activists be Environmentalists?" In Christine Pierce and Donald VanDeVeer (eds) *People, Penguins, and Plastic Trees*. Belmont, CA: Wadsworth, 2nd ed: 254–73.

Vitali, Theodore. 1990. "Sport Hunting: Moral or Immoral?, *Environmental Ethics* 12: 69–82.

Western, David. 1984. "Amboseli National Park: Human Values and the Conservation of a Savanna Ecosystem" in Jeffrey A. McNeely and Kenton R. Miller (eds), National Parks, Conservation, and Development: the Role of Protected Areas in Sustaining Society: proceedings of the World Congress on National Parks, Bali, Indonesia, 11–22 October 1982. Washington, D.C.: Smithsonian Institution Press: 93–9.

Westra, Laura. 1989. "Ecology and Ethics: Is There a Joint Ethic of Respect?" *Environmental Ethics* 11: 215–30.

ZIMTRUST. 1993. "Historical Overview and Background to CAMPFIRE." Unpublished report. Harare: Zimbabwe Trust.

Protectionism

60

⸺⸺✦⸺⸺

Gary E. Varner

"Can Animal Rights Activists be Environmentalists?"

Varner challenges the belief that individualistic perspectives such as animal rights and animal liberation are not compatible with anthropocentrism and ecocentrism. Using the case of species that can damage habitats for themselves and other species when they exceed the carrying capacity, Varner argues that biologically necessary hunting could be supported by all of these various perspectives. He then explores other avenues by which these philosophical perspectives can find common ground.

[. . .]

[E]nvironmental philosophers' antagonism to animal rights views grows out of their perception that the practical implications of such views would be antienvironmental in two basic ways.

1   With regard to wildlife population control the concerns are that:
    a   *hunting* would be prohibited, even when it is required to preserve the integrity of an ecosystem, and
    b   humans would have an obligation to prevent natural *predation* (including not restoring locally extinct predators).
2   With regard to preserving biodiversity the concerns are that:
    a   it would be impermissible to kill destructive *exotics*, and
    b   it would be impermissible to breed members of *endangered* species in captivity.

In what follows, I am going to begin with, and spend the most time on, hunting. Admittedly, this is the easiest case in which to reconcile the views of animal rights activists and environmentalists, but a careful treatment of this issue sets the stage for a careful treatment of the others.

[. . .]

Therapeutic hunting of obligatory management species

When teaching the hunting issue, I find it useful to distinguish among three types of hunting in terms of the purposes hunting is taken to serve. By *therapeutic hunting* I mean hunting motivated by and designed to secure the aggregate welfare of the target species and/or the integrity of its ecosystem (I'll discuss later the question of whether the two are separable). By *subsistence hunting* I mean hunting aimed at securing food for human beings. By *sport hunting* I mean hunting aimed at maintaining religious or cultural traditions, reenacting national or evolutionary history, honing certain skills, or just securing a trophy. Many would prefer to recognize a distinction within this third category between hunting for sport and hunting as a ritual. Although there may be some important differences, I class them together because both activities serve human needs (which is what distinguishes both sport and subsistence hunting from therapeutic hunting), but needs which are less fundamental (in the sense of universal) than nutrition (which is what distinguishes subsistence hunting from both ritual and sport hunting).

[. . .]

The thesis I wish to defend here is that environmentalists and animal rights activists can agree on the moral necessity of therapeutic hunting of *obligatory management species*.

I owe the term "obligatory management species" to Ron Howard of the Texas Agricultural Extension Service, who distinguishes between "obligatory" and "permissive" management species in the following way. An obligatory management species is one that has a fairly regular tendency to overshoot the carrying capacity of its range, to the detriment of future generations of it and other species. A permissive management species is one that does not normally exhibit this tendency. Examples of obligatory management species would be ungulates (hooved mammals like white-tailed and mule deer, elk, and bison) and elephants. Examples of permissive management species would be mourning doves, cottontail rabbits, gray squirrels, and bobwhite and blue quail.[1] It is not that permissive management species do not become overpopulated. They do every year, in the straightforward sense of producing more young than their habitat can feed through the winter. But they usually do not degrade their habitat in ways that threaten future generations of their own or other species. This is what makes their management environmentally optional, or "merely *permissible*" in Howard's terminology. By contrast, management of ungulates (and some other species) is environmentally necessary, or "*obligatory*" in Howard's terms.[2]

Environmental groups have taken great pains in recent years to distance themselves from animal rights groups, fearing that the widespread perception of animal rights activists as antiscientific romantics would rub off on them, and much of the distancing has had to do with the hunting issue. In 1990, *Audubon* magazine published an article with the scathing title "Animal Rights: Ignorance About Nature."[3] Also in 1990, the Wisconsin Greens adopted a resolution condemning Madison's Alliance for Animals for disrupting hunts in Blue Mound State Park.[4] And in 1991 a Sierra Club fund-raiser said in a phone conversation that the club was not "doing more to expose the enormous environmental damage caused by factory farming because they wanted to keep their membership as large as possible."[5]

Still, environmentalists do not uniformly support hunting. The Audubon Society and the Sierra Club both oppose hunting in the national parks, and the Texas chapters of both groups recently opposed a bill which opened the state's parks to recreational hunting.

[. . .]

Sierra's and Audubon's position on hunting in national and state parks shows that the only hunting environmentalists feel *compelled* to support is biologically necessary hunting, that is, *therapeutic* hunting, and therapeutic hunting normally is necessary only where obligatory management species are concerned. Officially, both organizations are noncommittal on sport hunting outside of the national and Texas state parks. This mirrors a difference of opinion within the environmental community. Many environmentalists would prefer that sport hunting which is not also therapeutic be stopped, and many would prefer that natural predators be restored to levels at which human hunting is less often biologically necessary. But many environmentalists are also avid hunters who attach great ritual significance to their hunting.

So the only hunting that environmentalists feel *compelled* to support is therapeutic hunting of obligatory management species. However, the received interpretation of the animal rights/environmental ethics split would have it that animal rights activists must oppose hunting even when it is biologically necessary. When we look behind the sound-bite quotations and political slogans of self-professed animal rights *activists*, and examine carefully formulated animal rights *philosophies*, we see that it is *not* necessary for animal rightists to oppose environmentally sound hunting. Animal rightists can support exactly the same policy in regard to hunting which environmental groups like Audubon and the Sierra Club support in regard to the national and state parks. The easiest way to bring this out is by making the now familiar and basic philosophical distinction between an animal liberation or animal welfare view and a true animal rights view, and by beginning with the former's application to the hunting question.

Animal liberation and therapeutic hunting

Peter Singer's 1975 book *Animal Liberation* has become the bible of the "animal rights movement."[6] Singer wrote that book for popular consumption and in it he spoke loosely of animals having "moral rights." But all that he intended by this was that animals (or at least "higher animals," like vertebrates) have some basic moral standing and that there are right and wrong ways of treating them. In later, more philosophically rigorous work (summarized in his *Practical Ethics*, which has just been reissued), he explicitly eschews the term "rights," noting that, as a utilitarian ethical theorist, not only does he deny that animals have moral rights, but in his view, neither do human beings.[7] In *Animal Liberation* Singer was writing in the vernacular in order to make his arguments appeal to the widest variety of audiences—he did not want to tie his critiques of agriculture and animal research to his specific moral philosophy.

When ethical philosophers speak of an individual "having moral rights," they mean something much more specific than that the individual has some basic moral standing and that there are right and wrong ways of treating him or her (or it). Although there is much controversy as to the specifics, there is general agreement on this: to attribute moral rights to an individual is to assert that the individual has some kind of special moral dignity, the cash value of which is that there are certain things which cannot justifiably be done to him or her (or it) for the sake of benefit to others. For this reason, moral rights have been characterized as "trump cards" against utilitarian arguments. Utilitarian arguments are arguments based on aggregate benefits and aggregate harms. Utilitarianism is usually defined as the view that right actions maximize aggregate happiness. In principle, nothing is inherently or intrinsically wrong, according to a utilitarian; any action could be justified under some possible circumstances. One way of characterizing rights views in ethics, by contrast, is that there are some things which, regardless of the consequences, it is simply wrong to do to individuals, and that moral rights single out these things.

Although a technical and stipulative definition of the term, this philosophical usage reflects a familiar concept. One familiar way in which appeals to individuals' rights are used in day-to-day discussions is to assert, in effect, that there is a limit to what individuals can be forced to do, or to the harm that may be inflicted upon them, for the benefit of others. So the philosophical usage of rights talk reflects the commonsense view that there are limits to what we can justifiably do to an individual for the benefit of society.

To defend the moral rights of animals would be to claim that certain ways of treating animals cannot be justified on utilitarian grounds. In the professional philosophical writings cited earlier, Peter Singer explicitly rejects rights views and adopts a utilitarian stance for dealing with our treatment of nonhuman animals. So the author of the bible of the animal rights movement is not an animal *rights* theorist at all.

When the views of animal rights activists are understood this way, in Singer's theoretical terms, animal rights advocates opposed to hunting actually have a lot in common with wildlife managers and hunters who defend hunting as a means to minimizing suffering in wildlife populations. Both factions are appealing to the utilitarian tradition in ethics; both believe that it is permissible (at least where nonhuman animals are concerned) to sacrifice (even involuntarily) the life of one individual for the benefit of others, at least where the aggregated benefits to others clearly outweigh the costs to that individual.

Relatedly, the specific conception of happiness which defenders of therapeutic hunting apply to animals is one which Singer himself uses, at least in regard to many or most animals. Since utilitarianism is the view that right actions maximize aggregate *happiness*, it is important for utilitarians to be clear about what happiness consists in. *Hedonistic* utilitarians define happiness in terms of the presence of pleasure and the absence of pain, where both "pleasure" and "pain" are broadly construed to include not only physical pleasures and pains (e.g. those accompanying orgasms and third-degree burns), but various kinds of pleasant and unpleasant psychological states (e.g., tension and nervousness, and glee and exhilaration). *Preference utilitarians* define happiness in terms of the satisfaction of preferences (conscious aims, desires, plans, projects), which can, but need not, be accompanied by pleasure.

In *Animal Liberation* Singer employed a strongly hedonistic conception of happiness. He admitted that, "to avoid speciesism," we need *not* hold that

> it is as wrong to kill a dog as it is to kill a normal human being. . . . [Without being guilty of speciesism] we could still hold that, for instance, it is worse to kill a normal adult human, [or any other being] with a capacity for self-awareness, and the ability to plan for the future and have meaningful relations with others, than it is to kill a mouse, which presumably does not share all of these characteristics. . . .[8]

For this reason he said that "The wrongness of killing a being is more complicated" than the wrongness of inflicting pain. Nevertheless, he there kept the question of killing "in the background," because

> in the present state of human tyranny over other species the more simple, straightforward principle of equal consideration of pain or pleasure is a sufficient basis for identifying and protesting against all the major abuses of animals that human beings practice.[9]

In *Practical Ethics*, by contrast, he devotes four chapters (almost 140 pages) to the "more complicated" question. There he stresses that, with regard to "self-conscious individuals, leading their own lives and wanting to go on living," it is implausible to say that the death of one happy individual is made up for by the birth of an equally happy individual.[10] That is, when dealing with self-conscious beings, preference utilitarianism is more appropriate than hedonistic utilitarianism.

An easy way to clarify Singer's point is with the following example. Suppose I sneak into your bedroom tonight and, without ever disturbing your sleep, kill you (by silently releasing an odorless gas, for instance). Since you led a happy life (presumably) and died painlessly, on a hedonistic conception of happiness, the only sense we can make of the harm I have done you is in terms of lost future opportunities for pleasure. In the case of human beings, who have complicated desires, intentions, plans, and projects, this seems an inadequate accounting of the harm I've done you.[11] For humans (and any similarly cognitively sophisticated animals) a desire-based conception of harm seems more appropriate. But, Singer argues, self-conscious beings are not replaceable. When a being with future-oriented desires dies those desires remain unsatisfied even if another being is brought into existence and has similar desires satisfied.

Singer cites research which he says clearly shows that the great apes (chimpanzees, gorillas, and orangutans) have projects[12] and, without saying what specific research leads him to these conclusions, that fish and chickens do not have projects,[13] but that: "A case can be made, though with varying degrees of confidence, on behalf of whales, dolphins, monkeys, dogs, cats, pigs, seals, bears, cattle, sheep and so on, perhaps even to the point at which it may include all mammals. . . ."[14]

Elsewhere I have characterized carefully the evidence I think shows that all mammals and birds have desires but fish do not.[15] However, I doubt that either birds or the "lower" mammals (by which I here mean mammals other than primates and cetaceans) have projects of the kind Singer is interested in, that is, desires that significantly transcend the present. Certainly the desire to go on living (which Singer mentions repeatedly as a sort of sine qua non of self-consciousness) constitutes a very sophisticated project. Dogs and cats almost certainly have desires that transcend the present. When a lion flushes a wildebeest in the direction of a hidden pridemate[16] (or, more prosaically, when my cat comes from the back room to where I am sitting and, having gotten my attention by jumping in my lap, leads me to the back door to be let out) it undoubtedly has a desire for something in the future. But it is a very near future about which cats and dogs are concerned. The desire to catch a prey animal here now, or even the desire to get a human being from the other room to come open the door to the outside, is not on a par with aspiring to longer life. Having the desire to go on living involves not only being self-conscious, but having concepts of life and death, and of self.

So I doubt that self-consciousness, as Singer conceives it, extends as far down "the phylogenetic scale" as Singer believes. But for present purposes, I will not try to settle this issue.

[. . .]

[L]et us consider therapeutic hunting from a hedonistic utilitarian perspective. The defense is obvious. Consider the following argument:

1   We have a moral obligation to minimize pain.
2   In the case of obligatory management species, more pain would be caused by letting nature take its course than by conducting carefully regulated therapeutic hunts.
3   Therefore, we are morally obligated to conduct carefully regulated therapeutic hunts of obligatory management species rather than let nature take its course.

Since premise (1) is just a (partial) restatement[17] of the hedonistic utilitarian principle, and the argument is valid, premise (2) is the obvious point of controversy. But premise (2) states an empirical claim. Thus Singer's disagreement with the hunters and wildlife managers is purely empirical. They agree at the level of moral principle; they disagree only about that principle's application in practice.

Specifically, Singer appears to believe that nonlethal means of population control are (or at least could be made) available, and that using them would minimize suffering vis-à-vis therapeutic hunting. Singer has very little to say about hunting specifically. However, in *Practical Ethics* he at one point clearly indicates that a hedonistic utilitarian could endorse hunting under some circumstances.

> [The replaceability argument is severely] limited in its application. It cannot justify factory farming, where animals do not have pleasant lives. Nor does it *normally* justify the killing of wild animals. A duck shot by a hunter . . . has probably had a pleasant life, but the shooting of a duck does not lead to its replacement by another. *Unless the duck population is at the maximum that can be sustained by the available food supply*, the killing of a duck ends a pleasant life without starting another, and is for that reason wrong on straightforward utilitarian grounds.[18]

Here Singer admits that the replaceability argument could be used to justify, not just therapeutic hunting of obligatory management species, but sport hunting of permissive management species. Ducks are not obligatory management species. Ducks do not, in the normal course of events, overshoot the carrying capacity of their habitat in ways that degrade that habitat for future generations of their own and other species. Their management is therefore environmentally permissible, but not environmentally obligatory. Nevertheless, a hedonistic utilitarian could endorse sport hunting of permissive management species when, as Singer indicates here, their populations are at or above the carrying capacity of their ranges. As noted above, permissive management species regularly overshoot the carrying capacity of their range, producing more young than their habitat can support. Where this is clearly the case, a painlessly killed individual is, in effect, replaced by an individual who survives as a result. So long as the average death that ducks suffer at the hands of hunters involves as little or less pain than the average death surplus ducks would have suffered in nature, pain is minimized.

However, in *Animal Liberation* Singer writes:

> If it is true that in special circumstances their population grows to such an extent that they damage their own environment and the prospects of their own survival, or that of other animals who share their habitat, then it may be right for humans to take some supervisory action; but obviously if we consider the interests of the animals, this action will not be to allow hunters to kill some animals, inevitably wounding others in the process, but rather to reduce the fertility of the animals.[19]

Here Singer is admitting that therapeutic hunting of obligatory management species is better than letting nature take its course, but he is arguing that there is yet a better option. Singer appears to be substituting into the above argument a different empirical premise:

(2′) By using nonlethal means of controlling populations of obligatory management species we would minimize suffering vis-à-vis both letting nature take its course and performing carefully regulated therapeutic hunts.

To reach a different conclusion:

(3′) We are morally obligated to use nonlethal means to control populations of obligatory management species.

When all of the learned dust has settled, the disagreement between the Peter Singers of the world and the self-professed advocates of animal welfare among hunters and wildlife managers boils down to an empirical controversy over the effectiveness of nonlethal wildlife population control measures. Both factions agree at the level of moral principle; they disagree over the facts.

My sense is that, at least in the current state of nonlethal wildlife population control, the defenders of hunting have it right. [. . .] For if, as the defenders of hunting maintain, hunting is in fact the only effective method of preemptive control, then both environmentalists and the Peter Singers of the world are compelled to support therapeutic hunting.

[. . .]

I do, however, think that eventually precision methods of nonlethal wildlife population control will be developed. Recently, extensive experiments with animals have validated the technique of using genetically engineered viruses to spread infertility among wild animals. By inserting part of the protein sheath from the species sperm into a virus which spreads easily in the population and then distributing food laced with the virus. Australian researchers hope to eradicate the rabbit, an exotic which has devastated their country. Trials of a similar technique to induce *temporary* infertility in other species are now under way.[20] The public in general and animal rights activists in particular are apprehensive of biotechnologies, but I think this method should, with appropriate caution, be embraced by the animal rights movement as a very promising approach to nonlethal control of wildlife populations.

The earlier discussion of environmentalists' ambivalent attitudes toward hunting suggests that if and when effective nonlethal alternatives to therapeutic hunting become available, environmentalists will be split. For some, the availability of nonlethal alternatives will strengthen their opposition to hunting; others will regard the choice between hunting and equally effective nonlethal means as morally moot. For present purposes what is important is this: animal rights activists operating from a hedonistic utilitarian stance will be compelled to support therapeutic hunting of obligatory management species in the absence of precision, nonlethal methods of wildlife population control. Only when such methods are available must such animal rights activists oppose therapeutic hunting, and then they will oppose it only in order to embrace a more humane alternative *with the same environmental effect*.

Animal *rights* and therapeutic hunting

Although Peter Singer's *Animal Liberation* has become the bible of the animal rights movement, Tom Regan's *The Case for Animal Rights* is the best defense available to date of a true animal *rights* position. It is impossible to do justice to the argument of a 400-page book in a few paragraphs. In what follows I will simply summarize the conclusions Regan reaches, without trying to reproduce his arguments in detail, and without critically assessing them apart from their application to the hunting controversy. It is my view that without resolving the theoretical question of which individuals (if any) have moral rights, we can still hope to make some progress on the practical question of which hunting policy to adopt. Specifically, I argue that in the absence of effective nonlethal means of population control, therapeutic hunting of obligatory management species *can* be defended from a true animal rights perspective.

According to Regan, there is basically one moral right—the right not to be harmed on the grounds that doing so benefits others—and at least all normal mammals of a year or more have this basic moral right. [. . .] Regan does not deny that any nonmammalian animals have rights. Although he does explicitly restrict the reference of "animal" to "mentally normal mammals of a year or more," Regan does this to avoid the controversy over "line drawing," that is, trying to say precisely where in the phylogenetic scale and where in their ontogeny animals' mental capacities become so impoverished as to make them incapable of being subjects of a life. And Regan clearly says that he chooses mammals in order to make sure that his arguments "refer [to] individuals *well beyond* the point where anyone could reasonably 'draw the line' separating those who have the mental abilities in question from those who lack them."[21] In thus restricting the reference of "animal" he is only acknowledging that the analogical reasoning which would establish that any nonhuman animal has moral rights is strongest in the case of mentally normal adult mammals and becomes progressively weaker as we consider birds and then reptiles, amphibians, and vertebrate fish.

Regan defends two principles to use in deciding whom to harm where it is impossible not to harm someone who has moral rights: the miniride and worse-off principles. The *worse-off principle* applies where *non-comparable* harms are involved and it requires us to avoid harming the worse-off individual. Regan adopts the kind of desire-based conception of harm discussed earlier in relation to preference utilitarianism. Regan measures harm in terms of the degree to which an individual's capacity to form and satisfy desires has been restricted. The degree of restriction is measured in absolute rather than relative terms. For if harm were measured relative to the individual's original capacity to form and satisfy desires, rather than in absolute terms, then death would be death wherever it occurs, but Regan reasons that although death is always the greatest harm which any individual can suffer (because it forecloses all opportunity for desire formation and satisfaction), death to a normal human being in the prime of her life is noncomparably worse than death to any nonhuman animal in the prime of its life, because a normal human being's capacity to form and satisfy desires is so much greater. To illustrate the use of the worse-off principle. Regan imagines that five individuals, four humans and a dog, are in a lifeboat that can support only four of them. Since death to any of the human beings would be noncomparably worse than death to the dog, the worse-off principle applies, and it requires us to avoid harming the human beings, who stand to lose the most.[22]

The *miniride principle* applies to cases where *comparable* harms are involved, and it requires us to harm the few rather than the many. Regan admits that, where it applies, this principle implies the same conclusions as the principle of utility, but he emphasizes that the reasoning is nonutilitarian: the focus is on individuals rather than the aggregate; what the miniride principle instructs us to do is to minimize the overriding of individuals' rights, rather than to maximize aggregate happiness. He says that the rights view (as Regan calls his position) advocates harming the few (at least where *comparable* harms are involved), because it respects all individuals equally. To illustrate the miniride principle's application, Regan imagines that a runaway mine train must be sent down one of two shafts, and that fifty miners would be killed by sending it down the first shaft but only one by sending it down the second. Since the harms that the various individuals in the example would suffer are comparable, the miniride principle applies, and we are obligated to send the runaway train down the second shaft.

Regan argues that the rights view calls for the total abolition of scientific research on animals, of commercial animal agriculture, and of hunting and trapping.[23] He contrasts his views to Singer's in this regard, stressing that because he is reasoning from a rights-based theory, his conclusions are not contingent upon the facts in the same way as those of a utilitarian like Singer.

At first glance, the prospects for convergence are slim when a true animal rights position like Regan's is opposed to the position of environmentalists. For if having moral rights means that there are certain things that cannot be done to an individual for the sake of the group, and a true animal rights position extends moral rights to animals, then the basic rationale for therapeutic hunting—killing some in order that others may live—appears to be lost. [. . .] Regan appears to be opposed even to therapeutic hunting, and his opposition appears to follow from the attribution of moral rights to the animals.

However, Regan never considers the applicability of the miniride principle to hunting. [. . .] Given Regan's conception of harm, death harms all normal individuals of the same species equally. So if it is true that fewer animals will die if therapeutic hunting is used to regulate a wildlife population than if natural attrition is allowed to take its course, then Regan's view implies that therapeutic hunting is not only permissible but a morally mandatory expression of respect for animals' rights.

Similar conclusions could, I think, be reached about certain kinds of medical research using the worse-off principle. Consider AIDS research, for example. Given Regan's conception of harm, the harm that death from AIDS is to a normal human being is noncomparably worse than the harm that death from AIDS is to a mouse or even a chimpanzee. So the worse-off principle would, if applicable, imply that nonhuman lives may be sacrificed to save human beings from preventable death.[24] Here again, however, Regan does not apply his principle.

With regard to medical research, Regan bases his abolitionist conclusion primarily on the "special consideration" that *"Risks are not morally transferable to those who do not voluntarily choose to take them,"* which, he claims, blocks the application of the worse off principle.[25] Returning to the hunting question, Regan might similarly cite a "special consideration" which blocks the application of the miniride principle. He might claim that a violation of an individual's moral rights occurs only when a moral agent is responsible for the harm in question, and that while hunters would be responsible for the deaths of the animals they kill in a therapeutic hunt, no one would be responsible for deaths due to natural attrition. Regan and Singer both give the following reason for thinking that natural predators do no wrong when they kill. They point out that only the actions of moral agents can be evaluated as right or wrong, and that presumably only human beings are moral agents (only human beings are capable of recognizing moral principles and altering their behavior accordingly).

But when a responsible agent knowingly allows nature to take its course, is he or she not responsible by omission for the foreseeable deaths which result? Regan's answer would presumably be no, but this does not seem to me to be a plausible position. In a recent article, Dale Jamieson presents a relevant counterexample. Suppose that a boulder is rolling down a hill toward a hiker and that you can save the hiker by calling out to her. Jamieson asks, does it make the slightest difference whether the boulder was dislodged by the wind rather than by a would-be murderer? If we are not responsible for allowing nature to take its course, then although you violate the hiker's rights by failing to warn her in the latter case, in the former case you would do her no wrong. But this seems implausible.[26]

There *would*, I think, be a good reason for not culling overpopulated humans: it is possible for any normal adult human to both understand the gravity of the situation and alter his or her behavior accordingly. A human being can recognize and act on the obligation of individuals to avoid contributing to overpopulation; a deer, an elephant, or a water buffalo cannot.

[. . .]

Endangered species, exotics, and natural predators

[. . .] Environmentalists recognize prima facie duties to remove exotics, to reintroduce locally extinct predators to their former ranges, and to captive breed critically endangered species. My thesis in this section is that a more critical understanding of animal rights philosophies shows how an animal rights activist could recognize each of these prima facie duties on one or the other of two closely related grounds: duties to future generations of animals and/or duties to future generations of human beings.

Let me begin with the latter ground. Singer and Regan both emphasize the formal moral equality of human and (some) nonhuman animals. Yet, as I had occasion to point out in previous sections, both think hierarchically in the last analysis. [. . .] Singer *clearly* states that it is *not* speciesist to hold that killing a normal adult human is as morally serious as killing a mouse,[27] and Regan *clearly* says that death is a greater harm to a normal adult human than it is to any nonhuman animal.

[. . .]

Although fair-minded scientists and agriculturalists will find this inegalitarian aspect of Singer's and Regan's views comforting, no doubt many animal rights activists will reject it. But this is not a point about which animal rights activists need be apologetic. [. . .] Any workable ethics must recognize some hierarchy of interests, and from this a hierarchy of life-forms follows, if it turns out (as I think it does) that only some forms of life have the favored kinds of interests.[28]

The point of this digression on moral hierarchies is this: if

1 we have a general duty to preserve the integrity of ecosystems as the necessary context in which future generations of humans can pursue their most important interests,
2 these interests are of overriding moral importance, and
3 safeguarding future generations' pursuit of these interests requires us to remove exotics, breed endangered species, and reintroduce predators,

then long-sighted anthropocentrists and animal rights activists can agree that these things should be done (or at least that there is a presumptive, prima facie duty to do these things).

[. . .]

If future generations of human beings can only fulfill their most important interests against a background of relatively intact ecosystems, then relatively intact ecosystems we must preserve. And if, as environmentalists claim, preserving relatively intact ecosystems necessarily involves (some) breeding of endangered species, (some) removal of exotics, and allowing (some) natural predation, then animal rights activists who acknowledge the primacy of humans' most important interests can agree with both long-sighted anthropocentrists and environmentalists that we have prima facie duties to do these things.

I said that animal rights activists could also recognize prima facie duties to breed critically endangered species, remove exotics, and reintroduce predators as duties to future generations of *animals* and I will end by very briefly outlining how this is so. If human flourishing requires a relatively stable ecological context, then so too, presumably, does the flourishing of the nonhuman animals with which Singer and Regan are concerned. [. . .] Certainly some species (e.g., coyotes and racoons) are opportunistic and can thrive in newly disturbed ecosystems. Others (e.g., beaver) must disturb ecosystems to survive at all. But only if a patchwork of habitats in various stages of succession is maintained in every region will the needs of such species be met, for cross-habitat diversity provides the species on which these animals' lives depend. Although any one species may require a specific habitat to survive, in the long haul, all species depend on an ecological background of cross-habitat diversity. So without invoking the interests of future generations of humans, an animal rights activist could defend captive breeding, removal of exotics, and reintroduction of predators where these are necessary to preserve the ecological background conditions on which future generations of animals will depend.

Notes

1   Ron Howard, personal communication, June 18, 1992.
2   It might be preferable to speak in terms of "necessary" and "optional" rather than "obligatory" and "permissible," because Howard's labels are intended to be descriptive rather than normative. Also, note the qualification, in the penultimate section of this paper, that even among obligatory management species, hunting is not *always* necessary to prevent environmental damage.
3   "Animal Rights: Ignorance About Nature," *Audubon* (November 1990).
4   Julie A. Smith, "Wisconsin Greens Support Hunting—The Alliance Wonders Why?" *The Alliance News* 8, no. 1 (February 1991): 1, 7.
5   Marian Bean, "Environmental Groups and Animal Rights," *The Alliance News* 8, no. 1 (February 1991): 6.
6   Peter Singer, *Animal Liberation*, 2nd ed. (New York: Avon, 1990).
7   Peter Singer, *Practical Ethics*, 2nd ed. (Cambridge: Cambridge University Press, 1993).
8   Singer, *Animal Liberation*, 18–19.
9   Singer, *Animal Liberation*, 17.
10 Singer, *Animal Liberation*, 125.
11 There are subtle but important differences among these terms. See Michael R. Bratman's treatment in his *Intentions, Plans, and Practical Reason* (Cambridge: Harvard University Press, 1987).
12 Singer, *Practical Ethics*, 111–16, 118, and 132.
13 Singer, *Practical Ethics*, 95, 133.
14 Singer, *Practical Ethics*, 132.
15 Gary Varner, "Localizing Desire," chapter two of *In Nature's Interests? Interests, Animal Rights, and Environmental Ethics* (New York: Oxford University Press, 1998).
16 See the anecdote reported by Donald Griffin, *Animal Minds* (Chicago: University of Chicago Press, 1992), 64–5.
17 Without the (possibly incoherent) obligation to maximize simultaneously two variables (minimize pain *and* maximize pleasure).
18 Singer, *Practical Ethics*, 133–4, emphasis added.
19 Singer, *Animal Liberation*, 234. Two points about this argument. First, with regard to obligatory management species, it is not just "in special circumstances" that a population of animals "grows to such an extent that they damage their own environment and the prospects of their own survival, or that of other animals who share their habitat." The regularity with which this happens with obligatory management species is what separates them from permissive management species. Second, the choice is not simply between "allow[ing] hunters to kill some animals, inevitably wounding others in the process" and "reduc[ing] the fertility of the animals" by nonlethal means. Hunting regulations could be radically changed to minimize the wounding of animals. For instance, hunting could (in principle) be confined to bait stations with nearby blinds, from which hunters with high-caliber, automatic weapons and telescopic sights would kill habituated animals in a selective way (e.g., only does and sicker animals).
20 Malcolm W. Browne, "New Animal Vaccines Spread Like Diseases," *New York Times*, November 11, 1991.
21 Tom Regan, *The Case for Animal Rights* (Berkeley: University of California Press, 1983), 78, emphasis in original.
22 Regan, *The Case for Animal Rights*, 285–6.
23 The phrase "*commercial* animal agriculture" is Regan's. It is not obvious why the qualification "commercial" is included.
24 See my "The Prospects for Convergence and Consensus in the Animal Rights Debate," *Hastings Center Report* 24 (January/February 1994): 24–8.
25 Regan, *The Case for Animal Rights*, 322 and 377, emphasis in original.

26 Dale Jamieson "Rights, Justice, and Duties to Provide Assistance," *Ethics* 100 (1990): 349–62, at 351ff.
27 Singer, *Animal Liberation*, 17–18, quoted above. See also *Practical Ethics*. chapter 3.
28 See, generally, my *In Nature's Interests? Interests, Animal Rights, and Environmental Ethics*.

Rehabilitation and Introduction of Captive Wildlife

61

Glenn Albrecht

"Thinking like an Ecosystem: The Ethics of the Relocation, Rehabilitation and Release of Wildlife"

Albrecht discusses justifications of wildlife rehabilitation and methods to evaluate the success of rehabilitation and release programs. He proposes evaluating rehabilitation programs based on biodiversity and ecosystem preservation, and concludes that rehabilitation and release programs are not successful unless there is adequate habitat in which these rehabilitated species can be released.

Human intervention in the form of the rehabilitation, relocation and release of wildlife seems, on the face of it, to be a good thing. It is an outlet for human compassion for species other than our own and is generally aimed at restoration of an environmental imbalance that humans themselves have caused. Similarly, research in the scientific community whose goal to captive breed and then release rare and endangered species back into 'the wild' seems virtuous in that it is meeting an important conservation need. However, it shall be argued in this article that such actions are self-contradictory in that they permit the continuation of the very conditions that led to their being undertaken in the first instance. While limited ethical justification can be made for rehabilitation, relocation and release of wildlife, it is not strong when faced with the claims of what might be called 'ecological justice' where the highest good equals the protection of the maximum amount of interconnected biodiversity in a given environment. The achievement of this higher good requires that our ethical attention and limited scientific and financial resources move away from supporting individual animals and species and be urgently redirected to the preservation and management of whole ecosystems.

The need to rehabilitate

[. . .]

The issue of human intervention in the natural order of things in the form of the rehabilitation, relocation and release of wildlife covers the full spectrum of intervention. The rehabilitation of sick or injured animals and their successful release back into their own habitat appears to maintain the complexity and diversity of ecosystems. [. . .] The same could be said for captive breeding programs that have as their goal, the release of rare and endangered species into 'the wild': it is better to have these programs than to see yet more of our native animals added to the 'extinct' list.

[. . .]

The evaluation of rehabilitation and release programs

The possibility of evaluating the options of rehabilitation, relocation and release depends largely on there being some evaluative standard measuring 'success' that all can agree on and the ability of science or some other institution to supply reliable data on whether the standard is being met. Conservation biologists have developed a set of practical criteria based on such factors as acclimatisation, medical and genetic screening, pre- and post-release training, provisioning and monitoring as a measure of the success or failure of reintroduction projects for captive bred populations.[1]

[. . .]

These criteria do not, however, address cultural and *ethical questions* about whether such projects ought to be undertaken in the first place. Cultural values are notoriously difficult to evaluate. In the domain of the cultural significance of animals it is evident that considerable disagreement prevails between those who value animals solely for their instrumental value (circuses, fox hunters) and those who value them for aesthetic (wildlife photographers) and 'spiritual' (indigenous Australians) reasons.

It is possible to develop evaluative frameworks for assessing relocation and release programs by undertaking a systematic examination of the models and theories of environmental value offered by contemporary environmental philosophers. However, such an exercise is likely to be of interest mainly to environmental philosophers and given the huge diversity of views on offer in environmental ethics, it is, in any case, a task beyond the capacity of a short article.[2]

I offer two related ways of avoiding this dilemma. The first is to propose a simplified schema for the evaluation of intervention based on some fairly uncontroversial knowledge that we have about the importance of biodiversity and its reliance on ecosystem preservation. The second is to generate an ethical framework by close examination of the outcomes of such actions on both the humans and animals involved in rehabilitation and release programs. If it can be shown that the commitments and actions of carers, researchers and policy makers are inconsistent with the interests of individual animals and species involved, then such commitments and actions are also self-contradictory for the person/group involved. This is the case if animals continue to suffer because of our interventions and if ongoing loss of habitat compromises the likely success of release and relocation programs.

Ecosystems and values

Biologists worldwide agree that the major contemporary factor driving species to extinction is anthropogenic habitat destruction.[3] [. . .] [If] we desire to see this trend stopped, then habitat protection in the form of ecosystem protection is needed. Value is then placed on total biodiversity and protection of ecosystems and habitat that contain it becomes the goal of human endeavor.

[. . .]

To think ecologically, we need to 'think like a mountain' and appreciate the full balance between predator, prey and habitat. This shift in thinking requires movement from attempting to value nature by assessing individual units, to valuing based on cumulative diversity and complexity. . . .[4]

Given the complexity of ecosystems it is not desirable or practical to assess the value of species or human actions in ways that are isolated from the system as a whole. Such a perspective is consistent with what we currently know about individuals, species and their relationship to their habitat. Animals exist by virtue of their dependence on a functioning ecosystem within which they survive and their survival is partly constitutive of that ecosystem at the same time. Species and habitat *co-evolve* and do so over millions of years. It is then impossible to disaggregate such interdependence and put values on so-called parts of what is an organically unified whole. It makes good ecological sense to value the whole, as it is the whole that ultimately supports life, including our own.

[. . .]

From the ethical perspective of ecological justice, the interconnected whole is the one that needs more attention focused on it and such a focus might mean that efforts to intervene at the level of individual animals or even individual species might be considered to be noble but misguided. Rather, resources that are scarce and valuable (including the resource of the community of research scientists and the rehabilitation community) should be redirected to the main problem confronting wildlife in Australia, fragmentation and complete loss of habitat.

The rehabilitation, relocation and release of individual animals

At one level of analysis, an ethic of compassion, care and concern, which is at the core of human involvement with animals in need of rehabilitation and or relocation, is an expression of the very best of human virtues. Individuals who selflessly devote time and their own limited finances to animals in need are indeed followers of St Francis of Assisi. Such selflessness is even more apparent when native wildlife-carers risk their own health in the support of some species. [. . .] So at the level of an individual human, we would want to support animal carers as humane and virtuous individuals. From the perspective of the animals that benefit from such care, the opportunity to 'have a life' where one was previously unlikely must be seen as something positive. Where such animals can be returned to their previous habitat, then it seems that complexity and diversity are maintained.

However, it is almost invariably the case that the primary cause for the need for an animal to be rehabilitated is a major perturbation to the habitat of that creature by humans. The case of Koalas in Eastern Australia is instructive. Koala habitat is contracting because of a large number of human development pressures.

[. . .]

It is apparent, however, that the very same pressures that lead to the need for rehabilitation in the first place have not been removed from the Koalas' habitat, indeed, they have most likely been magnified. All too often, animals are released, only to be found dead or in need of further help within a very short period of time. This problem is exacerbated by the fact that the animal has become habituated to humans and their environment and is thus more likely to place itself in a risky situation (for example, close to dogs) in the future. The ethics of this situation become less clear. A well-intentioned and virtuous act inadvertently causes continued suffering on the part of native animals.

[. . .]

A possible solution to this dilemma is to place rehabilitated animals back into 'safe' areas but increasingly for animals such as Koalas, such safe places are likely to be fragments of urban bushland that have a very finite capacity to hold a viable population. Supplementary feeding is necessary to hold a number of animals that exceeds the carrying capacity of the remnant patch. Overcrowding may in turn lead to social and health problems within the captive population as normal spaces between and within the generations and sexes become constricted.

[. . .]

Without expanses of habitat large enough for rehabilitated species to be safely released, the ethical impulse to care for animals is inexorably shifted from something unambiguously ethically good to something that has potentially undesirable consequences. I argue that such an outcome is the inevitable result of a focus on individual animals to the exclusion of ecosystems and the habitat requirements of the whole species. Where emotion overrides ecology, the result is likely to be negative for the species, and, in the medium to long term, negative for individual carers as their intensive efforts become increasingly failure prone. It is clearly contradictory to engage in emergency action that will inevitably lead to an even greater need for more of the same action in the future.

[. . .]

Notes

1   See B.B. Beck *et al.* 'Reintroduction of Captive-born Animals' in P.J.S. Olney *et al.* (eds), *Creative Conservation: interactive management of wild and captive animals* (Chapman Hall, London, 1994), p. 273.
2   See M. Zimmerman, *Contesting the Earth's Future: Radical Ecology and Postmodernity* (University of California Press, Berkeley, 1994) for a systematic account of such theories.
3   See Andrew P. Dobson, *Conservation and Biodiversity* (Scientific American Library, New York, 1996) for a very useful summary of the contemporary issues.
4   See Bryan Norton, 'On the Inherent Danger of Undervaluing Species' in B. Norton, ed., *The Preservation of Species: The Value of Biodiversity* (Princeton University Press, Princeton, 1986) on the importance of valuing total diversity.

62

Gary E. Duke

"Wildlife Rehabilitation: Is it Significant?"

Duke provides a justification for wildlife rehabilitation programs on the basis that they a) are humane to individual animals, b) provide the experience and develop the expertise necessary for treating less common or endangered species and allow the survival of a fully diverse gene pool with rare species, c) allow permanently crippled individuals to be used for education programs, zoos, etc., in place of healthy, intact animals, and d) provide the best evidence of the kinds of biomedical concerns encountered by wildlife under natural circumstances through diagnosis of medical problems in submitted wildlife.

This title poses a question frequently asked of wildlife rehabilitators, often more as a challenge than as a question. For this reason, rehabilitators need to be prepared to respond. Over the years, I've developed some of my own responses and collected some from others. The purpose of this short paper is to share these responses.

Most rehabilitation programs include wildlife education as well as rehabilitation, many also perform research or captive propagation and reintroduction. These additions certainly increase the significance of a rehabilitation program and we should all consider including them to the extent that we can, but they aren't absolutely essential.

Perhaps the most obvious significance of wildlife rehabilitation is that it is *humane*. There is a growing public demand for humane handling of injured wildlife and most people are offended if proper care cannot be provided for suffering animals. Humaneness may simply be swift and effective euthanasia for irreparable individuals for which there is no demand for captive propagation, research or education. Although many individuals of common species may thus be euthanized, if an individual has potential for release, rehabilitation should always be undertaken. This benefits not only that individual, but also provides the experience and develops the expertise necessary for treating less common or *endangered species*.

Care of the latter, wherein each individual animal is vital to the survival of the species, is the second great significance of wildlife rehabilitation. An individual need not be endangered, however, to be significant. Many individuals are significant because they are adapted to a research program, zoological garden display or captive propagation program. Frequently, the expertise of a wildlife rehabilitator is the best or only medical expertise available to care for these individuals.

Additionally, all individuals are significant in that each one contributes genetic diversity to its own species. A diverse gene pool is important to adaptiveness. I have been told that rehabilitators are tampering with natural selection, and that we should "let nature take her course." However, over 75 percent of our cases in Minnesota need rehabilitation because of an unfortunate contact with humans (e.g., hit by cars, shot, trapped, collision with a window.) Even house cats are human-introduced. Our North American songbirds didn't evolve with domesticated cats. This is not natural selection—it is unnatural selection as a direct result of humans. It is important to recognize that rehabilitators help animals who may be the best adapted of their species since they have learned to live in close proximity to humans. These tolerant individuals may be instrumental in the survival of their kind as the human population continues to increase in the future.

The third major significance of rehabilitation is that permanently crippled individuals can be made available for *education* programs, zoos, etc. This avoids capture of healthy, intact birds for such purposes. In our raptor rehabilitation program, approximately 75 percent of our admissions are injured due to contact with humans or human structures (powerlines, picture windows, etc.). (Redig and Duke, 1978; Duke, 1982). Therefore, educational programs help to avoid or reduce the negative impact of humans on wildlife populations. They can also help convince the general public of the importance of wildlife in our ecosystem. The use of live animals is a very effective educational tool as are the experiences of individuals dealing with man's direct impact on wildlife.

Lastly, and in my view most importantly, diagnosis of medical problems existing in cases received in rehabilitation programs provides the best *evidence of the kinds of biomedical problems faced by wildlife*. This evidence may provide direction for future research, for new legislation, and/or for wildlife management.

When our rehabilitation program discovered the extent and severity of accidental trapping of Bald eagles (*Haliaeetus leucocephalus*) in traps set for furbearers, state trapping regulations were changed to help reduce the problem. Our data on the extent of lead poisoning in Bald eagles has been used in arguments against lead shot at the state and national levels. Research in our laboratories on aspergillosis and lead poisoning arose because of the frequency of these problems in raptors (Duke, 1985).

The health of wildlife may be an excellent "barometer" of environmental health. If rehabilitators perform careful diagnoses and keep good records, they can alert governmental agencies to environmental problems. If all rehabilitators do this, and if data could be pooled from all over the U.S., we could have a significant impact on environmental policies and wildlife management as well as helping to save injured or ill wild animals.

Wildlife rehabilitators are often criticized by wildlife managers because they deal with individual animals rather than populations. Intensive management of individuals of common species, as is practiced by rehabilitators, is not *wrong*—it is not wrong to care for any creature. But, with the limited resources available for wildlife management, priorities must be established which usually result in ignoring individuals of common species. This is necessary and it is proper that public employees working on limited budgets observe these priorities. But in my opinion, rehabilitators working with little or no funding, or with funding not derived from sources competing with managers, should feel free to establish their own priorities.

As described above, diagnosis of problems faced by individuals leads to information about the health of populations and can be used by managers to help protect populations. While managers think in terms of wildlife populations rather than individuals, they manage populations so as to create a larger-than-natural surplus, then encourage hunting to "harvest" the surplus. The harvest then becomes similar to wildlife rehabilitation because it involves removal of one individual at a time from the population. Rehabilitators aim to return one animal at a time to the population. Both may be considered recreational but it is far easier to get a permit for harvest than for repair.

In the long run, good diagnoses of wildlife medical problems will provide significant input for management of wildlife populations and I predict that this will eventually be recognized by wildlife managers. I must emphasize *good* diagnoses and good rehabilitation practices. Each year a smaller proportion of our populace is involved in hunting and a growing proportion becomes more aware of the significance of a balanced ecosystem. I think that we will all ultimately work together to benefit wildlife and that many aspects of non-consumptive wildlife recreation will become more broadly accepted.

Literature cited

Duke, G.E. 1982. Philosophy and operation of the University of Minnesota Raptor Research and Rehabilitation Program. *Proc. Nat. Wildl. Rehab. Symp.*, Vol. 1, *Wildlife Rehabilitation*, Paul Beaver, ed., Exposition Press Inc., Smithtown, NY, pp. 1–10.

——. 1985. Research projects for rehabilitators. *Proc. Nat. Wildl. Rehab. Symp.*, Vol. 4, *Wildlife Rehabilitation*, Paul Beaver, ed., D.J. Mackey Pub., Coconut Creek, FL, pp. 9–12.

Redig, P.T. and G.E. Duke. 1978. Raptor research and rehabilitation program at the College of Veterinary Medicine. *Minn. Vet.* 18:27–34.

63

━━━◦◦◦◦━━━

Ned Hettinger

"Exotic Species, Naturalisation, and Biological Nativism"

Hettinger addresses arguments both in favor of and in opposition to the continued introduction of exotic species to many habitats. He concludes that there are good reasons for opposing their introduction; even the presence of species that are naturally dispersing and nondamaging leads to a loss of biological purity and to a greater global homogenization of plants and animals.

It is well-known that the spread of exotic species has caused—and continues to cause—significant environmental degradation, including extinction of native species and massive human influence on natural systems. What is less clear, however, is how we are to conceptualise exotic species. Consider, for example, [. . .] wild pigs (*Sus scrofa*) in the Hawaiian rainforest, whose ancestors were brought to Hawaii by Polynesians perhaps 1500 years ago. Are they still an exotic species or have they 'naturalised' despite constituting an ongoing threat to the native biota in this extinction capital of the world? One commentator put his finger on the problem of understanding exotic species when he said, 'The terms "exotic" and "native" . . . are . . . about as ambiguous as any in our conservation lexicon (except perhaps "natural")' (Noss 1990: 242).

This essay sifts through the mix of biological theorising and philosophical evaluation that constitutes this controversy over understanding, evaluating, and responding to exotic species. I propose a precising definition of exotics as any species significantly foreign to an ecological assemblage, whether or not the species causes damage, is human introduced, or arrives from some other geographical location. My hope is to keep separate the distinct strands typically woven into this concept while still capturing most of our fundamental intuitions about exotics.

[. . .]

What is an exotic species?

[. . .]

The fundamental idea underlying the concept of an exotic species is a species that is alien or foreign. Such a species is foreign in the sense that it has not significantly adapted with the

local species and to local abiotic environment. [. . .] Geographical considerations are typically taken as what distinguishes natives from exotics. [. . .] On this account, exotics are
species that originally evolved in some other place. Woods and Moriarty (2001) call this the
'evolutionary criterion'.

Specifying the natives of a region as those that originally evolved there is both too
stringent a requirement and perhaps overly broad. Too stringent because, by this criterion,
humans would be native only to Africa. But all species move around. Species evolve in one
locale, then migrate or expand their range to other places, and thrive for thousands of years
perfectly at home in these new regions. Few species in a region would be natives if we
accepted this evolutionary origin criterion of native species.

[. . .]

I do not think we should require that natives fit an ecosystem, much less be good fits.
There might be 'native misfits' as well as 'exotic fits'. [. . .] Consider that the Asian long-
horned beetle (*Anoplophora glabripennis*) recently discovered devouring trees in Chicago is
also an important threat to trees in its native range (Corn *et al.* 1999). Barnacles are an
example of species that proliferate wildly in their native ranges. [. . .] Unless one accepts an
idyllic conception of perfectly-harmonious natural systems, one must admit that native
species can wreak havoc in their native ranges.

Similarly, we should not assume that natives are well-integrated into 'balanced' and
'self-regulating communities'. [. . .] Presupposing a tightly integrated and balanced, community conception of natural systems is highly controversial given the recent emphasis in
ecology on disequilibrium, instability, disturbance, and heterogeneous patchy landscapes
(Hettinger and Throop 1999).

[. . .]

Native species will have significantly adapted with resident species and the local abiotic
environment, not in the sense that they necessarily have become good fits or are controlled by
others, but in the sense that native species will have 'forged ecological links' (Vermeij 1996:
4) with some other natives. Natives will have 'responded to each other ecologically' and
frequently evolutionary (Vermeij 1996: 5). Natives are established species (i.e., more or less
permanent residents) tied to some other residents via predation, parasitism, mutualism,
commensalism, and so on. Often native species will have affected the abundance of other
native individuals, perhaps altering the frequencies of alleles in the gene pool of native
populations and thus exerting selective pressure on other natives. A native species will also
likely have adapted to the abiotic features of the local environment.

Let me stress again that by 'adapted' I do not mean 'positively fit in'. A species has
adapted when it has changed its behaviour, capacities, or gene frequencies in response to other
species or local abiota. Aggressively competing is as much adapting as is establishing symbiotic relationships. By adapted, I also do not mean fit or well-suited to survive in an environment. Species that have historically adapted in my sense may go extinct and species that have
never actually adapted to a local assemblage may nonetheless be suited to survive there.

In contrast with native species, an exotic species is one that is foreign to an ecosystem in
the sense that it has not significantly adapted to the resident species and/or abiotic elements
that characterise this system and, perhaps more importantly, the system's resident species
have not significantly adapted to it. On the account defended here, species that are introduced to new geographical locations by humans, or that migrate or expand their ranges
without such assistance, may or may not be exotics in these new regions. Species are exotic in
new locations only when the species movement is ecological and not merely geographical.

That is, if a species moves into a type of ecological assemblage that is already present in its home range(s), then the immigrant species is not exotic (foreign) in this new locale: It will already have adapted with the species and types of abiotic features there. If, on the other hand, the species movement results in its presence in a type of ecological assemblage with which it has not previously adapted, then the species is an exotic in this new location.

[. . .]

When the first finches appeared on the Galapagos Islands, they were exotics because they had not adapted with the local species and to the local environment (Woods and Moriarty 2001). [. . .] In contrast, when bison (*Bison bison*) expand their range north or west out of Yellowstone National Park into the surrounding grasslands, they are not exotics because they enter a habitat with species with which they have adapted. [. . .] What counts is ecological difference, not geographical distance.

Whether a species is exotic to an assemblage is a matter of degree. The greater the differences between the species, the abiota, and their interrelationships in the old and new habitats, the more exotic an immigrant will be. After passing a certain threshold of difference, we can be quite comfortable with judgements about a species being exotic. [. . .] But there will be borderline cases where neither the designation exotic nor nonexotic is clearly appropriate. For example, the mountain goats that are moving into Yellowstone Park from the north would be neither clearly exotic nor nonexotic to the Yellowstone assemblages they join, if the flora, fauna, and abiota in their native habitat is somewhat but not all that similar to those they encounter in Yellowstone.

By requiring that a native species has actually adapted to (some of) the other natives in an ecological assemblage, we allow for the possibility of 'exotic fits'; that is, aliens that arrive in new ecosystems but are well-suited to them. Westman (1990: 254) calls this phenomenon 'preadaptation' and says it is possible because different species can play functionally similar roles. For example, even if Asian snow leopards (*Panthera uncia*) could play the same ecological roles that the restored grey wolves (*Canis lupus*) play in the Yellowstone assemblage, this would not make them native.

[. . .]

Exotics and human-introduced species

Although exotics are often defined as human-introduced species, the examples of cattle egrets moving to South America and the Galapagos' first finches show that exotic species need not be introduced by humans. Nor need human-introduced species be exotics. Species that humans place into an assemblage as part of a restoration project are often not exotics. For example, the restoration of grey wolves to Yellowstone Park is not exotic introduction, even though humans captured wolves from Canada and released them in regions (Wyoming and Montana) hundreds of miles south of their home. Despite the fact that the individual organisms involved were not previously in the recipient assemblages and despite the fact that they were put there by humans, on the account given here, the released wolves are not an exotic species.

[. . .]

Even human introduction of species to locations where they have never previously existed need not count as exotic introduction. As long as the resident species have adapted with the introduced species, the immigrant will not be exotic. Consider [. . .] introducing a fish species into a high mountain lake previously devoid of that species of fish because a waterfall blocks its dispersal pathway. This need not count as exotic introduction, if the life forms in the lake had adapted with that species of fish and if that species had adapted to abiotic conditions like those in the lake.

[. . .]

Disvaluing human-introduced exotics and U.S. park service policy

Although exotics need not be human introduced, recently many—likely most—are introduced by humans, including those that are the most exotic in their new habitats. Modern humans regularly transport exotics distances, with speeds, and between ecological assemblages that do not frequently occur (or are impossible) with naturally-dispersing exotics. When an exotic species is introduced by humans, whether directly or indirectly, intentionally or nonintentionally, this provides one reason for the negative appraisal commonly levelled at such species. This negative evaluation is justified independently of whether the human-introduced exotic causes damage. Negatively evaluating human-assisted immigrant species—and not those arriving on their own—is a controversial value judgement. It is supported by a number of reasons, briefly outlined below.

Massive human alteration of the earth is ongoing (Vitousek 1997). Perhaps half of the planet's surface is significantly disturbed by humans, and half of that is human dominated (Hannah *et al.* 1993). Humans are increasingly influencing, altering, and controlling the planet's natural systems. The result is a radical diminution in the sphere of wild nature on earth. An important reason to value natural areas and entities is because they are relatively free of human influence.

[. . .]

The presence of human-introduced species diminishes the wildness of natural systems and thus provides a reason for disvaluing exotic species when they are human introduced.

[. . .]

Some charge that there is misanthropy behind such a distinction in value between human-introduced and naturally-dispersed exotics (Scherer 1994: 185). But valuing humans, even loving humanity, is quite compatible with not wanting humans or their works everywhere, especially in National Parks and wilderness areas.

One of the mandates of U.S. National Parks like Yellowstone is to let nature take its course. [. . .] As a natural area where human influences should be minimised, the negative evaluation of human-introduced exotics is especially compelling and Yellowstone has a strong reason to remove human-introduced exotics. For closely related reasons, the Park has a strong rationale for welcoming naturally-dispersing aliens. The presence of such exotics is a manifestation of wild nature, a world that made us rather than one we have made. Removing naturally-dispersing exotics would (typically) increase human control and manipulation over natural systems.

[. . .]

[H]owever, [i]f naturally-dispersing exotics cause sufficient damage, they may warrant control. The policy of letting nature take its course is not absolute. Respect for wild natural processes can be outweighed by concern for certain outcomes in nature. For example, the protozoan parasite (*Myxobolus cerebralis*) that causes whirling disease (an affliction that cripples some fish species) is a recent European immigrant to Yellowstone's ecosystems. If this species somehow travelled from Europe into Yellowstone without the aid of humans, the Park would be hard pressed to justify welcoming such a naturally-dispersing exotic. If the parasite threatened to destroy the entire Yellowstone cutthroat population, the Park would have strong reasons not to let nature take its course.

Exotics and damaging species

Some define exotic species as those that damage the new regions they occupy (Scherer 1994: 185). Indeed, exotics have caused massive amounts of damage, both ecologically and economically. [. . .] Pimentel *et al.* (1999) estimate that there are about 50,000 species of non-U.S. origin in the country, a fifteenth of the estimated total of 750,000 species. [. . .] According to Pimentel *et al.*, the yearly quantifiable damage these species cause is at least $138 billion.

[. . .]

Exotics have caused the extinction of native species. [. . .] Approximately 40 percent of threatened or endangered species on the U.S. Endangered Species lists are at risk primarily because of exotic species (Pimentel *et al.* 1999).

Despite the massive ongoing harm such species cause, we should not identify exotics with damaging species. We have already noted that some native species also cause damage. Furthermore, not all immigrants to new ecosystems are harmful. Most get extirpated before they become established. [. . .] According to the 'tens rule', 10 percent of exotics that are introduced into an area succeed in establishing breeding populations and 10 percent of those will become highly invasive (Bright 1998: 25). Even if only 1 percent of exotics typically cause serious problems, this is of little comfort, for as Bright argues, 'since the global economy is continually showering exotics over the Earth's surface, there is little consolation in the fact that 90 percent of these impacts are "duds" and only 1 percent of them really detonate. The bombardment is continual, and so are the detonations' (1998: 24).

[. . .]

Exotics can even be beneficial in the new habitats they occupy. Vermeij speaks of the 'potentially crucial role invasions and invaders have played in stimulating evolution' and says that 'in the absence of invasions, communities and species and interactions comprising them may stagnate, especially if the economic base of energy and nutrients remains fixed' (1996: 7). Exotics sometimes provide habitat for native species. A species of *Eucalyptus* tree introduced into California from Australia over 120 years ago benefits Monarch butterflies (*Danaus plexippus*) who rely on them during annual migrations (Woods and Moriarty 2001). Eucalyptus also benefits native birds and salamanders (Westman 1990: 255). There are also examples of exotics benefiting endangered species: grizzly bears consume substantial amounts of nonnative clover in Yellowstone Park (Reinhart, *et al.* 1999) and, in some locations in the U.S., nutria (*Myocastor coypus*) (a South American relative of the beaver) are a principal food source for the endangered red wolf (*Canis niger*).

[. . .]

Still, there are good reasons for being suspicious of the disruptive potential of exotic species. Exotics often arrive without the predators, parasites, diseases, or competitors that are likely to limit their proliferation in their native habitat. Local prey, hosts, and competitors of exotics have not had a chance to evolve defensive strategies. Past experience, [. . .] is another reason for suspicion. Nevertheless, as with the connection between human introduction and exotics, one ought not to move from an empirical correlation between the presence of exotics and damaging results to a conceptual connection between exotic species and those that cause damage.

When an exotic species causes serious damage or harm, we have a reason for a negative appraisal of this exotic. When exotics cause harm to human interests, the ground for a negative evaluation of these exotics is fairly straightforward. [. . .] When exotic species harm or impoverish nonhuman nature, the justification for a negative evaluation is less straightforward. Many worry about whether it makes sense to harm natural systems and they challenge us to provide a principled distinction between harming a natural system and changing it (Throop 2000). (For example, in what sense did the chestnut blight harm or damage eastern U.S. forests as opposed to merely changing them?) But when an exotic species invades a diverse native community and changes it into a virtually uniform stand of a single species vastly diminished in suitability for wildlife habitat or forage (e.g., *Phragmites* in eastern U.S. wetlands, *Melaleuca* in Florida), a negative appraisal on nonanthropocentric grounds seems straightforward. Such an appraisal is also clearly called for when an exotic species, plentiful in its native habitat and present as an alien around the world, causes large numbers of extinctions of other species (e.g., brown tree snakes). The damage to humans and to nonhuman nature that some exotic species have caused is a significant reason to be worried about exotic species.

Naturalisation of exotics

[. . .]

I suggest that the process of naturalising and becoming native is neither arbitrary nor purely scientific. [. . .] To become native, an exotic species must not only naturalise ecologically (i.e., adapt with local species and to the local environment), but it must also naturalise evaluatively. This means that for an exotic to become a native, human influence, if any, in the exotic's presence in an assemblage must have sufficiently washed away for us to judge that species to be a natural member of that assemblage.

Ecological naturalisation

An exotic species naturalises in an ecological sense when it persists in its new habitat and significantly adapts with the resident species and to the local abiota. This is a matter of degree and typically increases over time. Immigrant species will immediately casually interact with elements of the local ecological assemblage, but significant adaptation between the immigrant and residents and between the immigrant and the local abiota takes time and increases over time. Exertion of evolutionary pressure between the immigrant, the residents, and the abiota will also not be immediate.

Determining what is to count as significant adaptation requires context sensitive judgement. Adaptation can continue indefinitely. Whether adaptation is sufficient for ecological naturalisation may depend on the adaptive potential of a particular species/ecosystem complex. If a great deal of adaptation is going to take place (perhaps including co-evolution of the exotic and several resident species), then until this occurs, we likely would not judge the exotic to have ecologically naturalised. On the other hand, if the exotic tends to employ resources and modes of living that were not previously exploited in the recipient habitat, then perhaps not much adaptation need take place before we judge the species to have ecologically naturalised. In highly individualistic and loose assemblages, where few ecological or evolutionary links exist between members and where many species have wide-ranging tolerances to a diversity of abiotic factors (and so are unlikely to have adapted much to local conditions), a newcomer may be no more exotic (that is, unadapted to the local species and abiotic conditions) than are the resident species. Perhaps very little adaptation is sufficient to ecologically naturalise to such an assemblage. Ecological naturalisation can also occur in assemblages where the vast majority of species are human-introduced exotics (e.g., Hawaiian forests, or cities and suburbs where people have eradicated the natives and planted exotics). Over a sufficient time period, a large group of exotics would ecologically naturalise with each other and the surviving natives would also adapt with the new assemblage.

[. . .]

Evaluative naturalisation

Should ecological naturalisation be all that is required before an exotic species is to be considered native? I think not. Many immigrant species have been in their new habitats long enough to ecologically naturalise (i.e., significantly adapt with local species) and yet we justifiably hesitate to consider them natives. Consider [. . .] Holmes Rolston's claim that mustangs on the western range are not natives even though they (and the ecological assemblages with which they interact) have had several hundred years to adapt. Many still consider Hawaiian feral pigs nonnative even after some 1500 years. It is hard to believe that significant ecological naturalisation has not occurred during that time span. The judgements that these species are not yet natives—despite having significantly adapted with resident species and to local abiota—can be explained by treating judgements about naturalisation and the resultant nativity as involving an evaluative component in addition to the ecological one.

Onetime exotic species that are judged to have naturalised and become full-fledged natives are ones that we take to be 'natural' members of their ecological assemblages. For this to be the case, we must judge their presence in these assemblages as not representing significant, ongoing human influence. [. . .] This is true even if the immigrant species has significantly ecologically naturalised and is thus no longer exotic.

We do not prevent human-introduced exotics from becoming native when we require that they not only significantly adapt but also become natural members of their new assemblages. For exotics can evaluatively naturalise as well as ecologically naturalise. Human influence on natural systems and species 'washes out' over time, like bootprints in the spring snow. Natural processes can once again take control, as when old mining roads erode and vegetation overgrows them. This washing away of human influence over time constitutes evaluative naturalisation and it allows human-introduced exotics that have ecologically naturalised to become full-fledged natives.

A number of factors affect the washing away of human influence and the resultant evaluative naturalisation (Hettinger and Throop 1999: 20–21). First, the greater the human influence, the longer it takes to wash out. Perhaps this is why we are reluctant to think of feral animals as capable of naturalising and becoming natives even over long time-periods. Domestication of animals constitutes significant human influence over them, and so even after several hundred years we might think that feral horses, for example, are still not native (fully naturalised) on the American range, despite having significantly ecologically naturalised. Withholding the judgement that they have evaluatively naturalised reflects the view that the human influence on those species is of ongoing significance.

[. . .]

Increasing temporal distance from human influence is another factor that contributes to the washing away of such influence. For an exotic species to naturalise ecologically, it must significantly adapt with other natives and the local abiota, and this ensures that it will have some temporal longevity in an assemblage. This longevity may—but need not—be sufficient to ensure evaluative naturalisation.

[. . .]

A third factor affecting the washout of human influence is the extent to which a natural system becomes similar to what it would have been absent that influence. [. . .] Mountain goats would be in Yellowstone if humans had not influenced natural systems. In contrast, [. . .] it is likely that Hawaiian nature would have remained without pigs virtually forever but for human intervention. Thus it is reasonable to view pigs on Hawaii as representing continuing human influence in this respect.

A fourth factor affecting washout of human influence is the extent to which natural forces have reworked a human-influenced system (independently of whether the result is similar to what it would have been absent human intervention). For example, if humans introduce coyotes into an area with significant wolf presence, human influence on the assemblage resulting from coyote introduction would be lessened quickly because wolves significantly dominate coyotes. When a human-introduced exotic has naturalised in the ecological sense, natural forces have reworked the affects of human action to some degree. Thus ecological naturalisation contributes to evaluative naturalisation in this dimension as well, though again there is no reason to think that it is sufficient for it.

[. . .]

Let me summarise the implications of my account of naturalisation for the distinction between exotics and natives. Exotics are species that have not significantly adapted with the local ecological assemblage. Once a species has significantly adapted (ecologically naturalised), it is no longer exotic. But such a species might still not be native. If it was human introduced and if its presence in the assemblage represents significant and ongoing human influence, then it is not a natural member of this assemblage and so is not native. Perhaps kudzu, western mustangs, and Hawaiian pigs are such examples of species that are no longer exotic (because they have ecologically naturalised), but are not yet natives either (because the human influence on their presence is still significant).

Although human introduction is not part of my account of exotics, it is a factor in my account of native species. Are the problems I identified with the human-introduced account of exotics applicable to my account of natives? Although I need not count the restored Yellowstone wolves as exotics (as must the human-introduced account of exotics), it might seem that I cannot say that they are natives either, given the significant human involvement in their return to Yellowstone. But because this is return of a species that humans had previously eradicated, the restoration of wolves to Yellowstone is, in one important respect, a lessening of human influence over both Yellowstone and the wolf as a species. Yellowstone with wolves is now like it would be had humans never eradicated them. Similarly, by returning the wolf to its former range, humans are, in one respect, lessening their overall impact on wolves. Thus, in these respects, wolves are natural and hence native members of Yellowstone, despite being restored by humans.

Xenophobia, biodiversity, and disvaluing exotics as exotics

Nativists are those who favour native inhabitants over immigrants and/or want to preserve indigenous cultures. Biological nativists favour native flora and fauna, and they combat the introduction and spread of exotic species in order to preserve native assemblages.

[. . .]

Such an opposition to exotic species has been compared to a xenophobic prejudice toward immigrant peoples. [. . .] Jonah Peretti argues that 'nativist trends in Conservation Biology have made environmentalists biased against alien species' and he wants to 'protect modern environmentalists from reproducing the xenophobic and racist attitudes that have plagued nativist biology in the past' (1998: 183, 191).

In contrast, David Ehrenfeld thinks that comparing the antagonism toward exotics with real biases such as racial profiling of African-Americans and Hispanics 'deserves ridicule'. [. . .] After noting some exceptions, Ehrenfeld concludes, 'There are more than enough cases in which exotic species have been extremely harmful to justify using the stereotype' (1999: 11).

Ehrenfeld is on shaky ground if the 'ten's rule' is accurate. If only one in one hundred exotics cause serious problems, then stereotypes about the damaging nature of exotic species may be no more statistically grounded than are some of the morally-obnoxious, racial, and sexual stereotypes about humans.

[. . .]

When exotics are also distinguished from human-introduced species (as I have done), what justification for a negative evaluation of exotics remains? Those who oppose naturally dispersing, nondamaging exotics seem to be doing so because these species are alien, and negatively evaluating a species simply because it is foreign does suggest a xenophobic attitude and a troubling nativist desire to keep locals pure from foreign contamination.

[. . .]

Biological nativists' opposition to exotic species can be defended by distinguishing between types of nativism and purism and the reasons for them. While nativisms based on irrational fear, hatred, or feelings of superiority are morally objectionable, I will argue that some versions of both cultural nativism and biological nativism are rational and even praise-worthy. For example, I believe the protection and preservation of indigenous peoples and cultures is desirable. This may involve favouritism for local peoples and opposition to the dilution of local cultures (a kind of purism), but it is based on an admirable attempt to protect the diversity of human culture. Similarly, biological nativism is laudatory because it supports a kind of valuable biodiversity that is increasingly disappearing.

It might seem strange to oppose exotic species on grounds of biodiversity, for the presence of alien species seems to enhance a region's biodiversity, not decrease it. [. . .] But this argument takes too narrow a view of biodiversity. Since the breakup of the supercontinent Pangaea some 180 million years ago, the earth has developed into isolated continents with spectacularly diverse ecological regions. Biological nativists value and want to preserve this diversity of ecological assemblages. This diversity is in jeopardy due to modern humans' wanton mixing of species from around the globe. The objection biological nativists can have to exotic species as exotics—at least in the current context—is that although they immediately add to the species count of the local assemblage and increase biodiversity in that way, the widespread movement of exotic species impoverishes global and regional biodiversity by decreasing the diversity between types of ecological assemblages on the planet. For example, adding a dandelion (*Taraxacum officinale*) to a wilderness area where it previously was absent diminishes the biodiversity of the planet by making this place more like everyplace else. Adding a mimosa tree to Sullivan's Island makes the Lowcountry of South Carolina more like some Asian assemblages. When this is done repeatedly, as humans are now doing and at an ever increasing rate, the trend is toward a globalisation of flora and fauna that threatens to homogenise the world's ecological assemblages into one giant mongrel ecology. Bright calls the spread of exotics 'evolution in reverse' (1998: 17) as the branches of the evolutionary bush are brought back together creating biosimilarity instead of biodiversity.

The loss of biodiversity resultant from the presence of exotics is greatly exacerbated by damaging exotics that invade, extirpate endemic species, or turn diverse native assemblages into near monocultures of themselves. But such causal diminishment in diversity is distinct from the conceptual diminution identified here: the mere presence of massive numbers of exotics in a great number of assemblages diminishes the diversity between ecological assemblages independently of whether they physically replace or diminish natives. Note that opposition to exotics on these conceptual grounds avoids the unfair stereotyping charge that must be addressed by those who oppose exotics because they are likely to cause damage.

It might be objected that presence of exotic species can enhance inter-assemblage biodiversity in certain respects, as well as decreasing it in others, and thus that the spread of exotics may not be a threat to overall biodiversity. For example, the movement of Asian snow leopards into Yellowstone Park would not only increase Yellowstone's species count but it would also make Yellowstone's assemblages differ from those of the Absoroka-Beartooth wilderness to the north in a way they previously did not: now they diverge in the types of mammals present. While snow leopards in Yellowstone would make Yellowstone's assemblages more like some Asian assemblages, it would also increase differences between Yellowstone and the wilderness areas to the north.

It is true that the presence of exotics can increase inter-assemblage biodiversity in the way suggested. More generally, species movement into new assemblages need not be a threat to overall biodiversity. In evolutionary history, such movement has frequently enriched ecosystems, brought on speciation, and enhanced global biodiversity. Careful planned and monitored human introduction of exotics into selected assemblages might be able to enhance biodiversity as well. But this is no defence for the blind and large-scale human introduction of exotics that is taking place on the planet today. In today's world, the increase in inter-assemblage diversity due to snow leopards' presence in Yellowstone would not last. Snow leopards would quickly find their way (or be introduced) into the Absoroka-Beartooth wilderness, and the increase in regional biodiversity would be lost. If we focus on individual cases of exotic introduction—without considering the cumulative impact of massive numbers of exotic introductions over time—we may be able to convince ourselves that the presence of exotics is benign (or even beneficial) in terms of biodiversity. But in the context of the current flood of exotics, such a focus is myopic. The logical end point of the ongoing, massive spread of exotics is that ecological assemblages in similar climatic and abiotic regions around the world will be composed of the same species. This is a clear case of biotic impoverishment.

[. . .]

In addition to this tragic loss in biodiversity, the spread of exotics also helps to undermine an important feature of human community. Globalisation of flora and fauna contributes to the loss of a human sense of place. As Mark Sagoff perceptively argues, native species 'share a long and fascinating natural history with neighbouring human communities. . . . Many of us feel bound to particular places because of their unique characteristics, especially their flora and fauna. By coming to appreciate, care about, and conserve flora and fauna, we, too, become native to a place' (1999: 22). Using knowledge of—and love for—local native species to help ground a sense of place will no longer make sense in a world where most of these species are cosmopolitan.

Just as the spread of exotic species threatens to homogenise the biosphere and to intensify the loss of a human sense of place, so too economic globalisation and the cosmopolitanisation of humans threaten to impoverish the diversity of the earth's human cultures and to undermine people's senses of community.

[. . .]

[T]he mass importation of exotics does significantly threaten biodiversity and biological nativists typically do not believe in the superiority of the species native to their lands. The charge that biological nativists are xenophobic ignores their admiration of foreign flora and fauna in their native habitats. Although biological nativists favour native biotic purity, they do so in the name of global biodiversity, the preservation of the spectacular diversity between Earth's ecological assemblages. Ironically, it is those who favour the cosmopolitanisation of plants and animals that support purity of an invidious sort: in that direction lies a world with the same mix of species virtually everywhere.

Opposition to exotics as exotic can thus be both rational and praiseworthy. Being a foreign species is a disvalue when humans are flooding the earth's ecological assemblages with exotics. Given the significant and ongoing homogenisation and cosmopolitanisation of the biosphere by humans, we may justifiably oppose exotic species even if they have arrived under their own power and cause no physical damage.

Conclusion

Exotic species are best characterised as species that are foreign to an ecological assemblage in the sense that they have not significantly adapted with the biota and abiota constituting that assemblage. Contrary to frequent characterisations, exotics need not cause damage, be introduced by humans, or be geographically remote. Exotic species become natives when they have ecologically naturalised and when human influence over their presence in ecological assemblages (if any) has washed away. Although the damaging nature and anthropogenic origin of many exotic species provide good reasons for a negative evaluation of such exotics, in today's context, even naturally-dispersing, nondamaging exotics warrant opposition. Biological nativists' antagonism toward exotics need not be xenophobic nor involve unfair stereotyping, and it can be justified as a way of preserving the diversity of ecological assemblages from the homogenising forces of globalisation.

References

Bright, Christopher 1998. *Life Out of Bounds: Bioinvasion in a Borderless World.* New York: W. W. Norton & Co.

Corn, M.L., Buck E.H., Rawson J., Fischer, E. 1999. *Harmful Non-Native Species: Issues for Congress.* Washington, DC: Congressional Research Service. Library of Congress. Available at http// www.cnie.org/nle/biodv26.html.

Ehrenfeld, David 1999. 'Andalusian Bog Hounds'. *Orion* Autumn: 9–11.

Hannah, Lee, Lohse, David, Hutchinson, Charles, Carr, John L., and Lankerani, Ali 1993. 'A Preliminary Inventory of Human Disturbances of World Ecosystems', *Ambio* **23**: 246–50.

Hettinger, Ned and Throop, Bill 1999. 'Refocusing Ecocentrism: De-emphasizing Stability and Defending Wildness', *Environmental Ethics* **21**: 3–21.

Noss, Reed 1990. 'Can We Maintain Our Biological and Ecological Integrity?' *Conservation Biology* **4**: 241–3.

Peretti, Jonah H. 1998. 'Nativism and Nature: Rethinking Biological Invasion', *Environmental Values* **7**: 183–92.

Pimentel, D., Lach, L., Zuniga R., and Morrison D. 1999. *Environmental and Economic Costs Associated with Non-indigenous Species in the United States.* Presentation at American Association for the Advancement of Science, Anaheim, CA, January 1999. For text, see http://www.news.cornell.edu/releasesljan99/species_costs.html.

Reinhart, D., Haroldson, M., Mattson, D., and Gunther, K. 1999. 'The Effect of Exotic Species on Yellowstone's Grizzly Bears'. Paper delivered at the *Yellowstone National Park Conference on Exotic Organisms in Greater Yellowstone: Native Biodiversity under Siege.* Mammoth Hot Springs. October 11–13.

Sagoff, Mark 1999. 'What's Wrong with Exotic Species?' *Report from the Institute for Philosophy and Public Policy* **19** (Fall): 16–23.

Scherer, Donald 1994. 'Between Theory and Practice: Some Thoughts on Motivations Behind Restoration', *Restoration and Management Notes* **12**: 184–8.

Throop, William 2000. 'Eradicating the Aliens', in William Throop (ed.) *Environmental Restoration: Ethics, Theory, and Practice*, pp. 179–91. Amherst, NY: Humanity Books.

Vermeij, Geerat 1996. 'An Agenda for Invasion Biology', *Biological Conservation* **7**: 83–9.

Vitousek, Peter 1997. 'Human Domination of Earth's Ecosystems', *Science* **277**: 494–9.

Westman, Walter 1990. 'Park Management of Exotic Species: Problems and Issues'. *Conservation Biology* **4**: 251–60.

Woods, Mark and Moriarty, Paul 2001. 'Strangers in a Strange Land: The Problem of Exotic Species', *Environmental Values* **10**: 163–91.

Annotated Further Reading

Bader, H. R., and Finstad, G. (2001) "Conflicts Between Livestock and Wildlife: an Analysis of Legal Liabilities Arising from Reindeer and Caribou Competition on the Seward Peninsula of Western Alaska." *Environmental Law* 31(3): 549–80.

Cartmill, M. (1993) *A View to a Death in the Morning: Hunting and Nature Through* History. Cambridge, Massachusetts: Harvard University Press.

Causey, A. 1989. "On the Morality of Hunting." *Environmental Ethics* 11: 334–5.

Clarke, C.H.D. (1958) "Autumn Thoughts of a Hunter." *The Journal of Wildlife Management* 22: 420–7.

Cohn, Priscilla (ed.) (1999) *Ethics and Wildlife.* Lewiston, New York: Edwin Mellen Press. A wide-ranging collection. Cohn provides a refutation of pro-hunting arguments.

Conover, M. (2002) *Resolving Human–Wildlife Conflicts.* Lewis Publishers, Boca Raton, Florida: CRC Press. 440 pp.

Curnutt, J. 1996. "How to argue for and against sport hunting." *Journal of Social Philosophy* 27(2): 65–89.

Curtis, J.A. (2002) "Ethics in Wildlife Management: What price?" *Environmental Values* 11: 145–61. Using a case of deer population management, argues that there may be instances where assessing wildlife for monetary valuation might be quite reasonable and useful for public policy, even when there are strong arguments against valuation of wildlife and nature.

Everett, J. (2001) "Environmental Ethics, Animal Welfarism, and the Problem of Predation: a Bambi Lover's Respect for Nature." *Ethics and The Environment* 6(1): 42–66. Disputes the views that animal welfarists must regard predation as bad or that they have a duty to intervene in wild predation. Asserts that a world without predation would be a better place than the present world.

Francione, G. L. (1999) "Wildlife and Animal Rights." Chapter II (pp. 65–81). In *Ethics and Wildlife*, Priscilla Cohn (ed.). Lewiston, New York: The Edwin Mellen Press.

Gish, R.F. (1992) "Songs of my Hunter Heart: a Western Kinship." Albuquerque, New Mexico: University of New Mexico Press.

Hooper, J.K. (1992) "Animal Welfare and Rightists: Insights into an Expanding Constituency for Wildlife Interpreters." *Legacy* 3(6): 20–5.

Houston, P. (1995) *Women on Hunting*. Hopewell, New Jersey: Ecco Press.

Kerasote, T. (1993) *Bloodties: Nature, Culture, and the Hunt*. New York: Kodansha.

Kleiman, D.G. (1989) "Reintroduction of Captive Mammals for Conservation." *BioScience* 39: 152–61.

Leopold, A. (1966) *A Sand County Almanac with Essays from Round River*. Oxford: Oxford University Press.

Lewis, D., Kaweche, G.B., and Mwenya, A. (1990) "Wildlife Conservation Outside Protected Areas—Lessons from an Experiment in Zambia." *Conservation Biology* 4: 171–80.

List, C.J. (1997) "Is Hunting a Right Thing?" *Environmental Ethics* 19: 405–16.

Lombard, A.T., Johnson, C.F, Cowling, R.M., and Pressey, R.L. (2001) "Protecting Plants from Elephants: Botanical Reserve Scenarios Within the Addo Elephant National Park, South Africa." *Biological Conservation* 102 (no. ER2): 191–203.

Luke, B. (1997) "A Critical Analysis of Hunters' Ethics." *Environmental Ethics* 19: 25–44.

Maehr, D.S. (1990) "The Florida Panther and Private Lands." *Conservation Biology* 4: 167–70.

Meche, L. D. (2001) "Wolf Restoration to the Adirondacks: the Advantages and Disadvantages of Public Participation in the Decision." Chapter Two, pp. 13–31. In *Wolves and Human Communities: Biology, Politics, and Ethics*, Virginia A. Sharpe, Bryan G. Norton, and Strachan Donnelley (eds). Washington, D.C.: Island Press.

Moriarty, P.V., and Woods, M. (1997) "Hunting/Predation." *Environmental Ethics* 19: 391–404.

Naess, A., and Mysterud, I. (1987) "Philosophy of Wolf Policies I: General Principles and Preliminary Exploration of Selected Norms." *Conservation Biology* 1: 22–34.

Posewitz, J. (1994) *Beyond Fair Chase: The Ethic and Tradition of Hunting*. Helena, Montana: Falcon Press.

Roleff, T.L. and Hurley, J.A. (eds) (1999) Chapter 3, pp. 97–146. In *The Rights of Animals*. San Diego: Greenhaven Press. Current controversies. A variety of perspectives addressing the pros and cons of hunting.

Sagoff, M. (1999) *What's Wrong with Exotic Species?* Institute for Philosophy and Public Policy. www.puaf.umd.edu//IPPP/fall1999/exotic_species.htm. Defends nonnative species.

Scruton, R. (1997) "From a View to a Death: Culture, Nature and the Huntsman's Art." *Environmental Values* 6(4): 471–82.

Shafer, C.L. (2000) "The Northern Yellowstone Elk Debate: Policy, Hypothesis, and Implications." *Natural Areas Journal* 20(4): 342–59. Intervention versus nonintervention in management of the northern Yellowstone National Park elk herd.

Shah, N.J. (2000) "Eradication of Alien Predators in the Seychelles: an Example of Conservation Action on Tropical Islands." *Biodiversity and Conservation* 10(7): 1219–20.

Stearns, B.P. and Stearns, S.C. (1999) *Watching from the edge of extinction*. New Haven, CT: Yale University Press. Stories and reflections from those watching extinctions.

Steinhart, P. (1990) "Humanity Without Biology." *Audubon* 92 (May): 24–6. Argues against wildlife rehabilitation.

Swan, J. (1995) *In Defense of Hunting*. New York: HarperCollins.

Vitali, T.R. (1990) "Sport hunting: moral or immoral?" *Environmental Ethics* 12: 69–82.

Wade, M. (1990) "Animal Liberation, Ecocentrism and the Morality of Sport Hunting." *Journal of the Philosophy of Sport* 17: 17.

Study Questions

1 Do you agree with Callicott that utilitarian and theocentric sources of inherent values for wildlife are outmoded? How would you support or contest these two as sources of inherent value?

2 Give two conditions under which you believe that sport hunting might be morally acceptable and two conditions where you believe it might not. Give your reasoning.

3 Do you believe the perspectives of Duke and Albrecht regarding rehabilitation and release of wildlife are compatible? Justify your position.

4 Do you agree with Gunn's assertion that trophy hunting is justified in Zimbabwe under the conditions he describes? Give your reasoning.

5   Based on Hettinger's discussion, do you agree with the notion of opposing exotic species, including those that are naturally dispersing and nondamaging? Explain your perspective.
6   What is your response to Varner's assertion that therapeutic hunting is compatible with an animal rights and an animal liberation perspective? Explain your reasoning.

Part VIII

Zoos, Aquariums, and Animals in Entertainment

Introduction

In this Part, the authors address some of the important moral issues associated with the long history of use of animals for purposes of human entertainment. In particular, there is a focus on marine mammal aquariums (Eaton), zoos (Regan, Hutchins *et al.*, Lindburg, Wemmer), and rodeos (Preece and Chamberlain, Rollin), with references to a few others.

Randall Eaton finds that animals in aquaria are often not well cared for and that the aquariums themselves are often under poor management. Tom Regan assesses the role of zoos in the context of several moral theories and finds that zoos are compatible with an anthropocentric perspective, but in conflict with holism (ecocentrism), utilitarianism, and the animal rights position; in particular, Regan finds that zoos conflict with the rights of these animals to be treated with respect. Michael Hutchins *et al.* and Donald Lindburg note that the entertainment value of zoos for the public is just one part of a larger set of values, including the scientific research conducted by zoos to gain greater knowledge of nature that is essential to wildlife conservation, particularly to endangered species management. Zoo and aquarium professionals tend to associate with ecocentric values rather than animals rights positions and generally place species, populations, and ecosystems' values above those of individual animals. Zoos also help educate the public about wildlife and help generate greater public interest in and support for wildlife conservation. Chris Wemmer goes on to assess the responsibilities and directions of zoos and aquariums in light of the global diversity crisis, and calls for a greater emphasis among zoo professionals on science and conservation efforts.

Preece and Chamberlain give an overview on other uses of animals for recreation, including cock-fighting, dog-fighting, bull-fighting, horse racing, and rodeos. They find little positive to say about the first three and associate the more cruel sports with cultures experiencing oppressive conditions and reduced educational opportunities. They note a number of abuses associated with rodeos over the years and support their abolition as well. Rollin acknowledges past abuses in rodeos, but points out that the moral issues with rodeos may be more complicated. He notes that western ranchers and cowboys have a long history of associating with and depending on these animals for their livelihoods, and commonly have developed a strong concern for their welfare. As they continue to become informed about animal welfare matters, they often have been strong supporters of changing or removing events and activities from rodeos that undermine the health and safety of the animals involved.

64

Randall L. Eaton

"Orcas and Dolphins in Captivity"

Eaton assesses public aquariums and finds them often affected by poor management, lack of imagination and creativity, politics, lack of openness to scientific research, waste, and inefficiency, among other problems. He provides a number of suggestions on how these aquaria can improve their care of marine mammals.

The exhibition of delphinids in captivity has done more to raise concern for cetaceans than everything else put together. [. . .] There are millions upon millions of people in North America, Europe, Japan, South Africa and Australia who visit aquariums and become turned on by dolphins and orcas.

[. . .]

More people in North America go to zoos and aquariums than take in all the college and professional athletic events combined. That says much of importance about man's desire to recover his soul. The animal is central to man's psyche, his origins, and his affections; thus, the zoo is much more than anyone has ever conceived. It is where we humans reconnect with our earthly kin, and where we share the common lament for another time and place. We visit the zoo to be inspired by the beauty, intelligence and wonder of nature. We also go there to know why we feel wistful about being caged with the animals in civilization, which, try as we may to deny it, is destroying us. The caged animal tells us that there is something fundamentally wrong with the way we and they live. So in this virtually religious homage that hundreds of millions of people annually make to the zoo the animal is not only an ambassador of good will for his still wild brethren, he speaks for their dubious condition, for ours, and also for the communal fact of all life.

Aquariums are significantly different than zoos for two reasons: a) the human's perception of the aquatic environment; and b) the nature of the creatures in the aquariums and what, as a consequence, they communicate to humans. When we humans, who are adapted by evolution and culture to live on land visit an aquarium, we perceive it to be a sizable body of water, what might constitute a very large swimming pool for us. If we saw two orca-sized land animals, say elephants, confined to an area the size of a typical aquarium pool used by orcas we might think that these behemoths have very little space. And if we had seen elephants in the wild or read that they often move over hundreds or thousands of square miles in a year then we would certainly wonder how extreme confinement might influence their behavior and needs. [...] Any reasonably thoughtful or empathetic person could easily wonder about a lot of the undesirable circumstances for elephants at the zoo, but few aquarium visitors ever see dolphins or orcas exhibiting what is the equivalent of pacing in a zoo animal.

An orca is adapted to move through huge expanses of water on a regular basis. Like elephants they have immense social tendencies and needs, as much, from all indications, as humans. In degree, each of these species has had to cope with the basic problems of all complex societies—finding food, cooperative foraging, protection of infants against predators, competition for limiting resources, balancing conflicts of interest, which exist for societies based on kinship, competition among polygamous males for females and the specter of violent warfare, and so on. An orca spends incredible portions of time and energy to locate, assess and capture food, and to do so they visit different environments which present different kinds of obstacles and demand variable strategies and solutions. Their feeding space is not only more variable in terms of factors like cover, prey species, and the like, it is three-dimensional, fluid and often dark, demanding the use of systematically more complex perceptual and communication faculties.

Contrast what altogether constitutes the most complicated niche occupied by any organism in the world with its life in what is for it something less than a bathtub. Compare living in a society of a hundred dolphins of every sex and age coordinating its cooperative feeding, defense, child-rearing, government, mating life and health in a dynamic, fluid ocean with living in a round, shallow tank with the company of three or four dolphins with nothing to do but make humans happy by repeating the same thing over and over, day in and day out, year after year. No catching of fish, no swimming at top speed or cavorting or playing at will through unlimited aquatic space, no diving deep or harassing sea lions or taking human children for tows in friendly harbors, no interaction with other groups of your kind, no cooperative anti-predator tactics, just the same old, easy-to-master job of jumping together through hoops for the enjoyment of enthusiastic onlookers. For the most curious, exploratory, mobile, playful creature on the planet, an aquarium must be very boring indeed.

All the evidence says so. Poor even by zoo standards, the dolphins and orcas have miserable records in captivity: lousy breeding success; much shorter life than in the wild; and, poor health in captivity—a lot of "brain disease." The stress engendered by boredom and lack of emotional needs being met should be nothing foreign to human consciousness in this day and age. [...]

That elephants don't attack humans far more often is actually a credit to their intelligence, and I mean that literally, besides which it should be mentioned that they are among the very large-brained creatures, right behind the toothed whales and man. That orcas don't attack humans in captivity is all the more remarkable considering their even greater ability to do so, their predatory nature, and their comparatively worse condition.

In 1979, we conducted a survey of the world's aquariums and learned that most aquariums had no more than a single orca. Here we have a large delphinid, with a tremendous repertoire of social expressions and, by inference, needs, being deprived of any social life save that with humans. Many aquariums do not let their personnel enter the water with orcas, which must make matters all the worse for the orcas, who, like the dolphins, seem to do their utmost to interact with humans as social surrogates. I wasn't surprised a few years ago when the male orca in San Diego's Sea World aquarium grabbed hold of the young woman's leg as she was trying to leave the pool after having made a commercial. She had been swimming with the orca for several minutes, and when she started to leave, he placed his jaws over her thigh. When she struggled, he wounded her. Flesh wounds only, the woman required stitches to mend. That the orca wanted her to stay and play with him seems likely; that he wanted to bite and hurt her seems unlikely. After all, had he intended to harm her, she would have had her leg snapped off, or worse. If anything he bit her very lightly; by orca standards, his may have been a love bite, intended perhaps to communicate affection.

Under captive conditions where dolphins are greatly loved, respected and admired, humans relate to them as persons, and enter the water to swim and play with them. In such circumstances the relationship between dolphins and humans is nothing less than beautiful and awe-inspiring, if not entirely incredible. There the humans have no doubt about the fact that they are dealing with creatures very like humans in some ways. And, I think it must be quite natural in these situations for deep, intimate affection to emerge between species, as has been described to me by experts with first-hand knowledge.

[. . .]

Orcas have survived about ten years on average in aquariums, no matter how old they are when captured. For reasons I discuss elsewhere, we know that one orca died in the wild at an age of at least 140 years, then by accident. Some estimates run 70 years for males, 100 for females in the wild. That they succumb to disease is not definite. Despite their authoritarian utterings, cetacean medicine men don't know much about whales or their maladies. Disease may result from stress, boredom and loneliness. (One must keep in mind that aquariums are not eager to retain marine mammal veterinarians who point to the conditions of captive life as the cause of whale disease, poor breeding and short life. Neither would most of these specialists want to admit it publicly.)

Breeding success is an indicator of how well a species tolerates captivity. In all the aquariums in all the years that sexually mature pairs of orcas have resided, only four births occurred before 1986, three of these to the same parents, all dead within a month.

[. . .]

Many public zoos and aquariums suffer from everything that any public facility does— poor management, lack of imagination and creativity, the horrible influence of politics, lack of spirit among employees, and all the rest of it, including waste and inefficiency. On the other hand are the majority of private zoos and aquariums which, despite claims and appearances to the contrary, are after profits. I say this knowing quite well that there are exemplary exceptions on both sides of the coin. Private aquariums may not be expected to sacrifice profits except for the sake of public relations. Their much publicized research programs or financial assistance to projects outside the aquarium itself are geared toward promotion, which is profitable for them, or for knowledge which may help protect their sizeable investment in expensive, hard to acquire animals such as orcas.

Fortunately, I also took considerable effort to communicate [. . .] how [. . .] to improve conditions for orcas, add to their longevity in captivity, propagate them successfully and curtail disease. I emphasized why all this would be profitable. At the time I was in the midst of orca studies in Puget Sound which had been associated with tremendous public disapproval of capturing orcas and placing them in captivity, and I argued that before long it might be impossible to capture additional orcas for aquariums, in which case, their big money maker would be lost, and their profits would plummet accordingly. Even if they could capture orcas in other places than Puget Sound, which they did for a while in Iceland after Puget Sound was declared off limits to them, they had to see the writing on the wall. Sooner or later the public would demand that all orcas, possibly all dolphins, be left in the sea. (I predict that this will happen unless we ruin the seas.)

I meticulously outlined the social needs of orcas—keeping a group of at least two males and three or four females from wild-living pods. Animals from the same region are already socialized to one another and most apt to interact well in captivity, and if adults, already could have bred. Such a group would provide each orca with "social security," fulfillment of social needs. And they would have to be kept in a pool or series of pools much larger than anything yet constructed in the world, though I urged them to consider developing a naturalistic aquarium.

It would be cheap to net off a bay or cove compared to building a concrete pool with all its expensive support facilities which include filtering systems, and such a setting would offer many of the sources of stimulation normally encountered by orcas in the wild, but not in captivity. Fish would swim into the cove or could be released there for orcas to catch their own food, or some of it anyway. Many tourists could be accommodated at numerous locales in easy access to major cities or travel routes on the east or west coast. Orcas would not have to perform for their dinner, and I am confident that the paying visitors would find a naturalistic situation more rewarding. Imagine walking on a floating boardwalk over a large cove by the sea watching a group of orcas with their young behaving naturally, compared with seeing an orca leap out of a small pool surrounded by concrete.

People prefer driving through a naturalistic wildlife park rather than seeing the same animals in a zoo because of the reversal of the role of animal and human. [. . .] Likewise, people would relish a sense of non-obtrusive intimacy with seemingly free, untamed orcas. No doubt the orcas would befriend people, but no matter how they would interact with human onlookers, the sight and sound of orcas themselves would be highly profitable. Why a counterpart to a drive-through wildlife park does not exist among seaquariums is a mystery; one with orcas, dolphins, and other sea mammals would be a gold mine.

[. . .]

In 1985 an orca was born. Able to feed from its mother in the largest aquarium in the world, it was the first to survive in captivity. Months later, the TV program 20–20 aired the events including the coaching by human wetnurses, the actual birth and the infant's behavior. [. . .] With proper care and wise management, that baby orca may become an ambassador for the orca nation, and more. Hopefully, its birth indicates the cessation of orca captures on the one hand, and the building of an intimate bridge between them and us on the other. Orcas are the world's leading attraction, and she became the most popular of orcas.

I wish [aquariums] would feed the orcas live fish so as to let them exercise in the proper manner as predators, a level of stimulation they may need. When we meet the natural needs of orcas we not only improve their health, we also make them more interesting to the public. From a research point of view, observations of orcas using communication to catch fish would be illuminating.

Imagine what the consequences would be if someone began to talk to an orca? What if, for example the orca said it wanted to return to the sea, to be free? That could be the end of profits, which brings us full circle back to the problem of self-interests: if the salvation of wild orcas, dolphins and other whales, possibly even the sea, were enhanced by deciphering orcanese, and humans could talk to them, the profiteers would perceive such a revolutionary breakthrough as a threat to their wealth. Profits and enlightenment don't mix when the latter must be given up for the former.

[. . .]

[John] Lilly and I agree on the short-sightedness of commercial aquariums regarding openness to scientific research. They fear poor publicity that could result from public knowledge of the abominable conditions and care received by most cetaceans in captivity.

Basically the same could be said of most commercial zoos. Overall, scientists could immeasurably improve aquarium conditions and operations in ways beneficial to the commercial interests of the aquariums, the visitors and the whales. Zoo standards have improved dramatically in the past twenty years due to a combination of increasing public interest in animal life and welfare, and increasing behavioral research in zoos.

My experience in aquariums indicated that the major obstacle is ignorance of the behavioral adaptations and needs of captive cetaceans, and too great an emphasis and trust in veterinary medicine, which, being so ignorant of cetacean biology and behavior, may kill more creatures than it aids. The real progress made in the health and medical treatment of wild animals in captivity has not come through advances in the traditional veterinary sciences such as anatomy, physiology or treatment but in behavioral understanding, which includes nutrition. I made these same criticisms of zoos, and though that meant ostracism by some of the old guard zoo directors, time has proved me right: the leading wild animal medicine specialists would agree that prevention of disease from accommodating behavioral needs of organisms has meant the most progress in zoos, and the same is possible for aquariums if they or the public expect the much needed improvements.

65

Tom Regan

"Are Zoos Morally Defensible?"

Regan assesses zoos against several moral theories. He concludes that zoos are not morally defensible based on the tenets of holism (ecocentrism), utilitarianism, or the animal rights view. Within the rights view, zoos violate the right of wild animals to be treated with respect.

Despite important differences, a number of recent tendencies in ethical theory are united in the challenges they pose for well-entrenched human practices involving the utilization of nonhuman animals, including their use in zoos. This essay explores three such tendencies—utilitarianism, the rights view, and environmental holism—and explores their respective answers to the question, Are zoos morally defensible? Both utilitarianism and holism offer ethical theories that in principle could defend zoos, but both, it is argued, are less than adequate ethical outlooks. For reasons set forth below, the third option—the rights view—has implications that run counter to the moral acceptability of zoos, as we know them. The essay concludes not by insisting that zoos as we know them are morally indefensible but, rather, by admitting that we have yet to see an adequate ethical theory that illuminates why they are not.

A great deal of recent work by moral philosophers—much of it in environmental ethics, for example, but much of it also in reference to questions about obligations to future generations and international justice—is directly relevant to the moral assessment of zoos. (Here and throughout I use the word "zoo" to refer to a professionally managed zoological institution accredited by the American Zoo and Aquarium Association (AZA) and having a collection of live animals used for conservation, scientific studies, public education, and public display.) Yet most of this work has been overlooked by advocates of zoological parks. Why this is so is unclear, but certainly the responsibility for this lack of communication needs to be shared. Like all other specialists, moral philosophers have a tendency to converse only among themselves, just as, like others with a shared, crowded agenda, zoo professionals have limited discretionary time, thus little time to explore current tendencies in academic disciplines like moral philosophy.

[. . .]

The growing philosophical debate over our treatment of the planet and the other animals with whom we share it is both a symptom and a cause of a culture's attempt to come to critical terms with its past as it attempts to shape its future.

At present moral philosophers are raising a number of major challenges against moral anthropocentrism. I shall consider three. The first comes from utilitarians, the second from proponents of animal rights, and the third from those who advocate a holistic ethic. This essay offers a brief summary of each position with special reference to how it answers our central question—the question, again, Are zoos morally defensible?

[. . .]

Utilitarianism

[T]he position of the influential contemporary moral philosopher Peter Singer can be seen to be an extension of the utilitarian critique of moral anthropocentrism (Singer 1990).

[. . .]

Like Bentham and Mill before him, therefore, Singer denies that humans are obliged to treat other animals equitably in the name of the betterment of humanity and also denies that acting dutifully toward these animals is a warm-up for the real moral game played between humans or, as theists would add, between humans and God. We owe it to those animals who have interests to take their interests into account, just as we also owe it to them to count their interests equitably. In these respects we have direct duties to them, not indirect duties to humanity. To think otherwise is to give sorry testimony to the very prejudice—speciesism—Singer is intent upon silencing.

Utilitarianism and the moral assessment of zoos

From a utilitarian perspective, then, the interests of animals must figure in the moral assessment of zoos. These interests include a variety of needs, desires, and preferences, including, for example, the interest wild animals have in freedom of movement, as well as adequate nutrition and an appropriate environment. Even zoos' most severe critics must acknowledge that in many of the most important respects, contemporary zoos have made important advances in meeting at least some of the most important interests of wild animals in captivity.

From a utilitarian perspective, however, there are additional questions that need to be answered before we are justified in answering our central question. For not only must we insist that the interests of captive animals be taken into account and be counted equitably, but we must also do the same for all those people whose interests are affected by having zoos—and this involves a very large number of people indeed, including those who work at zoos, those who visit them, and those (for example, people in the hotel and restaurant business, as well as local and state governments) whose business or tax base benefits from having zoos in their region. To make an informed moral assessment of zoos, given utilitarian theory, in short, we need to consider a great deal more than the interests of those wild animals exhibited in zoos (though we certainly need to consider their interests). Since everyone's interests count, we need to consider everyone's interests, at least insofar as these interests are affected by having zoos—or by not having them.

[. . .]

The task is simple enough to state—namely, to determine how the many, the varied, and the competing interests of everyone affected by having zoos (or by not having them) are or will be affected by having (or not having) them. [. . .] The hard (or impossible) part is actually to carry out this project. Granted, a number of story lines are possible (for example, stories about how much people really learn by going to zoos in comparison with how much they could learn by watching National Geographic specials). But many of these story lines will be in the nature of speculation rather than of fact, others will be empirical sketches rather than detailed studies, and the vital interests of some individuals (for example, the interests people have in having a job, medical benefits, a retirement plan) will tend not to be considered at all or to be greatly undervalued.

Moreover, the utilitarian moral assessment of zoos requires that we know a good deal more before we can make an informed assessment. Not only must we canvass all the interests of all those individuals who are affected, but we must also add up all the interests that are satisfied as well as all the interests that are frustrated, given the various options (for example, keeping zoos as they are, changing them in various ways, or abolishing them altogether). Then, having added all the pluses and minuses—and only then—are we in a position to say which of the options is the best one.

But (to put the point as mildly as possible) how we rationally are to carry out this part of the project (for example, how we rationally determine what an equitable trade-off is between, say, a wild animals' interest in roaming free and a tram operator's interest in a steady job) is far from clear. And yet unless we have comprehensible, comprehensive, and intellectually reliable instructions regarding how we are to do this, we will lack the very knowledge that, given utilitarian theory, we must have before we can make an informed moral assessment of zoos. The suspicion is, at least among utilitarianism's critics, the theory requires knowledge that far exceeds what we humans are capable of acquiring. In the particular case before us, then, it is arguable that utilitarian theory, conscientiously applied, would lead to moral skepticism—would lead, that is, to the conclusion that we just don't know whether or not zoos are morally defensible. At least for many people, myself included, this is a conclusion we would wish to avoid.

[. . .]

The rights view

An alternative to the utilitarian attack on anthropocentrism is the rights view. Those who accept this view hold that (1) the moral assessment of zoos must be carried out against the backdrop of the rights of animals and that (2) when we make this assessment against this backdrop, zoos, as they presently exist, are not morally defensible.

[. . .]

The rights view rests on a number of factual beliefs about those animals humans eat, hunt, and trap, as well as those relevantly similar animals humans use in scientific research and exhibit in zoos. Included among these factual beliefs are the following: these animals are not only in the world, but they are also aware of it—and of what happens to them. And what happens to them matters to them. Each has a life that fares experientially better or worse for the one whose life it is. As such, all have lives of their own that are of importance to them apart from their utility to us. Like us, they bring a unified psychological presence to the world. Like us, they are somebodies, not somethings. They are not our tools, not our models, not our resources, not our commodities.

The lives that are theirs include a variety of biological, psychological, and social needs. The satisfaction of these needs is a source of pleasure, their frustration or abuse, a source of pain. The untimely death of the one whose life it is, whether this be painless or otherwise, is the greatest of harms since it is the greatest of losses: the loss of one's life itself. In these fundamental ways these nonhuman animals are the same as human beings. And so it is that according to the rights view, the ethics of our dealings with them and with one another must rest on the same fundamental moral principles.

At its deepest level an enlightened human ethic, according to the rights view, is based on the independent value of the individual: the moral worth of any one human being is not to be measured by how useful that person is in advancing the interests of other human beings. To treat human beings in ways that do not honor their independent value—to treat them as tools or models or commodities, for example—is to violate that most basic of human rights: the right of each of us to be treated with respect.

As viewed by its advocates, the philosophy of animal rights demands only that logic be respected. For any argument that plausibly explains the independent value of human beings, they claim, implies that other animals have this same value, and have it equally. Any argument that plausibly explains the right of humans to be treated with respect, it is further alleged, also implies that these other animals have this same right, and have it equally, too.

[. . .]

By insisting upon the independent value and rights of other animals, it attempts to give scientifically informed and morally impartial reasons for denying that these animals exist to serve us. Just as there is no master sex and no master race, so (animal rights advocates maintain) there is no master species.

Animal rights and the moral assessment of zoos

To view nonhuman animals after the fashion of the philosophy of animal rights makes a truly profound difference to our understanding of what we may do to them. Because other animals have a moral right to respectful treatment, we ought not reduce their moral status to that of being useful means to our ends.

[. . .]

Thus, the central question: Are animals in zoos treated with appropriate respect? To answer this question, we begin with an obvious fact—namely, the freedom of these animals is compromised, to varying degrees, by the conditions of their captivity. The rights view recognizes the justification of limiting another's freedom but only in a narrow range of cases. The most obvious relevant case would be one in which it is in the best interests of a particular animal to keep that animal in confinement. In principle, therefore, confining wild animals in zoos can be justified, according to the rights view, but only if it can be shown that it is in their best interests to do so. That being so, it is morally irrelevant to insist that zoos provide important educational and recreational opportunities for humans, or that captive animals serve as useful models in important scientific research, or that regions in which zoos are located benefit economically, or that zoo programs offer the opportunity for protecting rare or endangered species, or that variations on these programs insure genetic stock, or that any other consequence arises from keeping wild animals in captivity that forwards the interests of other individuals, whether humans or nonhumans.

Now, one can imagine circumstances in which such captivity might be defensible. For example, if the life of a wild animal could be saved only by temporarily removing the animal from the threat of human predation, and if, after this threat had abated, the animal was reintroduced into the wild, then this temporary confinement arguably is not disrespectful and thus might be justified. Perhaps there are other circumstances in which a wild animal's liberty could be limited temporarily, for that animal's own good. Obviously, however, there will be comparatively few such cases, and no less obviously, those cases that satisfy the requirements of the rights view are significantly different from the vast majority of cases in which wild animals are today confined in zoos, for these animals are confined and exhibited not because temporary captivity is in their best interests but because their captivity serves some purpose useful to others. As such, the rights view must take a very dim view of zoos, both as we know them now and as they are likely to be in the future. In answer to our central question—Are zoos morally defensible?—the rights view's answer, not surprisingly, is No, they are not.

Holism

Although the rights view and utilitarianism differ in important ways, they are the same in others. Like utilitarian attacks on anthropocentrism, the rights view seeks to make its case by working within the major ethical categories of the anthropocentric tradition. For example, utilitarians do not deny the moral relevance of human pleasure and pain, so important to our humanist forebears; rather, they accept it and seek to extend our moral horizons to include the moral relevance of the pleasures and pains of other animals. For its part, the rights view does not deny the moral importance of the individual, a central article of belief in theistic and humanistic thought; rather, it accepts this moral datum and seeks to widen the class of individuals who are thought of in this way to include nonhuman animals.

Because both the positions discussed in the preceding use major ethical categories handed down by our predecessors, some influential thinkers argue that these positions, despite all appearances to the contrary, remain in bondage to anthropocentric prejudices.

[. . .]

Aldo Leopold (1949) rejects the individualism [. . .] of those who build their moral thinking on the welfare or rights of the individual. What has ultimate value is not the individual but the collective, not the part but the whole, meaning the entire biosphere and its constituent ecosystems. Acts are right, Leopold claims, if they tend to promote the integrity, beauty, diversity, and harmony of the biotic community; they are wrong if they tend contrariwise. As for individuals, be they humans or other animals, they are merely "members of the biotic team," having neither more nor less value in themselves than any other member— having, that is, no value in themselves. What value individuals have, so far as this is meaningful at all, is instrumental only: they are good to the extent that they promote the welfare of the biotic community.

[. . .]

Holists face daunting challenges when it comes to determining what is right and wrong. That is to be determined by calculating the effects of our actions on the life community. Such calculations will not be easy.

[. . .]

But perhaps the situation for holists is not as dire as I have suggested. While it is true that we often lack detailed knowledge about how the biosphere is affected by human acts and practices, we sometimes know enough to say that some of the things we are doing are unhealthy for the larger community of life.

[. . .]

Let us assume, then, what I believe is true, that we sometimes are wise enough to understand that the effects of some human practices act like insatiable cancers eating away at the life community. From the perspective of holism, these practices are wrong, and they are wrong because of their detrimental effects on the interrelated systems of biological life.

It is important to realize that holists are aware of the catastrophic consequences toxic dumping and the ever widening hole in the ozone layer are having on individual animals in the wild—on elephants and dolphins, for example. It would be unfair to picture those who subscribe to holism as taking delight in the suffering and death of these individual animals. Holists are not sadists. What is fair and important to note, however, is that the suffering and death of these animals are not morally significant according to these thinkers. Morally, what matters is how the diversity, sustainability, and harmony of the larger community of life are affected, not what happens to individuals.

[. . .]

Holism and the moral assessment of zoos

Holism's position regarding the ethics of zoos in particular is analogous to its position regarding the ethics of our other interactions with wildlife in general. There is nothing wrong with keeping wild animals in permanent confinement if doing so is good for the larger life community. But it is wrong to do this if the effects on the community are detrimental. Moreover, because one of the indices of what is harmful to the life community is a reduction in the diversity of forms of life within the community, holism will recognize a strong prima facie duty to preserve rare or endangered species. To the extent that the best zoos contribute to this effort, holists will applaud their efforts, even if keeping individual animals who belong to threatened species in captivity is not in the best interests of those particular animals. In that and other respects (for example, the moral relevance of the educational and research functions of zoos), the implications of holism are very much at odds with those of the rights view and much closer to those of utilitarianism.

Some people who accept a holistic ethic are skeptical of the real contributions zoos make to species protection. It is appropriate for all of us to press this issue since, despite the claims sometimes made on behalf of zoo programs whose purpose is to reintroduce endangered species into their native habitats, for example, the rate of success might be far less than the public is led to believe. Philosophically, however, there are deeper, more troubling questions that need to be considered. Of the many that come to mind, only one will be discussed here.

Holism—or, to speak more precisely, the unqualified, unequivocal version of holism sketched above—takes a strong moral stance in opposition to whatever upsets the diversity, balance, and sustainability of the community of life. Unquestionably, it is the human presence and the effects of human activities that have by far the most adverse effects on the diversity, balance, and sustainability of the life community. Now, as we have seen, the holist's response to such effects when these are allegedly caused by nonhumans (for example, by an overabundance of deer) is to recommend a limited hunting season, to cull the herd, and thereby restore ecological balance. Why, then, should holists not advocate comparable policies in the face of human depredation of the life community? In other words, why should holists stop short of recommending that the human population be culled using measures no less lethal than those used in the case of controlling the population of deer? Granted, the latter is legal, the former not. But legality is not a reliable guide to morality, and the question before us is a question of morals, not a question of law. And it is the moral question that needs to be pressed.

[. . .]

[E]ither holists mean what they say, or they do not. If they do not, then there is no reason to take them seriously. If they do, then they cannot avoid embracing the draconian implications to which their position commits them.

[. . .]

As was true in that earlier case, it is no good attempting to defend zoos in particular by appealing to a moral outlook that is morally unacceptable in general. Thus, because holism is not a morally acceptable outlook, it is not an acceptable basis for assessing the moral justification of zoos.

Those who believe that zoos, as they presently exist, are morally defensible, therefore, will have to find a moral outlook that parts company both with holism and with utilitarianism. The rights view, of course, is a third major option. But that view, for reasons advanced in the preceding, is highly critical of zoos, on grounds that they violate the right of wild animals to be treated with respect. This essay concludes, therefore, on the following cautionary note—if or as one hopes to marshal a moral defense of zoos, one will have to articulate, defend, and competently apply some theory other than the three surveyed on this occasion.

References

Leopold, A. 1949. *A Sand County Almanac*. New York: Ballantine Books.
Singer, P. 1990. *Animal Liberation*. 2nd ed. New York: Random House.

66

Michael Hutchins, Betsy Dresser, and Chris Wemmer

"Ethical Considerations in Zoo and Aquarium Research"

Hutchins *et al.* respond to the criticisms of zoos offered by the animal rights perspective. They note that scientific research is an important method to gain an understanding of the natural world that is critical to wildlife conservation, including preservation of endangered species. The authors also propose that the conservation ethic is generally compatible with an animal welfare ethic but largely incompatible with an animal rights ethic; they draw on arguments that the rights of individual animals should be secondary to those of populations, species, or ecosystems. They point out many of the tools implemented to maintain animal welfare and support species well being.

Although it is generally thought that public recreation was the primary impetus behind the initial development of zoos and aquariums, scientific investigation was an explicit objective of many early institutions.

[. . .]

In time, however, zoos and aquariums in industrialized countries became motivated more by the need for public recreation and civic pride than by the lofty ideals of these early zoos (Olney 1980). In the 1950s and 1960s comparatively little research was being conducted in North American zoological institutions. However, research is again being identified as one of the primary goals of zoos and aquariums, along with conservation and public education (Conway 1969, Hutchins 1988). In 1983, Finlay and Maple found that 70 percent of North American zoos and aquariums (out of a sample of 120) were conducting research of some kind, and 46 percent intended to expand their programs (1986). These efforts have continued to grow, but the need for and appropriateness of zoo and aquarium research, and of animal research in general, are being questioned by animal rights and welfare advocates (e.g., Regan 1983, Jamieson 1985, Fox 1990).

Our objectives are threefold: (1) to examine the types of animal-oriented research that takes place in zoos and aquariums today, (2) to discuss ethical issues related to research on captive animals, and (3) to outline ways of insuring that high standards of animal welfare are maintained during the pursuit of institutional and societal goals, including those of science and conservation.

An overview of research in modern zoos and aquariums

In the last decade, zoos and aquariums have been cast into a new role as conservators of wildlife (Conway 1969). In fact, many species [. . .] owe their existence to the cooperative

efforts of modern zoos (Tudge 1991). Along with this heavy responsibility has come a realization that little is known about the basic biology of many wild animals or about their
behavioral and environmental requirements in captivity. Zoo biologists are tackling these
challenges with a vengeance, and the quality of animal husbandry has rapidly improved.
Underpinning all captive animal management and breeding efforts are essential scientific
studies. Ongoing research in animal behavior, nutrition, reproduction, genetics, pathology,
and clinical veterinary medicine are conducted by zoo and aquarium scientific staff and by
collaborating scientists from local colleges and universities.

The investment of modern, professionally managed zoos and aquariums in conservation
science is vastly underappreciated. In 1992–93 alone, the American Zoo and Aquarium
Association (AZA) and its 164 accredited institutions initiated or supported nearly 1,100
scientific and conservation projects in more than sixty countries worldwide (Wiese *et al.*
1993). From 1990 to 1993, they also produced more than 1,300 technical and mainstream
popular articles on wildlife biology, conservation, and captive animal management, including contributions in respected scientific journals such as *Science, Primates, Endocrinology,
Biology of Reproduction, Journal of Mammalogy, Journal of Reproduction and Fertility,
Conservation Biology, Condor, Animal Behaviour, American Naturalist,* and *Heredity*
(Hutchins *et al.* 1991a; Wiese *et al.* 1992, 1993).

[. . .]

Since 1981, the journal *Zoo Biology*, produced by Wiley-Liss and Sons in affiliation
with AZA, has published twelve volumes containing more than 350 articles, all focused on
zoo and aquarium research. Additional papers have been published in other international
zoo publications.

[. . .]

Some larger zoos and aquariums [. . .] have, over many years, made substantial invest-
ments in conservation and science. However even medium-sized to smaller institutions [. . .]
now have full-time staff scientists and growing research programs.

Efforts to coordinate the research activities of individual zoos and aquariums are
improving. The AZA recently established a research coordinator's committee (RCC) and
seven scientific advisory groups. The RCC was established to address broad-based questions
concerning the conduct and administration of research programs in AZA institutions,
including ethical and organizational matters.

[. . .]

AZA's seven existing scientific advisory groups include those for contraception, animal
nutrition, behavior and husbandry, genome banking, reintroduction, small population
management (genetics and demography), and veterinary science.

[. . .]

Ethical issues in zoo and aquarium research

Animals are used extensively in both basic and applied research, but the appropriateness of
their use is being challenged by animal rights activists (Moss 1984). Proponents of animal
rights have traditionally opposed the use of animals in biomedical and toxicological studies,
especially when animals are caused to suffer pain or when their lives are sacrificed in order to
benefit humans (e.g., Singer 1975, Regan 1983, Ryder 1985, Barnes 1986). In *The Case for*

Animal Rights Regan states that "animals are not to be treated as mere receptacles or as renewable resources. Thus the practice of scientific research on animals violates their rights. Thus it ought to cease, according to the rights view" (1983, 385).

[. . .]

Studies conducted at zoos and aquariums generally fall under the umbrella of a relatively new scientific discipline known as conservation biology (Soulé and Wilcox 1980; Soulé 1985, 1986). The goal of this applied science is to preserve naturally occurring biological diversity. Conservation biology is one of the most interdisciplinary of sciences, encompassing not only the biological sciences but also economics and the social sciences. Conservation biology is the scientific foundation of the conservation ethic, the goal of which is much broader than either the animal rights or animal welfare ethics (Norton 1987). According to Ehrenfeld, the broad goal of conservation is "to ensure that nothing in the existing natural order is permitted to become permanently lost as the result of man's activities except in the most unusual and carefully examined circumstances" (1972, 7). It is therefore directly concerned with the rights of wild species to continue to exist in natural ecological communities.

It should be noted that unlike biomedical research, most zoo and aquarium research tends to be opportunistic, noninvasive, and nonterminal and does not involve large numbers of subjects. Often the subjects are endangered species. Rather than having a human-focused goal, it is aimed at improving conditions and ensuring a future for individual animals, populations, species, and even ecosystems (Hutchins 1988). Like any research conducted on animals, however, it does have the potential to violate the rights of individuals as defined by Regan (1983). In fact, the rights view would preclude all practices that "cause intentional harm." [. . .] But what are the consequences of this view?

If our interpretation of Regan's concept of intentional harm is correct, the animal rights ethic could preclude many practices commonly used by zoo and aquarium researchers and other conservation biologists, including but not limited to minor surgery to conduct reproductive studies (e.g., those related to experimental in vitro fertilization, embryo transfer, or artificial insemination procedures); any anesthesia or physical restraint solely to collect biological materials, such as tissue, blood, and semen; any testing of immobilizing drugs; and some forms of marking for individual identification (e.g., ear tagging, tattooing, and freeze branding).

[. . .]

Scientific research is one means by which humans gain an understanding of the natural world, and we believe that such an understanding is critical to wildlife conservation efforts. It is impossible to evaluate the ethics of zoo and aquarium research without placing it in this larger context. In fact, Poole and Trefethen have stated, "Knowledge is the essential prerequisite to making a management decision respecting a species, population or group of wildlife. A decision made in the absence of information about a species or population, depending on the result, is at worst, an act of ignorance, or, at best a stroke of good fortune" (1978, 344). Given the overriding goal of the conservation ethic (i.e., to conserve biological diversity), we cannot agree that all research on captive or wild animals should cease. In fact, in order to save endangered species, it is essential that such efforts be expanded as rapidly as possible (see Hutchins 1988, Roberts 1988, Mlot 1989, Soulé and Kohm 1989).

The development of innovative technologies and the attainment of new knowledge are critical for the future of endangered species conservation. It is estimated that as many as one million species of animals and plants could be lost in the next few decades, primarily through habitat destruction (Ehrlich and Ehrlich 1981). The implications of this impending loss are enormous, not only for natural ecosystems but also for the quality of human life and for the lives of millions of individual animals (Ehrlich and Ehrlich 1981, Regenstein 1985). What will it take to save wildlife in the context of growing human populations, habitat alteration and fragmentation, pollution, or even more pervasive ecological changes, such as global warming and holes in the ozone layer? Animal rights advocates believe that they have the answer. According to Regan, "with regard to wild animals the general policy recommended by the rights view is: let them be" (1983, 361). But what would be the consequences of such inaction?

Ecologists have noted that even the largest of national parks will lose much of their biological diversity in the absence of careful management (Soulé et al. 1979). For example, fragmented islands of habitat, no matter how large, can prevent normal gene flow from occurring, resulting in a rapid loss of genetic diversity (Shaffer 1978). This factor alone can lead to population and species extinctions. Small, isolated populations, however, are susceptible to a variety of other risks, including disease and various natural catastrophes (e.g., hurricanes, fires, or volcanic eruptions). Even if protection is successful, additional problems can develop. For example, local populations can become overabundant when predators or other natural checks and balances are removed. When this occurs, population pressures or social conflict may force animals to leave protected areas and therefore come into conflict with humans (Sukumar 1991). Densely populated animals can also alter their habitats to such an extent that they threaten their own existence or the existence of other species (Caughly 1981). Thus, the laissez-faire concept of wildlife conservation championed by Regan is unlikely to succeed, at least not in view of the political, economic, and biological realities under which conservation must occur (Hutchins and Wemmer 1987, Howard 1990).

Most conservationists, including those who work at modern zoos and aquariums, agree that habitat preservation should be our highest priority (see Hutchins and Wemmer 1991, Hutchins and Wiese 1991). Like it or not, however, the survival of many species, especially the larger vertebrates, is going to require unprecedented levels of human intervention (Hutchins and Fascione 1993). Intensive management actions, such as population culling, habitat modification and restoration, translocation, captive breeding for reintroduction, supplemental feeding, field veterinary care, and control or elimination of introduced or exotic species, will become increasingly necessary (Duffy and Watt 1971, Merton 1977, Wilbur 1977, Foose 1983, Younghusband and Myers 1986, Hutchins and Wemmer 1987, Cairns 1988, Conway 1989, Flesness and Foose 1990, Hutchins et al. 1991b, Diamond 1992, Packer 1992). Consequently, evolving technologies such as biotelemetry, reintroduction, embryo transfer, artificial insemination, antibiotics, immunization, contraception, sterilization, and chemical immobilization are likely to become important tools of wildlife conservationists (Cade 1988, Dresser 1988, Conway 1989, Hutchins et al. 1991b, Hutchins and Fascione 1993).

Some large African national parks have been completely fenced to protect both wildlife and humans, and have essentially become megazoos (Younghusband and Myers 1986). Thus, the technologies being developed by modern, professionally managed zoos and aquariums are directly relevant to field conservation efforts (Conway 1989, Hutchins and Wemmer 1991, Hutchins and Wiese 1991). A failure to conduct the needed studies and to take widespread and immediate action will almost certainly result in numerous species extinctions.

[. . .]

Zoo biologists have also developed or refined various technological advances that have the potential to make major contributions to wildlife conservation (Benirschke 1983). For example, reproductive technologies, such as cryopreservation, in vitro fertilization, embryo transfer, and artificial insemination will soon allow conservationists to move genetic material between isolated populations in captivity and in the wild and thus avoid the deleterious effects of inbreeding (Dresser 1988, Wildt 1989). Such methods may also allow zoo biologists to accelerate rates of reproduction or to stimulate reproduction in especially recalcitrant species (Dresser 1988, Wildt 1989, Cohn 1991). Disease is one of the most significant threats to the future of small, isolated wildlife populations. Advances in zoo veterinary medicine have helped to diagnose and treat various ailments in both wild and captive animal populations (Hutchins *et al.* 1991b). For example, veterinarians with zoo experience recently treated wild mountain gorillas (*Gorilla gorilla berengi*) for injuries and vaccinated them against disease, a practice that itself has stimulated numerous ethical questions (see Hutchins and Wemmer 1987). [. . .] [M]uch of what we know about the behavior of secretive, arboreal, nocturnal, and aquatic animals has come from zoo and laboratory studies (Hutchins 1988). In many cases, zoo and laboratory studies complement field studies and provide a more comprehensive picture of an animal's behavioral repertoire. Zoo and laboratory studies of animal behavior not only contribute to the welfare of captive animals (e.g., Maple and Finlay 1989, Shepherdson *et al.* 1993) but also help in formulating more effective methods of captive breeding and reintroduction (Eisenberg and Kleiman 1975; Kleiman 1980, 1992; Hutchins *et al.* in press).

[. . .]

It is also important to note that many kinds of research—for example, those that involve the routine collection of biological materials, such as blood, urine, milk, feces, semen, or tissues, or body measurements—can be conducted much more humanely in zoos and aquariums than they can in nature. Habituated animals are less likely to experience stress in the presence of humans (e.g., Frank *et al.* 1986). In addition, some captive animals can be easily trained to submit themselves voluntarily for sample collection, whereas the capture of wild animals can be an extremely stressful and risky procedure (Fowler 1978).

[. . .]

In some cases, zoo biologists have used common domestic or laboratory animals as models to develop techniques for application to endangered species. The World Conservation Union's policy on research involving species at risk of extinction encourages basic and applied research that contributes to the survival of threatened species, but opposes research that might directly or indirectly impair their survival (IUCN 1989). By inference, this encourages the use of common or domestic species as models for more endangered varieties. It also assumes, however, that endangered animals are more valuable than common ones, and that individuals can be sacrificed or caused to suffer for the greater good (i.e., to preserve a population, species, or ecosystem).

Animal rights advocates consider this view to be speciesist. They consider all sentient animals to be worthy of equal moral consideration and thus do not make distinctions based on the rarity of the species. Regan is very clear about this point. [. . .] One implication of Regan's viewpoint is that when a conflict of interest exists, humans should allow a rare species to go extinct rather than violate the rights of even a single individual of a common species.

Regan has labeled any attempt to subordinate the rights of individual animals to the species or ecosystem as "environmental fascism" (1983). From the perspective of the conservation ethic, however, the rights of individual animals must be viewed as secondary to those of the population, species, or ecosystem as a whole (Rodman 1977, Callicott 1980, Gunn

1980, Hutchins *et al.* 1982, Sagoff 1984, Hutchins and Wemmer 1987, Norton 1987). In fact, without the latter, there is no way that the former could even exist. [. . .] Proponents of the conservation ethic argue that endangered species should be given special status solely because of their scarcity and because their loss is irreversible (Gunn 1980, Rolston 1985, Hutchins and Wemmer 1987, Norton 1987). The underlying rationale of this view is that naturally occurring biological diversity is intrinsically good and that every effort should be made to conserve it. It also recognizes that species in an ecological community are often interdependent, so that the loss of one species may have detrimental effects on many others. Here the focus is on the population, species, or ecosystem as a whole, rather than on individual organisms (Rodman 1977, Callicott 1980, Sagoff 1984, Hutchins and Wemmer 1987, Norton 1987).

[. . .]

While we agree that a recognition of the value of wild animals and their habitats may be important to both the animal rights advocate's and conservationist's goals (see Leopold 1949, Stone 1974, Gunn 1980, Regenstein 1985, Rolston 1985, Norton 1987), we also stress that responsible stewardship can involve difficult decisions (Hutchins *et al.* 1982, Howard 1986, Hutchins and Wemmer 1987, Rolston 1992). In some cases, our actions may result in the death or suffering of other sentient beings. Of course, this does not imply that animals can be treated without care and respect. For example, when the need to study or manage a population of animals, whether in captivity or in the wild, has been identified, it should be accomplished in the most humane manner possible. However, when the purpose of such research or management is to conserve natural ecosystems or to protect endangered species of animals or plants, it should not be perceived as fascist or inhumane.

We conclude that the conservation ethic is generally compatible with the animal welfare ethic but largely incompatible with the animal rights ethic, except under very specific circumstances (Gunn 1980, Hutchins *et al.*, 1982, Hutchins and Wemmer 1987, Norton 1987). As Norton says, "When one justifies differential treatment of animals because of the status of their species, one treats individuals as a means to the preservation of species and denies that they are ends-unto-themselves. This is surely a damaging conclusion for anyone . . . who hopes to base protectionist policies on claims of intrinsic value of individuals" (1987, 165). He further states that "concern for welfare of individuals seems, in general, to be the wrong direction to look if the goal is to preserve species" (167).

Our intent in this section has been to show that the use of animals in zoo and aquarium science, and in conservation science in general, is a moral imperative if many species are to be saved from extinction. We do not wish to imply, however, that researchers have carte blanche to conduct science without taking ethical considerations, including the welfare of their subjects, into account. In the next section, we show how the design of zoo and aquarium research programs can help ensure that animal welfare and other relevant issues are taken into consideration and that various research projects will pròduce significant and meaningful results.

Animal welfare and the design of zoo and aquarium research programs

[. . .]

Any zoological facility that has an active research program should also have a mechanism for making decisions regarding which projects it will and will not support (Kleiman 1985,

Hutchins 1988). Typically this is accomplished by a zoological research committee composed of staff scientists, university scientists, veterinarians, zoo administrators, and animal curators. The functions of such committees are to (1) determine the institution's policies with regard to research; (2) review proposals made by staff or university affiliates to conduct research on the animal collection; (3) review manuscripts produced as a result of this research; (4) monitor compliance with the institution's research protocols and regulations, including its animal welfare guidelines; and (5) decide if funds will be used to support specific research projects. The New York Zoological Society (now NYZS—The Wildlife Conservation Society) has such a committee and has developed an effective model for the design of zoo and aquarium research programs (Hutchins 1988, 1990a, 1990b).

With regard to animal welfare, it is critical that individual zoological institutions develop written policies on the care and use of animals in research (Kleiman 1985, Hutchins 1988). United States institutions that receive federal funding for research are required to have an institutional animal care and use committee (IACUC). Such committees, which consist of both institutional and outside representatives, monitor researchers' compliance with established legal guidelines such as the Animal Welfare Act of 1970.

[. . .]

When developing a policy on the use of animals in research, zoos and aquariums can adopt guidelines prepared by other organizations, or portions thereof. A number of guidelines currently exist, and these focus on the care and handling of both captive and free-ranging animals. For example, the American Society of Mammalogists has produced a document titled "Acceptable Field Methods in Mammalogy" (American Society of Mammalogists 1987). Similar guidelines have been developed for other vertebrates, including birds (American Ornithologists' Union 1988), reptiles, amphibians, and fish (Schaeffer *et al.* 1992). Excellent guidelines for the care and use of laboratory animals have been produced by many professional and governmental organizations, including the National Institutes of Health (1985), the Sigma Xi Committee on Science and Society (Sigma Xi 1992), and the Association for the Study of Animal Behaviour and the Animal Behavior Society (ASAB, 1986). Some taxonomic groups may require special attention. For example, recent (1985) amendments to the Animal Welfare Act now contain some minimum standards designed to promote the "psychological well-being" of captive primates (Novak and Suomi 1988).

It should be noted, however, that zoos and aquariums differ from many other research institutions, especially biomedical laboratories. For example, animals exhibited in modern, professionally managed zoological institutions are usually maintained under conditions that far exceed the minimum standards for laboratory animals. In addition, the number of individual animals used in research is typically much smaller and the number and diversity of species studied are considerably greater than in biomedical or university laboratories. The diversity of animals maintained and studied by zoos and aquariums is not a trivial issue, with each species having its own specific requirements for care and maintenance. In addition, much of the research conducted in zoos and aquariums is focused on endangered or threatened species, and this can result in additional concerns. For example, research conducted on endangered animals should not threaten their ability to reproduce, particularly if such animals are involved in organized cooperative breeding or reintroduction programs, such as those coordinated under the AZA's Species Survival Plan (Foose 1983). The World Conservation Union has developed a policy on research involving species at risk of extinction to which all zoological institutions should conform (IUCN 1989).

The issue of what kinds of research should be allowed in zoos and aquariums is complicated. Research in zoological institutions should, of course, conform to all legal guidelines related to animal welfare (Kleiman 1985, Hutchins 1988). However, the question of whether certain kinds of research should be conducted must be left up to individual institutions. In short, each proposed project must be considered on a case-by-case basis, taking into account not only the potential benefits to be derived but also the costs to the individual subjects. In each case, every effort must be made to consider alternative approaches and to reduce, as much as possible, any pain, discomfort, stress, or loss of life.

Kleiman suggests that zoological research committees ask themselves the following questions when evaluating research proposals (1985): Are all federal, state, and local regulations being followed? Is the species being used the most appropriate for this study? Is the smallest number of animals required (for statistical analysis) being used? Are there alternative procedures available that might achieve the same goals? Are animals being maintained so that their species-typical and individual needs are being met? Does the scientific gain outweigh the cost to the individual animals or species in terms of unavoidable stress or discomfort? Has unavoidable stress or discomfort been minimized to the best possible extent?

In the case of laboratory studies, several decision–analysis models have been developed to assist review committees in their deliberations (Bateson 1986, Orlans 1987), and a similar approach might prove useful for zoos and aquariums. The most obvious projects to proceed with are those in which the amount of animal suffering is negligible, the quality of the research is high, and the benefit is certain. Conversely, proposals should be rejected when the potential for suffering is great and the quality of the work and the benefit are uncertain (Driscoll and Bateson 1988). We agree with Kleiman's statement that "all research supported by a zoo, whether using animals in the collection or in the field, must be conducted in as humane a manner as possible, in line with the zoo's mission to preserve and respect life" (Kleiman 1985, 97). We also note, however, that when the fate of populations, species, or ecosystems lies in the balance, the scales may be tipped in favor of a given project, regardless of its implications for individual animals.

[. . .]

Because of the nature of scientific inquiry, assessing the potential benefit of a project is not an easy task (Will 1986). Although a scientist typically starts with a working hypothesis or question, he or she does not know a priori whether the results of any project will actually be beneficial. Much of the research conducted by zoo and aquarium biologists is applied (i.e., aimed at finding answers to practical questions regarding animal care, breeding, and conservation).

[. . .]

While we recognize the necessity of some regulation, we are concerned that it might drown legitimate conservation organizations, including professionally managed zoos and aquariums, in a sea of paperwork. At present, federal permit regulations make it extremely difficult to conduct basic studies of protected species, and this could hamper long-term conservation efforts (Ralls and Brownell 1989). Similarly, the continual imposition of more stringent regulations on the use of laboratory and zoo animals may result in more paperwork for administrators and scientists, while making little, if any, difference in the care and treatment of animals (see Briefing 1992). We agree with Rowan, who suggested that the greatest advances might be made by training and sensitizing researchers and animal caretakers to welfare issues (1991).

Finally, the importance of communicating the role and methods of conservation science, including the role of zoo- and aquarium-based research, to the general public cannot be overemphasized (see Birke 1990). [. . .] We feel that very few animal activists and other laypersons currently understand the nature or scope of the problem or what it is going to take to find solutions. With more than 105 million visitors a year, AZA-accredited zoos and aquariums are in an excellent position to undertake this task.

Perhaps most important, it is critical that the public sees conservation biologists as they are—not as cold, calculating scientists but as sensitive, caring people, people who value the lives of individual animals and worry about the future of life on this planet (Ratcliffe 1976, Rowan 1991). As responsible stewards, we recognize that some difficult decisions will have to be made, but we feel we should also strive to be sensitive to people's emotional reactions and not condemn them for well-meaning intentions. In this context, and despite some fundamental philosophical differences, there may be much room for compromise and cooperation between conservationists and animal welfare and rights advocates (see Kellert 1982, Hutchins and Wemmer 1987, King 1988, Ehrenfeld 1991). We also feel, however, that the conservation issue presents a severe challenge for ethical theory and agree with E. O. Wilson, who wrote,

> In ecological and evolutionary time, good does not automatically flow from good or evil from evil. To choose what is best for the near future is easy. To choose what is best for the distant future is also easy. But to choose what is best for the near future and distant future is a hard task, often internally contradictory, and requiring ethical codes yet to be formulated.
>
> (1984, 123)

References

American Ornithologists' Union. 1988. Guidelines for use of wild birds in research: Report of the American Ornithologists' Union, Cooper Ornithological Society, and Wilson Ornithological Society, Ad Hoc Committee on the Use of Wild Birds in Research. *Auk* (Supplement) 105:1A–41A.

American Society of Mammalogists. 1987. Acceptable field methods in mammalogy: Preliminary guidelines approved by the American Society of Mammalogists, Ad Hoc Committee for Animal Care Guidelines. *Journal of Mammalogy* (Supplement) 68(4):1–18.

ASAB. 1986. Guidelines for the use of animals in research, Association for the Study of Animal Behaviour and Animal Behavior Society. *Animal Behaviour* 34:315–18.

Balls, M. 1983. Alternatives to experimental animals. *Veterinary Record* 113(7):398–401.

Barnes, D. J. 1986. The case against the use of animals in science. In *Advances in Animal Welfare Science 1986–1987*, ed. M. W. Fox and L. D. Mickley, 215–25. Washington, D.C.: Humane Society of the United States.

Bateson, P. 1986. When to experiment on animals. *New Scientist*, 20 February:30–2.

Beck, B. B., I. Castro, D. G. Kleiman, J. M. Dietz, and B. Rettberg-Beck. 1988. Preparing captive-born primates for reintroduction. *International Journal of Primatology* 8:426.

Benirschke, K. 1983. The impact of research on the propagation of endangered species in zoos. In *Genetics and Conservation: A Reference for Managing Wild Animal and Plant Populations*, ed. C. M. Schonewald-Cox, S. M. Chambers, B. McBryde, and W. L. Thomas, 402–13. Menlo Park, Calif.: Benjamin/Cummings.

Birke, L. 1990. Selling science to the public. *New Scientist*, 18 August:40–4.

Bogue, G., and M. Ferrari. 1976. On the predatory "training" of captive reared pumas. *Camivore* 3(1):36–45.

Briefing. 1992. Rat and mouse care. *Science* 255:539.

Cade, T. J. 1988. Using science and technology to reestablish species lost in nature. In *Biodiversity*, ed. E. O. Wilson, 279–88. Washington, D.C.: National Academy Press.

Cairns, J. 1988. Increasing diversity by restoring damaged ecosystems. In *Biodiversity*, ed. E. O. Wilson, 333–43. Washington, D.C.: National Academy Press.

Callicott, J. B. 1980. Animal liberation: A triangular affair. *Environmental Ethics* 2:311–38.

Caughly, G. 1981. Overpopulation. In *Problems in Management of Locally Abundant Wild Mammals*, ed. P. A. Jewell and S. Holt, 7–19. New York: Academic Press.

Cohn, J. P. 1991. Reproductive biotechnology. *Bioscience* 41(9):595–8.

Conway, W. G. 1969. Zoos: Their changing roles. *Science* 163:48–52.

———. 1989. The prospects for sustaining species and their evolution. In *Conservation for the Twenty-First Century*, ed. D. Western and M. C. Pearl, 199–209. New York: Oxford University Press.

Diamond, J. 1992. Must we shoot deer to save nature? *Natural History* 8:2–8.

Dresser, B. L. 1988. Cryobiology, embryo transfer, and artificial insemination in *ex situ* animal conservation programs. In *Biodiversity*, ed. E. O. Wilson, 296–308. Washington, D.C.: National Academy Press.

Driscoll, J., and P. Bateson. 1988. Animals in behavioural research. *Animal Behaviour* 36:1569–74.

Duffy, E., and A. S. Watt (eds). 1971. *The Scientific Management of Plant and Animal Communities for Conservation*. Oxford: Blackwell Scientific Publications.

Ehrenfeld, D. 1972. *Conserving Life on Earth*. New York: Oxford University Press.

———. 1991. Conservation and the rights of animals. *Conservation Biology* 5(1):1–3.

Ehrlich, P., and A. Ehrlich. 1981. *Extinction: The Causes and Consequences of the Disappearance of Species*. New York: Random House.

Eisenberg, J. F., and D. G. Kleiman. 1975. The usefulness of behaviour studies in developing captive breeding programmes for mammals. *International Zoo Yearbook* 17:81–8.

Finlay, T. W., and T. L. Maple. 1986. A survey of research in American zoos and aquariums. *Zoo Biology* 5:261–8.

Flesness, N., and T. Foose. 1990. The role of captive breeding in the conservation of species. In *1990 IUCN Red List of Threatened Animals*, pp. xi–xx. Gland, Switzerland, and Cambridge, U.K.: World Conservation Union.

Foose, T. 1983. The relevance of captive populations to the conservation of biotic diversity. In *Genetics and Conservation: A Reference for Managing Wild Animal and Plant Populations*, ed. C. M. Schonewald-Cox, S. M. Chambers, B. McBryde, and W. L. Thomas, 374–401. Menlo Park, Calif.: Benjamin/Cummings.

Fowler, M. E. 1978. *Restraint and Handling of Wild and Domestic Animals*. Ames: Iowa State University Press.

Fox, M. W. 1990. *Inhumane Society*. New York: St. Martin's Press.

Frank, H., L. M. Hasselbach, and D. M. Littleton. 1986. Socialized vs. unsocialized wolves (*Canis lupus*) in experimental research. In *Advances in Animal Welfare Science 1986–1987*, ed. M. W. Fox and L. D. Mickley, 33–49. Washington, D.C.: Humane Society of the United States.

Gunn, A. S. 1980. Why should we care about rare species? *Environmental Ethics* 2:17–37.

Howard, W. E. 1986. *Nature and Animal Welfare: Both Are Misunderstood*. Pompano Beach, Fla.: Exposition Press of Florida.

——— 1990. *Animal Rights vs. Nature*. Davis, Calif.: Published by the author.

Hutchins, M. 1988. On the design of zoo research programs. *International Zoo Yearbook* 27:9–19.

——— 1990a. Serving science and conservation: The biological materials request protocol of the New York Zoological Society. *Zoo Biology* 9:447–60.

——— 1990b. *New York Zoological Society Zoo and Aquarium Research Manual*. New York: New York Zoological Society.

Hutchins, M., and N. Fascione. 1993. What is it going to take to save wildlife? In *Proceedings: American Association of Zoological Parks and Aquariums Regional Conferences*, 5–15. Wheeling, W.Va.: AAZPA.

Hutchins, M., and C. Wemmer. 1987. Wildlife conservation and animal rights: Are they compatible? In *Advances in Animal Welfare Science 1986–1987*, ed. M. W. Fox and L. D. Mickley, 111–37. Washington, D.C.: Humane Society of the United States.

——— 1991. Response: In defense of captive breeding. *Endangered Species Update* 8:5–6.

Hutchins, M., and R. J. Wiese. 1991. Beyond genetic and demographic management: The future of the Species Survival Plan and related AAZPA conservation efforts. *Zoo Biology* 10:285–92.

Hutchins, M., V. Stevens, and N. Atkins. 1982. Introduced species and the issue of animal welfare. *International Journal for the Study of Animal Problems* 3(4):316–18.

Hutchins, M., R. J. Wiese, K. Willis, and S. Becker (eds). 1991a. *AAZPA Annual Report on Conservation and Science, 1990–1991*. Bethesda, Md.: AAZPA.

Hutchins, M., T. Foose, and U. S. Seal. 1991b. The role of veterinary medicine in endangered species conservation. *Journal of Zoo and Wildlife Medicine* 22(3):277–81.

Hutchins, M., C. Sheppard, A. Lyles, and G. Casedi. In press. Behavioral considerations in the captive management, propagation, and reintroduction of endangered birds. In *Captive Conservation of Endangered Species*, ed. J. Demarest, B. Durrant, and E. Gibbons. Stony Brook: State University of New York Press.

IUCN. 1989. Research involving species at risk of extinction, policy statement. Gland, Switzerland: World Conservation Union.

Jamieson, D. 1985. Against zoos. In *In Defense of Animals*, ed. P. Singer, 108–17. New York: Harper & Row.

Kellert, S. 1982. Striving for common ground: Humane and scientific considerations in contemporary wildlife management. *International Journal for the Study of Animal Problems* 3(2):137–40.

King, W. 1988. Animal rights: A growing moral dilemma. *Animal Kingdom* 91(1):33–5.

Kleiman, D. G. 1980. The sociobiology of captive propagation. In *Conservation Biology: An Evolutionary-Ecological Approach*, ed. M. E. Soulé and B. A. Wilcox, 243–61. Sunderland, Mass.: Sinauer Associates.

—— 1985. Criteria for the evaluation of zoo research projects. *Zoo Biology* 4:93–8.

—— 1992. Behavior research in zoos: Past, present, and future. *Zoo Biology* 11:301–12.

Leopold, A. 1949. *A Sand County Almanac*. New York: Oxford University Press.

Maple, T., and T. Finlay. 1989. Applied primatology in the modern zoo. *Zoo Biology* (Supplement) 1:101–16.

Merton, D. V. 1977. Controlling introduced predators and competitors on islands. In *Endangered Birds: Management Techniques for Saving Threatened Species*, ed. S. A. Temple, 121–34. Madison: University of Wisconsin Press.

Mlot, C. 1989. The science of saving endangered species. *Bioscience* 39(2):68–70.

Moss, T. H. 1984. The modern politics of laboratory animal use. *Bioscience* 34:621–25.

National Institutes of Health. 1985. *Guide for the Care and Use of Laboratory Animals*. Bethesda, Md.: U.S. Department of Health and Human Services, Public Health Service, National Institutes of Health.

Norton, B. G. 1987. *Why Preserve Natural Variety?* Princeton, N.J.: Princeton University Press.

Novak, M. A., and S. J. Suomi. 1988. Psychological well-being of primates in captivity. *American Psychologist* 43(10):765–73.

Olney, P. J. S. 1980. London Zoo. In *Great Zoos of the World*, ed. S. Zuckerman, 35–48. London: Weidenfeld & Nicholson.

Orlans, F. B. 1987. Review of experimental protocols: Classifying animal harm and applying "refinements." *Laboratory Animal Science* (special issue) January:50–6.

Packer, C. 1992. Captives in the wild. *National Geographic* 181:122–36.

Poole, D. A., and J. B. Trefethen. 1978. The maintenance of wildlife populations. In *Wildlife and America*, ed. H. Brokaw, 339–49. Washington, D.C.: Council on Environmental Quality.

Ralls, K., and R. L. Brownell. 1989. Protected species: Research permits and the value of basic research. *Bioscience* 39(6):394–6.

Ratcliffe, D. A. 1976. Thoughts towards a philosophy of nature conservation. *Biological Conservation* 9:45–53.

Regan, T. 1983. *The Case for Animal Rights*. Berkeley: University of California Press.

Regan, T., and G. Francione. 1992. The animal "welfare" vs. "rights" debate. *Animals' Agenda* 12(1):45.

Regenstein, L. 1985. Animal rights, endangered species, and human survival. In *In Defense of Animals*, ed. P. Singer, 118–32. New York: Harper & Row.

Roberts, L. 1988. Beyond Noah's ark: What do we need to know? *Science* 242:1247.

Rodman, J. 1977. The liberation of nature? *Inquiry* 20:83–131.

Rolston, H. III. 1985. Duties to endangered species. *Bioscience* 35(11):718–26.

—— 1992. Ethical responsibilities toward wildlife. *Journal of the American Veterinary Medical Association* 200:618–22.

Rowan, A. 1991. Animal experimentation and society: A case of an uneasy interaction. In *Bioscience/Society*, ed. D.J. Roy, B. E. Wynne, and R. W. Old, 261–82. New York: John Wiley & Sons.

Ryder, R. D. 1985. Speciesism in the laboratory. In *In Defense of Animals*, ed. P. Singer, 77–88. New York: Harper & Row.

Sagoff, M. 1984. Animal liberation and environmental ethics: Bad marriage, quick divorce. *Report from the Center for Philosophy and Public Policy* (University of Maryland) 4(2):6–8.

Schaeffer, D. O., K. M. Kleinow, and L. Krulisch (eds). 1992. *The Care and Use of Amphibians, Reptiles, and Fish in Research*. Bethesda, Md.: Scientist's Center for Animal Welfare.

Shaffer, M. L. 1978. Minimum viable population sizes for species conservation. *Bioscience* 31:131–4.

Shepherdson, D., K. Calstead, J. Mellen, and J. Seidensticker. 1993. The influence of food presentation on the behavior of small cats in confined environments. *Zoo Biology* 12:203–16.

Sigma Xi. 1992. Sigma Xi statement on the use of animals in research. *American Scientist* January:73–6.

Singer, P. 1975. *Animal Liberation*. New York: Random House.

Soulé, M. E. 1985. What is conservation biology? *Bioscience* 35:727–34.

—— (ed.). 1986. *Conservation Biology: The Science of Scarcity and Diversity*. Sunderland, Mass.: Sinauer Associates.

Soulé, M. E., and K. A. Kohm. 1989. *Research Priorities for Conservation Biology*. Washington, D.C.: Island Press.

Soulé, M. E., and B. A. Wilcox (eds). 1980. *Conservation Biology: An Evolutionary-Ecological Perspective*. Sunderland, Mass.: Sinauer Associates.

Soulé, M. E., B. A. Wilcox, and C. Holtby. 1979. Benign neglect: A model of faunal collapse in the game reserves of East Africa. *Biological Conservation* 15:259–72.

Stone, C. D. 1974. *Should Trees Have Standing?* New York: Discus, Avon Books.

Sukumar, R. 1991. The management of large mammals in relation to male strategies and conflict with people. *Biological Conservation* 55:93–102.

Tudge, C. 1991. *Last Animals at the Zoo: How Mass Extinction Can Be Stopped.* London: Hutchinson Radius.

Wiese, R., M. Hutchins, K. Willis, and S. Becker (eds). 1992. *AAZPA Annual Report on Conservation and Science, 1991–1992.* Bethesda, Md.: AAZPA.

Wiese, R., K. Willis, J. Bowdoin, and M. Hutchins (eds) 1993. *AAZPA Annual Report on Conservation and Science, 1992–1993.* Bethesda, Md.: AAZPA.

Wilbur, S. R. 1977. Supplemental feeding of California condors. In *Endangered Birds: Management Techniques for Saving Threatened Species*, ed. S. A. Temple, 135–40. Madison: University of Wisconsin Press.

Wildt, D. E. 1989. Reproductive research in conservation biology: Priorities and avenues for support. *Journal of Zoo and Wildlife Medicine* 20(4):391–5.

Will, J. A. 1986. The case for the use of animals in science. In *Advances in Animal Welfare Science 1986–1987*, ed. M. W. Fox and L. D. Mickley, 205–13. Washington, D.C.: Humane Society of the United States.

Wilson, E. O. 1984. *Biophilia: The Human Bond with Other Species.* Cambridge, Mass.: Harvard University Press.

Younghusband, P., and N. Myers. 1986. Playing God with nature. *International Wildlife* 16(4):4–13.

67

Donald G. Lindburg

"Zoos and the Rights of Animals"

Lindburg explores the need for zoo and aquarium professionals to respect both the needs of individual animals and the need of species to survive over evolutionary time, and how these needs might be integrated. He notes that zoo professionals are more strongly committed to animal welfare than animal rights and that when individual welfare conflicts with species preservation, zoo professionals normally give higher priority to species preservation.

Introduction

Many in our profession may harken back to a time when the welfare of their charges rested largely on their individual sensitivities. Concerns for humane treatment and quality of life within zoological institutions reflected the attitudes of society toward human–animal relationships at the time and were only modestly regulated by a professional code of ethics, largely unwritten. During the past three decades, however, we have witnessed the rise of philosophically driven activism that has profoundly altered the way society views these relationships. Where once such activities as feeding live prey or shipping a gorilla to another zoo fell largely within the purview of the profession, the reality of today is that the entire spectrum of zoo and aquarium activities is repeatedly held up to public scrutiny and judgment (Hutchins and Fascione, 1991).

[...]

It is widely recognized that the original objectives of zoos in maintaining collections of wild animals can no longer be condoned. Modern-day zoos, therefore, have redefined their missions in light of questions about the right to hold animals captive and the relevance and humaneness of this practice. They have done so by aligning themselves with conservationist objectives, a process that has entailed the investment of substantial resources in education, improved training of staff, modernization of exhibits, breeding, and, in some cases, reintroductions, and research designed to improve health, welfare, and propagation efforts. The modern zoo also takes note of the world-wide decline in populations and their habitats and increasingly envisions a time when at least some species will exist only within their confines (Soulé *et al.*, 1986). For the vast majority of those who labor in the profession, therefore, pride of achievement and a personal sense of fulfillment are commonly found. Indeed, for most it is a pursuit to be nobly and passionately held.

What, then, does the rights movement have to offer the zoo/aquarium community other than its condemnation? Can any agreement on principle be found? Can respect for different viewpoints be engendered, such that joint action on shared objectives may be realized? The need for improved welfare for animals within our institutions gets no argument (Fox, 1986; Gibbons *et al.*, 1995; Hutchins *et al.*, 1995; Mapie *et al.*, 1995; Shepherdson *et al.*, 1998), but more problematic for zoos and aquariums are the moral concerns flowing from the proposition that animals indeed have certain basic rights (Singer and Regan, 1976; Regan, 1983).

Taking as their major premise that animals do not exist to serve the interests of humans, true adherents to the animal-rights view oppose the use of animals for food, clothing, companionship, entertainment, sport, and experimentation of any kind. Actions that cause animals any measure of suffering, including research designed to benefit either humans or the animals themselves, are uniformly opposed.

[. . .]

It would be inaccurate to assert that all who are concerned with the humane treatment (welfare) of animals, including many who subscribe to vegetarianism, hold to the rights view. Nor would it be accurate to assume that all opposition to the keeping of wild animals in captivity arises only from this quarter. In an article entitled "Against Zoos," animal liberationist Dale Jamieson [1985] stressed human domination of animals and their loss of freedom during confinement in zoos, rather than a rights ethic, as presumptively wrong. He, and many others who are deeply committed to conservation, does not see zoos as offering viable alternatives to in situ efforts. Although critical of inhumane conditions, many animal welfare advocates nevertheless recognize a role for zoos (e.g., Grandy, 1989; Bekoff, 1995). In addition, some conservationists working in in situ contexts see zoos as anachronistic and inhumane (see Eudey, 1995; Loftin, 1995 for examples of critiques of captive breeding programs). However, because of their activist tactics, the zoo/aquarium profession is more concerned about animal rightists than about opposition from welfarists and conservationists.

Hutchins and Wemmer (1987), in reviewing areas in which animal rightists and conservationists (including zoo/aquarium professionals) are in substantial disagreement, also conclude that "the two views are not completely antithetical" (p. 131). They, and others (e.g., Ehrenfeld, 1991) called for united efforts between the two where there is common ground (see also Varner, 1994, and Jamieson, 1998). Although the intent of this commentary is to lay out some of the more salient issues in a non-advocative manner, my bias is that of the conservationist. There are zoo and aquarium professionals who believe animals have rights who also believe they should be conserved, and there are zoo and aquarium professionals who place a high value on animal welfare, yet hold rights advocates in utmost contempt. Despite deeply held positions for which no reconciliation is likely to occur, my objective is to increase understanding of the rights view and the zoo view in hopes of enhancing both welfare and conservationist prospects for endangered wildlife. To that end, I discuss animal rights as a political movement and as a belief system for that movement, and the implications of these views for zoo-based conservation efforts.

Animal rights as a political movement

Although many individuals in our society subscribe to the view that animals have rights, it is equally clear that this stance means different things to different people. For a majority, the intent in bequeathing rights on animals is to assert that they deserve humane, respectful treatment. Rowan (1992) states that this is the more common view held by the general public, 80 percent of whom believe that animals have rights. At the other extreme are those who reject the notion that only humans among living creatures can have rights. The basis for this view is variable, depending in some instances on animals' advanced social or rational capacities or on having the quality of sentience (the ability to experience pain and to suffer). Rightists stress the *similarities* between humans and animals, and granting rights to animals is but a logical extension of the struggle by humans to achieve social equality between races, classes, and genders as society becomes increasingly sensitized to its unprincipled biases against minorities.

However divergent the views of its adherents might be, the impact of the rights movement on how society interacts with both domestic and wild animals is far reaching. [. . .] In U.S. college newspapers, researchers using animals in experiments have seen themselves featured as "vivisector of the month," and in the aftermath of the destruction of a research laboratory at Texas Tech in 1989, university officials received over 10,000 letters opposing the work of the scientist in question (Herzog, 1993). Closer to home for zoos, in 1993 citizens of the city of Vancouver, British Columbia, Canada, voted by a 54 percent majority to close down its Stanley Park Zoo, founded in 1893. Although not listed in recent issues of the American Zoo Association (AZA) Directory of accredited institutions, and perhaps deserving of its fate, the important point is that the winning campaign was led by animal rights advocates whose principal argument was that wild animals ought not to be publicly displayed for the entertainment of people (Los Angeles *Times*, Oct. 6, 1995).

Unquestionably, the most significant indicator of the power of the animal rights movement in the United States is amendment of the Animal Welfare Act of 1985, requiring improved treatment of animals in laboratories and such other factors as the reduction of duplication in research and the consideration of alternative research methods to the use of animals. Although portions of the Act, such as improving the psychological health of captives, were initially resisted as undefinable and as requiring a huge outlay of money to implement, many labs were remodeled, and enrichment efforts on the part of laboratory staff are now routinely encouraged.

[. . .]

[T]he animal rights movement has significantly altered the views of society on human–animal relationships and on the ways in which scientists, doctors, veterinarians, zoo and aquarium managers, circus personnel, wildlife managers, agriculturists, pet owners, many corporate executives, and even hunters and fishers interact with members of the animal kingdom. There is no denying that much good has resulted from this effort. Although there are many among the ranks of scientists, for example, who have shown a lifetime of sensitivity to animal welfare, it took the passion of the animal rights movement to bring about widespread change in the ethical culture of the research laboratory. Few can deny, furthermore, that zoos and aquariums have made great strides in effecting more humane exhibitry and management, based at least in part on the impact of the rights movement on public sentiments (for further discussion of these points, see Geist, 1992; Herzog, 1993; Morrison, 1994; Norton *et al.*, 1995). The zoo/aquarium profession, nevertheless, finds itself at cross purposes with rightists on a wide range of issues from euthanasia policy to the validity of its educational, scientific, and conservation missions.

Animal rights as a belief system

[. . .]

Here, I examine the two main philosophies espoused by the movement, *utilitarianism* and *deontology* (also known as "the rights view"). [. . .] The utilitarian view justifies an action only if its good consequences outweigh its harmful ones. In identifying pain and suffering as harmful, Singer (1975) calculates that because the harm to animals used in research, for example, outweighs any resulting good, most animal-based research is immoral. This formula is applicable only to animals capable of experiencing pain or mental anguish, i.e., those described as sentient, and is today commonly used to deny the use of animals or their products for food, clothing, shelter, entertainment, and various other benefits to humans.

[. . .]

Although agreeing with his sentiments, Tom Regan [1983, 1995], a deontologist [. . .] rejects Singer's criteria for ethical treatment of animals since, under the utilitarian view, the benefits or harm to those humans interacting with them at the time must also be considered in deciding the morality of an action. [. . .] To Regan and his followers in the rights movement, exploitation of animals is wrong independently of the interests of their exploiters.

Alternatively, Regan believes it is the *sort* of individual, not the consequences of any act toward it, that defines morally acceptable behavior. In certain fundamental ways, some animals have the same qualities as human beings, i.e., they have interests, expectations, desires, perceptions, memories, a sense of the future, an emotional life together, and numerous other qualities that Regan (1983) terms "*the subject-of-a-life criterion*" that entitles an animal to the same respect we would extend to a fellow human. Stated another way, individuals meeting this criterion have *inherent* value, independently of the valuing agent.

[. . .]

This philosophy works only if one provides an "out" for animals that do things that, in human terms, would be immoral. A human who kills another human commits murder, whereas the lion that kills the zebra for food does not. Only humans can be *moral agents*. In contrast, animals are likened to "marginal" humans, i.e., infants or the mentally retarded who cannot be held accountable for their acts. They are, by contrast, *moral patients*. Animals, then, according to the rights view, have rights but not responsibilities. One can immediately perceive a certain inconsistency in the logic, namely, that it is their *likeness* to humans that enjoins our respect, but a profound *difference* from humans in terms of moral accountability that gives them special standing.

This point is further illustrated in rightists' approach to euthanasia, a procedure that, it is held, should be limited to circumstances in which it complies with the wishes of the animal in question. Animals suffering acute pain in the final stages of a fatal disease, accordingly, allow us to "do for them what they cannot do for themselves" (Regan, 1983, p. 114). By ending their misery, we are *complying with their will* and engaging in "preference-respecting" euthanasia.

[. . .]

Regan's "subject-of-a-life criterion" lies at the root of a recent proposal to bring the three great apes (orangutans, chimpanzees, and gorillas) into the human community as moral equals (The Great Ape Project (see Cavalieri and Singer, 1993)). In support of this proposal, a distinguished roster of scientists and philosophers wrote of the strong similarities between humans and apes in social, emotional, rational, and even incipiently moral capabilities, and used these to argue for an end to human dominion over the great apes, particularly those held in captive situations. Despite the obviously high level of sentience in these taxa and deeply felt concerns for their welfare, this case aptly demonstrates the difficulties encountered in finding a neat formula for action in moral philosophies that are based on arguments that "likes" ought to be treated alike (see discussion of "moral monism" by Norton, 1995). By wanting to do for apes what they cannot do for themselves, it must be asked if we can logically stress their continuity with humans in making the case for preferential treatment without at the same time highlighting their differential standing as moral patients. Put another way, it is a *discontinuity* between humans and apes that enables us to respect them for their *continuities*. In striving to increase respect for the apes, care must be taken not to draw oversimplistic depictions such as their having the elements of a social system that is socially transmitted across the generations (Noske, 1993), a "finding" that will come as no shock to any reputable zoologist. There are many welfare advocates on the other side of this issue who worry that such well-intentioned eagerness leaves us but a short step removed from a Disney-esque world of talking animals coming together to discuss the rules of the jungle. As Zak (1989) stressed, it is the unlikes between humans and animals and an infinite combination of likes and unlikes among non-human creatures that often leaves us on uncertain moral ground.

[. . .]

Animal rights and conservation

Many zoos and aquariums have had first-hand experience with members of the animal rights community. Perhaps the most common of these is some form of organized demonstration against a particular action, usually with advance notification to the television and print media. Representatives of zoos and aquariums have at times had to respond to media questions about charges emanating from these dissents. Among the issues that may be raised are

- the conditions under which animals are kept, often precipitated by some unusual event such as an escape or an accidental death, and commonly expanded into a challenge of the legitimacy of holding any animals captive
- euthanasia generally, but particularly as relates to the disposal of genetic surplus or highly sentient individuals
- the feeding of live prey and, in some cases, whole animal carcasses
- transfers of individuals between zoos, particularly when social relationships that are believed to have attributes in common with those of humans are ruptured as a result
- the use of animals in entertainment, especially performing animals
- bringing new animals in from the wild to augment captive holdings or to start new breeding programs
- the employment of invasive technologies such as embryo manipulation or exogenous hormonal stimulation in breeding efforts
- all research involving animals, even when it is the health and longevity of animals that stand to benefit.

We should be quick to acknowledge that protest is in many cases warranted. Dissent is among our most cherished constitutional prerogatives, and it often forces zoo personnel to examine the ramifications of their actions in ways that otherwise might not occur. There is, furthermore, a difference in views within the zoo community itself regarding the wisdom or legitimacy of a particular course of action, leading in some instances to staff having at least guarded sympathy with the positions of animal rightists. Far from wanting to stifle dissent, we are required to acknowledge that it often has a beneficial effect. Opposition to dissent arises, however, when there are sharp philosophical differences between positions taken by the institution and the dissenting group. It is therefore useful to consider how the philosophies driving the animal rights movement may differ from those underlying the conservation efforts of the zoo/aquarium profession, and how these may have a temporizing effect on certain of the latter's activities.

Attributes common to both Singer's utilitarianism and Regan's notion of inherent value are 1) a disavowal of moral anthropocentrism, 2) granting highest priority to the welfare of individuals, and 3) dependence on a single, fundamental principle such as sentience or self-awareness in granting animals equivalent moral standing with humans.

[. . .]

Although they as a rule give utmost respect to individuals, members of the zoo community are less inclined to grant them rights (Koontz, 1995) and side with holist philosophers in placing greater value on communities of individuals (see chapters in Norton *et al.*, 1995).

[. . .]

As noted in an earlier quote from Regan, once inherent value is granted, there is little ground for making distinctions between individuals. This applies to the distinction between animals that are rare or endangered versus those that are more common. According to the rights view, a rare individual has no higher moral standing than one that is common, since all share equally the basis on which they are granted inherent value. Regan (1983), in an oft quoted comment, states "That an individual animal is among the last remaining members of a species confers no further right to that animal, and its right not to be harmed must be weighed equitably with the rights of any others who have this right" (p. 359). Taken to its logical conclusion, this view allows for no special treatment in protecting threatened ecosystems by culling of unwanted animals (see Hutchins and Wemmer, 1987, for an extended discussion of this point), nor can it condone invasive technologies and the attendant suffering of individuals that are intended to secure their future as a taxon on grounds of rareness (Varner and Monroe, 1991, but see rejoinder by Hutchins and Wemmer, 1991). Animal rights philosophers do not oppose efforts to save endangered species, but neither do they single them out for special treatment. According to Regan (1983), "the general policy recommended by the rights view is: *let them be!*" (p. 361, original italics). In contrast, the zoo biologist or the park manager will usually opt in favor of steps that insure the survival of species over survival of its individual members (see, e.g., Lacy, 1991, 1995).

[. . .]

Norton (1995) points out that humans tacitly acknowledge differential obligations to animals according to context, and uses an example from interactions with wild versus domestic animals. One might chase off a house cat stalking a songbird in the back yard, for example, but would find it unthinkable to interfere with a wild cat's foraging activities. It is the *context* of the encounter that defines value and shapes the morally appropriate response. Furthermore, as this example shows, animals elicit different levels of responsibility from us, with emphasis on the individual when it comes to the community of domesticated animals but on populations, species, and generative processes in experiences of those in a wild state.

This contextual valuation may have particular relevance for the zoo profession. The animal taken into captivity, ostensibly to ensure its future survival, incurs increased obligations from the human community commensurate with its dependence on humans for food, shelter, psychological and physical health, etc. These obligations arise from valuing individuals as individuals, and in recognizing the moral requirement to treat them with respect. Left unsolved by the agreement that, as captives, animals should be granted heightened value, is the morality of taking them into captivity in the first instance. Here, a different value, operating on a different time scale, and at the level of the individual as member of a species or other collective comes into play. Norton suggests that all life forms are engaged in a struggle to survive—an individual striving—but are also engaged in a correlative striving to perpetuate their kind. This striving to perpetuate may fail, and the species is in danger of becoming extinct. At this point, because we value the taxon above the individual, we do for it what it cannot do for itself (notice the similarity in phrasing to the rightist's approach to euthanasia) and take the extraordinary measure of bringing it into the human community. A recent, widely publicized example of an apparent successful intervention illustrating this point is that of the California condor, whose last wild survivors were brought into captivity for protected breeding in 1987 (Toone and Wallace, 1994), and whose descendants are now being returned to the wild.

Although for their benefit, confining wild animals to a captive environment may be said to harm them (Jamieson, 1985, 1995). At this point, the concept of animal altruism is invoked, to wit, the wild animal taken captive sacrifices its freedom and sometimes its life for the good of its kind. By analogy, the soldier who gives his life for his country goes into the breech willingly so that others might live and is regarded as a hero. A difficulty with this analogy is the absence of volunteerism on the part of animals taken into captivity. Lacking the capacity to evaluate and to decide for themselves, their sacrifice on behalf of an abstract principle is without their consent. However, as noted by Norton (1995), an ethic that bases all moral decisions on a single criterion such as Regan's subject-of-a-life is "likely to conclude that sacrifice of individuals for species survival is always wrong because the individuals cannot fulfill the key requirement of voluntary acceptance of risk" (p. 113). This, he points out, is to define altruism in anthropomorphic terms, thereby disqualifying animals from ever acting altruistically in a cause implicit in their struggle to perpetuate their genes.

But, perhaps a slight modification of the analogy, not dependent on the element of volunteerism, is applicable. All-volunteer armies are probably fairly rare, and at least in recent history we have been made painfully aware of the process of conscripting soldiers to defend societies. Far from becoming voluntarily engaged, many conscripts would rather be at home with family than in a fox hole but heed the call when duty demands it. It would be inaccurate to say that acts of heroism are performed only by those who come into harm's way voluntarily. The conscript risking loss of life in battle would surely be severely punished if he/she deserted at that moment. But, self sacrifice would seem to be infrequently coerced by fear of the consequences of desertion. Though not in the situation voluntarily, the conscript accepts the obligation to stay and fight, even against his/her will. And we would see their self-sacrificing acts as no less heroic than those of the volunteer soldier. Following this analogy, the captive exotic is conscripted to sacrifice its freedom in the struggle to perpetuate its kind.

Defending one's country entails a context in which the usual rules of the game are suspended, and values undergo a change commensurate with the needs of society at the time. This, incidentally, may be one context in which having equal inherent value as envisioned by rights advocates does not hold. A rigid rank order, a chain-of-command, and a remarkable difference in rights and privileges are characteristic of all defensive entities, are sanctioned by society in the name of the discipline needed to mount protective actions, and are not to be measured in the same currency as differences in race, gender, and social class. Similarly, defending species from the finality of extinction may be said to have elements of a desperate struggle in which non-voluntary compliance with an extraordinary set of rules comes into play for certain individuals in the community under threat. Assuming captive animal "conscripts" are truly used to help save their kind in a significant way, the deprivation of freedom that is a major concern of rightists/liberationists (see Bostock, 1993, and Jamieson, 1995, for thoughtful discussions of this issue) may to some extent be ameliorated.

Conclusion

To summarize, the pluralistic ethic as set forth by Norton embraces a shifting value, depending on whether the animal is in the wild context, in which case we have a greater duty to collectives than to individuals, or in the community of domesticated animals, where individual welfare takes precedence. The community of zoo animals is, by contrast, a *mixed* community in which both the striving for life and for perpetuation over evolutionary time creates obligations to combine respect for individuals with respect for the process-oriented ethic that applies to preserving their kind. This mixed community is justified because the striving for preservation has taken on the aspects of a battle against global adversity, with attendant loss of freedom and even of life, involuntarily. It is these contextually relevant values that zoo and aquarium professionals readily invoke to justify ex situ conservation efforts.

Along these lines, and with some modification to allow for the special circumstance of the captive exotic, Callicott (1989) articulated a vision that has potential for reconciliation of the different ethics that today foster conflict among people everywhere concerned about the well being of our planet's inhabitants:

> If the case for animal rights would be theoretically restructured to divide animal rights holders from non-holders along the domestic/wild axis rather than subject-/ non-subject-of-a-life axis, then its reconciliation with environmental ethics could be envisioned. Both would rest upon a common concept—the community concept. And the very different ethical implications of either would be governed by the different kinds of communities humans and animals comprise—the "mixed" human-domestic community, on the one hand, and the natural, wild biotic community, on the other.
>
> (p. 47)

Reconciliation may also advance from the proposition that no animal lives wholly unto itself but is the "subject-of-a-group-life" or a "community-life," a concept introduced by Livingston (1994, as described by Noske, 1998) to counter the individual or self-centered focus of the rights view. Livingston's thesis asserts the participatory consciousness of wild animals flowing from everyday membership in entities greater than their individual selves and overcomes the problem of redefining animals in the human terms that attend the "subject-of-a-life" construct.

It is fair to presume that zoo professionals are strongly committed to animal welfare but less so to animal rights. Theirs is a profession that, by its very nature, shares the holistic ethic, viz., that preservationist goals can only be achieved by unfailingly giving highest priority to collections of individuals. Zoo professionals frequently find individual welfare and species preservation to be in conflict and in such cases will give higher priority to the preservation of species. It does not follow, as is often claimed, that there is indifference to the interests of individuals or lack of respect for them. In fact, goals of species preservation are more likely to be realized where the lives of individuals are given the highest respect (McManamon, 1993; Lindburg and Lindburg, 1995; Maple *et al.*, 1995), and where every effort is made to safeguard their interests. These dual concerns indicate that those who toil in zoos readily embrace the ethical pluralism that offers a basis for reconciliation with any who question the morality of their acts.

References

Bekoff, M. 1995. Naturalizing and individualizing animal well-being and animal minds; an ethologist's naiveté exposed? In: Rowan A.N., editor. *Wildlife Conservation, Zoos and Animal Protection*. Philadelphia: Tufts Center for Animals and Public Policy. pp. 63–115.

Bostock, S. St C. 1993. *Zoos and Animal Rights: the Ethics of Keeping Animals*. London: Routledge. 227 p.

Callicott J.B. 1989. *In Defense of the Land Ethic*. Albany, NY: State University of New York Press. 325 p.

Cavalieri P., Singer P. (eds). 1993. *The Great Ape Project*. New York: St Martin's Press. 312 p.

Ehrenfeld D. 1991. Conservation and the rights of animals. *Conserv. Biol.* 5:1–3.

Eudey A. 1995. To procure or not to procure. In: Norton B.G., Hutchins M., Stevens E.F., Maple T.L. (eds). *Ethics on the Ark: Zoos, Animal Welfare, and Wildlife Conservation*. Washington, DC: Smithsonian Institution Press, pp. 146–52.

Fox M. 1986. *Laboratory Animal Husbandry: Ethology, Welfare, and Experimental Variables*. Albany, NY: State University of New York Press, 267 p.

Geist V. 1992. Opening statement, panel discussion on "Wildlife conservation and animal rights: are they compatible?" In: *Proceedings of the American Association of Zoological Parks and Aquariums Annual Meeting*, Toronto, Canada. Wheeling, W.V.: American Association of Zoological Parks and Aquariums. pp. 10–2.

Gibbons E.F. Jr, Durrant B.S. Demarest J. 1995. *Conservation of Endangered Species in Captivity: an Interdisciplinary Approach*. Albany, NY: State University of New York Press, 810 p.

Grandy J.W. 1989. Captive breeding in zoos: destructive programs in need of change. *Humane Soc. News* summer: 8–11.

Herzog H.A. 1993. Animal rights and wrongs. *Science* 262:1906–8.

Hutchins M., Fascione N. 1991. Ethical issues facing modern zoos. In: *Proceedings of the American Association of Zoo Veterinarians*, Calgary, Canada, 1991. Philadelphia: American Association of Zoo Veterinarians. pp. 56–64.

Hutchins M., Wemmer C. 1987. Wildlife conservation and animal rights: are they compatible? In: Fox, M.W., Mickley, L.D. (eds). *Advances in Animal Welfare Science 1986–1987*. Washington, DC: Humane Society of the United States. pp. 111–37.

Hutchins M., Dresser B., Wemmer C. 1995. Ethical considerations in zoo and aquarium research. In: Norton B.G., Hutchins M., Stevens E.F., Maple T.L. (eds). *Ethics on the Ark: Zoos, Animal Welfare, and Wildlife Conservation*. Washington, DC: Smithsonian Institution Press. pp. 253–76.

Jamieson D. 1985. Against zoos. In: Singer P., (ed.). *In Defense of Animals*. New York: Harper and Row. pp. 108–17.

Jamieson D. 1995. Zoos revisited. In: Norton B.G., Hutchins M., Stevens R.F., Maple T.L. (eds). *Ethics on the Ark: Zoos, Animal Welfare, and Wildlife Conservation*. Washington, DC: Smithsonian Institution Press. pp. 52–66.

Jamieson D. 1998. Animal liberation is an environmental ethic. *Environ. Values* 7:41–57.

Koontz F. 1995. Wild animal acquisition ethics for zoo biologists. In: Norton B.G., Hutchins M., Stevens E.F., Maple T.L. (eds). *Ethics on the Ark: Zoos, Animal Welfare, and Wildlife Conservation*. Washington, DC: Smithsonian Institution Press. pp. 127–45.

Lacy R.C. 1991. Zoos and the surplus problem: an alternate solution. *Zoo Biol.* 10:293–7.

Lacy R.C. 1995. Culling surplus animals for population management. In: Norton B.G., Hutchins M., Stevens E.F., Maple T.L. (eds). *Ethics on the Ark: Zoos, Animal Welfare, and Wildlife Conservation*. Washington, DC: Smithsonian Institution Press. pp. 187–94.

Lindburg D.G., Lindburg L.L. 1995. Success breeds a quandry: to cull or not to cull. In: Norton B.G., Hutchins M., Stevens E.F., Maple T.L. (eds). *Ethics on the Ark: Zoos, Animal Welfare, and Wildlife Conservation*. Washington, DC: Smithsonian Institution Press, pp. 195–208.

Livingston J.A. 1994. *Rogue Primate: an Exploration of Human Domestication*. Toronto: Key Porter. 278 p.

Loftin R. 1995. Captive breeding of endangered species. In: Norton B.G., Hutchins M., Stevens E.F., Maple T.L. (eds). *Ethics on the Ark: Zoos, Animal Welfare, and Wildlife Conservation*. Washington, DC: Smithsonian Institution Press. pp. 164–80.

Maple T., McManamon R., Stevens E. 1995. Defining the good zoo: animal care, maintenance, and welfare. In: Norton B.G., Hutchins M., Stevens E.F., Maple T.L. (eds). *Ethics on the Ark: Zoos, Animal Welfare, and Wildlife Conservation*. Washington, DC: Smithsonian Institution Press. pp. 219–34.

McManamon R. 1993. The humane care of captive wild animals. In: Fowler M.E. (ed.). *Zoo and Wild Animal Medicine: Current Therapy*. Philadelphia: Saunders, pp. 61–3.

Morrison A.R. 1994. Animal rights and animal politics. *Science* 263:1073–4.

Norton B.G. 1995. A broader look at animal stewardship. In: Norton B.G., Hutchins M., Stevens E.F., Maple T.L. (eds). *Ethics on the Ark: Zoos, Animal Welfare, and Wildlife Conservation*, Washington, DC: Smithsonian Institution Press. pp. 102–21.

Norton B.G., Hutchins M., Stevens E.F., Maple T.L. (eds). 1995. *Ethics on the Ark: Zoos, Animal Welfare, and Wildlife Conservation*, Washington, DC: Smithsonian Institution Press. 330 p.

Noske B. 1993. Great apes as anthropological subjects—deconstructing anthropocentrism. In: Cavalieri P., Singer P. (eds). *The Great Ape Project*. New York: St Martin's Press, pp. 258–68.

Noske B. 1998. Animals as subjects-of-a-group-life. In: Beckoff M. (ed.). *Encyclopedia of Animal Rights and Animal Welfare*. Westport, CT: Greenwood Press, pp. 69–70.

Regan T. 1983. *The Case for Animal Rights*. Berkeley, CA: The University of California Press. 425 p.

Regan T. 1995 Are zoos morally defensible? In: Norton B.G., Hutchins M., Stevens E.F., Maple T.L. (eds). *Ethics on the Ark: Zoos, Animal Welfare, and Wildlife Conservation*. Washington, DC: Smithsonian Institution Press. pp. 38–51.

Rowan A.N. 1992. Opening statement, panel discussion on "Wildlife conservation and animal rights: are they compatible?" In: *Proceedings of the American Association of Zoological Parks and Aquariums Annual Meeting*, Toronto, Canada. Wheeling, W.V.: American Association of Zoological Parks and Aquariums. pp. 12–15.

Shepherdson D.J., Mellen J.D., Hutchins M. (eds). 1998. *Second Nature: Environmental Enrichment for Captive Animals*. Washington, DC: Smithsonian Institution Press. 350 p.

Singer P. 1975. *Animal Liberation*. New York: Avon Books. 320 p.

Singer P., Regan T. (eds). 1976. *Animal Rights and Human Obligations*. Englewood Clifts, NJ: Prentice-Hall. 250 p.

Soulé M.E., Gilpin M., Conway W., Foose T. 1986. The millennium ark: how long a voyage, how many staterooms, how many passengers? *Zoo Biol.* 5:101–13.

Toone W.D., Wallace M.P. 1994. The extinction in the wild and reintroduction of the California condor (*Gymnogyps californianus*). In: Olney P.J.S., Mace G.M., Feistner A.T.C. (eds). *Creative Conservation: Interactive Management of Wild and Captive Animals*. London: Chapman and Hall. pp. 411–9.

Varner G.E. 1994. The prospects for consensus and convergence in the animal rights debate. *Hastings Center Rep.* 24;1:24–8.

Varner G.E., Monroe M.C. 1991. Ethical perspectives on captive breeding: is it for the birds? *Endangered Species Update* 8:27–9.

Zak S. 1989. Ethics and animals. *Atlantic Monthly* March: 69–74.

68

Chris Wemmer

"Opportunities Lost: Zoos and the Marsupial that Tried to be a Wolf"

Wemmer assesses the responsibilities and directions of zoos and aquariums following identi-fication of the global diversity crisis. He contrasts the conflicting pressures between providing recreational opportunities for the public, providing education to the visiting public, and provid-ing a greater service to society through science and conservation activities; he advocates greater emphasis on using zoos to support science and conservation efforts.

In the archives of the National Zoo there is a story of an opportunity lost. As zoo stories go, it is not unique. There are many others like it. Such stories sometimes tell us about ourselves.

It started sometime in early 1902. Zoo director William Hornaday wanted to exhibit a thylacine: *Thylacinus cynocephalus*—the pouched beast with a dog's head. Depicted by Patterson as "a species perfectly distinct from any of the animal creation hitherto known . . ." (Quammen, 1997:281), the thylacine had been described almost 100 years earlier. Though sometimes called the Tasmanian tiger because of its striped coat, this strange mar-supial was actually a "wannabe" wolf. The long-muzzled head with its short ears, the deep chest, and the feet and legs were distinctly dog-like, but the rear end and long tail hinted of marsupial ancestry. True dogs can wag their tails. This one could not. All the same, the thylacine remains a remarkable example of convergent evolution, and the largest carnivorous marsupial to survive into the twentieth century.

[. . .]

In due course, a Tasmanian trapper caught a female, which was shipped to the states. [. . .]

Over a period of about 90 years some 13 zoos on three continents exhibited about 55 thylacines (Guiler, 1986) (Jones, personal communication). Farmers killed nearly 2,200 for bounties during a 21-year period starting in 1888. The last recorded shooting of a thylacine was in 1930. Six years later the last captive animal died in the Hobart Zoo (Beresford and Bailey, 1981). Even in recent times footprints allegedly have been sighted, but irrefutable evidence of the thylacine's survival is lacking. In reality, the thylacine seems to be gone forever (Quammen, 1997).

What did we learn from the thylacines that lived in zoos? Almost nothing. Guiler (1986:66) commented that "[t]here was an extraordinary apathy shown by the various zoos for the fate of the thylacine." String their lives together and you have more than 100 thyla-cine years in captivity—ample opportunity for some keen observer to note a few details. [. . .] But the zoo legacy to knowledge and conservation of this species is scant. It is recorded in some amateur movie footage, and a few photographs. The rest is stored in a few museum cabinets.

I feel a nostalgic longing when I think of thylacines. But I feel the same way when I visit a zoo and look at any mysterious creature or endangered species. Will they too become opportunities lost to the institutions that celebrate their uniqueness? How many species we now exhibit will share the planet with us in 25 years, when our numbers reach 10 billion? I don't believe zoos are apathetic about the fate of their charges, but I am concerned about their ability to have a lasting and meaningful impact in a rapidly changing world. The biodiversity crisis is on our lips, but our actions send another message. We know zoos can't change the world, but many of us believe we can have a far greater impact than we do at present.

Zoological institutions have clearly acted upon the calls of their visionary leaders to heed the global biodiversity crisis. In the 1980s, the conservation movement added a challenging new dimension to our profession. We saw a remarkable convergence of purpose among the rank and file of our association. Directors, curators, and keepers from different zoos found themselves working together on American Zoo and Aquarium Association (AZA) Species Survival Plan (SSP) committees. Talented keepers and curators discovered latent skills. For many curators, humdrum jobs suddenly became more interesting. New friendships emerged based on a shared vision. The movement grew into a groundswell. The AZA's conservation movement, embodied in the SSP, Taxon Advisory Groups, Scientific Advisory Groups, and Conservation Action Partnerships are extraordinary examples of planning and cooperation among institutions (Hutchins and Conway, 1995). The IUCN/Species Survival Commission's Conservation Breeding Specialist Group was born as a parallel movement in the international realm.

But not everyone was ready to ride the new wave. More midlevel zoo personnel were committed to the movement than directors, and some of the latter believed that "the tail was wagging the dog." When the AZA examined its mandate in the late 1980s, the board of directors consulted with institutional directors, and determined that the association's highest purpose was to provide members with services. While these services were seen clearly by the directors as serving the conservation mandate, the decision was disappointing for those who had been lifted by the surge of the new wave. Many midlevel members of the AZA had hoped for a declaration of commitment to a higher cause. They acknowledged that the AZA had made great advances in developing a conservation ethic, but their perception was that the organization's leaders were unable to agree that, as a unifying principle, conservation transcended the need for services.

[. . .]

Until we adopt a unifying philosophy for zoos and aquariums, our collective potential will not be achieved. We have all said it: "The public goes to the zoo to have a good time. Sure we 'do education,' but the hook is recreation." It's that familiar notion of service. We serve the public what it wants (entertainment) and at the same time we give it what it needs (education). But the word "entertainment" somehow doesn't do justice as a reason for keeping wild animals in captivity. Think about it. Isn't education the highest service zoos and aquariums can offer the visiting public? Surely, as a means of achieving conservation, it deserves to be our highest institutional mandate.

But there is another defect in what many perceive to be mainstream thinking about zoos and aquariums, and that is the notion that our visitors represent the ultimate target audience. Looking back, we can honestly say that the 18 zoos that exhibited thylacines certainly served their visitors, but did they serve society as a whole? They might have, had they been able to work together to prevent the thylacine's extinction. Serving society is a lot different from entertaining the public. Here is where science, captive breeding, reintroduction, education, and in situ conservation play a role. Unfortunately, the public doesn't always understand the benefits to society from zoos and aquariums. That's our responsibility, and that is what zoo and aquarium education should be all about.

Zoos and aquariums of the past didn't have the resources to study and conserve every species in their collections. The biodiversity crisis didn't loom darkly on the horizon. Nevertheless, people like Hornaday knew what was happening in the world, and took decisive action to save the American bison from extinction (Rorabacher, 1970). A lot has happened since then. Time is of the essence, and if we don't act soon, the world will lose much of its biota, including many of the most charismatic and engaging life forms we exhibit. Conway (2000) recently cited a prevailing excuse for inaction voiced by some of our colleagues: "Zoos and aquariums were not designed to be conservation organizations." Zoological institutions have unique and rich resources, staff with diverse skills and talents, and prominence in society. But do the leaders of our profession have the foresight and will to retrofit their organizations for a higher cause, and to make conservation and science their primary reasons for being? Let us think deeply about it, and resolve not to witness another opportunity lost.

References

Beresford Q., Bailey G. 1981. *Search for the Tasmanian Tiger*. Hobart: Blubber Head Press. 81 p.

Conway W.G. 2000. *The Changing Role of Zoos in the 21st Century*. AZA Communique, January: 11–12.

Guiler E.R. 1986. *Thylacine: the Tragedy of the Tasmanian Tiger*. Melbourne, Australia: Oxford University Press. 207 p.

Hutchins M., Conway W.G. 1995. Beyond Noah's ark: the evolving role of modern zoological parks and aquariums in field conservation. *Int. Zoo Year b*. 34:117–130.

IUDZG/CBSG (IUCN/SSC). 1993. *The World Zoo Conservation Strategy. The Role of the Zoos and Aquaria of the World in Global Conservation*. Brookfield, IL: Chicago Zoological Society. 75 p.

Quammen D. 1997. *The Song of the Dodo. Island Biogeography in an Age of Extinctions*. New York: Simon and Schuster. 702 p.

Rorabacher J.A. 1970. *The American Buffalo in Transition: an Historical and Economic Survey of the Bison in America*. St Cloud, MN: North Star Press. 142 p.

Rodeos and Other Entertainment

69

Rod Preece and Lorna Chamberlain

"Animals in Entertainment: Racing, Riding, and Fighting"

Preece and Chamberlain take a broad look at past human use and abuse of animals in a variety of entertainment activities, including cock-fighting, dog-fighting, bull-fighting, horse racing, and rodeos. They note abuses occurring in all of these activities and discuss some improvements that have been implemented as well as a number of changes they believe still should be instituted. They propose that more cruel sports tend to be associated with males in societies experiencing more oppressive economies, monolithic and rigid cultures, and reduced levels of liberal education.

[. . .] Throughout history animals have been frequently employed as a means to make that leisure time 'enjoyable'—from the circuses of the Roman Empire through bull- and bear-baiting, cock, dog, and bull-fighting, dog- and horse-racing, to rodeos, the modern circus, zoos and aquaria. Animals provide entertainment in films, television and on the stage.

No one could doubt that much of the 'entertainment' has been destructive—both of the animals and of all semblance of human decency. Yet the fact that animals in entertainment have frequently been demeaned, treated without consideration, and far worse, should not blind us to the fact that it is possible in principle for animals and human entertainment to be compatible. We do not hold to the view that animals should of necessity be left undisturbed by humans in their primordial natural habitat. In that case we would have to oppose the keeping of pets, which we believe can be of the greatest benefit to both human and animal. Certainly, other things being equal, the animal should be left to its primordial nature and its habitat, but we should not rule out a priori the possibility of a satisfactory human–animal relationship in the entertainment of humans.

Our experience, supported by an abundance of social science research, suggests that the more admirable of human characteristics are engendered and enhanced by contact with, and enjoyment of, the animal realm. If compassion, caring and a sense of veneration among humans toward animals and nature in general are encouraged by the entertainment then that entertainment has the most positive of values. It should itself be encouraged.

However, human entertainment, even if uplifting and worthwhile entertainment, is only valuable if it is neither cruel to the animals, nor disturbing to their dignity. Humans have a right to enjoy animals in entertainment only when there is a compensatory benefit to the animals—only when there is sufficient evidence that the animals derive a measure of satisfaction and enjoyment from the enterprise too.

If we lose animals from mutually advantageous entertainment we would also lose some of that potential for awe and reverence which contact with the animal realm gives us. Our sense of the community of sentient beings would diminish. We would lose an important element of that awareness which makes us better and more responsible human beings—a sense of ourselves as sharers of this planet with duties toward its constituents which go beyond our obligations to our fellow humans. Indeed, the entertainment must involve an earnest respect for the nature and dignity of the species employed, not merely for their sakes, but because to fail to do so would deprive us of the legitimate sense of well-being and sentience awareness. We would once again be exploiters. The question, of course, is whether there are entertainment activities which either do, or can, consider the interests of the animals as well as humans.

The antithesis to the question is easier to answer. There are undoubtedly many forms of 'entertainment' which are both utterly destructive of animal interests and are equally arousing of the most injurious and least healthy appetites among the human participants and spectators. We find it difficult to conceive of any explanation which would serve to begin to justify cock-fighting, dog-fighting, bull-fighting, or any analogous activities.

Yet in various parts of the world these 'sports' enjoy great popularity.

[. . .]

Cock-fighting remains a popular pastime in South America, Mexico, Puerto Rico and some of the Caribbean islands as well as the Orient. [. . .] The fighting cocks are routinely equipped with steel claws to maximize the injuries and contests are customarily conducted to a deathly conclusion, although local custom may dictate the refusal or inability to fight further as an acceptable finish.

[. . .]

Like cock-fighting, dog-fighting is frowned upon by all with even a vestige of sensitivity. [. . .] Certainly, a number of breeds have been wilfully developed for the sole purpose of fighting.

[. . .]

The reality is that organized dog-fighting and vicious dog attacks cannot be eliminated by the destruction of a breed or even of several breeds. Most dogs can become cruel and vicious either by being mistreated themselves or by being trained to be cruel. Certainly the power, arousability, and tenacity of some breeds make them potentially more dangerous, but all breeds can be further bred to reduce the likelihood of negative characteristics, and all breeds are potentially loyal, friendly and considerate. The potential viciousness must be instilled and brought out by their human owners, either intentionally or in ignorance.

Dog-fighting and viciousness against humans can only be effectively controlled at the level of the owners and the individual dogs. As long as certain breeds possess a ferocious image and as long as owners choose to project their own undesirable attributes through their dogs the problem will remain.

[. . .]

Bull-fighting was introduced to Spain by the Moors somewhere around the eighth century. From Spain it spread to Morocco, Southern France and Portugal. The Spaniards introduced the combat to South America where it remains popular in Mexico, Peru, Colombia,

Venezuela and Ecuador. *Banderilleros* or *peones* help picadors and matadors to kill the bulls. Around 4,500 a year are killed in the arena in Spain at the present time. An average of almost three bull-fights a day are held. These are the figures provided by Desmond Morris. "Each year more than 17,000 bulls are tortured to death in Spanish bull rings," is the claim of the World Society for the Protection of Animals—which adds, "Drugged, blinded, and repeatedly stabbed, the bulls suffer unimaginable pain in the name of entertainment." Again we encounter conflicting statistics. But even if we accept the more modest ones, the terror remains appalling.

The bulls are goaded, pierced by short lances, and finally killed by a swordthrust to the neck. In Spain today the height of ambition for a youth is still to be a matador. Indeed, the state provides free education and training for budding matadors who have shown significant promise. In Portuguese-style bull-fighting the animal is not put to death in the arena.

It could scarcely escape notice that the most obviously cruel "entertainments" are more pervasive in South America, Asia, and Southern Europe than in North America and Northern Europe. And that fact requires an explanation. Four factors apparently affect sensibility toward animals: economics, culture, socialization and rationalization. With regard to the exploitation of animals in "entertainment" economic conditions influence the amount of leisure time available and the disposable income to be expended. The less disposable income there is, the greater the likelihood of expenditures being devoted to the least expensive of "sporting" activities such as cock-fighting. However, it is the oppressiveness of the economy (or the society in general) which encourages those who are oppressed by the more powerful in turn to be oppressive of the less powerful. Those whose well-being is disregarded by economic iniquities are in turn likely to disregard the well-being of less powerful sentient beings. Oppression breeds resentment, which is in turn oppressive. However, economic oppression alone is an inadequate explanation, since women, who have been more oppressed than men, have customarily had a higher sensitivity toward animals.

[. . .]

Cultures in which the mastery of nature is considered laudatory will usually have an inherent disregard for the nature they master. Paradoxically, though, as mastery is achieved, they produce an embarrassment of riches which, having satisfied most needs and many wants, permits recognition of the rights of the oppressed—including oppressed animals—since the oppression is no longer as necessary to the satisfaction of needs. Moreover, the mastery of nature with the consequent satisfaction of needs—or perceived needs—permits far greater time for many to enjoy a liberal education in which moral sensibilities are heightened. It may also provide more time to engage in exploitative ventures. Thus within any one culture over time the attitudes to animals will vary considerably. The length of time they have prevailed will affect the difficulty or ease of changing them.

The culture of a society—which is in some significant respects a reflection of the economy—will promote a certain set of attitudes toward animals at any given time and will thus create the context, the boundaries, within which legitimate beliefs will operate. And since most of us most of the time want to belong, want to feel an integrated part of our society, we are constrained to maintain the beliefs accepted by our compatriots. Those beliefs will reflect a number of factors: the belief system conducive to the maintenance of existing economic and political relationships, the religious foundations of the society and the prevailing educational and moral myths. One's sense of acceptance, status and well-being within a society is affected by the degree to which one conforms. However, it is possible to achieve one's identity and status by belonging to a group whose norms do not correspond to the dominant values but which itself fulfils the function of integration for its adherents. While difficult, it is possible to step outside the dominant norms provided society is not monolithic but contains competing groups expressing different values. When acceptance of the diversity of legitimate values is itself a value of the society the psychological pressures to conform are somewhat diminished—or rather the pressures to conform to the predominant societal values are replaced by the pressures to conform to the values of one's parochial group.

When we are being socialized to a set of values by our parents or early school educators we are acquiring the context of our actions and beliefs. Parents and educators possess the esteem and authority to have us gladly accept the wisdom of the values they impart. If one's father enjoys "sport" fishing—or cock-fighting—or if one's teacher preaches the virtues of hunting—or the glory of bull-fighting—it would be most unusual to do any other than accept the imparted values. Of course, if there are effective competing agencies of socialization—as there frequently are in pluralistic societies—then the monolith is breached. If parents impart one value, teachers a second and the media a third then our own sensibilities develop independently.

Once one has come to engage in a particular activity, be it cock-fighting, hunting, fishing or whatever, then one is less likely to be convinced by argument or evidence which may otherwise be compelling. We rationalize by giving greater emphasis to evidence and argument supportive of our amusements. Sensibilities are thus acquired far more readily when one has nothing, or little, at stake.

Generally, then, we may expect that the more oppressive an economy, the more monolithic and rigid a culture and the lower the level of liberal education, the greater will be the tendency to cruel and invasive entertainment. Moreover, it is likely to be the most oppressed—at least of the males—and those with the least liberal education who will participate in these entertainments. As these conditions are changed so all societies and all individuals are more likely to respond to the empathetic sensibilities which lurk just beneath the surface of the human mind.

[. . .]

The racehorse gallops at speeds of up to 40 miles per hour. The heartbeat of a horse at full gallop can increase from 25 beats a minute to 250 beats a minute, an astounding tenfold increase. The human heart beats at around 72 times a minute and in a professional sprint rises to perhaps somewhat in excess of 200 beats, a mere three, occasionally four, times the norm. While human athletes adjust their training and restrict frequency of competitions so as to maximize the explosiveness of their performance on the most important occasions the restrictions for racehorses are far more severe. An over-raced horse risks an enlarged heart, serious health problems and an early demise. They are thus restricted for most of their day to a narrow stall, isolated from any relationship with other horses and are prohibited free exercise. To be sure, they are exercised, but it is a rigorously controlled exercise, designed not for the general well-being of the animals but solely to maximize their racing performance.

[. . .]

Why, for example, was the use of the whip not outlawed long ago? It is one thing to pat the rump smartly to give a direction, another to whip the horse painfully as it approaches the final furlong. Of course, the racers tell us that the whip is merely to encourage and does not hurt the horse. Yet one need only see the reaction of a horse to a whip cracked strenuously on the hide to know the pain that is felt. Surely abolishing the whip would be no detriment to the sport.

[. . .]

Even more disturbing is the condition of the horses once their racing days are over, unless they are able to command respectable stud fees. Customarily racehorses whose money-earning days are at an end are euthanized. The sole reward for perfectly healthy animals which have provided enjoyment for many thousands of spectators and no mean income for their owners, trainers and jockeys is an early grave. [. . .] This is not an unfortunately rare and random occurrence, but the decided policy of many owners which affects the majority of racehorses. What can one think of racing organizations [. . .] which do not require as a condition of membership and participation that healthy retired animals be put out to pasture as *minimal* common decency requires?

[. . .]

There is an unwritten rule among many Canadian Humane Societies that while rodeos may be generally criticized for the abominations that they are one should show some discretion in opposition in the west. They have become such an indigenous part of the culture, expressing the Albertan red neck self-image, that some Humane Societies consider only their grossest excesses subject to denunciation (although the Calgary Humane Society itself has shown great fortitude in its explicit opposition to the famous Stampede). Many Humane Society organizers think that to suggest that rodeos are destructive of the finer nature of both human and animal would be to risk losing sorely needed funds and general public support from Western sympathizers. 'Tradition' and 'cultural heritage' are concepts used not merely to justify aboriginal trapping practices but also to glorify the worst of the aura of the Wild West, although in fact very little which takes place in a rodeo bears more than a merely superficial resemblance to anything which ever happened in 'wild West' history.

[. . .]

'Rodeo' is derived from the Spanish noun meaning 'a going around', hence its use for a cattle-ring. The rodeo has its origins with the *vaqueros*, the sixteenth-century Mexicans who wore leggings and used ropes to herd their Spanish conquerors' cattle, a practice documented as far north as Santa Fe when it was a Spanish possession. [. . .] From an occasion for stocktaking the event turned into a celebratory event in which the participants demonstrated their prowess.

[. . .]

Unlike horse-racing and akin to bull-fighting the rodeo does not depend on any significant co-operation between man and beast but on brutal domination.

[. . .]

There are approximately 65 professional rodeos held annually in Western Canada involving the 700 cowboys who are members of the Canadian Professional Rodeo Association (C.P.R.A.), together with the American professionals who also take part in the events. Most of them are part-timers who make a slim living from their public appearances.

[. . .]

Not surprisingly, animal welfare advocates have been trying to outlaw rodeos for decades. They have provided us with lurid descriptions of the horrors perpetrated during these events. Rodeo organizers tell us that such reports are the wild-eyed imaginations of naïve animal lovers who have more concern with animals than humans and who lack both the knowledge and experience to make rational judgments about rodeos.

[. . .]

In 1990 a major rodeo was planned for Ontario, to be held at Toronto's Sky Dome. The Toronto City Council was inundated with many letters from individuals and several substantial briefs from animal welfare organizations demanding that the event not be allowed. Council was also briefed by the rodeo sponsors and organizers. The Neighbourhoods Committee of Council requested the city's Medical Officer of Health to "report back on rodeo practices, and whether such practices could be deemed cruel to animals."

[. . .]

In discussing the animals participation in the events and whether they involved pleasure, he noted that "In most rodeo events this is clearly not the case, since devices such as electric prods, sharpened sticks, spurs, flank straps and other rodeo tack must be used in order to induce the animals to react in a way that will make certain events 'exciting' for the spectators."

The Medical Officer recognized recent guidelines that have been instituted which are intended to prevent animal abuse but concluded that "even in some of the sanctioned rodeos these guidelines are at times deliberately and conveniently ignored." In discussing the broken legs incurred in calf-roping events, he added, "Unseen damage that is not obvious, i.e., injuries to the neck muscles, internal bruising, or haemorrhaging, or bruising of cartilage in the larynx and trachea, are not necessarily evident during the competition."

He describes the use of spurs "to stimulate a bucking behaviour" and of two cinches, the second of which is a belt "tightened around the flank and sensitive parts of the horse." His conclusion is that, "The flank strap tightly cinched provides pressure on the lumbar nerves, which are particularly sensitive, and to the groin. Frequently a shock or two from a 'hot shot' or cattle prod, together with the irritation from the flank strap, has the horse flying out of the chute." So much for the official rodeo claim that "Nobody knows what makes horses buck . . . they buck for the love of it." They buck in fact in an attempt to avoid the pain. All bucking events, according to Dr. Kendall, "use irritants of one form or another to make the animal buck."

[. . .]

In his summary, Dr. Kendall states that in terms of a dictionary definition of cruelty "one must conclude that most rodeo events have that potential [to cause injury, grief, or pain], therefore can be considered 'cruel'." He notes the option that "legal recourse exists under the Criminal Code which provides an opportunity to prosecute in the event that the legal definition of cruelty is met." Kendall does not say that such a definition is met, although he clearly implies that the limits are reached if not crossed.

[. . .]

70

Bernard E. Rollin

"Rodeo and Recollection: Applied Ethics and Western Philosophy"

Rollin assesses rodeos as a form of animal use and human entertainment. He notes that rodeos embody a broad range of Western U.S. values, including the capacity to manage animals, survival and success in a harsh environment, skills and traits essential to survival, and pride in a unique form of American culture. He also observes that cowboys and ranchers have a strong ethic of animal husbandry and generally have been receptive to instituting changes in rodeo practices to incorporate concern for animal well-being.

Like many other sports, rodeo can be understood on a variety of different levels. Although professional rodeos (those sanctioned by the Professional Rodeo Cowboy Association) recognize only a limited set of events as part of the sport—bull riding, steer wrestling, saddle bronc riding, bareback bronc riding, calf roping, team roping, and barrel racing—numerous other events are often included. These events are too diverse to list exhaustively but may include goat roping and barrel racing (women's events); wild horse races; wild cow races; chuck wagon races; cowboy bull fighting (in which the animal is not hurt); calf riding for small children; steer riding (less dangerous than bull riding); steer tripping (illegal in most states); rawhide racing; pick-up or rescue races; milk races (where nursing foals are separated from mares, and race back to mama); cow, buffalo, or horse turd throws: greased pig contests; cutting horse exhibitions; competitions involving dressing a wild cow in a negligee. Charro, or Mexican rodeos, which have recently garnered much publicity, featured horse tripping, an event now banned legislatively in most states.

The symbolic dimensions of rodeo are quite varied and many have been well-discussed by Elizabeth Lawrence, a veterinarian and anthropologist, in her *Rodeo: An Anthropologist Looks at the Wild and the Tame* (1). In my own experience, rodeos express a broad range of Western values relevant to our discussion:

1. *Management of Animals*: Historically, rodeo evolved from ranch practices that were commonly employed as a normal part of raising cattle under range conditions. Obviously, calves and steers often needed to be roped, horses broken, and steers sometimes were wrestled to the ground or tripped by solitary cowboys in order to be doctored. In justification of rodeo against attacks from people outside of the culture, participants and defenders often invoke the relevance of these practices to the cattle business. I shall discuss this point more fully later.

2. *Survival and Success in a Harsh Environment.* Western cattle ranching is a hard life, lived in an unforgiving, non-"user friendly" environment. Ranchers may control 250,000 or more acres with little help. The nearest neighbors may be 80 miles away.

In the New Mexico desert, each cow-calf unit may require 1,000 acres on which to forage; in Colorado or Wyoming this average can drop to between 20 and 50. Under the best of conditions, the land is harsh, subject to climatic variational extremes of over 100 degrees, seriously deficient in water, and intolerant of human errors.

[. . .]

3. *Demonstration and Extolling of Skills and Traits That Made Survival Possible.* Such skills embody primordial masculine virtues—physical strength, courage, quickness, independence (few events involve teams), and self-sufficiency. With the exception of specific women's events, such as barrel racing, rodeo participation is overwhelmingly male.
4. *The Uniqueness of Western American Culture and the Pride Taken Therein by Western Americans.* It is no secret that the United States has traditionally been politically, socially, and economically dominated by the urban East. [. . .] Westerners—and not just ranchers—feel an element of being neglected, misunderstood, and caricatured stepchildren. A good deal of these feelings are justified.

[. . .]

With the recent massive immigration of Easterners, Californians, and Yuppies into ranch states such as Colorado, Montana, Wyoming, Nevada, New Mexico, and Utah, there is a fear among Westerners of losing their culture. [. . .] This is compounded by environmentalist attacks on ranching; attempts to raise public land grazing fees or even to remove ranching from public lands; attacks on beef by physicians, feminists, and the Beyond Beef Campaign; attempts at gun control in a culture where gun ownership and handling is traditionally second nature; gobbling up of ranch land by developers; and revisionist accounts of Western American history. Outside attacks on rodeo, often based on urban ignorance, as when cowboys are accused of using leather vises on horses' testicles to make them buck, represent an example directly relevant to the topic at hand.

The result is something of a siege mentality. [. . .] And the more they feel besieged, the more Westerners flaunt their uniqueness. Rodeo is probably the strongest symbol of this uniqueness, to no small extent because it is so *prima facie* shocking to the current non-Western, Eastern-urban sensibilities that tend to view nature as good, not adversarial; the pet as the paradigm for all animals; violent sports as abhorrent; and the cowboy as a highly ambivalent figure at best and as an ignorant, know-nothing, brutal red neck shit-kicker at worst.

It is worth pausing here to elaborate on the last point, as it is directly relevant to social ethical concerns about rodeo. There is no cultural icon that is as iridescent as that of the cowboy. On the one hand, the cowboy is John Wayne, Gary Cooper, Jimmy Stewart—a gentleman, a protector of widows and orphans, slow to anger, resistant to authority, a loner, and an irresistible force once aroused. On the other hand, the cowboy is equally the reckless gunfighter, the outlaw who shoots up a town and makes tenderfeet dance, the lyncher of hippies and the shooter of eagles. [. . .] With the advent of the 80s and 90s, it is the latter take on the cowboy that has tended to predominate, and, while the urban public may thrill at bull-riding and bronc-riding, it is the roping of "cute little calves" that leaves the most indelible and negative imprint and feeds the negative image of the cowboy.

It is not therefore surprising that rodeo is a very plausible target for animal advocates. In the 1970s, a group of over 200 animal welfare/animal rights organizations signed a well-publicized document affirming that rodeo was absolutely unacceptable morally because of the pain and fear engendered in animals. Further, the groups claimed that rodeo could not be fixed or improved, it must be abolished. I was puzzled by this document, for it appeared to me that rodeo was amenable to very plausible modifications that would significantly improve the treatment of rodeo animals. To allay my curiosity, I phoned the vice president of one of the signatory groups, a very powerful organization, and queried him as to the claim that rodeo could not be improved. "Oh that," he said. "That's just fund-raising hype. Of course rodeo can be fixed. But why would we care about fixing it? Rodeo is an insignificant sport, practiced by an insignificant number of people in a few politically insignificant places. If we take a tough line on rodeo, we bring in a lot of contributions, and don't make any powerful enemies!"

This, then, is a sketch of the situation I walked into in the 1970s when I first confronted the ethical issues in rodeo as a spin-off from my work in veterinary ethics. My involvement with rodeo issues deepened considerably as I became increasingly occupied with ethical issues in animal agriculture, and particularly with Western ranching. This involvement in turn intensified as I was asked to lecture on the ethics of rodeo to rodeo cowboys, fair and rodeo managers, and others in the rodeo community. In what follows, I hope to show that the issues are far more complex and morally ambiguous than most people realize, and provide some indication of how what is today called "applied ethics" can play a constructive role in social ethics. [. . .] I have lectured to somewhere between 5 and 10,000 Western ranchers and rodeo people. [. . .] I have worked closely with the Colorado Cattlemen's Association on successfully eliminating mandated USDA face-branding of Mexican Cattle the first time an agricultural group has taken a pure animal welfare stand against practices allegedly implemented for their benefit. [. . .]

In the first place, cowboys and ranchers, as a group are the most fair-minded people I have ever dealt with. In my speeches and writings. I have often said that, of the almost 700 groups around the world to whom I have lectured on animal ethics and other bioethical issues, the best audience is one made up of Western ranchers. [. . .] The ranchers will hear what you say.

Second, and the importance of this point cannot be overestimated, ranchers and cow-boys are in fact the last bastion of the ethic of animal husbandry, which pervaded animal agriculture for all of human history until the advent of revolutionary changes in agriculture that took place in the mid-twentieth century. For all of human history, agriculture has represented the overwhelmingly predominant use of animals in society. The essence of trad-itional agriculture was husbandry, which meant first-rate care. (*Hus/band*, etymologically, is "bonded to the house.") Husbandry meant putting the animals one was raising into the most optimal environment possible, the environment in which the animal was best suited to thrive by natural and artificial selection, and augmenting those natural powers with the provision of food during famine, water during drought, protection from predation, medical care, etc.

[. . .]

Husbandry agriculture [. . .] was a win/win situation for both animal producer and animal. This is what Temple Grandin has called the "ancient contract" in which animals were better off in quality of life than they would have been on their own, and humans in turn harvested the animals' products or lives. Any harm done to the animals would as much harm the producer. This is why a minimalistic anticruelty ethic sufficed for thousands of years as the social consensus ethic for animals. Only a sadist or psychopath would hurt an animal intentionally for no good reason. To be sure, this ideal was clouded by relatively short-term insults such as branding, castration, and occasional rough handling, but wise husbandry people knew that "gentling was best." (Gentle handling has been demonstrated to correlate significantly with both milk production in dairy cattle and reproductive success in swine.)

Western ranchers still adhere to the ethic of husbandry, while the rest of agriculture has changed dramatically in the mid-twentieth century. The use of high technology-intensive agriculture (what the vernacular refers to as "factory farming") has broken the fair contract and turned agriculture into a patently exploitative activity, wherein the values of efficiency and productivity have replaced the values of husbandry. We are no longer constrained in our agricultural practices by the animals' biological natures. [. . .] Whereas no nineteenth century agriculturalist would have dreamed of crowding thousands of chickens in one building in cages, if only because they would all have died in a month of disease, we now have antibiotics and vaccines that allow us to effect such crowding, yet make a profit. Technology has, in effect, divorced animal productivity from animal happiness.

However, Western ranchers haven't changed their methods of raising animals. They still practice husbandry agriculture that respects the animals' natures. I have only to start the sentence "We take care of the animals . . ." and my rancher audiences chorus ". . . and they take care of us." My cowboy students invariably tell me the only time they ever "got whipped" by their dad was when they went off to a dance or ball game without taking care of the animals first. No one is likelier to report—and testify against—cruelty and neglect of animals than ranchers.

[. . .]

This, then, is the ethic that I can get ranchers to recollect. I go on to explain to them that, contrary to the propaganda they often receive from industry sources, the notion of animals having rights that need to be codified in law now that those rights are no longer guaranteed by a husbandry-based agriculture is a widespread social concern, and a conservative rather than a radical view. In fact. I point out, it is high technology agriculture and the attendant ability to respond to only those aspects of an animal's nature that are relevant to productivity, rather than all of the animal's needs constitutive of its nature, that is radical relative to the history of agriculture. Once I have explained this, over 90 per cent of the ranchers and rodeo people I address affirm that of course animals should have rights that are protected.

Since the overwhelming majority of rodeo people come from ranch backgrounds and have thus grown up with the previously described ethic, it is not all that difficult to get them to recollect that ethic, and apply it to rodeo, something they have typically failed to do on their own by compartmentalizing the two domains. Similarly, when I discuss this with ranchers, they often point out that they are reluctant to hire rodeo competitors, whom they see as athletes rather than husbandrymen. As one rancher said to me, "If I need to rope a calf, it is usually because the animal is sick or injured. If that is the case, the last thing I need is some rodeo jock running the animal hell for leather." Indeed I have heard cattlemen seriously discuss the need for distancing beef production from rodeo in the public mind.

[. . .]

It remains to ask where the animal welfare problems with rodeo really lie. And no one knows the answers to that question better than people who rodeo who have been stimulated to reflect on rodeo in terms of their own ethic for animals. The general consensus among such people I have dealt with is that the rough stock riding events—bull riding, saddle and bareback bronc riding—are not terribly problematic, provided that the animals are not hurt by spurring, and the bulls not agitated by electric shock "hot shotting." (This sometimes occurs before a bullride because the rider is judged by how difficult the bull is, and an angry bull is more difficult to ride.) Steer wrestling may cause some neck injury to steers, but that is probably rare and minimal. Calf roping is highly problematic, and that point is, as I suggested above, easily elicited from ranchers. In fact, even some people in the rodeo community have spoken against jerking calves to a stop and flipping them over. While the current PRCA rules mandate fines for jerking calves, that is largely ineffective. As one champion roper said to me: "The fine is $100, the purse is $5,000—you figure it out." A far better approach would be to disqualify any roper that jerked the calf. While it would slow roping times, it would affect everyone equally.

Steer tripping (or steer jerking or steer busting), which involves violently jerking a steer's legs out from under him, is, as mentioned earlier, illegal in all but a few states. In my experience, most rodeo cowboys and managers find it objectionable because of the very real chance of injury to the animals. [. . .] This event should be banned legally, ideally by legislation initiated by the rodeo community.

Many of the non-PRCA sanctioned events are morally problematic, both because they involve animals getting hurt or stressed (e.g., Chuckwagon races or wild horse races) and because they teach young people to take pleasure in an animal's fear (e.g., greased pig contests). Probably the best way to change these is through recollection.

The difference between urban ethical views of animals and the ethics of rodeo practitioners is usually seen by both sides as unbridgeable, and any attempt to bring them together is seen as impossible. The result is a "showdown mentality," with rodeo people unwilling to budge, and critics of rodeo demanding abolition. I hope I have shown that the tradition of husbandry and concern for animals built into Western ranching is in fact a significant potential bridge. But first, rodeo people must be willing to recollect their moral concern for animals, and critics of rodeo must be willing to acknowledge that moral concern, rather than dismissing rodeo people as a bunch of sadistic, redneck, uncaring moral troglodytes. Again, rodeo people must be willing to acknowledge the rational moral basis of social ethical concern for animals even among urban animal advocates, while urban critics must realize the strong symbolic and cultural dimensions of rodeo, and respect the role it plays in people's minds. Above all, moral dialogue should be seen as a creative challenge to achieving consensus through mutually respectful, rationally-based interaction.

[. . .]

Bibliography

1. Elizabeth Lawrence. *Rodeo: An Anthropologist Looks at the Wild and the Tame*. Knoxville: University of Tennessee Press, 1982.

Annotated Further Reading

Bostock, Stephen St C. (1993) *Zoos and Animal Rights: The Ethics of Keeping Animals*, London: Routledge. A comprehensive assessment focusing on English zoos. Bostock emphasizes the importance of zoos.

Cohn, J.P. (1992) "Decisions at the Zoo." *BioScience* 42(9): 654. Ethics, politics, and animal rights concerns affect the process of balancing conservation goals and the public interest.

Conway, W. (1995) "Wild and Zoo Animal Interactive Management and Habitat Conservation." *Biodiversity and Conservation* 4(6): 573–94.

Fiore, W.J. and Brunk, G.G. (1992) "Norms of Professional Behavior in Highly Specialized Organizations: the Case of American Zoos and Aquariums." *Administration and Society* 24(1): 81. Examination of professional ethics, organization, and responsibility of zoological managers to animals.

Hancocks, D. (2001) *A Different Nature: The Paradoxical World of Zoos and Their Uncertain Future*,

Berkeley: University of California Press. A sociological account of the history of zoos and an argument for new kinds of zoos.

Hardy, Donna Fitzroy (1999) "The role of domestic animals in the zoo." Online at: http://www.quantum-conservation.org/.

Hargrove, E. (1995) "The Role of Zoos in the Twenty-first Century." In *Ethics of the Ark: Zoos, Animal Welfare and Wildlife Conservation*, B.G. Norton, M. Hutchins, E.F. Stevens, and T.L. Maple (eds). Washington D.C., Smithsonian Institution Press.

Hosey, G.R. (2000) "Zoo Animals and Their Human Audiences: what is the Visitor Effect?" *Animal Welfare* 9: 343–57. The amount of control the animals have over their exposure to humans is a key element.

Hutchins, M. (2001). "Rattling the Cage: Toward Legal Rights for Animals (book review)." *Animal Behaviour* 61(4): 855–8.

Hutchins, M. (2001) "Animal Welfare: What is AZA Doing to Enhance the Lives of Captive Animals? *AZA Conference Proceedings* 1996: 77–86.

Hutchins, M. and Conway, W.G. (1995) "Beyond Noah's Ark: the Evolving Role of Modern Zoos and Aquariums in Field Conservation." *International Zoo Yearbook* 34: 84–7.

Hutchins, M. and Wemmer, C. (1987) "Wildlife Conservation and Animal Rights: are they Compatible? pp. 111–37 in *Advances in Animal Welfare Science 1986/87*, M.W. Fox and L. Mickley (eds). Washington, D.C.: Humane Society of the United States.

Hutchins, M., Smith, B., Fulk, R., Perkins, L., Reinartz, G., and Wharton, D. (2001) "Rights or Welfare: a Response to The Great Ape Project," pp. 329–66, in *Great Apes and Humans: Ethics of Coexistence*, B.B. Beck, T. Stoinski, M. Hutchins, T.L. Maple, B. Norton, A. Rowan, E.F. Stevens, and A. Arluke (eds). Washington, DC: Smithsonian Institution Press.

Hutchins, M., Wiese, R., and Willis, K. (1996). "Why We Need Captive Breeding." *AZA Annual Conference Proceedings* 1996: 77–86.

Jamieson, D. (1986). "Against Zoos," pp. 108–17 in *In Defense of Animals*, Peter Singer (ed.). New York: Basil Blackwell.

Jamieson, D. (1995) "Zoos Revisited." pp. 52–66 in *Ethics of the Ark: Zoos, Animal Welfare and Wildlife Conservation*. B.G. Norton, M. Hutchins, E.F. Stevens, and T. L. Maple (eds). Washington, D.C.: Smithsonian Institution Press.

Maple, T.L., McManamon, R., and Stevens, E.F. (1995) "Defining the Good Zoo: Animal Care, Maintenance, and Welfare." pp. 219–34 in *Ethics of the Ark: Zoos, Animal Welfare and Wildlife Conservation*. Washington, D.C.: Smithsonian Institution Press.

Masci, D. (2000) "Zoos in the twenty-first century." CQ Researcher, CQ on the Web: www.cq.com. 28 April 2000, pp. 355–64. Interviews to address important issues such as whether zoos help preserve endangered species in the wild or if keeping animals in zoos is morally defensible.

Midgley, M. (1999) "Should We Let Them Go?" Chapter 11, pp. 152–63 in *Attitudes to Animals: Views in Animal Welfare*, F.L. Dolins (ed.). Cambridge, U.K.: Cambridge University Press. A general discussion of keeping animals in captivity. Includes domestic animals and zoos.

Preece, R. and Chamberlain, L. (1993) "Animals in Entertainment: Zoos, Aquaria, and Circuses," Chapter 11 in *Animal Welfare and Human Values*. Waterloo, Canada: Wilfrid Laurier University Press, pp. 185–210.

Smith, B. and Hutchins, M. (2000). "The Value of Captive Breeding Programmes to Field Conservation: Elephants as an Example." *Pachyderm* 28: 101–9.

Stoinski, T.S., Ogden, J.J., Gold, K.C., and Maple, T.L. (2001) "Captive Apes and Zoo Education." Chapter 5 in *Great Apes and Humans: The Ethics of Coexistence*. B.B. Beck, T.S. Stoinski, M. Hutchins, T.L. Maple, B. Norton, A. Rowan, E.F. Stevens, and A. Arluke (eds), pp. 113–32. Washington, D.C.: Smithsonian Institution Press. Examines the ability of zoos to cause change in public attitudes, and assess needed improvements and future directions of zoos.

Weichert, J. and Norton, B. (1995) "Differing Conceptions of Animal Welfare," pp. 235–50 in *Ethics of the Ark: Zoos, Animal Welfare and Wildlife Conservation*. B.G. Norton, M. Hutchins, E.F. Stevens, and T.L. Maple (eds). Washington D.C.: Smithsonian Institution Press.

Study Questions

1 In light of Eaton's descriptions, what would be your response to a proposal to prohibit any future retention of marine mammals in captivity? Give your reasoning.

2   Regan and Hutchins *et al.* disagree on whether zoos are compatible with ecocentrism and an animal welfare ethic. Which perspective do you find most persuasive? Explain your reasoning.

3   Lindburg and Hutchins *et al.* argue that the rights of individual animals should be secondary to the care for populations and species, in contrast to Regan's view. What is your perspective? Give your reasoning.

4   Wemmer believes that zoo professionals, in contrast to continuing focusing a major emphasis on public recreation and education, should place greater emphasis on supporting science and conservation efforts. What is your position?

5   In comparing the perceptions of Rollin to those of Preece and Chamberlain regarding the propriety of rodeos, to what degree do they appear compatible and to what degree are they opposed? Justify your position.

Part IX

Animal Companions

Introduction

What moral responsibilities do we have to our animal companions? In the essay "Affections' Claim" Konrad Lorenz relates some wonderful stories of friendships between dogs and human beings, and asserts that a dog's fidelity imposes a responsibility upon us which is as morally important as our responsibilities to a human friend. Bernard Rollin and Michael Rollin address our responsibilities to our animal companions in a comprehensive way, arguing that we have obligations to all domestic animals because we have built a world in which they have no room to live on their own.

Paul Shepard describes the sequence leading from the sacredness of wild animal life in early human societies to our current situation, in which wild animals are confined in zoos and seen as equivalent to pets and stuffed toys. Pets were created by selective breeding and cannot restore us to wholeness with the natural world. They are "deficient animals," "monsters," "biological slaves." Wild animals, on the other hand, are the last remaining riches of the planet.

Sometimes the bond with a wild animal can approach that experienced with our domesticated animal companions. Anna Merz relates her remarkable experience of raising the wild rhino Samia in a rhino sanctuary in Africa. Merz and Samia experienced a bond of deep love, trust, and friendship over ten years, illustrating that beings of two wholly different species can reach out to each other for understanding.

Freya Mathews asserts that the company of both wild and domesticated nonhuman animals is a necessary part of human life, important for us and for our relationship with the environment. She defends domestication of animals and suggests that we need to find new ways to increase urban habitat for wildlife. Mathews describes her experience of how human psychological intimacy with the "unknowable subjectivity" of other animals helps open us to the world "astir with presence" vastly exceeding just human experience.

In "Protecting Children and Animals from Abuse" James Garbarino argues that child welfare and animal welfare ought to be natural collaborators, even though there have sometimes been divisions between these two caring communities in the past. There are empirical connections between cruelty to animals and cruelty to children. Garbarino points out that the persistent problem is not having too much empathy but having too little.

The final two selections in this Part concern our responsibilities to animals used to assist disabled or ill human beings. James Serpell, Raymond Coppinger, and Aubrey Fine point out several important sources of stress or suffering experienced by assistance and therapy animals. Stephen Brown and Val Strong describe the selection and reward-based training of dogs to assist people with epilepsy by providing advance warning of impending seizures. They report that they have observed no adverse health consequences to these dogs.

71

Konrad Lorenz

"Affection's Claim"

Konrad Lorenz describes several memorable dogs and affirms that he has always taken very seriously the responsibility imposed by a dog's fidelity and love. He believes that all love rises from instinctive feeling and that we have obligations to our dogs which are "no less binding" than those to our human friends.

> Knowing me in my soul the very same—
> One who would die to spare you touch of ill!—
> Will you not grant to old affection's claim
> The hand of friendship down Life's sunless hill?
>
> THOMAS HARDY

I once possessed a fascinating little book of crazy tales called 'Snowshoe Al's Bedtime Stories'. It concealed behind a mask of ridiculous nonsense that penetrating and somewhat cruel satire which is one of the characteristic features of American humour, and which is not always easily intelligible to many Europeans. In one of these stories Snowshoe Al relates with romantic sentimentality the heroic deeds of his best friend. Incidents of incredible courage, exaggerated manliness and complete altruism are piled up in a comical parody of Western American romanticism culminating in the touching scenes where the hero saves his friend's life from wolves, grizzly bears, hunger, cold and all the manifold dangers which beset him. The story ends with the laconic statement, 'In so doing, his feet became so badly frozen that I unfortunately had to shoot him.'

If I ask a man who has just been boasting of the prowess and other wonderful properties of one of his dogs, I always ask him whether he has still got the animal. The answer, then, is all too often strongly reminiscent of Snowshoe Al's story, 'No, I had to get rid of him—I moved to another town—or into a smaller house—I got another job and it was awkward for me to keep a dog,' or some other similar excuse. It is to me amazing that many people who are otherwise morally sound feel no disgrace in admitting such an action. They do not realize that there is no difference between their behaviour and that of the satirized egoist in the story. The animal is deprived of rights, not only by the letter of the law, but also by many people's insensitivity.

The fidelity of a dog is a precious gift demanding no less binding moral responsibilities than the friendship of a human being. The bond with a true dog is as lasting as the ties of this earth can ever be, a fact which should be noted by anyone who decides to acquire a canine friend. It may of course happen that the love of a dog is thrust upon one involuntarily, a circumstance which occurred to me when I met the Hanoverian Schweisshund, 'Hirschmann', on a skiing tour. He was at the time about a year old and a typical masterless dog; for his owner the head forester only loved his old Deutscher Rauhaar (German Pointer) and had no time for the clumsy stripling which showed few signs of ever becoming a gun-dog. Hirschmann was soft and sensitive and a little shy of his master, a fact which did not speak highly for the training ability of the forester. On the other hand I did not think any the better of the dog for coming out with us as early as the second day of our stay. I took him for a sycophant, quite wrongly as it turned out, for he was following not us but me alone. When one morning I found him sleeping outside my bedroom door, I began to reconsider my first opinion and to suspect that a great canine love was germinating. I realized it too late: the oath of allegiance had been sworn nor would the dog recant on the day of my departure. I tried to catch him in order to shut him up and prevent him from following us, but he refused to come near me. Quivering with consternation and with his tail between his legs he stood at a safe distance saying with his eyes, 'I'll do anything at all for you—except leave you!' I capitulated. 'Forester, what's the price of your dog?' The forester, from whose point of view the dog's conduct was sheer desertion, replied without a moment's consideration, 'Ten shillings.' It sounded like an expletive and was meant as such. Before he could think of a better one, the ten shillings were in his hand and two pairs of skis and two pairs of dog's paws were under way. I knew that Hirschmann would follow us but surmised erroneously that, plagued by his conscience, he would slink after us at a distance, thinking that he was not allowed to come with us. What really did happen was entirely unexpected. The full weight of the huge dog hit me broadsides on like a cannon ball and I was precipitated hip foremost on to the icy road. A skier's equilibrium is not proof against the impact of an enormous dog, hurled in a delirium of excitement against him. I had quite underestimated his grasp of the situation. As for Hirschmann, he danced for joy over my extended corpse.

I have always taken very seriously the responsibility imposed by a dog's fidelity, and I am proud that I once risked my life, though inadvertently, to save a dog which had fallen into the Danube at a temperature of −28°C. My Alsatian, Bingo, was running along the frozen edge of the river when he slipped and fell into the water. His claws were unable to grip the sides of the ice so he could not get out. Dogs become exhausted very quickly when attempting to get up too steep a bank. They get into an awkward, more and more upright swimming position until they are soon in imminent danger of drowning. I therefore ran a few yards ahead of the dog which was being swept downstream; then I lay down and, in order to distribute my weight, crept on my belly to the edge of the ice. As Bingo came within my reach, I seized him by the scruff of the neck and pulled him with a jerk towards me on to the ice, but our joint weight was too much for it—it broke, and I slid silently, head first into the freezing cold water. The dog, which, unlike myself, had its head shorewards, managed to reach firmer ice. Now the situation was reversed; Bingo ran apprehensively along the ice and I floated downstream in the current. Finally, because the human hand is better adapted than the paw of the dog for gripping a smooth surface, I managed to escape disaster by my own efforts. I felt ground beneath my feet and threw my upper half upon the ice.

We judge the moral worth of two human friends according to which of them is ready to make the greater sacrifice without thought of recompense. Nietzsche who, unlike most people, wore brutality only as a mask to hide true warmness of heart, said the beautiful words, 'Let it be your aim always to love more than the other, never to be the second.' With human beings, I am sometimes able to fulfil this commandment, but in my relations with a faithful dog, I am always the second. What a strange and unique social relationship! Have you ever thought how extraordinary it all is? Man, endowed with reason and a highly developed sense of moral responsibility, whose finest and noblest belief is the religion of brotherly love, in this very respect falls short of the carnivores. In saying this I am not indulging in sentimental anthropomorphization. Even the noblest human love arises, not from reason and the specifically human, rational moral sense, but from the much deeper age-old layers of instinctive feeling. The highest and most selfless moral behaviour loses all value in our estimation when it arises not from such sources but from the reason. Elizabeth Browning said,

> If thou must love me, let it be for nought
> Except for love's sake only.

Even to-day man's heart is still the same as that of the higher social animals, no matter how far the achievements of his reason and his rational moral sense transcend theirs. The plain fact that my dog loves me more than I love him is undeniable and always fills me with a certain feeling of shame. The dog is ever ready to lay down his life for me. If a lion or a tiger threatened me, Ali, Bully, Tito, Stasi, and all the others would, without a moment's hesitation, have plunged into the hopeless fight to protect my life if only for a few seconds. And I?

⟨⟩

72

Bernard E. Rollin and Michael D.H. Rollin

"Dogmaticisms and Catechisms: Ethics and Companion Animals"

Bernard Rollin and Michael Rollin enumerate the many ways in which companion animals are mistreated. They trace the source of this mistreatment to the invisibility of our treatment of companion animals. The solution is to examine our own behavior and to accept regulation of animal acquisition: a demonstration of knowledge should be required.

Welfare problems in companion animals, and the shortfalls of the social ethic

[. . .]

We kill somewhere between 10 and 20 million healthy dogs and cats a year (or between two and four million). (I am always astounded by the ferocity with which the exact number is debated and I am reminded thereby of a Marxist-Stalinist colleague who, confronted with the accusation that Stalin killed 50 million people, loudly proclaimed that he had killed no more than 20 million!) In addition, we treat them appallingly. We perpetuate dozens of genetic diseases of dogs through aesthetically-based dysfunctional "breed standards." The Bulldog's respiratory problems or the Shar-Pei's skin problems provide clear examples. We ignore the functionality of these animals and treat them as, in the words of one of my veterinary colleagues, "living statues." (Veterinary medicine should take a strong stand against this approach for reasons of preventative medicine alone!)

We acquire these animals while knowing nothing of their needs and natures, then get rid of them because they cannot help those needs and natures. We lavish affection on them—as a child does on a new toy—until familiarity or age takes the edge off cuteness. We adopt them on a whim, and get rid of them when it passes. And, exactly like the profit-motivated confinement agriculturalists most pet owners would profess to abhor, we alter them surgically to fit the truncated environments or hoops to jump we provide. Many trim beaks in chickens, crop ears and dock tails in dogs. Many castrate and sometimes spay, beef cattle without anesthesia, and do the same to companion animals without analgesia and sometimes with "anesthesia" that is in fact little more than chemical restraint—e.g. ketamine alone—for cat spays. Many owners train with shock collars and negative reinforcement, rubbing a puppy's nose in its feces when it does what comes naturally. Many find nothing problematic in crating a dog all day, while we profess to abhor the crating of veal calves. Where it is still legal, many declaw cats, yet let them go outside, robbing them of both defense and escape. Others "devocalize" dogs because they bark. These owners fail to understand and respect companion animal nature as surely as do those animal researchers or intensive agricultural-ists who see animals as tools, and keep them in a manner determined by our convenience, not by their needs or comfort. Rhinestone collars (or diamond collars), painted toenails, and birthday parties do not begin to compensate for days of neglect followed erratically by hours of child-substitute attention.

If ever any social use of animals does not warrant abuse, suffering, or death, it is animals as companions. After all, almost all of the pet-owning public will resoundingly declare that they see their animals as "members of the family," more perhaps, a bitter attestation to our growing numbers of dysfunctional families than a glowing tribute to our moral behavior towards our animal friends.

[. . .]

In our urban and suburban society, where *society* not *community* dominates—where we don't know our neighbors, and don't care to know our neighbors; where we stand in an elevator as far away from everyone else as possible; where so many marriages end in divorce; where inaugurating a conversation with a stranger is virtually unthinkable; where, if you fall down, people step over you—a companion animal is kept to give, and to receive, love, probably the ultimate human requirement. And, ironically, it is kept to bring us closer to other humans. In New York City, only people with dogs (or babies) get to talk to strangers without suspicion. Thus, as the phrase human–animal bond suggests, there ought to be an unbreakable contract between both parties, analogous to the one found in the best cases of husbandry agriculture.

[. . .]

I do believe, as I have affirmed for almost 20 years, that we have a contractual relation-ship with all domestic animals, but most clearly so with those who are totally dependent on us, and for whom we have left no room to subsist, let alone thrive, on their own. If the human animal bond is to be more than a slogan for the very lucrative pet industry, more than a marketing ploy for veterinary services, we must face up to the fact that animals are doing fine holding up their end of the bargain; it is we who should be ashamed.

For many years those who advocate for companion animals have promulgated the same solutions—spay and neuter, early spay and neuter, harvest gonads, or seek high-tech equiva-lents. Adopt, foster, euthanize. Yet while spay and neuter has reduced our killing of puppies and kittens, so that some humane societies must import litters, it has not stopped the killing of dogs and cats. If stray animals were the issue, the problem would have been resolved a generation ago through efficient animal control. The typical animal trashed is not a stray; but a young adult male dog or cat. Meanwhile, as a veterinarian friend once bitterly remarked, we kill them so nothing bad will happen to them, even though Alan Beck[1] and others have shown that at least some unowned dogs, even urban ones, would survive and thrive, while it is evident that large numbers of feral cats do as well or better. Indeed, it can be argued that feral dogs and particularly cats can be viewed as urban wildlife, and left alone, as Dr. Steve Frantz of the New York State Health Department has asserted to me in conversation. There is some evidence that aggressive destruction of feral cats leads to a rodent outbreak that is far more dangerous to human health than leaving the cats alone.[2]

A secondary tragedy, virtually unnoticed by society, is thereby perpetrated on those who care most about animals—they do society's dirty work at the expense of their physical, mental, and spiritual health. Be these people humane society volunteers, animal control personnel, or veterinarians, they suffer for our sins, as victims of what I have elsewhere called moral stress,[3] resulting from the constant tension arising out of what they believe they *should* be doing, in contrast to what they are doing. It is no wonder that, at the 1981 conference I helped organize with the Animal Medical Center and the Columbia University College of Physicians and Surgeons on client grief over pet loss, veterinarians wanted most to speak of their own grief at the constant assault on their souls occasioned by client requests for convenience euthanasia. It is no wonder that animal control people have told me repeatedly that they would do anything to make their own job obsolete. It is no wonder that humane society people "burn out."

[. . .]

Things can be invisible in two ways—either too remote or too familiar. We as a society are making it our business to ethically illuminate animal use that was historically remote—animal research, agriculture, genetic engineering—but we are not yet ready to criticize what is invisible to us because we take it for granted. We have not yet realized, as the comic-strip character Pogo wisely remarked, that we have "met the enemy, and they is us." Unwittingly, our shelters and humane societies have contributed to the problem—they have swept our dirt under the carpet, and sheltered us in the end from the truth more than they have sheltered the animals.

Extending the social ethic: regulation, education, and policy

[. . .] [All] societies must have a *social consensus ethic*, an ethic encoded in law and rules, and constraining everyone's behavior lest we degenerate into chaos and anarchy. Hence it is universally known that murder, rape, robbery and so on are seen as wrong, and "not in my opinion" does not exonerate you from the social consequences of such actions. On the other hand, much action of ethical significance is left to our individual views of right and wrong, our *personal ethic*. Such ethically significant issues as what we eat, what we read, what charity we contribute to or what religion we profess are all left to our personal ethic in our society, though not, of course, in all societies.

[. . .]

The treatment of animals—with the exception of social forbidding of cruelty—was for most of human history a paradigm case of that which was left to people's personal ethic. However, [. . .] it is ever-increasingly being subsumed by the social ethic. With the coming, for example, of solid empirical evidence that the research community was not doing right by animals in failing to control pain and distress, in failing to provide consistent high quality care, in failing to suit the environments of animals to their needs and natures (thereby both harming the animals and the scientific activity for which they were being used), society felt compelled to regulate something they didn't fully understand, for moral reasons.

As we have sketched, the suffering of companion animals is profoundly troubling morally. Essentially no benefit emerges from it, save for the emotional satisfaction of the owner; there is no claim comparable to that of the morally conscientious scientist who affirms that though there is ultimately no moral justification for harming innocent animals for human benefit, he or she will continue to uneasily do so for the tangible benefit it provides. Our injustice—for such it is—to companion animals cannot even be seen as constituting a moral dilemma, for what is the upside of our behavior? Indeed, there is a demonstrable down side—we treat irresponsibility as acceptable, the sidestepping of moral responsibility as inevitable, the bond to others who depend on us as revocable for convenience. If failing to check cruelty to animals inexorably leads to cruelty to humans, does something similar result from failing to honor our responsibilities to animals?

[. . .]

The only solution then is to shine our new social ethic on ourselves, to illuminate our own backyards. If the agricultural community were openly creating genetically diseased animals for profit (such as the genetically engineered super-pig) society would shut them down. Is doing it to our companion animals anymore justifiable morally? (Dozens of new genetic diseases in companion animals have been identified since I first wrote of this issue 20 years ago).

Recent work by Salman *et al.*[4] provides solid empirical grounding for what most shelter workers have known anecdotally—people relinquish animals to be trashed because they are cheap; they have no major investment in them (and they can always get another one). People relinquish animals because they have "personal problems," because they are allergic to them, because they cannot deal with their behavior, because they have no knowledge or false knowledge of what it takes to have and care for an animal and, above all, as Salman does not tell us but common sense does, because there are no consequences resulting from being irresponsible—not even social opprobrium or censure. Companion animals—easy come, easy go.

What can be done via the social ethic? Obviously, one cannot legislate responsibility as a character trait. But one can legislate responsible behavior, even as we can and do legislate morality—our whole social ethic embodied in law is in fact legislated morality!

Before discussing strategy, however, let me make a personal disclaimer. Philosophically, I tend to be an anarchist, and loathe regulation. I will not, for example, ride my Harley-Davidson in states with mandatory helmet laws. And I am very uncomfortable in general with being required to do things "for my own good." But just because we are over-regulated in some areas in a paternalistic way does not mean we are sufficiently regulated in others. In general, I believe that we are too paternalistic in dealing with rational adults, yet too lax in dealing with infractions against innocent objects of moral concern—infants, children, animals. I see great moral incongruity in people who batter babies and children to death or blindness or a permanent vegetative state getting their wrists slapped while those who swindle wealthy (and greedy) professionals go to jail for a decade.

The only solution to our widespread, systematic, and unnoticed moral irresponsibility towards animals is to regulate—i.e., encode in the social ethic—the acquisition, management, and relinquishment of companion animals. One cannot get a driver's license or a hunting license without (at least officially) becoming educated about the nature and rules of driving. One cannot own a car without permanently identifying it so that it is always traceable. And one cannot simply abandon a car or even simply park it on the street indefinitely. Creating a similar situation for companion animals seems to me a reasonable way to address the ignorance from whence flows our current irresponsibility. Animal "overpopulation" is not a birth control problem to be solved by high-tech gonad hunting—it is a moral problem, a problem of human behavior and abrogation of responsibility. In a responsible society, nothing more high-tech than a leash is needed for birth control. In fact, I believe that excessive gonad hunting has probably harmed the canine gene pool, with responsible people who acquire the best animals assuring that these animals' genes are not passed on, while clueless people happily breed disasters.

Currently an animal is often an impulse item. I see the Disney film "101 Dalmatians;" I want a Dalmatian. I see the film "Turner and Hooch;" I want a Tibetan Mastiff. Kittens are cute; I want a kitten. I want one, I get one. As Salman's[4] study indicates, most pet owners know very little about their animals. Philosophically, I cannot have a rational desire for a dog if I have no idea what owning a dog entails.

I would therefore argue that people wishing to acquire an animal should at least be compelled to demonstrate that they know what they are getting into. Licensing of owners should be a precondition of acquiring an animal; demonstrated knowledge should be a precondition of licensure. How one best acquires the knowledge is an empirical question. Perhaps a mandatory course in pet husbandry and responsibility (ethics) could become a staple of junior high or high school curricula. There is precedent here in the unparalleled growth of environmental awareness among young people in the late 1960s.

Alternatively, one could provide adult education and counseling for prospective pet owners. Although Americans resist jumping through bureaucratic hoops, they respect education. Many people seeking concealed weapons permits do not oppose mandatory shooting and safety courses—indeed welcome them—realizing that acquiring a gun is a major responsibility. So too is acquiring an animal. If one can't have an animal because of allergies, it would be good to know this *before* one gets an animal!

Such education could be undertaken, as I suggested years ago, by veterinarians, or by other trained animal behavior counselors. They ought to be paid, perhaps from the license fees, and will benefit by being exposed to members of the public they would not otherwise meet.

[. . .]

Obviously one cannot force such a policy upon society without risking the absurdity of Prohibition. Plato said that when dealing with ethics and adults, one must not teach, one must remind. In other words, one must show them that what one is trying to get them to do is implicit in what they already believe, only they don't realize it. So any law must be preceded by public education analogous to what convinced the public that the research community was not meeting its obligations to the animals it uses or that our environmental despoliation was intolerable. The public must be made to realize that "they is us," that often our treatment of companion animals is as egregious, shocking, immoral, and unacceptable—indeed more so—than any animal use in society. And this means telling the truth.

Finally, a system of permanent identification for companion animals must be put into effect, and humane societies and veterinarians positioned to reject convenience euthanasia for morally unacceptable reasons. (For example, pet owners could post a bond that they forfeit if they elect convenience euthanasia.) The technology is becoming increasingly available for trace-back of companion animals, as society demands irrefutable trace-back of food animals for reasons of food safety.

I do not propose legislation lightly, nor am I clear about what form it should take. This must evolve through public discussion informed by an awareness of the moral unacceptability—by society's own lights—of our current treatment of companion animals. As principal architects of 1985 federal law for laboratory animals, my colleagues and I faced a similar challenge—how does one legislate moral use of animals when the community using the animals sees no moral issues therein, and in fact further affirms that one must be agnostic about animal pain and that science is "ethics-free?" By legislating moral deliberation in animal care and use committees and mandating the control of pain and suffering, we were able to elevate the thinking of scientists beyond their ideological denial of the meaningfulness of these issues. Many believe that this has worked, as we raise a generation of young scientists to whom moral discussion and pain control are second nature. A good law, in the end, becomes an educational device, which, if it works properly, eventually vitiates the need for its own existence by creating a new culture in the regulated population.

I would very much like to believe that the society that has developed a new ethic for animals would have the moral courage to turn that ethic on itself. We who advocate for animals must therefore begin an educational campaign to force that dramatic turn. That, in turn, means not allowing people to escape the visible consequences of their own irresponsibility. We must cease to worry about offending the guilty; we must cease to be their sin eaters; we must cease battering the souls of those who care most. If we fail, we risk the moral revulsion of society as a whole, who could conceivably react by eliminating companion animal ownership altogether, as some societies have done. And this would be a great pity, for as both cowboys and Indians can tell you, we are irretrievably and mortally diminished if we must live without animals.

Notes

1. Beck, A. M. 1973. *The Ecology of Stray Dogs: A Study of Free-Ranging Urban Animals*. Baltimore, Maryland: York Press.
2. Personal communication, Dr. David Neil, University of Alberta.
3. Rollin, B. E. 1986. Euthanasia and moral stress. In *Loss, Grief, and Care* 115–26, ed. R. DeBellis. Binghamton, NY: Hawarth Press.
4. Salman, M. D., New, J. C., Scarlett, J., Kass, P., Ruch-Gallie, R. and Hetts, S. 1998. Human and animal factors related to the relinquishment of dogs and cats in 12 selected animal shelters in the U.S. *Journal of Applied Animal Welfare Science* 1: 204–26. See also Scarlett, J. M., Salman, M. D., New, J. C., and Kass, P. H. 1999. Reasons for relinquishment of companion animals in U.S. animal shelters: selected health and personal issues. *Journal of Applied Animal Welfare Science* 2: 41–57; and New, J. C., Salman, M. D., King, M., Scarlett, J. M., Kass, P. H. and Hutchison, J. M. 2000. Characteristics of shelter-relinquished animals and their owners compared with animals and their owners in U.S. pet-owning households. *Journal of Applied Animal Welfare Science* 3: 179–203.

73

Paul Shepard

"The Pet World"

Paul Shepard traces the dramatic change from wild and sacred animal life through domestication, stuffed animal toys for children, pet dogs and cats, and finally to zoos. He describes pets as "civilized paraphernalia," created by selective breeding and hence unable to restore us to wholeness with the Others. Pets only confuse our perception of the wild universe, an outer wilderness which we need to become aware of in our own selves.

[. . .] Against the indifference of the wild animals, the impetuous affection of our pets seems like an enormous boon. In a world so full of problems and suffering, only the worst curmudgeonly cynic would sneer at our indulgence, their simple pleasure in us, and our joy in them. Something, however, is profoundly wrong with the human/animal pet relationship at its most basic level. Given the obvious benefits of that affiliation, one has to poke very carefully into its psychology and ecology before its fragile core can be exposed.
[. . .]

During the rise of [the] biological void in urban existence in the industrial world from 1850 to 1950, the middle classes began to have fewer children, for whom the household could be a lonely place. In fiction, such a child who represented childhood without siblings and without easy access to street friends was Christopher Robin, for whom Winnie the Pooh was the substitute. Pooh Bear is an animated and storied teddy bear. In this way the Anglo-American concept of animal friends is prefigured in childhood, with the aid of "bedtime" stories, by pretending that one's stuffed toys are alive. This scenario creates a very different childhood orientation toward the living pets than in earlier times, when household animals like rabbits might be eaten, cats caught mice, and dogs served as guards or hunters. From Pooh Bear it is not very far to the doggy friend and but a step from the doggy friend to an imaginary relationship with or among wild animals—animals which, for the first time in history, are almost completely lacking in the child's experience. This sequence is a drama in five acts.

Act I is an outer circle of wild animal life which was a major focus of human attention, establishing the expectation of a rich, surprising, meaningful, and beautiful diversity of life around us. Some animals were sacred. All were conscious, unique, and different in spiritual power.

In Act II people took certain animals into captivity, manipulated their reproduction, and altered their biological natures to conform to human dominance, reconstructing them as members of the household. These became the domestic animals. The wild forms, reduced in number and diversity, literally receded.

Act III begins not with animals but with a class of things called "transitional objects." These are toted around by anxious three-year-old children who are having difficulty becoming independent from their mothers and who are comforted by a soft object that is subjectively intermediate between themselves and the outside world. The children who do not seem to require the security of such objects are those who are surrounded by abundant other forms of life. The exact reason for this is not entirely clear, but apparently animals in their diversity model a world of likeness and difference which makes the child's impending separation less frightening and also resonates with internal, psychic structures which can best be described metaphorically as a fauna. The stuffed toys are simultaneously huggable, transitional objects and "animals." They appeared in large numbers in the industrial, nuclear-family era, compensating children for their lonesome social and ecological situations and preparing them for lifelong pet keeping. The mode of this preparation is pretend-play, the self-dramatization of all life as a happy playground.

Act IV is the transfer of this affection from effigies to dogs and cats. As the toys had been pets, the pets became toys. Even "wild" animal manikins, such as stuffed bears and lions, are little people in the imagination, who participate in a household society, who have expectations, reasons, worries, expressions, voices, tastes, and complicated affinities and antipathies toward each other and their human companions.

Act V extends the equivalence of the living domestic pet and the stuffed wild toy to living nature. If the domestic forms have all along been substitutes for the wild and the latter have become unavailable and unknown, it is easy to fuse the domestic and wild. The wild are simply those potential pets who do not happen to live with us. They are each other's pets, or perhaps creatures whose friendship we have lost. Zoos seem to affirm this identity. The zoo has "toy verisimilitude," foreshadowing the modern child's menagerie of stuffed animals and friendly pets, each zoo creature enduring in blind lethargy, withdrawn except in moments of hyperactivity when the feeder comes, like the puppets waiting in the closet to be flung into tea parties or wagons by a child.

[. . .]

Pets are not part of human evolution or the biological context out of which our ecology comes. They are civilized paraphernalia whose characteristic combination of accompaniment and accommodation is tangled in an ambiguous tyranny. Constance Perrin, an anthropologist, calls it "attachment theory." The animal triggers nurturant behavior and serves as a kind of intermediate object between the owner and a more or less alien world, but at the same time it is dragged about like a tattered security blanket. Indeed, the domestication of animals has never ensured their tender care. In recent Anglo-American tradition the dog is "man's best friend," but it is abhorred in the Bible. In Muslim tradition the dog's saliva is noxious, and contact between people and dogs requires ritual cleansing. Over most of the planet the dog is a cur and mongrel scavenger, feral, half-starved, the target of the kick and thrown rock, often cruelly exploited as a slave. Although looked upon with affection, even modern pets are property that is bought, sold, "put down," and neutered. Pets are deliberately abandoned by the millions and necessitate city-run slaughterhouses, shelters, and "placement" services. This paradox of frenetic emotion and casual dismissal reveals our deep disappointment in the pet's ability to do something, be something, that we cannot quite identify. Yi-Fu Tuan considers our behavior to be exercises in casual domination that symbolize human control of nature.[1] In an earlier book I argued that pets were unacknowledged surrogates for human companionships or substitutes for the resolution of interpersonal social problems, and therefore impaired normal human sociality by enabling people to avoid mending, maturing, or otherwise dealing with their personal relationships.[2] Pets can cause family conflict, even divorce, and may become bridges of unhealthy transference relationships and regression to infantile human behavior.

Even so, I now see that the pet may be more than a human replacement. "Pet-facilitated therapy," casual or institutionalized, reduces human suffering. It is truly an astonishing solace. The "companion animal" is a medical miracle to which we should be kind and grateful. But like all psychotherapy its presence is not a true healing. It cheers, modulates pain, and helps the owner/patient to cope.

Domestic animals were "created" by humans by empirical genetic engineering over the past ten thousand years. They are vestiges and fragments from a time of deep human respect for animals, whose abundance dazzled us in their many renditions of life, helping us to know ourselves by showing all that we had not become. The pet cannot restore us to that wholeness any more than an artificial limb renews the original; nor can it do more than simulate the Others among whom our ancestors lived for so long, the Others that constituted for them a cosmos. They and all captive animals are like organ transplants: healthy for us but cut out of their own organic fabric.

What is wrong at the heart of the keeping of pets is that they are deficient animals in whom we have invested the momentum of two million years of love of the Others. They are monsters of the order invented by Frankenstein except that they are engineered to conform to our wishes, biological slaves who cringe and fawn or perform or whatever we wish. As embodiments of trust, dependence, companionship, esthetic beauty, vicarious power, innocence, or action by command, they are wholly unlike the wild world. In effect, they are organic machines conforming to our needs.

No one now doubts that pets can be therapeutic. But they are not a glorious bonus on life; rather they are compensations for something desperately missing, minimal replacements for friendship in all of its meanings. Mass society isolates us in ways and degrees that seem to contradict our population density. Pets occupy by default an equally great human need for others who are not part of our personal lives. The diversity that nourishes the mind extends to the whole realm of life and nature. Pets, being our own creations, do not replace that wild universe. But as living animals they confuse our perception and hide the lack of a wild, nonhuman comity of players on a grand scale—a spectacular drama of life to which our human natures commit our need and expectation.

Wild animals are not our friends. They are uncompromisingly not us nor mindful of us, just as they differ among themselves. They are the last undevoured riches of the planet, what novelist Romain Gary called "the roots of heaven." We cannot comprehend the world as it is experienced by a bat, a termite, or a squid; we cannot force them into barnyard conviviality or household banality without destroying them. More than bearded prophets and great goddesses they are the mediators between us and plants, the rock and suns around us, the rest of the universe. Wild animals connote the wildness in us which cannot be equated to our domestic affairs or reconciled with the petty tyrannies of "dwellers in houses," domesticates, from the same root word that gives "constrain" or "subdue." As a fauna only the wild are a mirror of the multifold strangeness of the human self. We know this. It is why we scrutinize and inspect and remark on them, make them the subject of our art and thought, and sometimes kill and eat them with mindful formality, being in place with our own otherness.[3]

Notes

1   Yi-Fu Tuan, *Dominance and Affection: The Making of Pets* (New Haven: Yale University Press, 1984).
2   Paul Shepard, *Thinking Animals* (New York: Viking, 1978).
3   James O. Breeden (ed.), *Advice Among Masters: The Ideal in Slave Management in the Old South* (Westport: Greenwood Press, 1980).

74

———— ✦ ————

Anna Merz

"Hand-Raising a Rhino in the Wild"

Anna Merz describes how she raised Samia, a female black rhino abandoned by her mother. The tiny baby rhino slept in her bed. When Samia matured and integrated with wild rhinos, she protected Merz in dangerous situations and returned to visit with her daily. Merz's story is so evocative that the reader grieves with her at the tragic death of Samia and her baby.

Samia, the female black rhino who was my pride and my joy, was born ten years ago in the Ngare Sergoi Rhino Sanctuary on the western side of Lewa Downs, a 45,000-acre cattle ranch situated on the northern slopes of Mt. Kenya. I have lived all my life with animals and I have handraised many, but Samia was truly unique. Between us there existed a love, a trust, a reaching out for understanding unlike anything I had known in a relationship before. With her there was none of the usual relationship between man and beast. I never tried to discipline or hold her; she lived as a wild rhino. Yet of her own free will, she kept alive with me the bonds of love, trust, and friendship until her death.

Early in 1984 the sanctuary received its first rhinos, including Samia's mother, Solia. At the present time there are nineteen white and twenty-two black rhinos. Twenty calves have been born here. Not all have survived, but those that died, died of natural causes; none have been poached.

On February 15, 1985, Solia gave birth to a calf, Samia, and promptly deserted her. At that time I knew virtually nothing about rhinos, and certainly nothing about raising rhino babies, not even the proper composition of black rhino milk. Over weeks and months I battled with Samia's unending bouts of diarrhea, dehydration, and abnormal temperatures. As a tiny baby, she slept in my bed, causing matrimonial complications with the amazing messes she produced. Raising her was a series of crises, but at about six months, she started to stabilize.

Each day I walked her over ever-increasing distances to introduce her to the world of which she would be a part and its inhabitants. I remember our first encounter with a group of giraffes; long black eyelashes aflutter, they peered at us with astonishment, this strange combination of old woman, baby rhino, and black dog. Samia didn't see them until they moved and then, in terror at their size, dashed between my legs for safety. This was not a practical proposition and I sat down with a thud. Unable to get under me she compromised by sitting on my prostrate form, snorting her disapproval.

Samia learned quickly that I did not really appreciate being knocked over, even in play, and as her strength grew so her gentleness with me increased. As we walked, she would, of her own accord, offer a helping tail to pull me up the steeper trails. When I weaned her at three and a half years, I expected the bond between us to loosen, as would be only natural, but it never did. For ten years, Samia and I were companions, and even when she was mature and integrated with the wild rhinos, she usually returned to visit with me at least once a day.

During our time together, she taught me so much about the world of the rhino that I could never have learned otherwise. I also tried to teach Samia what I thought she would need to know in order to survive. But I was not always successful. To help Samia develop her sense of smell, I hid, hoping she would put her nose to the ground and search after me. Instead, she went to the garden gate, opened it to let the dogs out, then galloped after them straight to me. By no stretch of the imagination can this be described as instinctive behavior.

Rhinos are not, as reputed, solitary, bad-tempered, stupid animals. I had been warned that after my experience with chimps in Ghana, I would find them dangerous and boring. Rather the opposite. Rhino intelligence is close to that of chimps and their outstanding characteristics are curiosity and nervousness rather than aggression. Through her incredible intelligence, Samia was able to reveal a great deal about the social structure of rhino society and much of the complex methods of communication her species uses, including a wide variety of noises and the regulation of breathing to form a sort of Morse code of sound.

In the beginning of our relationship, I was the teacher and the protector. As she matured our roles reversed, and she showed herself capable of teaching and protecting me. A few weeks before the birth of Samia's own calf, she joined me, which was not unusual, when I was walking the dogs one evening. The thick tropical dusk was falling when three rhinos emerged on the track ahead of us. To avoid them I would have to make a long detour through the thorny bush in the dark. Samia, sensing both my fear and my indecision, realized my predicament and took charge of the situation. She knew these three white rhinos well and would normally have ignored them. Now, she trotted up to them, ears laid flat, huffing and hurrumphing angrily, and they retreated in astonishment at her aggressive behavior. Satisfied that they were routed, she returned to me and the dogs and escorted us safely past where they had been. When she was satisfied that we were safe, she left us to resume her own affairs.

When Samia was mated it was by the wild and violent-tempered bull Kenu. He was a small but immensely powerful rhino and many times he came near my house. On one occasion, Samia saw I was in danger and moved very quickly between us with the intention of stopping his charge. Another day Samia and Kenu visited me together. I went to the gate to greet her not realizing he was there. She stood between us and I could sense his rage and hatred of me, his desire to obliterate both me and that gate that stood between us. For forty long minutes we three stood together and I could both see and hear the breathing patterns by which they were communicating with one another. I could literally see the control that Samia was exercising over his behavior. The first time she protected me, I thought it was chance and good luck, but the second and subsequent times revealed her focus and intention. From running to me for safety, she had come to act as my protector against buffalo and her own kind, but never had I expected her to actually protect me from her own mate.

On the morning of April 11, 1995, I learned, via a radio call, that Samia had had a baby. With both joy and terror, I and a tracker crept to where I could see her, feeding quietly. Deep in the long grass near her flickered the tips of two long ears. There was no sound but that of Samia's munching. I was relieved because I knew from painful experience that baby rhinos cry only if they are in trouble. Half an hour later, the tiny creature staggered to its feet, wobbled round Samia's hind legs, thrust its wee nose into her flank, and started to suckle. Samia stopped feeding and stood quietly while it drank from first one teat and then the other. There was no doubt that she had milk, nor was there any doubt as to the baby's sex—Samia had a son.

Two days later, I was watching her with two trackers and was so absorbed that I did not notice the change in the wind. The trackers moved back but she had got my scent. Now what? These long years of observation have taught me that rhinos are fiercely protective mothers and very solitary for the first year of their baby's life. My knees were shaking so much I had to sit down. Then Samia came to me and, as she had in the past, rested her great head in my lap. While her baby stood a scarce foot away wearing a bewildered expression, I rubbed behind her ears and gently told her how clever she was and how beautiful her son was with his huge ears, blunt nose, big feet, and pearl satin skin. Obviously the bond we had created over the past ten years had withstood his birth.

When Samuel was still a few days old, Samia came to me, leaving him sleeping under a nearby bush. She was standing beside me when he awoke and cried out in fear at finding himself alone. Samia's action was swift and wholly instinctive. She swiped me sideways with her head, knocking me to the ground, and ran to him. Seeing that no harm had befallen him, she returned to me, still sitting where I had fallen. She thrust her nose at me and I assured her that I was unhurt. Then she turned and, as often in days gone by, presented me with her tail for a pull up!

I never attempted to touch her baby, but slowly he got used to my scent and his inborn fear of me lessened. Almost daily at dawn, Samia would come to visit me with him at heel. Each day would start with the knowledge that they were well and safe and that she knew how to raise and protect her child. Frequently, hand-raised animals do not.

I had worried whether Samia would appreciate the dangers surrounding her baby; there was so much I had not been able to teach her. But after some time, I realized that these fears were groundless. Samia had also always been fully aware that I only pretended to eat thorn-bushes and had not been able to teach her how to manipulate the thorn in her mouth. But at four months, Samuel browsed on these same thornbushes alongside his mother. It was something very beautiful to behold. I watched Samia's affection for her baby, saw how the bond between them became stronger, and felt quite ridiculously proud of her.

Because our April rains virtually failed, I started to supplement Samia's natural browse with a small quantity of alfalfa so her milk wouldn't fail. Almost daily at dawn, she came to my garden fence with her baby. As soon as she heard me open the door, she called to tell me that she was there and hopeful of being fed. The rest of the day she spent in the bush. Seeing her thus was my greatest joy.

Then tragedy struck. Samia did not come to visit me one morning. I went down the valley with Patrick, a tracker, to look for her and found her dead. She was lying on her back below the cliff from which she and her child had fallen. Her death must have been instantaneous. Her baby lay nearby, still alive. I tried to help him rise, but being unable to do so, sent Patrick with the radio to call for help. For two hours, I knelt beside little Samuel, offering what poor comfort I could. Nearby a leopard was grunting, but I could not see it. The valley was beautiful, full of birds and color, and I thought of the many happy hours and days that Samia and I had spent there.

Ian Craig, who came with ropes and other people, realized what I had not, that the baby rhino's back was broken low down near his tail. A merciful shot ended his suffering. Later, after the local Game Warden had come to remove Samia's horns, the trackers laid Samuel beside his mother and I went to say good-bye to them and to cover them with a sackful of flowers.

Samia's death has to me been a tragedy. There was real love and friendship between us and I miss her all the time. Beyond that it was my dearest hope that through her life and that of her child, awareness of and caring for her species could be awakened. In her life, she had proved beyond all doubt that there can be a meeting between two wholly disparate species.

75

Freya Mathews

"Living with Animals"

Freya Mathews argues that we need to find ways to restore animals to our day-to-day urban reality and suggests ways in which we can increase the amount of urban habitat for wildlife. Mathews also recounts her own childhood, during which she learned to engage with the unknowable subjectivities of animals and found that this experience is "the principal bridge" to communication with the unknowable subjectivity of the wider world beyond human selfhood.

'Without animals,' says Peter, a Maasai nomad interviewed in the *New Internationalist*,[1] 'life isn't worth living'.

Sitting here in my inner-city backyard writing this, with a circle of attentive little upturned canine and feline faces surrounding me, and my cranky duck tugging at my shoelaces, I could not be in more heartfelt agreement. But how many people today would share this sentiment? For how many would it be football that makes life worth living, or cars, or opera, or ice-skating? Is there anything to ground the conviction that I want to defend here, that the company of non-human animals is a necessary part of human life, in a way that football, cars, opera and ice-skating manifestly are not, and that we relinquish or forego it at our peril?

There are two parts to this question. The first is, is it important for *us*, for our own well-being or the realization of our human potential, that we live in intimate commensal relations with animals? The second is, is it important for the *environment* that we live in such relations? Does the *world* need us to continue to live in our ancestral communalism with animals?

My view is that our present estrangement, as human beings, from both the natural world (as evidenced in the environmental crisis) and from ourselves (as evidenced in the intense neuroticization of life in contemporary "advanced" societies) is due at least in part to the progressive removal of animals from our day-to-day urban reality; consequently I shall argue that, in order to address both the environmental crisis and our own crisis of consciousness, we need to find ways of restoring animals to the human household.

[. . .]

If it is accepted that companion animals do induce in us a new moral seriousness about animals generally, then a question arises concerning the status of domestic animals used for productive purposes. Does this new moral seriousness condemn the utilization of animals for such purposes?

[. . .]

The short answer to this question is, I think, that such reconciliation of empathy and use is possible to the extent that utilization is of net benefit to the animals concerned.

[. . .]

To reconcile utilization with empathy, we need to be assured that the life that our exploitative intentions bestow on an individual domestic animal affords both the experiential opportunities and the requisite life span to enable it to achieve a significant degree of the form of self-realization appropriate to its particular kind. This implies that the use we may justifiably make of animals will vary according to their species.

[. . .]

In short, I think the fact that domestic utilization affords evolutionary niches for certain species, in a world of disappearing niches, is a prima facie reason for regarding such utilization as compatible with respect. However a full-blown attitude of empathy such as we develop through intimate association with animal companions—requires that the forms of utilization we countenance be compatible with the self-realization of the animals used, where this implies that different forms and degrees of utilization will be appropriate for different species. I would also add that, once we have acknowledged the subjectivity and moral significance of the animals we use, and the moral gravity of our practices of utilization, it becomes incumbent on us to develop cultural expressions of respect, gratitude and indebtedness for the lives we have thus dedicated to our own ends. In this way, our attitude towards domestic animals can develop more affinity with the familial attitudes of hunter-gatherer peoples towards the wild species that constitute their prey.

When domestic utilization of animals is subject to the qualifications I have outlined above, I think it is not only consistent with empathetic concern for the interests of animals: it is actually required by such concern. As environmentalists, committed to the maximal preservation of non-human life on earth, yet facing the cold, hard fact that in the twenty-first century, the processes of urbanization and industrialization that have been synonymous with the disenchantment and tragic devastation of the non-human world are only going to accelerate and intensify, don't we have to admit that one of our best chances for 'saving Nature' is by bringing Nature back into the human domain? We have, for the last few centuries, witnessed the runaway humanization of Nature; now let us inaugurate the wholesale naturalization of human habitat. Our cities are one of the major biological habitats of the future, and our task, as environmentalists, is to ensure that they provide the best opportunities for non-human life that we can devise. We can do this partly by increasing the amount of urban habitat for wildlife. Such habitat can be created by way of indigenous plantings and by permacultural programs of food production in the city. Buildings can also be designed or adapted to create, rather than exclude, habitat opportunities for wild animals (by way of stork-friendly chimneys, for instance, and roofs that accommodate bats and nesting birds). However we can also increase the urban opportunities for non-human life by finding new ways for animals to 'earn their living' in the city.

[. . .]

The possibilities for reintegrating animals productively into urban life are as limitless as our imaginations. However, the principal way in which animals can 'earn their living' in the city is still, I think, via their companionate role. The exclusive reign of the dog and the cat in this connection needs to be challenged, and the adaptability of other species to the human hearth and home investigated.

[. . .]

The 'green' city of the future, then, would be a mixed community rich in habitat opportunities for a great diversity of animal species. This reintegration of animals into human life would also help to expand human imaginative and empathetic horizons, undermining anthropocentrism and reinforcing commitment to the protection of the non-human world. At the same time, the multiple contacts with animals that it would afford would enhance the health and sanity of the human population.

[. . .]

These then are some of the reasons why I think that our living with animals is important both for us and for them. However, this commensality shapes not only our ethical attitudes towards non-human individuals and species, but our very sense of the world. I have not yet brought this larger significance of the relationship fully to light, nor can I hope to do so with any pretence of completeness. In order to capture a little of this cosmological significance however, I would like to recount, in these concluding pages, the experiential origins of my own conviction that 'without animals, life isn't worth living'.

I grew up surrounded by loving animals on what today would be described as a hobby farm, situated on the rural outskirts of Melbourne, Australia. These animals included dogs and cats, ducks, geese, hens, and, at one stage, a turkey. There were brief episodes with sheep and cows. The main focus of my entire childhood, however, was my ponies. My first pony, and the horses that came after her, were my day-long playmates and confidants. It was to them that I recited my earliest poems, and to them that I ran when I was hurt or excited. They nuzzled me in the same soft, considerate way whatever the occasion. I chose their company not for want of family and friends, but for its own sake. The form of intimacy that grew up between us was qualitatively different from anything that could have developed between myself and human persons. It was a kind of uncluttered closeness, or being-with, which existed despite the fact that our subjectivities were, in terms of content, mutually unknowable. We took it for granted, on either side, that this unknowability did not matter, that our psyches could touch and pervade each other, without need for explanations or self-disclosures, such as those conveyable by language. These animals were, for me, 'primary others', in the psychoanalytic sense; they were not substitutes for, but additional to, significant humans, nor could humans substitute for them. My subjectivity—my sense of self and world—was constituted through my 'object relations' with these animals just as fundamentally as it was through my relations with primary human others.[2]

[. . .]

Looking back on my early years now, it seems more plausible to me to assume that the ample opportunities for close communion with animals that were available to me throughout my childhood had opened me to a larger world, a world astir with presence or presences that vastly exceeded the human. It was this direct contact with unknowable but pervasive presence which instilled in me a sense of the sacredness or enchantment of the world, and the potentiality for 'magic' within it. 'Magic' was, in this context, just the possibility of the world's response—the possibility, indeed probability, that the world, when invoked in good faith, *will* respond, though not necessarily in the manner one anticipates or with the results for which one hopes. One should certainly not, in my view, rely on this world to fulfil requests or afford protection, but if one entreats it simply to reveal itself, to engage in an act of communication, then, in my experience, it will generally do so, though in its own ever-unpredictable way. I learned this as a child, through the receptiveness that my animal familiars created in me, and it filled my whole being with a sense of being accompanied, of never being alone, a sense of background love, akin to the background radiation of which physicists speak. This is a 'love' which has nothing to do with saving us from death and suffering, or with making us happy. From the viewpoint of the world, death and suffering are just inevitable concomitants of individual life. The point for individuals, from this perspective, is not to seek to evade these inevitabilities, but to reach beyond them—to call into the silence beyond human selfhood in search of a reply. This is the moment for which the world has been waiting, and in which it will rejoice: the moment when we ask it to speak. To receive its reply is to enter a love far greater than the kind of protection and indulgence that our traditional importunate forms of prayer expect, for that reply signifies that we belong to an animate order, a pattern of meaning, from which death cannot separate us, and to which suffering only summons us.

I offer these concluding reflections, not as argument, but as testimony relating to my own personal sense of the larger import of human-animal commensality, especially when that commensality is established in childhood. To engage with the unknowable subjectivities of animals, and to experience their response to us, is perhaps the principal bridge to communication with the unknowable subjectivity of the wider world. To experience the world thus, as an ensouled or spiritual thing, will not only direct the course of our own self-realization in the most fundamental way; it will also ensure an attitude of profound mutuality and awed protectiveness towards the world itself.

Notes

1   Nikkivan der Gaag, 'The Maasai and the Travellers', *New Internationalist*, 266, (1995), pp. 24–5.
2   The term 'object relations' is deployed in a branch of psychoanalytic theory, known as 'object relations theory', to designate the kinds of relations with primary others that an infant internalizes in the process of developing its individual sense of self. It is associated with the work of D.W. Winnicott, and later feminist theorists, such as Nancy Chodorow.

76

James Garbarino

"Protecting Children and Animals from Abuse: A Trans-Species Concept of Caring"

James Garbarino argues that empathy for animals and empathy for children are natural partners. The correlation between child maltreatment and animal abuse is well established by
social science research. We need to expand our empathy so that we treat both children and
animals with respect and caring.

Although my professional career has been spent seeking to improve the quality of life for
children, I come from a family of avowed and unabashed animal lovers. From my childhood,
I recall clearly that the greatest outrage arose in my parents and siblings from stories of
cruelty to animals. When the cowboys and Indians battled on television or in the movies, it
was for the wounded *horses* that the greatest sympathy was reserved. In fact, in the household of my childhood it was accepted practice to root for the animals whenever they were in
conflict with humans.

[. . .]

In this I am not alone. Josephine Donovan (1990) dedicated her analysis of "Animal
Rights and Feminist Theory" "to my great dog Rooney . . . whose life led me to appreciate
the nobility and dignity of animals." This is particularly interesting and important in the
present context, because in her article Donovan recounts the fact that one of the contributions of feminist theory to the formulation of animal rights is the assertion that it is from their
capacity to *feel* that the rights of animals derive. As outlined by psychologist Carol Gilligan
(1982), this orientation to feelings stands in sharp contrast to conventional masculine thinking, which sees the origins of animal rights either in the ability to think or in the use they
serve in the human community. I begin my analysis on precisely this issue, that any genuine
understanding of the rights of children and animals must arise out of empathy. *We (and they)
feel. Therefore we are entitled.*

[. . .]

But how far can we take this kinship? And what does it imply for the coordination of
child welfare and animal welfare programs and policies?

[. . .]

Child welfare and animal welfare ought to be natural collaborators, even if in practice
there have been historical wedges driven between these two caring communities. Certainly

the more we postulate the need for a general ethic of caring the more we can see a natural collaboration. What is more, the repeatedly documented correlation between child mal-treatment and the abuse and neglect of animals (Ascione 1993) warrants a synchronicity of effort. The fact is that professionals who uncover one sort of abuse in a household should be on special alert for the other. Thus, child protection investigators should be trained to be on the lookout for animal abuse—both as a condition bolstering their concern for the children and as a step in the direction of cost effectiveness by forwarding their observations to animal protection professionals. The reverse is true for animal protection officers as well, that is, using the occasion of investigating animal abuse as an opportunity to do an assessment of the quality of care for any children cohabiting with the animals in question. This sort of coordin-ation ought to be a matter of elementary human policy at the highest community and state levels. Rather than closing ourselves off to the suffering of beings beyond our professional or institutional mission, we should at the very least conceptualize a generic empathy for the victimized as part of our core missions.

Is a unitary approach to children and animals wise?

Despite the obvious need for a generic approach to protecting the vulnerable, we should consider the possible limits of this approach. Perhaps we can restate this question in the following way. Is it wise to have unbounded empathy? Certainly empathy is one of the foundations upon which to build morality in general, and a morality of child and animal protection in particular. *When we open ourselves to the feelings of abuse we create a prima facie case for protection.* Conceptual discussions of "aggression" or "punishment" may result in an abstract conclusion that children need discipline, that punishment is an accept-able strategy, and that under stress parents may engage in aggression. But look at a child who has been beaten or burned and the feelings create a powerful moral mandate. We reserve a special brand of judgment for those who inflict or profit from such violence to children.

But can we say the same of animals? Who can bear to look at a fox mutilated in a trap? Obviously the fox hunter can. Is he just an insensitive clod or a sadistic maniac? How is he different from the person who can tolerate or even enjoy being witness to or perpetrator of the suffering of an abused child? It is easy enough to see the similarities—unless you have known a hunter who cares for his children with gentleness and compassion.

Popular culture sometimes struggles with this issue. One recent example was to be found in the film *Powder*, in which a rather odd young man possesses the capacity for *imposing* empathy on others. At one point in the film he confronts a deer hunter by transmitting a wounded deer's feelings to the hunter. The hunter—regretfully and with reluctance to aban-don a way of life—disposes of his rifle collection and abandons hunting immediately. Who (other than a masochist who actually enjoys pain) could do otherwise? This, of course, is behind the oft repeated insight that if fish could scream there would be far fewer among us who would cast a baited hook into the water. I know that as I have expanded the boundaries of my own empathy there came a point where I could imagine the screaming of fish—and then ceased to be able to cast that baited hook.

Can we accommodate "human rights" and an "ethic of caring"?

In practice, this issue of unlimited empathy is not a matter of much concern in most situ-ations, most of the time. The more common problem, it would seem, is not too much empathy, but too little. Dealing with the most obvious cases of child and animal abuse and neglect already strains our response capacities to, and beyond, breaking point. Some of us, however, recognize that the foundation for *child* protection is *childhood* protection, because child maltreatment is at least in part a social indicator, that is, an indicator of deficiencies in the supportive quality of the social environment. Thus, by examining the values and policies that either support or undermine quality of care for children (childhood protection) we understand better the factors that generate the need for child protection among vulnerable families. This analysis leads to a focus on "social toxicity" in the community and the larger society (Garbarino 1995). Similarly, we can make progress in animal protection by focusing on the foundation for animal protection in the larger issue of the very concept of an ethic of caring for nonhuman life forms. This is where the animal rights movement intersects with animal protection.

Indeed, those of us who have worked with the most victimized among the human population (i.e., the most horribly abused who become perpetrators of heinous violence and end up in prison), see the loss of human dignity as the principal precipitator of "bestial" violence. I find this in my interviews with boys incarcerated for murder (Gabarino 1999). Psychiatrist James Gilligan (1996) worked with men in the Massachusetts prison system for a long period and from his experience learned that shame based upon denial of basic human rights is the engine that drives the violence machine. A rights-based culture is a culture that has a chance of establishing the reservoirs of self-worth and positive identity that promote high standards of care for children—and animals. An ethic of caring is the goal if we are to build the foundation for both child and animal welfare and protection.

[. . .]

We seek an expansion of caring, the progressive application of an ethic of caring that conveys respect within the terms available to us in our culture—both our local culture, and what the cultures of the larger world have to offer.

I believe we would do well to seek an ever-expanding ethic of caring, in part because dignity, respect, and caring knit together a social fabric that clothes all who are dependent upon the powerful. Desmond Morris (1967) observed, "The viciousness with which children are subjected to persecution is a measure of the weight of dominant pressures imposed on their persecutors." This seems true when we examine the socioeconomic and demographic correlates of child maltreatment.

But by the same token, the cruelty with which animals are treated seems a measure of the cultural foundations for cruelty in general. We know there is some empirical connection developmentally—cruelty to animals bears some correlation with subsequent cruelty to children (Ascione 1993). I hear it often in my interviews with boys who have committed acts of lethal violence.

In principle and in fact, when we say that someone is treating a child "like a dog" we tell a great deal about the person and the culture from which they come. Linking our animal protection efforts to a general ethic of caring for nonhuman life forms is, I think, a powerful strategy for elevating the quality of care for both animals and children.

Opening our eyes and hearts to the rights of animals to dignity and caring (even when we accept their use as instrumentalities under carefully controlled and evaluated conditions to meet the needs and improve the welfare of human beings) is one foundation for establishing the minimum standards of care for children. Animal protection and child welfare are natural partners.

References

Ascione, F. 1993. Children who are cruel to animals: A review of research and implications for developmental psychopathology. *Anthozoös* 6:226–47.

Donovan, J. 1990. Animal rights and feminist theory. *Signs: Journal of Women in Culture and Society* 12:350–75.

Garbarino, J. 1999. *Lost boys: Why our sons turn violent and how we can save them.* New York: The Free Press.

——— 1995. *Raising children in a socially toxic environment.* San Francisco: Jossey, Bass.

Gilligan, C. 1982. *In a different voice.* Cambridge, Mass.: Harvard University Press.

Gilligan, J. 1996. *Violence.* New York: G. P. Putnam.

Morris, D. 1967. *The naked ape.* New York: McGraw-Hill.

77

James Serpell, Raymond Coppinger, and Aubrey H. Fine

"The Welfare of Assistance and Therapy Animals: An Ethical Comment"

James Serpell, Raymond Coppinger, and Aubrey Fine identify the situations in which animals used to assist persons with disabilities or as therapeutic aides may themselves be harmed. Dogs can be harmed when they are kept too long in kennels or subjected to a succession of handlers. Capuchin monkeys may be harmed by the invasive measures needed to render them safe for people with serious disabilities. The authors also note that the assistance dog industry often fails to breed "in" desirable characteristics and that aversive conditioning is used for many assistance dogs.

Introduction

Ethical questions about the use of animals as therapeutic aides or for assisting persons with disabilities arise out of a tension between interests. Throughout history, people have used animals—whether for food, fiber, sport, adornment, labor, or companionship—as a means of satisfying human interests. But animals also have interests—in avoiding pain, fear, distress, or physical harm, and in pursuing their own needs, desires, and goals through the perform- ance of species-typical patterns of behavior. Relations between people and animals only become morally problematical where there is a conflict of interests between the two: where the human use either causes pain, fear, or harm to an animal, or it in some way thwarts or prevents the animal from satisfying its own needs and goals.

During the last 10 years, purveyors and proponents of animal-assisted activities and therapy (AAA/T) such as the Delta Society have made concerted efforts to professionalize the "industry," and establish selection and training standards that aim to minimize the risks of harm to all concerned, including the animals (Hines and Fredrickson, 1998). However, AAA/ T has experienced explosive growth within the last decade, and in many cases these stand- ards have been set in the absence of any systematic or empirical evaluation of the potential risks to animals imposed by current practices. Indeed, there is a general but unsubstantiated feeling across the industry that these are "good" activities for animals to be engaged in. The fact that a large number of animals fail to respond to the nurturing and training they receive has not generally been taken as evidence that they do not want to, or are unable to, partici- pate. Instead, practitioners tend to respond to failure by changing the selection or the train- ing procedures, as if the animals are theoretically capable of responding positively to any demands made of them.

[. . .]

[I]n this chapter [. . .] our goal is to reexamine the animal–human partnership from the animal's viewpoint to see what the benefits might be for the animal, or to see if the raising, training, and deployment of assistance and therapy animals is causing significant degradation in their welfare.[1] In doing so, however, we recognize that there is a shortage of reliable scientific evidence to reinforce some of our claims. Additionally, the authors want to make an impression for clinicians to examine their ethical responsibility for the welfare of their therapeutic adjuncts. Clinicians must respect the integrity of the animals and recognize that their involvement must be carefully monitored, so that their rights and safety are safeguarded.

The information that follows pertains more to the authors' concerns about the rearing, training, and expected responsibilities of service animals. [T]he term *service animal* is defined in the U.S. civil rights law (Americans with Disabilities Act of 1990), as "any animal individually trained to do work or perform tasks for the benefit of a person with a disability." However, some of the issues covered in this discussion have direct relevance to animals incorporated in AAA/T. When appropriate, the authors will also highlight their specific concerns for clinicians' considerations.

Possible sources of animal welfare problems with service animals and those incorporated in AAA/T

Failure to provide for animals' behavioral and social needs

In addition to having physical requirements for food, water, protection from the elements, etc., most animals have social and behavioral needs that should be provided for whenever possible (Dawkins, 1988). An understanding of these social and behavioral needs by primary caregivers is part of the ethical obligation attending animal ownership and use. Different species tend to have different social and behavioral needs (Mason and Mendl, 1993). Judging the value of a particular behavior or social interaction to an animal may sometimes be difficult. However, in general, if an animal is strongly internally motivated to perform a particular behavior or social interaction, and if its motivation to perform appears to increase following a period of deprivation, it is an indication that the activity or interaction is probably important to the maintenance of that animal's welfare. Common indications of deprivation include animals performing abnormally high frequencies of displacement activities, stereotypies, or self-mutilation (Broom and Johnson, 1993).

All animals need to be safe from any abuse and danger from any client at all times. The animal must be able to find a safe refuge within the working environment to go to if he or she feels exhausted or stressed. Throughout the day, the animal utilized in AAA/T needs to have a break from actual patient contact. Therapy and service animals must be free from pain, injury, or disease. All animals should be kept up to date on their inoculations. If the animal seems ill, stressed, or exhausted, medical attention must be given.

For assistance and therapy animals, welfare problems are most likely to arise in circumstances where animals are either residential within health care settings or spend large amounts of time in holding facilities such as kennels or stables. In the former context, inadequate advance planning, selection, and staff commitment and oversight can lead to animals being improperly cared for (Hines and Fredrickson, 1998). Small mammals, birds, and reptiles that are caged or confined are probably at greater risk of neglect or improper care, and nondomestic species that tend to have more specialized requirements than domestic ones are also likely to be at risk. "Improperly cared for" in these contexts should have the broadest definition. Most often it is defined as animals that are inadequately fed, watered, or cleaned. However, any failure to attend to individual needs should be regarded as improper care. Overfeeding animals to the point of obesity is just as negligent as underfeeding. Giving an animal the opportunity to exercise is not enough without ensuring that the individual takes advantage of the opportunity.

With regard to AAA/T, an additional challenge may arise when an animal begins to age. Naturally, the animal's schedule for therapeutic involvement will have to be curtailed. This may cause some disruption and adjustment to both the clinician as well as the animal. [. . .]

Welfare problems may be particularly severe where animals, such as dogs, have been reared in the enriched environment of a human foster home and then kenneled individually for months as part of their final training (Hubrecht, 1995). Such an abrupt change in social and physical environment appears to be highly stressful for some animals (Coppinger and Zuccotti, 1999) and may not only affect their immediate welfare, but also has the potential to foster obnoxious behaviors that might preclude successful training and placement.

Assistance animals may also be at risk because of the changing nature of their relationships with successive human owners and handlers throughout their lives. Most of these animals are picked because they are innately social—that is, they are internally motivated to seek social interactions with others—and because they form strong bonds of attachment for their human partners. Having to endure a whole succession of different handlers with different characteristics, experience, and motivations for "ownership" is likely to be particularly stressful for these individuals.

[. . .]

Selecting or breeding animals for assistance

Most domestic animals have been selected to show a higher degree of tolerance of stressful situations and stimuli compared with nondomestic species, even those reared entirely in captivity (Hemmer, 1990). Nondomestic species are also harder to train, and their entrained responses extinguish more quickly in the absence of appropriate reinforcement. Some species, such as many nonhuman primates, are also highly intelligent and socially manipulative (Cheney and Seyfarth, 1990), and this tends to make them potentially unreliable or unsafe as social companions for people. All of these factors make nondomestic species less suitable for use in AAA/T programs, and more likely to experience welfare problems if used.

This point is well illustrated by recent efforts to train and use capuchin monkeys to assist people with serious disabilities. In most cases, these programs have found it necessary to neuter and surgically extract the canine teeth from the monkeys before they can be used safely with such vulnerable human partners. Monkeys may also be required to wear remotely controlled, electric shock-collars or harnesses in order to provide the user with a means of controlling the animal's potentially aggressive and unreliable behavior. Clearly, the necessity of using of such extreme and invasive measures raises doubts about the practical value of such programs, as well as serious ethical questions concerning the welfare of the animals involved.

[. . .]

Some service dogs, such as the hearing ear dogs, are almost exclusively obtained from shelters. [. . .] In-house breeding programs are favored by guide dog and wheelchair dog organizations. [. . .] The history of dog breeding until modern times has been to create superior working animals through hybridization. [. . .] In the nineteenth century, a shift toward prezygotic selection began that has intensified ever since. The assumption behind this process is that excellence of form and behavior can be purified and preserved within a breed. Although such breeding practices do tend to produce uniformity of appearance and behavior within breeds, in the absence of periodic outcrossing, they also promote inbreeding depression, and the expression of various recessively inherited "genetic" diseases.

Unfortunately, the assistance dog industry has been slow to recognize these dangers. [. . .] Each generation gets more inbred because of the shrinking genetic variation, creating highly homozygous strains. In theory, dogs generated in these systems are more vulnerable to infectious disease, as well as being more likely to show phenotypic expression of deleterious mutant alleles.

[. . .]

There is another ethical issue buried within this production system. Creating large numbers of animals year after year with hip dysplasia or retinal atrophy is ethically questionable in itself, but ethical questions also attend the disposal of animals diagnosed with disease and dropped from assistance programs. Should these animals be euthanized or should they be put up for adoption? Overall, these kinds of issues raise certain doubts about the wisdom of maintaining purebred strains of dogs for assistance work.

Failure to take account of developmental events and processes

It is well established from research on canid development that early experiences have more profound and longer lasting effects on behavior than those occurring at later stages of the life cycle (Serpell and Jagoe, 1995).

[. . .]

Now consider where most service puppies spend the first 8 weeks of their lives: in a sterilized kennel being protected from any environmental insult that might challenge their little immune systems. The kennel is the equivalent of an orphanage.

[. . .]

These dogs are growing up on a fabricated diet, in a contrived and impoverished environment in which the handlers' motivations are primarily to do with health care and cost effectiveness. As a system, it pays practically no attention to neurologic and cognitive development. And yet the behavioral result of what happens to a pup during this period is largely permanent. Once the brain connections are made, there is no changing them. How and what a pup can learn is virtually fixed by 1 year of age.

[. . .]

Using inappropriate or inhumane training methods

[. . .]

[T]he reason dogs have been so successful as companions is that they are prepared to work for the reward of social interaction with people. Second, because particular dog breeds innately "like" to search for game, or like to herd sheep, it is not essential to reward such performance. Working dog specialists generally consider it impossible to train an animal that does not show the internal motivation to perform the specific task. Most sporting or trad-itional working dogs, such as sheep dogs or sled dogs, are not aversively conditioned nor are they given food rewards for proper performance.

[. . .]

In contrast, aversive conditioning is the primary method of instruction for many assist-ance dogs. It may be the only method that is practical because many assistance dog tasks are not discrete, nor is the significance of the task understood by the dog.

[. . .]

The attitude of many assistance dogs in public seems to reflect the aversive training techniques, and the internal confusion as to what is expected (Coppinger, personal observa-tions). This is probably more true of wheelchair than guide dogs. The high failure rate in AAA/T animals may in part be due to inappropriate training procedures. There has recently been some interest in "click and treat" methods using a variation of Pavlovian conditioning. This is a useful approach for "civilizing" assistance dogs and works reasonably well on hearing ear and therapy dogs. As yet it has not been demonstrated to work as a viable system for wheelchair or guide dogs. It may be that there is in fact no appropriate or humane training technique for dogs of this type, which might lead one to the ethical conclusion that animals shouldn't be asked to perform such tasks.

Use of badly designed equipment and facilities

By analyzing the "physics" of some of the tasks that service dogs are asked to perform, Coppinger *et al.* (1998) have recently drawn attention to inherent design flaws in some of the equipment used by persons with disabilities that may result in discomfort or injury to the dogs. Harnesses, for example, suggested that the designers did not understand the basic principles of harness design. Some had pulling webs which crossed moving parts, thus chafing the dog badly as it moved. Trying to get a dog to pull a wheelchair that is designed to be pushed forces the dog into awkward positions, increasing the difficulty of the task. Some of the tasks, such as pulling a wheelchair or pulling open a door with the teeth, reach the limits of what a dog is physically able to perform.

[. . .]

End-user problems

Although there have been no systematic studies of the problem, anecdotal observations suggest that some assistance dog users are insufficiently experienced with handling or training dogs. [. . .] Some agencies provide refresher courses for their clients with disabilities, or can send a trainer to the person's home to correct special problems. However, greater continuing education efforts by agencies would certainly help to ensure improved quality of life for animals used in this way.

[. . .]

Conclusions and recommendations

The concept of using trained and socialized animals to assist people with disabilities, or as therapeutic adjuncts, has great intrinsic appeal, exemplifying as it does for many people the ultimate in mutually beneficial animal–human partnerships. Nevertheless, while the advantages to the humans in these relationships may be obvious, the benefits to the animals are by no means always self-evident. Indeed, the use of animals for animal-assisted activities and therapy imposes a unique set of stresses and strains on them that the "industry" is only just beginning to acknowledge.

[. . .]

Note

1   The concept of welfare or "poor" welfare has been variously defined by animal welfare scientists. Some definitions stress the presence of unpleasant mental or emotional states such as pain, fear, frustration or suffering (Dawkins, 1980); some place the emphasis on impairments to an animal's biological fitness (McGlone, 1993; Broom and Johnson, 1993), while others refer to the extent to which environmental stresses and strains exceed the animal's ability to cope or adapt (Fraser and Broom, 1990). Rather than lend support to any one of these competing definitions, we will consider welfare as comprising elements of all of them.

References

Broom, D. M., and Johson, K. (1993). *Stress and animal welfare.* London: Chapman & Hall.
Cheney, D. L., and Seyfarth, R. M. (1990). *How monkeys see the world.* Chicago: Chicago University Press.
Coppinger, R., and Zuccotti, J. (1999). Kennel enrichment: Exercise and socialization of dogs. *Journal of Applied Animal Welfare Science.*
Coppinger, R., Coppinger, L., and Skillings, E. (1998) Observations on assistance dog training and use. *Journal of Applied Animal Welfare Science*, 1, 133–44.
Dawkins, M. S. (1988). Behavioural deprivation: A central problem in animal welfare. *Applied Animal Behaviour Science*, 20, 209–25.
Hemmer, H. (1990). *Domestication: The decline of environmental appreciation* (trans. Neil Beckhaus). Cambridge, UK: Cambridge University Press.
Hines, L., and Fredrickson, M. (1998). Perspectives on animal-assisted activities and therapy. In C. C. Wilson and D. C. Turner (eds), *Companion animals in human health* (pp. 23–39). Thousand Oaks, CA: Sage Publications.
Hubrecht, R. (1995). The welfare of dogs in human care. In J. A. Serpell (ed.), *The domestic dog: Its evolution, behaviour, and interactions with people* (pp. 179–95). Cambridge, UK: Cambridge University Press.
Mason, G., and Mendl, M. (1993). Why is there no simple way of measuring animal welfare? *Animal Welfare*, 2, 301–20.
McGlone, J. (1993). What is animal welfare? *Journal of Agricultural and Environmental Ethics*, 6 (Supplement 2), 28.
Serpell, J., and Jagoe, J. A. (1995). Early experience and the development of behaviour. In J. A. Serpell (ed.), *The domestic dog its evolution, behaviour, and interactions with people* (pp. 80–102). Cambridge, UK: Cambridge University Press.

78

Stephen W. Brown and Val Strong
"The Use of Seizure-Alert Dogs"

Stephen Brown and Val Strong report their experience of training dogs to assist people with epilepsy by providing warning of impending seizures. They have found no harm to the dogs and report that often the use of a seizure-alert dog resulted in reducing the frequency of seizures.

Hazards of untrained dogs

[. . .]

We have a number of anecdotal reports of dogs exhibiting particular behaviours during or after human seizures, and this behaviour is also reported in dogs that spontaneously anticipate human seizures[1]. These behaviours include attacking the person with epilepsy, helpers or passers-by. In some cases this may generalize so that the dog exhibits aggression to other similar humans, e.g. children. The general reaction seems to include elements of flight, fright, 'freezing', or appeasement. One dog choked on a lead with a flight reaction. It is not known how common this particular problem is. Of people with seizure disorders self-referring to the charity Support Dogs, only eight already had pet dogs. However, all eight had problems of the sort described above. We currently know of another 28 cases. It is not known how common this problem is, but if it is widespread, serious issues arise about the suitability of untrained pet dogs for people with epilepsy. We hope to complete a population-based study in the next two years to gain a clearer picture.

Can dogs be trained properly?

Questions arise as to whether pet dogs can be trained not to exhibit such deleterious behaviour, and furthermore whether they could be trained to produce alternative, helpful behaviours. Our experience is clearly that the answer to both questions is 'yes'.

Our *Seizure-Alert Dogs* are specially chosen for this work, and are not dogs that are already pets of people with epilepsy. They are socialized by working closely with a trainer and the person with epilepsy simultaneously. Their response to human seizures is modified by the use of an intensive reward-based operant conditioning regime. This starts in a specially controlled and monitored residential setting, and is later generalized to everyday life. So far 20 dogs have been trained, of which six have been reported previously.[2]

A trained dog can anticipate a seizure in a significant human, and provide a warning to the person 15–45 minutes beforehand, even if the human has no other warning. The dog is not stressed by the event if properly trained.

An unexpected finding in our early work was that with continued use of a seizure-alert dog, the person's seizure frequency was often reported to show an improvement.

Some frequently asked questions

Do dogs cause seizures in these cases?

The observation that human seizures may be preceded by a stereotyped canine behaviour raises a question about cause and effect. However, we feel that if dogs were causing seizures by raising an expectation in the humans, it would be very unlikely that seizure rates would reduce, although that is what was reported. Indeed it might be expected that seizures would increase in frequency in at least some instances, but no such case has been observed.

Are dogs harmed or stressed?

As far as we can tell from our work so far, properly trained seizure-alert dogs do not suffer any adverse health consequences from human seizures. We would suggest that this is because the operant conditioning programme involves associating a positive reward for the dog with a human seizure. Because our dogs are trained alongside the humans and have no previous experience of human seizures, their only association is a positive one. This is obviously an important issue, and we hope to address it in more detail in the future.

[. . .]

What is it that the dogs are detecting?

Our opinion, based on observation, and bearing in mind the training method that has been developed, is that the dogs detect subtle changes in the behaviour of the human subject that characteristically precede a clinical seizure.

Future plans

We are just completing a more detailed $n = 10$ study which will be reported in due course. This will provide more detail than our previously published preliminary report, which was based on earlier work. We are about to commence a new and much more comprehensive $n = 30$ study. This will include measurement of physiological responses in the dogs, as well as ambulatory EEG monitoring of a sample of the human subjects to confirm diagnosis. It will also incorporate measures of seizure frequency and severity, together with appropriate quality-of-life measures. Because of the potential adverse effects of human seizures on untrained dogs, we do not feel it is appropriate to include a control group of this type. Apart from this, we feel that we have set a higher standard for diagnosis and follow-through than in many antiepileptic drug trials.

Further opportunities

Recent changes in the UK quarantine law, and the introduction of animal passports, provide an opportunity for the work of support dogs to be extended beyond the United Kingdom. This would allow a standardized approach to training and would help to avoid hazards of untrained or inappropriately trained dogs.

A word from a customer . . .

One of our clients, whose trained support dog is called Rupert, said, '*Before I had Rupert, I had a lot of epilepsy and a little bit of life. With Rupert I now have a lot of life with a little bit of epilepsy!*'

Notes

1   Strong, V. and Brown, S. W. Should people with Epilepsy have untrained dogs as pets? *Seizure* 2000; 9(6): 427–30.
2   Strong, V., Brown, S. W. and Walker, R. Seizure-alert dogs – fact or fiction? *Seizure* 1999; 8: 62–5.

Annotated Further Reading

Allen, K. and Blascovich, J. (1996) "The Value of Service Dogs for People with Severe Ambulatory Disabilities: A Randomized Controlled Trial." *Journal of the American Medical Association* 275.13: 1001–7. All participants showed substantial improvement in psychological well-being and in number of assistance hours required.

Beck, A. and Katcher, A. (1996) *Between Pets and People*, West Lafayette, Ind.: Purdue University Press. Somewhat outdated but many useful ideas.

Beirne, P. (2000) "Rethinking Bestiality: Towards a Concept of Interspecies Sexual Assault." In A.L. Poderberscek, E.S. Paul, and J.A. Serpell (eds) *Companion Animals and Us: exploring the relationships between people and pets*, Cambridge: Cambridge University Press. As in the cases of abuse of infants and women, bestiality involves coercion, pain, or death.

Burgess-Jackson, K. (1998) "Doing Right by our Animal Companions." *The Journal of Ethics* 2: 159–85. Taking an animal into one's home generates duties.

Dresser, N. (2000) "The Horse *Bar Mitzvah*: a Celebratory Exploration of the Human–Animal Bond." In A.L. Podberscek, E.S. Paul, and J.A. Serpell (eds) *Companion Animals and Us*, Cambridge: Cambridge University Press. A wonderful essay discussing the inclusion of animals in religious and secular ceremonies.

Fine, A. (ed.) (2000) *Handbook on Animal-Assisted Therapy: theoretical foundations and guidelines for practice*, San Diego: Academic Press. Comprehensive.

Fleming, W.M., Jory, B. and Burton, D.L. (2002) "Characteristics of Juvenile Offenders Admitting to Sexual Activity with Nonhuman Animals." *Society and Animals* 10.1: 31–45.

Garrity, T.F. and Stallones, L. (1998) "Effects of Pet Contact on Human Well-Being." In C.C. Wilson and D.C. Turner (eds) *Companion Animals in Human Health*, London: Sage. A review of 25 studies between 1990 and 1995. The quality of life benefits are evident but only in certain situations.

Green, G.S. (2002) "The Other Criminalities of Animal Freeze-Killers: Support for a Generality of Deviance." *Society and Animals* 10.1: 5–30. Research on correlations between animal abuse and other criminal behavior.

Hien, E.D. and Bertrand, L. (1997) "Influence of Capuchin Monkey Companion on the Social Life of a Person with Quadriplegia: An Experimental Study." *Anthrozoös* 10.2–3: 101–7. The capuchin companion greatly improved the social environment of a person with quadriplegia.

Kellert, S.R. (1997) "Yearning for Kinship and Affection." In *Kinship to Mastery: biophilia in human evolution and development*, Washington, D.C.: Island Press. Includes several brief case studies.

Melson, G.F. (1998) "The Role of Companion Animals in Human Development." In C.C. Wilson and D.C. Turner (eds) *Companion Animals in Human Health*, London: Sage. Companion animals have positive effects on child development.

Podberscek, P. and Serpell, J. *Companion Animals and Us: exploring the relationships between people and pets*, Cambridge: Cambridge University Press. An excellent collection based on a 1996 conference, mainly for social scientists.

Schuppli, C.A. and Fraser, D. (2000) "A Framework for Assessing the Suitability of Different Species as Companion Animals." *Animal Welfare* 9: 359–72. Assessment to be used by pet retailers, animal adoption workers and potential owners.

Slater, M.R. (2002) *Community Approaches to Feral Cats*, Washington, D.C.: Humane Society Press. Well-written, comprehensive resource.

Sheldrake, R. (1999) *Dogs That Know When Their Owners are Coming Home and Other Unexplained Powers of Animals*, New York: Crown. Includes studies of animal empathy, telepathy and premonitions. Sheldrake invites the public to join in his research.

Study Questions

1   Konrad Lorenz, Bernard Rollin, and Michael Rollin maintain that "having" an animal companion involves serious moral responsibilities. What responsibilities do you believe should be associated with having an animal companion?

2   Do you agree with Paul Shepard that pets cannot connect us to the natural world? Explain why or why not.

3   How does Anna Merz's experience with a wild rhino affect your view of the intelligence or emotional capacity of wild animals?

4   Is Freya Mathews' description of the psychological intimacy she has experienced with animals supported by your own experience of animals? Explain any similarities or differences.

5   Do you believe that we should keep animals as companions? Explain the possible benefits and disadvantages to such animals, as well as to humans.

6   If you live in an urban setting, what are some interactions you have had with wild or feral animals? What recommendations might you suggest for changing urban habitat for the benefit of animals?

7   James Garbarino notes that people often have assumed that concern for animals means less concern for people. To what extent do you believe this is true?

8   Reflect on your experience of observing (or using) animals for assistance and therapy. Have you observed stress or suffering? What suggestions do you have to improve the welfare of animals performing these services?

9   Seizure-alert dogs are of definite assistance to persons suffering from epilepsy, according to Stephen Brown and Val Strong. Are there other medical conditions for which dogs or other species might be able to aid human beings?

PART X

Animal Law/Animal Activism

Introduction

Should animals have legal rights? How can the situation of animals be improved? Is civil disobedience morally justified? The authors in this Part present widely diverging answers to these questions. In "A Great Shout," attorney Steven Wise notes that we have assigned ourselves the exalted status of legal persons and consider every other animal as merely legal things which can be owned. Wise argues for fundamental legal rights for the great apes based on their possession of autonomy.

In a book review of Wise's book *Rattling the Cage*, Richard Posner critiques Wise's analysis. He points out that Wise does not show that having cognitive capacity is a necessary or sufficient condition of having legal rights. Wise downplays the fact that such legal rights would be a drastic departure from existing law. Posner argues that making wild animals property is the best way to increase animal protection, given that "aggressive implementations" of animal-rights thinking are not likely to prevail.

In "The Dangerous Claims of the Animal Rights Movement," Richard Epstein points out a number of important differences between human beings and animals which support the view that human welfare is more important than animal welfare. He maintains that treating animals as the moral and legal peers of human beings would undermine the liberty and dignity of human beings. It is appropriate that animals remain our property.

In "Every Sparrow that Falls," Wesley Jamison, Caspar Wenk, and James Parker analyze animal rights activism as a movement which functions like a religion, based on their research in Switzerland and the United States. They identify five components of animal rights activism which fulfill the definition of "functional religion" stated by the U.S. Supreme Court.

The four essays which conclude the Part discuss strategies by which to improve the condition of animals. In "Understanding Animal Rights Violence" Tom Regan explores the split between "immediatists" and "gradualists." The diversity of views within the animal rights movement means that it is accurately characterized neither as nonviolent nor as terrorist. Regan proposes incremental abolitionist change, in which one use of animals at a time is completely stopped.

Courtney Dillard examines the effectiveness of two organized protests and acts of civil disobedience against the largest pigeon shoot in the United States. Her findings suggest that the effectiveness of civil disobedience is increased when it is enacted in nonviolent and non-threatening ways and when participants demonstrate both a willingness to suffer for their beliefs and an interest in communicating that suffering to onlookers.

Chris DeRose describes his activism on behalf of animals in an excerpt from *In Your Face*. His willingness to be arrested and go to jail when he has broken trespassing laws is part of the process of civil disobedience. He maintains that animal slavery has to be abolished because it is wrong.

In "Ten Ways to Make a Difference," Peter Singer draws on the work of Henry Spira, an activist who has had remarkable successes in reducing animal suffering. He presents Spira's life as an example of finding meaning by living in accord with one's own values. The ten suggestions are the result of Spira's experience in changing public opinion.

79

Steven M. Wise

"A Great Shout: Legal Rights for Great Apes"

Steven Wise argues that legal rules that may have made good sense in the past may make good sense no longer. As the scientific evidence of the capacities of nonhuman animals such as the great apes continues to mount, it is apparent that treating animals as things is unjust. Wise argues on both legal and philosophical grounds that the "practical autonomy" exhibited by many animals is sufficient to justify the attribution of basic legal rights.

The earliest known law is preserved in cuneiform on Sumerian clay tablets. These Mesopotamian law codes, 4,000 years old, the Laws of Ur-Nammu, the Lipit-Ishtar Lawcode, the Laws of Eshunna, and the Laws of Hammurabi, assumed that humans could own both nonhuman animals and slaves (Wise 1996). It took most of the next 4,000 years for subjective legal rights to develop. Even in Republican and Imperial Rome, legal rights were understood to exist only in the objective sense of being "the right thing to do" (Wise 1996, 799). Subjective legal rights, claims that one person could make on another, first glimmered in twelfth-century writings. It was only in the fourteenth century that the notion that one's legal rights were one's property began to root (Wise 1996).

Not until the nineteenth century was slavery abolished in the West and every human formally cloaked with the legal personhood that signifies eligibility for fundamental legal rights. So the final brick of a great legal wall, begun millennia ago, was cemented into place. Today, on one side of this legal wall reside all the natural legal persons, all the members of a single species, *Homo sapiens*. We have assigned ourselves, alone among the millions of animal species, the exalted status of legal persons, entitled to all the rights, privileges, powers, and immunities of "legal personhood" (Wise 1996).

On the other side of this wall lies every other animal. They are not legal persons but legal things. During the American Civil War, President Abraham Lincoln was said to have spurned South Carolina's peace commissioners with the statement, "As President, I have no eyes but Constitutional eyes; I cannot see you" (*Oxford Dictionary of Quotations* 1979, 313). In this way, their "legal thinghood" makes nonhuman animals invisible to the civil law. Civil judges have no eyes for anyone but legal persons.

[. . .]

The legal thinghood of nonhuman animals has a unique history. An understanding of this history is instrumental to what Oliver Wendell Holmes Jr. called the "deliberate reconsideration" to which every legal rule must eventually fall subject (Holmes 1897). Alan

Watson has concluded from his studies of comparative law that "to a truly astounding degree the law is rooted in the past" (Watson 1993, 95). The most common sources from which we quarry our law are the legal rules of earlier times. But when we borrow past law, we borrow the past. Legal rules that may have made good sense when they were fashioned may make good sense no longer. Raised by age to the status of self-evident truths they may perpetuate ancient ignorance, ancient prejudices, and ancient injustices that may once have been less unjust because we knew no better.

[. . .]

To think about it was to condemn it

The wall's foundations have rotted. Because its intellectual foundations are unprincipled and arbitrary, unfair and unjust, its greatest vulnerability, at least in the English-speaking countries, is to the unceasing tendency of the common law "to work itself pure," to borrow a phrase from Lord Mansfield, the great eighteenth-century English judge.[1] Once a great injustice is brought to their attention, common law judges have the duty to place the legal rules that are its source alongside those great overarching principles that have been integral to Western law and justice for hundreds of years—equality, liberty, fairness, and reasoned judicial decision making—to determine if, in light of what are believed to be true facts and modern values, those rules should be found wanting.

[. . .]

Recall that the abomination of human slavery was finally abolished in the West little more than 100 years ago. It continues in a few countries to this day. The first thinking about the justice of the legal thinghood of nonhuman animals occurred just as slavery was flickering in the West. To date it has resulted mostly in the enactment of pathetically inadequate anticruelty statutes. But as the scientific evidence of the true natures of such nonhuman animals as chimpanzees continues to mount, that thinking will be its undoing. Because to think about the legal thinghood of such creatures as the great apes will be finally to condemn such a notion.

This process has begun. Modern law has begun slowly to disassemble the radical incommensurability said to exist between all human and all nonhuman animals from both the top down and the bottom up. The intrinsic value of human beings is now seen in law as commensurable with other legal values. This was reflected, for example, in the enactment in the English-speaking countries of wrongful death statutes in the middle of the nineteenth century. These statutes were intended to alter the ancient, and unfair, common law rule that the loss of human life, understood to be incommensurable with anything else, could never be compensated by money (Wise 1998b). The lives of at least some nonhuman animals have begun to be infused with a degree of intrinsic and not merely instrumental value. The preamble to the United Nations World Charter for Nature states that "every form of life is unique, warranting respect regardless of its worth to man" (World Charter 1982, 992). Respected international law commentators have argued that the legal right of individual whales to life may be becoming a part of binding international law (D'Amato and Chopra 1991). While interpreting the federal Endangered Species Act, the U.S. Supreme Court was guided in its decision by the declaration of the American Congress that endangered species were of "incalculable value."[2]

[. . .]

Liberty: the supreme value of the Western world

Today liberty "stands unchallenged as the supreme value of the Western world" (Patterson 1991, ix). Out of the more than 200 recorded senses of "liberty," Sir Isaiah Berlin famously identified two central senses: negative and positive (Berlin 1969). One's negative liberty, with which we are concerned, is often described as "freedom from" and depends on being able to do what one wishes without human interference (Berlin 1998). On the other hand, one's positive liberty may be described as "freedom to" (Berlin 1969, lvi; McPherson 1990, 61).

[. . .]

I refer to these fundamental negative liberty rights as "dignity-rights." International and domestic courts and legislatures around the world recognize that for a human being to have a minimal opportunity to flourish, such dignity-rights as bodily integrity and bodily liberty must be protected by sturdy barriers of negative liberty rights that form a protective legal perimeter around our bodies and personalities (Berlin 1969; Dworkin 1977; Feinberg 1966).

Anglo-American common law recognizes a general negative liberty right. The constitutions of most modern nations protect fundamental negative liberty rights (Allan 1991).[3]

[. . .]

Fundamental rights derive from a practical autonomy

It is true, as the Kansas Supreme Court has said, that "Anglo American law starts with the premise of thorough-going self determination."[4] But what kind of autonomy is required? Philosophers often understand autonomy to mean what the German philosopher Immanuel Kant intended it to mean 200 years ago. We will call Kant's notion of autonomy "full autonomy." Though whole books have been written about what Kant meant, I will try to catch much of his core meaning in a single sentence: I have autonomy if, in determining what I ought to do in any situation, I have the ability to understand what others can and ought to do, I can rationally analyze whether it would be right for me to act in some way or another, keeping in mind that I should act only as I would want others to act and as they can act, and then I can do what I have decided is right. My ability to perform something like this calculus is what makes me autonomous, gives me dignity, and requires that I be treated as a person. If I cannot do this, I lack autonomy and dignity and can justly be treated as a thing, according to Kant.

Whether I have summarized Kant's idea perfectly or not is irrelevant. What is important is that anything that resembles this analysis demands an ability to reason at an almost inhumanly high level. Perhaps our Aristotles, Kants, Freuds, and Einsteins achieved it some of the time. But it is only a glimmering possibility for infants and children, most normal adults never reach it, and the severely mentally limited and the permanently vegetative do not even begin. How did Kant deal with them? Well, he did not, and his "deep silence" on the moral status of children and nonrational adults has not gone unnoticed (Herman 1993). Even Aristotle and company pass significant portions of their lives on automatic pilot or often act out of desire, and not reason, which is precisely how Kant argued nonhuman animals act (Herman 1993; Langer 1997). Were judges to demand full autonomy as a prerequisite for dignity, they would exclude most of us, themselves included, from eligibility for dignity-rights.

Beings may possess a much simpler ability that allows them to act to fulfill their intended purposes. They may have varying capacities for mental flexibility and responsiveness.

Autonomy can encompass a range of capacities for consciousness from the most simple awareness of one's present experience to a much broader and deeper self-awareness, self-reflection, and an awareness of the past, present, and future. The full autonomy of, say, Plato might be said to approximate the high end of full Kantian autonomy, whereas the consciousness of a typical preschooler might approximate the low end of a practical autonomy.

A full Kantian autonomy is too narrow a prerequisite for dignity-rights. Not all humans possess it to any degree. Most possess it only in varying degrees. No humans possess it all the time and no one expects them to. Many more humans, though still not anencephalic or even normal infants, the most severely retarded adults, or adults in persistent vegetative comas, possess a practical autonomy than possess full Kantian autonomy (Russell 1996; Wright 1993). A practical autonomy merely recognizes that a being has a somewhat "less than perfect ability to choose appropriate actions" (Cherniak 1985, 5). Any being capable of desires and beliefs has a practical autonomy if she can have beliefs and desires and is able to make "some, but not necessarily all of the sound inferences from the belief set that are apparently appropriate" (Cherniak 1985, 10; Rachels 1990; Regan 1983; Wright 1993). A practical autonomy, therefore, much more closely coincides with the way in which human beings are normally understood to be autonomous.

Perhaps most important for our purposes, fundamental common law and constitutional rights were not designed to protect only the fully autonomous. Courts are exquisitely sensitive to autonomy's practical sense.[5] Once some minimum capacity is attained, courts generally respect the choices made within exceedingly wide parameters, at least with respect to human adults. Practical autonomy acts as a trip wire for dignity-rights. This is because a choice emanating from even a flickering autonomy is more highly valued, regardless of whether the actions are rational, reasonable, or even inimical to one's own best interests, than is any specific choice.[6] That is why the judges of the California Court of Appeals said that "respect for the dignity and autonomy of the individual is a value universally celebrated in free societies. . . . Out of fidelity to that value defendant's choice must be honored even if he opts foolishly to go to hell in a handbasket."[7]

American courts routinely hold that incompetent human beings are entitled to the same dignity-rights as competent human beings. For example, the U.S. Supreme Court held that a man with an I.Q. below 10 and the mental capacity of an 18-month-old child had an inextinguishable liberty right to personal security.[8]

[. . .]

Now comes the exceedingly odd part: Even humans who have always lacked autonomy and self-determination are said to possess the requisite dignity for legal personhood.[9] "Can it be doubted," state the judges of high courts rhetorically, "that the value of human dignity extends to both (competent and incompetent humans)?"[10] Undoubting courts grant competent, incompetent, and never-competent humans the same common law dignity-rights and the rights to protect their powers to use them as well.[11] The result is that humans with minimal, or even no, capacity for autonomy and self-determination, even terminally ill infants who lack all cognition, possess not just protected dignity-rights but the right to use their power to enforce them.[12]

[. . .]

Courts recognize human dignity-rights in the complete absence of autonomy only by using an arbitrary legal fiction that controverts the empirical evidence that no such autonomy exists. Conversely, courts refuse to recognize dignity-rights of the great apes only by using a second arbitrary legal fiction in the teeth of empirical evidence that they possess it (Nino

1993; Rachels 1990). But legal fictions can only be justified when they harmonize with, or at least do not undermine, the overarching values and principles of a legal system. Thus the legal fiction that a human who actually lacks autonomy has it is benign, for at worst it extends legal rights to those who might not need them. At best it protects the bodily integrity of the most helpless humans alive. But the legal fiction that great apes are not autonomous when they actually are undermines every important principle and value of Western justice: liberty, equality, fairness, and reasoned judicial decision making. It is pernicious.

[. . .]

Equality: likes should be treated alike

Equality is the axiom of Western justice that likes be treated alike. [. . .] Equality's logical component requires that dissimilar treatment rests on some relevant and objectively ascertainable difference between a favored and disfavored class with respect to the harm to be avoided or the benefit to be promoted (Simons 1989).[12]

[. . .]

Equality's normative component means that no matter how perfect the relationship between ends and means may be, some means and some ends are unacceptable solely because they are arbitrary, irrelevant, invidious, or are otherwise normatively illegitimate.[13]

Together, the logical and normative elements of equality mean that only qualities that are objectively ascertainable and normatively acceptable should be compared. Actual and relevant likenesses that are examined in light of current knowledge and normative understandings that are not false, assumed, unproveable, or anachronistic assumptions or contain "fixed notions" about likeness should be the measure.[14] These are the teachings of the fundamental value of equality.

Closely related to equality rights are proportionality rights. Proportionality requires that unalikes be treated proportionately to their unalikeness (Simons 1989).

[. . .]

At least three independent equality or proportionality arguments support fundamental legal rights for the great apes (Wise 1998a). First, great apes who possess Kant's full autonomy should be entitled to dignity-rights *if* humans who possess full autonomy are entitled to them. To do otherwise would be to undermine the major principled arguments against racism and sexism.

Second, great apes who possess a practical autonomy should be entitled to dignity-rights in proportion to the degree to which they approach full Kantian autonomy *if* humans who possess a practical autonomy are entitled to dignity-rights in proportion to the degree to which *they* approach full Kantian autonomy. Thus if a human is entitled to fewer, narrower, or partial legal rights as their capabilities approach the quality Q, so should nonhuman animals whose capabilities also approach the quality Q.

Third, in perhaps the clearest argument for equality, great apes who possess either full Kantian autonomy or a practical autonomy should be entitled to the same fundamental rights to which humans who entirely lack autonomy are entitled. Placing the rightless legal thing, the bonobo Kanzi, beside an anencephalic 1-day-old human with the legal right to choose to consent or withhold consent to medical treatment highlights the legal aberration that is Kanzi's legal thinghood.

Probably the strongest argument that just being human is necessary for the possession of fundamental equality rights has been offered by Carl Cohen, who has argued that at least moral rights should be limited to all and only human beings. "The issue," said Cohen, "is one of kind" (Cohen 1986, 866). He acknowledged that some humans lack autonomy and the ability to make moral choices. However, because humans as a "kind" possess this ability, it should be imputed to all humans, regardless of their actual abilities. But Cohen's argument can succeed only if the species, *H. sapiens*, can nonarbitrarily be designated as the boundary of a relevant "kind." That is doubtful. Other classifications, some wider, such as animals, vertebrates, mammals, primates, and apes, and at least one narrower—normal adult humans—also contain every fully autonomous human.

As well as being logically flawed, Cohen's argument for group benefits is normatively flawed. It "assumes that we should determine how an individual is to be treated, not on the basis of *its* qualities but on the basis of *other* individuals' qualities" (Rachels 1990, 187). Rachels calls the opposing moral idea "moral individualism" and defines it to mean that "how an individual may be treated is to be determined, not by considering his group memberships, but by considering his own particular characteristics" (Rachels 1990, 173). It is individualism, and not group benefits, that is more consistent with the overarching principles and values of a liberal democracy and that has the firmer basis in present law.

[. . .]

Will we affirm or undermine our commitment to fundamental human rights?

The destruction of the legal thinghood even of the great apes, our closest cousins, will necessarily involve a long and difficult struggle. It is the nature of great change to stimulate great opposition. But the anachronistic legal thinghood of the great apes so contradicts outright the overarching principles of equality, liberty, fairness, and rationality in judicial decision making that it will eventually be denied only by those in whom a narrow self-interest predominates.

[. . .]

Notes

1   *Omichund v. Barker*, 1 Atk. 21, 33 (K.B. 1744).
2   *Tennessee Valley Authority v. Hill*, 437 U.S. 153, 188 (1978). The Endangered Species Act, 16 U.S.C. §§ 1531–43 (1973).
3   E.g., *Youngberg v. Romeo*, 457 U.S. 307, 317 (1982); *Bowers v. Devito*, 686 F.2d 616, 618 (7th Cir. 1982).
4   *Natanson v. Kline*, 350 P.2d 1093, 1104 (Kan. 1960). *See also Stamford Hospital v. Vega*, 674 A.2d 821, 831 (Conn. 1996).
5   E.g., *Rivers v. Katz*, 495 N.E.2d 337, 341, *reargument denied*, 498 N.E.2d 438 (N.Y. 1986); *Schmidt v. Schmidt*, 450 A.2d 421, 422–23 (Pa. Super. 1983) (a 26-year-old woman with Down's syndrome with the mental ability of a child between 4½ and 8 years can rationally decide whether to choose to visit a parent).
6   E.g., *Thornburgh v. American College of Obstetricians and Gynecologists*, 476 U.S. 747, 778 n.5 (Stevens, J., concurring); *Application of President & Directors of Georgetown College*, 331 F.2d 1010, 1017 (D.C. Cir. 1964); *State v. Wagner*, 752 P.2d 1136, 1178 (Ore. 1988).
7   *People v. Nauton*, 34 Cal. Rptr. 2d 861, 864 (Ct. App. 1994).
8   *Youngberg, supra* note 3, at 315–16.
9   E.g., *Gray v. Romeo*, 697 F. Supp. 580, 587 (D.R.I. 1987); *Conservatorship of Drabick*, 245 Cal. Rptr. 840, 855, *cert. denied sub nom., Drabick v. Drabick*, 488 U.S. 958 (1988); *Superintendent of*

Belchertown State School v. Saikewicz, 370 N.E.2d 417, 427, 428 (Mass. 1977); *Eichner v. Dillon*, 426 N.Y.S.2d 517, 542 (App. Div.), *modified* 52 N.Y.2d 363 (1980); *see Conservatorship of Valerie N.*, 707 P.2d 760, 776 (Cal. 1985), citing *Matter of Moe*, 432 N.E.2d 712, 720 (Mass. 1982).

10 *Matter of Guardianship of L.W.*, 482 N.W.2d 60, 69 (Wis. 1992), quoting *Eichner, supra* note 16, at 542. *See also Gray, supra* note 16, at 587; *Matter of Moe, supra* note 16, at 719; *Delio v. Westchester County Medical Center*, 516 N.Y.S.2d 677, 686 (N.Y. App. Div. 1987).

11 *E.g., Gray, supra* note 16, at 587; *Conservatorship of Drabick, supra* note 16, at 855; *Foody v. Manchester Memorial Hospital*, 482 A.2d 713, 718 (Conn. Sup. Ct. 1984); *Matter of Tavel*, 661 A.2d 1061, 1069 (Del. 1995); *Severns v. Wilmington Medical Center, Inc.*, 421 A.2d 1334, 1347 (Del. 1980); *John F. Kennedy Memorial Hospital v. Bludworth*, 452 So.2d 921, 921, 923, 924 (Fla. 1985); *In re Guardianship of Barry*, 445 So.2d 365, 370 (Fla. Dist. Ct. App. 1984); *DeGrella by and through Parrent v. Elston*, 858 S.W.2d, 698, 709 (Ky. 1993); *In re L.H.R.*, 321 S.E.2d 716, 722 (Ga. 1984); *Care and Protection of Beth*, 587 N.E.2d 1377, 1382 (Mass. 1992); *Matter of Conroy*, 486 A.2d 1209, 1229 (N.J. 1985); *In re Grady*, 426 A.2d. 474–75 (N.J. 1981); *In re Quinlan*, 355 A.2d 647, 664 (N.J.), *cert. denied sub nom., Garger v. New Jersey*, 429 U.S. 922 (1976); *Eichner, supra,* note 16, at 546; *Matter of Guardianship of Hamlin*, 689 P.2d 1372, 1376 (Wash. 1984); *In re Colyer*, 660 P.2d 738, 774 (Wash. 1983); *Matter of Guardianship of L.W., supra* note 17, at 67, 68.

12 *E.g., In re L.H.R., supra* note 18 (4-month-old in chronic vegetative state); *Care and Protection of Beth, supra* note 18 (10-month-old in irreversible coma); *Strunk v. Strunk*, 445 S.W.2d 145 (Ky. 1969) (27-year-old with an I.Q. of 35 and a mental age of 6 years); *In re Grady, supra* note 18; *In re Penny N.*, 414 A.2d 541 (N.H. 1980); *Saikewicz, supra* note 16 (67-year-old with an I.Q of 10 and a mental age of 31 months); *Matter of Guardianship of L.W., supra* note 18, at 68; *In re Guardianship of Barry, supra* note 18 (anencephalic 10-month-old with no cognitive brain function).

13 *E.g., Logan v. Zimmerman Brush Co.*, 455 U.S. 422, 442 (1982) (plurality opinion); *Rinaldi v. Yeager*, 384 U.S. 305, 308–309 (1966); *McLaughlin v. Florida*, 379 U.S. 184, 191 (1964).

14 *E.g., Romer v. Evans*, 116 S. Ct. 1620, 1627–29 (1996); *Skinner, supra* note 34. *See Thoreson v. Penthouse International, Ltd.*, 563 N.Y.S.2d 968, 975 (Sup. Ct. 1990).

15 *E.g., United States v. Virginia*, 116 S. Ct. 2264, 2277–78 (1996), quoting *Mississippi University for Women v. Hogan*, 458 U.S. 718, 725 (1985); *Craig v. Boren*, 429 U.S. 190, 197 (1976). *See Romer, supra* note 35, at 1628.

References

Berlin, I. 1969. Two concepts of liberty. In *Four essays on liberty* (pp. 117–72). Oxford: Oxford University Press.
——. 1998. My intellectual path. *New York Review of Books*, May 14, pp. 53–60.
Cherniak, C. 1985. *Minimal rationality*. Cambridge: MIT Press.
Cohen, C. 1986. The case for the use of animals in biomedical research. *New England Journal of Medicine* 317: 867–70.
D'Amato, A., and Chopra, S. K. 1991. Whales: Their emerging right to life. *American Journal of International Law* 85: 21–62.
Dworkin, R. 1977. *Taking rights seriously*. Cambridge, MA: Harvard University Press.
Feinberg, J. 1966. Duties, rights, and claims. *American Philosophy Quarterly* 3: 37.
Herman, B. 1993. *The practice of moral judgment*. Cambridge, MA: Harvard University Press.
Holmes, O. W., Jr. 1897. The path of the law. *Harvard Law Review* 10: 457–78.
Langer, E. 1997. *The power of mindful learning*. Reading, MA: Addison-Wesley.
McPherson, J. M. 1990. *Abraham Lincoln and the second American revolution*. Oxford: Oxford University Press.
Nino, C. S. 1993. *The ethics of human rights*. Oxford: Oxford University Press.
Oxford Dictionary of Quotations. 1979. (3rd ed.). Oxford: Oxford University Press.
Patterson, O. 1991. *Freedom: Freedom in the making of Western culture*. New York: Basic Books.
Rachels, J. 1990. *Created from animals*. Oxford: Oxford University Press.
Regan, T. 1983. *The case for animal rights*. Berkeley: University of California Press.
Russell, J. 1996. *Agency—Its role in mental development*. Hove, UK: Erlbaum.
Simons, K. W. 1989. Overinclusion and underinclusion: A new model. *UCLA Law Review* 36: 447–89.
Watson, A. 1993. *Legal transplants—an approach to comparative law*. Athens: University of Georgia Press.
Wise, S. M. 1996. The legal thinghood of nonhuman animals. *Boston College Environmental Affairs Law Review* 23(3): 471–546.
——. 1998a. Hardly a revolution—The eligibility of nonhuman animals for dignity-rights in a liberal democracy. *Vermont Law Review* 22: 793–915.

Wise, S. M. 1998b. Recovery of common law damages for emotional distress, loss of society, and loss of companionship for the wrongful death of a companion animal. *Animal Law* 4: 33.

World Charter for Nature. 1982. GA Res. 37/7 Annex UNGAOR, 37th Sess. Suppl. No. 51, UNDO A/37151 (Oct. 28) (preamble). In H. W. Wood, Jr., The United Nations World Charter for Nature: The developing nations' initiative to establish protections for the environment. *Ecology* 12: 977–92.

Wright, W. A. 1993. Treating animals as ends. *Journal of Value Inquiry* 27: 353–66.

80

Richard A. Posner

"Book Review: *Rattling the Cage: Toward Legal Rights for Animals*" by Steven M. Wise

Richard Posner responds to Wise's arguments by pointing out that Wise has not shown that having cognitive capacity is necessary or sufficient for having legal rights. In Posner's view, Wise is not urging judges to develop doctrines already implicit in legal tradition, but rather to "set sail on an uncharted sea without a compass." Posner recommends instead that we build on the liberating potential of legal property, because people tend to protect what they own, and that we extend and more vigorously enforce laws designed to prevent cruelty to animals.

Rattling the Cage: Toward Legal Rights for Animals. By Steven M. Wise. Cambridge, Mass.: Perseus Books, 2000.

The "animal rights" movement is gathering steam, and Steven Wise is one of the pistons. A lawyer whose practice is the protection of animals, he has now written a book in which he urges courts in the exercise of their common-law powers of legal rulemaking to confer legally enforceable rights on animals, beginning with chimpanzees and bonobos (the two most intelligent primate species).[1]

[. . .]

If Wise is to persuade his chosen audience, he must show how courts can proceed incrementally, building on existing cases and legal concepts, toward his goal of radically enhanced legal protection for animals. Recall the process by which, starting from the unpromising principle that "separate but equal" was constitutional, the Supreme Court outlawed official segregation. First, certain public facilities were held not to be equal; then segregation of law schools was invalidated as inherently unequal because of the importance of the contacts made in law school to a successful legal practice; then segregation of elementary schools was outlawed on the basis of social scientific evidence that this segregation, too, was inherently unequal; then the "separate but equal" principle itself, having been reduced to a husk, was quietly buried and the no-segregation principle of the education cases extended to all public facilities, including rest rooms and drinking fountains.

That is the process that Wise envisages for the animal-rights movement, although the end point is less clear. We have, Wise points out, a robust conception of human rights, and we apply it even to people who by reason of retardation or other mental disability cannot enforce their own rights but need a guardian to do it for them. The evolution of human-rights law has involved not only expanding the number of rights but also expanding the number of rights-holders, notably by adding women and blacks. (Much of Wise's book is about human rights, and about the methodology by which judges enlarge human rights in response to changed understandings.) We also have a long history of providing legal protections for animals that recognize their sentience, their emotional capacity, and their capacity to suffer pain; these protections have been growing too.

Wise wants to merge these legal streams by showing that the apes that are most like us genetically, namely the chimpanzees and the bonobos, are also very much like us in their mentation, which exceeds that of human infants and profoundly retarded people. He believes that they are enough like us to be in the direct path of rights expansion. So far as deserving to have rights is concerned, he finds no principled difference between the least mentally able people and the most mentally able animals, as the two groups overlap—or at least too little difference to justify interrupting, at the gateway to the animal kingdom, the expansive rights trend that he has discerned. The law's traditional dichotomy between humans and animals is a vestige of bad science and of a hierarchizing tendency that put men over animals just as it put free men over slaves. Wise does not say how many other animal species besides chimpanzees and bonobos he would like to see entitled, but he makes clear that he regards entitling those two species as a milestone, not as the end of the road.

[. . .]

From his principle of equality Wise deduces that chimpanzees should have the same constitutional rights and other legal rights that small children and severely retarded adults have: the rights to life, to bodily integrity, to subsistence, and to some kind of freedom (how much is unclear), but not the right to vote. He does not discuss whether they should have the right to reproduce. But he is emphatic that since we would not permit invasive or dangerous medical experimentation on small children or severely retarded adults, neither can we permit such experimentation on chimpanzees, no matter how great the benefits for human health.

The framework of Wise's analysis, as we have seen, is the history of extending rights to formerly excluded persons. Working within that conventional lawyerly framework, he seeks to convince his readers that chimpanzees have the essential attribute of persons, which he believes is the level of mentation that we call consciousness, but (to avoid a *reductio ad absurdum*) that computers do not have it. In short, anyone who has consciousness should have rights; chimpanzees are conscious; therefore, chimpanzees should have rights.

How convincing is the analysis? [. . .] It is the major premise that presents the immediate difficulty with this syllogistic approach to the question of animal rights. Cognitive capacity is certainly *relevant* to rights; it is a precondition of some rights, such as the right to vote. But most people would not think it either a necessary or a sufficient condition of having legally enforceable rights, and Wise has not attempted to take on their arguments. Many people believe, for example, that a one-day-old human fetus, though it has no cognitive capacity, should have a right to life; and, after the first trimester, the Supreme Court permits the fetus to be accorded a qualified such right, though the cognitive capacity of a second- or even third-trimester fetus is very limited. And Wise is not distressed at the thought of destroying a "conscious" computer,[2] showing that even he does not take completely seriously the notion that rights follow cognitive capacity. Most people would think it distinctly odd to proportion animal rights to animal intelligence, as Wise wishes to do, implying that dolphins, parrots, and ravens are entitled to more legal protection than horses (or most monkeys), and perhaps that the laws forbidding cruelty to animals should be limited to the most intelligent animals, inviting the crack "They don't have syntax, so we can eat them."[3] And most of us would think it downright offensive to give greater rights to monkeys, let alone to computers, than to retarded people, upon a showing that the monkey or the computer has a greater cognitive capacity than a profoundly retarded human being, unless perhaps the human being has no brain function at all above the autonomic level, that is, is in a vegetative state. Cognition and rights-deservedness are not interwoven as tightly as Wise believes, though he is not, of course, the first to believe this.[4]

There is a related objection to his approach. Wise wants judges, in good common-law fashion, to move step by step, and for the first step simply to declare that chimpanzees have legal rights. But judges asked to step onto a new path of doctrinal growth want to have some idea of where the path leads, even if it would be unreasonable to insist that the destination be clearly seen. Wise gives them no idea.

[. . .]

But what is meant by liberating animals and giving them the rights of human beings of the same cognitive capacity? Does an animal's right to life place a duty on human beings to protect animals from being killed by other animals? Is capacity to feel pain sufficient cognitive capacity to entitle an animal to at least the most elementary human rights? What kinds of habitats must we create and maintain for all the rights-bearing animals in the United States? Does human convenience have *any* weight in deciding what rights an animal has? Can common-law courts actually work out a satisfactory regime of animal rights without the aid of legislatures? When human rights and animal rights collide, do human rights have priority, and if so, why? And what is to be done when animal rights collide with each other, as they do with laws that by protecting wolves endanger sheep? Must entire species of animals be "segregated" from each other and from human beings, and, if so, what does "separate but equal" mean in this context? May we "discriminate" against animals, and if so, how much? Do species have "rights," or just individual animals, and if the latter, does this mean that according special legal protection for endangered species is a denial of equal protection? Is domestication a form of enslavement? Wise does not try to answer any of these questions. He is asking judges to set sail on an uncharted sea without a compass.

The underlying problem is the practitioner-oriented framework of Wise's discussion, with its heavy reliance on argument from analogy and on the syllogism described above. Analogy gives him his major premise, and the syllogism takes him from there to his conclusion. Chimpanzees are like human beings; therefore, so far as Wise is concerned,[5] giving animals rights is like giving black people the rights of whites. But chimpanzees are like human beings in some respects but not in others that may be equally or more relevant to the question of whether to give chimpanzees rights, and legal rights have been designed to serve the needs and interests of human beings having the usual human capacities and so make a poor fit with the needs and interests of animals.

Wise's book illustrates the severe limitations of legal reasoning. Because judges (and therefore the lawyers who argue to them) are reluctant for political and professional reasons to acknowledge that they are expanding or otherwise changing the law, rather than just applying it, departures from existing law are treated as applications of it guided by analogy or deduction. Wise either is playing this game, or has been fooled by it. He makes it seem that animal rights in the expansive form that he conceives them are nothing new—they just plug a hole unaccountably left in the existing case law on rights. Animals just got overlooked, as blacks and women had once been overlooked. But correcting a logical error, removing an inconsistency—in short, tidying up doctrine—is not what would be involved in deciding that chimpanzees have the same rights as three-year-old human beings. What Wise's book really does, rather than supplying the reasons for change, is supply the rationalizations that courts persuaded on other grounds to change the law might use to conceal the novelty of their action. Judges are not easily fooled by a lawyer who argues for a change in the law on the basis that it is no change at all but is merely the recognition of a logical entailment of existing law. The value of such an argument lies in giving judges a professionally respectable ground for rationalizing the change, a ground that minimizes its novelty. But judges must have reasons for wanting to make the change, and this is where a lawyer's brief, of which Wise's book is an extension, tends to fall down.

[. . .]

There is a sad poverty of imagination in an approach to animal protection that can think of it only on the model of the civil rights movement. It is a poverty that reflects the blinkered approach of the traditional lawyer, afraid to acknowledge novelty and therefore unable to think clearly about the reasons pro or con a departure from the legal status quo. It reflects also the extent to which liberal lawyers remain in thrall to the constitutional jurisprudence of the Warren Court and insensitive to the "liberating" potential of commodification. One way to protect animals is to make them property, because people tend to protect what they own.

[. . .]

[. . .] Wise has overlooked not only the possibilities of commodification, but also, and less excusably, an approach to the question of animal welfare that is more conservative, methodologically as well as politically, but possibly more efficacious, than rights-mongering. That is simply to extend, and more vigorously to enforce, laws designed to prevent gratuitous cruelty to animals.

[. . .]

No doubt we should want to do more than merely avoid gratuitous cruelty to animals. [. . .] But neither philosophical reflection nor a vocabulary of rights is likely to add anything to the sympathetic emotions that narratives of the mistreatment of animals are likely to engender in most of us.

I close with a recent judicial opinion by one of our ablest federal judges, Michael Boudin, in a heart-rending "animal rights" case.[6] The plaintiff had rescued an orphaned raccoon, whom she named Mia and raised as a pet. Mia lived in a cage attached to the plaintiff's home for seven years until she was seized and destroyed by the state in the episode that provoked the suit. A police officer noticed Mia in her cage and reported her to the local animal control officer, who discovered that the plaintiff did not have a permit for the animal, as required by state law. The police then forcibly seized Mia from her cage after a struggle with the plaintiff, carried her off, and had her killed and tested for rabies. Testing for rabies in a raccoon requires that the animal be killed, and a supposed epidemic of raccoon rabies had led the state (Rhode Island) to require the testing of raccoons to whom humans (in this case the plaintiff) had been exposed.[7] Mia tested negative, but of course it was too late for Mia.

The plaintiff claimed that the state had deprived her of property, namely Mia, without notice and an opportunity for a hearing and thus had violated the Due Process Clause of the Fourteenth Amendment. Property for these purposes depends on state law, and the court found, undoubtedly correctly, that Rhode Island does not recognize property rights in wild animals unless a permit has been granted,[8] and fear of rabies had deterred the authorities from granting permits for raccoons. To be owned is the antithesis of being a rights-holder. But if Rhode Island had a more generous conception of property in wild animals, the police might have been deterred from what appears to have been the high-handed, indeed arbitrary, treatment of Mia. As the court explained, it does not seem that the plaintiff had been "exposed" to Mia in the relevant statutory sense: There was no indication that the raccoon had bitten the plaintiff or that its saliva had otherwise entered the plaintiff's bloodstream.[9]

And since Mia had been in a cage for seven years,[10] it was unlikely, to say the least, that she was infected with rabies. Moreover, from the standpoint of controlling the spread of rabies, there was no reason to worry about Mia infecting the plaintiff, since people do not spread rabies. Mia was dangerous, if at all, only to the plaintiff, who was happy to assume the risk. The refusal to allow her to keep Mia made no sense at all, but there was no constitutional issue because Mia was not the plaintiff's "property" within the meaning of the Due Process Clause of the Fourteenth Amendment.

This is just one example, and it does not prove that animals benefit less by having human-type "rights" and thus being "free" than by being "imprisoned" and by being "reduced" to "mere" property. I note in this connection that the average life span of an "alley cat" is only about two years, and that of a well-cared-for pet cat at least twelve years, but that is just another example, and against it may be placed the sad fate of the laboratory animal, who is the laboratory's property. The most aggressive implementations of animal-rights thinking would undoubtedly benefit animals more than commodification and a more determined program of enforcing existing laws against cruelty to animals. But those implementations are unlikely, so the modest alternatives are worth serious consideration. We may overlook this simple point, however much we love animals, if we listen too raptly to the siren song of "animal rights."

Notes

1. These are closely related species, and Wise discusses them more or less interchangeably. For the sake of brevity, I will generally refer only to chimpanzees, but what I say about them applies equally to bonobos.
2. *See* Steven M. Wise. Rattling the Cage: Toward Legal Rights for Animals (2000) p. 268.
3. *See* Richard Sorabji. Animal Minds and Human Morals: The Origins of the Western Debate (1993) note 3, p. 2.
4. E.g., Bruce A. Ackerman, Social Justice in the Liberal State 80 (1980) ("The rights of the talking ape are more secure than those of the human vegetable.") *But cf.* Wise, pp. 262–3.
5. *See* WISE, *supra* note 2 pp. 123–4.
6. Bilida v. McCleod, 211 F.3d 166 (1st Cir. 2000).
7. *Id.* p. 169.
8. *Id.* p. 173–4.
9. *Id.* p. 169 n.2.
10. *Id.* p. 169.

81

Richard A. Epstein

"The Dangerous Claims of the Animal Rights Movement"

Richard Epstein is unconvinced by the arguments of Wise and others for the personhood of great apes. Animals lack the capacity for higher cognitive language and thought that characterizes human beings as a species. Epstein points out a number of unfortunate consequences which would ensue if we accepted the claims of the animal rights movement. He concludes that it is appropriate for animals to be treated as property.

The separation of the species

Behind [the] traditional debates lies one key assumption that today's vocal defenders of animal rights brand as "species-ist." Descriptively, they have a point. Sometimes the classical view treated animals as a distinctive form of property; at other times animals became the object of public regulation. In both settings, however, the legal rules were imposed largely for the benefit of human beings, either in their role as owners of animals or as part of that ubiquitous public-at-large that benefitted from their preservation. None of our laws dealing with animals put the animal front and center as the *holder* of property rights in themselves— rights good against the human beings who protect animals in some cases and slaughter them in others.

Our species-ist assumption is savagely attacked by the new generation of animal rights activists, whose clarion call for *person*hood—the choice of terms is telling—is a declaration of independence of animals from their human owners. Their theme generates tremendous resonance, but it is often defended on several misguided grounds.

First, they claim that we now have a greater understanding of the complex behaviors and personalities of animals, especially those in the higher orders. Even though the fields of sociobiology and animal behavior have made enormous strides in recent years, the basic point is an old one. Descartes got it wrong when he said that animals moved about like the ghost in the machine. The older law understood that animals can be provoked or teased; that they are capable of committing deliberate or inadvertent acts. Sure, animals may not be able to talk, but they have extensive powers of anticipation and rationalization; they can form and break alliances; they can show anger, annoyance, and remorse; they can store food for later use; they respond to courtship and aggression; they can engage in acts of rape and acts of love; they respect and violate territories. Indeed, in many ways their repertoire of emotions is quite broad, rivaling that of human beings.

But one difference stands out: through thick and thin, animals do not have the capacity of higher cognitive language and thought that characterizes human beings as a species, even if not shared at all times by all its individual members. We should never pretend that the case against recognizing animal rights is easier than it really is. But by the same token, we cannot accept the facile argument that our *new* understanding of animals leads to a new appreciation of their rights. The fundamentals have long been recognized by the lawyers and writers who fashioned the old legal order.

Second, animal activists such as Wise remind us of the huge overlap in DNA between human beings and chimpanzees. The fact itself is incontrovertible. Yet the implications we should draw from that fact are not. The observed behavioral differences between humans and chimpanzees are still what they have always been; they are neither increased nor decreased by the number of common genes. The evolutionary biologist should use this evidence to determine when the lines of chimps separated from that of human beings, but the genetic revelation does not establish that chimps and bonobos are able to engage in the abstract thought that would enable them to present on their own behalf the claims for personhood that Wise and others make on their behalf. The number of common genes humans have with other primates is also very high, as it is even with other animals that diverged from human beings long before the arrival of primates. The question to answer is not how many genes humans and chimpanzees have in common; it is how many traits they have in common. The large number of common genes helps explain empirically the rapid rate of evolution. It does not narrow the enormous gulf that a few genes are able to create.

Third, Wise and other defenders of personhood for animals have line-drawing problems of their own. If that higher status is offered to chimps and bonobos, then what about orangutans and gorillas? Or horses, dogs, and cows? All of these animals have a substantial level of cognitive capacity, and wide range of emotions, even if they do not have the same advanced cognitive skills of the chimps and bonobos. Does personhood extend this far, and if not, then why does it extend as far as Wise and others would take it? The frequent analogy of chimpanzees to slaves hardly carries the day, given the ability of individuals from different human populations to interbreed with each other and to perform the same set of speech and communicative acts. Nor is it particularly persuasive to note that individuals with serious neurological or physical impairments often have far less cognitive and emotional capacity than normal chimpanzees or dogs. For one, we in fact *do* recognize that different rules apply to individuals in extreme cases, allowing, for example, the withdrawal of feeding tubes from individuals in a permanent vegetative state. In addition, important human relations intrude into the deliberations. These human beings, whatever their impairments, are the fathers, mothers, sisters, and brothers of other human beings in ways that chimpanzees and bonobos are not.

Fourth, the animal rights activists often attack the question from the other side by offering bland assurances that people today do not need to rely on animal labor and products in order to survive as human beings. Typically, animal rights activists put their claims in universalistic terms. But in so doing they argue as though in primitive times animals and agriculture fell into separate compartments, when in truth they were part of a seamless enterprise. Animal power was necessary to clear the woods, to fertilize and plow the fields, and to harvest the crop. Meat and dairy products were an essential part of primitive diets. The early society that did not rely on animals for food, for labor, for warfare was the society that did not survive to yield the heightened moral sensibilities of today. It was the society that perished from its want of food, clothing, and shelter—a high price to pay for a questionable moral principle. And, if this new regime is implemented, the animal rights movement condemns millions of less fortunate people around the globe to death today. Just this past March the *New York Times* ran a painful story about the question of whether the preservation of gorillas in Africa placed at risk the subsistence economies of the nearby tribes.

Today, perhaps people fortunate enough to live in prosperous lands could live without having to use animals for consumption or labor, but the long-term agenda, if not the immediate demands, of the animal rights activists cut far deeper. For activists such as Gary Francione of Rutgers-Newark Law School, the mere ownership of animals is a sin: no pets, no circuses, no milk, no cheese, no horses to ride, no dogs, cats, birds, or fish around the house. These relationships are condemned in good Marxist terms as being based on power differentials, and thus are barred: the animals who seem to like being pandered to suffer from, as it were, a form of false consciousness.

Fifth, more ominously, if pets are out, so too is the use of animals for medical science. In dealing with this issue, Wise is brutally explicit in describing what it is for chimpanzees to suffer in isolation the final effects of the ravages of AIDS. No one could argue that this conduct did not cry out for justification. Yet by the same token, the question is could the conduct itself be justified? To answer that question in human terms, one has to look at the other side of the equation, and ask what has been learned from these experiments, what wonder drugs have been created, what scourges of human (and animal) kind have been eliminated. I do not pretend to be an expert on this subject, but so long as the vaccine for smallpox comes from cows or the insulin for treating diabetes comes from pigs, then I am hard pressed to defend any categorical rule that bans all use of animals in medical experimentation. One has to have an accurate accounting of what is on the other side, and on that issue the silence of the animal rights activists is deafening.

The argument here has its inescapable moral dimension. No matter what one's intellectual orientation, no one would—or should—dispute the proposition that animals should not be used in research if the same (or better) results could be achieved at the same (or lower) cost by test tubes and computer simulations alone. Nor would any one want future surgeons to try out new techniques on animals if they could be risklessly performed on human beings the first time out. But, alas, neither of these happy eventualities come close to being a partial truth. It is easy to identify many situations where human advancement comes only at the price of animal suffering. How to proceed then turns on the balance between these two unquantifiable considerations.

[. . .]

Sixth, medical research is not all that is at stake once the asserted parity between animal rights and human rights is acknowledged. Our entire system of property allows owners to transform the soil and to exclude others. Now if the first human being may exclude subsequent arrivals, what happens when animals are given similar rights? Their dens, burrows, nests, and hives long antedate human arrival. The principle of first possession should therefore block us from clearing the land for farms, homes, and factories unless we can find ways to make just compensation to each individual animal for its own losses. But I fail to see how this system would work, for to transfer animals from one habitat to another only unlawfully displaces animals at the second location. The blunt truth is that the arrival of human beings necessarily results in the death of some earlier animal occupants, even if it increases the welfare of others who learn to live in harmony with us. So if prior in time is higher in right, then we should fold up our tents right now and let the animals fight it out for territory, just as if we had never arrived on the face of the globe.

[. . .]

The current legal scene

Animal owners have recovered large awards for the malpractice of veterinarians. The damages paid are meant to cover not only the market value of the animal, but the loss of companionship to the owner. This is simply solid economics—for what the defenders of animal rights do not tell is that this outcome derives its power from recognizing that the actual losses *to the owner* exceed the market value of the animal, precisely because they include these nonmonetary elements. [. . .] These cases therefore gain their resonance from a traditional property rights conception.

[. . .]

A similar logic also applies to a 1998 decision in the District of Columbia, *Animal Legal Defense Fund, Inc. v. Glickman*. Here a zoo visitor was held to have "standing" to sue under the Animal Welfare Act of 1985, which provided generally that animals' keepers must meet conditions of confinement that ensure "the psychological well being of primates." That objective is certainly laudable in simple human terms, even if the new animal rights activists would shut down all zoos. But allowing a zoo visitor to sue to protect the zoo animals made it crystal clear that the rights vindicated by the action were those of the individual plaintiff, and not those of the animal. And no one doubts that Congress could reverse that decision by a statutory amendment that allows only for public inspection and enforcement of the provisions of the Act.

In sum, no one can deny the enormous political waves created by animal rights activists. [. . .] It is, however, one thing to raise social conscience about the status of animals. It is quite another to raise the status of animals to asserted parity with human beings. That move, if systematically implemented, would pose a mortal threat to human society that few human beings would, or should, accept. We have quite enough difficulty in persuading or coercing human beings to respect the rights of their fellow humans to live in peace with each other. [. . .] We should not undermine, as would surely be the case, the liberty and dignity of human beings by treating animals as their moral equals and legal peers. [. . .] Animals are properly property. It is not, nor has it ever been, immoral for human beings, as a species, to prefer their own kind. What lion would deny it?

82

Wesley V. Jamison, Casper Wenk, and James V. Parker

"Every Sparrow that Falls: Understanding Animal Rights Activism as Functional Religion"

Wesley Jamison, Caspar Wenk, and James Parker have found that the goals of animal rights activists in Switzerland and the United States often require extremely high levels of commitment and conviction. An analysis of the movement as a functional religion demonstrates some of the sources of this commitment. The analysis uses Yinger's five categories: intense and memorable conversion experiences, newfound communities of meaning, normative creeds, elaborate and well-defined codes of behavior, and cult formation. The authors predict changes within the movement should it evolve into a mainstream political force.

The [. . .] goals of animal rights activists often require extraordinary levels of personal commitment and conviction (Jasper and Nelkin, 1992; Herzog, 1993; McAllister, 1997). What are the sources of this intensity and commitment? Once mobilized, what keeps an animal rights activist motivated toward the transformation of society's relationship with animals? And what course of action will the movement take should it fail to redeem society? A guide for activists who object in conscience to classroom vivisection and dissection advises that their objection is a constitutionally protected exercise of religious belief (Francione and Charlton, 1992). The authors' claim that such activists are acting out of religious belief may surprise many observers. Social science data indicate that most animal rights activists are not members of traditional churches; indeed, they think of themselves as atheist or agnostic (Richards, 1990).[1] Nonetheless, social scientists have argued that animal rights may serve as a cosmological buttress against anomie and bewilderment in modern society (Sutherland and Nash, 1994; McAllister, 1997; Franklin, 1999).[2]

Francione and Charlton (1992) argue that . . . "The law does not require a belief to be 'theistic' or based on faith in a 'God' or 'Supreme Being' " in order to be protected.

[. . .]

The United States Supreme Court, the authors point out, has adopted a "functional" definition of religion:

> The Court has recognized that in order to determine whether a set of beliefs constitutes a religion, the appropriate focus is not the substance of a person's belief system (i.e., whether a person believes in a personal God of the Jewish, Christian or Muslim traditions), but rather, what function or role the belief systems plays in the person's life. (Francione and Charlton, 1992, p. 4)

Yinger (1970) articulated the distinction between substantive and functional definitions of religion for social scientists. It is a distinction that allows us to analyze seemingly secular movements as religions because they function as religions; that is, they provide meaning around which individuals coalesce, interpreting life through a system of beliefs, symbols, rituals, and prescriptions for behavior. Indeed, Berger (1992; 1999) has noted the emergence of such functional, secular religiosity as an alternative expression of "repressed transcendence." Berger argues that in response to modernity's cultural delegitimization of traditional religions and objective truth, individuals, rather than ending their quest for religious truth, shift the foci of their quest toward other outlets.

[. . .]

We drew the data for this article from long interviews with informants in both the United States and Switzerland. Although the political manifestations of animal rights ideology are context dependent, social scientists have hypothesized that mass movement activism (e.g. animal rights) may be a reaction to sociological factors that transcend culture and thus share relatively uniform causes (Giddens, 1990; Giddens, 1991; Beck, 1992; Sutherland and Nash, 1994). Switzerland and the United States share similar representative, federal political systems that are highly decentralized and shunt many political issues toward the lowest levels of political participation where, over time, intensity in citizen involvement is emphasized. Likewise, democracy in the United States resembles Swiss democracy in that citizens have the opportunity to pass or amend legislation through direct democracy, and this similarly emphasizes political intensity among political participants. The Swiss and U.S. systems are similar in that multiple checks and balances thwart radical political movements and cause incremental change (Linder, 1994).

[. . .]

The animal rights movements in both countries differ in significant ways. The U.S. movement has diverged into a reformist arm that allows for humane use of animals and a radical arm that seeks to protect them from all human use through the extension of inalienable rights. In Switzerland, the *Tierschutz* movement similarly contains reformist and radical branches, but because of political history the Swiss movement tends to shy away from the language of rights. Another difference is that the U.S. system is intentionally confrontational, pitting interest groups against each other in perpetual conflict, whereas the Swiss system is by intent more consensual and cooperative (Berry, 1994; Linder, 1994). One manifestation of this difference is that in the United States the animal rights movement has sought confrontation outside the boundaries of political legislation both to shock citizens and to bring about strategic legislative change (Francione, 1996), while in Switzerland the animal rights movement has sought redress through primarily political means and has stayed relatively non-confrontational (Linder, 1994).

[. . .]

Results: the elements of functional religion

Conversion

Morally persuasive religious belief often originates in an experience of conversion. Coming from a biblical expression meaning "to be turned around," conversion can reverse a person's life.

[. . .]

Our informants reported having had formative events that sensitized them to movement rhetoric and images and began the process of dissonance. Our informants confirmed Jasper and Poulsen's (1995) hypothesis concerning activist recruitment. For our informants, awareness of incongruence between behavior and feelings remained a vivid but nebulous reality coupled to a vague sense of guilt over not doing more. Their unease grew until it eventually became manifest in a single emotional epiphany. One informant noted:

> I received literature, [that was] doing an exposé on dog-meat markets in Asia; I still remember it vividly. I was reading this mailing postcard while eating a ham sandwich. There was a picture of this dog, his legs tethered, a tin cup over his muzzle; then it hit me! I made the connection between the being in the picture and the being in my mouth. Before, everything seemed to be OK, but now, I realized that treating animals as objects was bad. It was like someone had opened a door. I felt incredible sadness, and at the same time incredible joy. I knew that I would never be the same again, that I was leaving something behind . . . that I would be a better person, that I had been cleansed.

[. . .]

Community

Converts create communities. [. . .] [One] informant experienced separation from her previous relationships: "I had a sense of being 'called out.' I had trouble relating to some people. People would stare when I would order [vegetarian food] in restaurants. It was embarrassing for me, and very uncomfortable." Indeed, some of our informants attributed their divorces to their newfound beliefs. After their conversion, our informants uniformly experienced feelings of social isolation, which in turn led them to seek out others who believed. Our informants often faced ostracism and scorn from family and friends as they tried to relate to their conversion.

[. . .]

Creed

Although most animal rights activists do not recite a formal profession of faith (Richards, 1990), they have beliefs that may be compared to traditional religious doctrines. At first glance, their creed seems obvious and simple: animals either have the right to live their lives without human interference or have the right to be considered equally with humans in the ethical balance that weighs the right and wrong of any action or policy (Singer, 1975; Regan, 1983). Nevertheless, the commitment of our informants to political guarantees of rights for animals is part of a larger system of beliefs about life and the human–nonhuman animal relationship. That system includes several beliefs about nature, suffering, and death and is typified by creedal doctrinaire beliefs. Our informants agreed that active inclusion in the movement carries with it certain proscribed beliefs such as the assertion of the moral righteousness of the movement and the necessity of spreading that revelation. Believing entails spreading the faith, and animal rights activists are proselytizers. Herzog (1993) has found that the involvement of almost all animal rights activists contains an evangelical component.

[. . .]

In our informants' creed, suffering is evil, and its alleviation is good; humans are at once derived from, and unique in, the natural world. In other words, people are related through evolution to animals but ethically constrained from using them because we, alone, are conscious of the suffering such use causes and can exercise free will to end it.

[. . .]

To our informants, nature acquires normative value and is the repository of nobility and virtue, while humans acquire negative and even evil attributes (Dizard, 1999; Chase, 1995). [. . .] Certainly, animals are part of nature, but to our informants their goodness lies in their perceived moral innocence. [. . .] Indeed, for our informants it appeared that people were the problem, that innocence could be found only in animals, and that humans just by existing—are detrimental to animals.

[. . .]

An all-encompassing statement of faith professed by some of our informants demon-strated the codified edicts of animal rights: "Animals are not ours to eat, wear, experiment on, or use in any way!" Finding its ultimate expression in the form of veganism, this lifestyle consciously forgoes the use of materials that have, in any way, caused animal suffering. Our informants defined vegans as "a person who doesn't use, to the greatest extent possible, any products that come from animals . . . it's impossible to get away from animal use . . . but if an alternative is available, they use it."

Unlimited in scope, veganism provides an elaborate superstructure with which activists support their lives. Bordering on asceticism, the constraints placed on personal behavior and the resultant emotional demands of compliance can be extraordinary (Sperling, 1988; Herzog, 1993).

[. . .]

Cult (collective meanings expressed as symbols and rituals)

Substantive religions often organize their worship around the teachings of sacred texts/ inspired narrative or the consumption of a holy food. Although nothing so formal as listen-ing to the inspired text or eating a sacred meal characterizes the gatherings of animal rights partisans, elements of those gatherings nevertheless resemble the ritual behavior of trad-itional religions. An informant reflected this repetitive reification of belief:

[I] was shy . . . I don't classify myself as an activist, but I went along with a friend. When we got there, the meeting began with people introducing themselves and talking about the problems [professing the creed and keeping the behavioral code] they had had.

[. . .]

Animal rights activists often share news clippings, letters, and personal stories that tell of recent conversions and encourage participants in their commitment. The introduction and welcoming of new and potential members often are an integral part of animal rights meetings.

[. . .]

During such moments of epistemological challenge, symbols helped to remind and rejuvenate our informants. [. . .] Animal rights activists use pictures of monkeys strapped in chairs, cats wearing electrodes and rabbits with eye or flesh ulceration in much the same way: that is, as symbolic representations of human values and the corresponding affronts to those values. Looking on and identifying with those innocent victims, just as Christians look upon and identify a lamb as the propitiatory sacrifice of Jesus, can bring about conversion and redemption (Sperling, 1988; Jasper and Nelkin, 1992). Indeed, most of our informants had such symbols in their social environments.

[. . .]

[T]he thesis may explain how our informants retain enthusiasm and how the movement retains its cohesion in the face of seemingly insurmountable obstacles posited by the incremental U.S. and Swiss political systems. Central to the stories of our informants was a profound sense of guilt at discovering personal complicity in the suffering of animals. The movement places moral culpability squarely upon their shoulders, and its rhetoric exacerbates this. Then, in the tradition of all purposive mass movements, it offers itself as the ultimate form of absolution. With a creed that presents a disheartening picture of their world and a code of behavior that at once is unattainable and noble, believers are drawn into further activism as a source of penance.

[. . .]

Predictive Power

[. . .] We can look to the course run by religious and secular movements to find answers to intriguing questions about the animal rights movement's future.

[. . .]

We might ask how the movement, should it evolve into a mainstream political force, might retain its distinctive redemptive flavor? First, while maintaining its transcendent goal, it could pick and choose its battles, settling for those it can win: not the end of animal use in agriculture, but the end of raising calves for veal; not the end of all animal products, but the end of wearing furs; not the end of using animals in medical research, but the end of research that can be presented as an affront to decency. Second, the movement might develop two distinctive and separable tiers of membership.

[. . .]

An elite would hold out for the original vision of societal transformation, keep themselves from any compromise, and pursue a prophetic course. Others entangled in earning a living, rearing a family, and enjoying friendships do what they can: adopt a dog, write a protest letter to a shampoo manufacturer or buy synthetic clothes.

A parallel with the early Christian church is instructive. The Church moved in this direction during the second, third, and fourth centuries. An elite chose to move into isolation and live by the evangelical counsels. With their vows of poverty, chastity, and obedience, they foreswore personal property and wealth, family responsibilities, and even personal autonomy. The way of these monks was declared the way of perfection. For those who were not able to live so purely a second tier of citizenship developed. Gradually, the word *laos*, which in earliest times referred to all Christians (as in the expression *laos theou* or 'the people of God'), came to refer to those who did not follow the monks—the laity. In other words, the animal rights movement may develop a secularized monastic system as a means to assuage the schismatic tension between pragmatism and purity implicit within an incremental political system.

[. . .]

It is no mistake that the movement has had success—although each of the informants was disheartened by the glacial rate of change. The modern movement to protect animals, whether it be in Switzerland or the United States, has, at the least, sensitized non-believers to the plight of animals and perhaps even continued to sow the seeds of epistemological discontent that led our informants to convert to the cause.

Notes

1   For a relevant discussion of animal rights as a derivative of modernity, see Franklin (1999).
2   It could be argued that cultural differences between the Swiss and Americans confound any useful examination of animal rights activism. On the contrary, a central theme in modernity and the study of pluralization is that 'modern' post-industrial Western nations are buffeted by the same effects of modernity. Our data showed little cultural differences between informants from the two countries.

References

Beck, U. (1992). *Risk society: towards a new modernity*. London: Sage Publishers.
Berger, P. (1992). *A far glory: the quest for faith in an age of credulity*. New York: Basic.
——— (1999). *The desecularization of the world: resurgent religion and world politics*. New York: Eerdmans Publishing Company.
Berry, J. (1994). *The interest group society*. Boston: Scott, Foresman/Little, Brown.
Chase, A. (1995). *In a dark wood: the fight over forests and the rising tyranny of ecology*. New York: Free Press.
Dizard, J. (1999). *Going wild: hunting, animal rights, and the contested meaning of nature*. Amherst: University of Massachusetts Press.
Francione, G. (1996). *Rain without thunder: the ideology of the animal rights movement*. Philadelphia: Temple University Press.
Francione, G., and Charlton, A. (1992). *Vivisection and dissection in the classroom: a guide to conscientious objection*. Jenkintown: The American Anti-Vivisection Society.
Franklin, A. (1999). *Animals in modern culture: a sociology of human–animal relations in modernity*. London: Corwin Publishers.
Giddens, A. (1990). *The consequences of modernity*. Stanford: Stanford University Press.
——— (1991). *Modernity and self-identity: self and society in the late modern age*. Stanford: Stanford University Press.
Herzog, H. (1993). "The movement is my life": The psychology of animal rights activism. *The Journal of Social Issues*, 49, 103–19.
Jasper, J., and Nelkin, D. (1992). *The animal rights crusade: growth of a moral protest*. New York: Free Press.
Jasper, J., and Poulsen, J. (1995). Recruiting strangers and friends: moral shocks and social networks in animal rights and anti-nuclear protests. *Social Problems*, 42, 493–512.
Linder, W. (1994). *Swiss Democracy*. London: Sage Publishers.
McAllister, J. (1997). *Hearts and minds: the controversy over laboratory animals*. Philadelphia: Temple University Press.
Regan, T. (1983). *The case for animal rights*. Berkeley: University of California Press.

Richards, R. (1990). *Consensus mobilization through ideology, networks, and grievances: a study of the contemporary animal rights movement*. Ann Arbor: University Microfilms.

Singer, P. (1975) *Animal Liberation*. New York: New York Book Review.

Sperling, Susan. (1988). *Animal liberators: research and morality*. Berkeley: University of California Press.

Sutherland, K., and Nash, W. (1994). Animal rights as new environmental cosmology. *Qualitative Sociology*, 17, 171–86.

Yinger, M. (1970). *The scientific study of religion*. New York: Macmillan Publishing Company.

83

Tom Regan

"Understanding Animal Rights Violence"

Tom Regan draws connections between two social justice movements: the nineteenth-century anti-slavery movement in the United States and the contemporary animal rights movement. Both exhibit the split between those who insist on the immediate end to unjust practice (abolitionists) and those who are gradualists or reformists. It is the abolitionists who include those who are willing to commit acts of violence. A second split is between those who work with the government and those who refuse to do so, and a third is between those who condone violence against property in defense of animals and those who do not. Regan recommends "incremental abolitionist change" as a shared agenda.

Those people who view themselves as advocates of animal rights—and I certainly include myself among them—also see themselves as part of a social justice movement: the animal rights movement. In this respect, animal rights advocates believe that common bonds unite them with those who have worked for justice in other quarters: for example, for women, people of color, the poor, and gays and lesbians. The struggle for equal rights for and among these people is hardly complete; the struggle for the rights of animals has only begun, and this latter struggle promises to be, if anything, more difficult and protracted than any of its social justice relatives. For while demands for equal rights for many historically disfranchised people face formidable obstacles, they have one advantage over the struggle for animal rights. None of the other movements I have mentioned challenges the conception of the moral community that has dominated Western thought and traditions, the one that includes *humans only*; rather, all these struggles work with rather than against this conception, demanding only (and I do not mean to minimize the enormous difficulties such a demand inevitably faces) that the boundaries of the moral community expand to include previously excluded human beings—Native Americans, for example, or humans who suffer from various physical or mental disabilities.

The struggle for animal rights is different; it calls for a deeper, more fundamental change in the way we think about membership in the moral community. It demands not an expansion but a dismantling of the for-humans-only conception, to be replaced by one that includes other-than-human animals.

Not surprisingly, therefore, any obstacle that stands in the way of greater justice for people of color or the poor, for example, also stands in the way of greater justice for chimpanzees and chickens, whereas the struggle for justice for chimpanzees and chickens encounters obstacles at once more fundamental and unique, including the resistance or disdain of people who are among the most enlightened when it comes to injustice done to humans. Any doubt about this can be readily dispelled by gauging the indifference and

hostility showered on the very idea of animal rights by both many of the leaders and most of
the rank and file in any human rights movement, including, for example, those committed to
justice and equality for women and racial minorities.

Despite these differences, those of us involved in the struggle for animal rights need to
remember that we share many of the challenges other social justice movements face. [. . .] By
way of illustration, I want to explore a few of the similarities between the nineteenth-century
antislavery movement in America and today's animal rights movement.

Before doing this, I want to try to defuse a possible misunderstanding. I am not in any
way suggesting that the animal rights movement and the antislavery movement are in every
respect the same (clearly, they are not), any more than I would be suggesting that all African
Americans must be either gay or lesbian because there are similarities between the movement
to liberate slaves, on the one hand, and the gay and lesbian movement, on the other. Similarities are just that: similarities. And one thing similarities are not is sameness.

[. . .]

Animal rights versus animal welfare

When it comes to what we humans are morally permitted to do to other animals, it is safe to
say that opinion is divided. Some people (abolitionists) believe that we should stop using
nonhuman animals, whether as sources of food, as trained performers, or as models of
various diseases, for example. Others (welfarists) think such utilization is permissible as long
as it is done humanely. Those who accept the former outlook object to such utilization in
principle and believe it should end in practice. Those who accept the latter outlook accept
such utilization in principle and believe it may continue in practice, provided the welfare of
animals is not unduly compromised, in which case these practices will need to be appropriately reformed. Clearly real differences separate these two ways of thinking, one abolitionist
at its core, the other not. Anyone who would deny or attempt to minimize these differences
would distort rather than describe the truth.

[. . .]

One area where these differences can make a difference is the particular matter before
us. For it is among abolitionists, not reformists—among animal rightists, not animal welfarists—that we find those willing to commit acts of violence in the name of animal liberation.
Nevertheless—and this is of great importance—not all animal rightists are prepared to go
this far. That is, within the animal rights movement one finds deep, protracted, principled
disagreements about the limits of protest in general and the permissibility of using violence in
particular.

Analogous ideological and tactical themes are to be found in the antislavery movement.
That movement was anything but monolithic. True, all abolitionists shared a common goal:
slavery in America had to end. Beyond their agreement concerning this unifying goal,
however, partisans of emancipation divided over a rich, complex fabric of well-considered,
passionately espoused, and irreconcilable disagreements concerning the appropriate means
of ending it. For my purposes, reference to just three areas of disagreement will suffice.

Abolition first versus abolition later

Following the lead of William Lloyd Garrison (1831), some abolitionists called for the unconditional emancipation of slaves, insisting as well that former slave owners not receive compensation for their financial losses. "Immediatists" (as they were called) wanted to end slavery first and then go forward with various plans to educate and in other ways prepare the newly freed slaves for the responsibilities of full citizenship. Other abolitionists (Channing 1835) favored a "gradualist" approach: complete emancipation was the eventual goal, but only after various alternatives to slave labor and improvements in the life of the slaves were in place. Thus, some gradualists sought freedom for slaves after (not before) those in bondage had received at least a rudimentary education or acquired a marketable skill or after (not before) a plan of financial compensation to former slave owners, or another plan calling for voluntary recolonization, had been implemented.

[. . .]

This split between slavery's immediatists and gradualists is mirrored in today's animal rights movement. Some people who profess belief in the movement's abolitionist goals also believe that these goals can be achieved by using gradualist means—for example, by supporting protocols that aim to reduce or refine animal use in a scientific setting, with replacement possibly achieved later on, or by decreasing the number of hens raised in cages today as a step along the way to emptying cages tomorrow. In this way, it is believed, we can succeed both in making the lives of some animals better today and in ending all animal exploitation in the future.

Other animal rights abolitionists are cut from more Garrison-like cloth. For these animal rightists, *how* we get to the abolitionist goal, not just *that* we get there, matters morally (Francione and Regan 1992). Following the higher moral law that we are not to do evil that good may come, these activists believe that they should not tacitly support violating the rights of some animals today in the hope of freeing others tomorrow. For these activists, as was true of their counterparts in the antislavery movement, it is not a question of first finding an alternative to the evil being done before deciding whether to stop doing it; instead, one must first decide to end the evil and then look for another way to achieve the goals one seeks. For these animal rights activists, then, our first obligation is to stop using animals as we do; after we have satisfied this obligation, there will be plenty of time to search for alternative ways of doing what it is we want to do. To end evil now rather than later is what conformity to the higher moral law requires.

Working with the government versus working independently

A second common theme concerns the role of government. The antislavery movement once again was sharply divided. Whereas Garrison and his followers refused to cooperate with the government, others insisted on the necessity of working with elected representatives; among this latter group, Frederick Douglass was unquestionably the most illustrious representative (see Douglass 1845).

[. . .]

The Constitution contains no ambiguous language concerning nonhuman animals that might occasion a split among today's animal rights advocates like that between Garrison and Douglass. Cows and pigs, chimpanzees and dolphins, ospreys and squirrels—all are total nonpersons as far as the Constitution is concerned. Even so, what we might term the *political sensibilities* of Garrison and Douglass live on in today's animal rights movement.

Douglass's faith in the role of government is represented by those animal rights advocates who look to the government—laws, enforcement mechanisms, and the courts—as essential elements in realizing the abolitionist goal for which they labor. In contrast, Garrison's disdain for the government is mirrored by today's animal rights activists who have lost faith in the progressive role current or foreseeable laws, enforcement mechanisms, or court proceedings might play in the struggle for animal liberation. For these activists, the government is not only historically rooted in and constitutionally committed to the ideology of speciesism but also daily subject to the influence of powerful special interests that perpetuate speciesist practices as a matter of law. These activists see the government as part of the problem, not part of the solution.

Violence versus nonviolence

Despite his belief in the necessity of working with the government, Douglass was to his dying day a staunch supporter of "agitation," a commitment poignantly captured by Philip Foner's description of a meeting that took place some weeks before Douglass's death. "In the early days of 1895, a young Negro student living in New England journeyed to Providence, Rhode Island, to seek the advice of the aged Frederick Douglass who was visiting that city. As the interview drew to a close the youth said, 'Mr. Douglass, you have lived in both the old and new dispensations. What have you to say to a young Negro just starting out? What should he do?' The patriarch lifted his head and replied, 'Agitate! Agitate! Agitate!' " (Foner 1950:371).

To our ears, Douglass's prescription might sound like a license to lawlessness, but this is not what he meant. For most of his life, Douglass, like the vast majority of abolitionists, favored only nonviolent forms of agitation: peaceful assemblies, rallies, the distribution of pamphlets and other materials depicting the plight of slaves, and petitions—measures that collectively were referred to as "moral suasion." People were to be persuaded that slavery was wrong and ought to be abolished through appeals to their reason, their sense of justice, and their human compassion, not coerced to agree through violence or intimidation.

On this point Garrison and Douglass, who disagreed about much, spoke with one voice. When Garrison said abolitionists were not to do evil that good may come, he meant that they were not to do evil *even to slaveholders, even in pursuit of emancipation.* As he saw it, respect for the higher moral law requires that all efforts made in the name of emancipation, whether immediatist or gradualist and whether in concert with the Union or apart from it, treat all persons respectfully and thus nonviolently.

[. . .]

On this matter, today's animal rightists, if not unanimously then at least solidly, align themselves with Garrison and Douglass. Evil, in the form of violence, should not be done to any human being, even in pursuit of animal liberation, and anyone who would perform such an act, whatever that person might say or believe, would not be acting according to the higher moral law that should guide and inform the animal rights movement.

This prohibition against violence to human and other forms of sentient life, however, does not necessarily carry over to property. Most of slavery's opponents understood this. If the cost of freeing a slave was damaged, destroyed, or in the case of slaves themselves, stolen property, then Garrison, Douglass, and most (but not all) of their abolitionist peers were prepared to accept such violence.

The same is true of many of today's animal rights advocates. Let me be perfectly honest. Some animal rightists obviously believe that violent acts against property carried out in the name of animal liberation, as well as the liberation of animals themselves (the theft of property, given current law), are perfectly justified. Other animal rightists disagree, believing that a principled commitment to the "higher moral law" of nonviolence must be maintained even in the treatment of property.

How many believe the one, how many believe the other, no one, I think, can say. What we can say, and what we should say, is this: it is just as false, just as misleading, and possibly just as dishonest to say that the animal rights movement is a nonviolent movement as it is to say that it is a terrorist movement.

[. . .]

How to lessen animal rights violence

This violence is something that everyone, both friend and foe of animal rights, must lament, something we all wish could be prevented. The question is how to do so.

[. . .]

My own (very) modest proposal is this. Although Garrison-like abolitionists cannot support reformist measures, they can support *incremental abolitionist change*, change that involves stopping the utilization of nonhuman animals for one purpose or another. One goal, for example, might be not fewer animals used in cosmetic or industrial testing but no animals used for this purpose. Other goals might be not fewer dogs "sacrificed" in dog labs, or fewer primates "studied" in maternal deprivation research, or fewer goats shot and killed in weapons testing, but no animals used in each of these (and an indefinite number of other possible) cases.

A shared agenda of this type could set forth objectives that animal rights abolitionists, scientific policy makers, and biomedical researchers, for example, could agree on and work collaboratively to achieve; as such, it would go a long way toward reducing animal rights violence. It would demonstrate that it is possible to achieve incremental abolitionist goals by acting nonviolently within the system. This in turn would help defuse the idea that such goals can be achieved only by acting violently outside the system.

[. . .]

[U]nless we practice preventive ethics in this quarter, animal rights violence will increase in the coming months and years. Indeed, as things stand at present, the wonder of it is not that there is animal rights violence but that there is not more of it.

[. . .]

Works cited

Channing, William Ellery. 1835. "Essay on Slavery." In *The Works of William E. Channing*, 6 vols., 2:123–33. Boston: Anti-Slavery Office.

Douglass, Frederick. 1845. *Narrative of the Life of Frederick Douglass, an American Slave. Written by Himself*. Boston: Anti-Slavery Office.

Foner, Philip S. 1950. *Frederick Douglass: A Biography*. New York: Citadel.

Francione, Gary, and Tom Regan. 1992. "A Movement's Means Create Its Ends." *The Animals' Agenda*, January/February, pp. 40–3.

Garrison, William Lloyd. 1831. "Immediate Emancipation." *The Liberator*, September 3, pp. 1–2.

—◦◦◦—

84

Courtney L. Dillard

"Civil Disobedience: A Case Study in Factors of Effectiveness"

Courtney Dillard presents her observations of two protests against the largest pigeon shoot in the United States. In the second protest activists lay flat on the ground, bound themselves to one another at the neck, remained silent, and remained calm. In being bound together they attempt to represent the helplessness of the birds. The onlookers who were interviewed indicated that this approach was very effective in changing attitudes.

Advocating for animals in this country dates as far back as the colonial period. In 1641, legal arguments were put forth that made cruelty to domestic animals unlawful in the Massachusetts Bay Colony. By the mid-1800s, several social movement organizations, such as the American Society for the Prevention of Cruelty to Animals (ASPCA) and the Philadelphia Society for the Prevention of Cruelty to Animals were created to advocate for animal welfare in the wider courts of public opinion. Over time, the numbers of people and organizations arguing on behalf of animals grew substantially. In addition, the tactics and strategies employed in such advocacy became more varied and creative.

Such changes perhaps are most notable in surveying the activities of social movement organizations in the last two decades. The 1980s witnessed not only major ideological shifts from welfare to rights but also tactical shifts from behind-the-scenes negotiation in the courtroom or legislative bodies to very public acts of protest and civil disobedience. As the media, particularly television, quickly became an essential part of educating and persuading the public on animal issues, tactics that gained media coverage were often employed. Because one of the enduring news values is controversy and conflict (Stephens, 1980), the potential for acts of civil disobedience often ensured media attention. Today, some activists and organizations wholly embrace the use of civil disobedience.

[. . .]

Instead of wrestling with the question of whether civil disobedience is an effective advocacy tool in general, I ask if the effectiveness of civil disobedience may be determined in part by the way it is enacted. To pursue this question, I analyze a specific case study of a long-term animal advocacy campaign—The Fund for Animals' campaign to abolish the Hegins pigeon shoot. In this article, I compare the enactment of civil disobedience in two years of protest that differed considerably from one another.

[. . .]

Hegins: a case analysis

The event

The Fred Coleman Memorial Shoot, the shoot's official name, began more than a half century ago in the early 1930s. Pigeon shooting is a rather common sport in the rural counties of Pennsylvania, but the shoot at Hegins quickly grew to become the largest event of its kind in the country. Each Labor Day weekend, people from a number of surrounding counties and states descended on the town to shoot over 5,000 birds. Funds from the event were used to raise money to continue maintenance on the park and subsidize such local services as the firehouse (B. Tobash, personal communication, February 20, 1997).

The rules surrounding the shoot and the manner in which it is conducted haven't changed since the event's earliest days. Organizers of the shoot purchase pigeons from breeders or those who have trapped the birds in the wild. They then keep the pigeons in cages, often cramped together for days or even weeks before the event. Participants in the shoot, limited to 250 at Hegins, pay an entry fee, typically $75, for a chance to shoot as many pigeons as possible. The shooter with the largest number of hits at the end of the weekend wins the event.

During the shoot, participants stand ready with their guns and then shout "Pull," ordering the strings tied to the cage doors to be pulled and the doors opened, releasing the pigeons one at a time. Pigeons either fly out or, having been weakened by their captivity, walk out of the cages. At that moment, the shooter fires, attempting to kill the pigeon (H. Prescott, personal communication, October 25, 1996). If the shooter misses, the bird may fly out of the park boundaries to safety. If wounded, the pigeon often lands in the shooting field. While the shooters aim to kill, they often only wound the birds. One field estimate suggested that only 30 percent of the birds died instantly (Fund Press Release, 1996). It is the duty of the trapper boys, typically about age 12, to retrieve the wounded birds from the shooting field and kill them by decapitating them over the rim of a barrel or with their bare hands. Although it is not advocated, birds also are killed by being jumped upon, left to suffocate in the barrel of bodies, or occasionally ripped apart. Once the shoot ends, the dead birds are thrown away as trash (Becker, 1996).

[. . .]

The protest in 1992

Before the event in 1992, The Fund encouraged activists to protest the shoot, running advertisements in animal activist magazines and networking through other national and local groups. The organization created a press release promising to stage "what is likely to be the nation's largest ever protest on behalf of animals" (Fund Press Release, 1992). The goal was to have as many people as possible engage in protest activities and willingly be arrested for breaking various laws. Though The Fund had been successful in attracting 1,500 protestors, it did little to organize protest activity before the event. A workshop in civil disobedience was optional, and no specific acts were arranged.

Because there had been no attempt to regulate the behavior of the activists, the overall context for the protest was one of chaos and tension. Several incidents led to a feeling of threat and anger. Videos of the event show the Black Berets, an animal rights militia of sorts, taunting spectators, calling them "pigeon sucking perverts," and trying to elicit a response.

All people interviewed, including Prescott, agree that there were obscenities, insults, and screaming matches "breaking out all over the park" (H. Prescott; Media representatives 1–4, personal communications, February 20, 1997). [. . .] Most of the 114 activists were arrested on charges of disorderly conduct, criminal trespass, theft and harassment (Helgeson, 1992).

Period of reconsideration

Following the protests of 1992, leaders at The Fund assessed their situation. It was clear that despite many acts of civil disobedience, they had not been able to gain much public support. The most disturbing trend that Fund leaders noticed was the media's approach to the protest. Only minimal attention was given to the actual plight of the pigeons. Reporters chose to focus on the more controversial conflict between supporters and protesters of the shoot.

[. . .]

In 1996, The Fund decided to reinstate some form of civil disobedience. Leaders at The Fund focused on developing an approach to civil disobedience that would better communicate their objections to the shoot and generally be more effective in persuading both the local and national audience to speak out against the event. In so doing, they tried to better understand their audience and more clearly represent themselves.

[. . .]

Protests 1996

The correspondence with activists before the event in 1996 differs notably from that in 1992. Instead of encouraging large numbers to attend, The Fund solicited only a small group of activists. As "peacekeepers," they were told that their job was to assure that "public attention—including media attention—is not distracted from the cruelty of the event by loud and potentially violent confrontations between activists and shoot supporters" (H. Prescott, personal communication, October 25, 1996).

[. . .]

In the midst of this context, those participating in the civil disobedience followed the plans that were carefully constructed prior to their arrival. Twelve activists in two groups of six entered the shooting fields before the event began. Locking steel bicycle locks together, they bound themselves to one another at the neck and then lay down. Their goal was two-fold: (a) to prevent the start of the shoot for as long as possible and (b) to make the argument, with their bodies, that the shoot was unjust and should be discontinued (H. Prescott, personal communication, February 21, 1997).

In conducting the civil disobedience, the activists remained silent and at a distance from the crowd. They lay flat on the ground, putting their "health and safety in jeopardy" (Police representative, personal communication, February 20, 1997). Even when the crowd tried to provoke the disobedients, they remained calm and did not respond in any way. When finally they were cut free from the kryptonite octopus, they did not resist arrest and were quietly removed from the field. The shoot was held up for close to two hours. The disobedients acted totally without violence (physical or verbal). In being bound together, they attempted to represent the captivity and helplessness of the birds. This small act of suffering was put forth as a type of representation for the ultimate suffering of the pigeons who were to be wounded and killed.

[. . .]

Discussion

At the protests of the pigeon shoot in Hegins, leaders of The Fund wanted to communicate a message about the suffering of the birds. Initially, this suffering aroused their anger, and they represented themselves in anger. At the protest in 1992, those involved in the protest often hurled insults at the crowd, which included a number of children. [. . .] In 1992, the protesters and those engaged in civil disobedience were neither nonviolent nor able to demonstrate clearly a willingness to suffer.

[. . .]

The most important aspect of civil disobedience that was recognized and respected by the activists in 1996 was nonviolence. The disobedients realized that their argument could not be put forth in violence, as those who were threatened would be unlikely to acknowledge some common ground and therefore could not be persuaded. Almost everyone interviewed agreed that the protesters were more effective when they engaged in "true" civil disobedience and abandoned the angry and violent tone set early on (Media representative 2, personal communication, February 20, 1997). One representative from the local media even suggested that if "they [the protesters] keep it toned down, at a low level, they can win over a good majority of the solid decent people in the town" (Media representative 2, personal communication, February 20, 1997).

The second key aspect of civil disobedience activists acknowledged in 1996 was a willingness to suffer for their beliefs and to communicate that suffering to onlookers. Instead of showing anger at the treatment of the pigeons during the shoot, the disobedients and other activists tried to represent the suffering of the pigeons through their own suffering.

[. . .]

In many ways, 1996 was the turning point in the battle over pigeon shoots in Hegins, Pennsylvania. In 1997 and 1998, The Fund basically stayed away from the event, choosing to capitalize on growing support for its position. The Fund pursued cruelty cases in court and lobbied for bills in the state legislature. After a series of legal rounds, supporters of the shoot agreed to discontinue the event. In 1999, and for every Labor Day since then, the shooting fields in Hegins have been silent. After 10 years and various approaches to the tactic of civil disobedience, the activists are finally sounding victory.

[. . .]

Civil disobedience can be an empowering activity for both activists and the general public. Activists join together and publicly advocate their position. The general public witnesses commitments and challenges to the system that extend beyond the voting booth and individual consumer choices. When civil disobedience is truly effective, it can change society's relationship to animals and even revitalize our public sphere.

References

Becker, C. (1996). [Videotape] *Gunblast, culture clash*.
Fund Press Release. (September 2, 1992). Silver Spring, MD: Author.
Fund Press Release. (September 6, 1996). Silver Spring, MD: Author.
Glaser, B. and Stauss, A. (1967). *The discovery of grounded theory*. Chicago: Aldine.
Stephens, M. (1980). *Broadcast news*. New York: Holt, Rinehart & Winston.
The Fund. (1996). *Guidelines for animal protection activists at Hegins, 1996*. Unpublished document.

85

———❦———

Chris DeRose

In Your Face: From Actor to Activist

Chris DeRose has been jailed and staged hunger strikes several times for actions he has taken on behalf of animal rights. He states that he is motivated by a hatred for injustice. He has never injured people in his activities. DeRose believes that animals are screaming for our help, and that most people want to know the truth about how their tax dollars are being used.

My name is Chris DeRose. By profession, I am a Hollywood actor. Not a superstar earning millions of dollars, but a working actor in films and television. At different times in my life, I've also been an altar boy, a black-belt in martial arts, a cop, an unofficial "big brother" to about two dozen tough street-kids, a private investigator, a pilot, a bouncer in a bar, and a TV reporter.

I still do some acting, but now I spend most of my time as an activist for social change, for justice, for the rights of the most oppressed and exploited of all populations on Earth: animals. I'm part of the growing movement for animal rights.

I've been arrested eleven times and jailed on four of those occasions for actions I've taken on behalf of animal rights. I'm not getting rich or famous by fighting for this cause. It's just what I believe in. Once I got shot in the back by a guy who had told me he believed in the same things.

I'm not talking about the roles I've played on screen. This is reality.

The most important reality for me is helping animals and exposing the people and institutions that profit from exploiting, torturing and killing animals. The group I head— Last Chance for Animals (LCA)—has been responsible for gathering the evidence that put some of the worst of these people out of business, and for sending a few of them off to well-deserved prison terms.

I'm no soft-hearted sentimentalist who just feels sorry for fuzzy, furry creatures. I have never even had a pet. But I hate injustice, and one of the greatest injustices in the world right now is how we treat animals.

A lot of people ask me why I got into this movement. Why did I let my acting career get sidetracked by a cause that has made me look straight at cruelty and suffering, at the most atrocious crimes human beings are capable of committing, at things so awful and ugly that I still sometimes have nightmares about them? Why did I decide to go to jail and stage hunger strikes when I could have stayed out of trouble and just issued a few good sound-bite protests against animal exploitation, from the safety and security of a successful and law-abiding career?

The answer is a principle that was eloquently expressed by Dr. Martin Luther King, Jr.:

"If a man hasn't discovered something that he will die for, he isn't fit to live." To me, the fight to save animals from torture and death is worth living for and, if necessary, dying for.

This principle doesn't make me a fanatic. Believing in something and being willing to act on that belief is not fanaticism. To me, fanatics are people who will commit acts of violence to further what they see as a just cause.

I'll tell you right up front that I've done some less-than-legal things on behalf of animals, but never anything violent. I've gone to jail for trespassing and other acts of civil disobedience, but I've never shot anyone or planted bombs or done anything that could endanger anyone's life.

Some people say, "Breaking the law is breaking the law." They don't see any difference between the nonviolent crimes I and some other animal rights activists have committed, and the shootings and bombings committed by fanatics devoted to other causes. What can I say? I *do* see a difference.

Someone once asked me, "Who appointed you God? Who gave you the right to decide which laws you'll obey and which ones you'll break?" Obviously, no one gave me any such right. That's why I willingly went to jail when I broke the law. That's what civil disobedience is all about.

But the most common question people ask me is, "Why animals, when there is so much human suffering in the world? Why not try to help human beings?" That's an easy one to answer. First, the plight of animals is far worse, and there are already a lot of people working for human rights. I feel I can do more good by working for animal rights, which doesn't yet have as much public support. Second, it's not an either-or choice. As Dr. King said, "Injustice anywhere is a threat to justice everywhere." And by showing how animal exploitation also harms humans, I believe I am helping people at the same time.

Some people try to analyze me, looking for some dark secret that would explain why I have chosen this path. Well, I don't need a psychology book to know why I do what I do. I can't not do it. And I don't need an excuse to rationalize fighting against injustice. The only time I'd look for an excuse would be if I *weren't* out there fighting. If you see injustice in the world, do you need to find a special reason to fight it?

There is nothing pleasant about struggling against the entrenched forces that profit from animal exploitation. I wish the fight were over. I'd like to do more acting, maybe get married and lead a normal life. But I can't and won't walk away from this fight. Again, to quote Dr. King: "I don't march because I like it. I march because I must."

How can people turn their backs on injustice and suffering? Saying the problem is too big to solve is bullshit. If enough people are determined to solve a problem, it will get solved. Saying that human concerns outweigh animal concerns is just more bullshit; the same changes that would help animals would also help people.

Look—if you heard someone screaming for help next door, wouldn't you try to do something? Sure you would. You'd come running even if you couldn't actually hear the screams, especially if you knew that the person was being tortured to death and needed your help.

The animals are screaming for our help right now. Each year, four billion animals scream to us from inside factory farms. Sixty to a hundred million a year from research labs. What am I supposed to do, just shrug at their screams? Would feeling indifferent to their needless suffering and death make me "normal"? If so, then I don't want to be normal. If it means not caring enough to try to do something to help, then normal must be another word for *dead*.

[. . .]

What makes the fight especially tough is that so many people have been led to believe that we have to choose between the needs of humans and the rights of animals. But that's false. A few people get rich from exploiting animals, but the rest of us always pay the cost. And we're not even talking about the suffering and death of the animals.

Factory farmers may make bigger profits by keeping cows, pigs and chickens in conditions you wouldn't want your worst enemy to suffer. But society pays the price in environmental devastation and avoidable illness.

Vivisectors get federal grants to do the same experiments hundreds of times, publishing hundreds of scientific reports detailing exactly how animals die under torture ("Canine subjects in restraint were sacrificed through introduction of saline solution into the bronchial passages" means "We took some dogs, strapped them down so they couldn't struggle, and pumped salt water straight into their lungs until they drowned"). But society pays the price—needless sickness and death—as people are misled into relying on high-tech medical salvation instead of learning to take responsibility for their own health.

I've spoken with doctors, scientists and environmentalists, and I've read thousands of articles and reports on how animals are abused and killed in laboratories, factory farms, circuses, rodeos and fur farms. I've gone into animal research labs where scientists are using our tax dollars to do things that anyone else would be arrested for doing. [. . .] I've seen and held animals dying in pain, fear and despair, and I swore that their suffering and death would never be forgiven or forgotten—*never!*

I've seen the horror first-hand, and I've committed my life to stopping it. It has to be stopped. Cruelty and exploitation are wrong, period. We can't justify injustice. We don't ask whether human slavery turns a profit, and we don't try to reform it by passing laws to make sure that slaves are treated humanely. It had to be abolished completely because it's wrong.

Same thing with animal slavery. It has to be abolished because it's wrong. And it doesn't help people, anyway. It's all useless, even if you don't care about animals.

I've written this book to tell you about these issues because the mainstream media won't touch them. But it's not a textbook. There are lots of books with loads of facts and statistics about the use and abuse of animals. To name just a few: On vivisection, a British scientist named Robert Sharpe wrote a great book called *The Cruel Deception*, which explains why animal experimentation doesn't benefit human health. On factory farming, you can read Jim Mason's classic work, *Animal Factories*, or John Robbins' *Diet for a New America*, which shows why vegetarianism is healthier for people and for the planet. On sport hunting (if ever there was a contradiction in terms, this is it), a guy named Ron Baker wrote *The American Hunting Myth*, which debunks the lies told to convince nonhunters which is most of the population that going into the woods to blow Bambi's head off with a high-power rifle is somehow natural and necessary as well as good fun.

This book is about my own experiences as an activist for animals. It is a highly personal account of what I've seen and done. If the language is sometimes rough, too bad. So is what happens to the animals. I won't try to soften it or make it any less ugly than it is. (In reconstructing conversations from years ago, I've tried to convey the content, tone, and actual language as accurately as I can remember, but these dialogues are not necessarily word-for-word transcripts.)

Some people don't want to learn the truth about how humans treat the nonhuman inhabitants of Earth. But I'm hoping that many more people want to know what's going on, how their tax dollars are being used and how their government sanctions cruelty and exploitation. Some people will even join in the fight to end it.

Maybe you will be one of them.

―――⟐⟐⟐⟐―――

86

Peter Singer

"Ten Ways to Make a Difference"

Peter Singer builds on the work of Henry Spira (1927–98) in suggesting ten effective strategies to use on behalf of animals. To many, Henry Spira was the most effective activist of the modern animal rights movement. He put the issue of cosmetics testing on the political map, and convinced the USDA to abandon a face-branding requirement slated to include all cattle imported from Mexico. His success shows that one person can still make a difference.

1 Try to understand the public's current thinking and where it could be encouraged to go tomorrow. Above all, keep in touch with reality

Too many activists mix only with other activists and imagine that everyone else thinks as they do. They start to believe in their own propaganda and lose their feel for what the average person in the street might think. They no longer know what is achievable and what is a fantasy that has grown out of their own intense conviction of the need for change.

[. . .]

Henry Spira grabs every opportunity to talk to people outside the animal movement. He'll start up a conversation with the person sitting next to him on a bus or train, mention an issue he is concerned about, and listen to their responses. How do they react? Can they feel themselves in the place of the victim? Are they outraged? What in particular do they focus on?

2 Select a target on the basis of vulnerabilities to public opinion, the intensity of suffering, and the opportunities for change

Target selection is crucial. Henry knows that he can run an effective campaign when he feels sure that, as he said about the New York state law allowing laboratories to take dogs and cats from shelters, "it just defies common sense that the average guy in the street would say, 'Hey, that's a real neat thing to do.' "

You know that you have a good target if, by merely stating the issue, you put your adversary on the defensive. During the museum campaign, for example, Henry could ask the public: "Do you want your tax monies spent to mutilate cats in order to observe the sexual performance of crippled felines?" The museum was immediately in a very awkward position.

Cosmetic testing made another good target, because you only had to ask, "Is another shampoo worth blinding rabbits?" to put Revlon officials on the defensive.

Keeping in touch with reality is a prerequisite for selecting the right target: If you don't know what the public currently thinks, you won't know what they will find acceptable and what will revolt them.

The other elements of point 2 suggest a balance between the good that the campaign can do and its likelihood of success. When Henry selected the cat experiments at the American Museum of Natural History as his first target, he knew that he would directly affect, at best, about sixty cats a year—a tiny number compared to many other possible targets. But the opportunity for change was great because of the nature of the experiments themselves and the location and vulnerability of the institution carrying out the experiments. In 1976, it was vital for the animal movement to have a victory, no matter how small, to encourage its own supporters to believe in the possibility of change and to gain some credibility with the wider world.

[. . .]

3 Set goals that are achievable. Bring about meaningful change one step at a time. Raising awareness is not enough

When Henry first took an interest in opposing animal experimentation, the antivivisection movement had no goal other than the abolition of vivisection and no strategy for achieving this goal other than "raising awareness"—that is, mailing out literature filled with pictures and descriptions of the horrors of vivisection. This was the strategy of a movement that talked mainly to itself. It had no idea how to get a hold on the levers of change, or even where those levers might be located. It seemed unaware of its own image as a bunch of ineffective cranks and did not know how to make vivisection an issue that would be picked up by the media. Henry's background in the civil rights movement told him that this was not the way to succeed:

> One of the first things that I learned in earlier movements was that nothing is ever an all-or-nothing issue. It's not a one-day process, it's a long process. You need to see the world—including individuals and institutions—as not being static but in constant change, with change occurring one step at a time. It's incremental. It's almost like organic development. You might say, for instance, that a couple of blacks demanding to be seated at a lunch counter really doesn't make a hell of a lot of difference because most of them don't even have the money to buy anything at a lunch counter. But it did make a difference, it was a first step. Once you take that first step and you have that same first step in a number of places, you integrate a number of lunch counters, you set a whole pattern, and it's one of the steps that would generate the least amount of resistance. It's something that's winnable, but it encourages the black struggle and it clearly leads to the next step and the next step. I think that no movement has ever won on the basis of all or none.[1]

Some activists think that accepting less than, say, the total abolition of vivisection is a form of compromise that reduces their chances of a more complete victory. Henry's view is: "I want to abolish the use of animals as much as anybody else, but I say, let's do what we can do today and then do more tomorrow."[2] That is why he was willing to support moves to replace the LD50 with tests like the approximate lethal dose test, which still uses animals, but far fewer of them.

Look for targets that are not only winnable in themselves, but where winning will have expanding ripple effects. Ask yourself if success in one campaign will be a stepping stone toward still-bigger targets and more significant victories. The campaign against Revlon is an example: Because it made research into alternatives respectable, its most important effects have been felt beyond Revlon and even beyond the cosmetics industry as a whole.

While raising awareness is essential if we are to bring about change, Henry does not usually work directly at raising awareness. (His advertisements against meat are an exception.) Awareness follows a successful campaign, and a successful campaign will have achievable goals.

4 Establish credible sources of information and documentation. Never assume anything. Never deceive the media or the public. Maintain credibility, don't exaggerate or hype the issue

Before starting a new campaign, Henry spends several months gathering information. Freedom of information legislation has helped enormously, but a lot of information is already out there, in the public domain. Experimenters report their experiments in scientific journals that are available in major libraries, and valuable data about corporations may also be a matter of public record. Henry is never content simply to quote from the leaflets of animal rights groups, or other opponents of the institution or corporation that he is targeting. He always goes to the source, which is preferably a publication of the target itself, or else a government document. Newspapers like the *New York Times* have been prepared to run Henry's advertisements making very specific allegations of wrongdoing against people like Frank Perdue because every allegation has been meticulously checked.

Some organizations describing experiments will conveniently omit details that make the experiments less shocking than they would otherwise appear. They may, for example, neglect to tell their readers that the animals were anesthetized at the time. But those who do this eventually lose credibility. Henry's credibility is extraordinarily high, both within the animal movement and with its opponents, because he regards it as his most important asset. It is therefore never to be sacrificed for a short-term gain, no matter how tempting that may be at the time.

5 Don't divide the world into saints and sinners

When Henry wants to get someone—a scientist, a corporate executive, a legislator, or a government official—to do something differently, he puts himself in the position of that person:

> [The question to ask yourself is:] If I were that person, what would make me want to change my behavior? If you accuse them of being a bunch of sadistic bastards, these people are not going to figure, "Hey, what is it I could do that's going to be different and make those people happy?" That's not the way the real world works.

Being personally hostile to an opponent may be a good way of letting off steam, but it doesn't win people over. When Henry wanted to persuade scientists working for corporations like

Procter & Gamble to develop nonanimal alternatives, he saw their situation as similar to that of people who eat animals:

> How do you change these people's behavior best? By saying you've never made a conscious decision to harm those animals. Basically you've been programmed from being a kid: "Be nice to cat and doggy, and eat meat." And I think some of these researchers, that's how they were taught, that's how they were programmed. And you want to reprogram them, and you're not going to reprogram them by saying we're saints and you're sinners, and we're going to clobber you with a two-by-four in order to educate you.

As Susan Fowler, editor of the trade magazine *Lab Animal* at the time of the Revlon campaign, put it:

> There is no sense in Henry's campaign of: "Well, this is Revlon, and no one in Revlon is going to be interested in what we are doing, they're all the enemy." Rather . . . he looks for—and kind of waits for, I think—someone to step out of the group and say: "Well, I understand what you're saying.[3]

Without this attitude, when Roger Shelley came along ready to listen to what Henry wanted Revlon to do, the opportunity to change the company's approach could easily have been missed.

Not dividing the world into saints and sinners isn't just sound tactics, it is also the way Henry thinks. "People can change," he says. "I used to eat animals and I never considered myself a cannibal."[4]

6 Seek dialogue and attempt to work together to solve problems. Position issues as problems with solutions. This is best done by presenting realistic alternatives

Because he doesn't think of his opponents as evil, Henry has no preconceptions about whether they will or will not work with him to reduce animal suffering. So he opens every campaign with a polite letter to the target organization—whether the American Museum of Natural History, Amnesty International, Revlon, Frank Perdue, or a meatpacker—inviting them to discuss the concerns he has. Sometimes Henry's invitations have been ignored, sometimes they have received an equally polite response from a person skilled in public relations who has no intention of doing anything, and sometimes they have led directly to the change he wanted without any public campaigning at all. But the fact that he suggests sitting down to talk about the problem before he does any public campaigning shows that he isn't just stirring up trouble for the fun of it, or as a way of raising funds for his organization.

Henry puts considerable thought into how the person or organization he is approaching could achieve its goals while eliminating or substantially reducing the suffering now being caused. The classic example of an imaginative solution was Henry's proposal to Revlon and other cosmetics manufacturers that they should fund research into alternatives to the Draize eye test. For more than a year before his campaign went public, Henry had been seeking a collaborative, rather than a confrontational, approach with Revlon. In the end, after the campaign finally did go public, Revlon accepted his proposal and, together with other companies, found that for a very small expenditure, relative to their income, they could develop an alternative that enabled them to have a more precise, cheaper form of product safety testing that did not involve animals at all.

Having a realistic solution to offer means that it is possible to accentuate the positive, instead of running a purely negative campaign. In interviews and leaflets about the Draize test, for example, Henry always emphasized that in vitro testing methods offered the prospect of quicker, cheaper, more reliable, and more elegant ways of testing the safety of new products.

[. . .]

In terms of offering a positive outcome, the difference between the campaigns against the cat experiments and those against the Draize test was one of degree, not kind. If your tube of toothpaste is blocked, whether you will be able to get any toothpaste out of it will depend on how badly blocked the tube is and on how much pressure is exerted on it. So, too, whether an institution or corporation will adopt an alternative will depend on how negatively it views the alternative and how much pressure it is under. The more realistic the alternative is, the less pressure will be needed to see it adopted.

7 Be ready for confrontation if your target remains unresponsive. If accepted channels don't work, prepare an escalating public awareness campaign to place your adversary on the defensive

If point 6 is about making it easy for the toothpaste to come out of the tube, point 7 is about increasing the pressure if it still won't come. A public awareness campaign may take various forms. At the American Museum of Natural History, it started with an article in a local newspaper, then it was kept up by pickets and demonstrations, and finally it spread through the national media and specialist journals like *Science*. The Revlon campaign went public with a dramatic full-page advertisement in the *New York Times*, which itself generated more publicity. The campaign continued with demonstrations outside Revlon's offices. The Perdue and face-branding campaigns relied much more heavily on advertising and the use of the media. Advertising takes money, on which, see point 8.

8 Avoid bureaucracy

Anyone who has been frustrated by lengthy committee meetings that absorb time and energy will sympathize with Henry's desire to get things done rather than spend time on organizational tangles. Worse still, bureaucratic structures all too often divert energy into making the organization grow, rather than getting results for the cause. Then when the organization grows, it needs staff and an office. So you get a situation in which people who want to make a difference for animals (or for street kids, or for rain forests, or for whatever cause) spend 80 percent of their time raising money just to keep the organization going. Most of the time is spent ensuring that everyone in the organization gets along with one another, feels appreciated, and is not upset because he or she expected to be promoted to a more responsible position or given an office with more windows.

Henry has been able to avoid such obstacles by working, essentially, on his own. That isn't a style that will suit everyone, but it has worked well for Henry. Animal Rights International has no members. It has a long list of advisers and its board consists of trusted close friends whom Henry can rely upon for support without hassles. Henry doesn't need a lot of money, but he does need some. He has been fortunate in finding two donors who support him regularly because they like to see their money making a difference.

When Henry needs more clout, he puts a coalition together—as he did on the repeal of the Metcalf-Hatch Act, in fighting against the Draize and LD50 tests, and now, to persuade McDonald's to take a leading role in improving the welfare of farm animals. Since his early success at the American Museum of Natural History, other organizations have been eager to join his coalitions. At their height, these coalitions have included hundreds of organizations, with memberships in the millions. Here, too, though, Henry keeps hassles to a minimum. Organizations are welcome to participate at whatever level they wish. Some get their supporters out to demonstrate or march, while others don't. Some pay for full-page advertisements, and others ask them to write letters to newspapers, where they may reach millions without spending a cent. What no organization can do is dictate policy. Henry consults widely, but in the end, he makes his own decisions, thus avoiding the time-consuming and sometimes divisive process of elections and committee meetings. Clearly, in the case of major disagreements, organizations have the option of leaving; but if the coalition is making progress, organizations will generally swallow the disagreements in order to be part of a successful team.

9 Don't assume that only legislation or legal action can solve the problem

Henry has used elected representatives in his campaigns to put pressure on government agencies and to gain publicity. But the only campaign in which he achieved his aim through legislation was the repeal of the Metcalf-Hatch Act. Here, since bad legislation was the target of the campaign, he had no choice. Otherwise, as far as he can, Henry stays out of conventional political processes and keeps away from the courts: "No congressional bill, no legal gimmickry, by itself, will save the animals." No doubt there are other situations, and other issues, on which legislation will make a difference. But on the whole, Henry sees laws as maintaining the status quo. They will be changed only in order to keep disturbance at a minimum. The danger of getting deeply involved in the political process is that it often deflects struggles into what Henry calls "political gabbery." There is a lot of talk, but nothing happens. Political lobbying or legal maneuvering becomes a substitute for action.

10 Ask yourself: "Will it work?"

All of the preceding points are directed toward this last one. Before you launch a campaign, or continue with a campaign already begun, ask yourself if it will work. If you can't give a realistic account of the ways in which your plans will achieve your objectives, you need to change your plans. Keeping in touch with what the public is thinking, selecting a target, setting an achievable goal, getting accurate information, maintaining credibility, suggesting alternative solutions, being ready to talk to adversaries or to confront them if they will not talk—all of these are directed toward creating a campaign that is a practical means of making a difference. The overriding question is always: *Will it work?*

[. . .]

Notes

1   "Singer Speaks with Spira," *Animal Liberation*, January–March 1989, p. 5.
2   Ibid., p. 6.
3   Susan Fowler, videotaped interview with author, New York, December 1996.
4   "Singer Speaks with Spira," p. 5.

Annotated Further Reading

Datta, A. (1998) *Animals and the Law: A Review of Animals and the State*, Chichester, England: Chichester Institute of Higher Education. History and the current state of English law concerning animals.

Einwohner, R.L. (1999) "Gender, Class, and Social Movement Outcomes: Identity and Effectiveness in Two Animal Rights Campaigns." *Gender and Society* 13.1: 56–76. Hunters make classist and gendered attributions about animal rights activists whereas circus patrons take their demands more seriously.

Favre, D. (1996) "Legal Rights for our Fellow Creatures." *Contemporary Philosophy* 28.4–5: 7–10. A brief, clear exposition.

Francione, G. (2000) *Introduction to Animal Rights: Your Child or the Dog?* Philadelphia: Temple University Press. Agrees with Tom Regan that we must abolish the institution of animals as property.

Garner, R. (1998) *Political Animals: Animal Protection Politics in Britain and the United States*, New York: St Martin's. Argues that both the British and American political systems have shown themselves reasonably responsive to change.

Jasper, J.M. (1992) *The Animal Rights Crusade*, New York: Free Press. Still useful though somewhat out-dated. A sympathetic treatment.

Jasper, M.C. (1997) *Animal Rights Law*, Dobbs Ferry, N.Y.: Oceana. A useful reference source covering both federal and state legislation.

Lowe, B.M. (2001) "Animal Rights as a Quasi-Religion." *Implicit Religion* 4.1: 41–60. A sociological argument that the animal rights movement functions as a religion.

Munro, L. (2001) *Compassionate Beasts: The Quest for Animal Rights*, Westport, Conn.: Praeger. Grassroots and organizational advocacy.

Singer, P. (1998) *Ethics into Action: Henry Spira and the Animal Rights Movement*, Lanham, Md.: Rowman and Littlefield. Spira combined persistence with intelligent thinking.

Wise, S.M. (2000) "Rattling the Cage: Toward Legal Rights for Animals." Cambridge, Mass.: Perseus Books. An important book, concentrating on the great apes.

—— (2002) *Drawing the Line: Science and the Case for Animal Rights*, Cambridge, Mass.: Perseus Books. Detailed consideration of a young child, honeybees, a parrot, a dog, a dolphin, an elephant, an orangutan, and a gorilla with respect to entitlement to basic rights.

Study Questions

1   Steven Wise and Richard Posner disagree concerning the role of an animal's cognitive capacity as a basis for legal rights. Which position do you find more convincing?

2   Wise proposes that we recognize "practical autonomy" as sufficient to justify the attribu-tion of basic legal rights. Do you support Wise's proposal? Do the positions of Gómez and Midgley in Part III support such a concept?

3   Richard Epstein discusses a number of negative consequences which follow from the recognition of animal rights. Do you agree that such consequences are likely? Give your reasoning.

4   Both Posner and Epstein point out that the current legal situation of treating animals as the property of human beings often has a positive effect on animal welfare. Does your own experience reflect this claim?

5   Which of the five characteristics of a religion discussed by Jamison, Wenk, and Parker are characteristic of the animal rights movement, in your experience? Which do not appear to

be characteristic? Justify your positions. Can you cite other social reform movements which also share some or all of these religious characteristics?

6 Tom Regan describes the current abolition/reform split in the animal rights movement. In your view, which approach is more effective? Do you believe that violence against property on behalf of animal welfare is morally acceptable?

7 Tom Regan proposes a solution to the abolition/reform split at the end of his article. Do you believe that his solution is workable?

8 Courtney Dillard analyses effective civil disobedience. How might the strategies she describes be used in social reform movements not involving animals?

9 Chris DeRose argues that direct action on behalf of animals with the possibility of arrest and jail time is warranted by the injustices suffered by animals. Under what circumstances (if any) do you agree?

10 Peter Singer recommends ten strategies in working to improve the conditions for animals. Which strategies do you believe to be most important? Are there others which Singer does not list?

Index